Butterfly Politics

From Nayoung
to Audrey
with love and
sisterhood ♡

Butterfly Politics

Changing the World for Women

CATHARINE A. MacKINNON

The Belknap Press of Harvard University Press

CAMBRIDGE, MASSACHUSETTS

LONDON, ENGLAND

Printed in the United States of America

First Harvard University Press paperback edition, 2019
First printing

Interior design by Dean Bornstein

Library of Congress Cataloging-in-Publication Data

Names: MacKinnon, Catharine A., author.
Title: Butterfly politics / Catharine A. MacKinnon.
Description: Cambridge, Massachusetts : The Belknap Press of Harvard
University Press, 2017. | "Encompassing legal and political interventions
from 1976 to 2016, this volume collects moments of attempts to change
the inequality of women to men and reflections on those attempts"—
Introduction. | Includes bibliographical references and index.
Identifiers: LCCN 2016040443 | ISBN 9780674416604 (cloth) |
ISBN 9780674237667 (pbk.)
Subjects: LCSH: Sex discrimination against women—Law and
legislation—United States—History. | Sexual harassment—Law and
legislation—United States—History. | Rape—Law and legislation—
United States—History. | Pornography—Law and legislation—
United States—History. | Women's rights—United States—History. |
Feminist jurisprudence—United States.
Classification: LCC KF4758 .M327 2017 | DDC 342.7308/78—dc23
LC record available at https://lccn.loc.gov/2016040443

for the last woman I talked with
and the next baby girl born

CONTENTS

Preface to the Paperback Edition   ix

Butterfly Politics   1

I. Change

1. To Change the World for Women (1980)   11
2. A Radical Act of Hope (1989)   23
3. Law's Power (1990)   28
4. To Quash a Lie (1991)   34
5. The Measure of What Matters (1992)   42
6. Intervening for Sex Equality (2013)   47

II. Law

7. Introduction, Symposium on Sexual Harassment (1981)   57
8. Sexual Harassment: Supreme Court Brief for
   Mechelle Vinson (1986)   63
9. Testimony on Pornography, Minneapolis (1983)   96
10. Testimony to the Attorney General's Commission on
    Pornography (1985)   99
11. Substantive Equality (1989)   110
12. On Torture (1990)   126
13. Rape as Genocide: Appellate Argument in
    Kadic v. Karadžić (1995)   140
14. Rape as Genocide: Summation to the Jury in
    Kadic v. Karadžić (2000)   152
15. Trafficking, Prostitution, and Inequality (2015)   162

III. Culture

16. Reality, Not Fantasy (1985)   183
17. To the American Civil Liberties Union on
    Pornography (1985)   189
18. X-Underrated (2005)   199
19. Gender: The Future (2007)   207

IV. Academy

20. Gender Literacy (1994)   217
21. Mainstreaming Feminism in Legal Education (2003)   225
22. On Academic Freedom: From Powerlessness to
    Power (2002)   242
23. Engaged Scholarship as Method and Vocation (2005)   263
24. Defying Gravity (2013)   278

V. Toward an Equal Future

25. Rape Redefined (2014)   285
26. Restoring Institutional Accountability for
    Educational Sexual Harassment (2013)   291
27. Toward a Renewed Equal Rights Amendment:
    Now More Than Ever (2014)   295
28. Sex Equality in Global Perspective (2015)   305

Intervening for Change, 1976–2016   325

Notes   333
Acknowledgments   473
Index   475

Preface to the Paperback Edition

The world's first mass movement against sexual abuse, #MeToo, took off from the law of sexual harassment, quickly overtook it, and is shifting cultures everywhere, electrifyingly demonstrating butterfly politics in action. The early openings of the butterflies' wings were the legal, political, and conceptual innovations of the 1970s,[1] but it is the collective social intervention of the #MeToo movement that is setting off the cataclysmic transformations of which a political butterfly effect is capable.

The legal breakthrough that defined sexual harassment as sex discrimination, a human rights violation, was a crucial precondition for #MeToo, despite the inadequacies of law that the movement has highlighted. Sexual harassment as experience and violation was exposed and defined as a vector and dynamic of sex inequality based on gender with major white racist and class-based dimensions. Legally framed as a deprivation of equality rights, sexual harassment stopped being something to just live through. This change broke through the age-old rule of impunity that the more power a man has, the more sex he can exact from those with less power. If all the sexual abuse reported in the #MeToo movement had remained legal for the past forty-some years—as most would have without sexual harassment law—this explosive movement against it would have been unthinkable. Without law delegitimizing sexual harassment, calling it what it is, powerful men would not be losing their jobs, political and academic positions, deals, and reputations today.[2]

But #MeToo has been driven not by litigation but by mainstream and social media, bringing down men (and some women) as women (and some men) have risen up. The movement is surpassing law in changing norms and providing relief that the law did not—and in some ways in its current form could not. Sexual harassment law prepared the ground, but #MeToo, Time's Up, and other similar mobilizations around the world—including #NiUnaMenos in Argentina, #Balancetonporc in France, #TheFirstTimeIGotHarassed in Egypt, #WithYou in Japan, and #PremeiroAssedio in Brazil among them—are shifting gender hierarchy's tectonic plates.

If sexual harassment law was necessary for this movement's butterfly take-off, until #MeToo, perpetrators could reasonably count on their denials being credited and their accusers being devalued to shield their actions. Many survivors realistically judged reporting to be pointless or worse, predictably producing retaliation. Complaints were routinely passed off with some version of "she isn't credible" or "she wanted it" or "it was trivial." A social burden of proof effectively assumed that if anything sexual happened, the woman involved desired it and probably telegraphed wanting it. She was legally and socially required to prove to the contrary. In campus settings at any rate, on my observation over time, it typically took three to four women testifying that they had been violated by the same man in the same way to even begin to make a dent in his denial. That made a woman, for credibility purposes, one quarter of a person.

Even when she was believed, nothing he did to her mattered so much as what would be done to him if his actions were taken seriously. His value, personal and political, outweighed hers. His career, his reputation, his mental and emotional serenity, his family, all his assets counted. Hers did not. A weird temporality set in. What he did was past so best forgotten and should not affect his future. She is entitled to recognition neither of her past injury nor of her past, present, or future trauma. In some ways, it is even worse to be believed and not to have what he did matter. It means you don't matter.

This precise choreography was retraced in the final Senate hearing for Judge Brett M. Kavanaugh's Supreme Court nomination. Dr. Christine Blasey Ford provided remembered facts of a sexual attack by him: He did this. When questioned on those facts, Judge Kavanaugh repeatedly provided . . . his resumé: I matter.[3] Many people seem to have believed her. Yet it/she became comparatively weightless, negligible; his future counted, heavily. His enraged display of toxic masculinity, coded as "strong" under male dominance—otherwise an unjudicial, even hysterical attempt at distraction—fooled just enough people just long enough. Senators who believed Dr. Blasey apparently did not recoil at placing someone on the Supreme Court who, therefore, must have been lying to them under oath. His value outweighed her violation. Dr. Blasey's cogent wrenching account, failing in traction the slut and nut riposte, was desperately shoehorned into the "so what" category.[4] These exact dynamics of inequality drive the system of sexual politics in which the more power a man has, the more sexual access he can get away with compelling. The hairline vote to confirm Kavanaugh[5] sandbagged that system against the MeToo tidal wave.

Over the prior year, during which long-buried reports of sexual abuse had exploded, the survivors speaking out cut across sex, gender, age, race, class, and politics, perfectly displaying the kaleidoscope that collectivities of butterflies are called. After four decades—or two thousand years, depending on when you start counting—the pervasive silence that has walled off reports of sexual abuse crumbled. What was previously ignored or attributed to lying, deranged, or venial discontents and whiners began to be treated as disgraceful and outrageous misconduct that no self-respecting entity, including companies or schools, could accept being associated with. This unprecedented wave of speaking out has actually begun to erode the two biggest barriers to ending sexual harassment and all forms of sexual abuse in law and in life: the disbelief and the trivializing dehumanization of its victims. Used to be, women accusing men of sexual abuse were the ones thrown overboard. Women's voices recounting sexual abuse being heard, believed, and acted on—and some men being thrown overboard, despite Kavanaugh's confirmation—is real change. The alchemy of #MeToo is beginning to transform what has been a privilege of power into a disgrace so despicable that not even many white upper-class men feel they can afford it around them. Maybe they have begun not even to want it there?

The #MeToo moment built on decades of collective work against sexual abuse, including Professor Anita Hill's foundational testimony in 1991 that Clarence Thomas, nominated and also confirmed to the Supreme Court, had sexually harassed her years before. Judge (now Justice) Thomas's testimony was far more effective than Judge (now Justice) Kavanaugh's, and far more dignified—as a Black man, it had to be—despite Professor Hill's unimpeachable credibility and unshakeable grace.[6] I believed her, but his anger at being held to a standard to which white men had not been held came from a real place. It was not a tantrum of entitlement.

In 2006, Tarana Burke laid a specific conceptual cornerstone for the current movement, applying the phrase "me too" to call out the widespread sexual and other domestic violence against women and girls and lift them up.[7] Some court cases reflected its impact by calling "me too evidence" testimony by women that the same thing had happened to them as was reported by a sexual harassment complainant.[8] In the decade following, in an independent vector, what was widely termed "campus sexual assault" combined legal initiatives with social media interventions, as survivors organized among themselves and inspired the Obama administration to investigate hundreds of schools for inadequate response to sexual abuse on campus.[9] This, too, was prepared by the legal recognition in the late 1970s that students had a right under sex equality law to an educational environment that is not sexually hostile and to a school's adequate, effective, and fair response to reports of abuse.[10]

Then on October 15, 2017, the actor Alyssa Milano, as part of her report of sexual abuse by Hollywood mogul Harvey Weinstein, created the Twitter hashtag, inviting survivors of sexual violation to join her and others on social media in reporting their sexual violation.[11] The numbers of those who provided their own accounts soon reached 1.7 million[12] before anyone stopped counting. Ashley Judd, the actor and activist, was perhaps the #MeToo movement's specific butterfly. Her willingness to be named alleging sexual harassment by Harvey Weinstein, as solidly reported by the *New York Times*,[13] followed swiftly by named allegations by others against him there and in the *New Yorker*,[14] produced the butterfly effect that is now the mass kaleidoscopic movement known as #MeToo, transnational in scope and showing no signs of slowing.

High-quality journalism, featuring in-depth, factually detailed reporting that was the product of years of investigative diligence, touched off this movement, followed by survivors in the millions taking to social media airwaves. Sexual abuse was finally being reported in the established media as pervasive and endemic rather than sensational and exceptional, disappearing after one oh-my-god blip on the public radar.[15] Women have been talking with each other about this outrage for millennia. Social media could have become just a digital echo chamber in which a million whispers of sexual mistreatment went to die. No small part of the cultural and legal changes that are occurring is due to mainstream media continuing its ethical, sometimes inspired, if not universally appreciated (what that matters is?) consciousness-raising focus on the topic. Journalists are persistently tracking down supporting evidence of the women's accounts, reporting survivors' own compelling voices, often accompanied by dignified and empowering visuals rather than the former cute flirty (wouldn't you do it to her if you could? wouldn't she like it?) girl paired with the grave silverback (would he do anything so cheesy? would he need to?) dude in a suit. And the journalists are following up—as if the reported events may have occurred and are worth serious consideration.

This extraordinary journalism unearthed sexual abuse in every corner of society—sports as well as entertainment, food as well as finance, tech and transportation as well as employment and education, children as well as adults. And, of course, in politics. Reporters and editors at long last have discovered that sexual abuse is a story, with legs even, and have refused to let that story and its telling voices die. Harasser prominence stoked some of this mainstream media fire, although anyone who sexually harasses a woman is plenty big to its target. As staggering as the scope and prevalence of the revelations have been to many who failed to face the long-known real numbers,[16] the structural and systemic depth and breadth of this dynamic has only begun to be exposed to general public view. Sexual harassment—as written in 1979, now revealed by this movement and finally being reported by traditional media—is "less 'epidemic' than endemic."[17]

Butterfly Politics, the activist collection, contains interventions that ground and predict such a development. The right small actions under the right conditions have indeed set off a political movement of systemic dimension. If one precondition for #MeToo was sexual harassment law, the other was the 2016 presidential election. Previously, complaints of sexual harassment had been linked for many to the left-right politics of the Clinton administration. In what Hillary Clinton called a "vast right-wing conspiracy,"[18] a popular president many Americans respected, whose politics a voting majority of the country had hoped to see enacted as policy, was derailed by sexual harassment charges.[19] The sexual politics of the complaint against President Clinton by Paula Jones, an Arkansas state employee when he was governor there, were also cross-cut by the simultaneous emergence of his ongoing affair with an intern in the White House who said she passionately desired the sexual relationship the two were having.[20] The immense inequality of power between them was thus clouded, if not obscured entirely, particularly because sexual relations characterized by dramatic inequalities of social power are common, perhaps normative, even as many participants in intimacy believe otherwise—or want to believe or purport to believe or believe of their current relationship if not of prior ones. In any event, sexual harassment as an issue became identified for many with the Right's exploitation for political gain, a morality crusade rather than a matter of coercion, one that moreover denied sexual choices to women who did not see themselves as victims at all, despite the wide disparities of power frequently involved.

The election of Donald Trump switched the relation of sexual harassment as an issue to conventional political alignments and redefined the democratic and liberatory potential of publicly claiming sexual victimization. Now it was an unpopular president[21] whose legitimacy was in question, one who had been caught on tape explicitly asserting that he could grab any woman by the genitals because he was the star of the show.[22] He did not repent. Many women were outraged by this and by the fact that charges of sexual abuse leveled against him by twenty-two women[23] did not matter enough to even jar, far less derail, his candidacy or his election. Legal scholar Kimberlé Crenshaw has brilliantly pointed out the direct line between disbelief of Professor Hill's sexual harassment allegations for combined reasons of racism and sexism and the election of Donald Trump.[24] That line runs straight through the undermining of electoral democracy by *Citizens United,* allowing the buying of elections in the dark, and the gutting of the Voting Rights Act, to both of which results Justice Thomas's fifth vote was crucial.[25] Intersectional politics are politics unmodified. Trump's right wing (not conservative), white supremacist, and xenophobic views and agenda inflamed much of the populace further and alienated people around the world.

The allegations against Harvey Weinstein threw a match into this tinderbox. Resisting sexual harassment by reporting its occurrence in one's own life became a means of resisting a president seen by many as a narcissistic authoritarian misogynist, the leading edge of fascism, as well as an unprincipled corrupt serial liar. Even as the movement revealed that perpetrators of sexual abuse were not just those men over there, but our men right here, this reversal of the conventional politics of the issue released a tsunami of enraged women, some of whom had been silenced by its prior political associations. Some had kept silent about their own abuse out of respect for Hillary Clinton, who had been put in a precariously difficult position by all of this, although who knows what confronting sexual abuse on behalf of violated women could have mobilized for her campaign. In any case, what contributed to creating Trump as president—indifference to reports of sexual abuse—fueled #MeToo, in no small part because of its role in creating Trump as president. If Hillary Clinton had been elected, #MeToo would not have occurred. While #MeToo unites survivors of all politics in a politics of its own, it is also a responsive backlash.

As #MeToo moves the culture beneath the law of sexual abuse to make it potentially a far more effective tool than it has ever been, early indications are that some conventional systemic legal processes may be shifting. In a kind of controlled experiment, the comedian Bill Cosby, accused of drugging and assaulting scores of women over decades, whose trial produced a hung jury in a case prior to #MeToo,[26] was then convicted several months after #MeToo broke. In the first trial, one woman was allowed to testify to similar experiences to support the single complaining witness; five were permitted in the second.[27] These *are* gender crimes, a point multiple victims make, despite this fact as yet not being recognized in domestic criminal law. Aaron Persky was removed from the Superior Court bench in California in a recall by the voters after sentencing a white Stanford swimmer to six months for committing three sexual assault felonies against an unconscious woman.[28] His victim's sentencing statement[29] inspired women worldwide and helped set off #MeToo. California made several legal changes in response to the case as well.[30] Larry Nassar, a doctor for Olympic gymnasts, was convicted of sexually assaulting scores of his young women patients over decades in the guise of treatment and was sentenced to more than a lifetime in prison.[31] Anyone who thinks that all the persuasive young women—breathtaking in number and compelling in voice—would have produced the same result without the #MeToo changes in climate is forgetting the multiple reports against Nassar over multiple years by some of these same young women that were utterly ignored. The ongoing surfacing of allegations against Catholic priests and bishops by adult survivors of childhood sexual abuse, many of them men,[32] which began before MeToo, increasingly including complaints of official cover-ups as well as direct acts of sexual aggression,[33] has arguably taken inspiration and heart and derived potency and momentum from adding its voices to a rising #MeToo.

Some courts are beginning to take explicit account of the cultural shift in what is "reasonable" to expect of a survivor who alleges sexual harassment at work, victim reasonableness having previously entered sexual harassment law at multiple junctures with no equality rationale. In one striking case, a Court of Appeals reversed a lower court's ruling for an employer and required a jury determination of fact as to whether a woman employee took reasonable care to avoid the harassment she alleged, and whether she reasonably did not report it over a period of several years.[34] In an innovative case, the British actor Kadian Noble sued Harvey Weinstein civilly for sex trafficking for forcing her to commit a sex act with him amid his fraudulent promises to advance her career. In fact, quid pro quo sexual harassment does amount to a form of commercial sex. The judge there held Noble could proceed to trial, saying that her reliance on his promises was reasonable because she actually did rely on them.[35] This is a whole new world. Harvey Weinstein has also been sued civilly by Ashley Judd for ruining her career opportunities[36] and prosecuted criminally by others. The Kavanaugh confirmation, which underlined authoritative indifference to allegations of sexual assault, may inflame rather than dishearten, making #MeToo electorally potent.

Time's Up, the organization sparked by the initial #MeToo reports of sexual harassment in Hollywood—the casting couch being Hollywood's version of quid pro quo sexual harassment—immediately opened its lens and arms to houseworkers, restaurant workers, agricultural workers, and many others.[37] Embracing the racial and economic dimensions of sexual subordination for women in the world of work up and down the class hierarchy deepened and broadened the group's analysis and reach, strengthening the movement immeasurably. The organization expanded its ambitions to end women's marginalization in private equity, high tech, and advertising as well as entertainment.

It has long been something of a miracle when anyone claiming sexual violation is believed, even if it takes multiple accusers. But the odds of being believed have just as long been irrelevantly improved by any kind of privilege—be it dominant race, ethnicity, religion, class, celebrity, nationality, caste, sexuality, age, gender, or combinations of these. An attack on these hierarchies is also an attack on the fact that women's work, like the rest of women's lives, is often denigratingly sexualized. Working for tips in a restaurant to make anything close to a living wage, for example, largely requires women in effect to sell themselves sexually. The entertainment industry also commodifies the sexuality of the women in it. It's no coincidence that so many of the exposed harassers in the entertainment field reportedly subjected their victims to a pornographic spectator sexuality, masturbating over them in real life like consumers do over women in pornography. This is what an endemic abuse, pervasively normalized, can look like. It also partly explains why Time's Up women—actors frequently used and abused to create the sexualized culture in which we are awash, who as working women, almost no matter how well-known or successful, must please powerful men to continue to get that work—are so perfectly positioned to attack it.

Once something is legally prohibited, it is often thought that it more or less stops. This may be true for exceptional acts, but it is not true for pervasive practices like sexual harassment, including rape, that are built into socially structural hierarchical relationships that are recognized as unequal only in islands of legal equality guarantees like employment, education, and federal housing. Equal pay has been the law for decades and still does not exist. Racial discrimination is nominally illegal in many ways but is still widely practiced against people of color, including in lethal forms. If the same cultural inequalities are permitted to operate in law as operate in the behavior the law prohibits—as exemplified by the rape myth that women who have had sex are inherently not credible, having somehow lost their credibility along with their virginity—equalizing attempts such as sexual harassment law encounter systemic drag.

This logjam, long paralyzing effective legal recourse for survivors of sexual harassment, is finally being broken, or starting to be, by the #MeToo movement. Structural misogyny, along with sexualized racism and class inequalities, is being publicly and persistently challenged by women's voices. The difference from prior attempts is that power is paying attention, at least sometimes. Powerful individuals and entities are taking sexual abuse seriously for once and acting against it as never before. No longer liars, no longer worthless, many of today's survivors are initiating consequences none of them could have gotten through any lawsuit—in part because the laws do not permit relief against individual perpetrators, but more because the survivors are being believed and valued as the law seldom has. Women have been saying these things forever. It is the response to them that is changing.

From experience, women often assume that any opposition to power will produce retaliation followed by retrenchment: not only that any progress made will be clawed back, but that those pushing for it will be punished. While often realistic, fear of blowback, as typifies battered women for example, can impede insistence on change and the collective mobilization it requires. Anxiety about backlash, however well-founded, endlessly keeps one's antennae attuned to giving power what pleases (and please pacifies) it. This can be more powerful than any real backlash. Dominance stays in place this way.

A related attitude that buys into subordination as if that will protect, even empower women has long fueled the belief that sexuality is a form of power, including at work, rather than a form of powerlessness. When I was working in the early 1970s to shape the concept and create the legal claim for sexual harassment when it did not exist, I called the organization 9-to-5 on the phone and explained to the woman who answered what I was trying to do, asking if she would be willing to talk with her members about my project on unwanted sexual attention and pressure at work. I was talking with anyone who would share experiences with me at the time. She finally called back, saying they could not help. Me: Why is that? Her: Our members think this would take away their only source of power. Me: I thought this was about a source of their powerlessness. Her: I understand what you're saying, but we can't help right now, maybe later. The organization grasped the issue shortly, but mistaking powerlessness for power hardly began recently and has hardly gone away. Among its underlying dynamics, together with maintaining an illusion of control when one is being controlled to hold onto self-respect, is a fear of the consequences of challenging a power seen as unchangeable, as inevitable. True, retaliation can be especially acute when one behaves as if one has rights. But #MeToo is giving a lie to the totality of male sexual entitlement and is exposing the price of *not* challenging its power and abuses of that power.

One measure of the success of #MeToo in its butterfly politics form to date is the muted presence verging on near impotence approaching absence of the usual deniers and apologists—opportunists, mostly women, who make their careers defending sexual abuse and abusers and attacking victims and their advocates. It has worked well for them. All has been quite quiet on that front since #MeToo began, allowing survivors an unprecedentedly clear public channel without that kind of static. So far #MeToo has not been denigrated as a "sex panic," the customary academic sneer that turns reports of sexual violation, with its actual harms, into moralistic crusades gone pompous and hysterical. In "moral panic" panics, rife disinformation and denigrating victim-blaming impel anyone with more practicality than principle to silence themselves and flee survivors. In these periods, no one wants to be identified as the dreaded "victim," a term that formerly meant only having been victimized, not a degraded existential condition of passivity. This backlash shoe has yet to drop. The formerly insatiable market in "feminists" attacking sexual assault survivors seems to have largely dried up for the moment. Closely connected is the relative absence of decrying #MeToo reports as "sex scandals." The moralistic conflation of sex considered inappropriate yet affirmatively wanted by both parties with sexual abuse, sexual exploitation, sexual violation, and predatory molestation is at last becoming disentangled.

Courts are typically more hidebound and less nimble than culture, although they are embedded in it and can and do change with it. The norms of rape culture continue to infuse much existing law. For instance, rape law still largely uses a "consent" standard often consistent with acquiescence to unequal power. Because it is an equality law, as rape law is not, sexual harassment law's standard is unwelcomeness. #MeToo is building a rich dialogue on lack of freedom under conditions of inequality, a neglected topic. Too, criminal law's burden of proof is often imported, tacitly or explicitly, into civil and administrative processes as a standard for the credibility of the victim when sexual abuse is investigated. Whatever a defendant stands to lose in these circumstances, it is not his liberty, making the criminal standard inappropriate, as is increasingly acknowledged.

Much more is needed. Investigative and adjudicative processes for sexual violation in most settings remain within the chain of command of the institution that is effectively being investigated rather than being independent of it. Even so-called independent investigations often are not. In any other setting, this would be recognized as corruption. Transparency is not the usual rule; secrecy is, protecting organizational brand, also known as cover-up. Liability standards for employers and educational institutions remain unrealistically stacked against sexual harassment survivors through standards of responsibility for perpetration that do not promote equality. Legal standards for retaliation—one of the biggest fears behind nonreporting—are not realistic in the sexual abuse context. Even before a case can get started, the federal law of discrimination has a statute of limitations of mere months, the shortest known in law, before almost any victim of sexual violation is past trauma, far less post-traumatic stress. No motion to change it exists in Congress.

Radiating out from sexual harassment to sex inequality as a whole, the #MeToo movement has stimulated a wider public discussion of equal hiring, equal numbers of women on boards, equal pay, and more women in politics, as well as brought further focus to the role of white supremacy in misogyny. Anyone who doubts that sexual abuse was central to the second-class status of women might consider what taking it seriously on a systemic basis has set off.

Sexual harassment encompasses, parallels, evokes, or echoes many other abuses of women and children from simple discrimination to other abuses of authority or trust or power, making it ideal for unifying across diversity. It is like sexual abuse in childhood in manipulating trust and dependency and institutionally betraying those who report. It often includes rape and raises all the issues of sex that is acquiesced to under conditions of unequal power. At work, sexual harassment makes all forms of women's work into a form of prostitution: coerced trading of sexual access for economic survival. In its fundamental dynamics, sexual harassment turns real work into an arm of the sex trade. The imperative to exchange sex for survival, or its possibility whether the survival is real or not, governs women's inequality, hence women's lives, worldwide. In prostitution, virtually all of women's and girls' options are precluded except for this one, making her consent to it, or choice of it, fraudulent and illusory. Women who supposedly have human rights, including equality rights in employment and education, are reduced to this floor of women's status when tolerance of sexual harassment, or sexual delivery in any form from objectification to rape, becomes a requirement in the paid labor force, including in paid housework, where sexual predation is widespread. The same applies to educational or career advancement. As one formerly prostituted woman colleague once cogently observed to me, ". . . and you have to do all that other work, too." Precisely this is what is being rejected by the #MeToo movement, even as an account of Kavanaugh's presence at gang rape parties— such parties are not unusual or extreme—was rejected because the lawyer representing the woman attesting to it is also the lawyer for a woman in pornography, who reported what amounts to quid pro quo sexual harassment by Trump in former years.[38]

If requiring sexual use as the price of survival is a human rights violation when combined with a real job or other entitlement, it certainly violates human rights all by itself, when it is the only thing a woman is permitted to be valued or paid for, even if her value approximates slime and the lion's share of the payment goes to others. Yet it is not effectively illegal to buy a person for sexual use in most places.[39] When will user men call forth revulsion and rejection when sexual harassment's dynamic in its pure form—prostitution—is exposed? Or will those who report it—women and girls, men and boys, transgender persons, disproportionately women of color and Native women—continue to be stigmatized, shamed, and blamed as their violators are vaunted and defended? When will this form of unequal predation be seen as the opposite of freedom, the men (as it almost always is) who outright buy others for sexual use be unmasked and penalized as the predators they are? That will be the transformation the present one has prepared.

Meantime, sexual harassment law can grow with #MeToo. Taking in #MeToo's changing norms could, predictably will, transform it. Issues being reconsidered have included the scope and content of nondisclosure agreements, independence of investigation and adjudication, equitability in procedures, and elimination of criminal law standards from civil and administrative adjudications. Some practical steps could help capture the movement's insights. Changes in institutional regulations, administrative rules, or statutes could include prohibitions or limits on various forms of secrecy and nontransparency that hide the extent of sexual abuse and enforce survivor isolation, such as forced arbitration, silencing nondisclosure agreements in cases of physical attacks and multiple perpetration, and settlements forcibly confidential. A realistic federal statute of limitations for all forms of discrimination, including sexual harassment, is essential. What does it mean, if not that legislators know discrimination is rampant and want to disappear it, that the statute of limitations for discrimination is the shortest in law? Damage caps for harassment minimize the extent of its harm by suppressing its measure and can discourage contingent representation. Being able to sue individual perpetrators and their enablers, jointly with institutions, could shift perceived incentives for this behavior. Evidentiary standards for reasonableness and unwelcomeness could alter. But the only legal change in U.S. law that matches the movement's scale would be the passage of an Equal Rights Amendment. That would, at minimum, expand the congressional power to legislate against sexual abuse. It could renovate the constitutional interpretations of equality in a more substantive including intersectional direction, reconfiguring the concept itself by guaranteeing sex equality under the Constitution for all for once.

Sincere revulsion against sexually harassing behavior, as opposed to revulsion at reports of sexually harassing behavior, could change workplaces and schools, even streets. It could restrain repeat predators as well as the occasional and casual exploiters. as the law so far has not. Shunning perpetrators as sex bigots who take advantage of the vulnerabilities of inequality could transform societies. Many social sectors are beginning to recognize their obligation to foster environments free from sexual objectification, pressure, or aggression, in which reporting of sexual abuse is welcomed rather than punished, accountability not impunity prevails for individuals and institutions that engage in or enable such abuse, and excellence and inclusion rather than hierarchy and fear operate as real rather than rhetorical standards. All this cuts to the core of rape culture so could change it. Simple linguistic shifts would also help. It is still generally said that women "allege" or "claim" they were sexually assaulted; those accused then "say" or "assert" it did not happen or "deny" what was alleged. Survivors could "report" sexual violation, or "say" they were sexually violated. The accused could then "allege" or "claim" it did not occur, or occur as reported. Rehabilitation needs to be discussed with, not without, reckoning.[40]

The #MeToo mobilization, this uprising of the formerly disregarded, has made increasingly untenable the assumption that the one who reports sexual abuse is a lying slut. That already is changing everything. A lot of the sexual harassment that has been a constant condition of women's lives is probably not being inflicted at this moment.

As butterflies take flight from beneath the shadow of the law, imagine the first rise in women's status since the vote. Conceive a revolution without violence against domination and aggression. Envision a moment of truth and a movement of transformation for the sexually violated toward a more equal, therefore more peaceful and just world. It is happening all around us right now.

Catharine A. MacKinnon
Cambridge, Massachusetts

———————————

Some of the themes and locutions contained in this Preface previously appeared in opeds in *The Guardian,* "How Litigation Laid the Ground for Accountability After #MeToo," *The Guardian,* Dec.

23, 2017, http://www.theguardian.com/commentisfree/2017/dec/23 /how-litigation-laid-the-ground-for-accountability-after-metoo and the *New York Times,* "#MeToo and Law's Limitations," *New York Times,* Feb. 5, 2018, https://www.nytimes.com/2018/02/04/opinion/ metoo-law-legal-system.html; Sarah Polley, Nona Willis Aronowitz, Katie J. M. Baker, Catharine A. MacKinnon, Stephen Marche, Shanita Hubbard, Daphne Merkin, Amber Tamblyn, and Roxane Gay, "'This Moment Turned Out to Be Fleeting': Nine reflections on #MeToo, one year on," *New York Times,* Oct. 6, 2018, https://www .nytimes.com/2018/10/06/opinion/me-too-weinstein-one-year.html; and in an interview in *Ms.,* Brock Colyar, "The Ms. Q&A: Catharine MacKinnon Weighs in on the #MeToo Movement," *Ms. Magazine Blog* (July 30, 2018) http://msmagazine.com/blog/2018/07 /30/ms-qa-catharine-mackinnon-weighs-metoo-movement/. A version was delivered as The Markowitz Lecture titled "Sexual Harassment: The Law, the Politics, the Movement," at Brandeis University on October 14, 2018.

Insightful comments from Lisa Cardyn, Diane Rosenfeld, Joy De Menil, Lori Watson, and Cass Sunstein sharpened it. Lori Interlicchio's assistance on the notes was skilled and creative. The support of the Cook Fund and the assistance of the University of Michigan Law Library was, as always, indispensable. Daysha Hampton, Diane Ellis, and Adolfo Rico made my life possible, no exaggeration, during its writing. They are angels. Each of them has my deepest gratitude.

Notes

1. See, e.g., Catharine A. MacKinnon, *Sexual Harassment of Working Women: A Case of Sex Discrimination* (New Haven, CT: Yale University Press 1979), laying foundation and chronicling early development.
2. The *New York Times* reported that since #MeToo began in 2017, "at least 200 prominent men have lost their jobs after public allegations of sexual harassment." Audrey Carlsen, Maya Salam, and Claire Cain Miller, "How #MeToo Realigned the Corridors of Power," *New York Times,* Oct. 24, 2018.
3. Nomination of the Honorable Brett M. Kavanaugh to be an Associate

Justice of the Supreme Court of the United States (Day 5): Hearing Before the S. Judiciary Comm., 115th Cong. (2018)

4. See Susan Estrich, "Teaching Rape Law," *Yale Law Journal* 102, no. 2 (1992): 509–520 (developing the "slut, nut, so what" analysis).

5. Sheryl Gay Stolberg, "Senate Confirms Kavanaugh to the Supreme Court," *New York Times,* Oct. 6, 2018, https://www.nytimes.com/2018/10/06/us/politics/brett-kavanaugh-supreme-court.html?action=click&module=RelatedCoverage&pgtype=Article&region=

6. For discussion, see Catharine A. MacKinnon, "Speaking Truth to Power," in Catharine A. MacKinnon, ed., *Women's Lives, Men's Laws* 277 (Cambridge, MA: Belknap Press of Harvard University Press 2005).

7. This initiative was for women and girls of color in particular but not exclusively. See Christen A. Johnson, KT Hawbaker, Randi Stevenson, Susan Moskop, and Lauren Hill, "#MeToo: A Timeline of Events," *Chicago Tribune,* Sept. 26, 2018, http://www.chicagotribune.com/lifestyles/ct-me-too-timeline-20171208-htmlstory.html; Tarana Burke, "The Inception," JustBEInc, accessed Oct. 4, 2018, http://justbeinc.wixsite.com/justbeinc/the-me-too-movement-cmml. (The Myspace page where the MeToo movement's information was originally created can apparently no longer be accessed.)

8. See Mandel v. M&Q Packaging Corp, 706 F.3d 157, 167 (3d Cir. 2013) ("[S]o-called 'me too' evidence in an employment discrimination case is neither per se admissible nor per se inadmissible," its relevance fact-based and depending on the closeness of its relation to plaintiff's facts and theory, finding the evidence properly excluded in that case (emphasis omitted)). See also Sprint/United Mgmt. Co. v. Mendelsohn, 552 U.S. 379, 388 (2008) (holding in age discrimination case, without using "me too" phrase, that such evidence is within discretion of trial judge depending upon proximity of alleged facts to plaintiff's case).

9. Although these numbers are a moving target, as investigations are closed when completed, as of September 22, 2017, there were 360 open investigations. Sarah Brown, "What Does the End of Obama's Title IX Guidance Mean for Colleges?" *The Chronicle of Higher Education,* Sept. 22, 2017, https://www.chronicle.com/article/What-Does-the-End-of-Obama-s/241281. See also Nick Anderson, "At First, 55 Schools Faced Sexual Violence Investigations. Now the List Has Quadrupled.," *Washington Post,* Jan. 18, 2017, https://www.washingtonpost.com/news/grade-point/wp/2017/01/18/at-first-55-schools-faced-sexual-violence-investigations-now-the-list-has-quadrupled/?utm_term=.15977fc8d3a1.

10. Alexander v. Yale Univ., 631 F.2d 178 (2d Cir. 1980).

11. Alyssa Milano (@Alyssa_Milano), "If you've been sexually harassed or assaulted write 'me too' as a reply to this tweet," Twitter, Oct. 15, 2017, https://twitter.com/alyssa_milano/status/919659438700670976?lang=en.

12. Andrea Park, "#MeToo Reaches 85 Countries with 1.7M Tweets," *CBS News,* Oct. 24, 2017, https://www.cbsnews.com/news/metoo-reaches-85-countries-with-1-7-million-tweets/. This article documents that as of October 24, 2017, "Twitter confirmed to CBS News that over 1.7 million tweets included the hashtag '#MeToo,' with 85 countries that had at least 1,000 #MeToo tweets." "[T]here were more than 12 million posts, comments and reactions regarding 'Me Too' in less than 24 hours [of Milano's tweet], by 4.7 million users around the world. As of Oct. 17, 2017, Facebook said 45 percent of users in the U.S. have had friends who posted 'me too.'" (A reaction is not a post but an interaction with one.)

13. Jodi Kantor and Meghan Twohey, "Sexual Misconduct Claims Trail a Hollywood Mogul," *New York Times,* Oct. 6, 2017, A1.

14. Ronan Farrow, "Abuses of Power: Stories from the Women Harmed by Hollywood's Most Influential Producer," *New Yorker,* Oct. 23, 2017, 42.

15. Twenty years ago, as keynote at the Journalism and Women Symposium (JAWS) on September 12, 1998, I urged journalists to do this. MacKinnon, *Women's Lives, Men's Laws,* 293 ("What women in the media can do, and sometimes win the fight to do, is place their stories of men's sexual mistreatment of women in real context. Sexual abuse is an everyday event—common, systematic, nonexceptional. Talk about it as if you know what you are talking about. Women in the press have been abused just as vast numbers of women in every profession have. Report and analyze events as if you live in the world we know we live in, in which sexual use, manipulation, and abuse can be believed to happen because they do happen. Talk about it as if it hurts and as if it matters because it does hurt and it does matter.")

16. Large-scale surveys of working women estimate that approximately 1 in 2 women will be harassed during their academic or working lives. See Louise F. Fitzgerald, "Sexual Harassment: Violence Against Women in the Workplace," *American Psychologist* 48, no. 10 (1993): 1070–76. When asked whether they have been "sexually harassed," fewer respondents answer affirmatively than when asked about sexual behaviors and experiences of the "has anyone ever" kind. See Vickie J. Magley et al., "Outcomes of Self-Labeling Sexual Harassment," *Journal of Applied Psychology* 84, no. 3 (June 1999): 390–402; Louise F. Fitzgerald et al.,

"Measuring Sexual Harassment: Theoretical and Psychometric Advances," *Basic & Applied Social Psychology* 17, no. 4 (Dec. 1995): 425–445. The same psychological damage is experienced by women who have harassing experiences but do not label them as such as those who do label them correctly. Magley et al., "Outcomes of Self-Labeling," 399. For more information on sexual harassment, see generally Catharine A. MacKinnon, *Sex Equality* (3rd ed., New York, Foundation Press 2016) 1002–1207.

17. MacKinnon, *Sexual Harassment of Working Women*, 55.

18. Hillary Clinton, interview by Matt Lauer, *Today Show*, NBC, Jan. 27, 1998, available at C-SPAN, video, 11:33, https://www.c-span.org/video/?99377-1/today-Tuesday.

19. For further discussion of this and the Paula Jones case, see Catharine A. MacKinnon, Afterword to *Directions in Sexual Harassment Law*, eds. Catharine A. MacKinnon and Reva B. Siegel, (New Haven, CT: Yale University Press 2004), 687–93.

20. For her updated reflections, see Monica Lewinsky, "Emerging from 'the House of Gaslight' in the Age of #MeToo," *Vanity Fair*, Feb. 25, 2018, https://www.vanityfair.com/news/2018/02/monica-lewinsky-in-the-age-of-metoo. We are all a work in progress.

21. "Trump Job Approval (Weekly), Gallup, accessed Oct. 5, 2018, https://news.gallup.com/poll/203207/trump-job-approval-weekly.aspx?g_source=link_newsv9&g_campaign=item_203198&g_medium=copy.

22. "Watch: Donald Trump Recorded Having Extremely Lewd Conversation about Women in 2005," *Washington Post*, video, Oct. 7, 2016, https://www.washingtonpost.com/video/national/watch-donald-trump-recorded-having-extremely-lewd-conversation-about-women-in-2005/2016/10/07/3bf16d1e-8caf-11e6-8cdc-4fbb1973b506_video.html?utm_term=.cf5903a3bb71.

23. Eliza Relman, "The 22 Women Who Have Accused Trump of Sexual Misconduct," *Business Insider*, Sept. 26, 2018, https://www.businessinsider.com/women-accused-trump-sexual-misconduct-list-2017-12.

24. See Jamilah King, "Kimberlé Crenshaw Reveals What Donald Trump and Clarence Thomas Have in Common," *Mic*, Dec. 13, 2016, https://mic.com/articles/161796/kimberl-crenshaw-nails-what-donald-trump-and-clarence-thomas-have-in-common#.j76Ix3IU9. I heard Professor Crenshaw discuss this analysis several times in public in 2018.

25. See Citizens United v. Federal Election Commission, 558 U.S. 310 (2010) (5–4 decision holding political spending is political speech for corpora-

tions or unions); Shelby County v. Holder, 570 U.S. 2 (2013) (5–4 decision striking down formula for determining racial discrimination in voting).

26. Tray Connor, "Cosby Trial: Juror Says it was a 'True Deadlock,'" *NBC News,* June 22, 2017, https://www.nbcnews.com/storyline/bill-cosby-scandal /cosby-trial-juror-says-it-was-true-deadlock-n775666.

27. Jen Kirby, "Cosby Defense Attorneys Used Personal Attacks to Try to Discredit Witnesses," *Vox,* Apr. 13, 2018, https://www.vox.com/2018 /4/13/17234172/bill-cosby-trial-accusers-janice-dickinson-testimony.

28. Maggie Astor, "California Voters Remove Judge Aaron Persky, Who Gave a 6-Month Sentence for Sexual Assault," *New York Times,* June 6, 2018, https://www.nytimes.com/2018/06/06/us/politics/judge-persky-brock-tur ner-recall.html.

29. Katie J.M. Baker, "Here's the Powerful Letter the Stanford Victim Read to Her Attacker," *Buzzfeed News,* June 3, 2016, https://www.buzzfeednews. com/article/katiejmbaker/heres-the-powerful-letter-the-stanford-victim- read-to-her-ra.

30. A.B. 701 (Cal. 2016); A.B. 288 (Cal. 2016); See also Astor, "California Voters," (Within four months of the sentence, California lawmakers "enacted mandatory minimum sentences in sexual assault cases and closed a loophole in which penetrative sexual assault could be punished less harshly if the victim was too intoxicated to physically resist.")

31. Christine Hauser, "Larry Nassar is Sentenced to Another 40 to 125 Years in Prison," *New York Times,* Feb. 5, 2018, https://www.nytimes.com/2018 /02/05/sports/larry-nassar-sentencing-hearing.html.

32. Sarah Hoye, "Man Sues Philadelphia Archdiocese, Claiming He was Abused as Teen," *CNN,* Mar. 7, 2011, http://www.cnn.com/2011/CRIME /03/07/pennsylvania.church.lawsuit/index.html; Al Goodman, "Catholic Sexual Abuse Case is Spain's Biggest of its Kind, Has Pope's Attention," *CNN,* Nov. 27, 2014, https://edition.cnn.com/2014/11/26/world/europe /spain-sexual-abuse-priest-charges/index.html.

33. See, e.g., Pascale Bonnefoy and Austin Ramzy, "Pope's Defense of Chilean Bishop in Sex Abuse Scandal Causes Outrage," *New York Times,* Jan. 19, 2018, https://www.nytimes.com/2018/01/19/world/americas/pope-sex-ab use-chile.html, and many more such reports into the present.

34. Minarsky v. Susquehanna Cty., 895 F.3d 303, 313 n.12 (3d Cir. 2018):

This appeal comes to us in the midst of national news regarding a veritable firestorm of allegations of rampant sexual misconduct that has been closeted for years, not reported by the victims. It has come to light, years later, that people in positions of power and celebrity have exploited their authority to make unwanted sexual advances. In many such instances, the harasser wielded control over the harassed individual's employment or work environment. In nearly all of the instances, the victims asserted a plausible fear of serious adverse consequences had they spoken up at the time that the conduct occurred. While the policy underlying [Supreme Court standards in] *Faragher-Ellerth* places the onus on the harassed employee to report her harasser, and would fault her for not calling out this conduct so as to prevent it, a jury could conclude that the employee's non-reporting was understandable, perhaps even reasonable. That is, there may be a certain fallacy that underlies the notion that reporting sexual misconduct will end it. Victims do not always view it in this way. Instead, they anticipate negative consequences or fear that the harassers will face no reprimand; thus, more often than not, victims choose not to report the harassment.

Recent news articles report that studies have shown that not only is sex-based harassment in the workplace pervasive, but also the failure to report is widespread. Nearly one-third of American women have experienced unwanted sexual advances from male coworkers, and nearly a quarter of American women have experienced such advances from men who had influence over the conditions of their employment, according to an ABC News/Washington Post poll from October of 2017. Most all of the women who experienced harassment report that the male harassers faced no consequences (citing ABC News/Washington Post, Unwanted Sexual Advances: Not Just a Hollywood Story, Oct. 17, 2017, www.langerresearch.com/wp-content/uploads/1192a1SexualHarassment.pdf).

Additionally, three out of four women who have been harassed fail to report it. A 2016 Equal Employment Opportunity Commission (EEOC) Select Task Force study found that approximately 75 percent of those who experienced harassment never reported it or filed a complaint, but instead would 'avoid the harasser, deny or downplay the gravity of the situation, or attempt to ignore, forget, or endure the behavior.' . . . Those employees who faced harassing behavior did not report this experience 'because they fear[ed] disbelief of their claim, inaction on their claim, blame, or social or professional retaliation' (quoting Chai R. Feldblum and Victoria A Lipnic, *Select Task Force, on the Study of Harassment in the Workplace* (EEOC, June 2016), at v, https://www.eeoc.gov/eeoc/task_force/harassment/upload/report .pdf (alteration in original); then citing Stefanie K. Johnson, Jessica Kirk, and Ksenia Keplinger, "Why We Fail to Report Sexual Harassment," *Harvard Business Review,* Oct. 4, 2016, http://hbr.org/2016/10 /why-we-fail-to-report-sexual-harassment (women do not report harassment because of retaliation fears, the bystander effect, and male-dominated work environments).

35. Complaint and Demand for Jury Trial, Noble v. Weinstein, No. 1:17-cv-09260 (S.D.N.Y. Nov. 27, 2017) at 27 ("In this context, Harvey's statements, while less than concrete, are highly material. When they are relied upon, such reliance is reasonable.").

36. Complaint for Damages and Equitable Relief, Judd v. Weinstein, No. 2:18-cv-05724 (C.D.C. June 28, 2018) (removed from Los Angeles Superior Court).

37. National Domestic Workers Alliance, "Nation's 2.5 Million Domestic Workers Applaud #TIMESUP," Jan. 2, 2018, https://www.domesticwork ers.org/release/nation%E2%80%99s-25-million-domestic-workers-ap plaud-timesup.

38. Peter Baker and Nicholas Fandos, "Show How You Feel, Kavavaugh Was Told, and a Nomination Was Saved," *New York Times,* Oct. 6, 2018, https://www.nytimes.com/2018/ 10/06/us/politics/kavanaugh-vote-confirmation-process.html.

39. The Nordic model, which does just this, is discussed infra in "Trafficking, Prostitution, and Inequality."

40. See Leah Litman, Emily Murphy, and Katherine H. Ku, "Opinion: A Comeback, but No Reckoning," *New York Times,* Aug. 5, 2018, https:// www.nytimes.com/2018/08/02/opinion/sunday/alex-kozinski-harass ment-allegations-comeback.html, opposing comeback without meaningful reckoning.

Butterfly Politics

Butterfly Politics

You don't see something until you have the right metaphor to let you perceive it.

—*Robert Stenson Shaw*

"The butterfly effect" was coined in 1972 by Edward Lorenz in a talk titled "Does the flap of a butterfly's wings in Brazil set off a tornado in Texas?"[1] It charmingly models (mathematically by many, not by me) how some extremely small simple actions, properly targeted, can come to have highly complex and large effects in certain contexts.[2] Yes: a butterfly opening and closing its wings in Brazil *can* ultimately produce a tornado in Texas, according to chaos theory's understanding of complex causality in dynamic unstable systems.[3]

Butterfly politics means the right small human intervention in an unstable political system can sooner or later have large complex reverberations. As an organizing metaphor and central conceit for this volume, it coheres forty years of flights of activism that, through recursion in a collective context, have eventuated or are eventuating in storms, sometimes tornados, in gender relations through law.

Encompassing legal and political interventions from 1976 to 2016, this volume collects moments of attempts to change the inequality of women to men and reflections on those attempts. As advocacy, many of the pieces mark the first time a particular idea showed its face in public, an idea that has now become established or at least familiar. The work on substantive equality, torture, and rape as a genocidal weapon are examples.[4] Other pieces initiate or urge changes that are still in process or have yet to take place, for example in the legal approach to prostitution, despite considerable social movement and momentum.[5] This also characterizes the initiatives against pornography and rape, and for a constitutional equality amendment.[6] Many of the discursive moments captured here proved decisively initiatory,

1

such as the testimony on pornography in Minneapolis.[7] The reverberations set off are still gathering force. Others reflect on and cohere
a series of such moments or consider their costs, attempting to grasp
the dynamic processes at work.[8] The waves of some moments captured here, especially those involving academia—a sphere more resistant to change than society or law—still reverberate almost silently
by most external measures.[9] Some of these talks are closer to pure
protest and dissent.

Almost all of these writings were spoken first; the remaining few
that were written first were dialogic in conception and written by
ear.[10] In terms of their resonating effects, their music—harmonies, dis-
sonances, rhythms—matters as much as their words. They retain the
interactive dynamics of their audiences. If the approaches to law in
this volume are in some sense deeply American, meaning they come
from everywhere, in their travels they have been deeply imprinted by
women everywhere, becoming collaborative with the audiences to
which they were, in the moments captured here, given. Even the pieces
in reflective mode were conceived as moving ripples on an ongoing
tide, aiming—hopefully including through this present iteration—not
to predict or describe but to alter their world. Some of the changes
undertaken here remain in glacial near-stasis, even if tectonic shifts
are gathering down deep. Some are in an ongoing process of being
accomplished. Some can be considered essentially achieved in the
sense of moving in the right direction. The project of every one is
change.

I am regularly asked, often with a tone of incredulity, how I do
what I do in law. Part of the puzzlement arises because it is apparently difficult to accept that some ideas, especially ideas that have
become common currency, had an actual origin. The butterfly theory
is a partial response. A butterfly politics highlights crucial dimensions
of legal political activism, including the domain of action, strategic
choice of moments of initiation, dynamics of intervention and blowback and its anticipation, and the collaborative effects of collective
recursion.

As to the nature of the domain, if any social system is complex and unstable, it is sex inequality. Complex, among other reasons, because of its simultaneous multiple interacting variables including race and class and sexuality and age. Intrinsically unstable, not least because it is predicated on the lie of women's natural inferiority to men and men's natural superiority to women, termed difference in ideological and legal and common parlance. Life, given half a chance, refutes it every day. The extraordinary tenacity of such a system for structuring and distributing power, including hierarchy of status—making it political—in the face of evidence and contestation of its false basis and some acknowledgment of its injustice has, when not taken for granted, frequently baffled analysts and frustrated activists. A major reason for its persistence is that dominant approaches to inequality have misdiagnosed the nature of the system, hence the necessary interventions to change it, including its structures, vectors, and trajectories, its flexible genius for indulgences and deprivations, including its rendering of the social status quo baseline as natural. By taking a different tack, some of the most substantial changes made in sex inequality through law—a number of which this book reflects and reflects upon—have occurred through unconventional and unprecedented approaches and arguments, usually with no institutional backing. A butterfly opening its wings can produce cyclones, or at least thunder claps, worldwide. The legal claim for sexual harassment,[11] with the substantive theory of equality embedded in it and growing out of it, exemplifies this dynamic in spades.

Butterfly politics is one way to understand how critical intervention can affect systemic transformation in the gender system. If the appropriateness of the metaphor is recognizable, its application to legal strategy for social change, specifically to a politics of action toward ending gender inequality through law, is new. Thinking about society and politics scientifically, producing the social sciences, is based on analogy to begin with, adapting to social life tools typically first developed in the physical sciences. Other scientific metaphors, such as evolution or path dependence,[12] have stimulated legal thinking rather than being used as rigid templates.[13] These metaphors can also help focus overlooked variables. For instance, Paul Ormerod usefully pointed out in his *Butterfly Economics* adaptation of the butterfly theory that existing economic models, because they failed to take account of the influence of consumers on each other, made accurate economic prediction difficult.[14] Relationships matter. They matter and can be overlooked in politics as well, especially given that men and women are often found in relationship with one another. Indeed, change in the patterns of those relationships is the goal of some sex equality initiatives.

If any analysis from the physical sciences resonates with efforts to change sex inequality for those who have engaged in those efforts, rather than observed them from armchairs or towers as bystanders on the sidelines, it is one of orderly disorder in complex systems of nonlinear dynamics producing difficult-to-predict outcomes initiated from unexpected small locales. Chaos does not mean chaotic in the sense of lacking any coherence or pattern. "Chaos here does not mean disorder, but that accurate predictions about where a system is headed are hard."[15] Complex patterns emerge in what initially appeared to be patternless. Chaos theory regards complexity and nonlinear causality's difficulty of prediction not as a failure of analysis but as the analysis itself. "Chaos theory does not merely recognize complexity but embraces it as the norm."[16] In physical science, some phenomena, classically weather patterns, have been more accurately captured as a result. Given that male dominance has historically been regarded as inevitable as weather, and that the weather has been changed by human societies more than male dominance has, there is a certain symmetry here.

Accurately identifying the substance of the system into which intervention is directed is obviously crucial. With weather patterns, it is environmental elements: air, water, temperature, motion, etc. In this respect, again by analogy, much work for sex equality has evidently failed. It has addressed some symptomatic outcomes but few causes. Conventional approaches usually do not face the key dynamic of sexism—hierarchy, specifically of men over women and other men— or its key site in my view, sexuality. Weather models would not work if scientists ignored small consistent rises in global temperature because they did not like thinking about climate change. Legal strategies that prefer to contend with dynamics that are not what is driving things, on terrain that is not where it is principally driven, because that produces less opposition or is more pleasant, can do some things but cannot hope to alter them, especially when they are structurally entrenched. As Leo Tolstoy once put it, "I know that most men, including those at ease with problems of the greatest complexity, can seldom accept even the simplest and most obvious truth if it be such as would oblige them to admit the falsity of conclusions which they have delighted in explaining to colleagues, which they have proudly taught to others, and which they have woven, thread by thread, into the fabric of their lives."[17] The fact that the career success, often survival, of individual intellectuals, academics, and lawyers, with other possible agents of change is substantially predicated on pleasing power provides a powerful incentive to keep one's wings folded.

Chaos theory's central notion of sensitivity to initial conditions resonates strongly with anyone who has worked hands-on with law to produce social change. Often called "sensitive dependence," it means that for systems of nonlinear nonmechanical dynamics, even the smallest shift in conditions at the outset, such as the facts of particular cases, can eventuate in dramatic changes in results in the long term. "[S]mall differences in initial variables will always produce dramatic variations in final outcomes."[18] As not linear and not mechanical, the common law can be a promising sphere of application for this model of complex recursion because of its rule of precedent. A single breakthrough iterated through many variations can open a complex flood tide in a distinctive direction, even as the precedential system resists an initial breakthrough for which there is no precedent. For agents of social change, acting consciously, knowing that extremely small initial conditions can be amplified exponentially over time through systemic recursion to radically shift the way a system behaves, presents the risk, the caution, and the hope.

The critical role of setting things up right from the beginning can be considered throughout the interventions that this book gathers.

One example is creating sexual harassment as a legal claim for sex discrimination. Making clear it is sexual and that means it is gender-based, because that actually is what the behavior is, rather than something else (say, biological) that the legal system might have more easily digested, means that recursion will be stimulated in the domain the problem actually inhabits. Over legal and political ups and downs, the basic paradigm of sexual harassment has held, changing society and politics.[19] Largely the right outcome will repeat, and it will extend, for example, to gay and lesbian and transgender rights,[20] in which students have participated in the butterfly effect, because the wing flap selected the accurate domain. Essential for accessing this dynamic is addressing in law what the problem actually is in reality. This is one reason abstractions do not work: there is no air under them. The definition of rape internationally predicated on coercion, with consent so irrelevant as not to require mention, has survived repeated attempts to replace it and has expanded its reach.[21] The development of the concept "gender crime" on the international stage, where it is now accepted,[22] further illustrates.

The specific tolerance built into nonlinear processes promotes course correction. "Simply put, a linear process, given a slight nudge, tends to remain slightly off track. A nonlinear process, given the same nudge, tends to return to its starting point."[23] Constitutional equality in Canada provides an example.[24] Originally accepting the substantive equality theory of hierarchy in historic disadvantage, the Supreme Court of Canada lost its way for a couple of decades, using the old equality model under the name of the new one, but proved capable of course correction, returning to the original breakthrough.[25] Remaining slightly off track is a charitable description of most attempts to change equality law and rape law in the United States. Engaging legal systems with linear strategies that participate in existing power dynamics and concede existing power structures reiterates them, proceeding even more determinately to paint us into a corner. The tendency of legal systems to reinscribe existing structures of power when confronted with challenges that do not actually face their problems could hardly be described more aptly. By contrast, a nudge that engages nonlinear process consciously, correctly begun, can be part of changing it. Any time can be a new beginning.

The theory that emerges from complex causality in the unstable, complex nonlinear nonmechanical system that is the law and politics of gender inequality is thus neither simply deterministic, as much legal realism would have it, nor cynically despairing, as critical legal theory could lead one to believe. By comparison, traditional theories, realism old or new, public choice theory, or pluralism for instance, tend to be reductionist, linear, unreflective of social complexity (which does not happen in a test tube and cannot be captured even in a multiple regression), and unadapted to the substantive realities of male dominance. Bemoaning unintended consequences, for example, reveals an unrealistic, mechanistic, and linear illusion about the nature of social life, legal change, and political activism.

By capturing practice in motion, as it is being engaged in, this collection, in light of its organizing concept, opens onto complicated perceptions and deep understandings in the moment of their unfolding. It may begin to explain how some changes can be ongoing, ready to erupt given sufficient momentum, as with the issue of pornography, even when the inequality it challenges has blocked their authoritative establishment. It exposes patterns where none were visible and may help reveal why certain arguments are persuasive, certain strategies worked, and some changes have seemingly come out of nowhere to suddenly be everywhere, for instance the Swedish model on prostitution, which decriminalizes people sold in prostitution and criminalizes sellers and, most distinctively, buyers.[26] The butterfly metaphor is not intended to apply to everything with complicated, seemingly inscrutable or illogical dynamics, or to be limited to sex inequality exclusively. It is offered as a useful image here, perhaps a heuristic elsewhere, beginning in other settings of inequality.

Butterfly politics, above all, is not an individual dynamic. The preconditions and subsequent pickups and recursions that produce the tornado, if one eventuates, are collective. Many of the pieces in this collection represent initial perturbations, unsettling the waters in what appeared to be an isolated local setting, such as the original proposal of the civil rights ordinance against pornography.[27] Some reflect later effects and subsequent attempts to amplify them. Some analyze change that has occurred in which prior interventions participated. Some are part of ongoing changes or propose changes that have yet to be realized.[28] Discursive moments in time are collected in which legal, social, and political change are urged or contemplated. Many more such moments occurred behind the scenes confidentially, even as some pieces in this volume discuss some of them through their public emergence.

The butterfly metaphor can animate political activism and support equality advocacy: small actions in a collective context can produce systemic changes. Butterfly politics encourages multidimensional political thinking, precise engagement, principled creativity, imagination, instinct, and adaptability. It inspires interventions, even tiny ones. It opens discussion and debate on strategy and substance as part of a disciplined process of transformation toward equality of the sexes. It envisions and joins hands with old and new forms of organizing. Equality seekers, spread your wings. You're stronger than you think. You never know what can happen.

I. Change

ONE

To Change the World for Women

An approach to activist law for women that is critical in theory yet engaged in practice was advocated here, then implemented between then and now. How effectively to approach change for women through law is the problem this talk takes up,[1] drawing on the analysis later published in *Toward a Feminist Theory of the State*.[2] Yet in retrospect, the substance through which this "how" question is explored surprisingly predicts a "what" agenda, as developed to the end of the century and beyond. Challenges to the law of sexual harassment, just established in the educational context,[3] are reflected upon. We still confront them in sexual harassment cases, which have exploded exponentially in numbers. The core theory of the civil remedy of the Violence Against Women Act[4] and of the antipornography civil rights ordinance[5]—neither of which had been conceived in those forms—is clearly anticipated. Although there is much water under both bridges, we still have neither law and need both. Themes revolving around rape in reality and under law, principally the lack of fit between the two, together with nascent understandings of the converged role of race and sex that, when subsequently brilliantly theorized, became intersectionality,[6] are foreshadowed in applied forms. Rape law reform has crawled in this direction but has not yet arrived,[7] nor have intersectional understandings yet fully reconfigured equality thinking. In other words, the specific concerns of this talk form a roadmap that can be seen to animate the direction of much work of the subsequent decades, extending into the present and beyond.

———————————

I went to law school because I wanted to change the world for women. One of the first things I learned there—something that pervaded my legal education whether my teachers, with exceptions, meant it to or not—was that in order to be a lawyer, it was necessary to strip oneself of passion, commitment, identification, feelings, community loyalties. Become objective, disinterested, fair, dispassionate. In a word: legal. The law is or should be neutral, was the idea, so a proper lawyer is a neutral instrument.

Together with this was a view that the law is everything. To change society—or what is responsible for society being the way it is—change law. John Stuart Mill's work illustrated the place of this idea in liberalism.[8] In this view, women were subjected in society because they were subjected in the law of the family. Implicit is a notion that law is all-powerful. Lawyers have a particular investment in this idea; it makes us the primary social activists.

Law school also taught the opposite idea: that the law is nothing. All law does is reflect the way society is. To produce social changes, work at a social level, abdicate the legal arena, because it is only a passive tool in the hands of society's manipulators. It merely reflects the way things are, the interests of those with power. Nothing can be done with it for the powerless.

Neither of these views seems adequate to the social system of women and law's relation to it. As legal advocates for women, we do not, I think, have a theory of what we are doing in the specific political context of sex inequality. Yes, the law is powerful in constructing social options. Yes, the law reflects forms of power that exist. But we need to devise what I would call a feminist theory of the state that looks at law from women's point of view, to see what can be done with it from there.

This may sound simple, but it is profoundly difficult and complex. Systematically, it has never been tried. Looking at the law from women's point of view has, of course, to embrace all women including all our sisters who are not with us today, each of us in our complexity, ambiguity, and divisions in our identifications, along with our attempts to reject the stereotypes we have been saddled with. "All women" includes not only those who do not identify as feminist but also those who deny that women and men are socially unequal. It includes women who embrace subordination to men. To have a feminist theory of law, hence a theory of our role as lawyers, we need to examine the law from the standpoint of this "all women." Quite obviously, this must encompass Black women, Latinas, all third-world women, including those, for example, who believe that if they still have a clitoris, they are ugly and unclean, and those who bound their own and each other's feet because they thought that it was (and it was) essential to their attractiveness and future. If they are not here, our equivalent to them is; participation and complicity in our own oppression is hard to avoid.

I pursue this task here through three issues: rape, sexual harassment, and pornography. These issues were chosen because I believe that women's sexuality is at the core of the way we are socially defined and therefore denigrated as women and because sexuality has been largely ignored as a factor in women's inequality to men. This means that the way the law treats issues of women's sexuality is a crucial indicator and determinant of women's status as a sex.

Over the past ten years, many women have attempted to pursue changes in the rape law and its administration. Rape is legally defined as sexual intercourse with force and without consent. The idea is to know it through its distinction from ordinary sexual intercourse, which is not forced and is consensual. Presumably, what makes it criminal distinguishes it from what most men do and from what most women experience.

Intercourse without consent—the one-sidedness is striking. Consent means somebody else initiates; you agree or not. But sexuality is supposed to be mutual. If rape means lack of consent, sex is apparently not envisioned to be mutual, but only consented to, acceded to. Equal initiation is not fundamental to the model. This is consistent with what has been found about much heterosexual intercourse. Women know from our own lives about the everyday construction of sexual intercourse. We are told that sex is something men do to women—men initiate it. Women at most approve that initiation or don't. At least, that is the dominant model, and it is built into the rape law.

Rape is also distinguished from sex by virtue of force. A fundamental question is whether the presence of force can be distinguished with a hard line from what ordinarily goes on between women and men under conditions of social inequality. As convicted rapists see themselves and are seen by other prison inmates, all they did wrong was get caught. They think that they are in prison for doing something that is little different from what most men do most of the time. Life taught them this. Add this to the fact that most rapes, it appears from studies, are not reported.[9] This indicates that women do not think the legal system will recognize their violation and vindicate their interests.

Many women who have gone through rape trials see the trial as an extension of the rape.[10] The burdens of proof, the legal assumptions, the disbelief they encounter, mean that their sexuality can be violated without consequences to the violator. The perspective they encounter is that what they said happened to them is not so different from what happens to most women much of the time. If this man is to be put away, the woman will have to show what happened to her is an extraordinary, exceptional occurrence. Often she cannot. If it is hard for a trier of fact to distinguish a rape clearly, perhaps that should indict the ordinary experience of heterosexual intercourse. Instead, it exonerates the rapist. Indicting intercourse does not directly help a woman who is trying, through the legal process, to establish that she has been raped, as the law defines it, either.

Discussing this analysis is sensitive in part because it can feed the implicit views of some judges and juries who converge rape with sex to let rapists off the hook. Men accused of rape often plead, in effect, that they did not use any more force than is usual during the preliminaries.[11] Studies show that most rapists are not psychologically abnormal men.[12]

Once a woman is married, unless she lives in a state with a still-exceptional marital rape statute, or with an interpretation of the rape law that extends to rape in marriage, any legal right to mutuality in a sexual relationship with her husband is given up, in the sense that the law does not stand behind her if she is not interested tonight. Under the pervasive assumptions about women's sexual availability, any woman who charges rape risks being undercut as a "whore," as someone who has had sex before, so cannot be violated. This assumption is used particularly invidiously against Black women, who are assumed, on a racist basis, to be hypersexual, labeled with one side of the madonna/whore distinction. When a Black woman who complains of sexual mistreatment is disbelieved, it is often because it is seen to be her nature to wish to be sexually used—she must have consented, so it was not a rape.

Women vote with our feet. We do not report rape because we do not believe we will get justice. The accuracy of this perception can be found in the animating requirements of the legal system on the issue of rape, which reflect rather than stand against the values of the unequal social system.[13] Those are male values, meaning values from the male point of view, unequal on the basis of sex.

Viewpoints don't have genitals. This refers to a social perspective in the interest and from the standpoint of a particular group of people. It doesn't matter whether members of dominant groups enjoy their position or not, although often they do. What does matter is that this system gives dominant groups social power to actualize themselves, to assert themselves at the expense of, over and against, other groups with impunity. To be white in a white supremacist society is to be a member of a socially dominant group. The phrase "from the experience and to the advantage of white people" describes a social standpoint—a dominant one that anyone can adopt if permitted to. Women, if permitted, can have male dominant attitudes. Men, with much struggle and perhaps decades of commitment, can learn women's standpoint. To speak of male attitudes is not to speak of the physical or the natural. That it does, is what *they* think.

With this state, as these fragments of evidence, logic, and experiences suggest, we are caught between letting rapists off the hook and demanding that they be energetically prosecuted. Successful prosecution means rapists go to jail, where they will likely be raped. They will be brutalized, at constant risk, much like what women experience every day walking down the street. Jail keeps them away from most women but changes nothing in the ultimate risk they pose to women. Men who go to jail and are raped do not usually come to identify with their victims. They cannot wait to get out, to be no longer the victim. Then they often rape again.[14] Women have no place to get out to. If we insist that the state protect us, we may get more rapes reported, but we do not seem to produce many more convictions. At the same time, Black men are often disproportionately convicted of rape, including those they did not commit, which is not in women's interest either. These initiatives do not change the predominately male behavior or attitudes of the society or the legal system. But what are our alternatives?

We are presented the choice of attempting to get the state to protect us, with dubious benefits, or abdicating the state as recourse and forum altogether. Back to the law as everything or nothing, no rights except those that power will accede or those that can be extracted or enforced socially. Abdicating the state altogether encourages rape. There would be even less risk in forcing a woman than there is now, men could rape with absolute, not just nearly total, impunity. That strategy leaves women, including Black women, to the rapists. There has to be a better way to use the state—maybe civil rights.

With sexual harassment, which has been pursued in this way, there has been more progress. Some of the same problems of credibility, and a similar set of social forces of gender and sexuality, animate this issue as they do the issue of rape. But this time, with sexual harassment women have so far defined the injury. The crime of rape was never defined by women but by male legislators and judges, who seem to have difficulty understanding that women are injured by sexual abuse. The rape law shows it; the damage to the victim of rape is nowhere central to it. What women lose when raped eludes it. The law of sexual harassment, by contrast, recognizes that this fairly standard set of social sexual behaviors is injurious. I am often asked what the difference is between sexual harassment and what goes on between men and women all the time. The answer is often very little. Their implication is, How can it be illegal to do something that goes on all the time? How can you be against it? The answer is, if it goes on all the time, maybe that is a reason to be *more* against it. That it is common supports the view that it is discrimination—implicit in discrimination is the notion that the behavior is pervasive, unlike the view taken by criminal law that the prohibited behavior is exceptional. Of course, particular acts of discrimination are often thought exceptional rather than systemic, but the concept makes it possible to argue that it is part of a larger phenomenon or pattern, shared by a group of victims who also share a lesser status.

Sexual harassment is the unwanted imposition of sexual attention on someone who is not in a position to refuse it. Now ask: In what circumstances do women tend to be in a position to refuse men's sexual attentions? In the workplace? Not usually. Women are systematically the structural subordinates of men in the workplace; therefore men can require pretty much anything, and hold women's jobs as hostage. Educational institutions? Some women are teachers, some women are in positions of power, but on the whole it is men who are at the upper reaches of that hierarchy too. Women students are not usually in a position to refuse men teachers' sexual attentions. Employment and education have been litigated because there are laws against discrimination there. But what about areas in which there is no equality law—say, the home? Women in the home are not necessarily in a position to refuse the sexual attention of their husbands either. The need to survive economically may make women who are beaten in their homes unable to leave or refuse the men who batter them. If women cannot avoid being beaten, then they are not in a position to resist sexual harassment—pinching, leering, unwelcome sexual acts—in the home either.

As a legal idea, it has been a struggle, but possible, to get legal actions for sexual harassment accepted. It has been a great deal more difficult to win individual women's sexual harassment cases. This dynamic is shared with rape cases. As an idea in the mind, everyone is against rape. Most men think of it as something they do not do. But most real-life situations in which women are raped, including many in which they charge rape, do not fit the male mental construct. When a woman presents herself in flesh and blood, in a real-life sexual situation involving a particular man, few realities look like the ideal outrages that those (mostly men) who make these determinations have imagined, what they are looking for and have distinguished themselves from. Many men can identify with the idea that sexual preconditions could prevent a woman from getting a job she should have. But real charges by women of propositions, pressure for dates, jokes, and cartoons at work engender disbelief and incredulity that this is an injury, similar to the disbelief women encounter that acts they call rape are injuries. Men who are accused of sexual harassment, like many imprisoned for rape, often also cannot see that they did anything very wrong, nor can their supporters. In their view, it was no different from what they, and other men, do all the time. They were just unlucky enough to get caught.

The point being, there is a difference between the ideal image of injury to the abstract woman and real injury to a real woman. Consider, for example, a faculty man saying to a woman student: "Sleep with me and I'll give you an A." This is what was alleged was said in *Alexander v. Yale*. The magistrate judge agreed with our theory that if these facts were proven, Title IX's prohibition on sex discrimination in education was violated.[15] But when the real woman actually walked into court and told what a man did, and he walked in and said I did not do this, the case lost at trial. The testimony of the real woman, who in this case is Black, against this white man was approximately as follows. I went to turn in my late paper, I sat down at his desk, he engaged me in discussion about my grade, mentioning that I might get a C. He asked me if I wanted an A in his course. I said I would like an A. He asked me how much do I want an A in the course. I said, I guess I could use one. Do I want an A in the course very, very much? Well, no, it really is not an insane desire, but I thought the final paper was a good paper. Then he said, God, you have a turn-on body. Stunned, she just looks back at him. And then she said he said (she was not believed at trial, so it is not a legal fact that any of this occurred, but I believe her), would she sleep with him? No, she said, no, no, no. (You should see this woman shake her head when she says no.) Then she ran out of his office.

He said that she did come there; she did turn in her paper. He was there. He made a phone call to his wife; it was on the phone bill. But what she said happened in that room did not happen and was not said. She complained orally and in writing shortly thereafter and tried to pursue her complaint persistently. Yale did little, having no procedure to follow in such instances. The trial judge believed the man.[16]

No explicit judgment about credibility or assessment of evidence was made. These facts were found so as to insulate them from appeal. The legal cause of action for sexual harassment under Title IX was recognized in this case for the first time, so anyone can now use it, but this plaintiff's appeal on her specific facts was lost a few days ago.[17]

The idea that sexual harassment violates women is easier to accept against a man's denials than the real violation of a real woman is. It seemingly does not matter how much women seek control over the reproductive consequences of sex or over the depiction of our bodies, itself a form of sexual access. No matter how much we argue that the real issue is altering our powerlessness, what is encountered is the use, meaning the withholding of the use for us, of male power. Will the courts protect us, vindicate us, or not? Protection is always on their terms. Being protected is not the same as having rights. Women who men think are worthy of protection, precious few who can be presented as having no sexuality, are most likely to be protected. But who is that? The minute a woman walks in and has a body, she is a walking provocation to rape and sexual harassment and a form of pornography. We are available to be taken as sexual beings, meaning as sexual objects who can properly be acted upon. As is clear from the *Alexander v. Yale* example, a woman can take this approach to women too. Take seriously that the woman judge in *Alexander* is white.

Sexual harassment is a new issue. In women's lives, it's been going on forever, but as a legal issue, it's emerged in the recent context of a women's movement. So there is still some potential to keep control over its definition. One way to do that is to be very careful and conscious about how we, as lawyers, use the law. The benefit of making sexual harassment illegal is not the progress of the law but the progress of women taking power over our own lives. Making sexual harassment illegal has legitimized women's discontent and dissent. It is changing women's feelings about what we have to put up with. It is redrawing dignity lines between and within people. As an example, in Minnesota's *Continental Can* case,[18] for the first time in a reported judicial opinion, persistent sexual harassment without indices of economic deprivation that most men understand was recognized as discrimination. The woman wasn't deprived of money or a promotion or a job. She was in a job situation, an environmental condition of work, that her tolerance of persistent sexual abuse was a precondition for keeping. She could have quit at any point—her option. To stay, she only had to put up with constant sexual byplay. This, exclusively a sexual injury, was found to be sex discrimination.

One concern is that, once law is used to legitimize women's discontent, the minute law cuts back, women's outrage will diminish to what the law says we can be outraged about. What will be found illegal will necessarily be narrower than what we want to protest politically and in our own lives. Women have not had, and still do not have, the resources, access, or authority to get our injuries, as we define them, recognized as abuses by courts. We need to keep control over our own outrage and the definition of our own injuries and never allow courts to tell us what constitutes our oppression.

Just as in law, rape is supposed to be distinguishable from intercourse, and sexual harassment is to be distinguished from ordinary sexual initiation, in obscenity law, pornography is supposed to be distinguishable from eroticism and art. As with the other issues, left out is, to whom? If pornographers were providing something found satisfying or gratifying or interesting or educational, women would not avoid it as most of us do. Men, mainly, buy it, make it, and sell it—or us—to one another at a phenomenal financial return. Over the last ten years, the success of the film *Deep Throat* showed that pornography could be conventionally lucrative; it legitimized it as a medium. Pornography, increasingly, is everywhere. Seen from the standpoint of the status of women, what is happening in pornography looks a lot like what is happening in many legitimate magazines, fashion, films, and advertising: the bondage, the violence, the bruises, being spread-eagled across car hoods like a bagged deer, the "I'm all black and blue from the Rolling Stones and I love it,"[19] the bloody-mouth and blackened-eye makeup, the "Hit me with a club" ad,[20] and so on. Women, like everyone else, are bombarded by these materials, but most women do not consume pornography itself if we can help it. If you do, you tend to know it means you. It targets women. It makes promises to men that women are expected to keep. Men we know consume it, not just other men. Whatever is available is what is allowed, is what in fact is not obscene, is what does not violate their community standards. It is what turns men on.

In the context of sex inequality, a hard line between obscenity and what is allowed as art and beauty is problematic. Hugh Hefner defends *Playboy* as just showing the natural woman's body and asks how looking at anything so beautiful can be exploitive.[21] Look at the pictures and ask whether you look like that or have ever found yourself in the normal pursuit of life, in such a circumstance or posture; or whether, if you had, you would feel about it the way the women in the pictures are said to feel. It is not that women do not have pornographic life experiences. It is not that these depictions of our bodies are pornography because they are always extraordinarily violent or exceptionally anything. It is that the material does not present what women experience under those conditions: the use, the abuse, the access, the humiliation, the violation. It is clear that men, not women, are its intended consumers. Is *that* what men want?

We are looking for a place and a way to confront this issue. When we consider the courts, we are effectively told it is not our place. What are women up against in using courts as forums? What social process are we a part of? What would it mean, for example, to expand the definition of obscenity through the courts? I do not trust this state to see obscenity from the point of view of women, and we do not have a definition of pornography from that vantage point. I am not against censorship of pornography as a First Amendment absolutist; the First Amendment, no matter how absolute, has not protected our right to speak. Women are silenced when we speak as and for women, as well as in pornography. To try to use obscenity law for these ends, though, would misunderstand the values and interest that this law has historically served.[22] A possible strategy lies in supporting pornography models who are coerced. Pornography means literally the graphic depiction of whores, historically the lowest class of women, whose sexuality is freely available to men. Consider those women who are forced to be there. We need to learn more from them and think about their civil rights and all of ours.

So, the legal system can be a means of legitimizing women's outrage and of promoting resistance to our status. If we are creative, it can be part of women's empowerment. But, as it stands, it also supports much of what we are attempting to change when we advocate for change for women. Men are allowed to get their sense of self out of women's selflessness, their sense of worth out of a projection of our worthlessness, their sense of power out of our powerlessness, their definition of beauty out of our degradation, their eroticism out of our denigration. Implicitly, we have been searching for a theory and practice of what this state is—the state that has supported and enforced these legal doctrines and social institutions—for those of us who want to change them.

We need to identify with the interests of women as a whole, so that each initiative we take as lawyers empowers women's resistance to this system. Only then will we recover our own passion, the passion many of us began this pursuit with, which we were taught in law school we had to abandon. We need to recover our identification as women, our commitment, our belief that we can and must be, as lawyers, committed to that in ourselves that is inseparable from that in the world that is all women. We need to develop an autonomous definition of our own direction, to search for forums and means and doctrines of struggle on behalf of women's equality that cannot be turned against us or taken away.

[TWO]

A Radical Act of Hope

Universities imagine themselves as open-minded places that value new ideas and serious questioning of accepted dogmas. My experience has largely been that attempts to change university contexts so that the content of study offered to students expands their minds and possibilities in the direction of a more inclusive and equal world have frequently produced uprisings of student discontent when unresponsiveness is encountered. Which it frequently is. Often universities recoil from challenges to power as currently distributed, and the concepts that support it, and punish those who call that into question.

At this Town Meeting, part of a Strike for Faculty Diversity at Yale Law School in 1989,[1] students staged an attempt to diversify the Yale Law School faculty, which was overwhelmingly white, male, and liberal. The law students spoke passionately and impressively about the relation between who the faculty members overwhelmingly were and the politics of the legal education they provided. Dean Guido Calabresi listened attentively, sitting on a chair as demonstrations swirled around him, taking detailed notes on the points made in the speeches. Despite the responsive intentions of some, little if any long-term change resulted in the faculty's composition, general ideological persuasion, politics, or course offerings. Present on one of several visiting teaching positions at Yale Law School, I was asked by the students to speak at this demonstration. I talked sitting on a table in the main hallway, students and faculty on the floor and arrayed up the central stairwell. Someone audiotaped it.

This strike for faculty diversity comes in a long tradition of student actions here and elsewhere, events in which students have been vessels and vehicles of a proud tradition of dissent and social change. In my experience of our history, I have seen strikes to change relations with other countries like Vietnam, and strikes to change relations between the university and the city, Yale and the City of New Haven. When I first arrived in New Haven in 1969, the cemetery entrance on

23

Grove Street where it is carved in stone "The Dead Shall Be Raised," had sprayed in white paint underneath, "If Yale Needs the Land." I have seen strikes to change the relations between Black people and white people, including one at Yale that closed down this entire university for many months. That strike from education as usual protested the relations between the University and the city, the genocide of people in Vietnam by the United States, the killings of peaceful student protesters at Kent State, and the lack of a fair trial for Bobby Seale, who at that time was chair of the Black Panther Party. There have been strikes for change in relations between employers and employees, otherwise called bosses and workers, in the attempt to get a union and decent wages and working conditions at this university.

Within all of these student strikes, the theme of the quality of education has always been raised, indeed central. The students always understood their education as connected with what our country was doing in the world, what our university was doing in the city, what white people were doing to Black people, what the university did to its workers. The strikes exposed the strategic power of people who didn't feel they had power, their power to withdraw their participation from the system even for a short period of time, exposing their place in it as crucial. Specifically about education, they delivered the message: we cannot learn in this narrow and unjust world, under these narrow and unjust conditions. We need to make this world bigger, broader, better, to make it a world in which we can learn.

In that context, this strike, while militant, is comparatively polite. It is subdued; it is verbal. It is also very, very short. You wouldn't know it from the prestrike anxiety barometer, though, which has also extended the norms for the usage of Yale Law School walls—a use that says "this is our place."

Speaking out is basic to defining the voice of the people, to taking back a reality that has been appropriated by those who have power to take it away. A "speak out," a town meeting, is a time to testify. Value this opportunity. You will be preparing *other* people to testify for much of the rest of your life. This is a time for the telling of tales, admitting the inadmissible, breaking silence, bearing witness, sharing grievances, shaping visions.

A town meeting is a profound moment of community struggling toward a direction for change. Not the kind of change that comes through entropy, where the system just winds itself down to a slow stop. Not the kind of change that comes from a centrifugal force or the force of gravity, or the change that comes when the fruit ripens on the tree and drops to the ground. Not the kind of change that comes with death as in that cemetery. Rather, it ushers in directed conscious human change: social change. Make no mistake about it. This, what we are doing here, is how that kind of change happens, if it happens.

From what I've learned over time—if these grey hairs entitle one to a little retrospect—I want to offer some observations phrased as cautions for your deliberations on diversity. They are titled "Mind Traps in Resistance to Diversity," or "Excuses for Leaving Everything Just the Same."

One, the entitlement assumption. As in, "Any change toward greater diversity could mean I won't get what I already have, what I got by excluding all those folks, so this diversity change cannot be right." Corollary: "merit works, see I'm here." The token's corollary: "others like me who are not here aren't as good as I am, that's why I'm here and they're not." Otherwise termed co-optation.

Two, unreal equations or the proportionality trick. This begins with equating Black and white, women and men, gay and straight as a standard for measurement, as if they are all the same. Sometimes it comes out "That wouldn't bother me, why does it bother you?" Another one is equating what people of color do to respond to what white people do to them with what white people do to people of color. Or equating anger against crimes against women with crimes against women, anger at rape with rape. You are upset by your rape; I am upset about your being upset about your rape. Another kind of example is: don't be so confrontational, you're alienating me. In other words, my discomfort at your point equals the discomfort that causes you to need to make your point. That is, if those who are now comfortable stay comfortable, the changes that you want will happen. That is, shut up, you're making me uncomfortable.

A subcategory of unreal equations might be called phony reversals or the neutrality trap or the "we're beyond all that" prophylactic. For example, thinking that taking race into account in order to solve exclusion or denigration based on race is equal to the problem of taking race into account to exclude and denigrate—as if the problem were race itself, or taking race into account, rather than exclusion or denigration based on race. Also called missing the point. Barbara Babcock once had the final word on this one. When asked "How does it feel to have gotten the job as Head of the Civil Service Commission because you are a woman?" she answered "A lot better than it would feel *not* getting the job as Head of the Civil Service Commission because I am a woman."[2]

Three, twisted causality: calling protest against the thing, the thing being protested. For example, this strike causes a "division" in the community, rather than reveals, responds to, and addresses a division in the community that already exists.

Four, moralism as a substitute for politics or the dissection and abstraction strategy. This is usually revealed by comments like the following: "that's terrible, but it's not racism"; or "that was incredibly rude, but it's not sexist." It's associated with what I call the guilt gambit: "I feel so good about myself because of how bad about myself I feel about racism, sexism, homophobia, that I'm doing what I need to do about it." Also called missing the point.

Five, the exception/exemption ploy. To put it simply and briefly: whatever is happening, this is not an instance of it; wherever it is happening, it is not here; whoever is doing it, it is not me or us. In other words, whatever it is, wherever it is, whoever it is this is happening to—the racism, the sexism—it is never me, now, here, this. If this were true for everyone who has ever said it, thought it, or meant it, there would be virtually no examples of sexism or racism left to protest. It would disappear.

Implicit in all of these evasions is seeing things from the point of view of power and not being able to see anything else. Additional features of the syndrome include relying on empathy and identification with a life one will never live as a basis for politics. "I'm so sensitive, I know everything." Another is metaphorizing harm, say, indignation about the rape of the land but not about the rape of women, which is no metaphor. Related is analogizing that gets more for those who benefit from the analogy than the analogized-to ever got. "You would never do that to Blacks, so don't do that to . . ." and the list goes on. Well, in fact they *do* do that to Blacks, usually. They do it all the time. And do nothing about it. The constant analogizing metaphorizing shifts keep the thing itself from being talked about.

And then there is the appropriation of pain and struggle device, the "I'm going to solve this" expression of authority. Taking over others' pain can be benevolently intended, but it is not the same as responsiveness or change or power sharing.

I understand this strike to be a protest against law faculties voting their comfort level as a proxy for quality. It is an act of resistance against the social club definition of law school faculties. It is an act of dissent against their conventionality and the core/periphery model implicit in their social design. It is also a clear statement of how deeply students value this place. They value it so much that they want to make it their place. They value it so much that they want to give it the very best thing they have: their own people. This is not what people do when they have given up on you.

This strike is a committed and radical act of hope: hope in teaching and learning, hope in speaking and listening, and an act of faith in the possibilities for change.

THREE

Law's Power

The graduating class at Yale Law School in June 1989 elected me as one of two speakers to address their commencement ceremony. Most memorably, after this rather harrowing speech, spoken from notes and audiotaped, a smiling young African American graduate approached me surrounded by his family to introduce his radiant mother. "Thank you for what you said," she said. "That was me you were talking about up there." It was a relief not to have spoiled her joy in the day. I did not know her situation in advance, but I did know what many students had told me of their experiences and how they felt about them, or I would never have blown the whistle this way.[1]

Dean Calabresi, members of the faculty, distinguished guests, our wonderful graduates, and all your friends: I must say, this is not something I ever imagined doing. Some of the graduates may share with me the sense of incredulity expressed by Cher when she won the Academy Award: "If I can get this, anyone can do anything."[2]

I want to talk with you about the nature of law in terms of some of the qualities shared by law in the academy and law in the world and about what it means to hold the power of law in your hands. Law is written by the powerful. You know that. But there is more. Law *is* words in power; it is written by power. Its power is not unlimited but it is real. This tends to mean that experiences that take place outside the routes in which power is socially negotiated do not make law because they do not count to power. Problems posed outside of power are outside the scope of legitimacy. They leave no trace. Law resists them because it does not know how to solve them or because it does not want them solved. When I say law is power, you are thinking "them." Of course, it's also us. And for you, the graduates, now, or soon, it's you.

I want to work this through with one example. I could have chosen the example of all people of color; I could have chosen the example of all working people; I choose the example of all women. Women, compared with men, have been historically deprived of the franchise, and still are deprived of income and adequate means of material survival and are systematically allocated to disrespected work.[3] Women are deprived of physical security through targeting for sexual assault in settings that range from the intimate to the anonymous.[4] Women are used in denigrating entertainment,[5] bought and sold on street corners for sexual use and abuse,[6] and deprived of reproductive control.[7] Women's authentic voice has been silenced, our culture taken away, our contributions often stolen when they have been recognized at all, and when not recognized, erased.[8] Women of color are intensively subjected to these denigrations, abuses, and humiliations that afflict all women.[9]

This is what it means to say that power takes a male form, specifically a white one, and that powerlessness takes a female form. This system has been supported by the notion that it is inevitable and somehow natural and fulfilling to women. It is also believed that the existence of this system of disadvantage is consistent with equality of the sexes.

This is not a problem law has solved; nor has law ever really apparently heard about it. Law in the academy and in the world actively collaborate in this situation through excluding women's point of view from the public realm and by denying women equal access to justice under law, pointedly by excluding harms that happen particularly to women from the legal definition of harm at all. Law collaborates by depriving women of credibility through the institutionalized belief that we are likely to lie about sexual assault and by legally defining sexual assault from the point of view of the perpetrator.[10] Law collaborates through the active protection of some forms of abuse of women, such as pornography, through affirmative guarantees to men of individual rights called, in this instance, speech.[11] Law collaborates through the elimination of the right to abortion for women who are least able to get access to it by depriving them of government funding;[12] and the law is working on eliminating that right for women who can pay for it as well.[13] Law also actively collaborates in women's status by defining sex inequality under law so that one virtually already has to have sex equality before the law supports your right to demand it.

Power's latest myth in this area is that the problem of inequality between women and men has been solved. Because now a few women can become lawyers, we all have sex equality. Yet, 44 percent of women are still victims of rape and attempted rape, at least once in our lives;[14] 85 percent of us are sexually harassed on the job;[15] 38 percent of us are sexually abused as children;[16] a quarter to a third of us are battered in our homes.[17] Women who are lawyers are exceptions to none of these.[18] Women still make around half the average male wage.[19] Thousands and thousands of women are still being bought and sold on street corners as and for sex.[20] Pornographers still traffic us and our children, making ten billion dollars a year.[21] We are told that sex inequality is over, when some proud mothers must, statistically, sit here at graduation next to their batterers; when some excited graduates must sit a row or two away from their rapists, relieved to be leaving their sexual harassers, trying not to think about those who molested them as children, who may also be celebrating this moment with them. Women especially must live with a division between what we know and what can be publicly acknowledged, between what we know and what the law will tell us back is true.

I want to talk about some of the professional pressures that help account for how those who have law's power in their hands have not changed this, and have not yet made it unnecessary to speak about such atrocities on joyful occasions like this one. I have identified three strategies for comfort, three deep mechanisms of power that, both with law in school and law in the world, conspire to keep situations like women's in place. They are the avoidance of accountability, the aspiration to risklessness, and the assumption of immortality. I want to challenge you, the graduates, to resist these pressures.

By avoidance of accountability I mean: you may have noticed in the legal academy a tendency to treat ideas as if they are just ideas, as if one can choose among them without consequence, as if they have no part in shaping or sharing power. You may also have noticed the use of neutrality as a norm and the way it hides its standards, obscures its reference point, and does not produce fairness, but rather derails accountability for the point of view being taken by presenting itself as no point of view at all. You may have observed, and learned to engage in, devil's advocacy: "Nobody really thinks this, certainly not me, but let me ram this particular point down your throat." Legal reasoning is presented in the hypothetical, the "as if" form, when law is not practiced nor is life lived in the hypothetical. There are also ethical norms in law that purport to protect the client from the lawyer, but as often or more protect the lawyer from accountability to the client. As to the practice of law, you may have heard that everyone has a right to counsel. The less-asked question is whether everyone has a right to counsel by *you*. I urge you to see through these devices and hold yourself accountable, including for the uses to which you are put.

There is a form of accountability that *is* encouraged in law school; one I know you are aware of having. When you came here you were chosen, not only for your academic achievements, for your demonstrated brilliance, but for your community ties, your commitment, and your diversity. These are not only qualifications but devices for accountability. At law school, you may have felt challenged, stimulated, expanded, elevated, rewarded, and prepared. If, however, you raised problems from your communities and from your experience that are not real to power, you may also at times have felt brutalized, humiliated, limited: as if you had wandered into some intellectual equivalent of boot camp. This was not because anyone on the faculty intended to do this, but because when you get an education in law, you get an education in power. Legal education works to attempt to make you accountable to power and not, for instance, to women. I urge you to keep your commitments, your communities, your accountability to who you are.

By aspiration to risklessness, I mean primarily a definition of effectiveness that ends contingency, makes everything certain. This comes out in all the energy lawyers put into figuring out ways to avoid telling the truth to power because they think power does not want to hear it. Typically, it is called litigation strategy. It would appear that some people believe that the Supreme Court is not old enough to hear the truth about women. There are so many ways to lie with law: not telling the whole truth, techniques of selection and obfuscation that make those who lie with statistics look like amateurs, making everything into a matter of interpretation so that in your hands A becomes not-A.

The voice of women in particular has been excluded or twisted by this process. One has to take risks to get it back in. Women's screams in pornography have, in law, become the pornographer's speech.[22] Few in power have heard them as anything else. Few will take the risk of siding with them. I am told that people can take only so much truth. I also think that people can take only so many lies. You will hear people's voices scratched from screaming as well as slippery with innuendo and luxury. I urge you to be selective and take risks in how you magnify them. You can affect how they are heard.

By the assumption of immortality, I mean living as if you have all the time in the world, as if you are awash in time, as if you will live forever. It's not true. This strategy for comfort is not, of course, peculiar to law, but it has consequences that are specific to it. The legal biography and legal norms seem designed to encourage putting off the real thing: the big issue, the major change. We get told change is gradual, small, slow. But many women's problems can be solved only by big changes. And even if you will live forever, other people won't. So do it now. Do it big. *Start* big. There are very few jobs in law where the norms include growth—the federal bench is one of them—and a great many jobs in law that make you smaller and smaller and smaller as your salary gets bigger and bigger and bigger. Speak and write as if it is the last thing you will ever say, the last chance you will ever have, as if it is the last thing that your audience is ever going to hear.

Now, or soon, you have this law in your hands, with all its pressures, undertows, and crosscurrents. The women among you have more power than any group of women has ever had in the history of the world. Remember that what all of you do with law takes a position: it either makes power more powerful or it redistributes and transforms it. I urge you to define principle in opposition to the pressures of power. A lot of people are waiting for your help.

If you take up this challenge, I am confident that the tradition of excellence, creativity, and originality that is encouraged at Yale Law School, the social and political engagement that is valued here, and the activism and even the militancy that is sometimes permitted, will assist you in these tasks.

You may even find the law unexpectedly receptive. For law is ultimately about accountability. It responds to risks and risk-takers; it can alter and reduce the social risks people have to face. And while law is thankfully not exactly immortal, in the shape we give it, it will outlast us all.

FOUR

To Quash a Lie

I attended a rural consolidated high school in a farming area where classes emptied out when rain threatened during late haying season. Being one of four alumnae to receive a Smith College Medal on Rally Day in 1991 was an astounding honor from my college that had already given me so much. The Smith College library alone had been nirvana. What struck me about this moment of recognition years later was the constraints that keep most women from doing the things for which I was being honored—things that so obviously had needed doing, things anyone could have done. What made them stand out as worthy of such a special award? The costs of acting and of not acting against our collective determinants, the punishments, came to me, looking into all those young women's upturned faces.[1]

What I'm wondering at this moment is what makes everything you were just told I've done stand out as worth recognizing. In particular, why did it take so long for someone, anyone, to have done them, because anyone could have. Thinking especially about the legal recognitions of harms to women, I want to speak with you about all the reasons I have ever heard for doing nothing about women's situation, including by law; why these reasons are so widely believed and practiced; what happens if you ignore them; and what this part of what we are up against means for the possibilities for all of our lives.

This subject, with many others, came into focus for me around the struggle for the civil rights antipornography ordinance that Andrea Dworkin and I conceived to make it possible for women who are hurt through pornography to do something legal about it.[2] We came up against something forcibly that we already knew, which is that we were not supposed to talk about the way pornography hurts women. The denial and censorship and cover up and retaliation we encountered were and are massive. Talking about what pornography really does to women and advocating a law—I mean, something that polite—against it would seem to be doing something about it. Pornography's actions are protected as speech,[3] but even our speech against it is silenced as action. Tell me if you figure that out. We were told to educate, at most, not legislate. Try educating an orgasm sometime. The real unthinkable thing was that the government, the state, would back us up, that there would be legal consequences—serious things, court orders, money damages—for what men do to women for sex.

You have never heard more reasons for doing nothing in your life. Liberal, conservative, radical reasons—you name it, they had them. It's more complicated than just what it does to women. It's been around too long. There's too much of it. It doesn't really do anything that isn't otherwise and already done. It isn't there anyway. Even if you can do something, it won't work. It might help one person, but this problem is bigger than all of us. It will only make men mad. It will backfire. It will hurt us more than it will hurt them. The courts can't be trusted. If we do this for women, we will have to do it for everyone else, who knows where it will end. Who do you think you are, anyway? What makes you think any woman matters more than any man's pleasure? Some women like it. I like it.

At times it seemed like the only people besides us who thought really quite a lot could be done with law were the ones who wanted to make sure that nothing was. This reaction was, for us, part of a larger process of making sure that what is done to women is never seriously challenged and that women never come first for anyone who could do anything to change it. Implicitly or explicitly, we were being told to shut up, lie down and take it and cooperate with the illusion that really we were having a wonderful time. Say anything, do anything, *just not this*. It does make one think one is onto something.

What is being done to women, this unspeakable, apparently irremediable something—the larger picture of which the particular process I've described is just a part of protecting—refers to an empirical reality. In this country, with parallels in other countries, it keeps most women poor, in jobs with low pay and less regard.[4] It targets us for rape, domestic battering, abuse as children, and systematic sexual harassment.[5] It is a reality that depersonalizes us, demeans our physical characteristics, punishes and stigmatizes our chosen relationships with each other and our love for each other. It uses us in denigrating entertainment.[6] It deprives us of reproductive control and forces us into prostitution.[7] These practices occur in many places and have occurred for a long time in one form or another, often in a context in which we were not allowed to vote, to go to school (which is why Smith was founded);[8] a context in which we are more likely to be owned as property than to own any; in which we are excluded from public life; kept so poor we have no alternative to dependence on men, in one form or another; a context in which our ideas and our children are stolen and our own worth and contributions to society are devalued. This subordination of women to men is socially and legally institutionalized. It cumulatively and systematically deprives women of human dignity, respect, resources, physical security, credibility, full membership in our communities, speech, and power.

This, I repeat, is an empirical description of a war against women. It is not a philosophical category, a construct, an abstract analysis, or any kind of universal essence. It describes a diverse and perverse concrete reality of social practices and social meanings, such that, in the words of Richard Rorty, to be a woman "is not yet a name for a way of being human."[9] This is the destiny we are all supposed to live out gracefully and quietly, to be fulfilled by, and, get this, to *like*.

So, what happens if this is not all right with you? What happens when women push back, even dig our heels in a bit, and what does the reaction to our resistance tell us about how this system keeps itself going? Most important here, as always, is what men do, but women's response to resistance is also a part of it. We're not all in this equally, but we are all in it.

In this system of inequality, a woman's first obligation is silence. Incest and child sexual abuse is not taboo. Exposing it is. Pornography is not forbidden. Saying what it does, is. Rape is not illegal. Trying to make the ways women are raped illegal apparently is. Because the voice of reality is silent here, no one knows what is happening to women, not even us, and so whenever it happens to you, it looks exceptional and it feels exceptional.

If you talk about all of this as if it is real, you are more likely to be punished than published. You learn that what you leave out is more important than what you put in. They may let you talk about female powerlessness, for instance, but not male power. The lines are really very clear. There is a huge body of suppressed writing out there that you will never read because of this. It's hard to talk about an absence, what isn't there. Here is just one tiny example that shows how the abuse is permitted, but resisting it is not.

The *New York Times* asked me to write an op-ed on Lois Robinson's case against Jacksonville Shipyards when we prevailed in it. She sued them for pornography as a form of sexual harassment and won at trial.[10] I wrote about what was done to Lois, which was an awful lot more than just "pin-ups," the media's cover-up term for what she had been subjected to. I included in the piece all the verbal abuse in quotes. The *New York Times* refused to print it, saying it was because of *those* words. So, I did something I've never done before. I censored myself. So it read, "Hey come here BLANK and give me a BLANK." "Black women BLANK like BLANK." And "BLANK me you BLANK dog BLANK." Then I said, in effect, that the *New York Times* would not let you read what really happened to Lois Robinson. Their censorship makes speaking of the harm of pornography look exaggerated because you are not permitted to know what was actually done to her. They are making you think it's all in her head because you have to fill in the blanks. They wouldn't print that either. This, a piece they had requested.[11]

The example is minor, but the implications are broad and pretty staggering. They mean that, other than in cases we win, like Lois's, abusers can *do* this to abuse women, and the press in general will be on the side of them doing it, and they will call *doing* it freedom of speech. But we can't *criticize* this abuse through *our* speech unless we first make it look nonabusive.

There is an even more massive body of work that will never be written as a result of this sort of thing. If you try to write the truth about the situation of women, you will be told by various authorities—advisers, editors, teachers, senior partners, judges, censors of all sorts—say it less directly. Say it in a more academic way. Be more strategic. Don't threaten the reader (gender neutral). It's not that it bothers me, don't get me wrong; it will bother other people. Say it in private and not in public. Don't be so confrontational, they won't like it, and they won't take you seriously. They won't like you, and they won't take you seriously. (As if them liking us has ever made them take us seriously.) It won't be effective. It won't sell. Tell the judge what he wants to hear the way he wants to hear it. Cave in. Don't disturb the surface. Let them keep thinking what they think and doing what they do. Just get by. We'll lose our advertisers. We'll get sued for libel. Wait until after you get tenure.

It is rare in my experience for anyone to stand up to this. On the effectiveness point, I do think it is worth noting that women are second to none in telling men what men want to hear, the way men want to hear it. So far as I know, we have been doing this for at least 2,000 years, and look at where it's gotten us.

After years of doing this, what gets male approval is all you know. You don't think anything else. You don't want anything else. You don't know that this is what's happened to you. If you never seriously step out of line, you will never know that this line is there, and you will reassure others that it doesn't exist. The process that we're dealing with here, I think, is that what can't be lived is hard to speak, and what can't be spoken can't be thought, and what can't be thought is hard to imagine. The result is, we almost never hear an uncompromised woman's voice in public. We are buried in imitative literature written by women with unlined faces and a scholarship on women written by strivers for tenure looking to carve out a niche, which by the way is a very small place.

There is no individual solution to this situation, only exceptions to it. Their exceptionality, however precious or exemplary, is tenuous, embattled, and a matter of degree or of time. All the ways of telling women to keep quiet and do nothing about the condition of women range from what's a nice girl like you doing studying a nasty topic like this through invisibility and shunning and hostility to poverty and death threats. Many people are all too willing to guard your prison in the guise of sincerely well-intended advice, and at least some of them are in the same prison you're in.

Whenever this doesn't happen, it is the kind of miracle that feels like freedom. For me, this first happened in Leo Weinstein's classes here at Smith College.[12] It changed everything. One point of the women's movement is to create this kind of space.

In most of the rest of the world, if you do not submit to these pressures, you will be reviled, lied about, ridiculed, isolated, ostracized, and targeted for slander and vilification and whispering campaigns. It seems to make an awful lot of people nervous if they think they can't control you. You may be considered unemployable, which means *being unemployed*. You may live at the poverty line for some time. Goddess forbid, should you speak the truth and survive, or maybe even succeed, you will become a target of competition, and proof that nothing that I have said is true, or at least is not fatal. They won't call you a role model; you will be resented for blowing the game. In particular, the horizontal hostility and resentment directed at women who prove that you do not have to fold to get by, that you can hold out for the integrity of your work and make a living, that you can tell the truth about women's lives and survive, is unrelenting and unforgiving. All this takes a huge intellectual, emotional, spiritual, and physical toll. This may be why more of us don't do it.

In academia, where I know it well, women who do not communicate that prized accessibility, who are too serious about doing something for women to waste what little life they have left on intellectual busywork, are called uncollegial, are not hired, are not promoted with fair regularity by faculties who vote their comfort level. If you do not conform socially, sexually, intellectually, politically; if you are not acquiescent and reassuring; if you do not dress right and smile at the right times—meaning all the time—you are punished economically and in every way that makes life worth living or liveable to most people. Even if you do manage to keep the integrity of your work, you will be supernaturally lucky to have a life. Need I add that such conditions do not help long-term relationships? That you can live with all of this and with yourself—with being who you have to become to get through it—does not necessarily mean that anyone else can.

Then someday you may miraculously appear on a platform. There she is. Standing. Smiling. Well-dressed. Published. Tenured. Without visible scars. And someone is giving her a medal.

What I want to know is this: What will it take, what does it take, for women to matter enough to put your life on this line, the line of the lives of our people—women? Too many of us are sacrificed on this line; I'm not talking about that. I'm talking about deciding over my dead body do you do this *to even one more woman*, and then figuring out what it's going to take to stop them, and doing it.

The other day while talking with my research student, Karen Davis, about a particularly discouraging feature of the record in a case that I'm involved in, I said, "I don't know if I'm going to make it through this world." She said, "I'm hoping this world isn't going to make it through you." Being on this line isn't about being heroic or self-righteous or thinking that you're so powerful or important that you can fix everything. I think it isn't really about courage, and it certainly is not about self-sacrifice. It's about recognizing that if you are serious about freedom, if you seriously value life, including your own, you really don't have any choice.

Now what do you do if you do what I'm suggesting, that is, take women's equality seriously? All the problems to be faced, they're all interconnected, so it really doesn't matter where you start. It does matter *how*. I think you listen to what is not supposed to be being said, but is. You do not forget. You resist this eraser that goes behind women, so that we leave no trace. You do not trivialize. If it hurts a woman, it's a *big deal*. You add it up so it does not end up amounting to nothing. You do not lie. I mean, you do not make nice and you do not shut up, so your silence means that nothing is there. And then you do what is in front of you, and believe me it becomes very obvious. You try to anticipate abuse because you will get it. And you figure out what you personally need to keep going, because you are going to need it, just to tell the truth of what women know in public even once. Telling the truth takes a lot of practice, but once you get the hang of it, all the rest is a lot easier.

Some people will support you, some only a little while, a few for a very long time. A lot of anonymous women will honor you by trusting you with their pain. You will touch a lot of lives, mostly people you never meet or don't know well. You will feel some self-respect, even some hope, and a sense of meaning and purpose, even if you won't see most of the results of what you are doing. It will matter that you were there.

What we are up against here is nothing less than women's survival in a world that wants us dead, whether messily and in public by an assassin's bullet like at the Montreal School of Engineering[13] or neatly and alone by our own hand. It is a world that deprives women of self-respect by predicating so much of its own on depriving us of the dignity of a whole life. I used to think that the slogan "Silence equals death" was a little exaggerated, or maybe best limited to the situation of AIDS.[14] My roommate at Smith, Heather McClave, took her own life about three years ago, and I don't think so anymore. She was a brilliant mind, a strong feminist, a superb scholar, a loving woman with a piercing eye and a passionate clarity, committed to life, to writing, to women, to change. She had a nuanced, subtle, disciplined, ironic intelligence and a macabre wit. She was the best there is. I knew her to fight for her life—hard. Then one day, she couldn't anymore. You know, it's easy to make someone's death a symbol of anything political that you want. But one thing I think I learned from this is that a person is a lot more likely to live through the consequences of speech than the consequences of silence.

I think, along with much I have talked about, that silence—her own and ours—killed her, and in different ways has killed many of the best minds of my generation, as much as anything has. I accept this honor today from our school in memory of her.

FIVE

The Measure of What Matters

Law school destroys much in its students that it valued in them when they were admitted. This is the first publication of a commencement address given at the University of California, Davis, Law School on May 23, 1992, encouraging its graduates to recover their path.

———————————

Think back to what was in your heart when you applied here, what you carried inside you the first time you walked into the doors of this law school. Not the intimidation, or your determination to persevere, or your thrill at getting here, but what brought you to law.

Among law students I have known, those moments have included a son watching his father beat his mother and not being able to do anything about it. For several, it has been watching their mothers descend into poverty after years of homemaking with nothing but their children to show for it. For others, it was watching their mothers disintegrate into advanced uselessness and depression after being trivialized all their lives. For one, it was learning his sister had committed suicide after several years in prostitution. For another, it was trying to explain to her puzzled five-year-old son what the pornography he just saw at his eye level at the 7–11 was. For many, it has been loving someone of the same sex and realizing they could be put in juvenile detention or fired from their job or kicked out of their apartment for it. For many men, they have told me, it had something to do with being sexually abused as children by men who had power over them. For one, it was watching the beer fall from her father's hand as he fell asleep in front of the television night after night after working three jobs just to keep food on the table. For one, it was seeing a picture of an empty swimming pool on the news and realizing that white folks would rather not swim at all than do it with you, no matter how hot it got. For one, it was seeing the Confederate flag still flying over his state capital.

For me, it started with pictures in, I think, *Life* magazine from the liberation of the camps at the end of World War II. My mother kept all of our magazines in a dirt cellar in the basement next to the barrels of wrapped apples from our orchard. My first conscious memory is of those twisted piles of bodies in a gash in the earth. Why? A picture next to it showed the ground there as it was long after, grass growing over a slight mound in the earth.

Some things you cannot live with knowing, or not understanding, and be the same. Some things take something away that change your life trying to get back, or give back, or stop. I am asking you to remember what is like that for you.

Having fixed that point, think ahead to the moment you die. What do you want to remember about your work as a lawyer? What will have been worth your time when it runs out? Will it be all the money you made? Your clever jibes and repartee or the blood on the floor when you ran that verbal rapier through the witness on the other side? Will it be that devastating brief that got a conviction reversed for years of brutal marital rape because of your argument that the jury was not instructed that the victim might have wanted it?[1] Will it be your balanced decision not to prosecute a man that many children said molested them because you did not "have enough evidence," that is, you did not believe the children?[2] Will it be your brilliant defense of four white police officers who beat a Black motorist to death?[3] Will it be the nine-figure real estate deals or the corporate mergers you put together or all the hours you billed for the firm? Somehow I don't think so.

At this moment, now, poised between what impelled you in this direction and where you are headed with it, surrounded by many of those who have come with you this far, implicit in these examples are some suggestions for your consideration.

First, make law fit life, not the other way around. If your training was anything like mine, we learned mostly how to bend facts to fit existing law. Most of the social problems that most urgently need attention, markedly those of social inequality, have no adequate legal approaches or they would have been solved by now.

Related to this is, call things what they are. Especially inequalities are being called other things, anything else; the legal set-up and the example seem not quite connected. One example that comes to mind is the criminal charge against a woman for years of back taxes on the proceeds of prostitution that she has handed over to her pimp. After lengthy attempts to conceptualize, a defense lawyer her family hired realized that it was not income to her, because it had never been her money.[4]

Related to this, if the law does not work for your clients, maybe it needs to change. For example, with sexual abuse of children, when it happens, many people forget it.[5] So statutes of limitations have to be changed to accommodate this.[6] When it happens, it is environmental, pervasive. So evidentiary and credibility requirements that value exceptional discrete incidents, with days and times attached, have to be transformed too. Just because it doesn't fit the law that exists does not mean it didn't happen. Every law was created for the first time, sometime, by someone. There is no reason that time cannot be now, and that person cannot be you.

Second, do not think that the way law approaches things is all there is to knowing about them. Many lawyers think that because they know a lot about the law of discrimination, they know about discrimination; because they know the law of obscenity, they know what pornography is; because they know poverty law, they know poverty. They could not be more wrong. The true experts are those who are hurt by these things, those on the receiving end: your clients. Get clients you believe in, then believe them. Don't limit yourself to court, either—with care, use legislation, the media, politics. Write, organize, speak out. Do not limit yourself to the United States. There is a whole world out there.

Third, do not be seduced by the notion that you will not be effective unless you compromise and cave in and lose your outrage and forget your dream. Little could have been less practical in 1974 than designing a new federal cause of action called sexual harassment.[7] It might have looked easier, for instance, to try to apply existing tort law—easier but and because it wouldn't have done anything, because torts happen to gender neutral individuals, and people are sexually harassed as members of gender-defined groups. It looks easier today to concede defeat to the pornographers, for instance when rapists are acquitted when juries, having seen home pornography of the defendant's wife being bound and tortured, believed it was a sex game.[8]

It looks easier to let all the women coerced into pornography—a process that passes for "consent" and "choice"—twist in the wind, as the products of their violation precede and surround them wherever they go, outlive them. It seems a lot easier not to even think about our sisters in involuntary servitude, being bought and sold on street corners of every city in the world, unable to get out, with no law yet invented to do anything for them.

About doing the easy thing, I have only one thing to say. Things will stay the same. We know what will happen if things stay the same. We often do not know what will happen if we challenge and change them, and to me that looks a lot like freedom.

Things can change awfully quickly when you work this way. It is said change is slow, but it is not. When change happens, it is breathtakingly fast. It is years of resistance to anything moving that gives the impression of slowness. Not long ago, few knew what the term sexual harassment meant, and a lot of men did not believe it happened, or that's what they said. Now there are thousands of cases at every level of the legal system, and sexually harassed women know their human rights are being violated by it.[9] Today, when I speak of snuff pornography, in which women or children are killed to make a sex film, many people say it does not exist. The time is coming when that world, too, will crack open, and what has been a secret horror will be exposed to the light of public scrutiny.

I have seen a lot of emptiness at the center of the lives of lawyers who are surrounded by money. The law is more than an instrument for redistribution of wealth from clients to lawyers. It is a tool for justice in many forms—accountability, revenge, and transformation among them. Many lawyers do things they are not comfortable with, that they know are wrong, because they are being paid. It eats you up eventually, or sooner. I am not suggesting you have to be poor or obscure or dramatically self-sacrificing. I am suggesting that you direct yourself to a meaningful life in the law, one that sustains you. I am not suggesting you never work for a corporate firm or that all your work be pro bono—although more would help, a lot. I am saying, use what you know to do something, for someone, sometime, who matters to you. You will find you have a lot more power than you thought you did.

Hold on to your vision, hold on to your voice, hold on to your community. Most lawyers do not go near enough or far enough in what they do. A Native American friend of mine tells me of a saying of his people: today is a good day to die. It means, do something that matters, be ready to do what it takes and to take what comes. If organized crime is on the other side, as with pornography, or your work is against a white supremacist group like Aryan Nation, one that maintains a point system and a hit list for people like you, maybe you are where it matters. I think this is the way to stay true to what brought you here, to live a life that will be worth remembering when your final day comes.

Congratulations on the accomplishment marked by this day. In an updated translation of *ave atque vale*: right on and go for it!

SIX

Intervening for Sex Equality

This talk congeals years of reflections on practicing law in the butterfly mode. National Taiwan University College of Law, supported by Formosa Transnational Attorneys at Law, a law firm, organized by Professor Chao-ju Chen, provided the opportunity in June 2013 to deliver three lectures. One was requested to be an interaction between a short talk reflecting on litigating and legislating for women with comments by Taiwanese activists and lawyers for women.[1] The speech needed to be in short sentences for simultaneous translation into Mandarin, which can be good discipline if a bit stilted in English. At these events, the massive auditorium of listeners barely moved for hours at a time. An unforgettable profusion of stunning orchids adorned me and the podium.

I was asked to talk about litigating for women's equality and to reflect on my experience having done so. I will do this in the form of a list of Ten Lessons Learned, which can be discussed and debated as best practices or not, depending on what you think of them.

This list needs to be understood in the context of my work with and for women primarily, which is centered on a gender inequality approach to issues of sexual abuse. That approach, by the way, has been adopted by the Committee on the Elimination of all Forms of Discrimination Against Women in its General Recommendation 19,[2] which I recommend be read. Although you don't report to that Committee, its general recommendations—a summary of its jurisprudence—are instructive. General Recommendation 19, adopting the theory that sexual abuse is a form of discrimination against women, explains how violence against women is covered by the equality provisions in The Convention on the Elimination of All Forms of Discrimination Against Women (CEDAW), although it was not originally mentioned in that Convention. The General Recommendation explains article by article the way domestic violence, rape, other forms of sexual assault, and pornography are covered. Their analysis of CEDAW in this area would be of real use to you in your advocacy of CEDAW domestically.

All my work involves litigation and legislation equally, so what I say covers both, if differently at times. The United States is thought of internationally as a common law country, but it really has a mixed civil law-common law system. We draw from the French and German systems to some degree, remaining rooted in British law, with particular American changes.

Here is a factual backdrop on my experience litigating and legislating for women's equality. I began with creating the legal theory for sexual harassment as sex discrimination.[3] Andrea Dworkin and I created the equality approach to pornography and racist hate speech, both of which were largely accepted by the Supreme Court of Canada,[4] as is my approach to equality in general there.[5] I conceived the Violence Against Women Act in the United States, legislation that was passed by Congress[6] and then, in my view, wrongly invalidated by the Supreme Court of the United States, because of their opinion that it exceeded the federal legislative power.[7]

From 1991, at the request of Bosnian and Croatian survivors of the Serbian-led genocide, I started working in the international legal system and with them conceived the concept of rape as an act of genocide and successfully litigated with co-counsel to establish it.[8] All of these developments have been made in connection with clients—particular people who have come to me asking for assistance. I helped the International Criminal Tribunal for Rwanda (ICTR) on rape and other issues.[9] I was involved in creating the language for the Palermo Protocol on international trafficking,[10] worked on drafting antitrafficking legislation in the United States, and with Andrea Dworkin conceived what has come to be called the Swedish then Nordic model for prostitution,[11] which I proposed in Sweden in 1990. Swedish women did the work that made it law there in 1999. That model decriminalizes prostituted people completely so that there can be no legal consequences to being prostituted, and criminalizes the sellers, that is, the pimps and traffickers, and, crucially, criminalizes the buyers. The innovation there, on a sex inequality analysis, is to strongly criminalize the buyers of people for sex, and go after them to enforce it. Many other countries have passed or are considering passing this law.

From 2008 to 2012, I was honored to be appointed the Special Gender Advisor to the first Prosecutor at the International Criminal Court (ICC), Luis Moreno Ocampo, the only actual boss I have ever worked for. The Rome Statute[12] of the ICC has in many ways embraced my concept of gender crime, which is now quite well accepted across international criminal law as well as international human rights law. All of the prosecutions Prosecutor Moreno Ocampo brought included gender crimes. (That hasn't always been the case since, as facts have varied.) Some of one's most important work as a lawyer cannot be publicly discussed because it is confidential, yet lessons learned are supported.

These developments provide the factual context that gave rise to the observations of practice that follow.

Not one of my ten rules, but crucial to all of them, requires attention to issues of race and racism, poverty, and all inequalities in any question of sex inequality. Women are half of most groups as well as a group of our own. Any inequality that affects any group in any way—sexuality, disabilities, age, crucially race, ethnicity, and economic class—affects women deeply and in distinctive ways. Most issues that affect women have dimensions of those inequalities built into either the problem or any proposed solution. You cannot work for women effectively unless you are aware of those issues, crucially race and class, at all times. These are all sex inequality issues.

Chao-ju asked me to consider why women should work with law. The reason is not because law is the universal solution to all problems. The reason is, we can't afford to ignore it because it does not ignore us. Women have not written the rules of law that powerfully affect our lives. Legal rules are not the only rules, but they do contribute to the structure of what we encounter in reality. Part of self-rule and democracy is that you get to have a voice in creating the rules that govern your life. Women historically have not had that voice, to our detriment.

I have never heard anyone ask why men should work with law. Men do everything and think about everything and work with everything, and what they think apparently matters to everything, including law, so the presence of their voice is taken for granted. Women should do everything, and what we think should matter to everything, including law, too. Our voices need to count. Andrea Dworkin once said that she learned from me that women have a right to be effective.[13] I did not even know that this was something I thought until she said it, but I do believe that. Then there is the question of what are the alternatives, and the limitations of those alternatives.

Much of what follows is personal and also doubtless cultural in part. You can take it for whatever use it may offer; we can begin our exchange here. Everyone's reflections, interventions, and challenges are welcome.

Rule Number One: Don't abandon your position before you start. Being practical and strategically smart doesn't mean that you begin by conceding whatever the other side is going to do or say. Your job is what *you* are going to do or say. Being a smart lawyer—I have learned in working with many—is often interpreted as taking the lowest risk approach. Given that law has not been written with women in mind, this generally means undermining yourself in advance, meaning even if you win, you win very little. Don't give up on your side because there is another side.

One good example, in my opinion, was the Equal Rights Amendment (ERA) in the United States, specifically the interpretation that was adopted for it in the last round. The amendment didn't pass. Its equality theory was the same old equality theory. The reason people used it then was likely that they thought it would be acceptable and would win. That didn't happen. The new amendment did not appeal to people as much as it might have. It could also be that they did not know there could be any other equality theory. By the time we lost ERA, and increasingly so in the ensuing years, it became clear that we didn't lose all that much, because the theory that was argued for it was already the theory of the Equal Protection Clause of the Fourteenth Amendment of the Constitution, and it expanded to encompass almost all the original reasons that had been argued for the new amendment. So much of what was said was the reason we needed a new amendment was proven untrue. If we do the ERA again, we won't begin by undermining the ground—new ground—we need to stand on.

Rule Number Two: Use everything you've got and create whatever else you need. The legal system we have, at its foundations, was not designed by women or for women. Sexual harassment law is the first law a woman ever created for women, I think. Existing laws certainly aren't designed on a sex equality principle. Do not hesitate to adapt whatever is already there, but do not feel confined to the tools that exist. We're trying to take down the master's house with the master's tools, to a considerable extent, but to rebuild it equally we also need new tools. Old tools can be used with ingenuity. But we have to forge new tools—legislation, litigation, organizing, media, pressure, psychology, poetry, plays, films. Every tool you can find, you're going to need. Many injuries to women as such are not yet illegal. We've only begun to bring them to the surface. So we need to be creative here. Sexual harassment is only one example. Rape as an act of genocide is another. Use everything you have, and failing that, invent.

Rule Number Three: Life is short. Go for central issues. Go for the jugular. I think sexual violation is a central issue, maybe *the* central issue, for women. Child sexual abuse and prostitution are the beginning and the end of the problem, with rape and sexual harassment in the middle. It's all there. People have a genius and a feel for what they experience as crucial. Whatever that is for you, make it the core of your work. Remember where you are headed. Keep a focus on your goals—your more distant as well as your more immediate ones. Keep the immediate goals consistent with your final goals.

Rule Number Four: What your woman client, or the victims in the situation, or the people you're working with in an attempt to legislate or litigate or agitate or otherwise create need, is likely to be what all women need. There is an idea in male law and philosophy that there is a conflict between what is good for one person and what is good for the group. This tension is greatly exaggerated, in my experience. What little has been done for all women has actually largely been done by doing something real for even one woman. Ask her: what do you want? If you really get what any one woman really needs, you will have done something for women. It will be a real change. Things are not arranged for even one real woman to get what she really needs. Figure that out, fight to get it, and you will have made a real change for women as a group. Do something real for whoever you are working for, and you are likely to do something real for all women. Do not underestimate the systemic value of work that serves individuals.

Rule Number Five: If you have something of value to offer, you will not have to look for clients. They will find you. You won't be able to keep them away. This was true before I was known. So-called "impact litigation," as it is largely done, is regrettably more often a stepping stone for the careers of lawyers than a benefit to other people. If people can find me from rural Bosnia and Herzegovina, if conservative Muslim women can find me and know that they want me to represent them, anyone can find the right person to represent them. It's a matter of having something real to offer, not of straining for "impact." If you really represent who you represent, you will have an impact. What is most innovative about a case is less what appears initially than what you make of it together.

Rule Number Six: Figure out what you need to sustain yourself in this work, how to recover from defeat and being attacked, including by women, and how to keep going. Because you are not likely to have much help. One needs an income that is separate from this work. The people who most need your help usually can't afford to pay for it. Accepting that means figuring out other ways to support yourself, and fancy foundations are unlikely to be that way. Figure out how to get the training you need and how to keep your health. It's your obligation—not that of a movement or anyone else—to become useful, to equip yourself with usable tools, and to keep yourself available. The work itself is sustaining in certain ways, but it is not your therapy or your meal ticket. Determination is a lot more important than optimism. Optimism is designed to be destroyed by cynicism or discouragement or burnout. Illusions are built for disillusion. Determination is realism that never quits.

Rule Number Seven: Stay grounded in what you're doing and for whom. Be open to learning and being led by what the women you're working with have to tell you. But do not romanticize them. Survivors give you what you need. But they're not always right, or nice to you, or easy to work with. Violently sexually abused people, specifically, are deeply harmed by what has been done to them by definition. They have real reasons not to trust others. There will be times when you are one of those others. Stay open to them but realize that part of this work is dealing with the conflicts, attacks, and difficulties that come from your own side. I also get a lot of what I need from the dead women I've represented.

Rule Number Eight: Each woman's case is her life. It is not your life. It is not about you. As her lawyer, you can't want a particular outcome more than she does. What you are there to do is representation, which is complicated but also simple. You're a medium, a channel, and a voice for her, but only to the degree that she gives you her voice. Actually, you're there to help give her *her* voice. This calls for humility. A lot of lawyers lack humility, particularly with clients. They instruct their clients. This is backwards. You are working for her; she is not working for you.

Rule Number Nine: Closely related to Rule Number Eight, sometimes getting something is better than nothing, especially when women have so little. This is up to her. I've had cases that would have been amazing if they went to trial or were appealed and established their theory. But the lawyers on the other side have begun to figure out that if I'm around, maybe they're in trouble, and they offer to settle, and our client takes their offer. It's her case, not yours. If she wants to settle, and needs this to be over, and feels that this is an acceptable end, it's over. Your beautiful theory, something that would also help many other women, is not the point. You accept what she wants and give it to her. If you take nothing because it isn't everything, and run the risk of maybe losing if you go forward, she might get nothing. Then she's left where she started; she came to you because she had nothing to start with. It's her decision.

Rule Number Ten: Fight to win. It really helps sometimes that, being women, we are often underestimated, even though it's insulting. And getting something done is more crucial than getting credit for getting something done. Working behind the scenes works. Other people publishing my work in their legal opinions without attribution, or in legislation, or in international protocols, is a fabulous way to get something done, because then it is in their mouth, not mine. They're in the position to do it. Recognize, too, that sometimes you will not win. This is inevitable when you fight for relatively powerless people. In my view, when it comes to sex equality, ultimately we can get this, we can do this if we do it in these ways, and we will win.

II. Law

prohibitions and a central dynamic of gender inequality, is to this extent illegal, women's resistance to it to this degree legitimized. But it took a feminist movement to expose these experiences as systematic and harmful in the first place, because feminism was the first politics to take women's point of view on our own situation as definitive of that situation. This volume documents and reflects the success, incompleteness, and potential limits on this attempt to embody women's point of view in the law of sex equality.

Sexual harassment, now a legal term of art, permits the claim that sexual initiatives are damaging to women that men may perceive as "normal and expectable"[7] sex-role behavior, just as men may see as intercourse the same encounters women experience as rape, or as erotic the same depictions women find violating. Doctrinal requisites responding to male perspectives on these injuries have been difficult to balance—at times, to identify. From the standpoint of a male harasser, there would be no harm if none was meant.[8] In the same view, damage and relief would implicitly be assessed according to what a male victim of heterosexual harassment might suffer and imagine being made whole by: pay, promotion, grades, and other concretia.[9] Burdens of proof would effectively presume a non-sex-discriminatory social universe (the one men largely occupy) and would require a plaintiff to prove herself exceptional.[10] Women who meet the "good girl" standard of asexual respectability would merit protection; "bad girls" would not be believed. These questions of the nature of sexual injury,[11] adequacy of remedy,[12] attachment and scope of liability,[13] and implicit standards for credibility at trial[14] are beginning to be adjudicated in the sexual harassment context. Advances reflect some acceptance of women's standpoint. Failures at the dismissal stage often reveal corresponding noncomprehension.[15] Losses at trial expose a lack of fit between the court's image of a proper victim and a real one.[16] The existence of a neutral ground between women's and men's perspectives on sexual issues, and the proper posture of the law, depend upon the relation between the sexes, the role of sexuality in work and education, and a theory of the state—substantive concerns that this symposium raises, explores, and furthers.

This volume provides an opportunity for progressed reflection upon the effect of the injection of the issue of sexual harassment into sex discrimination doctrine and equal protection theory. Whatever merit might exist in the Supreme Court's distinction between "differential treatment" and "disparate impact" as types of discrimination cases,[17] the division is inapt in instances of sexual harassment. The disparate treatment of an individual woman based upon a prohibited criterion (female sexuality as a badge or incident of gender) converges with the disparate impact of an arguably sex-neutral criterion upon one gender group (the requirement of sexual delivery sanctioned by material or other deprivations or threats, often supported by lack of an effective institutional remedy). This conceptual convergence occurs because of the social convergence of male sexual initiation toward women with the hierarchy between employers and teachers, who tend to be heterosexual men, and workers and students, who tend to be considered desirable sex objects on the basis of their femaleness.[18] Further, the distinction between treatment and impact relies upon an underlying sense that individual and group claims are somehow different. This difference is elusive under a legal theory of group-based injury in a legal system that requires representatively injured individual plaintiffs. Although sometimes injured one at a time, women are not discriminated against as individuals. Indeed, the absence of treatment based upon personal differential qualities is part of the harm of discrimination. At the same time, sexuality is no less individual to a particular woman for being an attribute of women as a gender. In short, there is no individual/group distinction here.[19] Although sexual harassment claims are implicitly brought under a "disparate treatment" theory, in which one must prove discriminatory motivation,[20] no court has required or inferred it in order to find the behavior sex-based. This doctrinal omission is appropriate and progressive from women's standpoint, since so much sex inequality is enforced by unconscious, heedless, patronizing, well-intentioned, or profit-motivated acts—acts which are no less denigrating, damaging, or sex specific for their lack of invidious sex-based motivation. To hold that a woman target of unwanted heterosexual advances would law and the unequal social reality to which it refers: when the two conflict, should law rationally reflect society or change it? From whose point of view? Sexual harassment law has avoided the doctrinal morass that failure to resolve this issue has produced. It may at the same time have avoided establishing clear policy connecting sexuality with gender that will survive continued attack and affect equally crucial areas for women, such as rape, abortion, gay and lesbian rights[24] and, potentially, pornography.

Remaining issues of prime importance addressed less fully in this volume include political concerns of trial strategy, racist abuse of the cause of action, and organizing in connection with legal initiatives.[25] Should plaintiffs be presented to finders of fact as exceptionally and uniquely abused by a deviant male? Or as examples of abuses common to women, the more outrageous for being pervasive, with which a properly selected jury is encouraged to identify? This is a question both of a plaintiff's facts and preferences and of political principle. The history of the racist use against Black men of vague sexual misdeeds, particularly with white women, raises problems of similar magnitude. This heritage haunts *any* attempt to use this state to support women's control over access to our sexuality. Even when white women are believed, should antiracist feminists support them? Is the question "did he do it?" decisive, irrelevant, or somewhere in between? What if Black women are sexually harassed by the same man but refuse to come forward—perhaps because of grounded apprehension of disbelief or insensitivity by institutions with a reputation for racism, or to protest the selective pursuit of a Black man for actions which white men get away with regularly. Institutions have been known to take the opportunity of a white woman's accusation against a Black man suddenly to support women's rights, however tepidly. What is it to win under such conditions—a victory against sexism or a victory for racism? Or, what is worse, both?

The question—can this state make change in women's interest—arises in some form for all feminist goals. The law against sexual harassment often seems to turn women's demand to control our own sexuality into a request for paternal protection, leaving the impression that it is more traditional morality and less women's power that is vindicated.[26] Can organizing prevent what has happened with rape, in which legal proof requirements reflect a vision of the injury that is far from the actuality of rape, yet women tend to feel they have not been raped if they could not prove it to the law's satisfaction? The law against sexual harassment has helped many women name their oppression and has reduced the stigma of victimization. Restrictions on the cause of action and losses at trial could take back this sense of legitimate outrage.

Creating and pursuing a legal cause of action for the injury of sexual harassment has revealed that different social circumstances, of which gender is one, tend to produce different stakes, interests, perceptions, and cultural definitions of rationality itself. This awareness neither reduces legal rules to pure relative subjectivity nor principle to whose ox is gored.[27] It does challenge the conception that neutrality,[28] including sex-neutrality, with its correlate, objectivity, is adequate to the nonneutral, sexually objectified, social reality women experience. It urges the priority of defining women's injuries as women perceive them. Andrea Dworkin has written: "One can be excited *about* ideas without changing at all. One can think *about* ideas, talk about ideas, without changing at all, people are willing to think about many things. What people refuse to do, or are not permitted to do, or resist doing, is to change the way they think."[29] Whether traditional legal approaches to discrimination are a way of thinking or something thought about, the law may need to confront not only what, but also the way, it thinks about women to achieve its commitment to sex equality.

EIGHT

Sexual Harassment:
Supreme Court Brief for
Mechelle Vinson

This brief argued the first case of sexual harassment to reach the Supreme Court of the United States—the first to reach an apex court anywhere in the world—for the plaintiff. The large number of rapes by her supervisor that Mechelle Vinson had sustained worried many lawyers on our side. The concern, not an unrealistic one, was that the Court would be persuaded that she was not raped at all. Apparently, the more you are raped, the more some think you consented. This, together with the fact that Mechelle had won in the Court of Appeals, were the primary reasons we opposed Supreme Court review.

But as Mechelle eloquently put it on the Supreme Court steps right after the argument, "If I fight, some day some woman will win." She did, that day. Her case unanimously established sexual harassment as a legal claim for sex discrimination,[1] setting a precedent that has reverberated at all levels of the nation and around the world.

We lost on the question of the irrelevance of dress; it seems many think women's clothing conveys consent to sex, or at least is a sexual communication. Making visible the fact that Mechelle is African American as part of her sex discrimination claim was controversial as well, especially because her accused perpetrator was also Black. That she could represent all women yet her racial specificity mattered materially to her injury of sex discrimination foreshadowed an aspect of what became the theory of intersectionality,[2] as well as embodied the politics of the women's movement.

Many people have asked me how on earth one can write to a court about legal concepts that do not exist. This brief illustrates that.

Supreme Court of the United States.
MERITOR SAVINGS BANK, FSB, Petitioner,

v.

Mechelle VINSON, et al., Respondents.

No. 84-1979.

October Term, 1985.

February, 1986.

On Writ of Certiorari To The United States Court of Appeals For
the District of Columbia

BRIEF OF RESPONDENT MECHELLE VINSON

Questions Presented

I. Whether the writ of certiorari was improvidently granted on
this incomplete and ambiguous factual record.

II. Whether sexual harassment as a condition of work, because it
is sexual, is less discriminatory than other forms of employment
discrimination.

III. Whether employers are liable for sexual harassment by supervisors that creates a discriminatory working environment.

IV. Whether evidence of plaintiff's dress and reported fantasies is
admissible in a sexual harassment case.

Summary of Argument

The present cloudy and incomplete factual record is inappropriate as
a vehicle for this Court's first decision on employer liability for environmental sexual harassment by supervisors. There are no factual
findings on whether sexual intercourse occurred between the parties,
or on whether the workplace was characterized by pervasive sexual
offense against women workers, including respondent, or on whether
Ms. Vinson was constructively discharged. The absence of a finding
on environmental sexual harassment renders hypothetical any con-

sideration of questions like whether the employer was told of the situation or should have known about it—hence whether notice and knowledge should matter for liability in environmental cases. Of what should the employer have been told? Of what should it have known? Further, without knowing the conditions under which the parties ended their employment relationship, it is unclear just what kind of sexual harassment case this will turn out to be on remand. As a vehicle for resolving issues of employer liability, such flaws render this record, upon re-examination, so inadequate to an adjudication of the legal issues raised that the writ of certiorari should be dismissed as improvidently granted.

Should this Court reach the merits, it should hold that conditioning economic survival on sexual submission is as invidious a practice of discrimination as any other. Its effect on the equal treatment of individuals at work without regard to sex is as destructive as any other. This is as true when employees *de facto* must tolerate a work-place setting permeated with sexual hostility and denigration in order to keep a job, as it is when exchange of sexual compliance for a job is overtly proposed. So long as abusive treatment is differentially based on gender and is employment-related, employers should receive no special latitude in liability because the abuse is accomplished by sexual means. Nor should the rules of evidence be rewritten because the discrimination is sexually inflicted, admitting plaintiff character evidence where it would otherwise be excluded.

Statement of the Case

Respondent Mechelle Vinson sued petitioner Meritor Savings Bank ("Bank") and her supervisor there, Sidney Taylor, for sexual harassment in employment under Title VII of the Civil Rights Act of 1964, as amended, 42 U.S.C. 2000e *et seq.* (1982) ("Title VII"). Ms. Vinson alleged that Mr. Taylor, who hired and supervised her, imposed unwanted sexual advances at work and unwelcome sexual activity as a requisite of her employment with petitioner. (Joint Appendix ("JA") 4–5.) She further alleged that Mr. Taylor altered her personnel records to cover himself and sexually harassed other women subordinates at the Bank. (JA 5.)

Ms. Vinson filed her complaint while still an employee of the Bank (JA 1), and one day after she (on advice of counsel) did not report to work and notified Mr. Taylor that she was ill and would be on sick leave indefinitely. (JA 1; Appendix to Petition for a Writ of Certiorari ("App.") 43a.) About a month later, the Bank sent her a letter (which she did not receive) stating: "In as much as you have refused to meet with me to discuss this problem, we assume that you have elected to voluntarily terminate your employment with the Association and we will consider you no longer employed as of this date." (JA 16.) In a letter of the same date, Ms. Vinson wrote the Bank stating that "due to the level of harassment and the unprofessional atmosphere that exists in my direction at your Northeast Office, I am forced to submit this letter of constructive resignation." (JA 17.)

Mr. Taylor denied that he sexually accosted or pressured Ms. Vinson or other women on the job. He denied that they had sexual relations. He denied doctoring her employment record. (JA 8.) The Bank, by contrast, took the position *arguendo* that any sexual relationship between Ms. Vinson and Mr. Taylor had been consensual. In any event, the Bank pleaded, it was not responsible because any such behavior was extracurricular and it had not known about it. (JA 11, 12.)

Ms. Vinson was denied leave to amend the complaint to add constructive discharge and other retaliatory acts, to add other victims of Mr. Taylor's sexual aggrandizement, and for reinstatement, declaratory relief, and tort claims for assault, battery, and intentional infliction of emotional distress. (Docket Sheet.) However, pretrial statements, trial briefs, and proposed findings of fact of all parties addressed termination and back pay. The district court's pretrial order specifically "incorporate[d] claims set forth in the respective pretrial statements" as triable matters.

At trial, Ms. Vinson testified to repeated outrages of sexual attention and aggression by her supervisor, including 40 or 50 episodes of undesired and traumatic sexual intercourse over a 20 month period between 1975 and 1977. (TR, Jan. 22, II, 51–59, 67–73; App. 32a.)[3]

Her physical and emotional suffering was testified to include bleeding and infections, inability to eat or sleep normally, loss of hair, and extreme stress and nervousness (TR, Jan. 22, II, 77–78; TR, Jan. 23, III, 51), with one attack so violent that she bled from the vagina for weeks. (TR, Jan. 22, 1980, II, 78.) Although Ms. Vinson testified she repeatedly pleaded with Mr. Taylor to leave her alone, her compliance with forced intercourse was exacted by his intimidation and threats of reprisals, including against her job. (TR, Jan. 22, II, 67, 73, 81; TR, Jan. 24, IV, 24–25, 28, 50, 65.) Mr. Taylor ceased forcing intercourse upon her after she acquired a steady boyfriend (TR, Jan. 24, IV, 88–89), but continued to impose himself upon her sexually at work in other ways. He still fondled her and molested her, exposed himself to her, and barged into the ladies room when she was there. (TR, Jan. 22, II, 64, 71, 80; TR, Jan. 24, IV, 65); *See also* TR, Jan. 21, I, 42–43 (Testimony of C. Malone).

Christine Malone and Mary Levarity, among other co-workers of the Bank, testified that they had seen Mr. Taylor sexually accost, abuse, and handle Ms. Vinson at work, that she repeatedly asked him to stop, and that she appeared upset by it. (TR, Jan. 21, I, 34–38, 40) (Testimony of C. Malone); (TR, Jan. 28, VI, 25) (Testimony of M. Levarity). They said he had committed similar transgressions against them as well. (TR, Jan. 28, IV, 9–14.) "Yes, it did come a time when he would put his hands on my breasts and he would put his hands on my backside and it was just disrespectful. That just tore me down. I couldn't stand it." (TR, Jan. 21, I, 21) (Testimony of C. Malone). Some of this evidence was admitted, and some of it was not. (E.g., TR, Jan. 21, I, 5, 20, 21, 25, 30 (Testimony of C. Malone)).

Ms. Vinson further testified that particularly after their sexual intercourse stopped, Mr. Taylor tampered with her personnel records, lodged false complaints about her with management, denigrated and abused her in front of other workers, entrapped her into work errors, escalated his campaign of fault-finding against her job performance, and threatened her life when she threatened to report him. (TR, Jan. 23, III, 50–52, 55; TR, Jan. 24, IV, 24–25.) She testified she was forced by the intolerable conditions to terminate her employment and was in effect constructively discharged. (TR, Jan. 22, II, 6; TR, Jan. 23, III, 55, 60, 64; TR, Jan. 25, V, 16.)

Also according to her testimony, Ms. Vinson did not report Mr. Taylor's misconduct to other employer authorities—other than to complain of his sexual harassment of two other women to David G. Burton, Vice President—because Mr. Taylor threatened to kill her or have her raped if she did so. (TR, Jan. 24, IV, 25.) "My life was put on the line. I didn't know what might happen to me. Christina was raped. She almost lost her mind. I saw things that went on in the bank and I didn't want anything to happen to me. My life was very valuable to me." (Objection sustained to strike reference to rape of C. Malone as to truth of matter alleged) (TR, Jan. 24, IV, 28). "I was always afraid of Mr. Taylor up until the day I left." (TR, Jan. 24, IV, 99.) Ms. Vinson's complaint to Mr. Taylor about his mistreatment of other women at the Bank supported her sense of the futility of reporting: "[he said] that was his way of relaxing them, and if they didn't like it, they can get the hell out and I can get the hell out." (TR, Jan. 23, III, 48) (Testimony of M. Vinson). Both Ms. Malone and Ms. Levarity testified that they told ("Q: And you used their terms, 'sexual harassment?' A: Correct") (TR, Jan. 25, IV, 56–57) (Testimony of M. Levarity) or tried to tell (TR, Jan. 21, I, 97–101) (Testimony of C. Malone) Mr. Burton of the situation, but he was unreceptive and took no action. (TR, Jan. 23, III, 76) (Testimony of M. Vinson); *See also* TR, Jan. 22, II, 8 (Argument of counsel for the Bank).

The Bank had a policy against sex discrimination headed by Mr. Burton with implementation delegated to "each officer and department head" rather than to any specific procedure. (JA 25.)[4] The Bank's general internal grievance procedure required an employee to "state his grievance in writing and present it to his supervisor . . . only after oral representation has been made and it is felt that the grievance has not been fully resolved." (Plaintiff's Exhibit 13, at 11.)

Mr. Taylor denied making sexual advances to Ms. Vinson and contended the suit was in retaliation for a business-related dispute. He said there had been no sexual relationship, consensual or otherwise, between himself and Ms. Vinson. The Bank also disputed Ms.

Vinson's allegations. One witness testified that Ms. Vinson, in her view, wore provocative clothing and said she fantasized about sex, testimony admitted over objection. (TR, Jan. 30, 14, 48.) The Bank also presented testimony that its corporate officers did not know of Mr. Taylor's alleged misconduct. (See generally TR, Jan. 31, VIII) (Testimony of D. Burton).

The trial judge denied relief. Neither plaintiff's proof of forced sex nor defendant's denial that any sex occurred was accepted. Instead, Penn, J., held that "*if* the plaintiff and Taylor did engage in an intimate or sexual relationship . . . [it] was a voluntary one by plaintiff . . ." (App. 42a) (emphasis added). The court found Ms. Vinson was "not required to grant Taylor . . . sexual favors as a condition of either her employment or in order to obtain promotion" (App. 42a) and no one properly reported the abuse alleged. (App. 43a.) The conflicting testimony on constructive discharge was not resolved. The Bank was held blameless, since "notice to Taylor should [not] amount to notice to the bank" (App. 41a.) In any case, no actionable events had occurred. (App. 43a-44a.)

The Court of Appeals for the District of Columbia Circuit, Robinson, J., reversed and remanded. *Vinson v. Taylor*, 753 F.2d 141, 152 (D.C. Cir. 1985) (App. 1a-21a, 21a). The Court of Appeals noted that unwelcome sexual advances and initiatives are actionable in themselves when they poison the workplace with a pervasive atmosphere of discrimination. 753 F.2d at 144-45 (App. 6a-8a) (citing *Bundy v. Jackson*, 641 F.2d 943-44 (D.C. Cir. 1981)). Sexual behaviors which create an "intimidating, hostile, or offensive working environment" 753 F.2d at 146 (App. 9a) (quoting EEOC *Guidelines on Discrimination Because of Sex*, 29 C.F.R. 1604.11 (a) (3) (1984) constitute sex discrimination separate and apart from ultimate sex acts to which a job is held hostage.

Since the trial court did not rule on whether the Bank condoned sexual innuendo and pressure as a condition of working there, the finding that the parties' sexual contact, if it occurred, was voluntary, did not dispose of all of Ms. Vinson's sexual harassment claims. This legal error might, further, have tainted the findings that were made. 753 F.2d at 145 n.32 (App. 7a-7b n.32). Further findings on the separate issue of the working environment created by the supervisor's sexual initiatives and advances were therefore required. Stressing the power of the supervisor in the workplace as well as the statutory language of Title VII, the court directed that on remand the employer be held liable if supervisorial sexual harassment created a discriminatory work setting. 753 F.2d at 150 (App. at 18a).

The Court of Appeals disapproved the possible role of irrelevant evidence of plaintiff's dress and alleged fantasies in the decision below. Finding that these matters "had no place in this litigation," they were directed excluded on remand. 753 F.2d at 146 n.36 (App. 9a n.36). In addition, clear error was found in the trial judge's exclusion of some evidence to show that Mr. Taylor sexually harassed other women at the Bank, 753 F.2d at 146 (App. 10a), a ruling not disputed here by petitioner. Amendments to the complaint were invited on remand by the court expressly "intimat[ing] no view on the disposition to be made should Vinson renew the motion on remand." 753 F.2d at 146 n.36 (App. 9a n.36).

Rehearing *en banc* was denied, 760 F.2d 1330 (D.C. Cir. 1985), with three judges dissenting, 760 F.2d 1330 (App. 22a-29a) (Bork, J.). In the view of the dissenters, the Court of Appeals' decision to exclude evidence of the victim's dress and fantasies would unfairly restrict defendants' ability to prove innocence of sexual force. 760 F.2d at 1331 (App. 22a). They also questioned whether acts that are so difficult to police and were here found to have freely occurred should make an employer liable for sex discrimination. 760 F.2d at 1331 (App. 22a).

Certiorari was granted.

Argument

I. The Writ of Certiorari Was Improvidently Granted on This Incomplete and Ambiguous Factual Record.

This is the first sexual harassment case to reach this Court. On certiorari this Court requires that cases present issues through factual records that are clear, reasonably complete, specific and unclouded by crucial ambiguities. By these standards, the present record is not a proper vehicle for resolving the legal issues it poses. Ambiguity in a key fact can "sufficiently cloud [] the record to render the case an inappropriate vehicle for this Court's first decision" in a new area. *Jones v. State Board of Education*, 397 U.S. 31, 32 (1970) (*per curiam*) (dismissing the writ).[5] In *Jones*, the record was clouded by a fact that might have presented an issue other than the one the petition sought to address. In the case at bar, the record is occluded by *absence* of facts necessary to present the issues petitioners raise.

The writ has been dismissed in prior cases for lack of "reasonable clarity and definiteness" in the facts, *Rescue Army v. Municipal Court*, 331 U.S. 549, 568 (1947) or when "the record does not adequately present the questions tendered in the petition." *Needelman v. U.S.*, 362 U.S. 600 (1960). Petitioners argue that environmental sexual harassment should not be actionable as sex discrimination. They argue that employers should not be responsible for such acts as do occur from supervisors to subordinates, especially if no employer authority other than the supervisor/perpetrator was told of the situation. Facts and factual inferences bearing on these issues include: whether the alleged sex acts occurred, and if so whether they were unwelcome; whether sexual harassment was a condition of the working environment, and if so whether the employer knew or should have known about it.

On this record, one still cannot say whether the sexual intercourse of which Ms. Vinson complained occurred. One key factual finding is that "if the plaintiff and Taylor did engage in an intimate or sexual relationship . . . [it] was a voluntary one by plaintiff . . ." (App. at 42a). The opacity and indefiniteness of this statement is so extreme that it finds no fact at all. To put it mildly, this creates "ambiguities in the record as to the issues sought to be tendered." *Mitchell v. Oregon Frozen Foods Co.*, 361 U.S. 231 (1960) (*per curiam*) (dismissing certiorari).

As the record stands, sexual intercourse may or may not have occurred, making purely projective any conclusion as to its welcomeness. Moreover, no finding even purports to be made on environmental sexual harassment by a supervisor. That also may or may not have occurred, making the welcomeness of advances wholly hypothetical and any consideration of notice, knowledge, policy or procedure, and obligation to cure wholly abstract. When "the facts necessary for evaluation of the dispositive . . . issues . . . are not adequately presented by the record," *Wainwright v. City of New Orleans*, 392 U.S. 598, 598–599 (1967) (Fortas and Marshall, J.J., concurring), the writ is properly dismissed. These lacunae leave open a disputed question of material fact, confound review for legal error, and make this case inappropriate as a vehicle for creating new law. Absence of facts is the most extreme violation imaginable of this Court's standards of clarity, specificity, and adequacy. It renders impossible a realistic assessment of the Title VII requirements that should attach in cases that *do* present these issues.

There is no finding of fact as to whether Mr. Taylor routinely initiated sex with the women under his supervision at the Bank, including Ms. Vinson. Therefore, no finding is possible on whether Ms. Vinson welcomed sexual by-play at work, precluding in turn any inquiry into whether the context was consensual or forced. The result is, this case has reached this Court, *not* on a motion to dismiss, and it is still correct, as petitioner does, to refer to the "alleged advances." (Brief of Meritor Savings Bank, FSB, ("Bank") 26). The Bank in effect seeks review as if on a motion to dismiss with the ground rules reversed: as if the plaintiff's original allegations can be taken as *disproven* and only issues of legal adequacy remain. To the contrary, at this point in the case, a ruling on whether or not environmental sexual harassment occurred as a matter of fact is essential to a decision on whether environmental sexual harassment is actionable sex discrimination under Title VII as a matter of law. One of the plaintiff's allegations and theories at trial—that unwelcome advances permeated the workplace—remain factual showings under a legal theory which the trial judge has not ruled upon one way or the other. The uncontested ruling by the Court of Appeals that it was error to exclude evidence of coercive advances to other women on the job highlights the inadequacy of any inference that could be made on this point at this time.

The lack of any finding on whether Mr. Taylor, through unwanted sexual mistreatment of women on the job, created a discriminatory work environment makes "this record too opaque to permit any satisfactory adjudication" *Wainwright v. City of New Orleans,* 392 U.S., at 598 (Harlan, J., concurring) of the question of the conditions under which employers ought to be held responsible for sexual harassment by supervisors in the workplace environment. Without a specific finding on the existence, pervasiveness, and welcomeness of Mr. Taylor's sexual initiatives, this Court cannot know if any advances were welcome on the one hand, unwelcome but permitted almost as a matter of policy on the other, *see Bundy v. Jackson,* 641 F.2d 934, 943 (D.C. Cir. 1981)—or unwelcome and by a supervisor, as yet a third legal possibility. Whether to require knowledge of the events by others in the employer hierarchy for corporate liability to attach might, according to the circumstances, be held to depend to some degree on whether the sexual atmosphere was so pervasive as to constitute an environment, ignorance of which was impossible. It might depend upon whether the terror created by the supervisor's advances was effective in creating an environment so pervasive and coercive that it was insulated from reports by victims. Both are possible readings of this trial transcript, but it would engage this Court in fact-finding to construe it. Yet petitioner seeks to litigate the triggers of employer liability for supervisors' environmental sexual harassment of subordinates in their absence.

The Court of Appeals properly found the claim of coercive advances as a condition of work to be raised by the case but unresolved by the trial judge, hence it remanded. If Ms. Vinson's constructive discharge continues to be an issue on remand, this case may yet turn out to be a *quid pro quo* in which sexual compliance is exchanged for a job, in addition to an environmental case. *See Henson v. City of Dundee,* 682 F.2d 897, 908 n.18 (11th Cir. 1982). Nor is there any finding on intent, also factual in nature, *Pullman-Standard v. Swint,* 456 U.S. 273, 287–8 (1982); *General Building Contractors Ass'n v. Pennsylvania,* 458 U.S. 375, 381 n.6 (1982); *U.S. Postal Service v. Aiken,* 460 U.S. 711, 715 (1983). This issue was raised for the first time (and doctrinally incorrectly, *see* n.16 *infra*) in the Bank's petition for certiorari. "We cannot decide issues raised for the first time here.

Cardinale v. Louisiana, 394 U.S. 437 (1969)." *Tacon v. Arizona*, 410 U.S. 351, 352 (1973) (*per curiam*) (dismissing the writ).

Granting certiorari prior to remand has rendered "the record ... n?? sufficiently clear and specific to permit decision of the important ... questions involved in this case." *Commonwealth of Massachusetts v. Painten*, 389 U.S. 560, 561 (1968) (*per curiam*) (dismissing the writ). These defects in the factual record may not have been "fully apprehended at the time certiorari was granted." *The Monrosa v. Carbon Black Export, Inc.*, 359 U.S. 180, 183 (1959). *See also Burrell v. McCray*, 426 U.S. 471, 472 (1976) (Stevens, J., concurring in dismissal of certiorari).

Taken together, the insufficiencies of this record reveal that the reasons for granting certiorari put forth in the petition are, on re-examination, not supported by the record in this case. *See Iowa Beef Packers, Inc. v. Thompson*, 405 U.S. 228, 230 (1972). The writ should be dismissed as improvidently granted.

II. Sexual Harassment, Simply Because It Is Done through Sex, Is No Less Discriminatory Than Any Other Form of Discrimination in Employment.

There is no disagreement before this Court that sexual harassment states a claim for sex discrimination under Title VII, a view which has been adopted by every Circuit that has considered the issue. (citations, n.3 *supra*.) Sexual harassment ranks "among the most offensive and demeaning experiences that an employee can have." Fryer-Cohen and Vincelette, *Notice, Remedy, and Employer Liability for Sexual Harassment*, 35 Lab. L. J. (May, 1984) at 301, 307. It damages individuals, *see e.g.*, *Stubbs v. United States*, 744 F.2d 58, 60–61 (8th Cir. 1984), *cert. denied,*—U.S.—, 105 S.Ct. 2113 (1985) (wrongful death action for suicide to avoid sexual harassment) and is economically costly, U.S. Merit System Protection Board, *Sexual Harassment in the Federal Workplace: Is It a Problem?* (March, 1981) at 14 (in two year period, sexual harassment of federal workers cost taxpayers $189 million in health costs, low productivity and job turnover). Yet the Bank argues for operative rules for adjudicating these claims that would make sexual harassment into a second-class discrimination claim. On the ground that "sexual activity is special," (Bank, 37) the Bank would render sexual harassment an injury especially difficult for victims to prove. By attenuating employer liability (see III *infra*), it would become an injury without effective remedy. In the case of environmental claims, the Bank (but not *amicus* United States, Brief for the United States and the EEOC as *Amicus Curiae*, ("US") at 15) would eliminate it from Title VII coverage altogether.

Each distinctive practice of, and basis for, claims under Title VII has recognized particularities. But if treatment is proven to be based on a prohibited classification,[6] and if it does damage in employment, it is employment discrimination and therefore illegal. The Bank argues for a legal double standard by distinguishing first between sexual *harassment* and other forms of sex discrimination, and second between *sexual* harassment and harassment on the basis of other protected classifications like race and religion. Sexual harassment as a legal claim would emerge eviscerated as a result.

Because sexual harassment is sexual, the Bank argues, it is not fully discrimination. Its inherently "personal" quality is said to distinguish it from other forms of purportedly anonymous gender-based treatment.[7] Whether a specific situation alleged to be sexual harassment is truly personal, as opposed to gender-based and work-related, is a question of fact not of law, as courts have uniformly held. *Heelan v. Johns-Manville Corp.*, 451 F. Supp. 1382, 1388 (D. Colo. 1978); *Tomkins v. Public Service Electric & Gas Co.*, 568 F. 2d 1044, 1047 n.3 (3rd Cir. 1977). *See also* C. MacKinnon, *Sexual Harassment of Working Women* (1979) ("MacKinnon") 83–90, 235–236 (appellate reversals of rulings that sexual harassment is "personal" as a matter of law). If a situation is found to be sexual harassment, it does not become *not* sex discrimination because it is sexual. Rather, it presents a form of discrimination which is particularly personally invasive.

Sexual advances and activities become talismanic in the Bank's perspective. It would impose greater burdens on a plaintiff when sex is involved than when discrimination is accomplished through other means. This approach turns on use of the phrase "sexual activity" to refer to welcome and forced sex alike, as if the two are properly indistinguishable for legal purposes. (Bank, 10, 13.) Whatever specialness inheres in sex, it inheres in sex freely chosen. To the degree that freely chosen sex is special, forced sex violates that specialness. Sexual harassment by definition is never wanted. 29 C.F.R. 1604.11(a) (sexual harassment is "unwelcome sexual advances" under certain conditions). If it may be said to be special at all, it is especially abusive. Yet both the Bank and their *amici* conflate unwanted forcible sexual initiation with welcome friendly suggestions. They equate forced sex with all sex, implying that if wanted sex has value, forced sex must also, a value to be recognized by special legal exemption. The value of something freely done, like philanthropy, does not undermine the culpability of the same act when it is forced, as with theft. The fact that episodes that are not sexual harassment do occur does not mean that episodes that *are* sexual harassment should not be actionable, with all other sex discrimination.

The Bank further argues that environmental harassment based on sex by supervisors of subordinates is not like harassment by identically situated persons when based on race or religion or national origin, because sexual advances may be wanted while racial invective is never wanted. Sexual *abuse* is no more wanted than racial abuse, and friendly discussions of race are no more inherently offensive than friendly discussions of sex. Similarly, one's ethnic identity is not inherently negative, but rather is a positive and personal (as well as collective) attribute. That does not render it a category open to special abuse under equal employment opportunity laws. Sexual characteristics, words, behaviors, or activities are no more or less inherently socially offensive or harassing than are corresponding racial or religious characteristics or designations or traditions.

The Bank further seeks to distinguish sexual harassment as an environmental condition of work from sexual harassment as a *quid pro quo*, arguing that a pervasive context lacks tangibility. (Bank 31, 37.) First, the Bank seeks to litigate this issue by proceeding as if it can assume that the environmental sexual harassment alleged in this case *did not occur.* There is as yet no factual finding to this effect, and there is substantial evidence to the contrary. Christine Malone testified that Mr. Taylor "would put his hands on my breasts and he would put his hands on my backside . . . ." (TR, Jan. 21, I, 21.) Asked how often, she responded, "He did it all the time. It was constantly . . . . It was every day. Every day we worked there." (TR, Jan. 21, I, 40.) Ms. Vinson testified that "he would touch me practically every day . . . . Whenever he felt like it." (TR, Jan. 22, II, 71.) "Each day was a touching day. Each day was a mental day." (TR, Jan. 22, II, 80.) "I felt humiliated. I felt powerless. I was afraid of him." (TR, Jan. 22, II, 66.) The witnesses also corroborated each other's reports, *e.g.*, "I observed Mr. Taylor touching Christina on her . . . rear end, touching her breasts and chasing her in the back . . . ." (TR, Jan. 22, II, 33) (Testimony of M. Vinson); "I heard him tell Mechelle that he wanted to fuck her." (TR, Jan. 28, IV, 25) (Testimony of M. Levarity); "He would often touch her body and fondle her." (Def't Ex. 43) (Affidavit of M. Levarity).

Sexual insult and aggression against women as a pattern in the working environment was an explicit part of counsel's theory of the case at trial: "overt acts of discrimination against other women in the environment [is] part of my *prima facie* case . . . ." (TR, Jan. 23, III, 45.) This evidence was argued to show that the advances against Ms. Vinson were based on sex, and also to show "the environment that Miss Vinson went into." (TR, Jan. 21, I, 21.) "Evidence of how he treated other women, that is members of the protected class, is admissible to prove that he in fact treated Miss Vinson in a discriminatory manner." (TR, Jan. 21, I, 16) (Argument of counsel for the plaintiff). One purpose of the remand is to allow evidence improperly excluded—*e.g.* objection sustained to evidence proffered to show "the daily environment . . . encountered whenever Mr. Taylor was . . . in that office" (TR, Jan. 23, III, 4)—with latitude to amend the complaint to conform to the proof, 753 F.2d, at 142 n.12 (App. 3a-4a, n.12), in order to rule on this issue.

Second, the two recognized forms of sexual harassment are not a hard distinction. Rather, they are more like poles of a continuum that operates on a time line. For instance, if a victim of environmental sexual harassment leaves the job for that reason, the resulting constructive discharge becomes a *quid pro quo*. Courts have recognized the insufficiency of a theory of sexual harassment that does not allow a context of unwanted advances to be actionable, effectively permitting all sexual harassment that stops short of the victim quitting or being fired, or other similarly aggravated thresholds. *Bundy v. Jackson*, 641 F. 2d, at 945–946; *Henson v. City of Dundee*, 682 F. 2d 897, 908 n.12 (11th Cir. 1982); *Jeppson v. Wunnicke*, 611 F. Supp. 78, 83 (D. Alaska 1985). The legal scholar who conceptualized the types of sexual harassment criticizes the construction that "no series of sexual advances alone is sufficient to justify legal intervention until it is expressed in the *quid pro quo* form. [This] forces the victim to bring intensified injury upon herself in order to demonstrate that she is injured at all . . . [if so] long as the sexual situation is constructed with enough coerciveness, subtlety, suddenness, or one-sidedness . . . while her job is formally undisturbed, she is not considered to have been sexually harassed." *MacKinnon*, 46–47.

Third, "Title VII's primary goal, of course, *is* to end discrimination." *Ford Motor Co. v. EEOC*, 458 U.S. 219, 230 (1982) (emphasis in original). Having realized that a rigid distinction between *quid pro quo* and environmental harassment is both analytically incorrect and undermines the purposes of Title VII, one court recently stated: "Preventing sex discrimination in employment is too important a goal to turn upon the vagaries of what does and what does not constitute a *tangible* job benefit as distinguished from what is evidently considered to be an *intangible* benefit such as psychological well-being at the workplace." *Jeppson v. Wunnicke*, 611 F. Supp. at 83 (emphasis in original). *See also*, Cal. Gov't Code Section 12940 (i) (West 1980 and Supp. 1983).

There is nothing ineffable about a daily gauntlet of vitriol. Nor does it take much sensitivity to recognize that being repeatedly called "slut" and "fucking cunt" on the job, *Zabkowicz v. West Bend Co.*, 589 F. Supp. 780, 789 (E.D. Wisc. 1984), *McNabb v. Cub Foods*, 352 N.W.2d 378, 381 (1984) is no less an injury of civil inequality than is being called "nigger" and "spook," *Taylor v. Jones*, 653 F.2d 1193,

1198 (8th Cir. 1981) or "Christ-Killer" and "Jew-boy," *Compston v. Borden*, 424 F. Supp. 157, 158 (S.D. Ohio 1976). In the instant case, Mr. Taylor "would make comments about my legs, said I had big hairy legs and he would like to get between them." (TR, Jan. 21, I, 21) (Testimony of C. Malone). "I observed him standing up by the wall in the bank with his penis showing through his pants showing it at Miss Vinson and myself there." (TR, Jan. 21, I, 34) (Testimony of C. Malone). He accosted the women employees, they testified, with statements like, "Come and get this. Come and get this dick. You want it." (TR, Jan. 21, I, 43) (Testimony of C. Malone).

Petitioner's contrasts between discriminatory environments based on race and those based on sex distort the clear parallels between them. The Bank states that "racially or religiously derogatory workplace activity cannot reasonably be conceived as occupationally neutral or desirable. Sexual activity, on the other hand . . . may be socially acceptable . . . ." (Bank, 10.) If the parallel were drawn correctly, it would state that sexually derogatory workplace activity cannot reasonably be conceived as occupationally neutral or desirable, but not all racially specific activity, including conversation, is socially unacceptable. Voluntary discussions of race and ethnicity, including use of racial and ethnic words and jokes, is not always socially problematic. For race as for sex, the same words that can be invective in one context can have a noninvidious meaning in another. Just as there is no value to racial invective, slurs, and harassment, *see e.g.*, *EEOC v. Murphy Motor Freight Lines, Inc.*, 488 F. Supp. 381, 384 (D. Minn. 1980) there is no value to sexual invective, slurs, and harassment. Eliminating existing Title VII claims for contextual harms which are, in the Bank's diminishing phrase, "unrelated to any loss or threatened loss of tangible job benefits" (Bank, 14), would, of course, sweep away claims on the basis of religion or race as well as sex. There is no principled distinction between them. The uniform gravamen of rulings in this area is that citizens do not have to endure these atrocities to have an equal chance to make a living. *Cariddi v. Kansas City Chiefs Football Club, Inc.*, 568 F.2d 87, 88 (8th Cir. 1977); *Firefighters Inst. for Racial Equality v. St. Louis*, 549 F.2d 506, 514–15 (8th Cir. 1977), *cert.*

denied, Banta v. United States, 434 U.S. 819 (1977); *United States v. Buffalo*, 457 F. Supp. 612, 631–35 (W.D.N.Y. 1978).

Although welcomeness was not here litigated as a fact between Vinson and Taylor, the unwelcomeness of a sexual encounter in employment is crucial to a sexual harassment claim. The Court of Appeals did not hold to the contrary. It is false that the Court of Appeals "eliminates unwelcomeness as an issue." (Bank, 14.) Perhaps the Bank perceives this because it does not distinguish, as do the Court of Appeals and respondent, between sexual *advances* that are welcome and sexual *intercourse* that appears voluntary. The Court of Appeals saw that sexual advances may exist, with or without intercourse, and sexual intercourse may *appear* voluntary even though the advances that initiated it were entirely unwelcome. This assessment cannot be made without looking at the advances separately, something the trial court did not do.

It should be underscored that unwelcomeness was not, as a factual matter, an issue between Vinson and Taylor. Mr. Taylor did not say that his advances were welcome, but rather that he did not make them, and not that the sex was voluntary, but rather that it did not occur. (JA 8.) The Bank denied the factual allegations concerning anything sexual between the parties on the ground that it knew nothing about it. (JA 10.) In its failure to find the facts and rule on the law of the wantedness of the advances separately, the trial court failed to rule on one of Vinson's legal claims. Moreover, it was a factual claim as to which defendant Taylor—other than Ms. Vinson, the only source of facts on most of the sexual intercourse—had apparently to some degree been disbelieved. This failure, in turn, gave rise to the further concern that *plaintiff's* evidence *that sex occurred* may have been misconstrued, affecting the ruling on voluntariness the lower court did make.

Each sexual harassment case is to be evaluated in light of "the totality of the circumstances," which include "the context in which the alleged incidents occurred." 29 C.F.R. 1604.11(b). In the case at bar, respondent maintains, and there is no factual ruling on the subject to disturb, she did not find Mr. Taylor's *advances* welcome. And she told him so. "I would always tell Mr. Taylor that I wished that he would stop, you know . . . Leave me alone, just leave me alone." (TR, Jan. 22, II, 67.) Other women supported this: "[Ms. Vinson] told him to remove his hands, to take his hands off her." (TR, Jan. 21, I, 36) (Testimony of C. Malone). Ms. Vinson testified, "I had no other choice." (TR, Jan. 24, IV, 50.)[8] It would be consistent with the environmental evidence to find that Ms. Vinson indicated her disinclination and repugnance to Mr. Taylor repeatedly, yet repeatedly submitted, rebuffing his attentions including those short of intercourse, but being unable to stop either the advances or the intercourse out of a combination of lack of power to make her wishes effective, lack of viable economic alternatives, and fear of reporting. "I was afraid. Fear is the wors[t] thing in the world." (TR, Jan. 23, III, 57) (Testimony of M. Vinson). This could create a pattern that, if evaluated at trial in the absence of assessing the welcomeness of the advances themselves, could appear voluntary on her part.

Since the trial court did not evaluate the atmosphere in which the advances occurred in light of applicable law, it could have interpreted plaintiff's account of the many acts of sex against a background of voluntariness and friendly mutuality, rather than against a background of hostility and force. Because the trial court did not evaluate the background at all, as under law it was obligated to do, remand was appropriate.

Thus the Court of Appeals did not hold voluntariness irrelevant nor does respondent argue that it is. Rather, the Court of Appeals correctly concluded that a ruling on voluntariness is ambiguous that does not distinguish between fearful compliance, i.e. unsuccessful resistance or hopeless nonresistance to each act at the time,[9] and mutuality of desire. Sex that kept occurring could be "a victim's 'voluntary' submission to unlawful discrimination" (App. 10a) and still be a fight repeatedly lost, or it could be free choice. Women often despairingly acquiesce in unwanted sex not only to keep their jobs at defined thresholds, but to keep their jobs on a daily basis, when the employment environment systematically requires tolerance of sexual harassment as a condition of being there. If the law of sexual harassment is unavailable to victims who have little choice but to comply, or who cannot make their rejection effective despite attempts, the consequence will be to protect all but those who need the protection the most: those who are so vulnerable that noncompliance is a physical impossibility or an unaffordable luxury. Respondent submits that if the law of sexual harassment is useless to her because of her lack of choices, it is of little use. *See Bundy v. Jackson*, 641 F.2d at 946 (resistance not required); *see also MacKinnon*, 46–47 (futility of resistance requirement).

In some workplaces, victims who resist and/or report are met with the hostility, ridicule, and disbelief exemplified by virtually every aspect of this record except the D.C. Circuit's sensitive rendering. Ms. Vinson may have perceived that, realistically, she had no alternative to acquiescence. Realizing that this possibility had not been ruled out, the Court of Appeals simply held that, absent a holding below on the wantedness of the *advances* in the case, a ruling that the sex, if it happened, was "voluntary" did not dispose of all of respondent's Title VII claims. Because the trial court applied the wrong segment of the right law, that also tainted its finding on the part of the law it did rule on. When reassessed and ruled upon under correct law, the previous factual ruling, undisturbed yet properly recontextualized, may prove not to have told the whole story about the relationship.

III. Employers Are Liable for Sexual Harassment by Supervisors Which Creates a Discriminatory Working Environment.

This is the heart of the dispute. It is not an abstract contest over whether sexual harassment is sex discrimination, which is undisputed. It is a concrete conflict over whether sexual harassment will be treated *as if* it is sex discrimination: whether the employer will be responsible so that its victims will receive relief. The current record, lacking as it does any finding on the occurrence of environmental discrimination, and lacking a resolution of the constructive discharge issue, is wholly inappropriate as a vehicle for deciding this crucial matter. Should the Court reach the issue of employer responsibility for the working environment on such an inadequate record, it should hold that when a supervisor in Mr. Taylor's position sexually harasses a subordinate in Ms. Vinson's position, making her working environment sex discriminatory, the company is accountable. This should be no less the case when sexual harassment is a constant of the work environment, with tolerance the price of job security, than it is when conditions reach a more definitive *quid pro quo.*

The Bank should not be permitted to carve out sexual harassment as an anomalous and unique claim for employment discrimination: one in which the employer is not responsible for the discrimination. The liability in question here is not, properly speaking, vicarious in any sense. The terms "strict" or "absolute" liability are tort analogies that do not exhaust the distinctive concept of liability in discrimination cases. Title VII's definition of "employer" *includes* "any agent" of the employer. 42 U.S.C. 2000e (b). Supervisors are "agents" in the supervising of employees. *Cleary v. Department of Public Welfare,* 21 F.E.P. 687 (E.D. Pa. 1979); *Kelly v. Richland School Dist.* 2, 463 F. Supp. 216, 218 (D.S.C. 1978). Liability here is thus not third-party; it is first-party or nothing. Under Title VII, by statutory design and by interpretation, so long as a circumstance is work-related, the supervisor is the employer and the employer is the supervisor. The employer does not become liable through the supervisor; for purposes of discrimination, the two are one. This has always been the case for purposes of employment discrimination litigation. *Anderson v. Methodist Evangelical Hospital,* 464 F.2d 723 (6th Cir. 1972); *Rowe v. General Motors Corp.,* 457 F.2d 348 (5th Cir. 1972); *Gay v. Board of Trustees,* 608 F.2d 127 (5th Cir. 1979); *Walthall v. Blue Shield,* 12 F.E.P. 933 (N.D. Cal. 1976).

It cannot be otherwise. When a supervisor discriminates, the subordinate has been discriminated against, whether anyone else in the employer hierarchy was told about it or not. For example, in *De-Grace v. Rumsfeld,* 614 F.2d 796, 803 (1st Cir. 1980), the employer was held responsible for discrimination in the constructive discharge of an employee who had been fired for absenteeism and abuse of sick leave. In fact, the employee had left the work-place due to racist threats and told the employer he was ill. Similarly, in *Young v. Southwestern Savings & Loan Assn.,* 509 F.2d 140 (5th Cir. 1975), a supervisor who did not have the power to hire and fire had required attendance of an atheist at a religious meeting against company policy. The employer was held responsible for discrimination by constructive discharge when she left. Few employees are sexually harassed *ex officio* by the chairman of the company on a majority vote of the Board of Directors. The EEOC Guidelines provide for employer liability for discrimination "regardless of whether the employer knew or should have known" of the events. 24 C.F.R. 1604.11 (c).

The Bank seeks to preclude corporate liability for sexual harassment as a working environment on the same grounds on which it attempts to trivialize its harm: by separating it sharply from other forms of sex discrimination, from *quid pro quo* sexual harassment, and from cases of racial or religious bigotry. If Mr. Taylor had set all women employees' wages at less than men's because they were women, he would have *been* the Bank. If Mr. Taylor had outright fired Ms. Vinson for her sexual non-compliance, he would have concededly been the Bank. If she had quit because of the sexual harassment, as she maintained through trial and still maintains that she did, Mr. Taylor would also perforce have been the Bank. If he had subjected Ms. Vinson to racial or religious invective, he would have been the Bank. But because the invective was sexual, not racial or religious, and because we do not yet know whether Mr. Taylor's alleged sexual advances against her on her job occurred, and because we do not yet know if a constructive discharge will make this a *quid pro quo* case, he is not the Bank, according to the Bank.

Ms. Vinson alleged discrimination by her supervisor in work and at work. She complained of damage through work, including the unspeakable violation of forced sexual access. Had Mr. Taylor not been her employing supervisor, and should his advances be found unwelcome, she arguably would not have had to "voluntarily" acquiesce in his demands for fear of job reprisals. The fact she was promoted on her merits, which is undisputed here, does not mean she *would have been* promoted on her merits had she not *also complied* with her superior's sexual demands.[10] Mr. Taylor was situated to make good on the power of his position, which he exercised for and as her employer. If he were found to have abused his position for sexual gain, whether he abused his role for his own sexual gratification at defined thresholds was his choice and irrelevant to employer responsibility. He may not have needed actively to use his power against specific indices of her employment *because* he had the power to do so at any time. Ms. Vinson was able to advance on her merits without the interference his advances may yet be found to have threatened (advances whose welcomeness as a matter of fact remains in dispute) because she complied. And she testified she complied because of his power as her supervisor, power he held because of his position at the Bank: "He said just like he could hire me, he could fire me . . . ." (TR, Jan. 22, II, 51.) "He told me that he was my supervisor. He gave me my pay check, and I had to do what he wanted me to do." (TR, Jan. 22, II, 59.) The minute she made her refusals effective, or his ardor cooled, he moved against her job.

The Bank accepts responsibility for sexual harassment in the hierarchical *quid pro quo* form, but not in the hierarchical environmental form. The line between the two can be as slight as the victim leaving the job, as may turn out to be the case here. Petitioner's position would mean that a victim must elect to injure herself more than she already is—forfeit her job because the perpetrator's conduct has made it intolerable—in order to be able to hold the employer liable for injuring her at all. She must make her situation worse so that she can use the law to make it better. The law of sexual harassment should encourage employers to discourage sexual harassment, to find out about it if it is occurring, and to act against perpetrators. The Bank's perspective, if permitted, would give the employer little incentive to do anything other than not to fire employees who are being sexually harassed when it is forced to their attention. The employer is in the best position to enforce a minimal standard of human dignity by power of position. *See* US, 26. Liability provides an incentive to do so.

The Bank wants two sets of rules, one for its hiring and firing decisions, which can include liability for *quid pro quo* sexual harassment, and another for its supervisors' sexual acts and the atmosphere their acts create in their places of work. Most of all it wants one for discrimination based on race and religion and another for discrimination based on sex. Uniquely in the case of environmental sexual harassment, the employer here seeks to hide supervisors' sexist abuses of power behind the corporate veil. *See Horn v. Duke Homes*, 755 F.2d at 604–5 (criticizing this evasion). The Bank purports to worry that the sexual harassment perpetrator is uniquely "motivated to keep his knowledge secret, not to disclose it and invite discipline for his indiscretions." (Bank, 12–13.) This is true for all discrimination, including *quid pro quo* sexual harassment. A supervisor who requires only his Black employees to clean his personal residence is unlikely to report it to the company. *Slack v. Havens*, 7 F.E.P. 885 (S.D.Cal. 1973), *aff'd*, 522 F. 2d 1091 (9th Cir. 1975).[11]

Further, petitioner argues that employers should not be liable when, as a practical matter, only the employer may be situated to provide adequate relief. At the moment, Mr. Taylor's behavior is discrimination in employment or nothing, given the trial court's denial of an attempt to amend to add tort claims. The Bank is concerned about being liable for acts it feels it did not do. Theoretically, if the Bank is not liable because the perpetrator did the act "as an individual," but the individual's liability is unclear because he is not, *as* an individual, the "employer" for purposes of Title VII,[12] some risk exists of creating a claim for employment discrimination for which nobody would be clearly liable if the injury were proved. Even individual supervisors who are held liable are less well situated than is the employer to provide make-whole equitable relief. Such relief is the primary purpose of Title VII. *Albemarle Paper Co. v. Moody*, 422 U.S. 405, 418 (1975).[13]

The distinctive statutory mandate of Title VII to end invidious group-based treatment is one under which ". . . Congress itself has concluded that classifications based upon sex are inherently invidious . . . ." *Frontiero v. Richardson*, 411 U.S. 677, 678 (1973) (for a plurality).[14] To prove that employment discrimination occurred in a workplace is to prove the employer liable for it. This is because Title VII distinctively exists to prohibit and rectify injuries to, in, and of *the employment relation itself*. For this purpose, while the facts of sexual harassment may be tortious, and torts are compatibly appended in a typical claim, sexual harassment as a term of art is not technically a tort any more than other species of discrimination in employment are technically torts. Because group-based bigotry is not accidental or individualized, as torts tend to be, tort tests tend not to fit.[15] Thus, whether events are "outside the scope of employment" (Brief of Equal Employment Advisory Council, *Amicus Curiae*, ("EEAC"), 6) in the tort sense has been supplanted by whether the events are "work-related" in the Title VII sense. Employers are not responsible for racial or sexual insults by employers to employees if they truly are non-job related. Similarly, while concepts like *respondeat superior* were sometimes used early and almost in an ordinary language sense or as an analogue, in order to make clear that employers could not evade responsibility for such acts by supervisors, *Miller v. Bank of America*, 600 F.2d 211 (9th Cir. 1979), later authority has tended to rest on Title VII statutory construction, implicitly rejecting any technical limitation that some views of *respondeat superior* might impose on employer liability for discrimination in Title VII areas.

When petitioner challenges whether Title VII was meant to regulate what is diminished as the "purely psychological aspects of the workplace environment" (Bank, 30), it also questions accepted authority that environmental sexual harassment by supervisors without further notice to the employer states a claim under Title VII. *Kyriazi v. Western Electric Co.*, 461 F. Supp. 894, 935 (D.N.J. 1978), *aff'd*, 647 F.2d 388 (3d Cir. 1981); *Flowers v. Crouch-Walker Corp.*, 552 F.2d 1277, 1282 (7th Cir. 1977); *Young v. Southwestern Sav. & Loan Assn.*, 509 F.2d at 144 n.7; *Rowe v. General Motors Corp.*, 457 F.2d at 359.[16] Further seeking to evade responsibility for its supervisor's conduct, the Bank seeks a ruling that, as a matter of law, employers must receive notice that supervisors are sexually harassing subordinates at work as a precondition for liability, and notice to the perpetrator can not be notice to the employer. (Bank, 22.) In other cases of employment discrimination, and by statute, the supervisor is the employer, and no further notice is needed.[17] Because a supervisor is an agent of the employer, an employee puts the employer on actual notice simply by notifying the supervisor. *See* Note, *Sexual Harassment*

Claims of Abusive Work Environment Under Title VII, 97 Harv. L. Rev. 1449 (1984) at 1460–1463. Respondent repeatedly, according to her testimony, told Mr. Taylor that she wanted him to stop, leave her alone, and let her work in peace. (TR, Jan. 22, II, 67; TR, Jan. 24, IV, 65.) Should Mr. Taylor's actions be found to constitute environmental sexual harassment on remand, even the existing evidence would support a finding that Mr. Taylor was on notice that his advances were unwelcome, because he was repeatedly told that they were. It is respondent's position that no more notice was needed, although further notice was attempted, to no avail.

The Bank attempts to use the EEOC Guidelines' requirement that co-worker (lateral) sexual harassment requires employer notice to undermine the Guidelines' position that supervisor (hierarchical) sexual harassment does not require such notice. 29 C.F.R. 1604.11 (d) (App. 54a.) In the Guidelines, liability follows power. Because coercion by a supervisor is derived clearly from the employment hierarchy, and is greater than that of a co-worker, the Guidelines attach corporate liability without a notice requirement for acts of supervisors, but not of co-workers. If co-worker sexual harassment is not reported to the employer, it is not clear that it is the *job* that holds the victim hostage to the differential treatment, because the perpetrator has no more employment power than the victim does. If the conduct is reported and nothing is done, then choice of perpetrator over victim puts the employer behind the conduct in a way it already is with supervisorial acts. With an unreported supervisor's act or a reported and condoned co-worker's act, the victim is in a position to tolerate it, risk firing, or leave. Once reported, co-worker sexual harassment becomes clearly "in employment" if the employer refuses to investigate or rectify it. Actual notice in co-worker cases serves to put the employer's power behind the perpetrator, invoking clout that a *supervisor already has* over an employee *as an employee.*

The *Barnes* dictum that in sexual harassment cases, "if the consequences are rectified when discovered, the employer may be relieved of responsibility under Title VII," *Barnes v. Costle,* 561 F.2d at 993, is twisted into its contrapositive by the Bank. (Bank, 18.) The *Barnes* court stated the obvious: employers who discover and fix the problem are not liable. It did not state, as the Bank would have it, that employers who do not discover the problem and do not fix it are not liable. Such a rule would reward employers for looking the other way "even as signs of discriminatory practice gather on the horizon." 753 F.2d at 151.

Inasmuch as nothing is yet found as to which notice should have been given, it is very odd to be considering standards of notice. *Bundy* is sought to be distinguished on this issue on the ground that the employer there, unlike here, had full knowledge of the harassment and chose not to act. (Bank, 19.) But constructive knowledge, a possibility the Bank does not mention, was inferred in *Bundy* from the fact that the harassment was "standard operating procedure." *Bundy v. Jackson*, 641 F.2d at 940. So the employer should have known about it. This determination requires a clear factual record on the flagrance and pervasiveness of the environmental harassment, if any. *See, Katz v. Dole*, 709 F.2d 251 (constructive notice inferred).

Respondent's experience suggests that a further notice requirement would place yet another gun at the head of victims. *Amicus* Boston University argues that forced reporting would enhance the goals of Title VII better than would giving the employer the incentive of potential liability for knowing what is happening in their places of work. Brief of Trustees of Boston University, *Amicus Curiae*, 14–15. It is difficult to avoid the sense that it is because employers know that this kind of discrimination is so pervasive, and the disincentives to report it remain so overwhelming (because victims are damaged more by reporting than by not reporting), they do not want to be held responsible for how people are treated in their institutions. Nor should an employer be insulated by the fact of having a procedure, simply because it looks good on paper. The reality of the case at bar is that Mr. Taylor *was* the procedure, although it dignifies their policy to call it one. The perpetrator was the procedure. (*See supra* 6–7.) In light of the fact that Mr. Taylor was the Bank's procedure, according to the procedure itself, it is particularly difficult to take that the Bank seeks to hide behind the existence of its procedure while maintaining that notice to the perpetrator is not notice to the Bank (*Accord*, US, 26).[18] This is not a situation in which there was an excellent procedure and an institutional commitment to making it work but the victim inexplicably chose not to use it. If procedures are viable and do not denigrate the victim, they will be used. Typically, too, an administrative complaint precedes suit, which provides the defendant ample opportunity to cure or settle short of liability. The available range of motion is far beyond the picture of virtual entrapment defendants and some *amici* portray.

The underlying issue here is the implicit "archaic and stereotypic notion," *Mississippi University for Women v. Hogan*, 458 U.S. 718, 725 (1982), projected onto Ms. Vinson, that some women lie about sex for money. It is apparently feared that women subordinates will entrap unsuspecting supervisors into sexual liaisons which women want and keep secret in order to sue the company: "Plaintiffs . . . may have initiated the relationship, but . . . later allege pain and suffering." (EEAC, 19.) *See also* 760 F.2d at 1330 (App. 23a-24a). Courts should have no more difficulty distinguishing fabricated cases in this area than in any other. In *Neidhardt v. D.H. Holmes,* 21 F.E.P. 456 (E.D. La. 1979), *aff'd mem.*, 624 F.2d 1097 (5th Cir. 1980), two women were, through application of conventional rules of evidence, found to have fabricated a sexual harassment claim.

The deeper fear seems to be that if a woman can sue for forced sex at work, there will be no voluntary sex at work, because she could always lie about it later. In this view, if women are given legal backing to decline unwanted advances, the only future will be an "entirely asexual" workplace, 760 F.2d at 1331 (App. 25a). If an employer can be sued for culturally biased acts and epithets, can cultural holidays not be celebrated or discussed? With all respect, it is difficult for respondent to believe that if forced sex is actionable, voluntary sex will become too big a risk to take. The contrary assumption, that only if sex can be forced with impunity, can it be had voluntarily, is perverse. Rape law poses the same issue, but it exists because rape exists. Moreover, the data suggest that at least statistically the problem is closer to the reverse: thousands of women like Ms. Vinson are sexually violated but do not complain officially in part because of the way they expect to be received. D. Russell, *Sexual Exploitation* (1984) 29–65, 269–271. Their apprehensions have not been unfounded.

IV. Evidence of Dress and Reports of Fantasies Was Properly Excluded on Remand.

Mr. Taylor said no sex occurred between him and Ms. Vinson. Ms. Vinson said it did, and moreover it was forced. The judge found that if sexual intercourse occurred, Ms. Vinson's participation was voluntary.

The trial judge ruled that "if the plaintiff and Taylor did engage in an intimate or sexual relationship . . . [it] was a voluntary one by plaintiff . . . ." (App. 42a.) This is not a finding of fact, it is a proposition of logic with a condition precedent verging on a conclusion of law. It amounts to an inference of consent although defendant Taylor did not plead consent and no one put on proof of consent. This may be the reason for the lack of factual support offered for the conclusion. Yet petitioner (Bank, 28–29) and some *amici* have contended that the Court of Appeals would exclude proof defendant offers that the relationship was consensual. Mr. Taylor offered no evidence that the relationship was consensual because he took the position that the relationship was not sexual. The Bank did not offer such evidence either.

How might one know that, if a sex act which may or may not have occurred, occurred, the woman did consent to it? This is a metaphysical riddle, not a factual finding. It is nothing other than a ruling that this is a woman who *would* have wanted it, whether it happened or not. As such it is not a finding of fact, it is an assassination of character. It is a reversion to an atavism from the law of rape that "a rape accusation . . . [is] the product of a woman's over-active fantasy life or . . . [the] consequence of a woman's communication of her sexual desires, subtly or otherwise, to a hapless male." L. Letwin, *"Unchaste" Character, Ideology and the California Rape Evidence Laws*, 54 So. Cal. L. Rev. 35, 35–36 (1980). While the ruling may express the factfinder's point of view on the plaintiff as a woman, it fails to enlighten reviewing courts on what Mr. Taylor did or did not do.

The trial judge's finding on this point led the Court of Appeals to suspect that weight may have been given to impermissible evidence, evidence admitted over plaintiff's timely objections on grounds of irrelevance. (TR, Jan. 23, 18, 23, 25) (Testimony of D. McCallum). The Court of Appeals thus noted, in distinguishing apparently voluntary compliance within a possible context of force from the unwanted environmental harassment that may have constituted that context of force, that although the District Court gave no basis for its findings, it "may have considered the voluminous testimony regarding Vinson's dress and personal fantasies." 753 F.2d at 146 n.36 (App. 9a n.36). Such evidence was directed excluded on remand.

Petitioner (Bank, 26–30) and the dissenters in the Court of Appeals, 760 F.2d 1330 (App. 24a-25a) fervently urge this evidence be admitted. They argue that defendants will be unjustly constrained in proving that their sexual behavior is welcome if they cannot introduce evidence of what the victim wore and what it was said the victim said she imagined. This constraint on perpetrators is not raised by this case. Mr. Taylor never sought to prove that the advances and intercourse alleged were welcome. He sought to prove that they did not occur. Ms. Vinson's dress and flights of fancy do not make them more likely to have occurred. Anyway, it was *her* contention that they *did* occur. Ms. Vinson's "sartorial and whimsical proclivities" 753 F.2d at 146 n.36 (App. 9a n.36) have equally little to do with whether Mr. Taylor assaulted her. It may put the Bank in an awkward position to have Mr. Taylor—who with Ms. Vinson is in the best position to know—argue that the sex did not occur, while the Bank seeks to argue *against both participants* both that consensual sex occurred and that it knew nothing about the whole affair. Clothing and fantasy evidence does not give probity to their position.

Neither the Bank nor the dissenting judges below offers legal support for the admissibility of this evidence. Respondent submits that there is none. To the extent analogies to rape law hold, unless the evidence was of previous consensual sex with the defendant, even evidence that the plaintiff voluntarily engaged in prior consensual sex with others would likely be inadmissible. Fed. R. Evid., Rule 412; 124

Cong. Rec. H 11944–11945 (daily ed., Oct. 10, 1978) and 124 *Cong. Rec.* S 18580 (daily ed., Oct. 12, 1978) (on passage of Rule 412). Such evidence is considered more prejudicial than probative. *U.S. v. Kasto,* 584 F.2d 268, 271–272 (8th Cir. 1978), *cert. denied,* 440 U.S. 930 (1979) (federal case prior to Rule 412, prior unchastity evidence more prejudicial than probative; reasons for exceptions (at 271) not applicable here). *See also State v. Bernier,* 491 A.2d 1000, 1004 (R.I. 1985).

In the leading case of *Priest v. Rotary,* 98 F.R.D. 755 (9th Cir. 1983), even evidence of a complainant's voluntary sexual activity with others was held not "reasonably calculated to lead to the discovery of admissible evidence" Fed. R. Civ. Pro. Rule 26(b) in a sexual harassment case. If anything, consensual sex acts are arguably more probative of other consensual sex acts than are dress or fantasies. If such evidence was not even discoverable where, as there, voluntariness *was* the defense, it is certainly less than admissible here. Women simply do not volunteer to be sexually harassed by their clothing or the purported content of their voluntary conversations any more than by consenting to sex with others.

Evidence showing that a relationship truly is voluntary would clearly be admissible. Apparel and reports of phantasms about others are *not that evidence.* No connection whatever between Ms. Vinson's choice of dress and a reported voluntary conversation and defendant's case has been offered. These are conversations not with the assailant about imaginations which do not include him. There is no evidence in this record that he overheard or even knew about them. The single purpose of this material is to provide a pornographic image of the kind of woman plaintiff is. Any plausible legal argument for its relevancy thus reduces to a violation of Fed. R. Evid. 404(a), which provides that "evidence of a person's character or a trait of his character is not admissible for the purpose of proving that he acted in conformity therewith on a particular occasion . . . ." Sexual character is not an exception.

Nor do any of the exceptions to this rule apply here. This evidence was not offered for the purpose of impeaching plaintiff's credibility. (Fed. R. Evid. 608.) One's choice of apparel or fantasy life does not make it more likely than not that one is telling the truth about a sexual relationship. The Bank offers that testimony that the plaintiff shared an imagined reincarnation of her deceased grandfather with a co-worker is probative of whether the events of which she complains might have been fantasized. (Bank, 28.) Petitioner does not argue that plaintiff mistook a purported fantasy about her grandfather for reality, nor does the testimony support such a conclusion. (*See* TR, Jan. 30, 62) (Testimony of D. McCallum). It is unclear on what petitioners base their inference that she may have mistaken fantasies about Mr. Taylor's behavior for the reality of his sexual aggression. Even if sexual freedom and sexual force were conflated here, the evidence sought to be defended is not remotely relevant.

Conclusion

This is an unusual case of sexual harassment—not in that it happened, but in that Mechelle Vinson sued. Even though resistance, far less successful resistance, is not required, most women, once forced to have sex, are too humiliated and intimidated to complain. The result is that most reported cases of sexual harassment involve victims who were able successfully to resist.[19] Unless rectified, this can mean that if a perpetrator can render a working situation sufficiently coercive to force the woman to have sex, by whatever means, he can then get away with anything, because the stigma of having had sex, i.e. the stigma *of having been injured in this way*, attaches to the victim. What was done to her is taken as testimony to her propensities, not the perpetrator's.

"Women are first excluded from employment opportunities free of sexual extortion and then stigmatized by having the behavior that the context produced in them (that is, their survival skill), singled out as the reason they are unfit for the guarantees of equality." *MacKinnon*, 196. This social fact has produced the vicious paradox that some of the least of sexual harassment's victims are the most likely to sue, leaving some of the most injured of women effectively outside the ambit of judicial relief. The more they are injured, the lower on

94

the scale of human value they are regarded as being, such that finally it is not believed that they were hurt at all.

All too often, it is Black women like Ms. Vinson who have been specifically victimized by the invidious stereotype of being scandalous and lewd women, perhaps targeting them to would-be perpetrators.[20] This is not to say that this is a case of race discrimination, but rather that minority race aggravates one's vulnerability as a woman by reducing one's options and undermining one's credibility and social worth. In the context of such beliefs, beliefs that animate this case, a picture can be painted that destroys the victim's ability to complain of sexual violation, such that sex acts can be inflicted upon her and nothing will be done about it.

The Court of Appeals saw through this and remanded for conscientious development of the factual record in light of applicable law. This Court should dismiss certiorari as improvidently granted for the same reasons, permitting the remand to proceed, or, in the alternative, affirm the Court of Appeals.

Respectfully submitted,

Dated at Grover City,   PATRICIA J. BARRY
California this 11th day   CATHARINE A. MACKINNON*
of February, 1986.

---

*Admitted to the bar of the State of Connecticut. The able assistance of Rachel Seidman is gratefully acknowledged.

NINE

Testimony on Pornography, Minneapolis

Andrea Dworkin and I were teaching a course on pornography together at the University of Minnesota Law School in the fall of 1983 when a citizen's group asked her to help them advocate with the city to keep pornography from being zoned into their working class neighborhood. In our discussion about how best to respond, I was unhappy about testifying against pornography to a legislative body without offering a legislative solution. So I proposed to Andrea that we adapt to legislation the legal idea previously conceived for a lawsuit for Linda Marchiano (Boreman), the woman who was coerced into sex acts for the pornography film *Deep Throat* against the pimps who forced her—a suit she had ultimately decided not to bring, due to the passage of time (expired statute of limitations). The legal concept was that pornography is a sex discriminatory practice, violating women's civil rights on the basis of their sex by inflicting sexual abuse to make it, in the case of coerced sex acts, or in the case of trafficked materials, by provably promoting the infliction of sexual violation and other sex-based denigration. We decided that, at the Zoning and Planning Commission hearing we had been invited to address, which proposed to zone pornography, an approach we opposed, Andrea would describe the harm of pornography, and I would sketch our proposed solution.

To say that our approach, once it got out, created a firestorm is an understatement.[1] The pornographers and their supporters, including consumers, immediately realized the civil rights antipornography ordinance was an extinction recipe for the industry. They could not make and use the materials without hurting people in the ways the law made actionable, for which it required compensation. With the fury of a knocked-down hornet's nest, they targeted its—and our—destruction with all the massive resources and forms of power at their disposal. Even as the ordinance's language and rationale has been refined and can be flexible, the approach retains validity and could be legislated.[2] With all the exposure this idea has received, much of it inaccurate, this transcript of what was said as recorded on October 18, 1983, the ordinance's butterfly moment, has never been published before.

I'm Catharine A. MacKinnon. I teach Sex Discrimination and Constitutional Law at the University of Minnesota Law School, 229 19th Avenue South, Minneapolis. I want to speak against this [zoning] ordinance. It seems clear from your remarks here that you have found that most of your people do not want pornography. What I think is the difference between the approach that I want to suggest to you, and what seems to be the approach of this ordinance, is that I do not admit that pornography has to exist. I assume I'm addressing a group that wants to do something about pornography but that, from the history of your attempts, you have been frustrated in the approach you have taken. I assume that you are searching for a jurisdictional and legal foundation or approach or concept that you can use. I assume, as Attorney Hyatt stated it, you've been looking for "a new concept—a different way of finding a constitutionally acceptable ordinance."

Following up on the comments that other women have made here, and that were also made by Steve Jevning, I want to suggest taking a civil rights approach. I suggest that you consider that pornography as it subordinates women to men is a form of discrimination on the basis of sex. You already have an ordinance against sex-based discrimination in this city. You have the jurisdiction to make laws against forms of discrimination. I suggest that you hold a public hearing on pornography to which you invite scholars whose studies now meet the First Amendment tests of even some of the most staunch skeptics as to the relationship between pornography as hate literature and violence toward women. The harm of pornography can also be documented by women who have been coerced into pornographic performances. You could hear testimony of women on whom sex has been forced who know that it comes from pornography that has been consumed by the men who force that sex on us, including husbands, bosses and strangers. We could also talk with prostitutes in this city, should a way be found to enable them to come forward, to address the connection from their standpoint between how they got into prostitution—an issue on which this state has done substantial research—and the existence of pornography. Then you can ask yourself about the connection between what you pointed out is the proliferation and extension of pornography represented by this proposed ordinance, and the proliferation and extension of prostitution, seen as an abuse of women.

I suggest that you inquire into the possibility of making an interpretive amendment to your existing ordinance that prohibits discrimination on the basis of sex, with a preamble of findings from such a hearing. I suspect it would provide a substantial basis for making an ordinance to prohibit pornography as a form of discrimination against women. You could consider a sex-specific ordinance to promote the valid governmental objective of eliminating the sex-specific civil rights violations your hearing documented. I would recommend a special subsection for coerced pornography models, with an injunctive remedy going to the pictures that were made of them while in a state of coercion, to cover their circumstance whether or not they were paid.

I am hoping that you will consider that the broad opposition to the zoning ordinance that you have heard from the people you represent is an expression of opposition to pornography that comes from something other than narrow-mindedness, anti-sex bigotry, and hysteria. Much of it represents a real concrete experience of sexual violation. Not just the desire to eradicate a bunch of bad ideas that are floating around in some people's heads, but some concrete violations of women's civil rights, as to which, to date, we have been entirely frustrated in our ability to be heard.

TEN

Testimony to the Attorney General's Commission on Pornography

One reaction to the civil rights antipornography ordinance and the debate it ignited was the creation of the Attorney General's Commission on Pornography in May of 1985.[1] Misnamed the Meese Commission by a press determined to stigmatize it through naming it after a widely hated Attorney General, the Commission was created by President Reagan's Attorney General William French Smith.[2] Its *Final Report* calmly, by unanimous vote of a diverse group, confirmed what any unbiased reading of the research and open-minded hearing of the testimony indicated beyond a shadow of a doubt, even at that time:

> [S]ince we believe that an increase in aggressive behavior toward women will in a population increase the incidence of sexual violence in that population, we have reached the conclusion, unanimously and confidently, that the available evidence strongly supports the hypothesis that substantial exposure to sexually violent materials as described here bears a causal (not casual, as some TV commentators read the word) relationship to antisocial acts of sexual violence, and for some subgroups, possibly to unlawful acts of sexual violence.[3]

The evidence for the relation between consumption of pornography and the infliction of sexual abuse and sexualized denigration of women, and for the removal or weakening of the Commission's caveats above, has become stronger with each passing year.[4] Here is my testimony, previously unpublished, to the Commission.[5]

Before you, this government has tried various approaches to the problem of pornography. Your predecessor commission believed that, although pornography may outrage sensibilities and offend taste and morals, it was harmless.[6] Nonetheless, the courts decided that, when materials violate community standards, appeal to the prurient interest, are patently offensive, and are otherwise worthless, they may be prohibited as obscenity.[7] State and local legislatures have tried to confine pornography by zoning,[8] to define it as a moral nuisance,[9] or to pay the pornographers to get out of town. Despite these attempts, the pornography industry has flourished, in part because it is so sexually and financially profitable that it effectively sets community standards.[10] But primarily pornography was allowed to flourish because its real harm was never identified: the violation of women and children that is essential to its making and inevitable through its use.[11]

This harm could be overlooked because pornographers, who are pimps, take the already powerless—the poor, the young, the innocent, the used, the desperate, the female—and deepen their invisibility and their silence. Pornography makes its victims so invisible that in years of inquiry, the only harm this government could see was sex it disapproved, not its most powerless citizens being hurt. Pornography makes its victims so silent that no official body heard them scream, far less speak.[12]

Recently, the U.S. Supreme Court admitted that obscenity doctrine had missed something—someone actually—for whose injuries it was therefore inadequate. Recognizing, finally, that child pornography is child abuse and whether or not it is obscene is beside that point, the Court found that the First Amendment allowed pornography made using children to be criminally banned.[13] Andrea Dworkin and I, with many others, have been working to expose the specific atrocities to women that have been equally hidden and for which existing law remains inadequate.[14] These abuses include coercion into performing for pornography,[15] the pervasive forcing of pornography on individuals,[16] the assaults it directly causes,[17] and the targeting for rape,[18] battery,[19] sexual harassment,[20] sexual abuse as children,[21] forced prostitution,[22] and the civil denigration and inferiority that is endemic to this traffic in female sexual slavery.[23] Pornography makes women what Andrea Dworkin (whom you owe it to yourselves to hear), in her testimony to the Senate, called the "sexual disappeared of this society."[24] Because these injuries are disproportionately inflicted upon women—but also on everyone whom it victimizes—on the basis of their sex, and because virtually nothing is being done about it, and because women matter, we have proposed a new approach: that pornography be civilly actionable as sex discrimination and recognized as a violation of human rights.[25]

In discussing this proposal, I will consider four points: the harm of pornography, the unique appropriateness of the civil rights approach to that harm, the First Amendment issues, and the reasons why the commission should take this perspective. I will begin with an analysis of the evidence that supports the civil rights approach, then show how the legal design of the ordinances we conceived and drafted at the request of the city councils of Minneapolis and Indianapolis, and the Commission for Women of Los Angeles County, pending elsewhere, respond to those injuries in a way existing law does not. Then I will present our constitutional argument, urge you to adopt this approach, and recommend this avenue for relief.

1. The Harm of Pornography

Women in pornography are bound, battered, tortured, humiliated, and sometimes killed. Or, merely taken and used. For every act you see in the visual materials, some of which I know you have seen, a woman had to be tied or cut or burned or gagged or whipped or chained, hung from a meat hook or from trees by ropes, urinated on or defecated on, forced to eat excrement, penetrated by eels and rats and knives and pistols, raped deep in the throat with penises, smeared with blood, mud, feces, and ejaculate.[26] Or merely taken through every available orifice, or posed as though she wanted to be. Pornography sexualizes women's inequality.[27] Every kind of woman is used, each one's particular inequalities exploited as deemed sexually exciting: Asian women bound so they are not recognizably human, so inert they could be dead; Black women playing plantation struggling against their bonds; Jewish women orgasming in re-enactments of Auschwitz; pregnant women and nursing mothers accessible, displayed; white women splayed across hoods of cars trussed like dead prey; amputees and other disabled or ill women, their injuries or wounds or stumps proffered as sexual fetishes; retarded girls presented as gratifyingly compliant; adult women infantilized as children, children presented as adult women, interchangeably fusing vulnerability with the sluttish eagerness said to be natural to women of all ages; so-called lesbians, actually women sexually arranged with women to be watched and claimed, bought and sold.[28]

The point is, because the profit from the mass production of these mass violations counts and women do not, because these materials are valued and women are not because the pornographers have credibility and rights and women do not, the products of these acts are protected and women are not.[29] So these things are done, so that pornography can be made of them. I call this a direct causal link between pornography and harm. The pornography industry is largely an organized crime industry in which overt force is standard practice.[30] Pimps are also known for their violence. But in a society whose opportunities for women are so limited that prostitution is many women's best economic option, even when explicit violence is not used,[31] the compulsion of poverty, of drugs, of the street, of no alternatives, of fear of retribution for noncooperation can be enforcement enough.[32]

Every act exacted from the women in pornography, who are typically made to act as though they are enjoying themselves, is acted out on yet more women integral to pornography's consumption. Such women are given no choice about seeing the pornography or performing the sex. Pornography is forced on them to destroy their self-respect and their resistance to sexual aggression, to terrorize them into compliance or silence, as a sex act in itself, or to instruct and season them for exact replication of the scripts and postures and scenes. Rapes are stimulated, inspired, fantasized, planned—and actualized.[33] The women are held down while the pornography is held up, turned over as the pages are turned over. As to pornography by our definition, which I will discuss in a moment, the evidence is consistent from social studies, clinicians who work with victims and perpetrators, battered women's shelters, rape crisis centers, groups of former prostitutes, incest survivors and their therapists, court cases, police and—in testimony that is typically devalued although it is the most direct evidence there is—from victims themselves, used on one end of pornography or the other.[34]

This evidence, together with laboratory tests in controlled experiments on nonpredisposed normals and recent correlational results, support the conclusion that exposure to pornography increases attitudes and behaviors of aggression and discrimination specifically by men against women—especially if you see administering electric shocks as behavior, and not seeing that an account of a rape is an account of a rape is discrimination.[35] The increment of increase varies according to type of pornography only in degree.[36] Sex and violence are inextricably interwoven in this harm, both in the material itself, which makes sex into violation and makes rape and torture and intrusion into sex, and also on every other level of pornography's social existence. In its making, violence may be used to coerce women to perform for materials which show violence, but also to perform for materials which are sexually explicit and subordinating but do not show violence, except perhaps for the bruises the makeup fails to cover.[37] In its use, women are forcibly compelled to consume pornography until they acquiesce without further complaint in sex that violates their personal dignity, their desires, and their bodies, not to mention their preferences, without the need for further force.[38] Subjection need not always be violent.

Further effects of exposure to pornography such as the trivialization and objectification of women, acceptance of rape myths, desensitization to sexual force, spontaneous rape—fantasy generation—these are so-called attitudes, so far from being considered violence that they are not even considered behavior.[39] But the only thing we cannot yet predict with exactness is which individual woman will be next on which individual man's list, and for what specific expression of his escalated misogyny. We do know these interactions will occur and that these materials contribute to them, causally to many. We also know that the more pornography is consumed, the less harmful these acts will be socially perceived as being. We also know that they will typically occur in contexts traditionally regarded as consensual if not intimate: in marriages, in families, in prostitution, on dates, among acquaintances, on the job, in churches, in schools, in doctor's offices. Most rarely, between strangers. Almost always, between women and men.

2. *The Appropriateness of the Civil Rights Approach*

On the basis of this analysis of its social reality, pornography, not alone but crucially, can be said to institutionalize a subhuman, victimized, second-class status for women in particular. If one can be denigrated and doing it is defended as freedom; if one can be tortured and enjoying it is considered entertainment; if the pleasure others derive from one's pain is the measure of one's social worth, one isn't worth much, socially speaking.[40] Tolerance of such practices is inconsistent with any legal mandate of equality or the reasons we protect speech. The civil rights approach to pornography is based upon the notion that this remains true even though the means are words and pictures, the enjoyment and pleasure are sexual and economic, and the victims are women.

Based on an empirical investigation of the materials actually available that do this damage, our law defines pornography as the graphic sexually explicit subordination of women through pictures and words that also includes women presented dehumanized as sexual objects who enjoy pain, humiliation or rape; women bound, mutilated, dismembered or tortured, women in postures of servility or submission or display, penetrated by objects or animals.[41] Men, children, or transsexuals, all of whom are sometimes violated like women are through and in pornography, can sue for similar treatment.[42] The term sexually explicit is an existing term with both legal and popular meaning that has never previously been considered ambiguous or problematic. A subordinate is the opposite of an equal. The term subordination refers to the active practice of making a person unequal. It can include objectification, hierarchy, forced submission, and violence, all of which are typical in the genre.[43] Presumably it is obvious that this is not the obscenity test.[44] To be pornography, materials must be graphic, and sexually explicit, and subordinate women, and also include at least one of the concrete list of particulars.[45] If they fit this definition, they do this harm.

But these materials, in themselves, are not actionable under our law. Victims of four activities only—coercion into pornography, forcing pornography on a person, assault, and trafficking (which is production, sale, exhibition, or distribution) can sue. Existing laws, abstractly extended, might be seen to cover at least some of these abuses. But no existing law adequately captures the specific social etiology of pornography and provides adequate relief. Laws against assault and battery or rape may, in theory, reach some of the acts, but they do not even in theory provide relief against the continued existence of the materials which re-enact those violations in public.[46] Privacy law, in theory, potentially reaches some of the materials, but most do not adequately address the abusive acts.[47] Not all states have such laws, and most that do have statutes of limitations that are not long enough to permit victims to recover their capacity for initiative and trust. These statutes have also proven hostile to women plaintiffs who have tried to use them to seek relief from sexual invasions of their privacy through media.

In theory, lynching was assault and battery or murder. But it did not begin to be effectively addressed in practice until the organizations that practiced it as concerted racism were accountable to federal civil rights law. In theory, sexual harassment could be a tort, or intentional infliction of emotional distress, or invasion of privacy. But it was not until it was recognized as sex discrimination that anything was done about it. In part, this was because existing law misdiagnosed and fragmented these experiences, producing legal requirements that did not fit the race-based and sex-based nature of these acts. Further as a practical matter, existing law exists and so do the harms of pornography.

Frankly, until the civil rights approach was proposed as law, most of pornography's concrete harms were not even publically noticed. Rather obviously, pornography—which is a trade in female flesh, with all its attendant abuses—coexists with existing law, realistically unthreatened. Perhaps it is not coincidence that those who want pornography also insist that existing law is adequate to any damage it does.[48] A peculiar complacency in the face of human suffering underlies reliance on this legal status quo, since it rather obviously has permitted the unrestrained existence of that suffering that constitutes the social status quo. As a practical matter, police and prosecutors look the other way and private lawyers recognize difficult cases to win because women are stripped of credibility and worth by the very practices that hurt them.

3. First Amendment Issues

Pornography, as defined in our law, undermines sex equality, a compelling state interest and legitimate concern of government, by harming people, differentially women. Under current First Amendment law, exceptions are recognized and speech interests are sometimes outweighed by other interests. The most common reason for this is harm: the harm done by some materials is more important than their expressive value, if any. Compared with existing exceptions and counterbalances to the First Amendment, the harm recognized by this law meets a higher standard than any of them have met or have been required to meet. It involves at least comparable seriousness of injury to massive numbers of people; its factual legislative basis is larger, more detailed, concrete, and conclusive; its statutory language is more ordinary, objective, and precise; and it covers a harm that is in some cases narrower, but never larger, than its findings substantiate.[49]

This is not a criminal law. It does not place more discretion or power in the hands of the police or prosecutors. It does place more power in the hands of those who are injured, providing a forum, legitimacy to speak, authority to make claims, and potential for relief. It does not provide sweeping bans, although it does provide injunctive remedies for proven harms.[50] It does not constitute prior restraint and it does not reach possession.

This is not an obscenity law. Pornography does harm, the harms of civil inequality, of sex discrimination, unlike obscenity for which no evidence of harm has been available or judicially required. But criminal bans on obscenity are constitutional under the First Amendment.[51] This is not a group libel law, either. A direct, not conjectured, connection has been established between the status and treatment of those who could act under this law and the materials it covers. But, however tenuously, group libel laws are constitutional.[52] This is not a libel law. But it does recognize, like the laws of libel and invasion of privacy both recognize, that words themselves can constitute harms. Laws against libel are constitutionally permitted, and privacy is constitutionally protected, in some tension with the First Amendment. Women are not children. But on the basis of the assumption that children in pornography are there by force, criminal bans on its production and distribution are constitutional.[53] It is true that some pornography has been found obscene, libels groups, lies about individual women and their sexuality, and destroys their repute and standing in their communities. It is also true that much pornography is produced under conditions of powerlessness (all of it under conditions of inequality). While our law does not strictly arise under any prior recognized theory, each of them evidences concerns and sensitivities and policies that provide the reasons why the First Amendment has been outweighed in each instance. These concerns and sensitivities and policies the civil rights approach shares, such that each of these theories provides a partial precedent for it.

Expressive values have also been qualified in the interests of unwilling viewers, captive audiences, young children, and beleaguered neighborhoods, for comfort and convenience, and to avoid visual blight.[54] If speech interests become comparatively less valued for constitutional purposes—when materials are false, obscene, indecent, lascivious, lewd, racist, provocative, dangerous, coercive, threatening, intrusive, inconvenient, or inaesthetic, we believe they should be able to be civilly actionable when they are—and can be proven to be—coerced, assaultive, and discriminatory. State interests in opposing sex discrimination have also prevailed over speech-interests in several recent Supreme Court cases.[55]

Coercion, force, assault, and trafficking are not ideas. They are not fantasies, representations, symbols, or advocacy either. Pornography is at the center of a cycle of abuse that cannot, our evidence suggests, be reached or stopped without reaching and stopping the pornography that is its incentive, product, stimulus, and realization. When speech interests are inseparable from illegal acts, as they are here, even justly stringent First Amendment guarantees have accommodated, without being seen as abridged. We believe that if existing legal standards for constitutionality are applied to this law as if women are human beings, recognizing that harm to women is harm, this law, which is under challenge in Indianapolis, currently on appeal here before the Seventh Circuit, will be found constitutional.[56]

4. Why the Commission Should Adopt This Approach

Many people enjoy pornography. In our view, that is why they defend it. That is also why there is so much hysteria over, and distortion of, the civil rights approach: it would work. The fact that some people like pornography does not mean it does not hurt other people. As in any instance of conflict of rights, the side one takes is a choice. We know that so long as the pornography exists, as it does now, women and children will be used and abused to make it, as they are now, and it will be used to abuse them, as it is now. The question is, whether we are willing to wait for each act of victimization that we know will occur to occur, relying on existing law to clean up after the pornographers one mind and body and devastated life at a time, never noticing the gender of the bodies, never noticing that the victimization is centrally actualized through words and pictures, never noticing that we encounter the pornography in the attitudes of the police, in the values in the laws, on juries, in court, every time we try to prove a woman has been hurt. It tells women how much we are worth that something that few have much good to say about is more important than we are.[57]

Many people do not want the problem of pornography solved. It is our view that if you want it solved, you will recommend this approach, and if you do not, you will not.

Full references are contained in:

EXHIBIT 1. The Reasons Why: Essays on the New Civil Rights Law: Recognizing Pornography as Sex Discrimination, reprinting A. Dworkin, Against the Male Flood: Censorship, Pornography, and Equality, Harvard Women's Law Journal, Volume 8, 1985 and C. MacKinnon, Pornography, Civil Rights, and Speech, Harvard Civil Rights-Civil Liberties Law. Review, Volume 20, 1985.

EXHIBIT 2. C. MacKinnon, Brief of Linda Marchiano and the Estate of Dorothy Stratten, Amici Curiae in Support of Appellant, Hudnut v. American Booksellers Assn., U.S. Court of Appeals for the Seventh Circuit, Docket No. 84-3147, March 1, 1985.

EXHIBIT 3. A. Dworkin, Brief Amicus Curiae of Andrea Dworkin, Hudnut v. American Booksellers Assn., U.S. Court of Appeals for the Seventh Circuit, Docket No. 84-3147, March 1, 1985.

EXHIBIT 4. Examples of laws based on the civil rights approach: Los Angeles County, Indianapolis, Minneapolis, and Pornography Victims Protection Act (the latter adapting the coercion section only and in part).

ELEVEN

Substantive Equality

A new approach to equality—the theory of substantive equality—was presented in public for the first time here to a meeting that brought together a diverse Canadian group of equality seekers. Subsequently, the factum the Women's Legal Education Fund (LEAF) embodied it in the first case argued under the equality provision of the new Charter of Rights and Freedoms in Canada. For the first time in history, it was largely adopted by a court when the Supreme Court of Canada embraced the essence of the approach in *The Law Society of British Columbia v. Andrews*,[1] repudiating the Aristotelian concept of formal equality, accepting what was, in the speech below, called "the dissident view" (termed "the inequality approach" in *Sexual Harassment of Working Women* (1979)[2]), predicated on concrete social grounds of hierarchical disadvantage. Following Canada's lead, other countries and the international community have since accepted many features of substantive equality.[3] This speech, transcribed from an audiotape, marks the first time this equality concept was publicly articulated in these terms.[4]

———————————

This morning I am going to be giving a critical overview of approaches to equality, directed toward developing an approach we can use to get equality under law in Canada.

In broadest terms, I am going to characterize what might be called the Anglo-Canadian-American approach to equality. This phrase is a bit of a misnomer. The approach I will discuss is definitely English; it also contains some of the worst tendencies of the American political system. But at least the mainstream approach to be discussed excludes some of the best tendencies in the American approach to equality developed primarily by Black Americans in the attempt to use the legal system to get legal equality as a means to social equality. It will also be informed by what Canadian courts and Canadian theorists have been thinking about equality. My main concern is what the Canadian legal approach to equality *will* be. So I will not only be describing, and at times criticizing, what courts in Canada have done with equality, but in a more open-ended way working to build a theory of equality for Canada under the new Charter of Rights and Freedoms that can be adequate to our aspirations and needs.

As to the session yesterday on our fears, hopes, and frustrations, my frustration is that there is not yet a meaningful approach to social equality through law. My fear is that there will never be one. My hope is that there will be.

With the law of equality, and other areas of law as well, the tools we are given are twisted, deeply flawed. This one is booby-trapped. Often we feel like we are digging ourselves deeper into the hole that they gave us this tool to dig ourselves out with. The notion of equality can capture some of our highest goals, but the law of equality does not correspond to those aspirations. In many respects it has made them incapable of legal achievement.

In the reigning legal or political theories of equality—because of course law is a species of politics—I see, basically, two kinds of thinking. One is accepted, the other isn't yet; one would work, the other doesn't. The one that would work isn't accepted and the accepted one doesn't work.

What it comes down to is that the mainstream approach to equality, as well as what I will call a dissident or alternate approach to equality, both give answers to two central questions. The first question is, what is an inequality question a question of? The second question is, what is a race or a sex or a disability question a question of? The mainstream answer we have had to live with in the received Anglo-Canadian-American tradition gives the same answer to both questions. The answer is: they are questions of sameness and difference. Inequality questions are questions of sameness and difference, and race and sex and disability questions are questions of sameness and difference.

The legal doctrine that corresponds to this says that what equality is about is treating likes alike and unlikes unalike. The main rule is, if you are "alike" you get equality, and if you are "unalike" you don't.

At the same time, the *social* definition of disadvantaged groups is based on their unlikeness to advantaged groups. In other words, we are told that to the extent you are disadvantaged you are different, and to the extent you are different you are not entitled to equality, because you are only entitled to equality if you are the same. The way one is socially defined and shaped is in direct conflict with what one needs to show legally to succeed in an equality claim.

The way this is embodied in law is something that you have all encountered: the "similarly situated" assumption. You have to be similarly situated with somebody who sets the standard that you must measure yourself by.[5] There is asymmetry built into this equality test. I am sure you have felt something false and funny about it. The law always seems to require you to deny or distort the worst facts of your social inequality to get access to its version of legal equality. It feels backwards. You always have to say, we are really the same as you, when in fact the very things that make one "different" in their terms are what make one "unequal" in our terms. Put another way, disadvantaged people tend not to be similarly situated to advantaged people because of their disadvantages. The very inequality that one experiences in social life is what passes for a "difference" in equality law, which in this approach means that one is not entitled to equal treatment.

Here are a few examples—not all the examples represented in the room, but enough to give a conception of what I am talking about. They may also give a broader sense of why many groups do not identify with the legal concept of equality or find it useful to them—why they feel suspicious about it, hesitant to use it, are uncomfortable making equality arguments, even though they have their own sense of equality with which they feel very secure.

What do we confront in this legal system? If a person is disabled in a wheelchair, we are encouraged to argue that whatever about that person is *not* disabled in a wheelchair is most relevant to an equality argument on their behalf, and whatever about that person involves being disabled in a wheelchair produces a compensatory argument about "reasonable accommodation." In other words, one needs to compensate for the equality concept, which on its own would not deliver what that person needs, by bringing in a notion of reasonable accommodation to get what that person needs to be treated equally.

Another example is a pregnant woman. No biological male under the current state of technology is about to experience pregnancy. Therefore, a pregnant woman is unlike a man, therefore different, just like being in a wheelchair one is unlike a person who is not in a wheelchair, therefore different. The mainline legal conclusion is, if you treat that person differently, even if it is to disadvantage them—say you don't have ramps, or don't get disability leave, or any other form of leave, for pregnancy—it can't be discrimination, because you are only being treated that way on the basis of your difference.[6] Unlikes unalike: equality. Different treatment for real differences is fine. If you are pregnant and not doing the work right now, you don't meet the standard of "worker" that sets the standard, even if all other health-related or reproductive reasons for not working for a while are covered.

Another example would be a Native person in prison who uses sweetgrass in religious observances. This is not to address the question of sovereignty, of why prisons or courts even have jurisdiction over Native people, which is a prior issue, but to consider just one dimension of racism in the situation. Under the conventional treatment of equality, we could be told that no white person gets what that Native person doesn't get, so there is no equality problem. No white person is allowed to smoke sweetgrass in this prison either, therefore when you deny that to a Native person, that is not an inequality. It is just that the Native person wants something different from what the person who sets the standards wants.

Another set of examples arise on the "what you compare with" dimension. Say a lesbian doesn't get medical coverage for her partner and their children through OHIP[7] or other means of coverage. She is told that this is not a question of inequality because gay men don't get covered either. The comparison is not between, say, her as a lesbian with all other individuals covered, or with all other women or her family unit with heterosexual family units. If you compare her with gay men, so the approach goes, there is no inequality because both similarly situated people are equally disadvantaged. It's as if, so long as there is any comparator with whom you are treated the same, even if there are others with whom you are not, it's not discrimination.

The question of racial segregation in the United States, as tackled legally, raised the symmetry question. White people were as segregated from Black people as Black people were from white people. Where's the inequality? If the segregation is the harm, meaning the harm of enforced separation on the basis of race, that harm equally describes white people and Black people. Both are equally kept in separate railway cars, or in the front or the back of the bus, at separate drinking fountains or swimming pools (actually, Black people did not generally have public swimming pools, but never mind.)[8] There were separate schools—Black people in Black schools, white people in white schools.[9] No legal issue was made about equal facilities. The facilities never were equal, but never mind that either; in the cases, it was stipulated that they were. So where's the harm? Different facilities for different people. Another level of example arises with language. In Canada, the notion seems to be that if equality arguments are to be made to reverse the disadvantageous treatment of the French language, the same arguments must or can be made to further advance the predominance of the English language.

All of this reveals that if one has a real social problem of inequality, a problem of disadvantage that one needs to overcome—in other words, one is "one down" socially speaking—one has problems using equality law to change it. How weird is that? The first problem is that, to the extent you're damaged by the inequality, you don't qualify for equal treatment; the second problem is, to the extent you're entitled to consideration, so is the dominant group. So the disadvantaged group runs the risk of empowering the advantaged group, or elevating their situation, just to get what the advantaged group already has, which it did not have to be the same as anyone to get. This built-in symmetry that magnifies the underlying asymmetry applies on whatever level the argument is used. In other words, equality arguments have a built-in bias against fixing inequalities because they are built to give to the disadvantaged only what the advantaged can also get. If the advantaged don't need it, the disadvantaged aren't permitted to ask for it, and if the disadvantaged are permitted to ask for it, the advantaged can also get it, or more of it, whether they already have it or not.

This equality doctrine is a precise device for maintaining the status quo. You can't change the relationship between those who are equal and those who are unequal, reduce or close the gap between them, if law provides each the same things or the same amounts of the same things. Either the people who are advantaged don't need the things the disadvantaged need because they already have it, or never will need it, or you give the advantaged the same additional increment of advantage you have just given the disadvantaged. This may raise the floor, which is fine in some ways, but the *relation* between the two stays the same. And it is that relation that defines the inequality between them.

What one starts to see in these examples, with their somewhat analytically disparate qualities but their common political thread, is that there is a group here that sets the standard. Then there is a group that is supposed to meet that standard. But the group that sets the standard is unlikely ever to be in the position that the group that needs something done is in. Whenever that occurs, whenever you have an inequality—because if you are disadvantaged, you are by definition not in the position that the advantaged group is in, in that inheres your inequality—you *don't* have an equality argument. The dominant measure is set by advantaged peoples. To the extent that a disadvantaged person is close to that measure, they are "the same;" therefore their unequal treatment is an inequality. But to the extent they are close to that measure, the same, they are far less likely to have an inequality problem that needs to be addressed at all. To the extent the disadvantaged person's situation is far from that measure, thus are likely to have an inequality problem that needs to be addressed, but they are likely to be considered "different." Hence not unequally treated. So if they are unequally treated, it's probably not discrimination, or at best you get access to one of the saving doctrines like reasonable accommodation or special benefits or affirmative action, with its denigration. At worst, you get treated worse, and equality doctrine is satisfied.

This legal approach begins to seem like an elaborate exercise in point-missing, one that has gone on for some time under the guise of fair treatment and equal standards and equal opportunity. What it misses is that sameness and difference is not the issue of inequality. It never has been. To make this the issue conceals, among other things, the way the dominant group becomes the measure of everything, including the measure of the disadvantaged group's entitlement to equal treatment. In other words, only when nondisabled people need ramps, only when men get pregnant, only when non-Natives take up the use of sweetgrass and are denied it in prison, only when English starts becoming in Canada what French in Canada still is, only when white people are segregated into inferior schools the way Black people still de facto are will this equality argument work for the disabled, pregnant women, First Nations and Black peoples, and the French language. In other words, only when some actual social parity between advantaged and disadvantaged occurs will this equality argument work to challenge whatever disadvantage remains. Only when it is not really needed will it be available. It's a trap.

I'm not saying there is anything wrong with saving doctrines like reasonable accommodation or affirmative action. They attempt to bail the doctrine out of the fact that it is basically set up wrong. If one had effective nondiscrimination policies, affirmative action would not be necessary, or not more than once. Because nondiscrimination doctrine does not work, affirmative action has to be done over and over and over and over again. This is because there is something wrong with the standards of merit being applied: they are discriminatory.

What I mainly want to say at this point is that one cannot take equal part in the game until one has equal say in the rules. And these equality rules are biased. With the existing mainstream doctrine, the consequences are that we can get nothing for women that we cannot get for men, we can get nothing for francophones we don't also get for anglophones, we can get nothing for Blacks that we cannot also get for whites or that whites don't also need. In other words, this law is a tool for maintaining subordination in the guise of promoting equality.

I think this is one reason disadvantaged peoples hesitate to use equality arguments. They know it denies reality. They feel misrepresented by it. This is also why we cannot use this equality law effectively until we are already equal socially—at which point, we don't need it.

Two main things are missing. Number one: the advantaged do not have to show they are the same as anybody to be entitled to fair treatment. Since they create the standard, this is only to say that there is a one-to-one relationship between "the standard" and the characteristics and qualities and values and situated advantages of advantaged people. In other words, the standards we live under—merit, excellence, qualifications, abilities—are coded versions of white, upper class, able-bodied, male, of a particular age and sexuality, qualities, or values. They are the product of the advantages people so described socially have. If you take the advantaged side of an inequality and describe who they are, what they value, what they get as a result of their advantages—namely to walk about in a society that is constructed for their access, to go to school in a way that has greased wheels for them to the top, that speaks their language, has job demands with their socially organized biographies and family roles in mind—those qualities are all implicitly described in the allegedly objective standards for merit and qualifications. All you have to do is to be such a person and you meet, or are given a more than fair chance to meet, those standards. You don't have to be the same as anybody else or anything else, because the standards are written for you. You are entitled to equality, essentially, because of who you are. If such a person is denied equality, they can successfully sue for it.

Number two, this whole approach misses that the advantaged are just as "different" from the disadvantaged as the disadvantaged are from the advantaged. Don't give me difference. The differences are equal. The issue is basically status and power, power to define standards, the dominant standard and the power to command the prerequisites for meeting the standards. Which is what is not equal. A particular standard is only "the standard" because it's dominant. In other words, to take the example of gender, men are as different from women as women are from men. So how come it is women who are "different"? The answer is that men set the standard, so women become the deviation. Men's differences do not make them "different" because men have power; they set the standard. What it means to set the standard is not to have inequality problems. What it means to set the standard is to be on the top of a hierarchy.

I'm suggesting we have to think about ways to define equality that are not limited by and to the dominant point of view, ways that bear some real relation to the qualities people bring that does not merely retrace the existing social reality of our inequalities. In other words, the existing theory of legal equality is designed to deal best with people who need it least; with people who are already most equal. It is not designed to deal with real inequality, or the worst of its consequences, at all.

How do we develop a theory for equality to deal with the real situation? There is a dissident undertone, an undercurrent and some cases in Canada as well as in the United States, that take another view of the problem. Let's call it the dissident or alternate view. A version of it came into prominence in the United States through the efforts of Black people, and is continuing to be used in the United States with somewhat less success than in the past. It's also being used by some women in the United States and more prominently in Canada. I think that what moves this approach is the reason why there is a law against inequality at all. In this approach, the answers to the two questions I posed at the outset—What is an inequality question a question of? and What is a race or a sex or an age or a sexual preference or a language a question of?, a question of poverty, a question of?—is not that they are matters of sameness and difference. The answer is: they are matters of dominance and subordination.

There is a big distinction between these two answers. Dominance and subordination is about power, its definition and distribution. Inequality is a question of hierarchy: who is on top and who is on the bottom. Only derivatively, within an already existing social hierarchy, does that become socially coded as sameness or difference. The sameness/difference approach derives from, and reproduces, the fact that some people have power and some people do not, or have a great deal less of it, while the dominance/subordination approach challenges that fact in order to change it. Where the mainstream approach to equality is bafflingly abstract, the alternate approach is concrete. Its goal isn't to make up legal categories that will reflect the status quo in law. The goal is to legally confront real social inequalities and conditions in order to end them. Its agenda is change.

I have been assuming that inequalities have certain things in common and at the same time that each inequality is unique. The tension between these levels of inequality's existence can be exacerbated by law if we aren't careful. We have to devise an equality law that will help us all. At the same time, we must get what we need for each group we work with. I think that there is no real tension between those tasks, but it is important to be clear that, with a law built on sameness and difference, the legal system may try to use differences between our inequalities as reasons why one inequality does not deserve what another inequality deserves, and may also try to use our similarities to deny benefits to any of us. I want to give a brief analysis of what I think all inequalities have in common, as a beginning way of developing a theory of equality that could work for all of us and get each of us what we need.

First of all, all inequalities share denigration, humiliation, disregard, degradation based on group membership. This happens with each inequality in a different way, but it is one of the cardinal qualities of every inequality as such. An inequality defines its victims as less than human, less than a full member of society, a second-class citizen. This is how you know an inequality when you see one. A second commonality of inequalities is that they exclude people from resources, respect, credibility, and power. One is not believed or respected because of one's membership in the disadvantaged group. Typically, one is also materially deprived. Resources include money; poverty is an expression as well as a basis of disadvantage.

A third commonality is that inequalities are collective. They may be visited on individuals one at a time but they are never isolated. Inequality means never being permitted to be an individual in the full social meaning of the word. We are always being told that something happened to a person who "happened to be" a member of such and so group. Things don't happen to happen to you just because you happen to be a member of a group. They happen determinately *because* you *are* a member of this group. It's collective. You don't have to be standing in a pack at the time you're hit by it, but it does happen to you as a member of a group.

Inequality also has a fourth commonality: it is systemic and systematic. It is not in any way accidental. Therefore, its incidents are cumulative. We are not dealing with marginal corrections needed at the edges of a fundamentally fairly ordered social situation. And finally, inequalities have in common the fact that each inequality is unique, concretely, and has to be understood first in its particularity. Each inequality is not a subcategory of the abstraction "disadvantage." It is the concrete specifics that give that term its meaning. Each inequality is first the status that it is, and later may be an example of something connected to other examples.

Section 15 of the Charter has done a number of interesting things. Everyone here, each in our own way, fought to be part of section 15 or is affected by the fights over section 15; each was given more or less under it. Section 15 puts us together under a list or set of terms.[10] As a result, it underlines the need to be clear on the tension between the commonalities of all inequalities and the concreteness unique to each. Section 15 is a lot more concrete than many constitutional equality mandates. It contains a list of bases for prohibited discrimination. It does not, however, list the concrete groups that are disadvantaged.[11] Then there is the unenumerated part.[12] It may submerge or obscure the qualities or characteristics or problems it does not mention, but it also makes it possible to surface and raise them. Section 15 imposes on us a special need to be clear about the particularity of each inequality by placing them on a list with commas in between. We can be sure that what is gained under one will be attempted to be gained under another, but also what is taken away from one or not given to one will be attempted, by analogy, to be taken away from or not given to another. Inequalities are always connected; section 15 connects them constitutionally. Then there's the tension between the concrete inequalities and abstract equality, between the particularities of each inequality and the generality of equality as it has previously been conceived. It is up to us to work with this.

The final thing I want to say about the commonalities of inequalities is that they are all connected somewhere. I do not mean on a level of abstraction or generalization or universality where obscure stuff goes on. I mean that fundamentally a hierarchical society needs to organize itself hierarchically. It's not only that the inequalities we deal with overlap, because of course they do phenomenally empirically in the world. For example, there is no woman without particularities besides gender. All inequalities interconnect and overlap in experience; to use a male metaphor, they interpenetrate. One could say, for example, that women are poor because they are women. That would be to analyze sex in a way to which poverty was essential, or one could say one is poor because one is a woman. That would be to analyze poverty in a way to which gender was essential. That's what I mean by interpenetrating. Somehow, in a way we have yet to understand fully, these things are all facets of one big thing, even as, at the same time, they are something very specific each in themselves.

All that is my contribution to our thinking about the big picture. There has never been a meeting like this in the United States—ever. I think it's partly because Canadians are better organized. It's partly because section 15 was created the way it was and is drafted the way it is. There is now such a thing in Canada as "the equality question," a question for each of us and for all of us. In the United States, the system has been much more effective in keeping equality-seeking groups separate. There is no equivalent to section 15 in the U.S. Constitution, nothing that lays out the specific bases, nothing that takes substantive disadvantage into account, nothing that by its terms invites disadvantaged groups to equality under law.

The alternate view that could change things is best pursued, crucially pursued, through a substantive analysis of each particular inequality. As to inequalities, the biggest trick of the system is to get you to be abstract. Don't fall for it. Define your inequalities the way you see them and stick to it.

Here is an example of how defining things one's own way works with women. A lot of things that weren't regarded as inequalities under the existing law of equality all of a sudden are. For example, questions of sexual abuse. Issues of sexual abuse have not been regarded as inequality questions. They have been implicitly regarded as questions of difference. Because of the sex difference, because women are different, it seems, we are sexually abused. Sexual abuse is then regarded as a question of community order or morality.[13] Anything but politics, anything but inequality. One of women's major experiences of inequality is sexual violence. The laws on sexual violence work as if they had been written not to work. An equality analysis suggests that what have been issues of criminal law in this area are issues of sex inequality in disguise. And because we know what we know, concretely, about the way women are socially subordinated, we know how to approach the criminal law through the Charter. We have to make equality meaningful in an area where it hasn't even been thought to have a place. Criminal law must promote sex equality or it violates the Constitution. The same goes for reproductive rights. Women know that social denial of reproductive control helps keep us second-class citizens because we are women. Therefore, legally, we must use sex equality guarantees to guarantee reproductive rights.

If you go through your own concrete examples, the situation you know best, think about what you need that you don't have, and then think about whether or how the law has even bothered to consider it. If it has denied it, you have a constitutional claim. But all kinds of things happen to the disadvantaged that the law has never even noticed. Most of what happens to the unequal isn't illegal anywhere. The next question is, how do you make *that* into an equality issue? Stay specific and concrete and insist that the legal system meet your needs, rather than cave in to the legal system's demands to begin with. Question the structure and assumptions of equality thinking in law. Don't just push to expand the content of existing doctrine.

As an example of structure that relates to the marginalization of most equality needs, take section 32 and the situation of women.[14] Women are subordinated socially, primarily, and only secondarily through law. That is to say, many of the most fundamental abuses of women as persons happen in private, where women are battered, raped, abused as children, prostituted, sexually harassed, and so on.[15] Those things happen prior to law. There are some laws against some aspects of them, but basically law permits them to go on. No law gives men the right to rape women. This hasn't been necessary, since no rape law has seriously undermined the terms of man's entitlement to sexual access to women in whatever way they choose, regardless of what women want.[16] No government yet, that I know of, is in the pornography business. This hasn't been necessary, since no law prevents men from getting access to it, regardless of censorship boards and customs restrictions.[17] These abuses are committed against women in society, not in the first instance by law, although law collaborates in it. No law gives men the right to batter their wives. This hasn't been necessary, because there really is no law to stop them.[18] No law guarantees that women are forever to remain the social unequals of men. This hasn't been necessary, because the law guaranteeing sex equality requires that before you can be equal legally, you have to be equal socially.

These inequalities occur on a social level. Then section 32 says that this constitutional equality guarantee only applies to the government.[19] Women are made unequal and kept unequal prior to any act of government, and then are told that the only way they can get equality is when government has made them unequal. You come to government unequal, and you are then, that premise undisturbed, guaranteed equal treatment.

How do we get at this? The unequal status quo is not only built into the equality argument substantively, it's built into the Charter structurally. There's this wall, this interface, called section 32. At that wall between law and society, that threshold of the legal system, the law collaborates in, is embedded in, the way the social system keeps women unequal. Work back from what you know about the social circumstances: the ways the law works, doesn't work, the way the police act, don't act. Governmental acts and omissions are so deeply involved in the society that it's something of a misnomer to say there is a private sphere. Government is already all over it. We have to work back from our social condition to expose the ways the law is involved in the structure, even if it tells us it is not. Equality law, correctly shaped, could do this.

To conclude, I would like to say a little about what they will say if we do this. We will be told that our approach to equality law is not neutral. But existing laws, and existing social reality, are already not neutral. The question is, on what side is the nonneutrality going to fall: to maintain inequality or to promote equality? The choice is between existing law—which is neutral from the standpoint of the advantaged and nonneutral from the standpoint of the disadvantaged—and the alternative, which, written from the viewpoint of the disadvantaged, may be considered nonneutral from the advantaged standpoint. The question is whether you want the problem of inequality solved. You can't solve the problem of disadvantage from the standpoint of dominance. You can solve it from the standpoint of the disadvantaged. In a hierarchical situation, neutrality really is not available.

It may also be said that the approach I have been advancing, get this, undermines the legitimacy of the legal system. But the legitimacy of this legal system is based on force at the expense of the disadvantaged. Its legitimacy is based on the exclusion of the majority of the population. It ought to have a big legitimacy problem now, to the extent that it is not responding to the needs of most of the people, who are being disadvantaged. Adopting this approach to equality strikes me as a real opportunity for the legal system to gain some legitimacy for itself for a change, by doing something for most people instead of for the tiny elite.

The next thing that will be said is that, if equality law is approached from the standpoint of the disadvantaged, it is particular pleading for a particular group, and where will it end? If we do it for some of them, then we'll have to do it for the rest of them. We are all supposed to say, just give it to us; you don't have to give it to them. They respond, this is a fair system, it's principled, it's abstract, it embodies the rule of law, which is a form of the equality ideal. If you apply it to one, you have to apply it to another, and if we start this who knows where it will end? To which we answer, it will end with equality. Give it to us *and* give it to them. Existing law is already special pleading for a particular group, the dominant group, where it has ended. They don't have any problem figuring out where advantage will end. They have given it to one group—themselves—and stopped. Somehow, the rule of law has not yet bound them to give all their legal advantages to the rest of us. If the rule of law worked in its vaunted everyday way, if the great slippery slope was slippery, we would all have slid into equality by now. We wouldn't be unequal, we wouldn't be disadvantaged through law, because what applied to one would truly apply to another, and there would be no such thing as the inequality problem. Our problem is the opposite. It is not giving it to one and where will it stop; it is getting anything for anybody except the ones who use law to keep it to themselves. They know how to stop. The question is, do they know how to start?

The other thing that will be said is that law on behalf of the disadvantaged can't win and won't work. This is your basic counsel from legal practicality: don't try. The law isn't for you. What made you think you really live here? Of course we will be strategic, intelligent, craft and couch arguments in ways that courts can understand and may appeal to them. But it is at the very least premature at this point in the assessment of the Charter, section 15 in particular, to say that this argument—an argument for real equality—can't win and won't work.[20] Its concrete possibilities can only be assessed in practice. The opportunity presented by the Charter is immense. Nothing this systematic, this concerted, this broad has ever been available, far less tried.

TWELVE

On Torture

During a dozen or so years of essentially making a living on the road, cobbling together speeches with short teaching hitches, I developed a practice of doing research for speeches in advance but preparing the talk itself on the way to the event, right up to the moment of delivery, and then reconfiguring it, sometimes completely, during delivery. A talk was ready to give when my notes became illegible. In this instance, I was trapped, fogged in, at Schiphol, Amsterdam, for nearly forty-eight hours, being told every few hours that the air would clear for takeoff. The conference I was aiming to attend generously rearranged itself to permit my speech later (in a kind friend's suit, my luggage marooned somewhere). The venue was a spectacular auditorium-in-the-round with vast windows overlooking a breathtaking view of the Canadian Rockies. With this transit time, this speech was pretty tightly wrapped by the time it was given.

With the rearranged timing, no dialogue after delivery was possible—especially unnerving as the full auditorium had fallen dead silent as I began reading Linda "Lovelace"'s words. Then we all flocked to the elevators. At the back of a packed one, I was obscured, everyone facing forward; several floors ascended in more total silence. In sudden daylight, someone got off. We rose in more silent darkness. Then a small grey-haired man in a suit at the front turned slightly to another small darker-haired man in a suit who was handling everyone's floor requests. "She's right, you know," the first one said quietly. "I know," the other responded. "Why didn't *we* think of that?" I knew I was home.

If anywhere in law, international law is where outrages are taken as outrages, where what happens to people who do not have power matters, and that is what law is for. (Might this be why the field traditionally has so little prestige in U.S. law and the U.S. legal academy?) From the moment of this speech, inside of a decade, beginning in a year or so—warp speed for legal embrace of a new theory—rape began to be recognized as a form of torture in international courts all over the world, where it is now accepted.[1] Rape is not yet fully embraced as a form of torture in the so-called private settings that formed the core target of this talk.[2] But there is motion. Internationally, domestic violence—probably because it is harder to defend overtly and its sexual dimensions are typically elided—has advanced the furthest. In some circumstances, the atrocity in the everyday is recognized as the responsibility of the state.[3]

Torture is widely recognized as a fundamental violation of human rights.[4] Inequality on the basis of sex is also widely condemned, and sex equality affirmed as a basic human rights value and legal guarantee in many nations and internationally.[5] So why is torture on the basis of sex—for example, in the form of rape, battering, and pornography—not seen as a violation of human rights?[6] When women are abused, human rights are violated; anything less implicitly assumes women are not human. When torture is sex-based, human rights standards should be recognized as violated, just as much as when the torture is based on anything else.

Internationally, torture has a recognized profile.[7] It usually begins with abduction, detention, imprisonment, and enforced isolation, progresses through extreme physical and mental abuse, and may end in death. The torturer has absolute power, which torture victims believe in absolutely and utterly. Life and death turn on his whim. Victims are beaten, raped, shocked with electricity, nearly drowned, tied, hung, burned, deprived of sleep, food, and human contact. The atrocities are limited only by the torturer's taste and imagination and any value the victim may be seen to have alive or unmarked. Verbal abuse and humiliation, making the victim feel worthless and hopeless, are integral to the torture having its intended effect. Often torture victims are selected and tortured in particular ways because they are members of a social group, for example, Jews in 1977 Argentina.[8] Torturers also exploit human relationships to inflict mental suffering; a man will be forced to watch his wife being raped, for example. Victims are forced to drink their own urine, to eat their own excrement.

Sometimes drugs are forcibly administered that alter personalities and make bodily or mental control or even self-recognition impossible. Torture is often designed as a slow process toward an excruciating death. Even when one survives, events move and escalate toward death, which is sometimes wished for to escape the agony. One is aware that one could be killed at any point. Many are.

What torture does to a human being is internationally recognized. Its purpose is to break people. People change under such extreme pressure, studied under the rubrics of brainwashing, post-traumatic stress, and the Stockholm syndrome. Long-term consequences include dissociation, which promotes survival but can be hard to reverse. What one learns being tortured, and what is necessary to survive it, can make living later unbearable, producing suicide even after many years. The generally recognized purpose of torture is to control, intimidate, or eliminate those who insult or challenge or are seen to undermine the powers that be, typically a regime or a cadre seeking to become a regime. Torture is thus seen as political, although it often seems that its political overlay is a facilitating pretext for the pure exercise of sadism, a politics of itself.

When these things happen, human rights are deemed violated. It is acknowledged that atrocities are committed.[9] While there is no ultimate answer to the question "Why do they do it?" and, in the context of torture, little agonizing over the question, nothing stops the practice from being identified and universally opposed as a crime jus cogens. With this framework in mind, consider the following accounts:

> "Linda Lovelace" was the name I bore during the two-and-one-half year period of imprisonment beginning in 1971. Linda "Lovelace" was coerced through physical, mental, and sexual torture and abuse, often at gunpoint and through threats on her life to perform sex acts, including forced fellatio and bestiality so that pornographic films could be made of her.[10]

Ms. "Lovelace" then describes encountering Chuck Traynor, a pimp, as follows:

> [W]hen in response to his suggestions I let him know I would not become involved in prostitution in any way and told him I intended to leave he beat me up physically and the constant mental abuse began. I literally became a prisoner, I was not allowed out of his sight, not even to use the bathroom, where he watched me through a hole in the door. He slept on top of me at night, he listened in on my telephone calls with a .45 automatic eight shot pointed at me. I was beaten physically and suffered mental abuse

each and every day thereafter. He undermined my ties with other people and forced me to marry him on advice from his lawyer. My initiation into prostitution was a gang rape by five men, arranged by Mr. Traynor. It was the turning point in my life. He threatened to shoot me with the pistol if I didn't go through with it. I had never experienced anal sex before and it ripped me apart. They treated me like an inflatable plastic doll, picking me up and moving me here and there. They spread my legs this way and that, shoving their things at me and into me, they were playing musical chairs with parts of my body. I have never been so frightened and disgraced and humiliated in my life. I felt like garbage. I engaged in sex acts for pornography against my will to avoid being killed. Mr. Traynor coerced me into pornography by threatening my life first with a .45 automatic eight shot and later with an M 16 semiautomatic machine gun, which became his favorite toy. I was brutally beaten whenever I showed any signs of resistance or lack of enthusiasm for the freaky sex he required me to act like I enjoyed. The lives of my family were threatened. Each day I was raped, beaten, kicked, punched, smacked, choked, degraded, or yelled at by Mr. Traynor. Sometimes all of these. He consistently belittled and humiliated me. I believed Mr. Traynor would have killed me and others if I did not do what he demanded of me. I didn't doubt he would shoot me. I made myself go numb as if my body belonged to someone else . . . Simple survival took everything I had. I managed to escape on three separate occasions. The first and second time I was caught and suffered a brutal beating and an awful sexual abuse as punishment. The third time I was at my parents' home and Mr. Traynor threatened to kill my parents and my nephew if I did not leave immediately with him. The physical effects of this are still with me. During my imprisonment my breasts were injected with silicone, which has since broken up and has been dangerous and painful. All of the surface veins of my right leg were destroyed because I used it to protect myself from the beatings. My doctor told me that because of the abuse, it was unsafe for me to have another child so I had an abortion when I

own. He cut off the phone, which was my only contact with the outside world. He would make me visit him when he finished his mailman routine and give him a blow job on the public street while people were passing by. I really wanted to die.[12]

Now consider this composite account of the systematic violation of a woman named Burnham by a man named Beglin, her husband: Beglin was watching an X-rated movie on cable television in the family room. He entered the bedroom, threw her on the bed, and bound her. He ripped off her clothing and began taking photos of her. He then sexually assaulted her. Crisis center workers and an emergency room doctor testified that her wrists and ankles were marked from being tied to the bed by ropes. He forced her sixty-eight different times to have sex with neighbors and strangers while he took photographs. She was forced through assault and holding their child hostage to stand on the corner and invite men in for sex and to have sex with the dog. He beat her so that she was nearly killed.

She testified to episodes of torture with a battery-charged cattle prod and an electric eggbeater. She was asked about photographs in an album showing her smiling during the sexual encounters. She said that her husband threatened her with violence if she didn't smile while these photographs were taken.[13]

In the accounts by these women, all the same things happen that happen in Amnesty International reports and accounts of torture— except they happen in homes in Nebraska or in pornography studios in Los Angeles rather than prison cells in Chile or detention centers in Turkey. But the social and legal responses to the experiences are not the same at all. Torture is not considered personal. Torture is not attributed to one sick individual at a time and dismissed as exceptional, or if it is, that maneuver is dismissed as a cover-up by the human rights community. Torture victims are not generally asked how many were there with them, as if it is not important if it happened only to you or you and a few others like you. With torture, an increase is not dismissed as just an increase in reporting, as if a constant level of such abuse is acceptable. Billions of dollars are not made selling as entertainment pictures of what is regarded as torture, nor is torture as such generally regarded as sexual entertainment. Never is a victim of torture asked, didn't you really want it?

A simple double standard is at work here. What fundamentally distinguishes torture, understood in human rights terms, from the events these women have described is that torture is done to men as well as to women. Or, more precisely, when what usually happens to women as these women have described it happens to men, which it sometimes does, women's experience is the template for it, so those men, too, are ignored as women are. When the abuse is sexual or intimate, especially when it is sexual and inflicted by an intimate, it is gendered, hence not considered a human rights violation. Torture is regarded as politically motivated; states are generally required to be involved in it. What needs asking is why the torture of women by men is not seen as torture, specifically why it is not seen as political, and just what the involvement of the state in it is.

Women are half the human race. To put the individual accounts in context, all around the world, women are battered, raped, sexually abused as children, prostituted, and increasingly live pornographic lives in contexts saturated more or less with pornography.[14] Women do two-thirds of the world's work, earn one-tenth of the world's income, and own less than one-hundredth of the world's property.[15] Women are more likely to *be* property than to own any. Women have not even been allowed to vote until very recently and still are not in some countries. Women's reproductive capacities are systematically exploited. While the rate and intensity of these atrocities and violations vary across cultures, they are never equal or substantially reversed on the basis of sex. All this is done to women as women by men as men.

Data contextualizes this, and a few selected examples show it with more texture. In the United States, 44 percent of all women at one time or another are victims of rape or attempted rape; for women of color, the rates are higher.[16] In 1988, 31 percent of murdered women were killed by husbands or boyfriends.[17] In egalitarian Sweden, one woman is battered to death every week to ten days.[18] Dramatic increases in the rate of reported rape are debated there; the debate is over whether the increases are "real" or "merely" reflect an increase in reporting. Where women are chattel or have only recently even legally emerged from the condition of being chattel, as is the situation in Japan, what can rape mean? If a woman exists to be sexually used, to what sexual use of her is the right man not entitled? Sweden, the United States, and Japan are all saturated with pornography. In the United States, women disappear on a daily basis—from their homes, from supermarket parking lots. Sometimes they are found in ditches or floating down rivers. Sometimes we dig up their bones along with those of ten or fifteen other women ten or fifteen years later. Serial rapists and serial murderers, who are almost always men, target women almost exclusively.

Why isn't this political? The abuse is neither random nor individual. The fact that you may know your assailant does not mean that your membership in a group chosen for violation is irrelevant to your abuse. It is still systematic and group-based. It defines the quality of community life and is defined by the distribution of power in society. It would seem that something is not considered political if it is done to women by men, especially if it is considered to be sex. Then it is not considered political because what is political is when men control and hurt and use other men—meaning persons who are deserving of dignity and power—on some basis men have decided is deserving of dignity and a measure of power, like conventional political ideology, because that is a basis on which they have been deprived of dignity and power. So their suffering has the dignity of politics and is called torture.[19] Women as such are not seen as deserving of dignity or power, nor does the sexuality that defines us have dignitary standards, nor is women's belief in our own dignity given the dignity or power of being regarded as a political ideology. The definition of the political here is an unequal one, determined on the basis of sex such that atrocities to women are denied as atrocities by being deprived of political meaning.

Often the reason given for not considering atrocities to women to be torture is that they do not involve acts by states. They happen between nonstate actors in civil society hence are seen as not only unofficial but unconscious and unorganized and unsystematic and undirected and unplanned. They do not happen, it is thought, by state policy. They just happen. And traditionally, international instruments (as well as national constitutions) govern state action.

First of all, the state is not all there is to power. To act as if it is produces an exceptionally inadequate definition for human rights when so much of the second-class status of women, from sexual objectification to murder, is done by men to women without express or immediate or overt state involvement. If "the political" is to be defined in terms of men's experiences of being subjected to power, it makes some (but only some) sense to center its definition on the state.[20] But if one is including the unjust power involved in the subjection of half the human race by the other half—male dominance— it makes no sense to define power exclusively in terms of what the state does when it is defined as acting. The state is only one instrumentality of sex inequality. To fail to see this is pure gender bias. Often this bias flies under the flag of privacy, so that those areas that are defined as inappropriate for state involvement, where the discourse of human rights is made irrelevant, are those "areas in which the majority of the world's women live out their days."[21] Moreover, the fact that there is no single state or organized group expressly dedicated to this pursuit does not mean that all states are not more or less dedicated to it on an operative level or that it is not a deep structure of social, political, and legal organization. Why human rights, including the international law against torture, should be limited by it is the question.

Second, the state actually is typically deeply and actively complicit in the abuses mentioned, collaborating in and condoning them. Linda "Lovelace" describes her escape from Mr. Traynor: "I called the Beverly Hills police department and told them my husband was looking for me with an M16. They told me they couldn't be involved with domestic affairs. When I told them his weapons were illegal, they told me to call back when he was in the room."[22] She testified before a grand jury in an obscenity case involving one of the films made of her. The grand jury looked at the films and asked her how she could have ever done that. She said because a gun was at her head. It did nothing.[23] As Linda Marchiano, she later tried to have an ordinance passed that would have made it possible for her to bring a civil action against the pornographers for damages for everything they did to her and to remove the pornography of her from distribution.[24] This ordinance, a sex equality law, was invalidated by the United States courts as a violation of freedom of expression, even though the court of appeals that invalidated it recognized all of the harms pornography did to women and agreed that it actually did those harms. This court held that pornography must be protected as speech in spite of its harm to sex equality—indeed, *because* of these harms, inasmuch as the value of the speech for purposes of protection was measured by the harm it did to women and to their equality.[25] When this result was summarily affirmed by the U.S. Supreme Court, the U.S. government legalized an express and admitted human rights violation on the view that the harm that pornography causes is more important than the people it hurts.[26] This is certainly state ratification of her abuse. It also raises the question, if someone took pictures of what happens in prison cells in Turkey, would they be sold as protected expression and sexual entertainment on the open market, with the state seen as uninvolved? The pornography of Linda continues to proliferate worldwide.

Jayne Stamen wrote her account from the Nassau County Correctional Facility in New York, where she was imprisoned. She was convicted of manslaughter in Jerry's killing by three men she supposedly solicited. Evidence of "battered women's syndrome" was excluded from her trial, to the reported accompaniment of judicial remarks such as "I'm not going to give any woman in Nassau County a license to kill her husband" and "Jerry Stamen is not on trial here but Jayne Stamen is."[27] Prosecution and jailing are state acts. Can you imagine a murder prosecution by a state against a torture victim who killed a torturer while escaping? If you can, can you imagine Amnesty International ignoring it?[28]

In the *Burnham* case, the conviction for marital rape that the wife won at trial was overturned on appeal because of the failure of the judge below sua sponte to instruct the jury that the husband might have believed that Ms. Burnham *consented*.[29] There was no standard beyond which it was regarded as obvious that a human being was violated, hence true consent was inconceivable. No recognition that people break under torture. No realization that anyone will say anything to a torturer to try to make it stop. When women break under torture, we are said to have consented, or the torturer could have thought we did. Pictures of our "confessions" in the form of pornography follow us around for the rest of our lives. Few say, that isn't who she really is, everybody breaks under torture. Many do say, he could have believed it; besides, some women like it.

This is the *law* of pornography, the *law* of battered women's self-defense, the *law* of rape. Why isn't this state involvement? Formally, its configuration is very close to the recent case *Velasquez-Rodriguez v. Honduras*,[30] in which a man was violently detained, tortured, and accused of political crimes by a group that was allegedly official but was actually a more or less unofficial but officially-winked-at death squad. He has never been found. What was done to him was legally imputed to Honduras as a state under international law mostly because the abuse was systematically tolerated by the government. The abuse of the women described was not official in the narrow sense at the time it happened, but its cover-up, legitimization, and legalization after the fact were openly so. The lack of effective remedy was entirely official. The abuse was done, at the very least, with official impunity and legalized disregard. The abuse is systematic and known, the disregard is official and organized, and the effective governmental tolerance is a matter of law and policy.

Legally, the pattern is one of national and international guarantees of sex equality coexisting with massive rates of rape and battering and traffic in women through pornography effectively condoned by law. Some progressive international human rights bodies are beginning to inquire into some dimensions of these issues under equality rubrics—none into pornography, some into rape and battering.[31] Rape is now more likely to look like a potential human rights violation when it happens in official custody.[32] A woman's human rights are more likely to be deemed violated when the state can be seen as an instrumentality of the rape. Yet the regular laws and their regular everyday administration are not seen as official state involvement in legalized sex inequality.[33] The fact that rape happens is regarded by some far-thinking groups and agencies as a violation of a *norm* of sex equality. But the fact that the *law* of rape protects rapists and is written from their point of view to guarantee impunity for most rapes is officially regarded as a violation of the *law* of sex equality, national or international, by virtually nobody.

High on my list of state atrocities of this sort is rape law's defense of mistaken belief in consent. This permits the accused to be exonerated if he thinks the woman consented, no matter how much force he used. This is the law in Canada, New Zealand, and the United Kingdom, as well as some parts of the United States, including California, where the *Burnham* case was adjudicated. Another example is abortion's unconstitutionality, as in Ireland. A further example is the affirmative protection of pornography in the United States, including under the case in which Linda "Lovelace" participated.[34] Of course, the United States, an international outlaw of major proportions, is not bound by most of the relevant international agreements, not having ratified them. But other countries where the pornography of her, and others like her, is trafficked are. I would also include in this list of state atrocities the decriminalization of pornography, first in Denmark, then in Sweden. Those were official state acts, however beside the point of the harm to women their prior pornography laws were. No pornography laws at all is open season on women with official blessing. So is the across-the-board legalization of all participants in prostitution.

Why are there no human rights standards for tortures of women as a sex? Why are these atrocities not seen as sex equality violations? The problem can be explained in part in terms of the received notion of equality, which has served as a fairly subtle cross-cultural template for the legal face of misogyny. The traditional concept is the Aristotelian one of treating likes alike and unlikes unalike—mostly likes alike. In practice, this means that to be an equal, you must be the same as whoever sets the dominant standard. The unlikes unalike part has always been an uncomfortable part of equality law, really an internal exception to it, so that affirmative action, for example, is regarded as theoretically disreputable and logically problematic, even contradictory. The Aristotelian approach to equality, which dominates worldwide, never confronts several problems that the condition of women exposes. One is, why don't men, particularly white upper-class men, have to be the same as anyone in order to get equal treatment? Another is, men are as different from women as women are from men: equally different. Why aren't they punished for their differences like women are? Another is, why is equality as well satisfied by equalizing down as up? In other words, if equality is treating likes alike and unlikes unlike, if you get somebody down in the hole that the unlikes are in, in theory that is just as equal as elevating the denigrated to the level of the dominant standard set by the privileged.

The upshot of this approach is what is called in American law the "similarly situated" test, a concept that is used in one form or another around the world wherever law requires equality.[35] As applied to women, it means if men don't need it, women don't get it. Men as such do not need effective laws against rape, battering, prostitution, and pornography (although some of them do), so not having such laws for women is not an inequality; it is just a difference. Thus are these abuses rendered part of the sex difference, the permitted treating of unalikes unalike. Because there are relatively few similarly raped, battered, or prostituted men around to compare with (or they are comparatively invisible and gendered female), such abuses to women are not subjected to equality law at all. Where the lack of similarity of women's condition to men is extreme because of sex inequality, the result is that the law of sex equality does not properly apply.

Sex inequality, in this view, is not simply a distinction to be made properly or improperly, as in the Aristotelian approach. It is fundamentally a hierarchy, here initially a two-tiered hierarchy. Inequality produces systematic subordination, as in the situations of the women discussed.[36] The Canadian Supreme Court in its *Andrews* decision and cases following has come closer than any other court in the world to beginning to recognize this fundamental nature of inequality, leading the world on the subject.[37] To be consistent with equality guarantees in this approach is to move to end sex inequality. Wherever the law reinforces gender hierarchy, it violates legal equality guarantees, in national constitutions and in international covenants as well.

Understanding inequality as hierarchy makes the torture of women because of sex an obvious human rights issue, obscure only because of its pervasiveness. In this light, laws that prohibit what women need for equality, such as restrictions on abortion, and unenforced laws, such as the law against battering, which can make violence women's only survival option, need to be rethought. They violate human rights. Laws that don't fit the violation, such as the law of self-defense, rape, and obscenity in most places, violate human rights. All are affirmative state acts or positive omissions that discriminate on the basis of sex and deny relief for sex equality violations. The lack of laws against the harms women experience in society because we are women, such as most of the harms of pornography, also violates human rights. Women are human there, too.

If, when women are tortured because we are women, the law recognized that a human being had her human rights violated, the term "rights" would begin to have something of the content to which we might aspire, and the term "woman" would, in Richard Rorty's phrase, "begin to become a name for a way of being human."[38]

THIRTEEN

Rape as Genocide: Appellate Argument in *Kadic v. Karadžić*

This case marked the first time rape was argued to be an act of genocide in a court of law.[1] For Bosnian and Croatian clients and their families, civil claims were brought in a United States federal court under the Alien Tort Act[2] and the Torture Victim Protection Act[3] for rape and other crimes committed in the genocide in Bosnia and Herzegovina and Croatia that had been orchestrated and led by Bosnian Serb leader Radovan Karadžić. On June 20, 1995, the appeal of the lower court's rejection of our clients' case, *Kadic v. Karadžić,*[4] was argued to a Second Circuit Court of Appeals panel in New York City. This is my part of that argument (the footnotes of course added).

By judicial fiat, our case was argued together with *Does v. Karadžić,*[5] in which rape as genocide was not the focus. Both cases also claimed rape as torture, which requires state action. After the panel gave Beth Stevens, counsel for Does, a very hard time about the role of the state actor—what remained of Yugoslavia—in the cases, Rhonda Copelon, advisor to the *Does* case, strongly pressured me at counsel table to abandon that claim in my argument. I refused.

The panel consisted of Chief Judge Jon O. Newman, Circuit Judge Wilfred Feinberg, and Circuit Judge John M. Walker, Jr. Judge Newman seemed to reify the public / private distinction, as if the real world is naturally so divided in places that can be physically found, rather than being a conceptual legal fiction to which facts can pertain.

We won this argument in every respect in a strong decision[6] that, once the U.S. Supreme Court declined to review the decision,[7] opening substantial subsequent use of the Alien Tort Act by victims of atrocities that violated customary international law, until this possibility was substantially eviscerated by the Supreme Court years later.[8] Karadžić was delegitimized when exposed by the proceedings, which on our initiative also produced the International Tribunal for Former Yugoslavia, before which he was eventually tried and convicted for rape and for genocide, although not precisely for genocidal rape.[9] Rape was subsequently recognized under international law by an international court, the International Tribunal for Rwanda, as integral to genocides when it is so weaponized.[10] *Kadic* has been a butterfly.[11]

NEWMAN, J: Good morning. As I think counsel know, and I see counsel know, we're going to defer the motion calendar, and turn immediately to Doe and Karadžić, and Kadic, is it? I'm not sure. . . .

CAM: Good morning. I'd like to reserve two minutes for rebuttal. I'm Catharine MacKinnon. I represent the Kadic plaintiffs, who are Bosnian, Muslim, and Croat women and children, named individuals and survivor groups, suing for damages and an injunction for violent torts that have been committed against them personally, prominently rape and murder, in this so called "ethnic cleansing" campaign, which is a euphemism for genocide through war, ordered by defendant Karadžić, in opposition to universally accepted international human rights of our clients. Our clients, who are judges, lawyers, mothers, factory workers, farmers, were violated in this genocidal war because they are women who are not Serbs. Karadžić, as has been stated, is the self-proclaimed president of the Bosnian Serb Republic. It is uncontested by either side in this litigation and by anyone in this world that he is official leader of this de facto regime and its army. The two federal statutes that we have sued him under were precisely designed, and have been consistently interpreted, to remedy harms like these, to people like ours, against perpetrators like this defendant.

WALKER, J: Let me ask you this. If we were to rule as you wish, wouldn't in effect the courtroom doors of the United States then be open to all sorts of lawsuits by foreign aliens, living in other countries, against individuals in other countries, who couldn't get redress in those countries, and you know, are there any limitations on that sort of situation? You have an internal conflict going on in Yugoslavia, where presumably, violations are occurring, according to your allegations, on a daily basis. That would, what you're basically saying is that anyone from those countries, uh, who is unable to achieve any kind of redress over there can come to the United States or find a lawyer in the United States, and simply bring an action here. And wouldn't that just open up the floodgates to a tremendously overcrowded court system that exists in this country?

CAM: It certainly is the case, your Honor, that one of the reasons the United States court system and individual human rights are respected worldwide, one of reasons that people respect this country, is that this is seen to be a place that respects human rights. And when the Congress has very specifically delegated, given, granted, ordered courts to permit people who are specifically described by the Congress as being aliens, when torts are committed against them in violation of international law, and, in addition, the most recent Congress, when forms of official torture are committed against those individuals, when Congress has made that decision, it's our position that it is not open to this Court, in order to deny them access, to consider that there may be a good number of people who may wish to make use of it. Now in addition, this Court in *Filartiga*[12] has further narrowed, to some extent, that, by laying out appropriate approaches to personal jurisdiction. That is, someone has to be found and served—as there is no factual issue that our defendant was served here, no factual issue. That has to be done. Our position is, so long as the legal requirements are met, yes, individuals will be able to use this law. That, however, has been the case for some time without there being a flood.

WALKER, J: But, in this case, most of the prior cases, excluding *Filartiga*, have on the facts of those cases, at least not had to face the question of individual liability as opposed to state liability, which you're asking us to face. Appropriately, you're raising the issue that many of these actions are, can be brought against individuals, against private actors. That uh, is uh, is a whole new area of possible litigation that could, that could occur, and, there's no limitation based on the head of, on the immunity for head of state under those circumstances, it would seem to me, where you're just bringing actions against private individuals so that the built-in limitations that may normally exist against a head of state wouldn't apply. And that, to me, changes the picture a little bit when taking an overview of the impact of this, or an interpretation such as you would seek from the court system.

CAM: We are suing an individual in his official capacity, so in that sense, cases against private actors—

WALKER, J: You're not seeking a ruling that would limit the doctrine to that—anybody—a My Lai massacre type kind of situation, anybody who commits an alleged war crime, would be a viable defendant under your interpretation. In this particular case may involve a person who's claiming to be a leader, but, you're not seeking such a restriction.

CAM: International law does provide specific limitations, both in what is customary international law and in defining what is a crime of war. Some of those go to private actors, but the law of the Alien Tort Claims Act has gone to private actors since the beginning. Pirates, slave traders, indeed in *Terrill* against *Rankin*,[13] an international war crime was the basis for private action against acts committed by a de facto regime member—

WALKER, J: Well, it's a statute, it's a statute that's on the books for sure, and yes, but we haven't, at least in my own personal experience, haven't seen too many slave cases or piracy cases. It's not really a common cause of action these days, and this would be a little different. It's just that it, I'm just raising it as more of a policy concern than anything else, but, uh, I'm not requiring you to go, I don't think that you should necessarily answer . . .

CAM: Well, pursuant to the policy concern, our particular position was that the possible scope, what is represented by your question is an important one. But it's not necessary to resolve that in order to make it possible for these plaintiffs to bring this action against this very particular defendant, under international law.

WALKER, J: Do you think that there should be some requirement in addressing this problem, that there be a U.S. interest? I'm not saying one doesn't exist here, but that there should be some sort of finding of that sort that there be an interest on the part of this country, that such lawsuits be permitted, um, as a possible limitation, and it may be that one exists here, I don't know.

CAM: There clearly is an interest that the United States has in torts that are committed against aliens, in violation of international law, I mean, in passing the Alien Tort Claims Act, the Congress has already made that decision.

WALKER, J: One might be able to discern torts in Tibet against the Tibetan minority over there by the Chinese. I'm trying to pick a spot as far from the United States as possible, and far less known, and not covered by the media and so forth, and yet we have international relations with China. What would prevent a Tibetan from coming in, if this case goes the way you would like to have it go, a Tibetan from coming in, and bringing a lawsuit against someone in China, uh perhaps an official from China, for some conduct that has occurred that uh is against U.S. interests, because we maintain relations with China?

CAM: Well, first of all, the acts would have to violate customary international law, or jus cogens, as genocide does. That is, genocide, in addition to being customary international law, is jus cogens, therefore non-derogable. Or, some other customary international law violations such as occurring in armed conflict, either internal or international—and it's our position that this is international—but that internal matters are also covered by that law. The individual who committed them would have to be found and served here. But going to the question of American interests. . . .

WALKER, J: I'm assuming all of that, I'm just seeing, trying to understand whether American interests are part of the equation here, part of the calculus. In Tibet, people have argued that a million and a half people have been killed by the Chinese, um, genocide by any stretch of the imagination. And, yet would this not open up the door to such a lawsuit?

CAM: Presumably in a case like that the defense would raise the issue, specifically doctrinally, of whether or not was a political question, as is not the case here. And presumably, in a case like that, there would be a question of running the risk of disrespecting a matter that was clearly reserved for a coordinate political department. There is no risk of that here.

NEWMAN, J: Your argument, I take it, is in the alternative—that he is an official state actor, either because of the self-proclaimed Republic or the relation with Serbia. And that, even if not, he's liable in tort as a private actor, isn't that so?

CAM: We do argue both of those your Honor, and, in a way, in fact, both of those are precisely accurate. That is, Mr. Karadžić—

NEWMAN, J: Well, is that so? They're both precise? . . . I mean, you accuse the Appellee of having it both ways, I wonder if there isn't a little bit of both ways argument in both sides of this case. Can he be both a state actor and a non-state actor?

CAM: Well, we're entitled to have it both ways because we're right both ways, judge, and (laughter in the courtroom), that is to say, we are precisely in the window—

NEWMAN. J: I'm not sure I know quite what that means. It may be that you're entitled to win on one or the other, but I've never heard that a pleading in the alternative argument means both ends of the alternative are right. That may be so, but that seems to me a novel approach.

CAM: Well, the Alien Tort Claims Act docs cover this kind of activity, whether it is private or not.

NEWMAN, J: It covers some of it, maybe, but does it cover all of it?

CAM: It covers private actors, and the specific acts we're looking at, that is genocide and war crimes, specifically make—

NEWMAN, J: But in the end, if we remand this as you wish, and it goes to some fact-finding, won't some of the issues turn on whether or not he is a state actor?

CAM: Well, our position is that—it isn't our position, that question is not contested between parties. Karadžić has never once said he is a private actor. He has said, and affirmed in affidavit, "I am president of a Republic."

NEWMAN, J: But you're saying he is a private actor for some purposes.

CAM: No, we are saying . . .

NEWMAN, J: You're not?

CAM: No, we're not.

NEWMAN, J: No, oh, then we should drop the . . .

CAM: We're saying that the law covers him, even if he were. We're saying he is amply official for any public requirement. . . .

NEWMAN, J: Can he be both?

CAM:—but he would be covered even if he were purely private.

NEWMAN, J: But can he be both?

CAM: Factually, no.

NEWMAN, J: All right.

CAM: But factually what he specifically is, is amply official to be reachable under the Torture Victim Protection Act, and nowhere near sovereign, immune, diplomatic, nowhere near that legitimate to be protected by any aspect of the doctrine that protects public figures when they are legitimate.

NEWMAN, J: If you're coming to court saying he is a state actor, and you say the defendant himself concedes he's a state actor, why should we even worry about what would happen if he were a private actor?

CAM: The only reason we're worried about it, your Honor, is because Judge Leisure was worried about it. He said, that international law. . . .

NEWMAN, J: Well, one of the issues is, was he right to worry about it?

CAM: No, he was wrong to worry about it.

NEWMAN, J: Well, then the fact that he worried about it doesn't sound like it should guide our thinking as far as you view the case, so that's, I mean, if you want to plead this case in the alternative, the federal rules let you. But it sounds to me, the way you're arguing it, you're not pleading it in the alternative, you're just noticing that if he were a private actor, he would nonetheless be liable. But, lots of things are so. And, we don't adjudicate the consequences of them normally, I won't say never, but normally. But if your position is, never mind what he might be, he is a state actor, and we'll hear in due course, I hope shortly from Appellee, if he thinks he's a state actor, then shouldn't we take the case as a claim about a state actor, and never worry what would happen if he weren't a state actor?

CAM: Yes, our . . .

NEWMAN, J: We should do it that way.

CAM: Yes, he is head of a de facto regime, and that's a very specific legal category.

NEWMAN, J: Well, I'm surprised to hear you narrow your claim that way, but you're entitled to if you wish to.

CAM: But our position is that even if he were deemed a private individual, that he would be covered by this law. The laws of genocide cover that, the war crimes laws cover that.

NEWMAN, J: But you say even if he were determined, lawsuits are framed by litigants.

CAM: Yes.

NEWMAN, J: So, when you say even if he were, you mean if somebody else thought he was. That's not our issue. Our issue initially is what does the plaintiff plead?

CAM: Well, we're happy to ignore the error of Judge Leisure in inventing private status for the defendant. He invented it, against the defendant's claims as to his status. He invented it against our allegations. And this is one of the problems with the procedural posture this case. . . .

NEWMAN, J: So you want this case to stand or fall on his being a state actor?

CAM: He is the leader of a de facto regime. We have pleaded it. The defendant has not contested it. . . .

NEWMAN, J: You're entitled to do it. I find it a very surprising tactical position.

FEINBERG, J: If you should be successful on this appeal, I'm not suggesting that you will be, but if you should be successful on this appeal, I take it that the tenor of the Chief Judge's questions to [you] are, is that the case would then be remanded. And he was inquiring whether one of the issues on which the court below would perhaps make a finding as to whether the defendant is a private actor or not. Are you saying that you would oppose such in inquiry?

CAM: We oppose it because it is resolved on the papers before this court.

FEINBERG, J: If the District Judge, or we, believe that it's not resolved on the papers before this court, would you oppose such an inquiry on remand?

CAM: Well, your Honor, there is no contest between the parties on that manner.

NEWMAN, J: You've already said that. We haven't heard from the other side yet.

CAM: Well, the other side's briefs never say that Karadžić is not the leader of a de facto regime. His affidavit clearly states that he is president of the Republika . . .

NEWMAN, J: If they try distinctions . . .

FEINBERG. J: If it turns out that there is a dispute, I repeat the question for the third time, would you oppose the district court making such an inquiry?

CAM: We oppose it, because it is our position that at this procedural point in the process, we are entitled to the benefit of our allegations. And to have these legal issues resolved . . .

FEINBERG, J: You're clearly entitled to . . .

CAM: . . . on the basis of the papers, and the record in this case, rather than inventions that are factual by the District Court Judge or at this stage . . .

FEINBERG, J: Ms. MacKinnon, you're clearly entitled to the benefit of your allegations. The issue we're putting to you, with little success, is whether you are burdened with their limitations.

CAM: If our facts as alleged, were taken as true, as we are entitled at this stage, there would be no factual issue as to this. And the remand would be for trial. Thank you, your Honors.

[Argument by Ramsey Clark] [Rebuttal by Beth Stephens]

REBUTTAL

CAM: I would like to clarify a response to Judge Feinberg's question, that as to Kadic, in our lawsuit, there are no factual issues on service of process. Process was served by U.S. marshals on the State Department individuals guarding the defendant, and was as reflected in the account by Agent Diebler for the State Department, immediately given to defendant Karadžić. Karadžić affirms that he received it, the papers, read them, and has kept them. So there is not a single factual issue there. Also it makes clear in that affidavit that at the time at which this was served, that the defendant was not at the UN, was not on any property other than in New York. He was, in fact, in New York.

WALKER, J: Well, he was on real estate in New York, somewhere. . . .

CAM: Yes.

WALKER, J: Perhaps a hotel?

CAM: No. In the street, your Honor.

WALKER, J: In the street.

CAM: Yes, and presumably even metaphysically, that's New York. (Laughter)

NEWMAN, J: Some would even say physically.

CAM: Yes. And Agent Diebler's affidavit to which I refer your Honors, once again, makes it entirely clear that this was specifically off the property of the Russian Mission, which is where the defendant was at the time, and then as he proceeded away from there and was well off that property, he was then handed these papers by the State Department agent. I would also like to clarify that, in addition to our allegations that this defendant is acting as head of a republic—and I will move to Judge Newman's question in just a moment, to take one more crack at it—we do allege most specifically that our defendant acts as an arm of Serbia and Montenegro, the remaining rump Yugoslavia. This is in our complaint at paragraphs 2 and 27,[14] and this point is discussed in our brief[15] beginning on page 39. So we argue that he acts under color of the law on two bases. The principal one, of course, is that which has occupied our attention here today.

That is, he is head of a de facto regime. But a secondary one is our clear allegation that he is also acting in concert with, in collaboration with, and as an arm of the Serbian regime in Belgrade, Yugoslavia. As to our position, which was just stated extremely clearly by my colleague, I think it is now indelibly clear that the defendant has never said he is a private actor. He does not contest that he is official in some way. It is the legal consequences of the specific office status that he holds that we disagree about, and that is for this court to resolve. That is, what are the legal issues involved in suing the head of a de facto regime. It is our view that clearly he is acting under color of law, and both actual and apparent authority, for purposes of the Torture

Victim Protection Act. That, with regard to the Genocide Convention, he could be private, he could be public. It doesn't matter. That is, without regard to the nature of his official status, he is liable under the international law against genocide. The same is equally true for war crimes. And, of course, a further corollary to our position is that none of these official statuses rise to the level of any particular immunity, that is either to be granted, which it has not been, or to be implied.

WALKER, J: Well, no head-of-state immunity . . .

CAM: No head-of-state immunity. He is not a head of state in the sense of the Foreign Sovereign Immunities Act, no.

WALKER, J: We've been arguing about immunity in a different context, and that is . . .

CAM: Yes.

WALKER, J: . . . any immunity accorded to people coming to the UN . . .

CAM: Yes.

WALKER, J: . . . or affiliated with the UN. And . . .

CAM: And he is not a foreign sovereign. He has not been argued to be in the sense of the Foreign Sovereign Immunities Act. It is also indelibly clear that, while acting under color of law, that he is entirely outside any scope of official authority, even of his own regime. That is, while his acts are official policy, it is not the official policy announced, acknowledged, and embraced of any regime in the world, including Republika Srpska, to engage in genocide. And that is the requirement for immunity: that it be the announced, accepted, official policy of the country that is being carried out for the activities of the sovereign. In addition, of course, we are not suing the official entity; we are suing this individual in his official capacity.

WALKER, J: I think you, too, will have to conclude.

CAM: We conclude by saying, your Honors, that there is no legal barrier to holding this defendant accountable that keeps us from going to trial. There is only the possibility of a generalized reluctance to get involved, as unfortunately manifested by the District Court, which I would characterize as a bystander mentality, which is not a legal reason not to hear this case. It's contrary to the intent of Congress, which committed these injuries to these people, to these federal courts in this country, at the founding of our nation, and once again, by the Congress of our time. Such a bystander mentality, I need not remind us, also violates the resolve of history that a genocide would never be permitted to happen again. Thank you.

NEWMAN, J: Thank you all. We'll reserve decision, we will take a brief recess. The court stands in recess.

FOURTEEN

Rape as Genocide:
Summation to the Jury in
Kadic v. Karadžić

Having won the legal argument on the civil claim for rape as an act of genocide, establishing that a United States court could try the defendant for what he was alleged to have done to the plaintiffs in Bosnia-Herzegovina, we could proceed to trial for genocidal rape. Before the trial, we had a right to question the defendant, Radovan Karadžić, leader of the Bosnian Serbs, on facts of which he had knowledge in a deposition. By this point, the case had participated in delegitimizing him to the extent that there was an international warrant out for his arrest. To our disappointment, but not surprise, he did not show up for his deposition. When Karadžić failed to appear upon repeated summons to his lawyer Ramsey Clark, the court decided the plaintiffs had won their case by his default.[1] However, their damages remained to be proven, which amounted to trying virtually the entire substance of the case. Karadžić declined to appear. Although we urgently requested Karadžić's lawyer defend his interests in our minitrial hearing on damages, Ramsey Clark said he best served his client's interest by not appearing. This left defense of his interests in the capable hands of Judge Leisure.

This case first established the legal recognition of rape as an act of genocide when it takes place within, and is linked to, a genocide by existing international definition, meaning the intentional destruction of a people as such on the basis of their race, religion, nationality, or ethnicity.[2] It has become common to contend that raped women are too afraid or ashamed to show their faces in public, including in court. My experience has been the opposite. Most survivors, including of mass sexual atrocities, seek conditions of security and respect in which to tell what happened to them that present a reasonable chance of their experiences being accurately named, understood, and believed. If they do not feel they can testify, that ultimately is an indictment of forums that often then hide behind their purported solicitude for survivors' sensitivities. I have seldom met a survivor who did not want to tell their story at some point, under the right circumstances.

In all, fourteen named plaintiffs testified, including one who obtained final judgments on her own behalf and as administratrix of her mother's estate, one who obtained final judgments on her own behalf and on behalf of her two infant children, and two group plaintiffs, one large and one small group. My colleague at Paul, Weiss, Rifkind, Wharton & Garrison, Maria Vullo, a brilliant trial lawyer, spoke for the survivors that she and co-counsel Liza Velazquez questioned. Taken from my notes, identities redacted for their continued protection, the statement below is my part of our closing to the jury in the trial on damages that ended on August 10, 2000, in their civil case for genocidal rape of our Bosnian Muslim and Croat clients pursuant to Radovan Karadžić's genocidal policies.

The Manhattan jury of eleven women and one man awarded this group of clients a total of $745 million, each award carefully quantified according to the injuries of each individual. After the jury was discharged, its members asked to meet the plaintiffs. With no common language, each juror hugged each plaintiff, crying. It was the first time one survivor had allowed a man to touch her since her captivity ended.

In closing this morning, my co-counsel Maria Vullo spoke with you about the Bosnian Muslim and Bosnian Croat women victimized by Serbian forces under control of the defendant in Omarska, the women she and her colleagues questioned, and of the defendant's responsibility.

I will be speaking with you about the other violated women and children in the order in which they testified—two in a shack on a remote mountain; three in their own homes; one in a rape/death camp underground, one son violated with her there, his twin previously murdered in her arms; and two in Croatia.

Imagine, if you can, looking out of these windows and seeing Manhattan taken over by a group of people who wanted to run the place for themselves and disagreed with the results of an election—an indigenous occupying political and military machine made up of certain of your neighbors, colleagues, the police, the Army, and various street gangs and assorted paramilitary cadres of thugs, armed, dangerous, united in a determination to claim your city and country for a single social group that is not yours. Something like this happening in Bosnia-Herzegovina is what was testified to here.

Imagine further, as testified to in this case, the people you had coffee next door with for years, celebrated holidays with, fed their children, worked with them, you saw in official positions, the cop on the beat on your block, headed up by a psychiatrist, turning on you. A boy you grew up with chasing you away from the front of your house because it was too late for people like you to be there; your secretary appropriating your apartment; a coworker locking you up or being locked up with you; a neighbor abducting you and your children and holding you captive for months; a neighbor killing your baby as you held him. For the plaintiffs in this action, as they testified, this happened.

You have heard from the victim's testimony, as we said you would, of systemic, relentless, and escalating acts of discrimination. Of white armbands and white sheets identifying Muslims and Croats as targets; of their firings from jobs on an ethnic basis; of signs that banned Croats and Muslims from certain places; of their movements restricted in the street through ethnically-selective curfews; of denial of all medical care on the basis of their ethnicity.

Then, as the evidence showed, this escalated into a full-scale genocide, the ultimate inequality, through which a minority, the Bosnian Serbs, tried to destroy the majority, Bosnian Muslims and Bosnian Croats, and claim Bosnia-Herzegovina and parts of Croatia as parts of Serbia under their own domination and control, under the political and military leadership of the defendant. This genocidal policy, as testified to, included saturation propaganda in the media, pretextual searches for weapons, house-to-house terror, homes looted and sacked and torched, people driven out and killed, beaten and humiliated, hounded, hunted, captured, tortured, and eventually liquidated.

I submit that the twisted reversals—Serbian radio saying the Serbs were protecting Muslims from attack when, in fact, as our evidence shows, the Serbs were attacking the Muslims; Serbian soldiers making rape propaganda of a Croatian woman, saying that the rapists were Croatian and the raped woman was Serbian—with other evidence, testifies that these acts were conscious, and shows how reality was manipulated to try to cover them up.

At the heart of this case, you have heard evidence of rape as a weapon in genocide, evidence of how sexual assault destroys a people. You have heard in detail how rape was systematically used by the Bosnian Serbs under the control of the defendant in an attempt to destroy Muslims and Croats in Bosnia-Herzegovina and Croatia by destroying the women of those ethnicities. Dr. Loncar testified as an expert that sexual assault destroys the self. We submit that the self, as it lives in human society, has a sex and an ethnicity, and that we have shown how, when sexual assault is based on sex and ethnicity, it destroys that self and those identities as well as the relationships of intimacy, family, culture, of group that make up a people, from which the self is inseparable. Not only does rape make women want to leave where they were raped and never go back, making selective rape an effective tool to clear a territory, as Professor Bassiouni testified it was intended to be by the Bosnian Serb leadership. Rape also, as you heard directly from the women's testimony, shatters women themselves. The plaintiffs told you—and, we submit, eloquently showed you by their bearing, gestures, and by feelings that come across in any language—how being raped because they were Muslim women or Croat women or both, their minds and bodies, their individuality and social existence violated at once, took away from them their sense of self-worth, dignity, respect, and safety—taking from them nothing less, we submit, than their equal stature as human beings in a human community, to destroy that community.

Our evidence has shown, we submit, rape as a weapon in a genocide, euphemistically called "ethnic cleansing." As the evidence showed, rape by defendant's genocidal policy served to terrorize, exile, claim, divide, and reproduce all at once. When you destroy women of a community, we submit, you destroy that community. Now, their communities scattered, their families devastated if they remain at all, their capacity for intimate connections damaged or destroyed, what they survived is, our evidence showed, precisely an attempt to destroy peoples as such.

At this point, I cannot do better than their own voices. I can only remind you of the unforgettable and ask you to consider, as Karadžić's forces did not, the individual experiences of our plaintiffs in this mass sex and ethnic atrocity.

[Plaintiff #1] testified to her Muslim family living in a village in rural Bosnia-Herzegovina, she working principally as a mother and homemaker, her community's customs including men not visiting women at home without the husband present or the wife coming along. When her husband was away working in Croatia, and the Serbs took over the town, Serbian soldiers, she testified, abducted her and her children and locked them into a remote private concentration camp—a shack for animals in which she and they were the animals, ringed by hostile armed forces she saw and heard. There, she was repeatedly raped for months, in front of or in view of her children, who were terrorized and starved and beaten with her, her thirteen-year-old son so humiliated that he didn't speak for two years after.

She was taken there by a Serbian neighbor she knew, she testified, who returned to the shack to violate her regularly, bringing different Serbian military men with him. Other men came on a regular basis and raped her over and over again. She testified to her fear then and now, her physical pain then that has not gone away, to facts from which a pregnancy can be inferred, to her blackouts at reliving the threat of the Serbian soldiers to rape her daughter, [plaintiff #2], age 8 at the time. The mother testified that it was early summer when she was taken, and snowing when a renegade Serb freed her, swearing her to secrecy as to who he is—showing, we submit, that the genocide, including the genocidal rape, was ordered by making clear to her that he was disobedient in freeing her.

[Plaintiff #1] had a normal life of stability, warmth, prosperity, and hope. It was taken from her in the most ruthless and vicious way. She lives far from her house, her garden, her town, her country. She, her children's lives, her relationship with her husband are scarred, likely forever. She testified to being unable to imagine any future at all.

[Plaintiff #3], like the others, was in the middle of her life, a mother, having been a housekeeper and dishwasher, of Croat ethnicity, having, she testified, gone back to where she grew up to visit her parents in Bosnia-Herzegovina. She got caught in a war that was a genocide, and then an occupation, and didn't return until three years later, having been interned in camps, released, only to be raped in her home by Serbian soldiers and denied an abortion of the resulting conception by Serbian doctors under the occupation. She bore the so-called "chetnik baby" the Serbian soldiers, carrying out defendant's policies, threatened our clients with.

[Plaintiff #3] testified to the terror, degradation, mutilation of the rape itself on her. She also testified to a reality she had never dreamed of: being surrounded all the time by the memory of what was done to her, being faced by its reality every day, embodied in the form of a little girl who, she said, she can love, a little; can't hate; and may be able to care for.

Sixteen years old at the time, [Plaintiff #4] was blissfully unaware, she testified, of the discrimination she said she now sees was building around her, then unprepared for what was to come, was growing up as a Muslim teenage girl in Doboj, with school, friends, family, wanting to learn Arabic, with a mother who wanted to join her husband at his work abroad. When her city was occupied—as we know from her and other witnesses—indigenous Serbian military and paramilitary forces organized and turned against their neighbors and multiethnic communities. Serbian soldiers came to her house when her father was away working. As she testified, they intimidated her, her younger brother, and her mother, and threatened to take either her or her mother to what she understood was a place to be raped. Then they left. When they came back, as they held her, lying on top of her younger brother at gunpoint, they raped her mother and then murdered her, slaughtering her like [our lead plaintiff] said they had slaughtered her baby: like an animal.

This young girl courageously fled for her life, moved to the United States, married, and is building a new life. But I submit, as you saw her hand to her throat as she struggled to tell you about what she saw, you felt her suffering, her anguish, her grief.

A proud mother of twin sons, living independently, working in a house she owned, [our lead plaintiff], whose father was Muslim and mother was Croat, had her hands full with two babies, her partial disability, her job, and looked forward, she testified, to seeing her children grow up. The war entered her life abruptly and early when, as she told you, a Serbian soldier came to her door and slaughtered one of her babies, as she held him in her arms. She fled with his brother only to be picked up by more Serbian soldiers and taken underground to a reality so horrific it almost defies description. In what had been a mine, she testified, a makeshift theatre, with lights and camera and chairs had been set up, where women were raped and otherwise sexually tortured so Serbian military, some of them high ranking, could watch. Held in a compartment with bars like in a zoo, she witnessed the rape to death of woman after woman, Muslim and Croat women, mostly young Muslim women, as she herself was taken to be raped day after day, day blending into night underground in one continuous horror. Women, she testified, were called out by number on a loud-speaker system, examined and tortured including by forced abortions in a room across the tunnel from her location, and murdered and discarded. She also testified to "weekend Serbs" coming in, in civilian clothes, to money changing hands, and to the unspeakable injuries to her baby boy.

She, like the first three I discussed, is now, she testified, living in exile in another country. That she is even alive, able to speak to you, is testimony to her phenomenal strength and determination, as is the case with all our plaintiffs. But make no mistake about the extent of her harm. As a result of what she experienced in that rape/death camp, as she testified, her disability has progressed dramatically; her body hurts all the time; she is bulimic; she is often terrified; she struggles to work but lives on social welfare, fighting self-loathing, flashbacks, and suicide attempts. As she testified, all that happened, for no other reason than that she was Muslim, Croat, disabled, and a woman.

Our [two Croatian women] clients, you have heard from only through their doctor because they are too destroyed by what was done to them to come here and testify. Their abuse speaks eloquently of their demise. Through [the doctor's] account you learned of the rape [of one] in internment in southern Croatia at the hands of the Bosnian Serbs, and her resulting psychological and physical problems, including frequent hospitalization, depression, and aggravation of asthma and heart complications. Her prognosis, he testified, is that she will continue to deteriorate. [The other,] an older Croatian woman, as he told you, was forcibly interned, forced to fellate young Serbian guards, burned and penetrated by electric cattle prods, and raped by them in front of a camera, wearing Croatian army hats to make it appear that Croatians were raping a Serbian woman. If you lived in a world that contained a film of you being raped, would you go out of your yard either? Now in her mid-sixties she is, [her doctor] testified, waiting to die.

Our clients share many things apart from being Muslim or Croat or both, apart from being women or their children, apart from having been put into concentration camps, which is enough suffering in itself for anyone's lifetime, and apart from their will to survive and bear witness. They share, I submit, being most deeply moved not by what was done to them but by the injuries of others, injuries that they carry with them that never change. They share, as you have seen and heard, being often most moved, most haunted, awake and asleep (which they testified they seldom do), not by the unspeakable atrocities committed against them personally, but by the screams of the tortured and the dying, who are not here to speak to you themselves, but whose voices they never stop hearing. This is unbearable, living being a witness for the dead, of the women left behind. This harms them every day. It never ends.

They see, as they testified, the innocent face of their baby, severed on the floor; they hear the head bumping down the stairs as the body of their tortured colleague is dragged out; they see their once smiling mother with her throat slit, hear her dying scream; their dreams echo with the pleas of their friends and colleagues, who they keep trying to help but can't reach.

Many Americans hear about atrocities like those our clients have testified to, never seeing the faces or hearing the voices of women like our clients, and wish there was something they could do. You have seen their faces, heard their voices. And for you, here and now, there *is* something you can do. You are in a position to do something very real. To compensate them justly and fairly for their emotional and physical damages, and to punish the defendant for what he did to them.

As you take up this task and ask yourselves how possibly to quantify the harm before you, as you take this opportunity you have been given to assess their damages, exercising the responsibilities his Honor will define for you, I ask that you consider: how much would it be worth, paying in advance, knowing what you know, to keep this from happening if you were in a position to do so? I ask you, in your answer to this question, to give them, after what they have been through, some real measure of the justice that is within your power to give. You have become witnesses to their suffering as they have been witnesses to the sufferings of so many other people. I ask you to return their generosity to others with your generosity to them.

What would justice look like for these women? This forum and your attention and kind listening while they testified, have provided a real part of it. But now is accountability time. Until Karadžić is held accountable directly to them, in real and tangible terms, there will be no justice, and no possibility of an end to this suffering.

You have the opportunity placed in your hands, the rare chance to act both for them and against what happened to them. By awarding substantial damages, you can believe them. [Our lead plaintiff] was told by the guards in that underground rape/death camp that no one would believe her. Make them wrong, for her and all the others. You can stand up against what was done to them, against Karadžić and, by expressing your outrage and making him an example, with punitive damages, for anyone like him. Perhaps most importantly, with your award of damages, you can value these women, you can make the one who is responsible for what you heard here in their voices, saw on their faces, take responsibility for that damage, and in so doing, you can promote their survival, and begin to change their lives. Our clients will never have the lives they would and should have had; they cannot go back to what they were; they cannot, as [one plaintiff] said, start over. But they can, with your help, go forward from this courtroom better, more whole, than when they entered it.

We place them, their pain, their memories, their possibility for hope, and the recovery of their futures, in your hands.

FIFTEEN

Trafficking, Prostitution, and Inequality

The civil rights ordinance against pornography was inspired and largely initiated by formerly prostituted women. Through the insight and dedication of the same people, the Swedish model applies the same concept of equality to prostitution, although it is a criminal law. This talk, in the form of an assessment of the debate over prostitution, argues for the Swedish model, which strongly criminalizes those who buy people for sexual use, and does not criminalize those who are bought and sold in prostitution. This speech was originally given al fresco not far from Forbesgunge, Bihar, India, on January 4, 2009, to a group that included many prostituted and formerly prostituted women associated with Apne Aap, an organizing group that supports women leaving prostitution. I can still see the women's bright saris and erect carriages, holding their children. The thoughts were carried forward, enriched, reshaped, and deeply imprinted through connecting with women in prostitution surrounding its delivery in South Africa, Argentina, Taiwan, Israel, China, and in the form in which it appears here from an audiotape, in Australia.[1] Every country thinks their prostitution is unique. Prostitution takes many different cultural forms all right, but it does the same harms everywhere to prostituted people. The Swedish model has since been passed in Norway, Iceland, Canada, in France, and is being considered in many other places around the world.[2]

This will be an assessment of the state of the debate around the world as it has developed in the last decade or so—its empirical, philosophical, psychological, political, legal, and rhetorical dimensions—on the intersection of trafficking, prostitution, and inequality. And an engagement with that debate.

No one defends trafficking. There is no explicit pro-sex trafficking position. It is hard to find overt defenders of inequality. Prostitution is not like this. It is contested. Some people are for it and affirmatively support it. Many more believe it politically correct to tolerate it and oppose doing anything effective about it. Most people assume that, even if it is not quite desirable, prostitution is necessary, harmless, and most of all inevitable. On my analysis and observation, views about prostitution structure the debate on trafficking. This remains the case whether prostitution is distinguished from trafficking or seen as a form of it, whether it is seen as a human right or a denial of human rights, and whether it is seen as a form of sexual freedom or its ultimate violation.

Wherever you are in the world, the discussion on prostitution is organized by five underlying moral distinctions that divide what is regarded as the really, really bad from the not-so-bad. Adult prostitution is distinguished from child prostitution, indoor from outdoor, legal from illegal, voluntary from forced, and prostitution itself from trafficking. In the moralist view, which again pervades this debate (people don't seem to be able to think about this subject without their moral crutches), child prostitution is always bad for children. Adult prostitution is not always so bad. Outdoor or street prostitution can be pretty rough. Indoor prostitution, house or brothel, less so, and maybe even can be sort of good. Illegal prostitution has problems that legal prostitution is imagined to solve. Forced prostitution is very bad. Voluntary prostitution can be not so bad. Trafficking is really, really bad. Prostitution, if voluntary, indoor, legal, and adult, can be a tolerable life for some people.

Measured against the known facts, these supposed distinctions emerge as largely illusory. In reality, they occupy points on a continuum, overlap substantially, and despite being illusions, have very real consequences in law, policy, and life.

Within and across nations, the two fundamental positions in this debate—to polarize somewhat, but this is a remarkably polarized debate—are: the sex work model, and the sexual exploitation approach.[3] When prostitution is termed sex work, it is usually understood as the oldest profession, a cultural universal, consensual because paid, stigmatized because illegal, a job like any other denied that recognition, sometimes a form of liberation.[4] Sex workers are expressing what its academic advocates term "agency." Of the many meanings this slippery piece of jargon has, "agency" here appears to mean freely choosing, actively empowering, deciding among life chances, asserting oneself in a feisty fashion, fighting back against the forces of femininity, and resisting moralistic stereotypes, maybe a kind of model of sex equality. In this view, these agentic actors called "sex workers"—most of them women—control the sexual interaction, are compensated for what is usually expected from women for free, and have independent lives and anonymous and autonomous sex with many partners—all behaviors usually monopolized by men. Hence . . . liberating for women.

By contrast, the sexual exploitation approach sees prostitution as the oldest oppression, as widespread as the institution of sex inequality, in which it is foundational. The noun "prostitute" here is seen as misleading as well as denigrating, equating who people are with what is being done to them. The past participle term "prostituted" is used instead, to highlight the people and social forces acting upon them. Not an a priori attribution of victim status, this term is based on considerable information on the sex trade from the women themselves[5]—when they have left prostitution, termed "exited" women, who often help design and conduct the research. In this view, people are empirically found to be "prostituted" through choices precluded, options restricted, and possibilities denied.

Prostitution in the sexual exploitation analysis is observed to be usually a product of lack of choice, the resort of people with the fewest choices or none at all. The coercion behind it, both physical and not physical, produces an economic sector of sexual abuse in which the majority of the profits go to other people. Prostituted people frequently gain nothing or little by it. The money in these transactions coerces the sex, it does not guarantee consent to it, making prostitution a practice of serial rape. There is nothing equal about it. Prostituted people pay for paid sex. The buyers do not pay for what they take or what they get. People in prostitution, in this view, are wrongly saddled with a stigma that properly belongs to their exploiters.

Each account has its corresponding legal approach. The sex work approach favors across-the-board decriminalization with various forms of legalization, usually with state regulation, sometimes with unionization as a first step. The goal is to remove criminal sanctions from all actors in the sex industry so that prostitution becomes as legitimate as any other livelihood—as in the Netherlands, Germany, New Zealand, parts of Australia, and ten counties in Nevada, although some of these, including the Netherlands, citing harms they never intended and none of the benefits they did intend, are retreating from it.[6]

The sexual exploitation approach seeks to abolish prostitution. The best way is debated. Criminalizing the buyers, the demand for prostitution, as well as the sellers, the pimps and traffickers, while eliminating sanctions of any kind for prostituted people, "the sold," and providing them with the services and job training they say they want—is the approach pioneered in Sweden.[7] Also adopted in Iceland, Norway, and largely in South Korea, being considered in Israel and South Africa, debated in the Scottish Parliament, adopted in the lower house in France and headed for the upper house, it is sweeping the world.[8]

For the Swedish model, at least as crucial as criminalizing the buyers and enforcing it is decriminalizing prostituted people, removing all penalties against them.[9] This model, having shown real and now well-documented promise, is increasingly favored by abolitionists at the principled and practical forefront of this movement.

You will make up your own mind on this question. But apart from preferences, commitments, values, politics, and experiences you bring, each position can be measured against a body of evidence on the sex industry, much of it uncontested, most of it provided by survivors, on the conditions of entrance, realities of treatment, and the possibilities for exit.

Everywhere prostituted people, with few exceptions, are overwhelmingly poor, normally destitute. There is no disagreement on this. Urgent financial need is the most frequent reason mentioned for being in the sex trade.[10] Having gotten in because of poverty, almost no one gets out of poverty through prostitution.[11] It is not unusual for the women in the industry to get further into poverty and deeper in debt. And they are lucky to get out with their lives, given the mortality figures. In Canada, one study estimated a mortality rate for prostituted women of forty times the national average.[12]

Disproportionately, people in prostitution are members of socially disadvantaged racial or ethnic groups or lower castes.[13] In Vancouver, Canada, prostituted people are First Nations women, indigenous women, in numbers that far exceed their proportion of the population.[14] In India, although caste is illegal, there are prostitute castes. Women members of the Nat caste, for example, are selected by men in their families to prostitute; Nat men are expected to pimp Nat women to higher caste men.[15] No one (*pace* Gandhi) chooses poverty. No one chooses the racial or ethnic group or caste they are born into. Based on who is in prostitution, these circumstances—the ones that most powerfully determine who is used in this industry—are not chosen by any of them.

Another global commonality of prostitution, the accuracy of which no one contests, is that people typically enter prostitution when they are young, most frequently well below the age of majority.[16] Most women I met in India were first prostituted at age ten. This is not a time when you are fully empowered to make a choice about the rest of your life, or when you have much power to stop adults from doing things to you. In most places, sexual abuse in childhood, usually in one's intimate circle, is a major precondition for prostitution.[17] In India, the women told me their first sexual abuse, actually their first sexual experience, occurred in prostitution at age ten. If they resisted then or later, they said they were gang raped and tortured. Extreme abuse by pimps—in this case he can be your father—typically occurs at the beginning. Caste and sexual abuse in childhood function similarly here: they tell you what you, your life is for.[18] In Kolkata, scores of girls around thirteen years old line the streets of the red light area. Once when I was there, I glanced down a narrow alley, and saw a tiny naked girl with her legs being spread wide, tiny crotch out toward the street. So when exactly did she choose?

Given the terms on which prostitution is defended, it dawned on me that this might be a good time to define sex (after about forty years of not needing to). Let's say that sex as such is chosen and wanted and uncoerced. Presumably this is the reason prostitution's supporters defend prostitution in sexual terms. When you are having sex with someone you want to be having sex with, I would hazard that you aren't generally paying each other. Being one of those things that money cannot buy, the real thing is neither bought nor sold. In this light, if sex is for survival—the term "survival sex"[19] is sometimes used as a synonym for prostitution—*the sex is coerced by the need to survive*. Where women have sex equality rights, the law of sexual harassment recognizes this transaction as a human rights violation.[20] The point is: what you get out of sex as such is that you are doing it. Just as I was beginning to wonder if no one thought this but me, if this was hopelessly naïve and sentimental in an unequal world, I encountered a study of the law of Namibia that crisply defines prostitution as sexual acts for consideration that is nonsexual.[21] How simple! The consideration for sex is sex. This is what sex as a human right could look like: the right to have sex that is mutual, so equal that it is its own reward. Apparently, at present, there are a good many men out there with whom sex is not its own reward. We know this because they are going around buying mainly women and girls, sometimes men or boys, for sexual use, mostly for proceeds that line the pockets of other men.

As to magnitudes, women in prostitution in Kolkata—in numbers not that different in the United States—told me they service twenty to thirty men a day on average, with no choice over the sex or the men. Assuming two days a week off, a mercy that few are shown, each woman services as many as 8,000 men a year, perhaps a few less for repeat customers.

I speak here of the demand. They are why the sex industry exists.[22] Some are aggressive. Some are contagiously ill.[23] All are invisible in the sense that they can go anywhere in the true privacy of anonymity and not stand out as buyers of women. In most languages, they have the dignity of an identity with no unique nonslang descriptor noun. All the words that are applied to them—customer, client, buyer, date, guest, my favorite (the Nat women use the Hindi word) passenger—are shared with nonpurchaser-users of women. So in the United States, he has been given a real man's name. We call him "john." Johns make prostituted women's lives unhealthy and dangerous.

In addition to the sexual transactions that are paid for, many prostituted women are raped by johns, meaning here *not* paid.[24] They are beaten by criminal gangs or by pimps and landlords if they show any resistance or express a desire to leave, or by buyers when abuse is the sex that the buyers want to buy.[25] Far from having police protection, in most places police sweep in on raids from time to time to arrest—get this—the women for whatever reasons are invented at the time— arrested because they are being victimized:[26] guilty of the crime of being forced. Even prostituted children, are still typically regarded not as victims but as criminals, including in many U.S. jurisdictions, although this is changing.[27] In many places, she is not old enough to have sex, it's called statutory rape, but when found being sold for sex, she is arrested and booked as a criminal.

Prostitutes of color in racist cultures may be disproportionately likely to be arrested.[28] At the same time, police are routinely paid off in many places to protect the sex business. Consider how many women pay for the money used in this corruption, and how. Then, when the women are arrested, they typically fall even further into debt to the pimp who bails them out or pays their fine.[29] This official contribution to her bondage, this official net of sex discrimination from a constitutional and international law perspective, makes it even harder to leave, because now she has an official criminal record.[30]

Proponents of sex work often insist that indoor prostitution in a house or brothel gives the prostitute more control. (They sometimes also contend, with no factual support, that criminalizing the buyers makes prostitution more dangerous because it drives it indoors, hence underground.[31]) In reality, any protection or power from being indoors is a delusion. It's reversed.[32] Street women are definitely at the bottom of the sex industry's transnational hierarchy, the call girl and escort and courtesans at the top for men who can pay more for the upscale packaging. This class structure of prostitution has some reality,[33] but the distinction between indoor and outdoor is a poor proxy for it. It isn't the weather that puts them in danger. Although street women do not have much choice over johns, women in brothels usually have no choice at all. They are lined up for selection; the men pick them. The video surveillance in the brothels—yes, pimps do watch this live pornography—and the panic buttons positioned in the rooms (four is de rigueur in the higher end houses) often fail to get her help soon enough.[34] Indoor prostitution, the dominant form that proliferates in red light districts, tends to mean more pimp control and even less accountability.

The indoor-outdoor distinction also functions ideologically to feed the illusion, beloved by moralists of all conventional politics, that the women in prostitution who appear classy really do have upper-class options: that they are exercising free choice—perhaps a bad one—are being well paid, enjoying themselves (some women being "like that"), could leave anytime they want, are relatively safe if they are careful, and are not being compelled or hurt, at least not very much. Apart from reading the empirical studies,[35] my feeling is that the moralists should try it sometime.

Not long ago, sex work proponents denied that there is any harm in prostitution at all.[36] Overwhelmed by the reality that prostituted women and survivors have revealed, showing them subject to more violence than any group of women in the world (so far as we know), these days a small amount of harm is at times recognized, usually attributed to its illegal status, in the "harm minimization" or "harm reduction" (prominent in New Zealand) approach.[37] Note, the terms concede that some harm will remain. The imperative is to clean up the harms so prostitution itself can stay, as if you can separate the two.

Groups dedicated to this notion suck up vast amounts of international funds devoted to addressing HIV/AIDS.[38] When prostitution is seen as commercial sexual exploitation, resulting cases of AIDS are understood as a symptom, the cause of which is prostitution itself—sex with thousands of men a year under conditions you cannot realistically control. The sex work perspective, by contrast, protects the buyers from the women so they can keep using them without getting sick, rather than protecting the women from the buyers, who are making them lethally ill. Everyone supports less harm to the women.

But harm elimination is not part of the sex work agenda because it is inconsistent with sex for sale, and they know it.

Whether on the street or in a whorehouse, legal or illegal, the majority of prostituted women's measured level of Post Traumatic Stress (PTSD) is equivalent to that of combat veterans, victims of torture, or raped women.[39] PTSD results from atrocities you cannot mentally sustain. Understandably, it often produces dissociation: you put the violation away, leave mentally because you cannot leave physically, forget or repress or deny it or act like it is not there inside you, although it is. You disappear the self who knows about this, the one who goes out and does it, in order to get through the day or the night.[40] Often drugs or alcohol are used for similar reasons, partly numbing the pain of the trauma that is constantly being re-inflicted, distancing the body and the mind somewhat from what is being done, while also making her dependent on the pimp for the next fix.[41]

The abuse that is constant in prostitution, indeed endemic to it, requires dissociation from oneself and the world to survive.[42] You may create another self, give her another name. She does this, and may defend doing it. If you cannot live inside your own head and be who you are—is that what freedom looks like to you? Being subjected to constant rape, beaten to stay, prevented from looking into other options, sustaining the trauma of a torture chamber, needing drugs to get through it—is this what you mean by employment?

Across cultures and at all levels of economic development, street or house, legal or illegal, union or not, when asked what do you need most, the spontaneous answer of an average of 89 percent of people in prostitution is: to leave prostitution but I don't know how.[43] Whether you are in your own country or another, however you entered the sex industry, being in a situation of prostitution that you cannot get out of has been aptly defined by Kathleen Barry as sexual slavery.[44]

Many women are prostituting in their country of origin, but many in richer destination countries are from destitute, poverty-stricken families from other countries. Someone said they could get them a good job and they woke up locked in a brothel. Someone sold them to someone else who bought them.[45] They are then owned by someone who rents them out as property to others who use them sexually. These events and dynamics are not limited to exotic far-away places; they are paralleled and reproduced all over the United States and, I suspect, Australia as well.[46]

Slavery is internationally defined as the exercise of powers of ownership over a person.[47] When pimps sell you for sex to johns who buy you and you want to leave but cannot, you are a sex slave by international legal definition, whether you have ever been beaten or crossed a border.

So far, I have been analyzing prostitution as an institution of class, race, caste, and age inequality. Men and women both are poor, young, and members of disadvantaged classes, racial groups, and scheduled classes. Yet men are not found selling sex in anything like the numbers that women are, although sometimes they do. So we arrive at the question: why are prostituted people so often women?[48] The answer—and this also produces surprisingly little disagreement in an otherwise contentious debate—is sex inequality. Some women rank higher within the female sex caste[49] than other women on the basis of race, ethnicity, religion, or class, as well as in the terms of their sexual use. Women try to work their way up in this caste called women, to avoid it, deny its existence or its application to them. Those who fail and fall to its floor are in prostitution, where those who are used for and defined as being used for sex reside. No one fights to become a prostitute against all the odds. She is in prostitution when the odds beat her.[50]

If prostitution were a choice, one would think that more men would be found exercising it.[51] But boys, even sexually abused or prostituted boys, grow into men, with the options of men, which are better than most women's, even when they are not always good. Nobody chooses the single attribute that most prostituted people share, the single most powerful determinant for being sold for sex: the sex they were born with. Or, if transgender, the sex they transition to or affirm combined with the discriminatory inability to be gainfully employed as who they are.

Worldwide sex inequality gives most members of the male sex group the privilege to have being bought and sold for sex NOT defined as your destiny. At least it is recognized that something must have gone wrong for you, rather than having your circumstance define the realization and fulfillment of your true character and worth. Men also have the privilege of choosing to sell and buy women, and also men and children of both sexes. This is a real choice. The sex industry exists because millions of men, whom no one is forcing, are exercising this free, if conditioned, choice.[52] This seems a good time to point out that no one ever died from lack of sex.

So, what exactly is this that is bought and sold in prostitution? (Interesting that when you say "selling herself," everyone knows what you mean.) In prostitution, it is mainly some men selling women to other men for intimate access to and power over them. It is "you do what I tell you to do" sex.[53] They are buying the sex of no backtalk, of not having to relate to her as a person, of being served and serviced, of being in the privacy of anonymity with a switched-off, dissociated person who is not really there. This gaze of prostituted women, by the way, is the look of women in pornography: the blank, gone—what men call "sexy" look. These women are counting the cracks in the ceiling, watching the clock, thinking of England.[54] This is the sex of not doing anything real for the woman sexually, as he kids himself that all she wants is to be there doing exactly this for big sexy irresistible him.[55]

To be fair, most johns know the women don't enjoy the sex. We've studied them and they talk a lot. They know the women are there out of economic necessity for the most part.[56] But get this: "consenting" is what he thinks she is doing, even though he knows she doesn't want to and is doing it because she has no viable alternative.[57] *This* is an ideological position. Consent in liberal philosophy is the term used to legitimize the rule of the rulers over the ruled, specifically to legitimize the state, although women, for instance, had no say in it whatever. The ruled are deemed to perform this "consent" just by not rebelling and not leaving, whether dissent or exit are possible or not. In law, one "consents" to something that may be necessary but would be harmful without agreement, or is inherently dangerous, like having your body cut into. Sex is not like this, but men apparently think that, for women, it is. Get real. "We consented" is not how anyone describes a glorious sexual interaction. Consent is a pathetic standard for sex between free people. What it is doing in the debate over prostitution is making men feel better about sex they know women do not sexually want, which makes it good for business (as well as for male dominance, i.e. rule). For her, she is having the sex of the sexually abused child, that is, sex that you would never be having except that he has more power than you do.

Consent is intrinsically an unequal concept. A lot of sex, such as in marriage, may be unequal, although the old rule of deeming consent to sex via consent to marriage is not respected in many places anymore. There is an exit built into marriage, it's called divorce, for which there is no parallel in prostitution. Sex that is unequal by force, we have decided we can do something about. It's called rape. Sold sex that is unequal by third-party constraint, we have decided we can do something about that, too. It's called trafficking and pimping. Sex that is unequal by economic survival in the paid labor force—sexual harassment—we do something about that, it's called sex discrimination. Sex for survival pure and simple—prostitution—I'm saying, we can do something about that too.

Prostitution is not just like every other job. Setting limits on the intimacy and intrusiveness on the demands that can be made on a person is the whole point and purpose of human rights law and labor law. No place I am aware of that legalizes prostitution partly on the rationalization that it is a job requires that women "work" at a legal brothel, or anywhere else in the sex industry, before they can receive unemployment compensation benefits, although most jurisdictions require that recipients be willing to accept available work.

Yet in this debate, the notion that prostitution is work generates no end of illuminating parallels; the same ones seem to spring spontaneously to the minds of people all over the world. What's the matter with prostitution that isn't also wrong with cleaning toilets? disposing of hazardous waste? losing your hand in a factory accident perhaps?

dying building a bridge abutment? These people have never defended these jobs or conditions before or since. I suspect the people who are implicitly defending them by suggesting prostitution is a sad but kind option for poor and unfortunate women—an option they are being so enlightened, tolerant, and considerate to defend as a matter of policy—would be among the first to identify the human rights violations involved if everyone who was doing these things was of one race, or all were undocumented immigrants, far less if 89 percent wanted to leave but could not. None of these jobs is prepared for by sexual abuse in childhood (maybe academia is?). None produces prostitution's PTSD rates. The operative shared underlying assumption is "someone has to do it." Without passing on the need for clean toilets or factories or bridges, the fact is, no one has to do what is done in prostitution. Without it, some men would just not get laid today. People, this is conceivable. It is even possible. And no sympathetic subgroup of men, such as disabled men, has a right to keep a whole other group available for bodily invasion just for their sexual satisfaction. Prostitution is not any more inevitable than rape is.

If the line between sex and labor can seem indistinct at times, it is not because being sexually violated is a job, even if money is thrown at the person when it's over. And it is not only because a lot of women's work is sexualized, to our disadvantage, which gives a lot of steam to the indistinguishability notion. It is because a lot of labor also includes sexual exploitation, and many people who are trafficked for labor end up in the sex industry.[58]

The work analogy also overlooks the relations involved, which, this being sex, is the whole problem. Slavery doesn't make the work involved not work, but the relations involved don't make it just a job, and the work in slavery IS work. Nor does unionization change who is used and how, or make it easier to leave. If prostitution is work, a human right, so is debt bondage. Debt bondage involves work, and choices are made every step of the way. Does that mean it is just a job, an alternative to the welfare state, and not a human rights violation?

Finally, in the analogy department, with all respect to my academic colleagues who contend that prostituting is not all that different from thinking and writing[59]—we all sell some part of ourselves, they say—prostitution in the real world is not an abstraction or a metaphor for their appropriation. Apart from the differing assault and mortality rates—rather a lot to put aside, even given the pervasiveness of sexual harassment in education—and the hopefully differing roles of explicit sexuality in the activity; apart from the fact that no one has ever put a gun to anyone's head to make them be a law professor, some of us, anyway, do not do "you do what I say" scholarship.

Amnesty International take note: nothing in reality transforms this human rights violation into a human right.[60]

Proponents of the sex work model sometimes suggest that anyone who is against prostitution is against sex.[61] The sex they are talking about is the reality of abuse I am describing. It is like saying that being against rape is being against sex. Indeed, it actually *is* saying that. The same group sometimes also insists that all of the abuse, rape, and beatings are invented or exaggerated by us ideologically motivated, repressed, sex-panicked Victorian prudes and whiners who just don't have what it takes to make it as whores.[62] The pimps are invented too, apparently. Prostituted women, in their view, are independent entrepreneurs; well, maybe some have managers.[63]

Then along came HIV/AIDS, and even this crowd discovered a harm along with a lucrative profit center in purporting to address it.[64] How handy, this disease that sickens the men who use the women as well as the women whose faces they explode all over. How refreshingly gender neutral and symmetrical. Now the pernicious brothel system in India must stay in place, or where would the condoms be distributed? Sex trafficking in India is up 300 percent since Bill Gates spent his thirty million on condoms.[65] Who is keeping track of whether the women can actually use these condoms, or the skyrocketing prices for the women next door who have no choice but not to use them?[66] I have come to think that these condoms are emblematic of the prophylactic sex work idea that proposes to make the world safe for prostitution by containing and covering up its violations one at a time.

The first fault line in the denial of prostitution's intrinsic harm came when it was conceded that children should not be prostituted, a concession the sex work approach now routinely makes.[67] No one ever says precisely what is wrong with buying and selling children for sex. Just that it is "wrong." Well, if prostitution is freedom, equality, liberation, and empowerment, if it makes a woman's life more autonomous and independent, and its harms are occasional or negligible and can be minimized and contained, do tell what on earth is wrong with children doing it or seeing it being done. Nobody says. And whatever is wrong with children being involved in prostitution, they also don't say what precisely changes suddenly when she's seventeen years and 366 days old. The fact is, and everyone knows, if no one could enter commercial sex as a child, the sex industry would be depopulated overnight (making a look-back provision attractive). Few try to deny that most women enter the sex industry as children with previously violated childhoods. What is denied is that defending the prostitution of adults supports their continuous violation on the rationale that they are no longer little girls.

Adults and children in the sex trade are not two separate groups of people. They are the same group of people at two points in time. One consequence of childhood sexual abuse, fought by women in or outside prostitution, is feeling valued and approved when you are being sexually violated, while also feeling fundamentally ashamed, humiliated, and worthless.[68] Sexual abuse in childhood makes it seem that prostitution is where you belong, while law, policy, and popular culture just wait for you to live long enough to be written off as a consenting adult. Recognizing prostitution's harms in this form is a strategic retreat to allow its intrinsic harms to continue.

The second concession by the sex work defenders has been to criticize sex trafficking while defending prostitution. But what is trafficking? Internationally, the Palermo Protocol definition,[69] which has been sweeping the world—even adopted in the United States—includes being sexually exploited through force, fraud, or coercion for commercial sex. That definition and the industry's reality also include sexual exploitation through "abuse of power or a condition of vulnerability."[70] Caste, race, or age can be conditions of vulnerability, as, actually, can poverty, sex, and gender.[71] Sex trafficking is transportation, transfer, harboring, or receipt of a human being for purposes of sexual exploitation, so defined. This is simply what pimps do. Movement across jurisdictional lines is not, and has not been, an element of the international definition of trafficking since at least 1949.[72] The sine qua non of trafficking is thus neither border crossing nor severe violence. It is *third-party involvement*. You cannot traffic yourself, which distinguishes trafficking, in theory, from some prostitution. Sexual exploitation can also be slavery: internationally, exercising rights of ownership over a person.[73] You cannot enslave yourself either.

While most places make prostitutes criminals because they are being victimized, those who victimize them are typically let off the hook in law or fact. What Sweden has done is see that prostitution is violence against women[74] and strongly criminalize the buyer: make purchasing sex a crime and enforce it.[75] It has extended some help to those who want to leave, although more could be done.[76] (France's bill has much more of this support, thankfully.)[77] Eliminating her criminality raises her status; criminalizing him lowers his privilege. That makes it a substantive sex equality law in inspiration and effect.[78] It has cut street prostitution in half or more, reduced prostitution overall dramatically, and produced the lowest trafficking rate in Europe.[79] After ten years of being in effect, the Swedish government concluded that this law is working as hoped.[80] The stigma of prostitution may be shifting to the johns. Despite the lies being circulated about it, as the sex industry goes into panic mode, this model is the only legal approach to prostitution that has ever worked against the sex industry in the history of the world.[81]

When prostitution is legalized, by contrast, as documented in some of the excellent Australian scholarship, trafficking goes through the roof.[82] It makes economic sense. Once the women and children are installed, the profits from operating in the open are astronomical. Illegal prostitution also explodes under legalization, also visible in Australian venues.[83] Legal brothels require protections the johns do not want, so they go next door to the illegal brothels and pay more.[84] This makes life even more dangerous for the often illegal and immigrant women who are in more danger to begin with.[85]

Legalization, the sex industry's main goal for obvious reasons, is a failed experiment.[86] The German government has concluded that legalizing the sex industry there failed to deliver any of its promised benefits: It hasn't reduced organized crime's hold; it hasn't reduced trafficking; it hasn't made prostitution more transparent or less underground; it hasn't made it easier to leave, healthier, or safer.[87] It does corrode any law enforcement apparatus that previously existed and leads society and popular culture to believe that there is nothing wrong with it. The New Zealand government committee inquiring into prostitution laws in 2008 similarly found that violence against women in prostitution and the social stigma surrounding the sex industry continued despite decriminalization.[88]

One reason legalization doesn't work, apart from the obvious economic incentives involved, is that most women in prostitution do not want to think that this is all their lives are ever going to be, and becoming legal requires using a real name, registering, creating a paper trail. Being a legal prostitute means deciding that prostitution will be part of your official life story. Most prostituted women, even if they have to do this right now, have dreams.[89] So to be able to leave prostitution someday, they resort to the illegal prostitution that flourishes under legal prostitution and receive few if any of its purported benefits.

In light of all this evidence, the moral distinctions that structure law and policy on this topic, those I began with, emerge as ideological, confused, and confusing, making more socially tolerable and endlessly debatable an industry of viciousness and naked exploitation. Most adult women in prostitution are first prostituted as girls and are just never able to escape. As they age out, they retain the adult vulnerabilities of class, sex, and often race, often combined with a criminal record and almost always the psychological devastation of having been prostituted. Traffickers and pimps are incentivized to grab girls when they are most powerless, hence most desirable to the market; then, with each day that passes, their exploitation is more blamed on them. When used indoors, prostituted women are industrially accessible to pimps and johns and invisible to most everyone else. Legal and illegal regimes inflict the same harms and pathologies, many of which get worse with across-the-board legality. At the core of prostitution are forms and amounts of force that make it hard to believe that a free person with real options would ever voluntarily elect it.

Perhaps the deepest injury of prostitution—evidenced by its material basis in inequalities and concrete harms—is that there is no dignity in it.[90] Attributing "agency" here as if it means freedom can be a desperate grab toward that lost dignity, as well as a cooptation for the sex industry of the dignity that the exploited never lose.

An adequate law or policy to promote the rights of prostituted people has three parts: decriminalize and support people in prostitution, criminalize the buyers strongly,[91] and criminalize third-party profiteers. To promote equality, the violators have to be closed down, the world has to be opened up to the violated. This is what they are asking for. Not one woman in prostitution I have ever met wants her children to have that life. What does that say, except that prostitution chose her?[92]

Some people who have the choices that women in prostitution are denied cannot seem to imagine prostituted women's lives outside of prostitution. The ones I know—my colleagues, friends, those I work with and for—have no such trouble. They see real work, real love, dignity, and hope.

III. Culture

The *Voice*'s journalistic angle on our story, which you present as fact, concerns our alleged relationship with the Right. Our legal approach to pornography grew out of the concern of neighborhood groups in Minneapolis who saw pornography first as a class issue. Poor and working people, because of their lack of power, had the pornography forcibly zoned into their neighborhoods, making their lives a particular kind of hell. They asked us to work with them to tell the city how pornography hurts women in particular. The ordinance we wrote was supported by many progressive groups in Minneapolis, and by no conservative or even traditional interests of which I am aware. (Local Morality in Media spoke in favor of it tentatively in the hearings, then reversed its position in a written statement, saying we were trying to redefine obscenity, which they thought had already been properly defined—a position later taken by Mayor Fraser, hero of the liberals because he vetoed the ordinance.) Some of those who voted against the bill were Republicans, including conservative ones. An almost entirely Democratic City Council passed the bill the second time, with one Republican and one lapsed Republican among those voting against.

If the Right as such supports our bill, we have not seen this support. The conservative legislator(s) in Suffolk County who tried to make our bill a vehicle for conservative values had to change it substantially even to attempt to do so. (The fact that we worked to defeat that bill did not appear in your pages.) The only conservative who has actively worked with us is Beulah Coughenour, the Indianapolis city councilwoman who skillfully managed the bill there. Your accounts minimize the progressive neighborhood groups who supported the bill there and omits the Blacks who voted for it. The law in Indianapolis— they asked our help, we did not initiate contact with them—is a feminist law. Not a single legislator among the many now considering introducing our bill in governments throughout the country is, to my knowledge, conservative, although some may be. Achieving sex equality is not, you may have noticed, high on the Right's agenda.

Our experience is that the issue of pornography is producing a breakthrough for feminism with some women on the Right. Where they used to see obscenity as a violation of their moral code, they are now considering that pornography is sex discrimination. They are beginning to notice that the logic of obscenity law harmonizes public repudiation with private use, that many of the men who designed and defend obscenity as an approach use pornography themselves, and that obscenity law keeps it available to them. A concept of sex equality that opposes the intimate violation of women for the sexual pleasure of predators speaks to something real in these women's lives that the aspiration to live a male biography did not. As feminists, we are inspired by their motion. We see it as a movement among women.

To those who see politics as a static process in which power circulates among elites in fixed blocs, this movement is apparently sinister. To those who decide what they think by seeing who is on what side of conventional alignments, such transformation gives vertigo. I, myself, am waiting for someone, anyone, to ask me how I can possibly ally myself with the liberals—you know, those people who keep defending the Nazis and the Klan? And since guilt by association seems to be your approach to analysis (I had thought that was a right-wing tactic), you might clarify that *we* are not the ones who are tying in with organized crime.

I find it very strange that when we propose an initiative that divides the Republicans, divides the Democrats, divides the working press, divides the gay and lesbian communities, divides those who identify as feminists, divides the ACLU, and divides the Right, the *Voice* terms it a right-wing thing. To put it to you directly, I think that the only reason you take us seriously at all is because you think the Right (read: other men) does. Feminists cannot have done anything of this significance, surely not on feminist terms. Before you discovered this angle, we were not even worthy of coverage. We have found, in working with this issue, that masculinity knows no left and right, but is itself a politics, a sexual politics. We have had to answer the same questions, respond to the same charges, deal with the same objections to our law, in conservative Indianapolis and progressive Minneapolis, from left women and from Jeremiah Denton and from *Playboy*. The reason is that our law draws a clear line that divides the defenders of male supremacy from those who seriously want it ended. We take this line to be a feminist line.

Decoding the opposition has been instructive. Many of those who oppose our approach know absolutely nothing about the pornography itself, essentially have never seen it or think we are talking about *Esquire* around 1953. This includes some of the scholars the *Voice* references. The only examples that apparently come to their minds when reading our law are materials they *have* seen—hence the tortured and often ludicrous misapplications you report. That our definition[3] simply and accurately describes an $8 billion-a-year industry that they (unlike many women) have been privileged to maintain an ignorance of, goes right by them. By contrast, many of our opponents know all about the pornography, because they are users. To them, its indistinguishability from anything else is a matter both of material interest and conditioned incapacity. Add to this the fact that those who know the least about pornography often act as though they know all about it, and those who know all about it act as though they have no idea what we are talking about, and you begin to see some of what we are up against. Let me know when you figure out which is Nat Hentoff.[4]

Whatever the reason, Hentoff measures his freedom by the pornographers' freedom to abuse women. Our pain is his free speech, our bodies his chosen words, our agony his grammar, our second-class status his self-expression.

Richard Goldstein comes close to getting this. If Jews were being strung up on street corners and it was an entertainment industry making $8 billion a year, or if people sold gay bashing as a business, it might be difficult for people like Richard Goldstein to feel safe walking down the street, and he might think something should be done about it. But being as it's women . . . His article,[5] like many that have appeared in your publication, relies on sexual stimulation to evoke the complicity of male sexual arousal in readers for the views he espouses. *Playboy* magazine has used this strategy for some time. (Feel that erection? They're trying to take *that* away from you.) Because the *Voice* exploits the conditioned viciousness of much of

your audience in this way, you can count on built-in bigotry to increase your credibility as you increase the scope and violence of your
lies. Your lock-step liberalism sees only risks in our initiative to empower women. We see risks, too—including risks that, like any law,
it could be abused. Some of your writers concede that pornography
is not an entirely good thing, but it is those who are trying to do something about it who are positively dangerous. You never seriously ac-
knowledge that the status quo has risks, risks run by all women who
are targeted for use and abuse on the basis of a condition of birth.
When that use and abuse is found pleasurable it is called "sex" and
thereby exonerated. When it is done through words and pictures it is
called "speech" and thereby canonized. Women are now being tortured,
humiliated, played with, patronized, forced, violated, and killed in part
for this reason, and really nothing is being done about it. The risks of
your legal approach are the risks women run daily. It is this status quo
you defend as freedom.

Because they were not allowed to learn to read and write (a fact
the First Amendment did not address), Black slaves in this country
did not leave as full a record as they otherwise might have of the difficulties of organizing their own communities. There were those who
counseled that to resist their status—the status itself, not just its
excesses—was to rock the boat. There must have been those who saw
themselves only in terms of the way the powerful saw them, who
valued themselves only as the powerful valued them. There must have
been those whose fear, fear that the radicals were going to make life
even more dangerous than it already was for those who submitted
and made the best of it, looked like practicality, looked like avoiding
the risk of making things worse. Now people know when they see an
Uncle Tom shuffle.

If you think the analogy is strained, I bet you don't think sexism
is based on force. Look at the pornography. As one woman said in
our hearings "Everything you see in the pornography is being done
to a real woman right now." Now look at the data on rape, child
sexual abuse, sexual harassment, forced prostitution, and battery. It
is being done. Understand that this is the condition of women, such

SEVENTEEN

To the American Civil Liberties Union on Pornography

By invitation, this talk ventured into the belly of the beast. The American Civil Liberties Union (ACLU), representing pornographers in public or through its members or allies in court, was everywhere the tip of the spear of opposition to civil rights for those pornography's harms. The atmosphere in which the debate over the civil rights ordinance took place was created, there and elsewhere, by the mainstream press reporting as news the results of a public relations campaign undertaken by the Media Coalition,[1] the group of trade publishers and distributors, including some pornographers, substantially funded by *Penthouse*,[2] that was behind the litigation against the ordinance in Indianapolis and in Bellingham, Washington, which had passed it by public referendum. In 1986, a memo leaked to us from the public relations firm Gray & Company proposed the press campaign for the Media Coalition to "discredit the Commission on Pornography" and stop "self-styled antipornography crusaders" from creating "a climate of public hostility toward selected publications."[3] Their proposed contract budgeted about a million dollars to pursue their recommended lines of attack, which were to claim, contrary to well-established scientific research, that there is no evidence that pornography does harm, and to falsely cast opposition to pornography as "being orchestrated by a group of religious extremists."[4] These lies became common knowledge, and to a considerable degree still are. The ACLU of the time was the organization that remained after it lost members following the Skokie case,[5] in which it successfully defended the speech rights of Nazis marching in an area selected because of its large population of Holocaust survivors.[6] Those who could live with that invasion being defended as freedom of speech were my audience. The spring flowers nodding on the surrounding sunny mountains contended with the group's icy hostility.[7]

Sometimes, when people are tortured and violated, it is seen as torture and violation. In the prisons of South and Central America, when people are imprisoned and abducted, when they are hung up, confined, tortured with cattle prods, when they are disappeared, the atrocity is acknowledged—at least, it is here and now.[8] In South Africa, when the same things are done to Black people; in Auschwitz and in Dachau, when they were done to Jews and others. In the American south, when they were done to Black people under slavery, the atrocity is now acknowledged. It is understood that some people have been selected for torture and violation on the basis of who they are, their group status—and within that group selected essentially at random—and that this is a very effective method of terrorizing and controlling that group.

Torture because of who you are is understood as a method of keeping people in submission, acquiescent, terrorized, and compliant, although they also resist. In the incidents that I have mentioned, the force, at least now, is acknowledged. And rights—civil liberties—are recognized as being violated. At times other than when it happens, and in their places and by other people, there is another recognized feature about systematic torture: the inequality of which it is a part is seen to be pervasive and acknowledged as political. It is understood that it is possible to do *these* things to *these* people, even though there may even be laws against doing them, because of an unequal social context that gives permission for *these* people to be stigmatized, singled out and tortured on the basis of a condition of birth. Even though we may lack a final answer, still, to the agonizing ultimate question of why things like this happen, not having that answer does not lead most people to think that the atrocities should be allowed to go on and on and on.

But when these same acts are done in this country today, in basements or in studios, by men holding cameras up to women against whom they are committed, the atrocity is denied. It is not considered torture; it is considered sex. By many, it is even considered freedom, equality, and love.[9] It forms an eight-billion-dollar industry in entertainment.[10] It is enjoyed; it is considered fun; it is a consumer choice, not to mention a constitutional right. Its relation to social inequality is denied or minimized. When it is done through pictures and words it is passionately defended by the ACLU.[11] It is allowing those to whom it is done to *do* something about that is seen as the civil liberties violation.

When the denial of what is really being done is stripped away from pornography, what we see, very simply, is women being bound, battered, tortured, humiliated, and sometimes killed.[12] Or, to be fair to what is termed the "soft core," merely being taken and used. This is being done to real women right now.[13] In hundreds and thousands of magazines, pictures, films, and so-called books now available in this country, women's legs are splayed, presented in postures of sexual submission, display and access—those that *Newsweek* recently wryly referred to as the gynecological shots.[14] We see women becoming pussy, beaver, chick, cunt, named after parts of our bodies or animals, cut up into parts of our bodies or mated with animals. We are told this is a natural woman's sexuality, but as women who tell us about being in it know, it is elaborately contrived.[15] The photographs are retouched, but even when they are not, often the bodies are.

We see children presented as adult women, adult women presented as children.

We see so-called lesbian material, which is how men imagine women touch each other when men are not around, so men can enjoy watching. Pornography is a major medium for the sexualization of racial hatred; every racial stereotype is used. Black women are presented as animalistic bitches, bound, bruised, bleeding, and struggling; Asian women are presented as so passive, so bound, they cannot be recognized to be human. You cannot tell if they are dead or alive. They are hanging from light fixtures and trees and clothes pegs in closets. We see amputees, sick people, the disabled, their illness or disability sexually fetishized. In some pornography, women and/or children are actually tortured to death, murdered, in fact, to make a sex film.[16]

This is all being done for a reason. The reason is that it gives sexual pleasure to its consumers and therefore profits to its providers. When you look at a system like this, it becomes clear that some people matter and some people do not. Those who want the profits—including the money and the pleasure—they matter. What they like and want is called a constitutional right. But to the women and children who are the victims of its making or use, that constitutional right means being bound, battered, tortured, humiliated or killed, or merely taken and used, and used, and used until you are used up or you can get out. Because someone with more power than you, someone who matters, gets pleasure from seeing it done to you, or doing it to you, or seeing it as a form of doing it.

Since Andrea Dworkin first started talking about the harm of pornography to women, joined later by the rest of us, we have been deluged by evidence and documentation of that harm. In the hearings on our proposed law against pornography, we heard testimony that it does take coercion to make some pornography.[17] We have come to think of those women as our "disappeared." We heard how pornography is forced on women and children in ways that give them no choice about viewing the pornography or performing the sex.[18] We heard about the use of pornography to break women's self-esteem, to train them to sexual submission, to season them to forced sex, to intimidate them out of job opportunities, to blackmail them into prostitution and keep them there, to terrorize and humiliate them into sexual compliance, and to silence their dissent.[19]

In private, we have heard from thousands of women in whispers, in desperation, remembering the camera, describing the pictures, remembering every detail of how the knots were tied according to the magazine, what the expression on their face should be according to the film, how they were forced to re-enact the photographs, how the abuse was created with the pornography as the man's main instrument of arousal, inspiration, energy, and technical advice. We have heard about women who have been raped every way with every object and device that will fit and many that will not, by animals, and all of that filmed, and the photographs of the rapes now being sold as protected speech. We have heard transgenerational stories of mother-daughter abuse premised on pornography and in which pornography is centrally used. We have heard of *Playboy* and *Penthouse* rapes of children, boys and girls in which the children are first shown the materials and then raped, or told to emulate the pictures they are shown while being raped. We have heard of hundreds of women being violated, used on one end of the pornography or another. We have heard how pornography stimulates and condones all of those acts it took the feminist movement so much effort to discover and make public and break silence on: the rape, the battery, the sexual harassment, the child sexual abuse, and the forced prostitution, not to mention the rest of the just plain denigration and discrimination.

We observed how the pornography contains all these abuses. All these acts of sexual violence are presented in the pornography, not as rape but as sex, not as battery but as sex, not as sexual harassment but as sex, not the sexual abuse of children but the sexual fulfillment and sexual expression of children. The forced prostitution is presented, of course, as consent. We have come to think that the sex-violence distinction so central to the way many people have thought about this question is false: that violence is sex when it is practiced as sex. What we have found here is a whole world of sexual abuse, silenced previously.

Because the pleasure pornography gives is sexual, it has been considered exempt from scrutiny and repressive to question. Because it is considered speech—because it is done at some point through words and pictures—it has been considered repressive to do anything about it, even to question, because it is thought that all speech is somehow at stake. I want to suggest to you that because the pornography is sexual, and works *as* sex, it is not even like the "literature" of other inequalities. It works differently. It works as a direct behavioral stimulus, conditioner and reinforcer of a very specific, compelling, and distinguishable kind. It is unique. What it does, and nothing else does, is make orgasm a response to bigotry. Thus dominance and subordination, the daily dynamic of sexual inequality, is enjoyed and practiced as well as learned in the male body.

You know already that sexism is a lot of things. It is profitable; it is pervasive. I am suggesting you face the fact that it is also sexy, and that pornography is a big part of what makes it that way.

On the basis of this analysis, Andrea Dworkin and I have proposed that pornography—not abstractly, but in the particular forms in which it is practiced, and the harms it does—should be considered a violation of the civil liberties of women and children primarily, but of anyone who is hurt by it on the basis of their sex.[20] Pornography is a major institution of a subhuman, victimized, and second-class status for women. We think this is inconsistent with any serious legal mandate of sex equality and with the reasons speech is protected.

As to why our ordinance is constitutional, I am not going to argue the existing law of speech to you, although it supports us, because many of you disagree with it. Instead I want to talk about why you should agree with us, why you should want our proposed ordinance to make the harm pornography does actionable as sex discrimination.

Our ordinance defines pornography as the graphic sexually explicit subordination of women through pictures or words that also includes women presented dehumanized as sexual objects who enjoy pain, humiliation or rape—I am truncating it slightly—woman bound, mutilated, dismembered or tortured, in postures of servility or submission or display, being penetrated by objects or animals.[21] Men, children or transsexuals, all of whom are sometimes violated like women are, in and through pornography, can sue for similar treatment.[22]

The term "sexually explicit" is an existing term with a legal and social meaning that has never before been considered vague or problematic. It refers to sex being explicitly shown. Sex exists objectively in the world, unlike, for instance, obscenity's sex term "prurient interest."[23] Subordination is a term that is often used politically when the people who are being put down or in a position of loss of power are considered real, and fully human. It refers to *actively* placing someone in an unequal position. Presumably, people know that to be a subordinate is not the same as being an equal. When we say that pornography is the graphic sexually explicit subordination of women through pictures or words, it means the subordination must be proven to be *done*, either through the making or use of the materials, or it does not fit the definition.

This definition is not actionable in itself. There are four harms through which, and only through which, it is actionable. Our civil rights law allows victims of four activities only—coercion, force, assault, and trafficking—to sue those who hurt them.[24] "Coercion" means someone is coerced into acts to make pornography.[25] "Force" means somebody has pornography forced on them.[26] "Assault" means someone can show that they were assaulted in a way that is directly caused by a specific piece of pornography.[27] "Trafficking" covers production, sale, exhibition or distribution—the activity of saturating a community, of pushing, of purveying pornography in the world.[28] Coercion, force, assault, and trafficking are not ideas. They are not fantasies. None of them, as such, is speech.

I understand that this organization is on record in opposition to all four harms of pornography being actionable to their victims.[29] I am going to focus on the trafficking provision, because I understand it gives most of you the most trouble.

Our hearings in Minneapolis produced overwhelming evidence of the harm of pornography. This evidence has changed and magnified and grown the more we have talked about pornography in public; the less silence the pornography has been able to impose, the more we have heard about its effects. In addition to the testimony mentioned before, we have heard from researchers and clinicians documenting the conclusion that women know from life: that pornography increases attitudes and behaviors of aggression and other discrimination, principally by men against women, and that this relation is causal. This evidence is better, more, and much more direct than existing exceptions to the First Amendment—although I recognize you may not care. It is also far better than correlations many people live by, like the smoking and cancer correlation or the data on drinking and driving. We have social studies as well as lab studies and other expert testimony documenting the laboratory predictions of increased aggression toward women.[30] It does happen, both in real life and in the laboratory, by men who use these materials.

The most accurate thing I can say about the state of the research on the broad social harm we have here at this point in its development is that we may or may not be able to predict what particular individuals will do to what other particular individuals, although we can do that to some degree. But we *do* know that if men in a population consume pornography, more and more acts of sexual aggression and discrimination against women will occur, and less and less will be done about them, because those acts will be experienced sexually as more and more enjoyable and less and less violating. We know that so long as the pornography exists as it does now, women and children will be used and abused to make it, as they are now, and it will be used to abuse them, as it is now.

Those of you who want us to "go after the acts and not the speech," and don't consider that coercion, force, and assault are acts, consider that the so-called speech can be the predicate for the acts. Someone rapes so they can take a picture of it. As to the much-loved causal connection between pornography and harm, between the acts and the speech, how about: *they did the act so they could make the so-called speech.* Is that causal enough? If it hadn't been for making the "speech," *this* rape would not have happened. Is that a strong enough connection for you?

Those of you who want us to "enforce existing law" against these acts, I would like you to try to explain to me the difference between the real rape rate, the real child abuse rate, the real sexual harassment rate and the reported rates, the prosecution rates, and the conviction rates.[31] Tell us why we should use or rely on the system that produced them. *Why* are those laws not enforced? Why it is, for instance, that *the* most taboo thing, one of the most illegal things in virtually any society, the sexual abuse of children, yet it is also the most done, the most common?[32] Maybe one reason is that those with power don't see those acts as a very big problem. We think that the ways women are used and presented in pornography, creating legitimacy for sexual abuse, may have something to do with why so little is done about it and why we are making so little progress in getting real sex equality.

I hope you have observed that our law is not an obscenity law. Pornography does harm, unlike obscenity, for which no evidence of harm has ever been available or required. Obscenity doctrine has never defined a harm, although it has been looking for one for a long time. The closest it could come was offensiveness.[33] Offensiveness is not our harm; *sex discrimination* is. It is not our fault that obscenity law is vague. It is not our fault that it is available for police state repression. It is not our fault that it is anti-gay and defines women's body parts as filth. It is not our fault that when legislatures and courts look at women being used and hurt, the most they have been able to see is sex they don't want to say they want to see. And finally it is not our fault that civil libertarians move to enact stricter obscenity laws, your policy against them notwithstanding, and move to get stricter enforcement of them by the police, in other words move to police state repression, the minute something effective—our law—might be able to be done about the real pornography, which obscenity law never gets near. It is not our fault that the police crack down on those who are least responsible, and on those who are most vulnerable, and that the pornography and its real harm goes on and on.

There *is* an issue of speech here. I want to speak briefly about the silence of those on whose inequality First Amendment jurisprudence—and with all respect, the ACLU's policies—have been based. The First Amendment was written by those who had speech. They also had slaves, many of them, and a lot of them owned white women as well.[34] They made sure, in their design of the Constitution, to keep their speech protected from what they thought threatened it: the federal government. You first have to *have* speech before keeping the state from taking it away from you becomes your problem. Knowing that they have the speech and every other form of slaver's power, the pornographers have taken the position that they are the political rebels: they are the disenfranchised and the hated. But they are the practitioners of a ruling ideology of misogyny and racism and sexualized bigotry. It is ludicrous to say that something that is consumed more than *Time* and *Newsweek* is hated and outcast.[35] It is ridiculous to say that an industry is disenfranchised that makes eight billion dollars a year[36]—some of which they give to this organization, which makes sure they have a voice.

I wonder if the screams of the victims, of the tortured, are inaudible to you, or if they are sex to you. I wonder if you will continue

EIGHTEEN

X-Underrated

This piece reflects on what has changed and what has not changed in the law and culture of pornography, its social conception and material existence, since it was first confronted with real evidence of its harms through the butterfly of the antipornography civil rights ordinance over twenty years before, which the pornographers and their minions have been determined to smash.[1] Since I was asked to write this essay, another decade passed until anyone asked me to contribute in public about pornography again—in Iceland. Although "worse and more of it" describes the trajectory of the materials, proliferated on the Internet, only ineffectual approaches to it, window dressing at best, are typically considered anywhere. The reflexive fear that is inspired in anyone who seriously considers opposing pornography might be a clue.

———————————

The belief that pornography inhabits its own physical and mental world is an illusion. Nothing restricts its effects. Yet the protective myth of its spatial separation and cognitive confinement endures, even as pornography visibly takes over more and more public and private space, invading homes and offices and transforming popular culture.

There is such a thing as pornography, as its producers and consumers well know. No one is making tens of billions of dollars from,[2] or masturbating to, the Bible, for example. This is only to notice that the pornography industry and mass media have long operated in separate spheres defined by content. In the name of taste, values, or division of labor, legitimate cinema, books, and media have traditionally eschewed or coyly skirted the sexually explicit. The "adult" movie industry, cable television, and "men's entertainment" magazines have frontally specialized in it. This mutually clear line, quite precisely and effortlessly observed in practice, coexists with the common cant that pornography cannot be defined or distinguished from anything else.

Pornography is increasingly breaching this divide, making popular culture more pornographic by the day. This effect is routinely observed and sometimes deplored, whether for sexually objectifying women yet more inescapably or for taking away the sexiness of the forbidden. But if this movement is rarely documented, and even more seldom explained, the fact that pornography itself has been a popular feature of culture—the most mass of media for some time—is never faced.

Society's ideology of compartmentalization—that the rest of life can go on unaffected—never seems to be embarrassed by pornography's ubiquity. It has been in plain sight all along. In reality, pornography's place is just down the street, right there on the rack in the convenience store, not to mention in the bedrooms and bathrooms of homes where its users seldom live alone. Yet even as the industry has burgeoned, taking over more public space and penetrating more deeply into private life at home and at work with each advance in technology, it is considered to be somehow not really there.

The same dissociative logic structures the legal regulation of pornography. Obscenity, one meaning of which is "off stage,"[3] is located in some neighborhoods and not others. The question of where to put it is politically fought over locally like the placement of noxious waste, as if its effects can be so confined. Pornography has to be somewhere, the attitude is, the only question is where. (One reading of the law of this subject in the United States revolves around how far a man has to travel to get his fix before it becomes unconstitutional.) Pornography is considered addressed by the legal sleight of hand through which it is imagined placed in some demimonde: over there rather than right here.

Beyond the geographical, the psychological disconnect is perhaps most socially potent: the delusion that pornography is "fantasy." No woman was ever ruined by a book, as the slogan goes.[4] This gives using pornography a certain deniability. Never mind that someone has to be sexually used to make the visual materials that form the vast majority of the industry's output. Never mind that among the first and most robust of the results of consumption is the spontaneous generation of rape fantasies, or that people often do what they imagine they want to do.[5] Never mind that "fantasy" is the word used by a man convicted of being about to make a snuff film of a boy to describe the detailed plans he was intercepted discussing, or what the media reported a man was having with a prostitute he drowned in a bathtub.[6]

One telling episode in these annals of denial arose in the publication of *American Psycho*, an upmarket high-concept work of fiction in which one woman after another is sexually slaughtered.[7] Women are skinned alive, mutilated, raped and one dismembered head is used for oral sex, all in graphic and explicit terms.[8] Simon and Schuster, in an exceptional move, rescinded its contract of publication shortly before the book was due out.[9] It was rumored by insiders that women on the staff refused to have it published in their house.[10]

The publishing industry has long coexisted with—at times affirmatively defended—the pornography industry.[11] This includes the film *Snuff*, a sex movie available since 1972 right down the street from Simon and Schuster, in which a woman is shown being disemboweled while alive.[12] The shock of, hence the opposition to, *American Psycho* was apparently that it was here, in mainstream publishing. As long as sexual killing is happening "over there," it is as if it is not happening at all. *American Psycho* seemed to shatter that illusion of context for some people, at least momentarily. The book was quickly bought and published by Vintage, a division of Random House.[13]

A similar magical framing move occurred in connection with the scandal surrounding Abu Ghraib. The photos of naked Arab men being abused by American soldiers while in their custody were routinely termed pictures of torture and sexual humiliation in the press.[14] If the fact that the photos were identical to much pornography (although mild by its standards) was noticed at all, it was more often to excuse the crimes than to indict the pornography.[15] Then a mass-market U.S. newspaper was duped into publishing photos said to be of an Iraqi woman being raped by American soldiers that turned out to come from pornography.[16] The public was upset by the pictures—until they found out that it was pornography.[17] The newspaper apologized for not properly authenticating the picture.[18]

The photos, had they been what they were thought to have been, would have documented criminal atrocities. The identical picture, framed as pornography, became masturbation material that a legitimate outlet had been cleverly tricked into putting on its front page in another blow for sexual freedom of expression. As pornography, the conditions of its making—who was she? how did she get there? was she being raped?—were not subject to inquiry. They never are.

The assumption that the violence, violation, and abuse that is shown in pornography is somehow "consensual" is just that: an assumption. It coexists with much evidence of force and coercion, beginning with the materials themselves. Mass emails advertising photos of "hostages raped!" are spammed to Internet accounts without generating inquiry into whether they are either. A website called Slavefarm offers women for sale as "sexual slaves," complete with contracts signing away all human rights and explicit photographs of the slave being tortured.[19] Authorities stonewall. Live feed provides direct sexual use of prostituted women onscreen. No matter how real and harmful it gets, pornography, in reality a form of trafficking in women, is this parallel universe in which everything that happens becomes harmless and unreal.

Long overlapping sub rosa with legitimate entertainment, pornography has been a criminal underworld pursuit. Making it still is. But as it has exploded—the industry was said to gross $4 billion a year in the 1980s, between $10 billion and $14 billion in 2001, and by 2005, adult video rentals alone were estimated to earn $20 billion a year in the United States, $57 billion globally—its distributors no longer live under rocks.[20] Legitimate corporations now traffic pornography, often through subsidiaries, their financial stake as immense and established as it is open.[21]

Certainly the level of threat and damage to women's status and treatment and to equality of the sexes worsens as pornography goes mainstream and becomes seen as more legitimate. Venue does matter.

That does not mean that pornography has not been a dangerous, damaging, and real part of social life all along. If its effects do worsen the more widespread and visible pornography becomes, the view—as tenacious and pernicious as it is baseless—that it has no effects as long as it stays underground has made its march into the open possible. If the spatial separation of pornography into its own little world has been dubious, its mental isolability is pure delusion. Pornography changes its consumers, who then go everywhere under its influence. Nothing zones them.

Excellent social science research over the past 25 years has documented the effects of exposure to pornography, providing a basis to extrapolate the predictable consequences of mass social saturation.[22] The catharsis hypothesis—the notion that the more pornography men use, the less abusive sex they will seek out elsewhere—has been scientifically disproved.[23]

Closer to the reverse has been found: it primes the pump. As women have long known, use of pornography conditions consumers to objectified and aggressive sex, desensitizing them to domination and abuse, requiring escalating levels of violence to achieve a sexual response.[24] Use of pornography is also correlated with increased reports by perpetrators of aggressive sex and with increased inability to perceive that sex is coerced.[25] Consumers thus become increasingly unable to distinguish rape from other sex. Some become addicted, virtually no one is unaffected, the evidence as a whole suggests.[26]

Consuming pornography, with some individual variation, produces attitudes and behaviors of discrimination and violence, particularly against powerless others.[27] By extension, the more pornography is consumed, the more difficult it will become, socially, to tell when rape is rape, even for some victims. An increase in sexual assault, accompanied by a drop in reporting and low conviction rates, is predictable. All this has happened.[28]

Mass desensitization of a major segment of the viewing public has a corresponding effect on the rest of popular culture. The audience for popular culture is the same as the audience for pornography. Ten winos in raincoats are not producing the pornography industry's revenue figures. Popular culture, from advertising to legitimate film and books, has to become correspondingly more explicitly sexual—specifically more sexually aggressive and demeaning to women—to get the desired rise out of the same audience. Advertising is a particularly sensitive barometer of this effect.

How that public buys, what it demands, how it responds, and what it wants to see are being significantly controlled, skewed by pornographers. Soft pornography blurs into light entertainment. The powerful conditioning of huge proportions of the male public makes them demand that the women around them look and act in conforming ways. We increasingly live in a world the pornographers have made.

High culture is affected as well. Women writers who present young girls loving being sexually initiated by old men, daughters feeling ambivalent about sex with their fathers, pornography being part of the old world of freedom rather than a future dystopia of totalitarianism, rocket to success.[29] It is not that they are not fine writers. It is the fact that their work converges with pornographic conditioning, affirms it in a classy woman's voice, that catapults them to the top, makes their work suddenly catch on as exciting. It is the moment of and precondition for their success. Academic women who breathlessly defend pornography benefit from the same response. Criticizing pornography, or writing so that rape is experienced by the reader as abuse, produces the opposite reaction: detumescent shunning. When feminists unmask pornography effectively, those who support it suddenly become favorites du jour. It works for men, too. Excuse sexual assault ever more openly, present women who oppose pornography as befuddled if well-intentioned moralists, attack serious approaches to the problem as evil censorship, and you too may receive a Nobel prize for literature.[30]

Tracking the escalation in sexual explicitness and sexual violence in mainstream cinema is child's play. More to the point, why was Sharon Stone's vaginal flash in *Basic Instinct* so electrifying, such a sensation?[31] Far more than that was available in any softcore pornography film or magazine right down the street. It was context: a mainstream actor, doing it here, in a mainstream film in a family cinema. Breaking the frame on sex gives a frisson of power, it seems, for which you first have to believe that the frame is there. Why was it shocking when Janet Jackson's breast popped out in a dance-attack on her in the Super Bowl halftime show?[32] *Playboy* has scores monthly, page three in England at least two a day. Context: a mainstream singer, here, in family time during one of masculinity's public ritual events. Audiences are thrilled, scandalized, titillated. Barriers broken. Pundits juiced. Territory gained. Freedom reigns.

Who pays? Stone was told when she shot that scene that the footage would not be used (hence its grainy first-take outtake quality); she reportedly suffered considerably when it was.[33] Jackson more or less apologized for the "wardrobe malfunction."[34] However they felt, they had to be good sports for the sake of their careers, just as Paris Hilton did when pornography of her was released.[35] Pornographic portrayals of feminist antipornography writer Andrea Dworkin lowered the floor on how she was seen and treated for life.

In pornography, women are publicly construed as members of an inferior sex-based group and constructed, some individually, before they are ever known personally. Sexual arousal, excitement, and satisfaction are harnessed to that portrayal, reinforcing it, naturalizing it, making it unquestionable and irrefutable. So, too, for all the nameless women used in pornography—society's "whores." Pornography is a mass instrument for creating how women in general, specific women and groups of women in particular, are seen, treated, and received. It constructs their status as unequal and their reputation as inferior. Few weep for a "whore's" reputation.

Meanwhile, progressive people, whatever they really think, defend pornography's right to exist and other peoples' right to use it, in tones pious and terms high minded.[36] Esoteric debates about aesthetics and causation take place amid periodic convulsions of moral fervor, producing occasional convictions for obscenity or restrictions on indecency. The industry shapes itself to law, and, more crucially, law to it.

Most fundamentally, pornography changes culture to protect its existence and extend its reach, so finally it will be true that there is no distinction between pornography and anything else. The best camouflage of all is being able to lie around in plain sight.

People who do not want to be accosted by pornography visually are expected to avert their eyes. Having fewer and fewer places to avert their eyes to, with fewer means of escape in public and none in private, women specifically—who are most endangered by these materials and often know it—are segregated, painted into ever smaller corners. The female version of the male compartmentalization myth is "pornography has nothing to do with me." Pornography is thus at once increasingly everywhere and yet protected from direct scrutiny and effective abolition by seeming not to be there at all.

In 1983, Dworkin, who died recently, and I proposed a civil law that would empower anyone who could prove they are hurt through pornography to sue the pornographers for human rights violations.[37] We defined pornography as what it is—graphic sexually explicit subordination of women through pictures and words that also includes specified presentations—and defined causes of action for coercion, force, assault, and trafficking.[38] We documented its effects and predicted its impact if nothing was done.[39] Our law was found unconstitutional in a ruling that held that pornography had to be protected as "speech" because it is so effective in doing the harm that the opinion conceded it does.[40] Since then, although the law could have been repassed and this blatantly wrong and arguably illegal ruling challenged, pornography has not only exploded, it has changed the world around us. Even the determinedly blinkered cannot evade noticing. It is colonizing the globe.

The pornography industry is a lot bigger, more powerful, more legitimate, more in everyone's face today than it was a quarter of a century ago. To the degree that it cannot exist without doing real damage, it could still be stopped in its tracks anywhere by this law. Sexual objectification and violation does not happen all by itself. Real social institutions drive it. Pornography does, powerfully, in capitalist mass mediated cultures.

If nothing is done, the results will keep getting worse. We told you so.

NINETEEN

Gender: The Future

The butterfly effect is not clearly predictable. Apart from the question whether the mode of intervention is the right kind, or the domain so engaged is unstable, it does not proceed determinately in a simple far less linear way; that is what makes its pattern distinctive. In social settings, including law, predicting its trajectory and alchemy is as much a matter of intuitive sense—perhaps accessible through the wisdom of experience on the ground—as it is of trained expertise. It certainly is as political in the largest sense as it is narrowly legal. Since many powerful forces converge in the complex multidimensional dynamic that is gender inequality, intensified inequality could result from a considered challenge when those who have long been devalued and disempowered attempt to assert their value and power within a still unequal system. It might even be the case that the more appropriately-targeted the intervention, the stronger the push-back. In this talk, two diametrically opposed futures for sex equality are faced, turning on the role of pornography, with no assurance as to which one wins.[1]

In 1976—around the time when many of us learned what some of us have not forgotten, and the world hasn't been the same since—Marge Piercy published a novel called *Woman on the Edge of Time*.[2] The titular woman, Connie Ramos, was a sane woman trapped in an insane place (who among us hasn't felt that way); hers was a mental hospital. Through a neurological torture experiment, she kept being thrown into the future. But there were two of them. Sometimes she is in this androgynous loving place where men are kind and gentle, reproduction is nonexploitive, sexuality is about intimacy and communication, and the word "equal" is redundant. Other times she is projected into this pornographic nightmare where women are sex, televisions everywhere simultaneously watch you and bombard you with sexualized abuse, and life corresponds to it. Some thirty years later, we are poised ever more sharply on the edge of these two futures. One of them is winning, and I wish it was unnecessary to tell you which one. In which one our children's children live, lies the future of gender.

Since gender was "discovered" some thirty years ago,[3] through the efforts of many women in and outside the academy, this regularity of status, with half the population supreme and half the population subordinated, has been altered, or at least challenged. As a result, the lives of some women are better, more in some ways and places than others, especially in developed countries and among economic and racial elites.[4] Yet it is hardly controversial to observe that women as such—women as a group, women as women—are not free and equal anywhere.[5] So the question asked by the women's movement—the movement critical of gender as it is practiced—remains: why?

The major obstacle to the liberation of women—the central problem we confront and the fundamental reality that we still need to change—is what women need liberation from: male dominance. In the past few decades, the many interlocking dimensions of this social system—economic, political, legal, cultural, religious—have been exposed, analyzed, and organized against. They have been the subject of educational campaigns, of international conventions and agreements, of legislation and litigation and policy development within states and between states. Male supremacy has been hammered and chipped at, blasted through on occasion, circumvented periodically, eroded at its foundations in places, tunneled beneath, and at times catapulted over. Yet the global institution of male dominance remains.

One reason is that a fundamental, pervasive, and tenacious form male power takes is still evaded or denied by many. Thinking about it is widely resisted, even by those whose situations are comparatively secure. Talking about it directly can make men edgy, angry; some women deny its reality with bravado or derision. Confronting it is called "depressing" by people who have no problem thinking about nuclear war for a living. Most academics, notably including the post-modernists (especially the American stripe), have yet to address it—which alone might be a clue to its importance.

Power is even more sexualized all around the world than it was thirty years ago. The sexualization of power—this drug of male supremacy, this third rail of social life, this profit center for capitalist global media, legal and illegal—is particularly visible in prostitution and pornography, which increasingly are setting the terms of popular culture around us.[6] As the decades of empirical studies of pornography consumption document beyond cavil, exposure desensitizes consumers to violence and abuse, requiring escalating intrusiveness for continued excitement and stimulation. In order to catch the attention of pornography-saturated consumers, mainstream media and advertising ignores the racism, economic desperation, and sexual abuse in childhood that impels most women into the sex industry. Glorified, whitewashed, or covered up are the sadism, the relentless abuse, violation, and horror, the physical and psychic violence that are endemic to sex for sale.[7] Despite some official attention to violence against women in the areas of rape, battering, and sexual harassment, and despite important legal initiatives against various cultural forms of sexual objectification of women, women's status and treatment around the world has observably regressed in this area.[8] Thus is gender—that is, gender hierarchy—recreated daily in the magma of popular culture.

Prostitution and pornography feed off of, exist because of, and promote the combination of sex-based poverty and gender-based violence. Women need to be kept poor so that they will be compelled to be available for money to any man who wants to buy them for sex. That availability, that survival necessity, is called "consent." Women have to be seen as sexual things so their sexual use can be normalized as what women are for. Those qualities, displayed, are called femininity; given (or in some cultural settings sold) to one man for life, as Simone de Beauvoir observed over half a century ago, are called marriage;[9] sold to many men, they are called prostitution. Women's options need to be precluded by discrimination so that, when they are found prostituting as the one thing men will pay them for, it can be called "her choice." In Western capitalist countries, where media dictate consciousness, many are fooled. What was "soft-core" pornography when our movement began is now mainstream entertainment. Legitimate corporate giants now cash in on what used to be controlled nearly exclusively by organized crime.[10] Gender inequality is a booming business, even as much business is failing.

Concretely speaking, most people who are used in the sex industry were sexually abused in childhood,[11] often beginning in their families, where power and access are unquestioned, abuse that escalates in frequency and visibility when done by strangers, including, for example, during armed conflicts among men.[12] The war on women that is gender starts here, and it is a sexual war.

The consequences are as widely ignored as they are far-reaching. More of this dimension of gender inequality can be explained by the single fact of the high prevalence of sexual abuse of children than by any other single fact.[13] Girls who are sexually abused, most of them by adult men, learn femininity, that is, how to give men the active sexual passivity men crave to feed their sense of entitlement to supremacy. These girls learn that male power is real and requires appeasement. They learn that their life chances improve to the extent they give men with power over their lives what those men want sexually, whatever that is. They learn that men want women to want to be used. So they learn to convey that they enjoy giving men whatever they want. When women do this, having internalized as children to sexualize being sexually used by someone more powerful than they are, part of them experiences being loved, approved, and valued. What has become their identity is validated. Many women fight this, even successfully; many more do not.

Less is known about sexually abused boys,[14] although it appears that many more are violated than is formally documented, and that they, like the girls, grow up to become everyone. Certainly formative sexual experiences can shape sexual orientation, straight as well as gay.[15] To the degree that facts are known, many serial killers, rapists, child molesters, and pedophiles were abused [as] boys, many sexually.[16] It would make sense that raped little boys would be well-represented among torturers and terrorists like those who carried out the September 11th atrocities—misogynists who dissociate, never

wanting to be in a woman's position again, turning their own violation into the pleasure of dominating and hurting another, a well-trod
path to recovering their own value.[17] Each violated boy who walks
this road violates many others. Sexual abuse of children thus predictably geometrically increases the incidence of sexual abuse in society.
How male sexuality is shaped in this context can go in either of two
directions. Some men who were abused boys want to make sure
nothing like that ever happens to anyone again, including to girls and
women. Others embrace as their own the sexuality of force that was
forced on them. Some girls and women are doubtless valued because
men sexually desire them. Some are raped and killed for the same
reason. The pornography of this sexuality is "snuff."

Sexually abused girls, over a third where good studies have been
done, often grow up to be abused further;[18] so do some of the boys.[19]
How many of these boys—at least a quarter, which one suspects is a
vast undercount, particularly in societies where same-sex contexts for
boys are the norm—grow up to abuse, or at least to discriminate, has
not been studied. Both sexes tend to identify their own sexuality with
its long-term effects. Men often identify with their abusers, so with a
dominant sexuality. Women often identify and eroticize the subordinated sexuality imposed on them. The scripts can last at least as long
as the post-traumatic stress.

Sexuality is the perfect vector for male supremacy. It gives everyone
an identity stake in their socially designated position of power, or
lack of power, together with a visceral sense that this arrangement is
not only right but natural and their very own. As my client Linda
Boreman, forced as "Linda Lovelace" to perform sex to make the
pornography film *Deep Throat* put it: "You do it, you do it, and you do
it. Then you become it."[20] What is oppression feels like freedom. This
is gender feminine.

When one's fundamental sexual experiences are imposed in a context of inequality of power, sex itself becomes imposition on those
with less power. This sexuality is necessarily unequal. This hierarchical dynamic fundamental to male supremacy defines girls as for
sexual use, boys as sexual users. What these boys were subjected to

gives them a strong incentive to despise girls and the powerlessness they stand for and to opt for the alternative society gives them: masculinity—their way out, that is—siding with the abusers. This is gender masculine.[21] The sexual politics of this process, superimposed on conventional lines, divides between left and right: the right repressing any sexuality of equality, the left liberating the sexuality of inequality.

This model of sexuality—the one produced by and enacted through the sexual abuse of children—is quintessentially expressed in prostitution and pornography. Pornography embodies this abusive sexuality by eroticizing the inequality it relies upon and exploits in order to be made. When consumed—and more of it is consumed every day, as it is aggressively pushed and trafficked worldwide[22]—pornography promotes this sexuality as a cultural norm, expanding its profits, with destructive and violent consequences for women and children in particular[23] and for the equality of the sexes generally. Pornography makes gender inequality—the inequality that is gender today—sexy. And so long as it is sexual, it will be hard put to be equal.

Although the women's movement has been instrumental in exposing this reality, its academic arm especially has often hesitated to trace and face its consequences. Often pornography and prostitution are defended through standard liberal abstractions like freedom of expression or freedom of choice, as if one can be free while being unequal. Many of the results are romanticized and analyzed as aesthetics or difference rather than identified as the products of inequality. Many men aggressively resist confronting this reality of their conditioning and compulsions, but so too do a good many women. Facing these facts does not produce *jouissance*, apparently, although it feels a lot like the beginning of real empowerment to many of us. One is often punished professionally and personally for addressing this problem squarely. Complex psychologies to invalidate resistance and encourage adjustment are based on denying it. Sexuality is thus allowed to remain imbricated with power, gendering male and female into masculine and feminine, defining men and women, driving male dominance.

This sets the sexual floor that permits male dominance to reproduce and expand unimpeded. This is why we are closer to Piercy's pornographic hell than anyone (except me and Andrea Dworkin, who predicted it precisely in 1983) thought possible in 1976.[24]

It is this sexual floor on relations between the sexes, one that can also operate between women and between men, that determines relations that most people believe both that they are free of and that cannot be changed. Both of these are unlikely to be true at the same time. But those who know that gender is not sex, rather sex is gender, know that gender is not natural, it is social; it is not inevitable; and it is not immutable. Addressing prostitution, for example, as is now being done in Sweden following Andrea Dworkin's and my proposal—where "johns" are assertively criminalized along with pimps and traffickers and prostituted people are decriminalized[25]—moves against this model in a way that provides one concrete step toward real equality. Giving prostituted people human rights, including people used in pornography and violated as a result of it, would be further steps in the same direction. Civil remedies like those Andrea Dworkin and I proposed[26] would provide the ability to act on our own to take back from the pimps and predators what is ours: the piece of our humanity that is our own sexuality. The point of such steps is not only what they would accomplish materially, although that is crucial, but what they would mean: women are not sex and are not for sale. Women would be, finally, human. Gender would be so transformed as to be effectively abolished. In the process, solidarity would be achieved among all women, across race and class and culture and religion, a solidarity that has largely eluded our movement to now. Hope for equality would be re-lit among those for whom it has by now nearly gone out.

Which of Marge Piercy's futures will we have? I do know we don't have much more time; today, it really is time that we are on the edge of. We can win, but not for much longer. In her benign future, one of Piercy's characters put it this way: "at certain cruxes of history, forces are in conflict. Technology is imbalanced. Too few have too much power. Alternate futures are equally or almost equally probable . . ."[27]

The odds were closer to equal in 1976 with a smaller pornography industry.

Today, we can choose to cheer pornography's death-in-life and be validated, supported, embraced, and funded by power. We know where that leads. Or we can choose equality for real, the end of gender as we have known it, and at least you will know which side you were on.

For moments like this, a fable attributed to many different cultures, but I first heard credited to a nation of peoples native to the territory now called the United States, tells of an old blind sage known far and wide to be wise and to see and know what no one else did. To show she was not so powerful, two young men came to her with a bird they had caught. Their plan, a sadistic one, was to ask her if the bird was dead or alive. If she said alive, they would kill it on the spot. If she said dead, they would let it go. Power holds two futures in its hands: tell the truth, it crushes you; cave in and lie, you live but have abdicated your power. So, they asked her, "Oh wise one, is the bird alive or dead?" She sat for long moments, still and silent. Finally, she said, "I don't know. I only know it's in your hands."[28]

IV. Academy

be gender literate is to possess a general working grasp of what is known about sex inequality in one's field, in this case, the body of information about the differential ways women and men are treated by law and society, with links and discontinuities with race, class, age, sexual orientation, and varying abilities. The body of information encompasses all legal fields, from constitutional law to the tax code—otherwise quite a reach. Education of judges to these facts and perspectives on sex bias contends against the systemic assumption that the law is gender neutral, that the rule of law as such means that there is and should be no particularity on any group basis.

In gender bias work, neutrality—as ideal and certainly as reality—takes a real trouncing. It was criticized at this conference in areas as potentially unlikely as estate planning, where Mary Lou Fellows asked the stunning question: "If a couple comes in and asks you to plan their estate, do you wonder if there is domestic violence going on?" Beverly Moran illuminated the racism and gender bias of the home mortgage deduction, as well as the ways in which it is surprisingly not class biased. Kathleen Mahoney dismembered the criminal law of self-defense. To summarize: a lot of legal even-handedness was not found.

What is this thing we call bias? It is a tilt, the uneven ground we stand on or try to climb up, this slope under our feet that only slips going up, that refuses to slide us into equality, as it should have long ago. This bias, in Lynn Schafran's terms, includes malice, ignorance, and lack of resources. It ranges from the misogyny—an interestingly underused term—of the *Peacock* case[3] to women's special invisibility in many legal doctrines—as illustrated by the insightful discussion of nonpecuniary loss damages in tort by Lucinda Finley—to the gender-blindness through which law can be applied in a far-from-gender-blind world, an analysis particularly well furthered by Cass Sunstein's analysis of the anti-caste principle in equal protection law.[4]

Most women, if they encounter the law directly at all, face it in the law of the family. For the most part, gender is not even a doctrinal category in family law, unless a legislature misspeaks. The "mother" and "wife" of family law are just facts, seldom meeting the "woman" of equal protection fame, with the result that sex equality is almost unheard of as a legal standard in this area. Analysis for gender bias reveals that those areas of law that are most discretionary, including child custody, affect most women most directly and are also considered the least "legal." Those areas of law that most affect women in their roles as women are most governed by the logic of the "personal," so are least subjected to principle, including the constitutional equality principle.

So, no, Professor Schulhofer, bias does not only mean motive. It does not mean only disregarding what you know. We do not need to learn to move from bias to harm. We know the harm is there, and also that, where harm is differential, there is likely to be bias. And no, Professor Epstein—a useful example and exponent of neutrality—we are not surprised to hear that there is another side to these issues of sexual harassment and paternity. Until we came along, your other side was the only side there was, and it is no more neutral now than it was then. I will take this as a transition to the central strategic question for educating against gender bias: Can men learn?

As a corollary, I suppose it is necessary to ask, can some women learn? To the degree the damage of male dominance hasn't happened to them, or in some cases to the degree it has, will they see it or will they deny it? Sadly, because most women are not in the positions of power men are, asking this question about women may not yet be as urgent in the present context as asking it about men is. Lucky, because it is a lot more painful. Just raising this question reveals the targets of this particular sort of education as elite in many senses of the word.

I frame the question "can men learn" with real apologies to Cass Sunstein's beautiful point about gender being a put-up job, an analysis made even more appealing by the fragility and tentativeness with which it was advanced. Andrea Dworkin once called this point "the delusion of sexual polarity."[5] They are right. Having said that, I will continue to refer to men and women as gendered, to this deeply unreal thing with profoundly real consequences.

Gender bias in law is maintained by a mix of ignorance—which includes prejudice, determined ignorance—with interest. Interest means people know what they are doing, want to do it, and do not care who gets hurt so long as it is not them. A character of Lily Tomlin's said it best: "We don't care. We don't have to. We're the phone company."[6] To all defenders of male supremacy who are convinced of its monolithic hegemony and permanence, I offer the example of the dismemberment of AT&T.

The biased include those who know what they are doing and don't care because they don't have to. They also include those who don't want to know because it will undermine their sense of the legitimacy and merit of their position; those who don't want to know because they will feel they have to do something about it that they don't want to do, or don't want to be seen doing. There are those who can't seem to get it, despite genuinely trying. There are those who are torn between knowing everything and pleasing everybody—is gender literacy even sort of beginning to be included in the "everything" someone who knows everything needs to know?—and looking bad to power by even giving that much ground. We all know examples.

Education exposes bias. Considering the nature of the bias we are trying to educate people out of, and the interest that lies beneath it, raises the next question: can male supremacy survive exposure? It seems no. But why, I am unsure. It may be because male supremacy has been saying that it is neutral for so long, has built so much of its own sense of legitimacy on its professed neutrality, that showing how it is not neutral—meaning unequal—is experienced as severely undermining. It has, however, managed to survive its real lack of neutrality, which a lot of people are quite realistic about, for quite some time. If it cannot survive having said aloud what most people already know on some level, educating against gender bias is a powerful tool. Illuminating this issue, Dean Sheilah Martin discussed the role of men's assertion of a right not to know. Ann Scales argued that ignorance is central to this system. Validating ignorance about the reality of sex inequality appears to be central to the claim to authority on which male supremacy in part depends. The twin examples of law school and military school—in which people become ever more learnedly stupid by learning to disregard their experiences—suggested that legal thinking is to thinking as military music is to music. Not coincidentally, both are gender illiterate.

Examination of the role of male ignorance in law reveals that ignorance often provides legal deniability as a doctrinal matter. Cass Sunstein reminded us of the role of intent in equal protection law. To capsulize that area: what *he* doesn't know can't hurt *her*, or *them*. Equal protection of the laws cannot be violated by someone who doesn't know what he is doing. Kathleen Mahoney deconstructed the similar doctrines of mistaken belief in consent and the *mens rea* requirement in the rape law: a man isn't raping you unless he knows you didn't want it. That certainly provides an incentive to male ignorance. So does the *scienter* requirement in U.S. child pornography law: if a pornographer is ignorant that a girl is underage, the sex pictures he makes using her isn't child pornography.[7] Since she isn't a child if you can want her like a woman (a gender illiterate court will find this assertion credible), any girl with breasts is fair game, regardless of age. In these crucial areas, ignorance provides a complete defense to harm. It doesn't prevent it, far from it, it just precludes accountability for it. In the absolutist approach to the First Amendment, ignorance becomes a constitutional principle in trafficking pornography. So long as they are pornography, what is actually in the materials is irrelevant, so ignorance of their contents is the most principled posture in which to decide protection. Never was justice more determinedly blind.

Part of our job is to remove the validation on gender ignorance across the law and make gender literacy a standard. Many bigots don't know what they're doing; many do. The problem is the privileging of the ability to escape accountability by credibly asserting ignorance. We need to make ignorance of harm to women less credible as well as to make it no longer a defense.

Implicit in the gender bias work is an affirmative answer to the question of men's ability to learn and to be changed by what they learn. In the sexual harassment area, Judge Posner's moving opinion in *Carr*, "of course she didn't want it,"[8] and much of the U.S. Supreme Court's decision recognizing sexual harassment as a legal claim for sex discrimination in *Vinson*,[9] provide examples. We know men can learn because they have. There is also the example of our men students, human beings of the male persuasion who get it every year in real numbers. In some ways, men can be better situated to learn certain difficult things about the gender system than women are, because they get punished less for it. Which is far from saying they don't get punished at all.

Moreover, there is a material basis for men's ability to learn about gender in the fact that gender itself is learned in the first place. Beneath these veils of ignorance men hide behind as principle, as philosophy, as defense, as doctrine, lies how men learn to be men. Many learn through being sexually abused as children. This happens to a lot of men; no one really knows how many.[10] From it, they learn that sex is hierarchy and abuse, just as sexually abused girls learn the same lesson. When they grow up, the boys have different options, but when it is happening to them, they don't. Men also learn masculinity through having it denied them based on race, some of the consequences of which are acted out on women of color. Men also learn to be men through athletics, which can be as brutalizing and humiliating as it is risky, demanding, identity forming, and solidarity producing. Men learn to be men in what are euphemistically called playgrounds, where boys beat each other up. They learn in fraternities and in schools like the Citadel, and in police academies in rituals of hazing. The hazing would be clearly seen as sexual abuse and harassment, as sexual sadism, if the same acts were done to women. Men become men by going to war, by raping women together, by going to prison and getting raped by other men. Through homosocial subordination, men create hierarchies among men, including employer/employee and, yes, teacher/student. The process may be responsible for much of the groveling, posturing inauthenticity that sets the standard for public life. Just don't let me be humiliated is its bottom line. At the end, some men get to be men, meaning many men and all women are beneath them; a few men are above them. They can be dominant, if they choose—so much the better for them if they are white and upper class and straight, the top of the top of this pile.

The gender literate answer to why gender bias exists is: so some men can get the rewards of male dominance. But we may have overlooked part of this answer: so they don't have to have this done to them anymore. That is, so they don't have to be women. Those who do well under this system want to validate the process because it got them where they are and kept them safe from where they don't want to be. The details, they want to deny, forget, cover up, sexualize.

This analysis includes men along with women as subordinated under it but would not be mistaken for any kind of soppy gender neutrality. Men's treatment of men as men sets a sorry standard for humanity by any definition. The payoff does not make it less violating, dehumanizing, and deeply humiliating. Men's stake in male dominance, in not being women, is very real, but it is not without cost. This brings us to the deepest strategic question we have to confront in the area of gender bias education, a tragic third question: can we compete with this?

We are trying, with determination and humor. After listening to our colleagues, clearly being a law professor doubles as being a stand-up comic, if not always "the fun kind."[11] What Tracy Meares said about the price of talking about certain things being too high, and the pain and restraint that animated Larry Lessig's comments, made me want to lower that price. I think that is something we can do. Perhaps we made a step in that direction in drawing not only on our legal learning but also on our own experiences. I was compelled to confront my own when Ann Scales said law school was divided between the people who were at home there and the people who were not. I have learned to be at home with not being at home there, which was excellent preparation for over a decade of unemployment by America's law schools. When Judge Ilana Rovner sat down after her moving remarks last night, she said in a stricken voice to no one in particular, "Oh dear, I didn't mention the loneliness." As if she had sworn to tell us the whole truth, not just nothing but the truth.

Gender literacy has also produced many concrete solutions, so many and so concrete that they cannot be briefly summarized. We, the people who brought you the antipornography ordinance, are the Department

TWENTY-ONE

Mainstreaming Feminism in Legal Education

Rethinking the legal curriculum from the ground up, Dean Naya of Meiji University Law School asked me what should be the role of feminism in legal education. What an inspiration of a question! I certainly had never been asked it before by anyone considering acting on the answer. The first school in Japan to educate women in law celebrated the 120th anniversary of the admission of women to its Law Department and the creation of its Law School in January 2001.[1]

I have come to think that there is something deceptive about terming this exercise a feminist one, or at least I have come to tire of being the only one in the discussion seen to bring a politics, particularly when that cabins its ambition or contribution in ideological and political space, or suggests that its insights only make sense from this particular point of view, or need be taken seriously only by those who take feminism seriously or see themselves as feminists. It is as if existing reality has no politics, only a critique of it does. Mainstreaming feminism in this sense is less an ideological or political exercise, certainly not a partial or sectarian one, than the revelation and rectification of one.

Nothing short of everything will really do.

—*Aldous Huxley*[2]

In 1988, in an elevator in Washington, D.C., a federal judge, a very nice man who not long after was elevated to the United States Supreme Court, congratulated me warmly on recently publishing *Feminism Unmodified.*[3] As the elevator descended, he looked at his feet and reflected, "It's amazing how much you can accomplish if you stay focused on just one thing!" A few floors went by in silence; the topics in the book—including rape, obscenity, athletics, Marxist theory, discrimination, the First Amendment—went through my mind. As we jolted to ground, I said, "Yes, actually, the whole law library testifies to that. One ought to be able to accomplish at least as much by staying focused on the other 53 percent of the population." He took it well. I did wonder to myself whether Alexander Pope's admonition that "the proper study of mankind is man" had ever been described as focusing on just one thing.

In 2001, a distinguished and congenial law professor in charge of curriculum talked with me about what seminar, in addition to my lecture course on Sex Equality, might be best to offer. Possibilities included Sexual Harassment, Feminist Legal Theory, Women's Human Rights, and The Law of September 11th, the last focusing on the law of war and the international humanitarian law questions raised by the atrocities of that day and its unfolding aftermath. My interlocutor said he thought the 9/11 seminar would be best. It would, he said, pausing for the right word, expose students to me "on a . . . broader range of questions." Sex Equality raises some issues that overlap with the September 11th seminar, but certainly he was right that their legal focuses are different. Then, too, both Sexual Harassment and Women's Human Rights overlap with Sex Equality only a little. I wondered to myself whether addressing gender issues in the September 11th seminar would be seen to narrow it.

I.

The assumptions afoot in these conversations illustrate some common misconceptions about feminism in general, its role in law and legal education in particular. It is often thought to involve a narrow, one-dimensional, one-note, geographically limited, thin set of problems, questions, and people. Traditional subjects, by comparison, are not imagined to be limited or narrow when they do not consider women or men as such, or the relative status of the sexes, in their fields. When vast ranges of materials are scrutinized and reconfigured through a gendered lens, it seems only the lens is seen, even though most people accept that there is no such perspective as no perspective, while traditional subject frames are seen as imposing no point of view, certainly not a gendered one, when they never consider sex or women at all. It is thought possible to know a subject while maintaining illiteracy on questions of gender and the relation of the status and treatment of the sexes to that subject. Focusing on women and gender is seen as narrow. Excluding women and gender is not.

Which raises the now well-tilled question of what feminism—in raising questions on women and gender—means.[4] Feminism entails a multifaceted approach to society and law as a whole, a methodology of engagement with a diverse reality that includes empirical and analytic dimensions, explanatory as well as descriptive aspirations, practical as well as theoretical ambitions. It lays the whole world open in new ways, offering fresh vistas and angles of vision. Pursuing its leads is a complex adventure—vast, deep, rich, and open—of reexamining existing legal and social reality in light of women's exclusion from, and subordination within, nothing less than life, law, and scholarship. Women are over half the world's people; men are the rest. How could studying them as such ever be "just one thing"? How could it be narrow?

Feminism starts with the simple observation that women are people. It moves into the more complex observation that they have been denied that simple recognition to their disadvantage. Then it gets complicated. Feminism exposes the reality that men as well as women have a sex and are variously gendered, and that the male sex and masculine gender have largely been unrecognized as such, having been merged with humanity and merit and superiority, to men's social advantage. In this way, feminism reveals that women have a universality that has been denied, as well as a contribution to make to universality that has been overlooked, while men have a particularity that they have denied in themselves in defining their particularity as the universal. These attributions and denials converge into a socially stratified system of deference and command that plays out in law and the legal academy as elsewhere.

As has now become familiar, this does not assume that women and men are the same, quite the contrary. Nor does it assume that all women or men in all cultures, or across history, have been in an identical position, especially on the basis of race and class. It is to say that the experience of women as women, and men as men, in all its multiplicity and variety, exists in social space in the real world. Recognition of women's experience of systematic disadvantage relative to men is at the basis of feminism,[5] a theory that began not in academia but as a movement for liberation. Feminist theory remains no self-referential theory-for-theory's-sake theory. It comes from social reality and goes back into social reality, disciplined by that relation.[6] Its project fits its ground: to expose unequal social status on the basis of sex in order to change it.

Framing feminism's point of departure and return this way focuses the question of what women's experience concretely is. Transnational and cross-cultural patterns within nations, including on the basis of race and class, have emerged from asking feminist questions.[7] Women, the least privileged more than the more privileged, tend to be segregated into forms of work that are paid little and valued less, their material contributions, including as mothers and homemakers, devalued. Women's status is enforced by demeaning women's physical and social characteristics, often through stereotyping and relegation to disfavored roles, even as their entrance into some conventionally more favored roles diminishes their status as well as their compensation or standard of living. Across cultures, women are subjected to domestic servitude and battering in their homes. They are often forced to become mothers in a setting of lack of reproductive choice. Sometimes they are sterilized against their will, sometimes forced to have children they do not choose and cannot care for. Unwanted sexual attention that women are in no position to refuse is commonly inflicted on them. Women are, worldwide, sexually abused and assaulted as children and as adults, in war and in peace. They are sexually objectified, reduced to things for sexual possession, use, and abuse. Women of every racial, national, sexual, and aged specificity are bought and sold for denigrating entertainment and trafficked in prostitution, sometimes by their own families, within and across jurisdictional boundaries. They are transferred for intimate sexual access like chattel, sometimes in marriage for a long time, sometimes in prostitution for a short time.

Sometimes men pay for them, sometimes men are paid for them; in either case they are considered his. In some places, being female means not being permitted to be born. It can mean less food, less education, having one's genitals sliced out, being stoned to death for sex outside of marriage, or being incinerated because a dowry is too small or a man feels like moving on unburdened.

Through experiences like these, and in being socialized and targeted for them, and because of the status they represent, women are socially deprived of respect, personal security, human dignity, access to resources, speech, political representation, and power—in a word, equality. It is common across cultures to attribute this subordinate status to nature and body. Evidence and analysis support the conclusion that this attribution is an ideological excuse and rationalization, not a preexisting natural reality.[8] Together, these experiences and others like them become a pervasive social system through which women are gendered, hence made into a sex. Together with other practices and mechanisms of enforcement, they form an unequal status on the basis of sex.

Women as a gender group can, then, be observed to be used, violated, demeaned, exploited, excluded, and silenced—whatever else does or does not happen to them as individuals, however these effects are muted or evaded by luck, chance, resistance, or privilege. When they happen, these acts are inflicted on women by men who, socialized to masculinity, can decide to do them or not. Not all men do them, or are in an equal position to do them. Whether or not individual men do these things is largely their choice, though, depending on factors that include their relative status among men. As men, most men benefit from not being the people to whom these things are done (although they are done to some men) and can be done with relative impunity (although some men are held accountable for them, actually, whether they do them or not). They also benefit from being in a position to decide to do these things or not to do them, a power men have to varying degrees. Ultimately, women are able to choose precious little about whether these things happen to them. Attempts to avoid them, often through restrictions on liberty, do not necessarily mean they will not happen anyway. This is what it means to speak of the inequality of the sexes in terms of male power. To be a member of the social group women, as a condition of birth, means that any one or more of these things can happen to you, and little will be done about it, whether these acts are formally illegal or not.

Many legal problems are generated by, and interact with, this treatment and its status outcomes. The question of the role of feminism in legal education can thus be reframed as: What can legal education do to prepare lawyers to intervene in this situation—women's inequality to men—in order to change it?

II.

Around the world, people—some men as well as many women—working with law, who want to end this inequality, in confronting these realities have produced and are producing new knowledge, new approaches, and new law. Legal education has responded to some extent with specific courses centered on the status of women, including courses on sex equality, violence against women, women's legal history, women's human rights, feminist jurisprudence, sexuality, intersectionality (race, sex, nation), and women and the law, to name a few. Subjects centered on sex, gender, and people so modulated create new unities and reveal deeper structures across and beneath conventional legal topics. They can alter not only what people think about but how they think.[9] These courses need to continue.

Legal education faces a challenge on another level as well: mainstreaming gender[10] in the entire law curriculum, integrating it into how teaching is done and what is taught. Because women are everyone, everywhere, doing everything, done to in distinctive ways—the latter being what law primarily exists to address—attention to women, and to men as a sex, and their inequality, raises far-reaching questions for the content of existing legal subjects. Many specific topics within conventional legal subject areas have been richly explored by feminist legal scholars over the past three decades; slowly and in fragments, they are making their way into standard courses and casebooks. What has not been done is to rethink conventional courses and curriculum in light of the implications of these investigations for core premises of fields and courses. The task, building on existing insights,[11] is to pave the way to broader, deeper change in the law curriculum, equipping lawyers to work toward social equality under law—all law.

In light of the reality of women's conditions as described, consider first the structural division in the curriculum (and most legal systems) between public and private law—tort, contract, and family law deemed private; criminal and constitutional law considered public. Does this structural division in the curriculum (one many scholars already bridge) need rethinking in light of women's unequal status? The status of women is a public reality that largely constructs the private realm, and a private reality that deeply structures the public order; each cuts across, inflects, and partially underpins the other. How, then, other than by being formally so divided, does private law remain meaningfully separate from public law where questions of sex inequality arise? Once law is involved in and affects an area, the sense in which that law or area remains meaningfully "private" is an open question in any event. Making constitutional and international guarantees of sex equality effective surely implicates private law, hence teaching as policy and practice. Should the public/private deck of legal cards be reshuffled on a curricular level?

In light of constitutional and international guarantees of sex equality, consider the implications of situating torts in the context of the status of women as such for its concepts of injury, of damage, and of individuals relative to groups. Women, like men, have accidents. But if society is organized to insulate some people from some forms of risk and concentrate them on others, producing systematic, cumulative, and determinate injury to some people because they are members of one sex-based group from which the other sex-based group is largely exempted—indeed injuries that are largely inflicted on members of one group by members of another—then those injurious acts are not very accidental. It is one thing to create new constitutional torts (which require governmental, i.e., public action) or pass new discrimination statutes recognizing new so-called private injuries by some people to others. It is another to ask systematically what existing torts are systemic and effectively social and public, masquerading as haphazard and essentially private. As new public patterns become visible, what duties arise? Are negligence concepts sufficient? What causation theories are appropriate for liability? Should systemic sex-based torts need to be intentional in the willed conscious sense to be actionable? Once new patterns are discerned, does the foreseeable change? While some scholars have productively considered such questions, knowing that tortfeasors and victims are often not as gender neutral as tort's traditional persons,[12] asking whether accidents are standing in for more determinate injuries of inequality has not been central to most tort teaching. It is one thing to look at women's injuries as women as a special area of tort, another to look at torts as such in a gendered light.

Consider the way inequality causes harm, not a subject typically taught as part of tort law's concepts of causality. If all women are members of the group "women" in ways that variously (including varying by race, by class) target them for injury (as previously described), and some torts are inflicted on some women systemically as a result, it does not make sense to consider such torts as done to them as unique individuals in the one-at-a-time sense that still tends to predominate in the law of tort. Group injuries happen not only as mass accidents or toxic contaminations, in which a lot of people become a group by being hurt by the same agent or at the same time. Group injuries also happen through bias, harming members of preexisting collectivities as such. Collective injury due to membership in a group thus often happens to one person at a time without happening to them "as" individuals. The group ground or combined grounds for the harm preexists the injuries for which members are differentially singled out for particular forms of it. If legal education is to mainstream feminism, a sustained examination of the implications for tort of this disparate reality that preexists specific cases is needed—a reconsideration that calls for reassessment of mental elements among other things. Are the substance and ranking of the familiar trilogy of intentionality, recklessness, and negligence adequate to all women's experiences of sex-based tortious harm? Work on the gendered meaning of the "reasonable person" has broken some of this ground.[13] Damage assessments are being reconsidered in light of the related realization that women's lower social worth has been built into tort law's measures of damages for their injuries.[14] Pointed particular questions have been raised. But tort teaching as a whole has barely begun to consider the larger implications of situated social inequality in the hierarchical sense, in order to illuminate the meaning of the existence of unequal social groups for its subject.

A similar set of questions can be and has been raised about contract law,[15] beginning with the assumption that parties to contracts are meaningfully "individuals" and can be assumed to operate at what is called arm's length, as equals. Absent duress or fraud or unconscionability or other recognized caveats, it is thought parties contract freely. But whether social unequals, including sex-based unequals, can be assumed contractual equals remains largely unexamined in basic contracts courses. It is one thing to look at prenuptial agreements when they are contested, for example, another to ask whether the marriage contract (probably the most common contract people make or, rather, find themselves in) would be enforceable in any other setting, and what the answer reveals about contract law's assumptions. It is one thing to ask what contract concepts are best applied when a surrogacy contract is disputed, another to ask whether surrogate childbearing can be validly contracted under unequal conditions, which dramatically encompass race and class with sex, and what the answer means for what a contract is. If concepts of consent from contract law were applied to consent to sex, how often would it be valid?[16] A full investigation into the meaning of the inequality of sexes for these and other contractarian concepts might benefit the first-year curriculum.

The law of civil procedure offers similar opportunities for gender critique that have yet to be widely pursued in teaching. The idea of standing to sue, for example, generally embodies a notion of differential harm: a person hurt in an exceptional, not standard or everyday way, and more than others. If all women are hurt by the status of women in one way or another, even if some more than others, if this injury of status is defined by what women share with other women, even if in differential ways, what are the implications for standing doctrines? What are the implications for class actions requirements of this potentially largest plaintiff class action in history? Leaving aside who the defendants would be, whether the law is constructed to deny such a legal injury and to preclude such a class seems worth asking in teaching both doctrines, to reveal their basic assumptions if nothing else.

Jurisdiction divides power, making it unlikely to be unaffected by gender, itself a power division. From the standpoint of women, socially speaking, jurisdiction might be seen as first divided between the law of force, which operates socially, and the force of law, which operates legally. (Sometimes the two are not so different, but moving from the first to the second is widely regarded as an improvement for women, as it has been among men.) Different fora are governed by, and sensitive to, different laws, communities, and political pressures. The domestic sphere—home—operates as a kind of primary jurisdiction where questions affecting women are concerned. As with men, this is then followed by local law, national law, and international law. Gender highlights the fact that jurisdictional rubrics tend to prefer courts closest to home for resolving conflicts, which for women is a sphere of structural inequality (however favorable a personal arrangement individual women manage). Domestic resolution is preferred: by states within nations, by nations internationally. This tropism for the forum close to home is arguably not favorable to women's interests, in that women as a group tend to be most oppressed and furthest from independent recourse the closer to home they are.[17] The structural doctrines of privacy for home, federalism for states, and sovereignty for nations have all been deployed to deny women equal access to rights. The closer to the control of immediate men they are, the less likely women have been to get relief from inequality, yet jurisdictional doctrines structurally prefer the local. Such gendered questions about jurisdiction—whether jurisdiction as structured serves male dominance, for example—might be incorporated into civil procedure classes.[18]

Similar questions concerning the criminal law could, if pursued, be integrated more fully into courses in the upper-level curriculum. For example, the purposes of the criminal justice system classically include prevention, deterrence, and punishment. As tort law does, the law of crimes tends to assume that crimes are unusual. However, not only exceptional men commit all the crimes of violence against women described earlier, and the rates of the crimes make them more pervasive than exceptional. Most violence against women is committed by men whom the victims personally know, often with whom they are personally intimate, and who are documentably little different from the male statistical norm.[19] Combining this with the staggering nonreporting rate,[20] it makes sense to ask, when considering the purpose of deterrence, whether incarcerating those convicted of violence against women makes sense. This is not only a question about violence against women; it is a question about the efficacy of the criminal law. If jail does not reduce these crimes, and perpetrators and crimes are ordinary rather than exceptional, criminal justice needs fundamental rethinking—and where better to start than in law school?

As with torts, it is also a good time and place to ask whether many traditional crimes are really injuries of sex inequality in disguise, misconceived because their roots in sex and gender, often combined with race, have been ignored. Is rape an act of sex discrimination? Is prostitution serial rape? Is battering a domestic crime against humanity on the basis of sex and a one-on-one form of terrorism? Does child sexual abuse underlie all of them, as femininity's underpinning? These questions draw attention, potentially, to the lines between criminal and civil law, and between international and national law with curricular as well as practical implications. Might empowerment or social change be a goal for criminal law? What would it take to pursue it? What role should victims have in the criminal process? Unlike in civil law, in criminal law victims have no formal control over their own cases. Should they have more voice? If so, how might this be institutionalized, relative to the "community" or "people" that criminal law purports to speak for? How the teaching of criminal law and its place in the curriculum might change if these issues—which include accountability, alternate dispute resolution mechanisms, attention to race- and class-based injuries and systemic biases, and creative sentencing options among others—were part of it, is a relatively open question.[21]

Other substantive issues of criminal law with curricular implications to which the experience of women is relevant range from statutes of limitations to the death penalty. On the substantive end of this spectrum, the death penalty, which has long raised racial issues of the greatest importance, also raises the largely neglected issue of whether women should be executed when they have not been equally represented in creating the system and rules under which they are judged.[22] This question, even in less apocalyptic settings, remains largely unasked in law school. In an issue considered procedural, statutes of limitations for sexual crimes against children, for example, are arguably impossibly short. Some children are sexually assaulted from a very young age; sometimes they remember it, sometimes their memory only surfaces later, sometimes decades later.[23] Perpetrators are skilled at persuading their victims of the calamities that will befall them if they tell. Legislatures are beginning to recognize that the factors that produce nonreporting—including a sense of despair and inefficacy due to systemic unresponsiveness, personal shame, and desire to protect one's family and reputation—require more time, if children are to proceed to justice for these injuries. Nonreporting does not mean nothing happened. The changes in criminal law in this area raise the question of how many other injuries might fit this model, and how many other injuries of sex and gender have been exacerbated rather than solved by criminal procedure. It could be asked in teaching.

Gender status questions have been asked more systematically in constitutional law and incorporated into the curriculum. This process might go further, exploring for instance the assumption underlying most constitutions that society is free and equal unless law and the state intervene in it—the notion of the negative state. Can such constitutions adequately address social inequalities? The more familiar form of the question is whether constitutions should be interpreted to provide affirmative rights actionable by individuals against other individuals (often called horizontal rights) as well as restrictions on law's intervention into society (often called vertical rights) policed by the state action requirement. Some societies such as South Africa have taken up the challenge of this public/private question in their constitutions and enable direct suit among individuals for violations of certain constitutional provisions.[24] Very few constitutional law courses make this question central in how constitutional rights are taught.

Similarly, most constitutions use a neutral approach to questions of gender and race, favoring the notion that treating people the same is what treating them equally means. Feminists have both used gender neutrality and criticized its limitations. A deeper critique leads to a criticism of neutral principles in constitutional law generally in favor of substantive contextualized approaches.[25] While critiques of neutrality are commonly recognized in specific areas, most constitutional law courses continue to be structured around doctrinal neutrality as a methodology for thinking, as if neutrality is what legal doctrine, by definition, requires. How constitutional law, and law in general, would be taught if doctrine was *substantively* reevaluated across the board is unexamined. For example, is respect for precedent neutral? The erstwhile "new equal protection" emanating from the *Carolene Products* footnote began with the realization that African-Americans had been excluded, substantively, from political representation;[26] this shifted the ground under their constitutional inequality claims. Well, the common law foundation of torts and contracts and crimes and procedure was laid when women were not even allowed to vote. Under these conditions, there is little gender neutral about fealty to precedent.

Other examples can be found in the law of evidence. Evidence law lays down what the legal system will take to be real. As law's epistemology, the rules of evidence embody assumptions about reliability and credibility and common knowledge. Often they do not accord with women's experiences at all. Consider, for example, the hearsay rule in light of my Bosnian women clients' experience in genocide.[27] The hearsay exclusion is based on the idea that: if you say you heard someone say something happened, that is not reliable evidence that it happened, certainly not as reliable as if you said you had seen that same thing happen yourself. My Muslim and Croat clients in Bosnia-Herzegovina survived on something like the opposite rule. What was done to other Muslims and Croats could and would be done to them, so what was said happened was taken by them as having happened. If they had waited to see for themselves that the Serb army was coming, instead of relying on hearsay that it was coming, they would likely have been exterminated. Hearsay was not only reliable enough to take action; taking it as true of the matter alleged often made the difference between life and death. When a community is subject to group-based inequality, of which genocide is an extreme, such that what happens to one group member may happen to any other, hearsay may be the most reliable evidence there is, if you are going to live to be a witness.

This does not mean that hearing about a rape is as reliable evidence concerning that rape as having seen it or having been subjected to it. Apart from the fact that being subjected to rape is often tacitly treated as producing subjective bias, rather than information and expertise as well as up-close first-person reliability, this example serves to raise the contextual question of how much of evidence law—including crucial notions of relevance and burdens of proof—is predicated on the notion that group experience as such does not exist, hence builds in dominant group experience, the members of which are more likely to have the power of individuation. How much does ignoring group experience as valid ignore how inequality constructs legal concepts of reliability, making collective experiences of subordinated groups incredible, as well as assume a uniformity of experience across (and within) inequalities that conditions of inequality refute? What would it do to teach evidence law by asking "to whom?" on the basis of sex, race, class across the board and in combination?[28]

One could go on to family law,[29] labor law,[30] tax law,[31] corporate law,[32] wills and trusts, legal ethics,[33] and many other conventionally defined legal subjects. In teaching the law of property, ownership of people—slaves and women—in diverse social forms might be more centrally considered.[34] You get the idea: basic principles need scrutiny in light of women's experiences of gender inequality. International law needs it as well.[35] On another level, women have a special stake in the infusion of international and comparative law within and across the legal curriculum. Women are a transnational group, existing in all societies with a diverse experience of inequality that crosses national boundaries. At the same time, as the discussion of jurisdiction intimated, women have rights, actual and potential, under international law and in the international system that they do not yet have in national systems—a realization that opens crucial avenues for advocacy and creativity in curriculum as well as practice.

Finally, in light of the long but still unsettled experience of clinical education in U.S. law schools, it is not original to say that the relation between legal education and law practice could use rethinking. Students in the United States still learn how to practice law largely from law firms and judges. Perhaps this is how it should be; perhaps not. This fact is related to the comparatively marginalized status of clinical legal education within law schools; clinical teachers, who are often women, tend to have lower status on faculties. The idea seems to be that they are contaminated by mucking around in a real world instead of inhaling the thin air of ideas. Apart from being injurious in itself, this is a destructive attitude to convey to students who are about to enter the practice of law themselves. Too, women practitioners often make creative conceptual contributions to law precisely because they are closest to women's most urgent problems. Perhaps some of the insights from women's lawyering, applied, would transform clinical education.[36] The theory/practice split inherited from male dominance has not served women conceptually or practically. I doubt it serves legal education either.[37]

III.

Consideration of the place of feminism in legal education must include concerns of process—the how as well as the what. Women have historically been excluded from legal education as well as from the rest of the legal profession. The fact that so few women are professors of law, still, particularly in the higher reaches, means that, despite real improvements, women who teach law remain tokens. We experience a vexing combination of presence and absence: exaggerated attention combined with near total invisibility, seldom seen but always center stage.[38] Many self-censor, trying to please authority that remains male. This survival response often means that women stifle their voices and genius and never do their best work. Most abandon women's issues in order to be perceived as serious; some neither say what they have to say nor survive in legal academia. The related comparative silence of women students in legal education is pervasive and well documented.[39]

Less well documented is sexual harassment of law students by other students and faculty members, and what happens in such cases. The perpetrators are almost never held accountable, and if so rarely in public, while the rumors that hurt their targets almost always get out. It is impossible to think and learn under these conditions. In part because individual students come and go and the faculty remains, faculty tend to be more institutionally valued as individuals than students are. Also because they are gone after three years, students have group amnesia. Perpetrators gain access to an ever-young crop to prey upon while their victims cannot know what is happening to them because they have lost their history.

The so-called Socratic method is still widely used in legal education in the United States. Socrates was a great teacher. His method, premised on knowing what one knows not,[40] sought truth through dialogue, exchange among intellectual equals with varying levels of information and experience. What passes for the Socratic method in law school is more often a humiliation ritual of adversarial interchange predicated on "guess what I'm thinking." At its worst, the process embodies all the vices of inequality. Students are motivated by fear; infantilized, they learn the opposite of respect for their own thoughts. In this tacit curriculum, law students are schooled in hierarchy, taught deference to power, and rewarded for mastering codes for belonging and fitting in. By imitation, as in the military, they learn to inflict the same when their chance comes. Conflict and confrontation modes of teaching and learning are particularly inhospitable to women's development. I personally think that their enforced masculinity and hazing psychology is unhealthy for young men's education and independence of mind as well. Studies have shown that the impact on women students of these experiences can be crushing,[41] presumably regardless of the intentions of the faculty, many of whom know that hierarchy is hostile to freedom of thought. Abusive teaching needs to change.

I have a short list—the more I think about it, the longer it gets—of what it will take to make feminism real in legal education.[42] Feminism will be real in legal education when gender literacy is a requirement for everyone in their own subject, an essential part of doing what they do well.[43] When women are no longer marked on law faculties. When women and women's points of view and experiences and those of all excluded groups are represented and respected in texts and in class. When women students speak up with a comparable ease and presumption of place and entitlement to take up public space that men students do (and when there are no more vicious impossible-to-convict explicit rape hypotheticals on 100 percent exams). In addition, it will be real when students are taught that most everything they do is on one side or another of a real social divide that includes sex, with material and differential consequences. When listening to clients, and responsiveness and accountability to them, is taught in all courses and informs all legal analysis of the case law that is created from their lives. When women faculty, staff, and students are no longer sexually harassed in law schools, and when something serious is done about it when the few are. When there are as many men secretaries and librarians as women, and they are paid a living wage, and as many women faculty members and deans as men. When men, too, make tea and coffee for everyone, childcare is available on site, and everyone has and uses family leave. And when women's intellectual and personal integrity is not something that has to be chosen at the price of a life as a legal scholar—in other words, when it no longer takes courage to be a feminist in the legal academy.

TWENTY-TWO

On Academic Freedom:
From Powerlessness to Power

I wish this speech was out of date. Instead, since 2002, the trajectory of this issue has continued in the direction criticized: the attempt to use academic freedom to crush rights for students resisting racism and misogyny. The lecture series of which it was a part was created because of a reversed configuration of power and powerlessness. In 1954, the University of Michigan suspended then terminated two tenured professors, and suspended then reinstated a third, for their refusal to give testimony to a group from the U.S. House Committee on Un-American Activities. After unsuccessful attempts at amends to the three from the Regents, the Senate Assembly in November, 1990, passed a resolution deeply regretting "the failure of the University Community to protect the values of intellectual freedom" in 1954, and established the annual University of Michigan Senate's Davis, Markert & Nickerson Lecture on Academic and Intellectual Freedom.[1] My previously unpublished contribution to this series in 2002, here from a transcript, confronted attempts to use the assertion of academic freedom to protect sexual harassment of students by professors.

When he observed, in asking me to give this lecture on this crucial subject, that much of the literature on academic freedom is "preaching to the choir," Ted St. Antoine was right. Those who write it are generally academics, tenured, and think they are free. So it is a form of self-dealing; surely, not many are against it. Let's say that this literature is not the most robust example of the critical thinking that the notion of academic freedom was created to protect. The subject could use more examples of academic freedom in discussions of it.

The core principle of academic freedom centers on safeguarding freedom of thought. But complacently, in my view, it proceeds on the assumption that academic freedom and intellectual freedom are one thing: if we have the first, we have the second. The basic view seems to be that, unless interfered with from the outside, the academy is free, and safeguarding the academy's freedom safeguards freedom of the intellect, freedom of the mind, freedom to think. Seldom considered is whether any element of the opposite might also be the case: whether academic freedom, as culturally ingrained, socially invoked, academically defended, institutionally practiced, legally deployed, and legally protected, functioning as it does to insulate the academy from external accountability or even transparency in many instances, might—by and when functioning as it is designed to function—fail to serve intellectual and political freedom, and even in some ways affirmatively obstruct it. How do we know that the university axiomatically safeguards it and the government always stands to threaten it?

As a tonic to the often cloying self-congratulation and self-righteousness that pervades a literature paved with platitudes and pieties, I will begin by observing an overlooked paradox. Evaluated from the standpoint of the values that justify it, academic freedom is both under-used and over-used. Under-used, it is seldom practiced, meaning actually deployed as a shield from the enforcement of orthodoxy, because academics so seldom question orthodoxy. Their work more often defines the orthodox, and—including in the name of academic freedom—enforces it. The appeal to academic freedom is also over-used. Here can be found a discernible shift in the center of gravity in reported and unreported cases invoking it. Increasingly frequently, academic freedom is wielded as a sword against students on the basis of their sex, sexuality, race, and ethnicity. Students assert their equality rights; universities oppose them in the name of academic freedom.

My thesis here is that, as a guarantor of intellectual freedom, academic freedom is often not being used as it should be, for the purposes that its original goals support. And it is increasingly being misused as it should not be, for ends far from its original goals. To develop this, I'll trace a shift from its original invocation *against* power to some of its more recent uses as an instrument *of* power, *for* the powerful. This shift parallels larger developments in the law of the First Amendment, of which academic freedom is, legally speaking, a "special concern."[2]

The original purpose of academic freedom was to protect those who challenge the power of orthodoxy and the orthodoxy of power. Built into the cornerstones of liberalism, the familiar Millian "search for truth"[3] and the Miltonian notion of liberty as founded on freedom in the pursuit of truth,[4] increasingly built on the notion of tolerance for diversity of views, it did serve this purpose in the original academic freedom cases during the McCarthy period and the Red Scare, when the legal status of academic freedom was first enshrined.[5] In those cases, the principle took root in dicta to become less than a freestanding First Amendment right but more than just a policy norm. It was during that period that the events took place that inspired this lecture series.

The concrete factual setting for entrenching academic freedom included experiences like those of Tom Emerson, my teacher and friend.[6] It was born when the interests of people without power, specifically workers, were articulated and spoken for and about by teachers and scholars pursuing their vision of the truth in and outside classrooms, sometimes taking a position against the exploitation of the working class through the dominant economic system, and sometimes just being said to have done that. Thereby, they incurred sanctions, sometimes negatively life-changing ones, by universities and states—those who had more power than they did. In eventually disallowing these kinds of sanctions, academic freedom was recognized as a legal right to the extent that it is. As Justice Brennan, writing for the majority in *Keyishian*, said in dictum:

> Our nation is deeply committed to safeguarding academic freedom, which is of transcendent value to all of us, and not merely to the teachers concerned. That freedom is therefore a special concern of the First Amendment, which does not tolerate laws that cast a pall of orthodoxy over the classroom.[7]

The other dimension of academic freedom recognized in the early cases was the value of individual free expression of ideas, especially, the Court said, in the social sciences.[8] The Court also reiterated in *Keyishian* that "[t]he Nation's future depends upon leaders trained through wide exposure to that robust exchange of ideas which discovers truth 'out of a multitude of tongues, [rather] than through any kind of authoritative selection.'"[9] Academic freedom protected diversity of thought. The "multitude of tongues" strand was strengthened by the *Bakke* plurality's recognition of academic freedom as the legal basis for affirmative action, allowing schools to take race into account in selecting among qualified students in educational admissions.[10] Academic freedom, in this instance, was used for equality-promoting purposes.

Academic freedom's evil twin has grown up next to these positive functions. Consider the extent to which universities have become bastions of orthodoxy, including and while affirming that they are bastions of freedom of thought and models of the search for truth. This orthodoxy is not imposed by law but is reinforced in large part through the doctrine of academic freedom itself, including its legal practice, entrenching academic exceptionalism and exemption from external scrutiny. This produces part of the paradox of academic freedom: many people who could and would most use it seldom have it, and those who have it seldom use it.

On my observation, orthodoxies are seldom challenged in the academy because they are not allowed to be. Conformity and consensus are enforced. Uniformity of thought on the fundamentals of fields—in this I suspect my own, law and politics, which have been at the core of the Supreme Court's concern for academic freedom, are not unique—is policed by the grading of students, by hiring committees, and by tenure determinations, to cite a few major techniques of gatekeeping. It is termed merit. This is how authoritative selection is done in fields with trends that, again in my fields, bear a remarkable resemblance to trends and fashions in media, politics, and the world at large. One way to test this proposition in the United States is to ask: where *did* the left go? And when?

Paradigm smashers, and in some cases even paradigm questioners, are told they don't know what they're talking about. Instead of saying that they don't agree with certain scholarly work, teachers and committees say it is not good work. This is not to say that every time teachers and committees say work is not good, it is because it is paradigm challenging and they don't agree with it. It is, rather, to point to a systemic reality that is so built in and pervasive and taken for granted that it is virtually invisible, and little publicly questioned or even consciously recognized. By design, to ensure its freedom, we are told, the academy has to be unaccountable to anything but itself.[11] In democracies, among social institutions, only the family otherwise operates like this. Beware the parallel.

It is arguable that as long as one's intellectual views remain within a certain consensus that is virtually never questioned—examples are the sanctity of the First Amendment as interpreted and of sexuality as currently lived, related fundamentalisms—and as long as your work doesn't challenge the settled social distribution of power, especially as long as you do not mess around in the real world and there are no uncomfortable practical implications in what you think, you are perfectly free to think whatever you want. You are even free to say it. In my observation, keeping disagreements narrow and shallow rather than broad and deep, marginal but competently done, preferably highly competently done, is lavishly rewarded. Pursuit of questions outside or beneath the consensus or with practical implications for the distribution of power can be viciously punished.

It is no news that there are crushing pressures for conformity in academia. It's a common observation that almost all original contributions, far from being welcomed in most fields, have at some point encountered very heavy going for their proponents.[12] But it may be news that academic freedom supports rather than counters this, that one function of academic freedom amounts to silencing dissent through exclusion and threats to one's livelihood, not to mention denigration and shunning. That is, if your work crosses the line from the stimulating to—heaven forfend—the controversial, particularly if it raises hard questions without answers that can easily be implemented without making real change, especially if you lack powerful constituent backers already in place in the academy and a supportive built-in conventional cohort, and if your work undermines myths that keep the dominance of socially dominant groups in place, the more so if it engages the real world in a practical way that could change things, your career as an academic is in trouble. Big trouble.

This is only to say what most academics know but few will admit in public. It is not to say that this is all that happens in academia, or that all original thought is ruthlessly crushed, or that academic freedom is a pure shibboleth. Rather, it is to say that this does happen, and its happening is precisely what academic freedom, as institutionalized, guards, rather than guards against.

Academic freedom, then, is the freedom exercised by academics to decide who will be free to be an academic and what, within the bounds and bonds of academia, will be freely considered. If your work is rejected in the academy, say, based on widely repeated lies about its content, or bigotry towards you and your work that is trumped up by members of society who have a lot staked on defaming what you have to say and need to destroy it and your credibility to save their own status or profits, good luck, especially if you have no powerful built-in conventional constituency that watches your back. It can help a little to do it historically, because at least that is over, or to do it in places far far away in cultures the consensus regards as other, where those whose power is threatened are beyond arm's length. But it only helps a little; frequently not at all. Stakes are guarded there, too.

Of course, there are exceptions to this, due mostly to luck and patronage by exceptional powerful individuals who, it turns out, believe in the ideals of academic freedom more than in its norms as more commonly practiced: people who are willing to expend at least some credibility to act on those ideals. These people are rare and threatened. If they do it once, they are unlikely to do it twice. The risks they run, the blowback even they face, and their exceptionality highlight the backdrop reality I am describing.

Legally, discrimination is an exception to some legal deference to academic decisions. In 1990, the Supreme Court ended a series of cases in which academic freedom was asserted to preclude access to evaluations leading to tenure rejections challenged on grounds of sex or race-based discrimination.[13] When the Equal Employment Opportunity Commission (EEOC), investigating charges of discriminatory tenure decisions, asked to access peer review materials, universities argued they were protected by the right to academic freedom under the First Amendment. The Supreme Court rejected their argument, adding to the few notable instances in which equality claims have been found to outweigh First Amendment ones.[14] Had the universities' academic freedom argument carried the day, it would have become impossible to effectively investigate race or sex discrimination claims in academic employment. They are hard enough to pursue as it is.

Academic discrimination claims, which actually are almost impossible to win, are no substitute for academic freedom working the way it's supposed to work, either. Discrimination cases have to be brought on a group ground that does not so far include bias against the politics or content or angle of vision of scholarly work. Or sometimes—this is the real dirty laundry—the bias against some scholarship is based not even on not understanding it, but on not having read it. (That Michigan is *known* for reading the work should tell you something.) Academic freedom should be a guarantee against this, but it usually is not. And there is little or no recourse otherwise, particularly given that academic settings repel troublemakers.

In this context, only certain kinds of views are regarded as being political in the sense that academic freedom protects. Feminism, for example, is not generally considered political in the protected sense,[15] although some of us consider it a politics. Nor is discrimination against feminist work considered anti-woman, hence a form of discrimination based on sex, although a couple of cases have tried to broach this.[16] At the same time, feminism is not regarded as having the intellectual legitimacy of being nonpolitical, as one methodology or philosophy to be assessed in the academy based on, say, its explanatory power or the scholarly merits of its deployment. Rather, feminist work is often dismissed as being merely political. So it is too political to be considered scholarly but not political enough to be protected as a politics. It also has little established constituency as a field or within most fields. It is often maintained in the literature and case law on academic freedom that academic decisions should not be reviewed by judges,[17] because judges might tend to protect points of view with which they are sympathetic, and not protect those they do not find congenial. Seldom is it said that academic decisions themselves may not be free from this tendency, a tendency that appeals to academic freedom insulate from scrutiny.

The empirical reality here is unlikely to readily produce hard data, being difficult although not entirely impossible to research for obvious reasons. So one story is going to have to stand for many. One of the most original, analytically and intellectually brilliant and inventive minds I know was being interviewed for a legal teaching job in what some call the meat market, the American Association of Law Schools (AALS) job fair. He mentioned sex inequality in the context of a discussion of rape, drawing a parallel with lynching. His interviewer opined sanctimoniously that the difference between sexism today and racism under slavery is that relations between women and men are "built on love." Not missing a beat, my friend responded that actually, on the contrary, slaveholders of yore would have found that rationale for male-female relations to be highly congenial to their views of black-white relations. Needless to say, there was no academic job offer—not then, not ever. Some of the most interesting writings on law I have ever read lie in this man's drawer, as he practices law, brilliantly. Who can even imagine what else he might have written? Count him among the academy's structural unemployed.

Academic freedom is typically defended as necessary to prevent academic work from being censored, usually by the state. There is no vibrant strain in the academic freedom literature on avoiding the self-censorship that makes aspiring academics parrot orthodoxy to get and keep academic jobs. Keeping governmental officialdom out works to some degree, no doubt, and the aspiration is a good one. But who would know, as it is so seldom put to the test. What about academic officialdom? My own observation, again of my own fields, is that almost no one who *has* academic freedom seems to think thoughts, or say or publish them anyway, that challenge the structure of power or the orthodoxy in their fields. What people do tends more to uphold, rationalize, and justify that structure and orthodoxy. In other words, the assumption that protecting academic freedom protects freedom of thought is far short of the mark when it comes to how academic work is actually censored.

In the academy, being too challenging, too original—the phrase "prematurely anti-fascist" comes to mind—what is its equivalent now? Telling too much of the truth so as to expose the naked hand of power and its interests, calling things finger-pointy descriptions like male dominance, white supremacy, capitalism (I repeat, where *is* the U.S. Left? Did all these people really just disappear with the collapse of the Soviet Union?), going too much against the grain, especially against views embraced by the mainstream media—which has taken over much of the function of credentialing the intelligentsia that the academy used to exercise—this is the danger zone. Calling out power makes well-trained academics reflexively uncomfortable, and they certainly are not in the academy to be unsettled.

So aspiring young academics, not being stupid and having survival firmly in view, learn through observation and exposure to consistent patterns of indulgence and deprivation to gravitate in other directions. More bluntly, the most perceptive and creative minds are repelled by the strictures of universities and run screaming in any other direction. To law firms; believe it. To, yes, business, institutes, the creative arts, journalism, publishing, even government. Courts have been more receptive to my work sooner, more responsive to the new ideas in it, than the academy ever has. While courts are off adopting or implementing it and thinking through the questions it raises, a good many academics are still looking over their shoulders to see whether other academics are going to take it seriously, meaning whether they can afford to be seen reading it or citing it without denigrating and distancing qualifiers.

If you think merit overcomes all of this in the marketplace of ideas, consider that intellectual work is also effectively censored when competence in challenging established ideas is threatening to the self-image of the established. That is, censorship happens not only by the familiar discrimination of having to be twice as good to get half as far, but also in a form less spoken about: punishment by ostracism, the better you get at what you do. Ideally, to be good enough to be noticed, but not so good that you're threatening, is the point. I submit it is impossible to walk that line and think any thought worth thinking. Put yet more directly, if you question precepts that are basic to the structure of power, particularly if you are a member of a socially subordinated group, there is special punishment reserved for you for being good at it. Academics do not want you around, a good many of them, because you overshadow them and they can't control you. One can be unemployed a long time this way.

This form of prison-guarding keeps women and people of color in particular—note their continued underrepresentation in the upper reaches of academia[18]—contained and shut down in subtle but potent ways that get inside your head to a degree that most of us never realize, far less able to effectively combat. There is nothing in the theory of the marketplace of ideas or the literature on self-censorship, far less the famous "chilling effect,"[19] that has the faintest clue about this deep freeze dynamic. It is a consequence not of a failure of academic freedom to operate, although it certainly is in tension with its high ideals, but of the working of the doctrine of academic freedom as it is supposed to work, by keeping the academy impenetrable and unaccountable. In this respect, as in others, self-regulation does not work.

Tenure is justified as a bulwark for academic freedom, so academics can pursue truth. Yet few orthodoxies are ever seriously challenged, especially by the tenured. Might this be because the tenure process deselects for challenging orthodoxy as a precondition for receiving it? Put narratively, people often don't say what they think, or do the work they most want to do, in order to get good grades, so they can enter academia. The grading process is completely insulated. Don't even go there. Its insulation is called academic freedom. Then, people don't say what they think in order to get an academic job, that is, to be approved by the guardians and gatekeepers of the field. And to be published. Publishers also don't want to publish what makes them uncomfortable, especially those who do it for money, who think if they don't like it, other people won't like it, so they won't buy it. Typically, academic publishers ask other academics if a given manuscript is worth publishing. If the work to be evaluated calls into question the evaluator's own work, especially if it does so very well, what do you think they are going to say? Then people don't say what they really think in order to keep an academic job and be promoted. Then they don't say what they think in order to get tenure in an academic job. Then once they have tenure, and have academic freedom, voilà, they can finally say what they really think. By this point, a good many people don't even know how to think anything other than what will be approved by power, because that is all they have ever had any practice doing, having spent years fitting themselves into existing boxes and walking these very thin lines. In other words, the deepest violations of academic freedom happen before you ever get it to exercise.

One fundamental aspect of this picture was once acknowledged in passing in a typically smug formulation by Ronald Dworkin when he observed that academic freedom, compared with other free speech rights, is "less clearly a right, because no one is morally entitled to the status which brings that extra protection."[20] As usual, eliminate the term moral and you have the same point. That is, being in a position like his is a privilege, not a right, meaning it is for the privileged. This hardly calls up the absence of constraint that "unfettered expression"[21] is supposed to invoke. The upshot is that academic freedom is very often simply not there for the people who need it most, when they most need it, because other academics are exercising it over them.

Academic freedom, to sum up this part of the analysis, is the freedom to be academic. Only those in the higher reaches of academic status have it. You can only be one of the people who have it, if those who are one say you are one too, in a way that the norm itself insulates from review. Unless you're within the magic circle, to enter which often comes at a high price of conformity to orthodoxy, you have no academic freedom to exercise. Thus, it is rare that anyone who truly needs academic freedom has it, and that anyone who has it truly needs it. In other words, it's far from democratic, can work at times affirmatively to stifle the search for truth, and is a lot more academic than free.

On this analysis, academic freedom functions more in line with the rest of the First Amendment than is usually recognized. Just as the First Amendment guarantees from official suppression only the speech that is socially powerful enough to be expressed, those who are silenced by academics exercising academic freedom not only have precious little recourse to equality law or due process law in most instances, but neither academic freedom nor the First Amendment more broadly helps them. On the contrary. In other words, you have to first get what the law supposedly guarantees you, in order to have its deprivation be considered a violation of your rights.

While academic freedom is off not promoting freedom of thought in ways that it should be—even as there is this whole underside to the academy where intellectual freedom is urgently needed and nonoperative—there is another site where academic freedom is being vigorously and muscularly asserted: as a defense to student claims of discrimination in sexual harassment cases. If academic freedom is underavailable to those who need it, at a point that is very close to its original purpose, it can be found becoming overly available for a purpose very far from its original one: to be exercised against those with less power within the academy.

The legal picture is that through the sixties, seventies, and eighties, academic freedom was at times used to defend student speech against restrictions by schools.[22] Since then, although cases remain that claim academic freedom in its original form—more of these may arise as the security environment of the so-called war on terror picks up steam—in the nineties, we saw a shift in the center of gravity in academic freedom cases to situations in which students claimed they were sexually harassed by professors in class.[23] The professors they accused claimed that the sexual statements were protected both from student claims and university processes siding with the students, or even investigating those claims, by the professors' First Amendment right to academic freedom.[24]

The larger legal context for this confrontation is unsettled. The law on what teachers can say in class has as yet no definitive Supreme Court ruling. But given its existing rulings on the general topic and decisions in lower courts, this debate over sexual harassment, including in class, walks into a legal discussion that is framed as follows. We who thought from *Keyishian* et seq. that teachers had academic freedom to teach in schools what and how we want have essentially been relegated to a status similar to that of those who think the First Amendment gives them the freedom to speak in the press: nice idea, legally naïve.[25] When the Court said "our nation is deeply committed to safeguarding academic freedom, which is of transcendent value to all of us and not merely to the teachers concerned,"[26] we somehow thought that included the teachers concerned. And when the Court described the classroom as within "the marketplace of ideas,"[27] we did not think it meant that teachers and their ideas were to be bought and sold in classrooms by universities.

Come to find, after the 1977 case of *Mt. Healthy v. Doyle*,[28] which protected some speech rights of teachers from firing, the possession of the protected rights—the ones who own the speech—are the universities. Some violation of the speech of some teachers is actually allowed. The Third Circuit articulated this bluntly: "we conclude that a public university professor does not have a First Amendment right to decide what will be taught in the classroom."[29] The Eleventh Circuit, in a suit for a First Amendment violation by a public university professor against his employer for restricting the extent to which he could proselytize his Christian religious beliefs in class, found that the public university's restrictions on this professor's in-class speech "implicated First Amendment freedoms."[30] One would think. That is the good news in the case from the First Amendment standpoint. The rest of the news is, when the university and the professor disagreed about the content of the courses he taught, the university legally was given the final say in the dispute.[31]

Given the relative absence of legal protections for in-class speech by public university professors, it then becomes all the more striking that in cases in which students claim sexual harassment by teachers in class, a good number of the professors are found to be protected by academic freedom for those statements. Consider three reported cases—reported cases stand for many that never get anywhere near courts—two in which academic freedom won, one in which it lost. *Silva*, in which it won,[32] became a distorted media cause célèbre.[33] Silva was a college writing instructor who used fairly explicit sexual language in class. In one instance he paralleled sexual intercourse to focus in writing, saying: "Focus is like sex. You seek a target. You zero in on your subject. You move from side to side. You close in on the subject. You bracket the subject and center on it. Focus connects experience and language. You and the subject become one."[34] To summarize his parallel as we might have in the sixties, you fuck reality to write about it. Since then, we have had reason to consider the sexes that his description of the writer ("you") and the written-about tend to fit, and how much it sounds like stalking deer. Silva also discussed a vibrator in the context of metaphor,[35] and made sexualizing comments to specific students outside of class.[36] The court found that the university's application of its sexual harassment policy to Silva's classroom speech "was not *reasonably* related to legitimate pedagogical purposes of providing a congenial academic environment."[37] Which I simply find incomprehensible. On the vibrator point, the Court said it wasn't sexual,[38] as to which they are sadly uninformed.

The university's application of its sexual harassment policies and procedures to sanction Silva were found to violate his academic freedom, as defined and protected in his AAUP tenure contract.[39] The case was not appealed. This becomes particularly interesting in light of *Bethel*, a Supreme Court case in which a student who used an extended sexual metaphor in what the Court described as a "lewd and indecent" speech could be suspended for disruptive conduct without violating the First Amendment.[40] Finding the pervasive sexual nuance in the student's speech "plainly offensive," the Court said: "By glorifying male sexuality and in its verbal content, the speech was acutely insulting to teenage girl students . . . [and] could well be seriously damaging to its less mature audience."[41] Some of the students were, um, "bewildered" by the speech.[42] *Silva* and *Bethel* are hard to explain together without noticing the respective location in the power hierarchy of the legally unprotected student speaking in *Bethel* and the legally protected teacher speaking in *Silva*.

An outcome similar to *Silva* occurred in *Cohen*, another faculty-student case in which, in the court's sanitized rendering of the facts, we learn that students complained of "the sexual nature of [his] teaching material and his frequent use of derogatory language, sexual innuendo, and profanity."[43] Among other things, Cohen told his class that he wrote for *Hustler* and *Playboy* magazines and read some articles to the class.[44] He repeatedly focused, the court said, on "topics of a sexual nature," used "vulgar terms," and (law professors take note) played "devil's advocate" in discussing topics such as obscenity, cannibalism, and consensual sex with children.[45] On the testimony of students, the college found that his "sexually oriented teaching methods" violated the college's sexual harassment policy.[46] The Ninth Circuit, however, in a weird legal move, found the sexual harassment policy vague by First Amendment standards as applied to Cohen. The policy defines sexual harassment, among its terms, as behavior that "has the purpose or effect of unreasonably interfering with an individual's academic performance or creating an intimidating, hostile, or offensive environment."[47] This language is verbatim from federal regulations[48] and has been quoted approvingly in U.S. Supreme Court cases.[49] Cohen's behavior was permitted on what is essentially an equitable estoppel theory: that he had been doing this for years.[50] Because of what the court called "a legalistic ambush" of Cohen—is it odd for a court to make an epithet out of applying the relevant law to someone?—the Ninth Circuit found his First Amendment rights were violated.[51] I guess someone got around to applying law for the first time to behavior he had become accustomed to getting away with for a long time. Then they were told they couldn't.[52]

Standing in contrast is *Rubin v. Ikenberry*.[53] In a class on elementary social studies, Rubin inquired about celibacy and preference for husband, taught about love making and birth control, and spoke of cooking breakfast in the nude.[54] He observed one female student was smart "for a woman."[55] Rubin asked a student if she would marry a paraplegic "with no vital functions from the waist down" and then polled the class on their opinion; remarked that if he were king, female teachers would daily go on a canoe with a drunken sailor on a moonlit night; called Indian women "stupid enough" to follow some of the customs described; and joked that teachers would make good prostitutes because they encourage their students/customers to "do it again and again until they get it right."[56] He addressed his female students as "Babe," and expressed unconditional love for one of them.[57] Rubin argued that his teaching style treats his students as "serious, open-minded contemplative seekers after wisdom."[58] He said he knew some of what he said was sexist but—in perhaps the final recourse of scoundrels these days—said it was meant as "irony."[59]

Based on the students' grievances, the school found Rubin had committed sexual harassment. He argued that his classroom speech rights were violated, chilling his speech and imposing political correctness.[60] The court invoked academic freedom as judicial abstention: not to interfere in the determination of the university. Where did this go in the two prior cases? Now academic freedom means that the university gets to make its own determinations, not that Rubin gets to say whatever he wants. In *Silva* and *Cohen*, the university's determinations were completely overridden in the interest of Silva and Cohen saying whatever they wanted in class.[61]

On substantive inquiry, the *Rubin* court found no First Amendment violation because Rubin's comments did not constitute "a matter of public concern,"[62] a central legal issue in this area. The ruling distinction is that schools are permitted to control speech that is part of employment, such as teaching; that is, the academic freedom belongs to the school. Speech made as a citizen on matters of public concern, within limits, is First Amendment protected, even for employees.[63] In

Rubin, the court found his comments "exceedingly remote from the First Amendment's concern with protecting 'socially valuable' expression."[64] So can we conclude that students can be found injured in a way that could restrict Rubin's academic freedom only if what he said was intellectually and socially trivial? For those of us who think that sexuality is serious and political, although Rubin's treatment of it exploited, rather than exposed and explored, these features, what he said was, by this standard, far from lacking in public concern. Which does not make what he said socially valuable. It certainly does not make it harmless. It also does not make it outside the course of his employment. But the alignments in this concept are peculiar, to say the least.

A deeply unsettling aspect of these cases is that the equality interests of the young women students are totally ignored by these courts, even when the claim is sexual harassment, which makes the behavior being adjudicated a potential violation of Title IX, the law against sex discrimination in education.[65] The equality dimension is ignored both when the universities lose, even though they have the obligation to guarantee an equal learning environment, and when they win—when they were backing up their own students claiming an equality violation. It is hard to grasp why. Equality is an affirmative claim the students have in this context. Surely the legal basis for their claim is relevant.[66] Instead, when grounds for discrimination—a/k/a "viewpoints;" since when is being a woman a point of view?—are used as the basis for restricting harassing behavior, including verbal harassment, the First Amendment takes up all the air in the room.[67]

For our purposes here, note that academic freedom is being asserted as the right of teachers verbally to sexually abuse students, potentially in violation of their ignored equality rights, and in some cases winning. This happens even though the teachers in these cases have fewer First Amendment rights, as public employees in public universities, than they would have in other settings. But *this* is a right they have. Specifically, teachers having a right to do what they enjoy doing through words sexually as men to young women students is conflated with, and protected under, the academic freedom mantle to teach what and how they choose. Even when the latter right is already a limited one. Apparently the teachers in these cases can't tell the difference between these two things, and the law that governs their assertion, and sometimes courts can't either.

Notice the shift in the hierarchical location of the assertion of academic freedom. Both in process and in substance, it has moved from bottom up to top down. It has moved from a claim by teachers to be free of silencing by hierarchical superiors of institutions and states to a claim by teachers to be free to silence their students in and outside class. Substantively, it has gone from an act of standing up to power by speaking out on behalf of the silenced and dispossessed to an act of abusing power by talking down and intruding on and shutting up those who have less power than you do. The assertion of academic freedom has gone from the powerless to the powerful, from powerlessness to power.

One cannot think freely and learn—that is, have intellectual freedom, freedom of mind—while being sexually harassed. So these are not necessarily inconsistent values at all. But in the proud line of standard-bearers of academic freedom, it is a long way from Davis, Markert, and Nickerson[68] to Silva, Cohen, and Rubin. The *Silva* and *Cohen* decisions were framed as if the issue was the state against the teacher, in line with the original tradition and the original hierarchy, when in fact it was the teacher against his students. It is hard to say that the district court was wrong in *Rubin* in standing up for his students against what he asserted as his academic freedom to impose on them sexually in the guise of educating them. The relative lack of protection for public employee speech makes it all the more remarkable when a university like New Hampshire responds to student complaints of sexual harassment in class, as it did in *Silva*, and the public employer's decision by the university on behalf of the students is found to violate the teacher's academic freedom. The students have no academic freedom to be free from sexual harassment; the university has no academic freedom to remove a sexual harasser; in fact, it seems that a sexual harasser has academic freedom to sexually harass, so long as he does it in class. If you compare this with the invalidation of a statute mandating teaching creationism if evolution is also taught,[69] and cases finding that teachers have no right to indoctrinate students in their religious beliefs in class,[70] it appears that you can't lead your students to what by your lights is eternal salvation, but you can intrude and impose on them sexually for your own pleasure in the here and now.

My own view is that the standards for public employee speech[71] are miscast when applied to teacher classroom speech, even in a public university, and that, at the same time, the law of sexual harassment in the workplace is miscast when applied to student-teacher relationships. To begin with, it seems to me bizarre that the government can restrict your speech as your employer in ways it could never as your sovereign. I think, in general, that teachers should have stronger speech rights, including in class,[72] but that the equality rights of students should also be stronger in the educational setting, and not regarded as per se viewpoint-based by virtue of opposing race or sex discrimination. Among other considerations, the requirement that speech be of public concern to be protected—meaning outside what we do when we teach!—is off the point as well as elastic and ham-handed when applied to teaching, where human minds and scholarly and intellectual exchange and integrity and growth, not goods and services, are the products. And the validity of appearing loyal to the employer or the government is at best attenuated.

Sometimes ideas are disruptive, but the existing standard is not sensitive to the requisites of anyone's academic flourishing. At the same time, a sexualized environment that would never be judged hostile in the workplace might very well interfere with a student's ability to learn and find their own path. The workplace standard of employment is not sensitive enough to faculty flourishing and the workplace standard for sexual harassment is not sensitive enough to student learning. Students are not guaranteed the equal benefit of an education, Title IX's distinctive mandate, when they are sexually aggressed-against in class.[73] So as to the law, the real speech issues and the real equality issues both lie beyond where it has gone. It also seems to me that, certainly for students, in this area, equality is closer to protecting the original goals of academic freedom than the First Amendment is.

One final illustration. Not long ago, I was told that an eminent professor of English literature typically began his signature graduate course annually with: "Will the ladies please cross their legs? Now that the gates of hell are closed, we may begin." This has it all. Academic sexual harassers tend to harass their own professional way: the psychologists mess with your mind, the musicians feel your breathing, the literati leave you insinuating little quotes, the philosophers argue you into tight corners, the coaches and dance instructors correct your physical form, and so on. This professor points to genital markers of female sex in a literary way. He moves you into his position at the front the class and says, essentially, I'm looking up your skirt. It is your responsibility to block the male gaze. The sexualizing comment heightens gender visibility and intellectual erasure at the same time, both spotlights and negates a sexual body part of a woman before "we" can begin to think about the subject at hand without being threatened with eternal damnation. To bracket a female sexual body part as a predicate for the entry into literary discussion is a fancy way of saying that women as such, with their sexual equipment, don't belong in that discussion. It effaces female sexuality by reducing women to it, defining every woman in the room in terms of it. It is an amazingly powerful and economical way of putting women in a sexually subordinated place at the threshold of scholarly inquiry. Do you think women in this class are more or less likely to feel at home in the academy? Will they feel free to challenge literary orthodoxy? Who can stand up with their legs crossed?

Whether or not this comment would be found protected or prohibited employee speech, of public concern or trivial, sexual harassment or not (by itself, it would not, under workplace standards), is this what academic freedom is for? It and worse is the kind of thing that academic freedom is being asserted to protect, in and out of court.

At this point, it helps to return to the original principles of the AAUP from 1940:

Institutions of higher education are conducted for the common good and not to further the interest of either the individual teacher or the institution as a whole. The common good depends upon the free search for truth and its free exposition. Academic freedom is essential to these purposes . . . Academic freedom in its teaching aspect is fundamental for the protection of the rights of the teacher in teaching *and of the student* to freedom in learning.[74] (Emphasis added.)

I don't think students have freedom to learn in an environment like those in the *Silva*, *Cohen*, and *Rubin* classrooms, any more than they do in a class that teaches as fact socio-biological so-called proofs of the inferiority of some racial groups or of the female sex.

So speech seeking protection under the banner of academic freedom has gone from speaking for the powerless to speaking against the powerless. In this, it parallels the more general trend in the First Amendment over the past same three quarters of a century, which has gone from defending those who spoke out on behalf of the dispossessed and silenced, to defending not only media giants and other corporate entities, which are neither dispossessed nor silent, but the so-called speech of the Klan, the Nazis, and the pornographers—that is, defending in its expressive forms the silencing and subordination of already subordinated peoples on behalf of structures of dominance.[75] Our challenge is to reshape academic freedom so it extends to the people who need it and would use it, those largely kept out of its charmed sphere so far and for so long, and to reclaim it from those who would use it to deprive others of the values and opportunities that, rightly understood, it exists to protect.

TWENTY-THREE

Engaged Scholarship as Method and Vocation

For better and worse, law perforce engages and affects its world, making butterfly effects to some extent inevitable. It is my view that legal scholarship must therefore embrace rather than pretend to detach from this engagement. After Gerald Torres was elected president of the American Association of Law Schools (AALS), I was requested to speak on the method of my work at a Plenary Session at the annual meeting in 2005. This broader reflection on the enterprise of legal scholarship resulted.[1]

For the engaged scholar to talk about engaged scholarship is something of a contradiction in terms. A scholarship that is engaged is a scholarship of doing it, rather than talking about doing it: scholarship as action. The difference between doing it and talking about doing it is the difference between scholarship that enjoins us, say, to attend to race in feminist scholarship—which it may be an action to say once—and addressing issues and solving problems from a Black feminist perspective, which can be done for at least as many lifetimes as it has been ignored. This difference is not one of voice or subject or politics, ultimately, although all can be involved, but one of stance in relation to substance, and ultimately one of substance itself.

Having somewhat repudiated my task in order to frame it, let me start this comment on what we all do by asking, if "engaged scholarship" is not redundant, what about "scholarship" doesn't already mean "engaged?" If adding "engaged" adds something—as I thought something was added by subtitling *Feminism Unmodified* "Engaged Discourses in Life and Law" in 1987, a battle lost with the publisher[2]—what does it add? Under prevailing academic norms as practiced, focusing here on legal academic norms, there is tension between the two terms. Engagement pulls in one direction, scholarship in another.

Scholarship as such, its epistemological roots in the nineteenth century's separation of knower from known, fact from value or opinion, and law from politics,[3] is ideally imagined to be, in a word, disengaged. Its disengagement is believed to conduce to objectivity, meaning beginning from no preconceived position, taking no sides, pulled by no consequence or advocacy necessity, making no judgments of value. The value dimension of the problem has been extensively ventilated in moral philosophy in particular and has especially concerned liberals who pursue the "good." My opinion is that bad views are so not the problem and good views are so not the solution, particularly where women are concerned.

Being more interested in the prior question of "what is," i.e., the real, I will focus on the dimension of knowing it that separates knower from known. Its traditional goal is finding "truth," ultimate verity; its narrower purpose is creating authority by producing scholarly work that is universally acceptable and indisputable, qualified neither by subjectivity (the bugbear of the nineteenth century) nor relativism (the challenge of the twentieth). Under this standard, involvement in the world of one's subject, especially its social world, is widely supposed to be constraining and contaminating rather than a source of knowledge and foundation for insight. Experience, rather than helping you know what you are talking about or serving as a source of insight, is seen to produce partiality, bias. It gets you dirty. To be on a side is thought to make the work slanted, nonscholarly—in law, a brief, not an article. Exposing the experiential roots of academic work is a common means of challenging its accuracy and reliability: its authority. Since law is a form of power, created by authority and creative of authority, this cognitive situated dimension is an especially sensitive one in legal scholarship.

To be engaged in the sense I mean—conscious of location and clear about position, open to the world of the known both going in and coming out, grounded in substance—centers on having and affirming direct involvement with the reality of the subject matter. Doing this violates the traditional academic *Grundnorm* of above-it-all/out-of-it-ness. Most with-it scholars won't admit adhering to it when bluntly stated, even as they respect it like an invisible fence. Many would own it if more congenially coded, though. Say: from the Greeks forward, method is a way to truth, which since Descartes has become both a stance and technique of scholarship that serves as a shortcut to reliable knowledge and helps prevent error. In one contemporary instance, take Paul Kahn's (unacknowledged) reinvention of Karl Mannheim's free-floating, socially detached observer[4] in his requirement of "[d]istance from one's own beliefs,"[5] and the related imperative to "abandon the project of law reform" as methodologically necessary for reconstructing legal scholarship.[6] As Kahn puts it, "This imaginative act of separation, of creating a distance between the subject and his or her beliefs, is the model of understanding that I want to offer in place of the normative, practical reason that has informed both law and legal scholarship."[7] He is advocating what is actually an entrenched element of the status quo's intellectual maintenance as if it would be a positive or even radical change.

In my experience, one can tell that disengagement, as a tacit model for what is aimed at, is being enforced when it is said that your work is not scholarship, it is just politics (or, if your field is politics, it is just journalism; or if your field is journalism, it is just activism), or you are not committed to scholarship or do not belong in a university. Not hiring practitioners, including the rule of thumb that a person is ruined for the scholarly life if they practice law for more than a couple of years, is another way. Not considering work in practice as bona fide "professional activity" for purposes of tenure, promotion, and merit salary increases in law school employment is another. Kahn could not be more wrong in his claim that law reform and law practice are the central projects of today's legal academy. Actually doing something in the world of law—making legal change being proof that you had intercourse with the real world much like pregnancy proves you had sex, both being a bit of a public embarrassment—can be virtually disqualifying for the serious scholar in some quarters. In our time, the resolution of the tension in the legal academy over whether the study of law is an intellectual discipline or an arm of the legal profession has tended to be resolved in favor of the desirability of legal academia being its own world, at least in its upper reaches. At the core of the tension is a stigma of appearing to be on a side—as in, resembling the adversarial legal system.

It is not news that people tend to conform to the shape of what they are rewarded and respected for: the process is called socialization when we study it being done to other people. Nor is it news that this tendency shapes the mind and reproduces itself through what and how we teach, including by example. There are of course many exceptions to the norm sketched; opposition to it has a long and strong history among scholars who respect and engage in practice. And it may be shifting. Surely it is increasingly acknowledged among philosophers, especially where social scholarship is concerned, that objectivity as a norm is not only inaccurate as description, it is incoherent as theory, naïve as sociology and psychology, and unachievable as method.[8] There is even doubt as to whether it is desirable to try. This is not to embrace relativism, cognitively meaning that anything and its opposite can be equally accurate, but to admit the overwhelmingly obvious: scholarship doesn't come from nowhere.

The scholar's choice of topic, because it is about something rather than everything, is a choice of agenda and priorities based on some ranking. Because it is done by a person situated in a context, speaking a language, with a history and a culture, professional training, and personal experience, employing concepts and following habits of mind, it is intrinsically a social endeavor. It has ideas, usually, and ideas do not come from nowhere. In a materialist perspective, they are based in reality; in social disciplines, that makes them based to some degree in the same reality being studied. Trying, in order to strike the pose of disengagement, to deny scholarship's antecedents in intercourse with reality does not make it come from the stork.

Once it is realized that point-of-viewlessness is an illusion, that Paul Kahn's "separation" is not possible and clinging to the illusion of it promotes an unconsciousness that is treacherous and even delusory, the question becomes not whether scholarship is engaged or not, but *with what* is it, in fact, engaged. Kahn's scholarship, for example, is engaged with the male liberal academy. Tilting against a notion of "practical reason" that is scarcely practiced, it seems unaware that the hermeneutical theory of law's culture he calls for—looking into the roots and meanings of the rule of law as such—has been going on over here in the land of engaged scholarship for some time.[9]

Engagement with women's lives has produced new scholarship on women across the academy, including in law. Its embrace of engaged method, the openness to and visibility of that engagement within the work, has made its method—its relation to reality—appear new. Maybe it is. Its consciousness of its relation to what it studies may be what is most new about it. Certainly its substance is new. But it should be recognized that men scholars have always been and still are engaged with certain things and in the lives of some people—rape law, underpinned as it is by the treatises of Blackstone and Hale, is not nearly unenforceable for nothing—just not these things, these people, in *this* way.

Where social topics are concerned, choice of topic, angle of vision, approach, and methodology are variously affected by the life of the scholar, otherwise termed personal. This is almost trivially true, but it opens onto something more contested and profound. In my experience, people feel your biography offers insider information on your work if you write about some subjects, say discrimination or sexual abuse. But this is no more true of these subjects and no less true of others, occupational choice research suggests, although it may be more obscure in antitrust or the UCC. If Lasswell's insight that much of politics involves the displacement of private problems onto public objects is true of politics,[10] it is no less true of political science. If not everything the scholar thinks can be reduced to individual biography, what they have been through and seen is variously relevant to what they know or want to avoid or what they have a genius for illuminating or what field they choose to spend their lives tilling. Whether they will say what they know is another matter. That something real shapes the work is the at-once denied and almost trivially true point.

In other words, what Jerome Frank and the other realists observed of legal decisions—that they are made by humans in context—is no less the case of legal scholarship about those decisions.[11]

Underlying even the most abstractly-presented thesis—perhaps most especially that one—is the elementary fact on which the sociology of knowledge is predicated: life motivates scholarship, social circumstances shape it, even as we reach beyond our limits. This dynamic has heightened visibility in highly contentious areas, but it is not confined to those areas. We all know instances. Someone who adopts a child of another nation or ethnicity becomes an expert on transcultural adoption. Desire to marry one's same-sex partner generates new discrimination theories. Pornography users create First Amendment scholarship that ensures they can keep using it. A parent who molests a child develops law to stop suits against parents for child abuse. Someone abused as a child litigates against abusers or tries to prove there is no such thing as repressed memory. The relation between experience and scholarly position, this is to suggest, is not always linear, far less always clear. That Heidegger was engaged with the Nazi party and wrote *Being and Time* does not make the relation between that life and that text a simple one.[12] Whether one's scholarly work is propaganda is, I think, ultimately less about voice and method (although demagoguery and lies, even with footnotes, are scholarly flaws) than it is about substantive content. For present purposes, it is enough to observe that it is thought crucial in the academy that only the work part of scholarship, not the life part, be visible. The common advice to young women not to do scholarship on women, certainly not to make it the center of their professional work, offered with their best interests at heart, is a case in point.

If the dichotomy between engaged and disengaged scholarship is a false one, devolving into the question of what the scholarship is engaged with, that does not mean that there is no such thing as scholarship doing its best to be as disengaged as possible. This is *alienated* scholarship, fleeing as far from anything real as it can, strenuously appearing committed to nothing outside itself. These days it often seems driven by style and posture for its own sake and theory for abstraction's sake, alternately pervaded by a sense of no one at home or navel-gazing self-involvement (what might be described as only the author at home). Such scholarship, I hazard, is often engaged with impressing an academic in-group or with career promotion, especially with getting tenure. It is driven more by its relation to an academic social world and its byzantine rules, and anxiety about them, than by its topic. If its ostensible subject matter is quite incidental, the work is far from truly disengaged; it is merely engaged other than with its subject. To the existentialist's question, "What is your project?" it answers (as hilariously parodied in Kingsley Amis's *Lucky Jim*):[13] to be seen to do successful academic work as the academy defines it. Successful scholars in this vein say more and more about less and less, until finally they've said everything about nothing.[14] Defending this orientation, Stanley Fish described it as proceeding from "[t]he near-sighted situatedness of those who remain within the borders of the academy."[15] I have never heard it said that this stuff does not belong in a university.

Put another way, in an irreducible epistemic sense, all scholarship, especially on social topics, is ineluctably participant observation, it is just a question of what it is participating in when it observes. Engaged scholarship is far from uncritical of its determinants; rather, instead of denying or pretending to repudiate them, it consciously takes them on board as not only awareness of limitations but also as an opportunity for access to knowledge. Once you see that the pose of the less point of view the better, the less visible the better, is a shared illusion, you see that that illusion has a politics.

By the norm of disengagement, scholarship is most successful when it does not challenge the reality it studies in any basic way. To illustrate by counterexample, feminist scholarship came from women living under male dominance becoming conscious of it and determined to end it. Its view from inside and underneath, far from limiting the work, required that the fish become critically conscious of the water. This challenged the dominant ecology—something that wasn't even supposed to be there—a tall order for method and career. As there was little to no scholarship for this departure to base itself on, this work *had to be* engaged with its world to have anything to study. And it has had (no coincidence) a serious struggle establishing itself as academically legitimate—a challenge that, in my view, has largely swamped it over time, making it more disengaged by the day. But feminist scholarship is, in actuality, no more engaged in the methodological sense than standard male-dominant scholarship is; it only appears to be. Indeed, it only appears to be coming from an angle of vision to the degree that it stands out from the angle of vision of the social and scholarly background by contrast.

The norm of disengagement demands that the scholar leave the status quo of the subject fundamentally untouched, as Paul Kahn recognizes when he advocates the necessity to abandon the task of legal change. This *is* a relation to reality. For that feeling of absence of authorial presence that gives legal scholarship its special authority, it helps to affirm the arrangement of power as it is, which is why it is easier for some political persuasions to appear to be disengaged than for others. It helps if the ideological paradigm being used reflects the ideology that shapes the subject the scholar is investigating.[16] Law reform work can be engaged but, from the standpoint of academic norms, it preferably does not challenge the lineaments of social power that underlie the law it would reform. Being Kuhn's paradigm worker, tinkering at the margins, helps immeasureably.[17] The norm of disengagement thus becomes a tool for disciplining the unruly academic or silencing opponents. Its voice of presencelessness, the voice that never speaks an ordinary language—the language of social reality—and cannot be distinguished from anyone else's, submerged in the philosophical "we," enhances that authority that keeps academic work from being marginalized or dismissed. This also makes it rare in the academy "to find," as Robert Frost once put it, "[o]n any sheet the least display of mind."[18] He was watching a mite crawling across a page.

Another indicator of legal scholarship in the putatively disengaged mode is the pains taken to appear to spring only from the law of, rather than the life of, its subject—meaning the doctrine on the face of the text, preferably in a commentator or bystander role. Better still is when its context is other legal scholarship. This contortion is often painful to watch as well as doomed. Law, the subject of legal scholarship, although written in books, exists in constant and intimate engagement with its world: social reality. Among academic subjects, law is uniquely alive in this way. It is words in power; its texts live in social space, ordering and reflecting structures of power, even lying there on the page. Unlike other literature, real heads roll directly depending on what is inscribed there. This makes legal scholarship not an intellectual discipline in the usual sense; legal scholarship is not to law as literary scholarship is to literature or historical scholarship is to history or political science is to politics. Law is always already real. Whenever you deal with it, including in scholarship and teaching (even, yes, at conferences), you are taking some part in that reality. Because law itself *is* engaged, legal scholarship is always already engaged. This does not make bias more inevitable than usual. It does make disengagement epistemically impossible, the illusion of its pursuit as a high calling arrogant, and the self-conscious embrace of engagement appropriately humble as well as productive, despite the fact of it being ineluctable.

As a result, while professors of English do not usually write novels (at least not very good ones), and historians as such rarely change the course of history (regrettably), and political scientists do not generally run for office (no loss, I suspect), law professors not only consult confidentially with judges and provide them judicial clerks who draft their opinions; they become judges and legislators with some regularity. And legal scholarship is cited in legal decisions (at least by the Supreme Court) and sometimes ghosts them in that plagiarism we call victory. Barbara Johnson can with some plausibility say in the literary context, "It is a grandiose fantasy of omnipotence to fear that by forgetting reality, a person might damage reality."[19] But for a judge or a legislator or a lawyer to forget reality is incompetent, even vicious. Legal professionals, including legal academics, indulge a fantasy of impotence if they think that, when they forget reality, they do no damage. I'm not at all sure he is right about this, but Stanley Fish can plausibly say of literary scholarship that, "Politics does not need our *professional* help; texts do."[20] Now really: what is law, text or politics?

For these reasons, it takes affirmative effort to try to kill off legal scholarship's intrinsic engagement with legal and social practice. The tip of this intrinsic iceberg can be seen in civil law countries, where commentaries of scholars are used to interpret law, and in the doctrine of customary international law, which predicates the universality of a legal norm (a practically powerful conclusion) on the practice of states, opinions of jurists, and the work of scholars alike. Most legal practitioners in the United States do not read law reviews, although they ransack them on occasion for bits of some use for strategic deployment—most often (and ironically in light of my argument) when they are deliberately trying to change the status quo and have no more presentable authority at hand. But my point is larger: legal scholarship participates in historical and social life whether legal scholars try to or want to or not, not only as grist for its mill, but inexorably through what it does. Read Weimar legal scholarship if you doubt it. In our realm, to attempt to be truly disengaged is to strain to say so little that one's scholarship weighs nothing at all on the scale of the legal quotidian. What an ambition. Imagine not only what is ossified but what is lost because of it.

In conforming to the disengagement norm, diligently emptying one's scholarship of signs of interest in real life also helps, encouraging the substancelessness of so much legal scholarship, a pose that is all too successful much of the time, an unreality that has very real results. The effort recalls a story one philosopher told about another, a rational choice theorist, who was agonizing about whether he should take a job at another institution. The hassle of moving, his wife's feelings, his children's school, his future prospects, what to do? Mischievously, the first philosopher, modeling the second's scholarly theories of rational choice, said, "Hey, Tom, it's easy, just write down all the positives in one list, all the negatives on another, see which list is longer, voilà." To which guy two snapped peevishly, "Come on, Dick, this is serious." Disengaged scholarship, you see, affirmatively needs not to take its subject seriously, meaning not to treat it as you would treat something that was real to you. Far from impossible, this is all too possible. It spells much academic success and siphons off much mental energy. But what must the world be like for this knowledge of it to be possible, one wonders? What is legal knowledge by this definition? In a mortal context, the question it raises is, why bother?

Disengaged scholarship, in the sense I have been discussing it, seeks to cover up who and what it is engaged with, its real project and raison d'être. The project of denying that one's work has a project, particularly when its driving force is reflexively academic, comes from and results in a solipsism that, in my view, undermines more than enhances its fairness and balance, which are accuracy norms. Being serious gives you every incentive to be accurate. Disengagement twists work by imperatives that have nothing whatever to do with what it purports to be about in ways that, deflected by dead-handedness or fancy footwork on the surface, are hard to get at by design. But disengaged scholarship is no more ultimately possible of realization than is disinterested adjudication. The tilt of the work—inevitable even if it says next to nothing, since it leaves the world of its subject alone—is just made less rather than more accessible and transparent. This way of approaching the subject is arguably responsible for the utter contempt (on my observation unique in degree if not kind, compared with other professions) in which most practitioners hold most legal scholarship, particularly the high-end sort, one defining characteristic of which is its ever-shrinking audience. This is not at all the same as disagreeing with it. It is my impression that both this kind of work and practitioner contempt for it are becoming more rather than less prevalent.

Practicing the law of the subject of one's scholarship is, in my view, indispensable to engagement. The impulse of law and economics, however abstracted its intellectual apparatus can be, is fundamentally highly engaged with the real social world, although one keeps wanting to urge its practitioners to get beneath their assumptions and closer to the street. My work with Bosnian women, embodied in litigation, prosecution, and adjudication, is generating new definitions of and accountability for rape, new understandings of its place in conflict, and new models for victim participation in defining and vindicating international human rights.[21] It all emerged from women close to the ground in war and genocide. Andrea Dworkin's and my work, which proposed to legally empower people abused through pornography, emerged directly from their experiences and moved the theory of a subject stuck for centuries.[22] By contrast, much legal scholarship, from the doctrinal to the postmodern, makes an effort to be as distant from the real world of the law's lived roots and impact as it possibly can. Its above-the-fray stance defines the fray as akin to the medieval rabble, the perceived low-lifes who, however fashionable as objects of study, remain, along with the grittier and more unpleasant realities of their lives, decidedly unfashionable as members of the faculty. By distinction, from corporate litigation to state department advising, the breath of real air blows through engaged work.

For life to make new law, forge new understandings of law's meanings, and create new theories, the life of the problem and the life of the law of the problem must both be engaged, in practice, directly. This method is risky in a hostile professional atmosphere but the upside gains can be big. The legal claim for sexual harassment as sex discrimination, for example, emerged from immersion in women's experiences of sexual abuse in hierarchical contexts, about which nothing was being done. It became a law school paper that was used as the basis for rulings establishing the claim, which turned into a book analyzing the reality of the experiences and the theory behind the rulings that the paper had participated in creating.[23] So now there is a law against sexual harassment and (oh yeah) theory books too. Notice, the trajectory was not to think up an idea from reading books, scan the horizon for victims to use to test it out, and then to write about the results of test cases brought. It was being picked out to listen to victims to address an urgent problem that had yet to be solved, to have to create the theories that adequately responded to their situation because existing theories did not, and thereby to create legal change and new legal theory.

To connect these points to conventional politics, it is my observation that, in the legal scholarly world, liberals and conservatives tend to relate differently to reality and to ideas. Conservatives are more open to reality; liberals are more open to ideas. Conservatives are more interested in reality so are better at seeing how things are. Liberals are more interested in thinking about whatever it is they think about (usually the ideas of other liberals), so tend to be better at that. Methodologically, conservatives are thus grounded but stuck in the mud, and liberals soar in flight but are unable to land. In the terms of this talk, conservatives tend to be characterized more by engagement with the world, legal and social, as liberals have become ever more engaged with the academy. Hence the liberals' children, the postmodernists.[24] And the hiring practices of most top law schools. And many elections. But I digress.

Engaged scholarship at its best is both grounded and theoretical, actively involved in the world of its subject matter, and for that reason, able to think about it in fresh ways. The work may be "relevant," or involved in "law reform," the typical catch phrases, or not. Submersion in the real-world reality of its subject makes it better, deeper, broader as scholarship; its walk on the street teaches what no book yet does. On the cognitive level, to be engaged in the sense I mean is to take the inevitability of location and the self-conscious immersion in reality as a source of knowledge and inspiration rather than as a barrier to thought and action. Being shaped by the social reality being studied—being consciously up close and personal with it—is its method. Paradoxically, just as claiming the particularities of the self who works can make the work less self-involved, immersion in the constrictions of the world can give the work a wider vision. At this point, it becomes unnecessary to discuss feminism as method. It works for over half of humanity. Wouldn't you think it might work, self-critically, for the other half?

Grounded theory of this sort is involved with the world of its subject as well as with creating the law that refers to and emerges from its world. From practice in at once the Marxist and legal senses of the word, you know what is real, because you know what the world was like before your piece of its practice was there. The discipline of reality born of engagement, including responsibility for consequences, sharpens the faculties, a bit like knowing you will be shot at dawn. The self-imposed uselessness of disengaged method, the superiority of its Olympian pose, offers a false freedom, and it is predicated, I will again hazard, on a fear of mattering, which cannot be avoided for fear of mattering. The pose of disengagement protects ignorance, ensures aridity, and virtually guarantees that nothing much, surely little new, will come from the legal academy—not to mention its destructiveness to diverse creativity. Grounded involvement, I am saying, is where real theory comes from, where new ideas are running around on the hoof, as well as how you know what you know and what you don't know, hence how you come to have anything worth saying.

I am not saying that the only test of value in legal scholarship is value in use. I am saying that there is real value, including scholarly value, in being real. A key methodological difference between scholarship that embraces its engagement, and scholarship that keeps trying to disengage from the sticky grasp of the real world, can be seen in contrasting a 1920 poem by Robert Frost with another written around 1976. You know that one by Robert Frost where he kneels at wells and sees only his own reflection? Then one day, just when he thinks he actually sees something down there at the bottom of that well, a drop ripples the water. "What was that whiteness?/Truth? A pebble of quartz? For once, then, something."[25] Did he see it? Was it really there? At least he knows that his image, before, wasn't "something." Something, for once, was out there.

About all that, with the law in mind, this other poem by legal scholar Gerald Torres says this:

> *Why the World Ain't Obvious*
>
> and Robert Frost
> gazed upon the well
> water—
> he sat and saw or
> thought he saw or he
> sat and thought he thought
> about seeing or
> he

> thought about others who
> thought about him
> seeing and
> spied a pebble
> smooth white stone
> with breeze
> the quiet rippled pond
> disfigured his face.[26]

Frost's project here was seeing his own reflection framed by ferns and sky, reminding one again of how un-new the American postmodernist self-involvement is. Gerald's project was to see through the water to the stone at the bottom. He observes the world seriously, not as a pretext to look at himself. When you are serious, neither the looker nor the looked at, Heisenberg-like, stay the same, and you know it. You are engaged. This does not prevent error; nothing does (I'm sorry to be the one to tell you). It does not end debate or guarantee that your politics will be my politics, but why should it? Of course I think reality is on my side, but whether it is or not is a question of substance, not reducible to stance. Because the knower is inseparable from the known, the world ain't obvious, but it sure exists out there and will change the shape of your face.

Gerald's poem—this rebuke to solipsism, this pithy forerunner of post-postmodern method, this spur to and embrace of practical action, this reminder that whatever goes on in your head, that rock, this breeze, is out there, the breeze changing how you can see the rock but not whether it is there, this recognition that the world engages you whether you face your engagement with it or not, this orientation, this inspiration, this challenge to keep looking deep into that well—has been sitting, since it was written, on my desk behind a shard of slightly stained glass from the Yale Law School's front door.

TWENTY-FOUR

Defying Gravity

It was literally incredible for me to be awarded the Ruth Bader Ginsburg Lifetime Achievement Award from the Women's Section of the American Association of Law Schools (AALS) on January 3, 2013. Among the several hundred law professors who attended was one man. The quotations from experience recalled verbatim in this transcript as delivered are from Yale, Stanford, UCLA, and a past AALS meeting. (Who said them, where, and when was unforgettable. You know who you are.) The song of Elphaba—stigmatized in *Wicked* as the Wicked Witch of the West, who sided with the animals being denigrated and escaped on a levitating broomstick she created after discovering that the Wizard of Oz was not the benevolent all-powerful figure she had believed—captures years of animating spirit:

> I'm through with playing by the rules
> Of someone else's game
> Too late for second-guessing
> Too late to go back to sleep
> It's time to trust my instincts
> Close my eyes and leap!
> It's time to try
> Defying gravity
> I think I'll try
> Defying gravity
> And you can't pull me down![1]

This experience is like walking into some alternate universe. If anything could be more surprising than my selection for this award, standing me next to Ruth Bader Ginsburg—and it could be that nothing is—it is the award itself: by women for legal scholarship and practice, including activism, that "impacts women and . . . the issues that affect women." In a profession that often considers mixing in reality on the ground to be beneath it, here legal scholarship is valued for its impact on the world: women's world.

My gratitude to those who supported this work when it was anything but inevitable could take hours. Doug Rae admitted me to graduate school late and against all odds. Bob Dahl defended me from being kicked out, sent me to his publisher, and advised my dissertation on women's relation to the state. Jim Thomas strategized my fifth application to Yale Law School so it actually got to the Admissions Committee. Bob Stein hired me at Minnesota. Canada gave me a real job and a real listen when the United States wouldn't. Lindsay Waters insisted on first reading, then publishing, the pile of papers ("what *is* that stuff?") that became *Feminism Unmodified*. Lee Bollinger, an authentic First Amendment practitioner, decided to hire me at Michigan. Joseph Weiler, then Chair of Appointments, figured out that the key was getting people to read the work (now there's a concept) and made it happen. Each of them reached out and kept my work for women from being washed away in the tsunami of trivialization, lies, stigma, jealousy, and poverty. This award is their achievement, along with my teachers Leo Weinstein, Bob Dahl, Tom Emerson, and Burke Marshall, who recognized something here and gently and generously nurtured it.

In retrospect, work that impacts women is attributed a curious temporality. We start impossibly post-revolutionary, so radical we can't possibly be taken seriously, then suddenly we're at post-feminism— always too early or too late, ahead of or behind their curve. The individual academic version takes us from "the work up to now is great, but we're not sure where it's headed" until "her best work is behind her" arrives. As we morph from avant-garde to passé, from enfant terrible to éminence grise, now is never our time. This award marks a present moment that has come.

Now that we're celebrating, I'd like us to think together about what it will take to lower the cost for our students and younger colleagues to give their lives to what this award honors. I don't know—only that it will take all of us. I'm thinking of the ones who come to law school on fire with the desire to change the world for women and often reach graduation cherishing the same commitment. To put it bluntly, what will make that no longer academic suicide?

What do we need to do to lower the probability that the Ruth Bader Ginsburg awardee of twenty years from now—when, unfortunately, she or he will still have been needed—will not still have been told that race and sex are "vanity subjects." Or, "we agree that the work you do is at the highest level in the country, maybe the world, we just don't want it done here." Or, observing the record of work in litigation and legislation, "we're not persuaded you're really committed to scholarship."

What will have kept the head of recruitment from opining, in discussing over coffee the emphasis in work on sexual abuse of children, that "the moment that girl is being abused by her father, she has the most power she will ever have in her life." What will change so the chair of appointments, as he sits down with our candidate at what is euphemistically called lunch, won't begin the Greek salad with, "So, now, tell me again just what is wrong with liberalism?" Will the dinner in the dimly lit wood-paneled room with all the heavies someday not feature the Dean repeatedly insisting that a man—ever the hypothetical man—sexually enjoying being diapered and spanked by a woman, must be approvingly exempted from the candidate's analysis? Will it have become impossible for the national meeting to turn our person into a thinly veiled ethical hypothetical for law faculty: "A visit is proposed of someone whose writing is absolutely first rate but contains the most extreme possible views on every imaginable subject. How should you vote?" You all have your own stories.

Granted, some of these topics could be discussed, if discussion rather than "shut up and go away" were their point; the questions have answers, should answers matter. But presumably there is little doubt in this room as to the drift of the sexual politics of these examples, far less the consequences of standing one's ground in such situations. No one should have to survive the resulting years of effective unemployment while litigating path-breaking Supreme Court cases with no library while writing some of the most widely cited scholarship on law at the same time.

My question is: what can we do, what are we doing, to change the dynamic that the more and deeper the truth you tell about women's lives, or (horrors) try to do something about it—especially about sexual abuse, which raises male hackles—the less our profession wants you in the room, far less at the table? Why do so few of us do the work lifted up in this award, fewer still make it central to our legal agenda? With all the women in law school, who have burgeoned, and all the problems of women that need solving, which have escalated, neither pipeline nor progress explains it. Perhaps it is the punishment: the discrimination against taking the subject and reality of women's status and treatment seriously, particularly in the upper reaches of a status-obsessed profession.

Any one of the experiences mentioned could make anyone with a practical bone in her body, far less responsibilities and a survival sense, rethink their direction or at least trim their sails. The shame of such incidents, like the shame of rape, sticks to the person they are done to who exposes them, not to those who do them. The point is to scare and humiliate, what we in the women's movement used to call to "guard our prison." Along with sexual harassers and pornographers' lawyers in powerful positions, treatment like this continues to flourish in silence beneath the myth of merit hiring in the least transparent employment market on the planet.

This is not only about accountability (but, hey . . .), but normativity. We need to change the hostility, the isolated ghettoization, at best the poisonous jellyfish form of respect that makes all but the most intrepid younger people avoid doing "work that impacts women, on issues involving women," just in order not to be academic road kill. Why shouldn't they spend their lives on technical issues in intellectual property—not, apparently, a vanity subject—instead? They are owed better. And the women of the world are owed their genius.

I do know one thing. If sisterhood is powerful, horizontal hostility is even more so, given the wind of misogyny at its back. We may be tokens but we don't have to be used as tools against each other. This award—by the women's section, for work for women—stands strikingly against this dynamic. If we keep at this, maybe our awardee twenty years from now will have a stellar list of women supporters who were in a position to put out a hand that will be as recognizable a list as my initial one of exceptional men. As a step, maybe we could inaugurate an annual Ann C. Scales[2] Memorial Grit Award: for the person starting out most likely to achieve a lifetime of work that impacts women, to support the brilliance and risk-taking of, say, a young Jane E. Larson.[3]

Defying gravity is a collective project. Survivors of sexual abuse trust me with their pain, or I would have nothing to say or do. My sister the incomparable Andrea Dworkin is always in my soul and by my side. Natalie Nenadic and Asja Armanda opened the world to me. Jessica Neuwirth and I need several more lifetimes to achieve our shared agenda. Kent Harvey has been my best friend on the long road. There are so many more, including Ruth, who broke the waves, Ann Bartow, among those who nominated me for this singular honor, and the award committee who stood up to everything just mentioned and more to choose me for it.

What really matters is our work itself. I inherited my mother's dream and vision of something none of us has ever seen, but is yet somehow there in and around all of us: sex equality. Because we keep working toward it together—and thank you for all you do—it is coming within our reach. We will get there.

V. Toward an Equal Future

TWENTY-FIVE

Rape Redefined

For over forty years in various settings, I've proposed the ideas advanced here, thinking others would pick up and develop or challenge them. As this has largely not happened, a twelve-minute speech in Malmö, Sweden, at Nordiskt Forum on June 13, 2014, provided an opportunity to put them across in a context in which they might be taken seriously. The thousands of Nordic women in that stadium in which, from a couple of minutes in, you could have heard a pin drop, were an inspiration. The later published version that developed these ideas benefitted from the remarkable research and often appalling discussions of the American Law Institute (ALI) process redefining rape for the Model Penal Code in 2015–2016, in which a serious attempt was made to give consent meaning.[1]

Rape is recognized in international law as a "gender crime," meaning it happens to women because we are women.[2] It is a crime of gender inequality. This analysis, partly operationalized in international law, for instance by the International Criminal Court,[3] is not implemented in any country's domestic law. So, what would a rape definition governed by sex equality principles look like?

Rape is generally defined in Western countries as sexual intercourse by force or without consent or both.[4] It is without consent in the UK.[5] It is by force or violence in France.[6] Most U.S. jurisdictions require both: by force and without consent.[7] None of these has a good track record even for reported rapes, which are a small percentage of actual rapes. The conviction rate for reported rapes in the UK is around 6 percent.[8] In France, it is a breathtaking 2.6 percent.[9] The conviction rate for reported rapes in the United States, where most states require some version of both force and nonconsent, is between 12 percent and 25 percent.[10] Especially given that in the United

States about one out of every ten acts of rape or attempted rape is reported that essentially fit the legal definition,[11] this is pretty appalling.

Consent definitions—in which the prosecution has to prove nonconsent—require a woman be believed concerning a sexual fact that is by its nature subjective. *This is why it puts the victim on trial.* Essentially, it attributes victimization to the victimized. It makes the case be about what she was thinking, or what he thought she was thinking, rather than about what he did. It makes rape occur in someone's mind, not by his body on her body.

It is therefore no surprise that, in legal application, consent has been found when women are married,[12] drunk or drugged, repeatedly said no,[13] were asleep, comatose, just seen to be raped by several other men, threatened with deportation[14] or false criminal charges[15] or loss of her job. In legal operation, consent to sex is routinely found in situations of despairing acquiescence, frozen fright, terror, absence of realistic options, socially situated vulnerability, and even death. Prostituted sex is regarded as consensual because it is paid.[16] All this is what consent actually means legally, not mistakes in what it legally means.

The often accompanying standard of mistaken belief in consent means that if the accused is found to have believed she consented, whether she did or not, it is not rape.[17] In societies saturated with pornography, a lead pipe over the head can sincerely be believed to produce consent to sex. This makes it further no surprise that "rough sex" is such an increasingly effective consent defense.[18]

In other words, consent is often found in situations where considerable force was used, building into law the misogynistic assumption that women want to be forced into sex. This is the real meaning of requiring a showing of both force and nonconsent, as prevails in U.S. state laws. The same assumptions tend to be attributed to a gay man when he claims another man raped him. He is feminized, reduced to his gendered violation.

If sex occurred, her consent is typically presumed on the most minimal of acquaintance between the parties. If sex happened, or if a woman had ever had sex before, especially with the accused, consent is effectively assumed. She has to disprove it. It's a social burden of proof women enter the law burdened by. Consent in law is consistent with economic, psychological, and hierarchical threats, so long as physical injury or life are not threatened, for which purpose rape itself is not generally considered a physical injury.

Although the history is unclear to me, it seems that consent as a concept was not originally most strongly developed to apply between two people in civil society. It was given its current dominant meaning in Western liberal philosophy, hence Western law, as the basis for legitimizing the obligation to obey the laws of the state.[19] Even as a fiction,[20] it never envisioned equal parties. It exists to rationalize the exercise of dominant power—the state—over its subordinates—the governed. Applied to sex, he is the government, she is the governed. Whose bright idea was this anyway?

Its purpose is to attribute and justify the requisite obedience of the powerless to the rule of the powerful. It is about compliance. One is regarded as tacitly consenting, for example, to whatever one does not leave;[21] you consent because you are there, whether leaving is a realistic option or not. Silence in sex, as in governing, is deemed consent, not dissent.[22] These assumptions, along with the presumption in the sexual setting that the two parties involved are somehow axiomatic equals—an assumption never articulated far less sought to be justified in theory or law—operate powerfully in sex-unequal circumstances, contrary to its realities, and remain invisible as assumptions under even the best of consent standards.[23]

Attempts to correct for this social burden of proof, the assumption of yes, women being walking consent—attempts women are often seduced by as well—involves adding additional words to make consent mean anything at all, such as full and free, positive, chosen, affirmative, autonomous, unequivocal, freely willed, etc.[24] Look how many words you have to add to make it mean anything at all like freedom. These modifiers can be helpful, but they cannot be relied upon to overcome what consent fundamentally means. Requiring a woman to say yes before sex is rape—and there is a lot of not-yes-saying out there—is not enough. If you can get a woman to suck an employer's penis weekly to keep her job, or to have sex with a dog, I would suppose you can get her to say yes. Pornography is full of yes. "Consensual" is a fallback stand-in for "it wasn't so bad" in societies like ours, in which sex by definition fulfills you, it doesn't violate you, because sex is what women are for.

Fundamentally, it needs to be faced that consent is not an equal concept. It is an intrinsically unequal one, a hierarchical idea that presupposes an actor and an acted-upon—the purported form of power of the acted-upon being acceding to the actor's actions, meaning doing what you are told to do—with no guarantee of equality of circumstance. That it might make sense in a society of actual social equality does not mean that it will get us there, because it silently presupposes that the parties are already equals whether they are or not. It relies on an illusory image of a woman's "agency" under conditions of inequality, as if one can be free without being equal. The corresponding fantasy—one that well-intended, strong progressive women often accept politically and argue for, not knowing what it has actually meant legally—is that if consent is the legal standard, what the woman says, even what she actually felt she wanted whether she said it or not, will be believed and will carry the day, determining in a criminal trial whether sex was rape. This reliance is profoundly misplaced, unrealistic, and impractical.

Apart from the problem of relying for incarceration on a victim's subjective state of mind, including when unexpressed, which can play into racism and has, the concept of consent relies for its social appeal on the assumption that it stands in for desire. This is its credibility cover, but nothing limits it to that. In social discourse, the crucible of its meaning, sex that is actually desired or wanted or welcomed is not termed "consensual," because it does not need to be. Its mutuality is written all over it. Sex women want is almost never described by them or anyone else as consensual, as in, "We had a great hot night last night, I consented."

Although the European Court of Human Rights in *M.C. v. Bulgaria*[25] and the CEDAW Committee in *Vertido v. Philippines*[26] have said that consent is the core of an equality approach, for reasons of principle and practicality, it is not. Far from it. These cases unintentionally endorse the active/passive model of sex and social conditioning to trauma and the acquiescence that goes with it, and call that equality. Under unequal conditions, many women acquiesce in or tolerate sex they cannot as a practical matter avoid. That does not make the sex wanted. It certainly does not make it equal. It does make it legally consensual in most jurisdictions. This is the wrong road. Consent is a pathetic standard of equal sex for a free people.

Force definitions have also been problematic. The main problem has been that they have been largely confined to physical force and typically require an excessive and unrealistic amount of it, often with weapons, in a standard that seems to have in mind a fight between two men.[27] In addition, it tends to require proof of resistance as evidence that force existed, even if the law has eliminated the resistance requirement.

On the view that a rape is about what (usually) a man did, mostly to women and children, sometimes to other men, a useful legal starting point is the *Akayesu* decision from the International Criminal Tribunal for Rwanda where rape is defined as a "physical invasion of a sexual nature committed on a person under circumstances which are coercive."[28] The notable features here are the absence of nonconsent, seen as essentially redundant—coercion is present because consent is absent—and the exclusive use of coercion, which can be circumstantial as well as physical. The definition is on the force side but is not limited to physical force. In international criminal law, when a nexus with war or genocide or campaigns of crimes against humanity is established for a sex act, such that sexual assault is weaponized, those circumstances of coercion make it arguably unequal, vitiating consent of any operative meaning. Which is why it isn't in the definition.[29] In settings outside recognized zones of armed conflict or genocide, "circumstances" adapted to domestic settings of so-called peacetime could include psychological, economic, and hierarchical forms of coercion—which, in limited ways, some jurisdictions already recognize in the sexual assault context.[30]

Survivors of prostitution often cogently describe it as serial rape,[31] let's say sex unwanted for itself that is coerced by multiple circumstances of inequality.[32] With this in mind, consider the international definition of sex trafficking, the destination of which is prostitution, from the Palermo Protocol (2000).[33] It prohibits the use or threat of use of force or other forms of coercion, abduction, fraud, deception, or abuse of power or a position of vulnerability for purposes of sexual exploitation. And, where any of these means is used, the consent of a victim "shall be irrelevant."[34]

So, here is a proposal to redefine rape. Suppose we combine the best of the international definitions to redefine rape domestically as "a physical invasion of a sexual nature under circumstances of threat or use of force, fraud, coercion, abduction, or of the abuse of power, trust, or a position of dependency or vulnerability."

Then it is essential to *explicitly* recognize that psychological, economic, and other hierarchical forms of force are coercive, including age, mental and physical disability, and other inequalities, including sex and gender, and that states like drunkenness and unconsciousness are positions of vulnerability. Inequalities would be recognized as a form of coercion when mobilized to force sex in specific interactions. As in the international context with war and genocide, for a criminal conviction, it would be necessary to show the exploitation of inequalities, their direct use, their nexus with the act, not merely the fact of them.

And, where any of the listed means is used, the consent of the victim is irrelevant.

Apparently it is difficult to think about sexuality in equal terms. The Swedish model of prostitution is educating the world that paid sex is forced sex, engaging in world leadership by setting a standard for what violence against women includes.[35] This proposed definition of sexual assault in terms of circumstances of coercion could do the same. Let's think together about it. "It all starts somewhere."[36]

TWENTY-SIX

Restoring Institutional Accountability for Educational Sexual Harassment

Once the argument that sexual harassment is a form of sex discrimination was won as a matter of law, so that in theory sexual harassment in education was covered under Title IX, cases started to be brought on live facts in real numbers. The legal attempt to avoid responsibility shifted to whether and on what terms institutions should be liable for it. When the U.S. Supreme Court exempted schools from accountability as long as they did something more than nothing in each instance,[1] schools realized they were effectively off the hook. The old rule that sexual abuse is prohibited by law but winked at in reality was, in effect, reinstated. Lack of responsiveness returned in most educational environments. This testimony, previously unpublished, was one attempt to reconfigure the law of institutional liability to hold schools accountable for their own environments, by changing the liability standard to promote the educational equality that schools that receive federal funds are legally obligated to deliver.[2]

PROPOSAL:

To amend Title IX to provide as follows:

Section 1. All education institutions and programs receiving Federal financial assistance must exercise due diligence to prevent sexual harassment and all other forms of sexual violence in education, protect its targets and victims, and punish its perpetrators, including by promptly investigating all reports however informal and by providing effective remedies for all resulting harms.

Section 2. A private right of action is granted in the United States district courts for equitable relief, compensatory and punitive damages, and reasonable attorneys' fees for all failures to adhere to Title IX of the Education Amendments of 1972, including the standard in Section 1 of this amendment.

RATIONALE:

The liability standard of "deliberate indifference," invented to govern sexual harassment cases by the Supreme Court in *Gebser*,[3] was predicated on a reading of Congress's choice to structure Title IX through a contractual framework under the Spending Clause.[4] Inappropriate for an equality law, especially one so affirmative as to guarantee "the benefits of . . . any education program" free from sex discrimination,[5] this flaccid liability standard in practice has seriously undercut Title IX's effectiveness in the sexual harassment area, drastically reducing institutional incentives for voluntary compliance, harming individual students and their educational environments with nonresponsive, ineffective, or nonexistent complaint processes for incidents of sexual abuse. It needs to be replaced.

Beginning with *Alexander v. Yale*, sexual harassment has been recognized as a violation of the educational sex equality rights guaranteed under Title IX.[6] In the wake of *Alexander*, many steps forward in policy and culture began to be made as educational institutions reasonably recognized that they faced exposure to substantial liability if they failed to address sexual harassment that occurred on their campuses.[7] The *Franklin* case—in which monetary damages were authorized against a school district that took no effective action against sexual harassment of a student by her coach and teacher—sustained and supported this progress.[8] When *Gebser*, and then *Davis*, subsequently held that schools were not liable for sexual harassment in faculty-student or peer situations unless they were "deliberately indifferent" to the incident,[9] schools relaxed. To avoid a finding of "deliberate indifference," a nominal investigation or a hearing suffices, even if no relief or sanctions result.[10] In fact, the "deliberate indifference" standard creates an incentive for institutions not to know about sexual atrocities, since any indifference can then not be deliberate.[11] With little liability to fear and only conscience to govern, perceiving a low probability of loss of all federal funds, schools effectively have become largely unaccountable once again.

Since 1998, all a school has had to do about sexual harassment, including rapes in education reported directly to them, has been something more than nothing. This may help explain the documented lack of sexual assault response policies, inadequate sexual assault training and response, and underreporting of campus crime statistics to federal education officials found by the National Institute of Justice as of 2005.[12]

"Deliberate indifference" is not an equality standard.[13] It was lifted from due process, embodying a low standard for a knowing failure to proceed. The affirmative guarantee of equal benefit of an education under Title IX calls for a more substantive, more affirmative, higher standard of duty and care than conscious disregard by institutions that receive federal funds, to which attendance by our children is essentially compulsory. Due diligence to prevent injury to equality rights, to protect victims of equality rights violations, and to promote equality, capable of implementation by individual litigants, is such a standard.[14]

Accepting the *Gebser* Court's explicit and repeated invitation to Congress to "speak[] directly on the subject,"[15] this amendment would affirm Congress's intent, as originally found by the Court in *Franklin*, that the private right of action under Title IX includes the availability of money damage remedies for sexual harassment in education.[16] Such an addition to Title IX's existing enforcement tools would supplement the withholding of federal funds (helpfully present if seldom exercised[17]) and the imposing of fines. Strong back-up would thereby be provided to the recent legislative changes passed by Congress in the Campus SaVE Act,[18] building on prior administrative developments.[19]

Although it is essential that victims have access to the federal courts for enforcement, Section 1 of the above proposal could alternatively, as explained by my colleague Diane Rosenfeld,[20] be employed as an administrative guideline in a properly coordinated federal approach.

This proposal has no budgetary implications.

The incentive for educational institutions to address rape cultures as well as sexual assault reports on campus would be restored and significantly strengthened under this proactive provision. It would make real and effective action against sexual harassment a required part of the funding contract between the government and its educational institutions, putting the obligation to provide an equal education in the hands of those with the power and the duty to provide it.

Due diligence places the responsibility where it belongs—on the schools—to end impunity for sexual harassment in their educational environments. May they rise to the challenge.

TWENTY-SEVEN

Toward a Renewed Equal Rights Amendment: Now More Than Ever

The revived effort to give women's equality rights explicit constitutional status in our time would be one of the biggest butterflies ever. Or actually, the efforts over many decades to give women's equality explicit constitutional status is part of an extended butterfly effect that produces ever-building storms. This is a brief introduction to this renewed effort, embodying an updated theory for ERA, reconfiguring constitutional equality.[1] New constitutional provisions are allowed, even expected, to do new things, otherwise why would they be needed? Before we die, women of my generation want to leave an institutional foundation for real legal sex equality to those to come, unto the eighth generation.

The sexes are human equals. Yet women, on the whole, are not men's legal equals[2] or, by most any standard, recognized as men's social equals.[3] The laws that guarantee against discrimination—mainly the Fourteenth Amendment Equal Protection Clause[4] and Title VII of the Civil Rights Act of 1964[5]—have, I argue, gone about as far as they will or can to produce equality of the sexes in life. An Equal Rights Amendment (ERA) is urgently needed, now as much as or more than ever.

The provisions we have can, of course, still be used, including more creatively, in litigation and as the basis for legislation. But the way sex equality has been approached under U.S. law has, I think, essentially run its course. Most of the issues that were the focus of the last ERA debate in the 1960s and 1970s have been largely addressed, in some cases solved, under the Fourteenth Amendment, by executive or legislative action, or through social change.[6] Two major issues that were not central to the prior ERA discussion remain basic in women's second-class status: economic inequality and violence against women. Both the 1972 ERA language, prohibiting discrimination "on account of sex,"[7] and Carolyn Maloney's bill's proposed addition of "Women shall have equal rights,"[8] could, if correctly interpreted, remedy the effective shut-out from the legal system most women still face today on these two fundamental engines of sex inequality in a way that existing law, interpreted as it has been, is intrinsically incapable of doing.

The existing legal interpretation of the sex equality principle guides both its Fourteenth Amendment application, where sex is given "intermediate scrutiny"[9] in the rationality review structure, and its Title VII usage. On my analysis, even if sex was granted strict scrutiny[10]—long the Holy Grail of constitutional sex equality litigation—this approach is not, has not been, and will not provide what women need. Even at its apex, this interpretation applies a form of rationality review. Rationality review with this content, at whatever level of scrutiny, inherently reflects the status quo because the operative meaning of "rational" is "reflects sex as it is." That is, to see if a law or policy is equal, this method looks around at "sex" as it socially exists to see if the distinction being challenged reflects present reality. Apart from the fact that "rational" is not in the Constitution and "equal protection" is, this approach does not grasp that reality may be systemically and systematically sex biased. It is asking the wrong question. The "sex" this method finds is sex inequality, but it is legally considered the sex difference, essentializing sex discrimination. On this logic, the more sex-unequal social reality is, the more sex-unequal law can be, and be considered equal, because the law reflects the reality.

Legal equality guarantees have been in effect in the United States for a long time without producing equality in social life. Suppose that the existing legal approach, predicated on Aristotle's formulation of equality that calls for treating "likes alike, unlikes unalike,"[11] is consistent—determinately connected—with the outcomes it produces or fails to produce. Perhaps, then, it is the approach itself, rather than a failure to apply it, that is responsible for the tenacious persistence of inequality? Most people who need equality aren't empirically "the same" as, or in doctrinal terms "similarly situated" to, those who already have it. The damage of inequality ensures that "difference." Moreover, requiring sameness with a comparator who dominates is inegalitarian, frequently odious, and arguably undesirable, as well as usually impossible. But the result of this approach is that imposed inequalities, reconfigured as unalikeness or dissimilarity based on the damage they do, are treated as, at best, ignored or denigratingly compensated for, in order to try to produce equal results.

The notion that people can be different from one another yet still be equals, entitled to be treated equally, simply does not compute in the Aristotelian equality framework used in U.S. law.[12] Far less does affirmative diversity—treating people alike based on their unalikeness. The point is not that there are no sex differences. The point is that they are virtually irrelevant to sex inequality. Women are not inferior to men, men superior to women; yet that is how the two are socially ranked. Sex itself is neutral so far as inferiority and superiority are concerned. But society is organized (in general, and among other ways) by gender hierarchy: less and more, better and worse, above and below, valued and devalued, with the male (sex), masculine (gender) and men (people) superior, the female (sex), feminine (gender), and women (people) inferior. Sex inequality, as socially organized, is not and never has been based on sex differences but on hierarchical orderings of gender supported by ideological rationalizations that naturalize it as difference, as sex. The resulting theory, turning on sameness and difference, observably resists transforming entrenched hierarchical rankings of material resources and social status that have been systemically socially entrenched. Aristotelian equality—regarded in U.S. law as equality's common sense meaning—has thus not generally been useful in situations in which social equality does not already exist, which is where an equality law is needed.

This analysis explains why women largely already have to have achieved equality before they have a legally assertable claim to equal treatment. It is why existing law, pursuing this method—particularly under the Fourteenth Amendment—works best for men, who are the equal sex, next best for elite women. It works best for those who, usually due in part to some form of privilege such as race and class, have been most able to achieve an exceptional status more similar to more privileged men than to other women. It does not work at all for problems like sexual violence, the victims of which are overwhelmingly women and girls, or yet for reproductive rights. It is also why the existing approach tends to invalidate affirmative action: the use of the classification, especially one that fits the social reality, is prohibited, not the hierarchical disadvantage predicated on it. And when it is permitted, it is stigmatic for those who benefit from it because it is seen as treating unlikes unalike: second-class equality. Combined with the lack of an explicit sex equality guarantee, this analysis explains why the Constitution has neither required nor permitted the initiatives most women most need. It is also why the Fourteenth Amendment has achieved most of the gains sought under the prior ERA: the two adopt essentially the same approach to the equality problem. And it is why existing law has gone as far as it can go, which is not far enough. It has not, will not, and cannot produce equality.

If this approach were not sufficient to make equality unachievable by current law, on top of it are intent requirements.[13] Other than under Title VII's disparate impact dimension—which is in the process of being undermined, nearly demolished, by burden of proof standards, the requirement to specify the exact practice causing the disparity, and any other technique imaginable to make it unworkable—intent under the Fourteenth Amendment, and motive and purpose under Title VII, do not address how discrimination mostly works in the world. The vast majority of sex inequality is produced by structural and systemic, thus unconscious, practices in a context of the absence or abdication of laws against them. Most sex discrimination is done not by people thinking bad thoughts about women, as the Fourteenth Amendment requires for discrimination to be proven, but by people following schemas and routines and habits and biases ingrained for centuries, seldom challenged, and not yet changed. The existing economic market and the present norms of sexual interaction were created when women were chattel who could not even vote. It is unnecessary for anyone to consciously intend anything to keep those biases operative, legally and socially. And even when discrimination is intentional, it is very difficult to prove, because the challenged activity occurred within the mind of the defendant(s), and its revelation as evidence is almost always in their complete control. The invention of the intent requirement under the Fourteenth Amendment, as it has operated in constitutional sex equality law since 1979, and its devastating result for effective redress for most sex discrimination (of which domestic violence is one crucial instance),[14] was unforeseen and unforeseeable at the time the prior Equal Rights Amendment was proposed to be interpreted.[15]

Two key areas—economic inequality and violence against women—were not central to the legal debate then but have come into sharp focus since. When the Equal Rights Amendment was introduced, its companion Economic Equity Act proposed to legislate economic equality as a package.[16] Some of the contents have been legislated; most have not. Doubtless largely also because of the perception that the Constitution addresses state action while economic inequality is mainly produced by (what is regarded as) private action, the Equal Rights Amendment debate was not clearly centered on economic inequality.

The large sex-based pay difference of around one quarter per dollar has remained essentially stable since 2002.[17] Although it has been smaller at certain points in time, that has been largely because men's wages have risen at a slower rate.[18] Women's pay on average remains largely stagnant at around three quarters of comparable men's income and is unlikely to move without further intervention. Most people in poverty are women and their children, with households headed by single mothers being especially vulnerable.[19] Forty-one percent of adult women live in households that are economically insecure at this time, meaning they face falling below the poverty line within the next year.[20]

The cause of a vast amount of economic inequality is the structurally segregated workforce: women remain locked into lower-paying jobs filled overwhelmingly by women.[21] Many women in elite, professional, and blue collar jobs are paid less than their male counterparts and are otherwise discriminated against based on sex,[22] but a substantial portion of the wage gap is accounted for by women doing what is called "women's work."[23] Legally, it is regarded as different work. Gender neutrality, the main standard in the existing standard of constitutional review, will not fix this problem because gender neutrality means same treatment for sameness, on the assumption that this will get women what we need. But women who are segregated into lower-paying job categories are not in the same situation as men. Often, there are few, if any, men there for comparison, and the men who are there are often treated as badly as the women, because the women's treatment sets the standard. Less pay is different treatment for different work.

The rationality review of the Supreme Court's equality jurisprudence, with its gender neutrality, could work in a more equal world. But it will not get us to that world. If the workplace is segregated, producing unequal results—that is, "differences" in work and pay and respect—and that inequality is assimilated with "sex" per se, as if poverty is a sex-linked trait, this legal tool will not produce equality. If rationality is the standard for equality, and rationality is mobilized by seeing if the law reflects the reality, and if the reality is unequal, the law will be unequal too, while meeting the legal equality standard. The unequal status quo is so far built into the baseline of existing equality doctrine that employers are permitted to predicate women's present unequal pay on their past unequal pay, terming this an acceptable reason for accomplishing business objectives under the Equal Pay Act.[24] Put another way, the equal opportunity approach does not address structural inequality.

Childrearing is another major engine for impoverishing women up and down the wage scale, producing the endless "work-life balance" discussion. So is the treatment of pregnancy in the paid workforce. Given the different-treatment-for-differences view of equality, nothing requires accommodation for pregnancy-related needs, such as temporary lighter duty assignments that are available for other reasons,[25] or something as simple as a water bottle to maintain hydration.[26] No paid pregnancy leaves are legally guaranteed, and new mothers often do not receive comparable jobs on return from unpaid leaves, not to mention the subtler discrimination against the possibility of pregnancy. Divorce, a process controlled by courts, also remains a major driver of the mass impoverishment of women in many states.[27] Attempts to address all this by law have not succeeded. Women, especially women with children, are being kept poor as a result.

Providing women equal pay for work of comparable worth is one essential: economic equality in place. Title VII has been interpreted not to require it.[28] Where divorce systematically disadvantages women economically through state action, however legally unintentional, it must be rectified. Pregnancy,[29] although its treatment has been improved by the Pregnancy Discrimination Act (PDA)[30] and will be further addressed by the Affordable Care Act,[31] raises a serious series of issues that affect women's economic status, yet reproduction is constitutionally treated as a "difference" for which different treatment is not considered to be sex based, so cannot produce discrimination. An ERA could give women a fighting chance in all these areas in ways no existing law, or laws based on existing constitutional provisions, have or are likely to.

The physical security issues have a similar structure. Violence against women was for the most part invisible in the prior ERA debate. Rape and prostitution were discussed to some extent but were not fully developed as sex equality issues, nor have they been resolved since. Without additional legal tools, one doubts they will be. Domestic violence vividly demonstrates the prevailing unequal protection of the laws not recognized as such.[32] When the failure to effectively enforce laws against violence because it occurs between intimate partners is brought to the attention of the courts, women are told either that their neglect is not based on sex, usually because it is not proven intentionally so based, or there is otherwise no valid constitutional claim. Women have been shut out of the legal system on this issue. So, since the criminal justice system was not providing it, women decided to try to get justice ourselves through the passage of the civil remedy provision of the Violence Against Women Act (VAWA).[33] We did finally get it passed by Congress: zero tolerance was established for rape and domestic violence as gender-motivated violence was recognized as a practice of sex discrimination. The Supreme Court then invalidated the VAWA—not because violence against women was not sex discrimination, but because Congress assertedly had no authority to pass it.[34]

As things stand now, neither rape nor domestic violence are remotely redressed by law in any proportion to their occurrence. Systemic rape attrition begins with nonreporting: only 9.5 percent of rapes committed outside marriage are ever reported.[35] This happens because women know that their reports of sexual assault will likely not be taken seriously, and they are more likely to be punished than vindicated. Further falloff occurs in prosecution decisions, fewer still result in convictions, fewer yet receive more than token sentences. Depending on the study, 0.1, 0.5, or 5 percent of reported rapes that fall within the ambit of the legal definitions result in a conviction.[36] And there is no relief in sight and no sex equality oversight on this process at all—even though once there is a report to an official, every bit of what happens is indisputably state action. This is massive unequal protection of the laws. It occurs because rape plain doesn't matter under this legal regime. Even as tens of thousands of rape kits sit untested in jurisdictions throughout the country,[37] probably nobody is consciously deciding that women will be raped and nothing will be done about it because they are women and men want to keep doing it, or whatever a showing that this malignant neglect is intentional, constitutionally, would look like. Systematically not caring if women get raped with impunity apparently does not meet the intent standard, far less provably so, because the disparity in numbers sure is sex discriminatory. And it has never been said that rape is not sex based.

A new ERA can be a new departure. An ERA, as a new constitutional amendment, would expand the congressional authority to legislate. Both versions of an Equal Rights Amendment, the original one and the proposal adding Carolyn Maloney's new first sentence to it, have the possibility of being interpreted in new ways. Since so much of the older interpretation has either been achieved by law—the older interpretation being essentially the same as the Fourteenth Amendment approach—or changed by life (we have not been sitting still), here is an opening to go farther. Carolyn Maloney's proposal has as its second sentence the 1972 Equal Rights Amendment: "Equality of rights under the law shall not be denied or abridged by the United States or by any State on account of sex,"[38] a fabulous sentence. Her new proposal has, in addition, a new first sentence, providing that "Women shall have equal rights in the United States and every place subject to its jurisdiction."[39] Women begin the amendment, with the second sentence on "sex" as backup and floor. The second sentence, of course, applies to everybody: men, transgender persons of whatever sex if not covered by the first sentence, on my analysis to gay and lesbian issues,[40] as well as to women for whatever "sex" does to them.

From a legal standpoint, Carolyn Maloney's formulation offers certain additional benefits. Her new proposed text, "women shall have equal rights," addresses a concrete group of people, not an abstract right. It heightens the possibility of guaranteeing rights to all women even when the discrimination against them isn't exclusively based on sex. With the phrase alone "on account of sex," a comparative abstraction, discrimination against women of color could be said to be based on their sex but also on their race,[41] as it actually often is, thus possibly evading coverage of women of color by the ERA. Substantively, women of color are obviously "women," so this proposed sentence indisputably covers them, whatever the grounds for discrimination against them.

There is no state action requirement in this new sentence. One could say that "rights" by definition look to the state. But that only says who has to provide the rights, not who has to deprive the victim of such rights in order for plaintiffs to have a viable constitutional claim. Nothing in the text makes this guarantee exclusively vertical.

The new sentence is a positive guarantee. It does not direct that states stay out, on the view that society will automatically provide equally for women unless government intervenes to prevent it—the concept of the negative state. Our Constitution is largely a negative one, and would remain so, except for this sentence in Carolyn

Maloney's proposed ERA. This positive right to equality is, I think, what we have meant and needed all along, given that society and law have combined to the present to bias legal and social entitlements against women. By its language, it encourages legislation for equality rights. This sentence provides directly what an equal rights amendment can help give women: freedom from sex discrimination.

Neither ERA has an intent requirement. A lot of noise would be needed on this during ratification to make clear that a key reason existing law is inadequate, and a new departure needed, is the existing constitutional and statutory intent requirements. Our possibilities for real equality under the Fourteenth Amendment were decisively blown in 1976 when the intent requirement was first explicitly attached to race, then later to sex.[42]

On my count and analysis, gender equality exists in some form in some 184 out of the 200 written constitutions in the world.[43] Of those, only eight have the U.S. model. One hundred thirty-nine have express sex or gender equality or express nondiscrimination provisions on the basis of sex—the word "sex," or "gender," or women and men are in them.[44] At least in language, most other countries have legal guarantees of sex equality that are far superior to ours. Its absence in the United States provides such basis as exists for traditional literalists like Justice Antonin Scalia to opine, "Certainly the Constitution does not require discrimination on the basis of sex. The only issue is whether it prohibits it. It doesn't."[45]

Whatever can be said against this as things stand, his reading needs to be made an explicit textual nullity. At least as importantly, an ERA would provide an inspiration and impetus for public policy and a powerful symbolic support for women's equality at all social levels at the apex of the legal system in a culture in which law has power and meaning, and sometimes leads. It is long past time for the United States to join the world and high time American women became full citizens under our own law.

TWENTY-EIGHT

Sex Equality in Global Perspective

Violence against women, much if not most of it sexual, is at the core of the organized, practiced, pervasive inequality of the sexes. It is also extremely unpeaceful. Yet equality and peace are seldom connected. Peace is not simply the absence of men fighting each other, as is often thought, any more than sexual assault is biological or a criminal exception to a peaceful norm. Equality is a powerful and necessary precondition for peace. The architecture of real social equality is the requisite design of social peace, primarily between women and men but also, arguably, among men.[1] Ending rape and prostitution builds a more peaceful world as it constructs a more equal one.

Equality is valued nearly everywhere, seldom practiced, and nowhere yet achieved. As an ideal, equality can be passionately sought, widely defended, legally guaranteed to varying degrees in diverse forms, sentimentally assumed, complacently taken for granted, or largely ignored. As a legal guarantee, sex equality has been in effect for a considerable period all over the world. None of this has observably produced sex equality in social reality. In lives lived or institutions run, so far equality does not exist anywhere. Although inequalities between the sexes display remarkable similarities across history and cultures, they do take culturally and historically specific forms and are inflected and valanced and powerfully shaped by interaction with class and race hierarchies. One can throw up one's hands[2] and conclude that all this shows the limits of law in the equality area. Or, asking why this gap between law and life exists, one can look into the framework, the concepts, and their implementation more deeply, on the view that the legal approach taken is consistent with its results or lack of them.

Traditional formal equality theory, predicated on Aristotle's formulation calling for treating "likes alike, unlikes unalike"[3] or "[e]quality consists in the same treatment of similar persons"[4]—in the grip of which United States law remains mired with much European law— is more tenacious elsewhere than is usually recognized, predominating legally within most nations, including Australia,[5] revolving around sameness and difference. The substantive equality alternative instead aims to eliminate systemic patterns of group advantage and disadvantage—i.e. hierarchies of social dominance and subordination—on the concrete often intertwined bases like sex and race that have historically been their grounds. Despite considerable advances, the legal systems of Canada and Israel,[6] for example, both of which claim to embrace substantive equality, have understood and effectuated it less well than is usually realized. No domestic legal system applies equality principles to sexual violence, even as the recognition that ending sex discrimination in the form of violence against women with impunity drives many substantive equality developments internationally.

International law, combining human rights concepts with international criminal and humanitarian law, has made considerable substantive equality strides in opposing violence against women analyzed as "gender crime," a theory first developed in sexual harassment law in the United States[7] and further pioneered in the Canadian courts,[8] but not yet applied to crimes of gender in either country. By exposing and recognizing the gender hierarchy in sexual aggression, international criminal law, the European and Latin American regional human rights systems, the International Criminal Court, and some international treaty bodies[9] are converging to become the cutting edge of substantive equality law around the globe.[10]

Along with these advances, failures to fully grasp the substance of gender inequality remain. Two key instances focus on the mediating concepts of dignity and consent,[11] notions often regarded as equality promoting but in my view impeding its substantive realization. The Supreme Court of Canada for a time[12] contended that deprivation of dignity was the essential meaning and fundamental essence of inequality, then saw the error of its ways. Israel's approach to equality is formally reversed but closely related, such that its legal sex equality principle is interpreted as derivative of dignity under the Basic Law.[13] In some international bodies, consent has recently been seen as central to an equality approach to sexual assault.[14]

My central critical arguments will be, first, that dignitary deprivation is often a major part of the injury of substantive inequality, but it is seldom if ever all of it. Inequality includes indignity but is not reducible to it. Inequality is frequently undignified. But reducing its injury to the feeling of indignity in the subordinated person makes it all mental within the unequally treated person, which tends to cover up, even trivialize, the coercive and injurious external conditions and systemic acts usually involved—the material deprivations and physical harms inflicted by dominant groups that at the least contextualize it—along with the resources and status they benefit from. Indignity is a part of most inequality, not its whole. It thus cannot substitute for the harm of inequality on its own terms, which includes the material as well as the psychological. Arguably, inequality is relentlessly material first, a system of hierarchical social meanings second. At least, its demeaning meanings cannot be ended without also ending its material deprivations. The harm of unequal pay, for instance, is not only that it deprives one of dignity, although it can, but that it deprives one of money. Reducing inequality to its dignitary dimension misses too much, is too airy, to be able, upon remediation, if that is possible, to produce equality.

Second, consent will be argued to be intrinsically unequal and inappropriate to an equality framework. Consent, pervasively masquerading as "wanting it" in the law of sexual assault worldwide, ranges in applied meaning from affirmative desire (which anyone who has ever felt it or seen it felt will realize is virtually never seen in cases of claimed sexual assault) to being dead in some jurisdictions. It works to attribute acceptance of victimization to the victimized. Like the dignitary notion, it acts as if the harm of inequality occurs in the mind of its victim, not in the external world of actions by its perpetrator—in this case, by his body onto and into hers. It makes the injury be what she is thinking, not what he is doing. Consent is an intrinsically unequal concept; indeed it exists to rationalize inequality. It presupposes an actor and an acted-upon, active and passive, paying no attention to unequal circumstances. It includes what women want, but under that cover encompasses what they are coerced through multiple forms of circumstanced inequality into accepting, what they resign themselves to because they have no choice, what they give up on fighting because they cannot avoid or stop. Its fundamental dynamic is acquiescence. As is well understood in the international law of sexual assault and sex trafficking, sex acts imposed through coercive means can never be meaningfully consensual. Again, accepting unequal pay does not make it equal. One does not meaningfully consent to inequality; one is just run over by it.

1. Formal Equality

The reasons formal equality has been rejected where it has been expose its deceptive attractiveness and some reasons for its continued persistence in most places. The more extreme and pervasive a social inequality is, the less useful this approach has been, and is, in rectifying it. This makes the approach work the interest of dominant groups. It can grant equality of social status where it already exists but has been denied in exceptional cases, but on principle resists transforming entrenched rankings of material resources and social status that have been systemically precluded. Simply put, where one already has equality, and inequality is a marginal exception, the traditional approach can work. Otherwise not. Most leading U.S. cases on sex equality can be characterized this way, making formal equality generally unuseful in situations in which social equality does not already exist, which is where an equality law is needed most.[15]

This standard equality approach, which generally prevails in Europe's employment law as well, seeks to rationally mirror the reality of sex. The point of reference for the "sex" it seeks to mirror turns out to be, in fact, the existing social reality of sex inequality. For example, a small number of exceptional girls being admitted to elite (male) schools or women being promoted or hired at work when they qualify by the tacitly male standard are successful; this is treating "likes alike." Those who are in a position to benefit from this will be the few, elite, largely white in the United States and in Australia, and relatively privileged, but they will be women. The approach of courts giving women what society hasn't been able to stop them from qualifying for, or from already taking on their own, always puts me in mind of the Women of the Wall cases in Israel,[16] so far resolved on the ground that the women have been praying there for thirty years. I call this de-factoing your way to equality.

Most women do not inhabit de facto equality. They are not permitted to—for instance, the large nonelite group of victims of battering or rape with legal impunity. Under formal equality, it is legally rational, hence equal, to do nothing for them: it is treating "unlikes unalike." Apparently the gender chasm between perpetrators and victims is so vast, it looks like the reality of sex, so that it has traditionally been inconceivable to consider violence against women a sex inequality area at all. The same for women in most countries who are trapped in sex-segregated jobs that pay less, discrimination against pregnancy which is legal in most places, not Australia (she's different, surprise!),[17] and women's lesser status in the family and on dissolution of marriage. The more reality looks like a "difference," and sex is socially constructed as a difference, the more sex inequality is pervasively real rather than an illusion, the more it looks like the social ideology of sex, so the less likely equalization will be seen to be called for in this equality approach.

To simplify, this approach is looking for real sex and, finding real sex inequality, thinks it has found it. In the United States, the closer this approach looks—termed "scrutiny"—the more equality it is supposed to produce. But in fact, the higher its level of scrutiny, the more sex inequality it is deigned to ignore.[18] This is perverse even before law reaches the purported heights of affirmative or positive action, which shows the problem in high relief. The more a classification is known to be a ground of inequality, the less can legally be done about it, because it is subjected to the highest level of scrutiny or prohibition.[19] So affirmative action is either unprincipled discrimination, undignified and stigmatic, or marginally tolerated as a form of discrimination for which we regretfully make time-limited exceptions. As we will see, the substantive equality approach, by contrast, regards affirmative action as not discrimination at all, because it promotes equality. In some contrast, I've never before seen "special measures," a term with a legal meaning close to affirmative action, used to disadvantage a disadvantaged group, making a unique Australian contribution to this discussion.[20] At this point, one wonders what, if not equality, formal equality has been promoting. Inequality, perhaps?

Under formal equality rubrics, many forms discrimination takes do not look like discrimination to the law. Specifically, sex discrimination frequently takes the shape of legal absence. Absent are laws that address crimes of misogyny the way they occur in life. Absent is enforcement or interpretation of laws that do exist that might help. Absent are applied legal standards that find these absences discriminatory. Absent is any sense that the presence of some rights that mainly men exercise, such as freedom of speech or right to fair trial, could embody and perpetuate discrimination against women. Absence of accountability for violence against women is so reliable it becomes the presence of impunity. So in the United States, for instance, a father murders his three little girls over a mandatory order of protection their mother could not persuade the police to enforce, no equality argument is even made, and the Supreme Court provides no relief. In the same case, an international forum applying substantive equality principles finds a denial of equal protection of the law based on sex.[21] Failure to act is one of the most potent forms of discriminatory action women encounter in law. Many sex equality rights are imagined in Israeli law since 2000, for instance, yet the remaining gender gap places it 53rd in the world, without even accounting for sexual violence.[22] Australia, similarly, is 24th in the world, despite all its equality laws.

The formal equality approach is also incoherent, capable of concluding both A and not A with equal logical consistency. It can equally well, for instance, support the analysis that a gay marriage prohibition does *not* discriminate against gay men and lesbian women based on sex—because both men and women equally cannot marry persons of their own sex—and that it *does* discriminate based on sex, because each person could marry the person they want to marry but for their sex.[23] This is beyond indeterminacy. Coming to opposite determinate conclusions with equal logical consistency in situations of conflict makes it no legal doctrine at all. Further, pretending that absence of substantive content is what makes this approach fair and unbiased, its abstract emptiness biases it toward upholding the status quo. Unless a legal rule—say, a same-sex marriage prohibition—is found legally unequal, it will be left as it is. An approach that can go either way will support existing arrangements, that is, the status quo that social power has constructed. Where social inequality exists, where unequal power constructs reality, this test will tilt toward the unequal, having no tiebreaker between the power of the status quo and the powerlessness of equality-seeking challengers. Being neutral between equality and inequality makes it no equality rule at all. Yes, inequality is what it promotes.

This, I think, is the reason it is so commonly observed that equality imperatives in the hands of this ahistoric acontextual approach reduce to the politics and perceptions of those who decide the cases. This is why proponents are reduced to arguing not a legal rule, not a factual recognition—that a group that is humanly equal is being treated socially as if it is not—but a moral imperative: something it would be good or nice to do. When you feel like you're crawling on your knees, begging for the equality you are supposed to be guaranteed already, this is why.

In order to produce an equal outcome, in other words, equality-seekers are reduced to arguing that equality is a moral rule, the right thing to do, against an equality logic that is looking to see if the law matches existing empirical conditions, when usually it does. Most people who need equality aren't empirically "the same" as the people who already have it. The damage of inequality typically ensures at least that "difference." Moreover, why women should have to be like men before we can be considered equally human is a mystery lost in the mists of misogyny. So inequalities have to be ignored, we have to not know what we know, in order to produce equal outcomes—hence "colorblindness," the foundational supposedly neutral rule in U.S. race equality jurisprudence,[24] which is not even cognitively possible in a racist social order, and far from neutral. Hence gender blindness, the foundation of gender neutrality, the ruling doctrine in sex equality jurisprudence, which is highly unlikely to be possible in most social circumstances either, and means that women have to look like men, as well as be like men (a dubious aspiration to many of us), before they can be seen as human equals. Men don't have to be like women to get anything they have.

That refusing to perceive inequality is not a promising approach to ending it might go without saying. Apparently not. That people can be different from one another yet still be equals, entitled to be treated equally, simply does not compute in the Aristotelian equality framework, far less does diversity: treating people alike based on their unalikeness. All this is why substantive equality was created—not to vaunt difference but to end the social hierarchy based on it.

2. Substantive Equality

Substantive equality doctrine requires that equality be promoted. Equality first began to be understood as substantive in law in 1989 in Canada, replacing the Aristotelian calculus with a substantive test of historical disadvantage predicated on enumerated and akin concrete grounds of discrimination, open to reality and envisioning the need for change.[25] Substantive equality grasps that inequality involves treating people as if they are less and more, inferior and superior, supreme and subjected based on their membership in social groups historically so designated and treated. It centers on social hierarchy, which is material before it is psychological. The actual substance of each inequality constructs the law's response to the claim on each ground. The first question is whether a legally challenged inequality is part of a socially pre-existing disadvantage. For evidence of this, look out the window.

For a while, after its breakthrough, Canada lost its way, performing formal equality in the name of substance,[26] while granting the substance of an equality result in case after case without bringing itself to say so. The Supreme Court of Canada spent these years mired in a well-intended but vacuous and damaging focus on dignitary loss as the sine qua non of inequality. Having wriggled at least nominally free of Aristotle, it fell into the grip of Kant. Then, in a 2008 case, noting that dignity is "abstract and subjective,"[27] can "become confusing and difficult to apply,"[28] and creates unintended additional barriers for disadvantaged groups seeking equality, Canada returned to the recognition that inequality is concrete and material, equality rules prohibit the perpetuation of practices of disadvantage or prejudice and stereotyping based on enumerated or analogous grounds, and "different treatment in the service of equity for disadvantaged groups is an expression of equality, not an exception to it."[29] No doubt the facts of that case helped, twenty-four hours of fishing devoted to First Nations people being difficult to construe, either in inclusion or exclusion, in dignitary terms.

The lesson here is: when courts fail to grasp inequality's nettle of hierarchy, they cast about, at sea for what oh what can be unequal about inequality. *Hierarchy* being missed, distracting and desperate concepts like dignity fill the void, becoming doctrine.

Yes, deprivation of dignity is often a powerful dimension of the substance of inequality; it does some of its work. But it is not all there is to it, always its irreducible core or floor. The Kantian conception of dignity[30] that has implicitly dominated in some law, which has its moments, essentially presupposes equality as a precondition. Apart from assuming what needs to be created in inequality cases, this dignity is absolute and intrinsic, not allowing comparison or price, which makes it uniquely unsuited to legal situations of inequality, which are intrinsically comparative and often call for material reparation and damage awards. Since it has no social grounding, hence none of the context so crucial to substantive equality functioning in law, this notion of dignity is also susceptible to culturally gender-biased standards that cannot be decoded without a grasp of substantive inequality's context and meaning. What would be regarded as decidedly undignified for a man is often not regarded that way for a woman, even if it may well be highly problematic when seen through a substantive equality lens. A lot of sexual harassment could fall into this category: not seen as undignified, hence not discriminatory, because women are commonly so treated, and the society does not find women deprived of dignity, just treated like women. It becomes another way of saying women are not unequally treated, just different. When inequality is understood through its specific hierarchical substance, with comparative measures in the world, this problem disappears.[31]

Dignity in courts' hands is envisioned as the subjective experience of being treated as a lesser human, not as the material reality of such treatment or the fact of the social status ranking imposed. Put another way, it is like saying that the real problem of the Shoah was indignity rather than extermination. Seeing genocide as the ultimate form of discrimination, there is a lot more than a loss of dignity in being forced to live on 200 calories a day because of who you are. Simply being treated as if one is a lesser human is definitely integral to hierarchy, but it is usually materially manifested, including verbally, as well as measurable, even if the loss cannot ultimately be fully compensated. That material expression is evidence needed in court. Genocide, the ultimate inequality, is defined as the intentional destruction of a people as such, not as inflicting indignity on them. The core of the diminution of equal humanity is the unequal treatment itself. The subjective impact that is the dignitary violation is a partial precondition as well as one consequence, but it is neither the whole cause nor the whole consequence. Indeed, sometimes their dignity is all subordinated or violated people have left.

For another example, *Brown v. Board of Education* found that the harm official racial segregation did to African American children, stipulated as occurring with equal material facilities, was this: "To separate them from others of similar age and qualifications solely because of their race generates a feeling of inferiority as to their status in the community that may affect their hearts and minds in a way unlikely ever to be undone."[32] If dignitary loss were needed to do any work in the equality context, this is where it would have been. It was not necessary because the inequality—the segregation—was grasped for the harm that it was. The sense of inferiority was a consequential harm of inequality for Black children, a key measure of that harm, but it was not the discrimination, i.e. the inequality, itself. Where the harm of hierarchical ranking was grasped—even as white children were equally segregated from Black children without apparently teaching them that they were inferior—calling the racial segregation "inherently unequal" was enough.[33]

Substantive equality is not a variant of mainstream equality. It is a new start. It changes not only results but the understanding of the circumstances that give rise to equality questions in the first place. Its core insight is that inequality, substantively speaking, is always a material or social value hierarchy—higher and lower, more and less, top and bottom, better and worse, clean and dirty, served and serving, appropriately rich and appropriately poor, superior and inferior, dominant and subordinate, justly forceful and rightly violated, commanding and obeying.[34] Its injury is not confined to the indignity of the position in which one is placed, although it encompasses that, but extends to all its unequal dimensions, which are physical and concrete as well as perceived, attributed, and psychological. The injury involves material treatment and social standing simultaneously. And the inequality exists whether the person subjected to it experiences a loss of dignity or not.

Put another way, dignity is a value or a feeling. Equality is only secondarily a value or a feeling. Primarily, equality is a fact. Inequality is also a fact. If sex equality is seen as a value, it can be accepted or rejected as one side in a normative discourse. In policy, a fact can either be faced or denied; a value can be debated endlessly. A feeling can be regarded as trivial or subjective, as with *Plessy* and Herbert Wechsler's "the construction [African Americans] put upon"[35] the segregation. If the sexes are human equals, the social inequality of the sexes is a monumental inaccuracy. Only if the sexes are not seen as being human equals ontologically, in their being as members of groups deemed presumptively equal, is it necessary to argue that it would be normatively positive (read nice) to treat them as if they were. In the customary approach, equality becomes a giant hypothetical. In the substantive equality approach, sexism is not at base a bad idea, although it is not a good one; it is a factual lie. Put another way, sex is not unequal; gender, the social meaning of sex, is. The injury of inequality is not reducible to feeling bad at its indignity, although we often do. The injury is the harm of the fact of one's equal human status being denied realization in the world. Fixing the world will fix the way we feel about it.

The law of prostitution is a great example for all of this. Formal equality asks whether the law treats men and women the same. Typically, the law treats all prostituted people more or less equally badly, because the person being sold as and for sex is treated according to the female standard without regard to sex, just as whoever—rich or poor—begs for bread under bridges is treated the same. Hence equally. In the mainstream sameness/difference approach, the fact that most pimps and johns are men would legally be treated the same as the fact that most prostituted people are women: as a sex difference, not a sex inequality.[36] The gendered hierarchy between the two is rendered invisible and irrelevant.

In a substantive equality perspective, the social institution of prostitution—selling people for sexual use—is a gendered activity that is fundamental to male dominance. It violates people, most of whom are women, most of the rest of whom are feminized, as objects for sexual sale and use, expressing their socially inferior status as it treats them as—and makes them be—social inferiors, stigmatizing them as human dirt, trashing their human dignity as it severely harms them physically, psychologically, spiritually, and economically. Laws against pimping are largely unenforced and the laws against buying—an activity overwhelmingly engaged in by men, always masculine, and the reason prostitution exists—have been largely nonexistent or unenforced. It is to remedy this inequality that the Swedish model was enacted, in effect also in Norway and Iceland, largely in Canada, in the process of adoption in France, and repeatedly considered in Israel.[37] This approach, arresting the buyers and sellers and decriminalizing the sold, raises the status of prostituted people, most of them women, and lowers the status of their violators, most (not all) of them men, producing a law that is sex-equal in outcome, equalizing against an unequal reality.[38] The Swedish model aims at abolishing prostitution as an institution of sex inequality, with all its material harms and dignitary violations. Under the substantive equality approach, this is what promoting sex equality looks like.

3. International Law

If much of the substance of sex equality has gone missing in national laws,[39] the international order is beginning to find it. Over the last two decades or so, attention to crimes committed against women in peace and war, including prostitution, under international humanitarian and criminal law has combined with a muscular pursuit of violence against women as a violation of human rights to produce the converged concept of "gender crime." In a parallel dual motion, United Nations treaty bodies and regional legal systems, with governments as defendants, have begun to recognize violence against women (including by nonstate actors) as gender-based violations and sex discriminatory when tolerated, at the same time international criminal justice tribunals have been coming to see prosecuting the individual perpetrators of those same crimes as a tool for vindicating the human rights of their victims.

The first large step was taken by the CEDAW Committee in 1993, interpreting its prohibition on discrimination against women to include gender-based violence—violence that is directed against a woman because she is a woman or that affects women disproportionately.[40] Over the following decade, international criminal prosecutions have increasingly become instruments for vindicating human rights on the basis of gender by the International Criminal Court, along with proceedings against states for ignoring such crimes in the Latin American regional system, under the African Protocol,[41] and a new European protocol on violence against women and domestic violence that came into force in August 2014.[42] All recognize violence against women as "a manifestation of the historically unequal power relations between women and men," as a distinctive human rights violation "based on gender, which causes death or physical, sexual or psychological harm or suffering to women, whether in the public or the private sphere."[43] This is some essential substance of a substantive equality approach.

The European Court of Human Rights has distinguished itself in a trio of cases on rape, domestic violence, and trafficking for prostitution, using equality concepts in varying ways. The most instructive and farthest-reaching of which, *Opuz v. Turkey*, found the state responsible for the murder of a woman by her daughter's husband, whose violence against the two women had been repeatedly reported to the authorities, under the European Convention's guarantee of equal protection of the laws on the basis of sex.[44] The women repeatedly reported the staggering violence and repeatedly withdrew their charges, no doubt in fear of the perpetrator. Batterers are also notoriously manipulative. "Bearing in mind its finding [that] ... discriminatory judicial passivity in Turkey, albeit unintentional, mainly affected women," the Court said, "the violence suffered by the applicant and her mother may be regarded as gender-based violence which is a form of discrimination against women."[45] Moreover, it found that the "overall unresponsiveness of the judicial system and impunity enjoyed by the aggressors ... indicated that there was insufficient commitment to take appropriate action to address domestic violence."[46] It is hard to overstate the importance of a ruling that held the state accountable for the loss of life of a woman at the hands of her nonstate actor son-in-law as a violation of her guaranteed sex equality rights.

In a similar finding, in 2011, the Inter-American Commission on Human Rights found the United States failed to guarantee equal protection of the laws to Jessica Gonzales and her daughters in their father's actions resulting in the girls' murders, discriminating against them based on sex under the preamble of the American Declaration through its sex-based, and sex- and ethnicity-based, systemic neglect of law enforcement against domestic violence.[47] The United States courts had done nothing for her.

International criminal law, beginning in the ad hoc tribunals, has also embraced these human rights rulings to further build substantive sex equality from the criminal side. Under the Rome Statute of the International Criminal Court, gender crimes are recognized as crimes against humanity, war crimes, and acts of genocide.[48] Its sources of applicable law specify interpretation in conformity with international human rights standards.[49] So far the strongest substantive contribution in this regard has been made in the trial decision by the International Criminal Tribunal for Rwanda in the *Akayesu* case, in which rape was defined as "a physical invasion of a sexual nature, committed on a person under circumstances which are coercive,"[50] recognizing that "coercion may be inherent in certain circumstances."[51] The hierarchy built into the context of domination intrinsic to genocide and campaigns of crimes against humanity was recognized as coercing sexual acts when there was a nexus to them. In the presence of such coercion, for acts linked to genocide, consent was so irrelevant as not even to be mentioned, just as it is never mentioned for torture or war crimes. When rape is weaponized, circumstances of coercion in war or genocide or crimes against humanity to which a rape is linked make it so unequal that consent has no operative meaning. Coercion, defined to include all forms of inequality including gender, not lack of consent, is thus the essence of gender crime, including rape.

Rather than adapting this insight to nonwar settings—asking what nexus to inequality would make the circumstances of alleged sexual violations be coercive, recognizing gender as a potential civil conflict—some international human rights authorities have instead reintroduced consent into their inequality determinations. One example is *M. C. v. Bulgaria*,[52] in which the European Court of Human Rights—in the second of its trio of cases—reached the right result using the wrong equality analysis. There, a fourteen-year-old girl who had not had sex before, frozen in fright, saying no, pushing back and sobbing, was raped twice on the same night by several men who offered to give her a ride home or from whom she sought help. Bulgaria found insufficient evidence for conviction. The ECHR required that the state enforce its rape law, which it had not done, and found consent to be the essence of an equality approach to rape. The result was good, this aspect of the rationale unfortunate. Under unequal conditions, many women acquiesce in or tolerate sex they cannot as a practical matter avoid but do not want. That does not make the sex wanted. It certainly does not make it equal. It does make it legally consensual in most jurisdictions. Apart from the judicial impracticality or even injustice of having a subjective state of mind of a victim determine whether an act by another person is a crime, and the difficulty of such a determination, consent is an autonomy (freedom) concept, not an equality concept. How one can be free without being equal has never been explained. If, instead, the European Court had applied a coercion standard, on the understanding that sex inequality can be coercive in specific circumstances, it would have found ample evidence of it in M. C.'s case.

A similarly correct outcome was generated by the same misguided concept before the CEDAW Committee in *Vertido v. The Philippines*.[53] There, a woman had accepted a ride home from a workplace superior who raped her, despite her declining, struggling, running away, and repeatedly attempting to escape him. He was acquitted in the Philippine court on grounds that the evidence left too much doubt for conviction. The CEDAW Committee brilliantly identified sex stereotypes in virtually every dimension of the case, accurately finding the Philippine ruling inadequate by sex equality standards. But rather than analyzing sex inequality as the form of coercion that the perpetrator relied upon to force sex on his victim, mobilized by the stereotypes it so clearly saw, with which the state then collaborated in acquitting him, consent was recommended as the essence of inequality in the rape context. The Committee required the Philippines put "consent at [the] centre" of its rape law to be in compliance with CEDAW.[54]

Consider how this analysis goes off the substantive equality rails. Consent standards, ubiquitous in countries colonized by the English, put the woman on trial. Consent fundamentally presupposes a dyad of acting and acted-upon; the acted-upon is imagined as acceding to the actor's actions, as if this makes them equal, whether the equality of conditions that would make such assent meaningful is present or not, unasked. Even where consent is elaborately defined or qualified— with terms like free ("freely given" in Israeli law[55]), positive, voluntary, affirmative, and autonomous being added to give the term any meaning at all—its use relies upon imagining that courts will find credible and decisive a woman's assertion that the sex was not something she wanted, whatever she said or did or did not say or do. Even if the woman is believed—for which history provides scant assurance—courts tend not to permit women's subjective lack of desire for sex to control whether a man loses his liberty. To imagine to the contrary under conditions of sex inequality is a fantasy. I also do not think it probably should. Consent is a subjective fact, ultimately. Such a posture invites the racist use of the rape charge as well as requires courts to believe what a woman says now she felt then, regardless of what she said or did at the time. This may explain the few convictions for rape in Israel, its law being predicated on consent virtually entirely, although rape attrition data does not seem to exist. It also helps explain high rates of rape attrition elsewhere, meaning the fall-off between rapes reported, charged, prosecuted, convicted, and significantly sentenced. The world model (perhaps origin?) of consent-only rape law is the UK, an approach spread worldwide with empire, which has a conviction rate of 6 percent of reported cases.[56]

Look. As a concept, consent in Western liberal philosophy became the basis for legitimizing the obligation to obey the state after the fall of the divine right of kings. Even as a fiction,[57] it never envisioned equality among parties. It exists to rationalize the exercise of dominant power over subordinates, to attribute the rule of the powerful to the acquiescence of the powerless. It exists, in other words, to justify dominant rule, which has been male rule. One is regarded as tacitly consenting when one does not leave,[58] because you were there, whether leaving is realistic or not. Being paid means consent, even if one would not survive otherwise. Silence is deemed consent. Consent also has no dignity, should anyone care.

In legal operation, consent to sex is routinely found in situations of despairing acquiescence, frozen fright, terror, trauma, absence of realistic options, socially situated vulnerability, drunkenness, coma, and even death.[59] Consent is often found in situations where considerable force was used,[60] building in the misogynistic assumption that women want forced sex. If virtually any domestic criminal law of sexual assault had to meet substantive sex equality standards, something never yet done anywhere, it would fail. Consent is a pathetic standard of sex for a free people. It has no place in a substantive equality analysis.

Consent is also no defense to sex trafficking, defined as sexual exploitation under conditions, inter alia, of abuse of power or conditions of vulnerability.[61] The European Court of Human Rights, in the third of these European cases, failed to see the inequality in a situation of trafficking for prostitution in *Rantsev v. Cyprus & Russia*.[62] Oksana Rantseva of Russia, a young girl who was the sole support of her family at the time, had fled her placement in a situation of apparent prostitution in Cyprus after three days, was recaptured by her "manager," and taken to the police. The police returned her to this "manager," since she had committed no crime on which she could be held, who took her to the apartment of a male employee. She was found dead in the street in front of that apartment building some hours later, a sheet hanging from a balcony above her body. Autopsies found she fell to her death. The Cypriot inquest found, if one can call it a finding, that "in strange circumstances, [she] jumped into the void as a result of which she was fatally injured . . . in circumstances resembling an accident, in an attempt to escape from the apartment in which she was a guest."[63] As the ECHR dryly observed, most guests leave by the front door.[64]

The police's decision to hand Ms. Rantseva over to the "manager" was found to deprive her of her protected liberty under the European Convention; she was also found to have been enslaved and/or trafficked.[65] Failing to apply a substantive equality analysis, however, the Court found that while the investigation had been inadequate, depriving her of procedural rights, Oksana's substantive right to life was not violated, since no specific indication was given that her life was immediately threatened.[66] My point: had the Court been as clear on the unequal gendered realities of trafficking for prostitution as they were on battering in *Opuz*, seeing the one as systemically and structurally integral to sex inequality as the other, and as such well-known to be life-threatening, they might have found the state substantively responsible for Oksana's death, as they did for Mrs. Opuz's. Oksana died trying to flee prostitution, a substantively gendered practice of sex inequality, risking death to get away; perhaps she risked dying rather than staying under such conditions; perhaps she chose death to prostitution's dishonor. On this view, the state that colluded with her traffickers through its visa system and documented police corruption was responsible for her death whether she jumped or was pushed, whether she was murdered or committed suicide. Either way, they killed her.

In substantive equality light, M. C., Oksana Rantseva, and the Opuz women resemble each other, looking like the same woman at different points in time. As a child, she is raped, then prostituted, then married to a batterer or indentured to a trafficker, likely a rapist also, who kills her mother who was trying to protect her, then she is also killed. The perpetrators converge, too. Many batterers and pimps start out as rapists of girls and use the same violent and controlling manipulations on the women in their "stable" as they do on women family members. The "manager" in *Rantsev* may be a murderer, along with the son-in-law in *Opuz*. The dignity of none of these women was respected by the nonstate-actor men charged or by the men of their states. But the atrocities of sex inequality committed against them hardly ended there. Battering and rape can keep women so traumatized in prostitution or family that they wind up dead.

In law too, on a substantive equality analysis, there is little distinction between the rape of M. C., being around the age (often younger) most prostituted women enter the sex industry, the battery of both Opuz women in marriage and the family, and the apparently forced prostitution of Oksana, who was either had done to her or avoided having done to her by buyers what was done to M. C. and potentially to Mrs. Opuz in her marriage, as Oksana's "manager" collected payment for it. Two of the three women were victims of femicide, gender-based killing.[67] All three were too traumatized by their abuse to make effective use of the legal system by presenting themselves credibly to authorities by the authorities' standards. When each woman did come to the attention of officials, each state sided with violent men against them. Each woman was faulted for not falling apart enough. Had she done so, she would likely have been considered hysterical. Each woman likely felt ashamed, possibly blaming herself or thinking, with reason, she would be blamed for what was done to her. Until Europe interceded, she was not wrong. All are victims of gender crimes, in need of a substantive sex equality analysis for remedy. This was embraced in *Opuz*, glimpsed to some extent in *M. C.*, and partially grasped in *Rantsev*.

The converging international frameworks also include the U.N. Security Council, which, for its part, is taking an increasingly substantive sex equality approach in its declarations on violence against women in promoting international peace and security. Building on years of reports and declarations focused on the role of gender inequality in conflict, and of the pursuit of gender equality as key in achieving and maintaining international peace and security, the Security Council in 2013 issued a resolution that locates gender inequality at the roots of conflict.[68] It in effect went to war in Congo, in major part because of the rapes there.[69] Monumentally, the Security Council has identified the empowerment of women and girls, and an end to impunity for sexual and gender-based violence, as critical to efforts to achieve security and sustainable peace. Joining hands across the jurisdictional divide, in a document issued the same day, the CEDAW Committee's General Recommendation 30 centered its comprehensive approach to women's role in preventing conflict, and in conflict and post-conflict settings, on sexual violence, an analysis described in terms of "substantive gender equality."[70] Neither document mentions consent.

The goal and hope of substantive equality theory, in recognizing the irrelevance of difference and countering the mainspring of dominance, in giving dignity its proper place and refusing to be distracted by consent under conditions under which it is meaningless, is to close the gap between legal promise and social reality in the equality area. A legal regime capable of ending conflict between the sexes by producing equality of women to men—ending this longest and most pervasive of conflicts in its pervasively sexual forms—may prove capable of producing equality and peace among men as well.

Intervening for Change, 1976–2016

Thinking about making basic social change through law, in 1976 I wrote a student paper titled "Political Lawyers: Theories of their Practice."[1] It laid the failure to achieve equal justice at the feet of lawyers: "the failure of equal justice under law is inequality under lawyers."[2] The anatomized skepticism about the use of law for real change provides a benchmark against which to measure the next forty years of practice "tread[ing] what turns out to be a very thin line between the inevitable and the hopeless."[3] Meditating on the dilemma on the Left between the activist's push of the freight train of history on the one hand and the pull toward quietism of history's determination on the other, the paper pondered the conundra presented by "law as a response to social needs versus as an index to the system's readiness to recognize and respond to them."[4] Law leading social change as opposed to following it was also pondered. Political lawyers were observed to be "persistently suspicious that whatever concessions or relief the courts grant cannot be systemically significant or they would not grant them, yet they continue to push the law as far as it will move and call it political work."[5] Whatever you cannot get must be what really matters, and what you can get must ipso facto not be worth getting. The young writer, not yet admitted to the bar, did know that the thinking on this subject was necessarily "abstract until given concrete content,"[6] and that the criticisms leveled and questions raised could not ultimately be addressed in theory, but only in practice.[7] Not prematurely resolving a question—hanging onto what you do not know—can be far more instructive than what you do know.

Based in existing literature and a little experience, the paper confronted a conflict framed as one between the politics of political lawyers, "which are critical of the establishment, and their role as lawyers, which derives its power from the establishment."[8] I have come to think that this framing of the tension is wrong on a number of levels, and would only be seen that way by someone who had not yet been engaged on a practical level with moving anything significant through law. Law's power to make the kinds of changes I have wanted to make—for instance, recognizing sexual abuse as abusive and discriminatory—does not derive from law's place in the existing order per se. In addition to the aikido moves of using power against itself, law's power comes from its hermeneutic location in social life: what it means to people, even when all people are not equal. The lawyer's power to work such changes does not derive from their role as a lawyer in any simple sense but from the alchemy of the relationship between the people represented, their lived facts, the location of their facts in social reality and consciousness, and the acuity of their legal representation. Therein lies the politics.

Law can change reality, in other words, not because of its place in a structure of force or even authority, or because it establishes precedents to be applied in future cases. Not because it is backed by the police power or fronted by legions of propagandists for the status quo. These features of law as much work to prevent reality from being changed. It can change reality because of the meaning with which people invest it, including those whom it has not represented. If people did not believe in it, did not believe it could be—against all odds, despite much experience—an instrument of remedy, of healing, of restoration of humanity, of empowerment—it would not work for change, or I suspect actually at all. Because and when they do, it can. This is why even a small percentage of women report their rapes to their legal system. It is why they feel vindicated when the law believes them and shattered when it doesn't. This is not naïveté or trust or the illusion that one lives in a just world. It is a determination to stand and fight with an inkling that law can be a weapon in their hands, even if it has not been before, and an insistence that law represent them and people like them for a change, as it says it does.

You saw this meaning on the faces of Black community members in Jasper, Texas, when the white supremacist murderers who dragged James Byrd Jr., an African American, to death behind their pickup truck on an asphalt road were convicted and two of the three were sentenced to death by juries of eleven white people.[9] You saw it on the faces of survivors that former Chilean dictator Augusto Pinochet had ordered tortured when he was to be extradited from London to face charges for that torture.[10] Both outcomes were unprecedented. Look for it on the faces of families when the murderer of their child is felt rightly convicted, or in the eyes of women when their rapist is found guilty and appropriately sentenced. It is not triumph or vengeance. That their lives or honor might matter after all, that justice might exist in this world and law be its instrument, is the miracle they glimpse. This is what gives law the power to change.

Put another way, what was missing in the understanding of the relation of law to social change in my 1976 paper and its sources—what is generally missing in discussions of what can be done socially with law—is not just lived experience and not just a feel for reality, although those definitely tend to go missing. Missing most was women, substantively:[11] women's location in the existing social, political, and legal order; women's experiences of violation, especially sexual violation, women's exclusion from full lives and full citizenship; women's creative insubordinate determination to fly free. Overwhelmingly missing tends to be any sense of the sweep of women's existence across the globe, the vicious attacks and unrelenting exploitation met by unbending valor and unending dignity, eyes on their children and the horizon: women's pain, wisdom, and grace. Over one half of humanity, essential to all of it, women as a group continue, overwhelmingly, to be treated as not human at all, as if we do not matter, as if we are not even there, except for the ways we can be used. This is not like anything else. It calls for its own analysis and its own strategy for change through law. This has been the work of my life, side by side with so many others. When women enter, everyone enters.

Looming over the 1976 analysis was an understanding of law as resistant to change in the distribution of social power, given that law is a product of that same distribution, making the "need to judge the distance between the status quo and a proposed change one factor in deciding whether law can be used to accomplish it."[12] Along these lines, existing theories of the relation of law to social change, building on Marx, suggest that the more basic the change, the more the legal system will resist making it. There is truth in this, but practice has shown it is a limited truth. The legal system may not resist some changes because it does not know they are basic to women, not having given women much conscious systematic thought. Until we did, who had? Law may not resist some important changes out of institutionalized hubris, tending to regard women as trivial and beneath notice in a kind of noblesse oblige. You can afford this. Law may assume that women cannot succeed, underestimating us, until we do. Those who control law may reflexively think that whatever law says, the real social rules to the contrary will prevail anyway, as with sexual harassment, and sometimes they do.[13] Or an initiative for women will win because there is also something for men in it, as with abortion.[14] Legal systems may not have arranged themselves to keep women down because it has not been necessary, as social systems accomplish that so effectively already. All these provide openings.

Other gains for women, such as what civil rights against pornography would provide, can be successfully resisted by law because law provides male dominance a seemingly principled cover—"speech" in this case—to shift the issue from sex-based harm to constitutionally protected expression. This example further reveals that social change through law for women is not what the extrapolations of Marx believe: that the worse it gets, the more likely a system is to be forced to change it. Women's reality, under the heel of male dominance for millennia, is more straightforward: the worse it gets, the worse it gets. It becomes harder to change, not easier, the more entrenched it becomes. It was less difficult to address the pornography industry in 1983 than it is today, virtually nothing having been done. The fact that pornography is financially lucrative, unlike sexual harassment or domestic violence or rape, as well as ever-more-widely consumed and ever-more-widely legitimated and normalized, supports the continued evasion of legal accountability for its harms. Which is not to say that it is impossible. Similarly, paying women for work of comparable worth, which would contribute to a major extent to ending women's poverty, would also cost some people (who are mainly men) money that they are used to keeping for themselves. The legal system, and conventional theories of change, know that money is crucial to power; sexual access, not so much. At least that knowledge is not overt, although the continued virtually total impunity for sexual abuse of children and the widespread support for the sexual use of prostituted people, combining the money with the sex, suggests that it is systemically deeply rooted.

Before being involved in the initiatives in this volume, and many more behind the scenes, I did not think of substance as the key to process. Now I do. The main lesson learned from practice on the question of how to produce social change for women through legal activism is that the who and the what are utterly crucial to the how. Content—the content of each situation, in context—is key to strategy. In trying to move the plate tectonics of the world, knowing where to insert the lever matters more than anything; the relation of the substance of the political analysis to the effectiveness of the legal strategy is what makes for effectiveness. This is absolutely not about figuring things out intellectually and then putting them into effect, as conventional idealism would have it, any more than it is about the search for test cases or the invention of impact litigation. It is about the reality you confront with those who need the change made. In other words, the power of political law for women comes less from the law than from the women and the politics. My suspicion is that this is the case for other systemic change as well. It is the reason there is no prescription for it and why each intervention has its own imperatives.

Substance is why talking reality to judges about sexual assault has proven so effective. Exposed to the light of day, having been almost entirely blinkered, sexual assault looks like what it is: denigrating, devastating, destructive, and denying of the victim's humanity, defended as if the perpetrator has a right to do it, as if freedom itself looks like this. Substance is the reason that a legal system imagining that legal equality on the basis of sex already exists, staking its legitimacy on this illusion, becomes vulnerable to challenge based on the demonstrable nonexistence of this imagined fact, its substantive lack of congruence with evidence to the contrary. This is not to say law is an empty vessel, amenable to infusion with any substantive content. It is to say that law can be a way to fight for change, that every situation is specific, and that in its specifics lie the keys both to the change needed and the change that can be made through it.

In 1976, a law student noticed that legal interventions could at times derail the development of other forms of power that could be more effective in both the long and short run, as well as produce less dependence on elites.[15] This was predicated on a fairly mechanistic notion of law's relation to the reality in which it intervenes. In any case, the opposite has proven true of the legal work on sexual harassment, genocidal rape, pornography, and prostitution, which—win or lose, actually—have been empowering, not disempowering. And what lawyers contribute is not just another skill, like plumbing, a canard rightly rejected back then: "To participate in this interface between the coercive powers of the state and the life of the people is not the same as fixing their plumbing."[16] I actually decided to go to law school because I did not believe male lawyers I watched enjoying their godlike position of saying "no, that's impossible" to most things women wanted law to do. Some of the necessary competence is mechanical; some, like intuition and empathy and tenacity, is more spiritual. Years of observation of male lawyers went into the 1976 description that "becoming a lawyer elevates argument over feeling, interrogation over receptivity, combativeness over cooperation, grandstanding over self-expression, smokescreening over openness, 'just being careful' (and millions for insurance) over trust, tact over sensitivity, self-control over self-mastery, and always being right over self-change."[17] You don't have to be that kind of lawyer.

Law means community: your people stand behind you, hear you, support you. It means reality: what you say happened, happened, your knowledge is valid. It means vindication: it is wrong that you were wronged; someone took something that belongs to you; you count. It means hope: what happened to you might not happen to someone else, or to you, again. That law is invested with this meaning—not that it can provide closure, because it can't; not per se that it can order incarceration, because that does so little right and so much wrong; not that it provides money damages, however deserved, because no amount fully compensates. It cannot bring back a murdered child or un-rape a woman or girl. Law's power to change lies in its capacity to restore some of the humanity their victimization took away.[18] This possible piece of wholeness is what lawyers for violated people—the wrongfully convicted and the rightfully vindicated, including through guilty verdicts against their perpetrators—hold in their hands.

In isolation, in image, butterflies are delicate, vulnerable, even fragile. They can be reduced to decoration or flit by overlooked. In life, their endurance and power lies in collectivity. On its journey, a butterfly can be smashed against a windshield or die of lack of nutrition or be collected and categorized, pinned in a box. But what butterflies together—sometimes even one—can set in motion cannot be stopped.

NOTES

BUTTERFLY POLITICS

Epigraph: Robert Stenson Shaw quoted in James Gleick, *Chaos: Making a New Science* 262 (New York: Viking 1987).

1. Robert C. Hilborn, "Sea Gulls, Butterflies, and Grasshoppers: A Brief History of the Butterfly Effect in Nonlinear Dynamics," 72 *American Journal of Physics* 425 (2004) ("Sea Gulls").

2. A proximate intuition drives only a superficial similarity in Ray Bradbury's 1957 story in which time travellers, in their trip to the past, accidentally kill a butterfly. When they return to the present, history has changed. "A little error here would multiply in sixty million years, all out of proportion . . . . A dead mouse here makes an insect imbalance there, a population disproportion later, a bad harvest further on, a depression, mass starvations, and finally a change in social temperament in far-flung countries." Ray Bradbury, "A Sound of Thunder," in *R Is for Rocket* 61 (New York: Bantam 1962). Everything everyone does matters, including upholding sex inequality every moment every day by everyone's actions. The general drift would not be unfamiliar to Foucault. See generally Michel Foucault, *The History of Sexuality*, vol. 1, *The Will to Knowledge*, Robert Hurley, trans. (New York: Pantheon Books 1978). The butterfly effect has a set of precise requirements that every example that would fit Bradbury's image does not fit. With Bradbury, everything matters as much as everything else; not so Lorenz, nor me. Not just any dead mouse will do.

3. The following sources were instructive on chaos theory: James Gleick, *Chaos: Making a New Science* (New York: Viking 1987) ("*Chaos*"); Celso Grebogi and James A. Yorke, eds., *The Impact of Chaos on Science and Society* (New York: United Nations University Press 1997); Hilborn, "Sea Gulls,"; Stephen H. Kellert, "Extrascientific Uses of Physics: The Case of Nonlinear Dynamics and Legal Theory," 68 *Philosophy of Science*, S455 (2001); L. Douglas Kiel and Euel Elliott, eds., *Chaos Theory in the Social Sciences: Foundations and Applications* (Ann Arbor, MI: University of Michigan Press 1996); Vincent Di Lorenzo, "Legislative Chaos: An Exploratory Study," 12 *Yale Law & Policy Review* 425 (1994) ("Legislative Chaos"); Dragan Milovanovic, ed., *Chaos, Criminology, and Social Justice: The New Orderly (Dis)Order* (Westport, CT: Praeger Publishers 1997);

Paul Ormerod, *Butterfly Economics: A New General Theory of Social and Economic Behavior* (New York: Pantheon Books 1998) (*"Butterfly Economics"*); Glenn Harlan Reynolds, "Chaos and the Court," 91 *Columbia Law Review* 110 (1991); Diana Richards, "Spatial Correlation Test for Chaotic Dynamics in Political Science," 36 *American Journal of Political Science* 1047 (1992); Mark J. Roe, "Chaos and Evolution in Law and Economics," 109 *Harvard Law Review* 641 (1996) ("Chaos and Evolution"); Robert E. Scott, "Chaos Theory and the Justice Paradox," 35 *William & Mary Law Review* 329 (1993) ("Chaos Theory"); Laurence H. Tribe, "The Curvature of Constitutional Space: What Lawyers Can Learn from Modern Physics," 103 *Harvard Law Review* 1 (1989) ("Curvature"); Christopher R. Williams and Bruce A. Arrigo, *Law, Psychology, and Justice: Chaos Theory and the New (Dis)order* (Albany, NY: State University of New York Press 2002).

4. See numbers 11 (substantive equality), 12 (torture), and 13 and 14 (on rape as genocide).

5. See number 28 (trafficking, prostitution, and inequality).

6. See Part III (on pornography), number 25 (on rape), and number 27 (on ERA).

7. See number 9 (on pornography).

8. The pieces in Part I and many in Part IV exemplify this.

9. See all the pieces in Part IV.

10. All the pieces in this collection except numbers 7, 8, 16, 18, 26, this introduction ("Butterfly Politics") and the conclusion (Intervening for Change 1976–2016) were initially spoken. Footnotes have been added to the spoken interventions. For previously published pieces, footnotes have been updated where that seemed helpful, others are left as they were at the time of the talk, especially where their specifics were mentioned in the text. Sometimes the original factual assertion is documented as of the delivery date as well as updated to the present, particularly where much has changed in the interim in either the world or the research environment.

11. Discussed here in numbers 7, 8, and 28, as well as throughout.

12. Roe, "Chaos and Evolution."

13. See, e.g., Tribe, "Curvature."

14. Ormerod, "Introduction," in *Butterfly Economics* xi.

15. Roe, "Chaos and Evolution" 642.

16. Di Lorenzo, "Legislative Chaos" 427.

17. Tolstoy is tellingly quoted in Joseph Ford, "Chaos: Solving the Unsolvable, Predicting the Unpredictable!" in Michael F. Barnsley and Stephen G.

Demko, eds., *Notes and Reports in Mathematics in Science and Engineering,* vol. 2, *Chaotic Dynamics and Fractals* 1 (London: Academic Press 1986). For another translation of this quotation, see Leo Tolstoy, *What is Art?* 143, Aylmer Maude, trans. (New York: Funk & Wagnalls 1904) ("I know that most men—not only those considered clever, but even those who are very clever and capable of understanding most difficult scientific, mathematical or philosophic problems—can very seldom discern even the simplest and most obvious truth if it be such as to oblige them to admit the falsity of conclusions they have formed, perhaps with much difficulty—conclusions of which they are proud, which they have taught to others, and on which they have built their lives.").

18. Scott, "Chaos Theory" 348.

19. Catharine A. MacKinnon, "Afterword," in *Directions in Sexual Harassment Law,* Catharine A. MacKinnon and Reva B. Siegel, eds. (New Haven, CT: Yale University Press, 2004).

20. Actually, Oncale v. Sundowner Offshore Servs., Inc., 523 U.S. 75 (1998), in which sexual harassment prohibitions were extended as a matter of law to men sexually abusing another man, was the first Supreme Court recognition of sex equality rights in a same-sex context. Transgender rights are moving in the same direction under sex equality rubrics. See Schroer v. Billington, 577 F. Supp. 2d 293, 306 (D.D.C. 2008) ("The evidence establishes that the Library was enthusiastic about hiring David Schroer—until she disclosed her transsexuality. The Library revoked the offer when it learned that a man named David intended to become, legally, culturally, and physically, a woman named Diane. This was discrimination 'because of . . . sex.'"). See also Baldwin v. Foxx, EEOC Appeal No. 0120133080 (July 16, 2015) (footnote omitted) (quoting Heller v. Columbia Edgewater Country Club, 195 F. Supp. 2d. 1212, 1222 (D. Or. 2002)), https://www.eeoc.gov/decisions /0120133080.pdf ("Interpreting the sex discrimination prohibition of Title VII to exclude coverage of lesbian, gay or bisexual individuals who have experienced discrimination on the basis of sex inserts a limitation into the text that Congress has not included. Nothing in the text of Title VII 'suggests that Congress intended to confine the benefits of [the] statute to heterosexual employees alone.'"); Catharine A. MacKinnon, *Sex Equality* 1041–1044 n.3 (3rd ed., New York: Foundation Press 2016) ("*Sex Equality*").

21. The *Akayesu* definition, Prosecutor v. Akayesu, Case No. ICTR-96-4-T, Judgement, ¶¶ 687–688 (Int'l Crim. Trib. for Rwanda Sept. 2, 1998), http://unictr.unmict.org/sites/unictr.org/files/case-documents/ictr-96-4 /trial-judgements/en/980902.pdf, is discussed in Catharine A. MacKinnon,

"Defining Rape Internationally: A Comment on *Akayesu*," 44 *Columbia Journal of Transnational Law* 940, 942–943 (2006), and here in number 28, "Sex Equality in Global Perspective." See also Prosecutor v. Kunarac, Case No. IT-96-23 & IT9623/1A, Judgement ¶¶ 132–133 (Int'l Crim. Trib. For the Former Yugoslavia June 12, 2002), http://www.icty.org/x /cases/kunarac/acjug/en/kun-aj020612e.pdf ("Such detentions amount to circumstances that were so coercive as to negate any possibility of consent . . . . In conclusion, the Appeals Chamber agrees with the Trial Chamber's determination that the coercive circumstances present in this case made consent to the instant sexual acts by the Appellants impossible.").

22. See the discussion in number 28.

23. Gleick, *Chaos* 292.

24. This is discussed in numbers 11 and 28.

25. The original analysis was first laid out in Canada in "Substantive Equality," number 11 in this collection, embodied in the factum in *Andrews*, Women's Legal Education and Action Fund, "Factum of the Women's Legal Education and Action Fund (LEAF), Andrews v. the Law Society of British Columbia and the Attorney General of British Columbia," in *Equality and the Charter: Ten Years of Feminist Advocacy Before the Supreme Court of Canada* 3–22 (Toronto: Emond Montgomery Publications Ltd. 1996), largely embraced in the decision in *Andrews*. Andrews v. Law Society of B.C. [1989] 1 S.C.R. 143 (Can.). Losing its way and returning is traced in MacKinnon, *Sex Equality*. The Court re-embraced the approach in R. v. Kapp, [2008] 2 S.C.R. 483, ¶¶ 41, 55 (Can.).

26. As argued for in number 15, this approach was proposed in Sweden in 1990 after the notion was alluded to in the speech recorded at Catharine A. MacKinnon, "On Sex and Violence: Introducing the Antipornography Civil Rights Law in Sweden," in Catharine A. MacKinnon, ed., *Are Women Human? And Other International Dialogues* 100 (Cambridge, MA: Belknap Press of Harvard University Press 2006).

27. See number 9 infra. The arguments and observations in numbers 10, 17, 18, and 19 expand upon it.

28. See the pieces in Part V infra.

1. TO CHANGE THE WORLD FOR WOMEN

1. This talk was given at The Midwest Regional Women and the Law Conference, University of Minnesota Law School, Minneapolis, Minnesota on October 11, 1980. Its transcript is published here for the first time.

2. Catharine A. MacKinnon, *Toward a Feminist Theory of the State* (Cambridge, MA: Harvard University Press 1989).

3. Alexander v. Yale University, 631 F.2d 178, 185 (2d Cir. 1980).

4. The civil remedy section of the Violence Against Women Act, 42 U.S.C.A. § 13981, was held unconstitutional by United States v. Morrison, 529 U.S. 598, 627 (2000) for exceeding Congress's legislative power.

5. See, e.g., Andrea Dworkin and Catharine A. MacKinnon, *Pornography & Civil Rights: A New Day for Women's Equality* 31 (Organizing Against Pornography 1988); Catharine A. MacKinnon and Andrea Dworkin, eds., *In Harm's Way: The Pornography Civil Rights Hearings* 426 (Cambridge, MA: Harvard University Press 1998).

6. See Kimberlé Williams Crenshaw, "Demarginalizing the Intersection of Race and Sex: A Black Feminist Critique of Antidiscrimination Doctrine, Feminist Theory and Antiracist Politics," 1989 *University of Chicago Legal Forum* 139–167 (1989); Kimberlé Williams Crenshaw, "Mapping the Margins: Intersectionality, Identity Politics, and Violence Against Women of Color," 43 *Stanford Law Review* 1241 (1991). For updated analysis, see the entire symposium issue, 38 *Signs: Journal of Women in Culture and Society* (2013).

7. Redefining rape along the lines of the analysis sketched here, and developments accordingly, are traced in Catharine A. MacKinnon, "Rape Redefined," 10 *Harvard Law & Policy Review* 431 (2016) ("Rape Redefined").

8. John Stuart Mill, *The Subjection of Women* 30 (Cambridge, MA: M.I.T. Press 1970) (1869) (arguing that women are subjected through society because they are unequal in the law of marriage).

9. Diana E. H. Russell, *Sexual Exploitation: Rape, Child Sexual Abuse, and Workplace Harassment* 31 (Thousand Oaks, CA: Sage Publications 1984) (documenting 9.5 percent of rapes reported); National Victim Center, Crime Victims Research and Treatment Center, *Rape in America: A Report to the Nation* 5 (1992) (finding 16 percent of rapes reported); Catharine A. MacKinnon, *Sex Equality* 854 (3d ed., New York: Foundation Press 2016) (compiling research to date).

10. This report was taken directly from women's experience as reported at the time. Subsequent research proved it to be widespread. See generally Lynda Lytle Holmstrom and Ann Wolbert Burgess, *The Victim of Rape: Institutional Reactions* (1991); Lee Madigan and Nancy C. Gamble, *The Second Rape* (New York: Lexington Books 1991); MacKinnon, *Sex Equality* 866 (compiling research to date).

11. At the time this talk was given, support for this observation was mainly anecdotal. For a reasonably contemporary instance, one case that was discussed in the press at the time held that acts of a defendant wrestling, kissing, and pressing himself against the victim without her consent "when such acts are merely the preliminaries to consensual sexual intercourse" are not enough to put a reasonable person in fear of bodily harm, hence are not a lesser included offense of assault. State v. Jeffries, 291 S.E.2d 859, 861 (N.C. App. 1982). Actually, the State's evidence here showed that the defendant grabbed the victim, pulled her onto his lap despite her telling him "No," whereupon she burned him with a cigarette and tried to break away; he held onto her and threw her on the bed and started kissing her and pressing his body down on her despite her crying and pleading that he stop, after which he forcefully wrestled with her, and despite her continued resistance and threats to prosecute, forcibly removed her clothing while she continued to try to push him off her; she hit him in the face with her fist, he struck her back, and he eventually had sexual intercourse with her. Id. at 860. (His testimony was that she hugged and kissed him and then he hit her while they were having sex. Id. at 861.) He was convicted of second degree rape; that conviction was upheld. Id. at 864. In other words, the jury did not believe his version. Regrettably, substantial case law support for this kind of judicial normalization of forcibly abusive sexual initiation being deemed even potentially consensual—the *Jeffries* court actually said that the acts mentioned above "may constitute assault," but when they initiate sex, they don't, id. at 861— has developed substantially since. See MacKinnon, "Rape Redefined," 459–462.

12. At the time of delivery, this fact was supported by Richard Rada, ed., *Clinical Aspects of the Rapist* (New York: Grune & Stratton 1978); Clifford Kirkpatrick and Eugene Kanin, "Males Sex Aggression on a University Campus," *American Sociological Review* 22, 52–58 (1957); Neil Malamuth, Scott Haber, and Seymour Feshbach, "Testing Hypotheses Regarding Rape: Exposure to Sexual Violence, Sex Differences, and the 'Normality' of Rapists," 14 *Journal of Research in Personality* 121 (1980). Soon after, it was further documented by James Check and Neil Malamuth, "An Empirical Assessment of Some Feminist Hypotheses About Rape," 8 *International Journal of Women's Studies* 414, 415 (1985), Diana Scully, *Understanding Sexual Violence: A Study of Convicted Rapists* (Boston: Unwin Hyman 1990), and others.

13. Much later, the process described here came to be termed "rape attrition" by researchers. For extensive documentation of it, see MacKinnon, *Sex Equality* 854–855.

14. These rates, known from experience at the time, have been variously documented since. See, e.g., Vernon L. Quinsey et al., "Actuarial Prediction of Sexual Recidivism," 10 *Journal of Interpersonal Violence* 85 (1995).

15. Alexander v. Yale University, 459 F. Supp. 1, 5 (D. Conn. 1977) (adopting the ruling of Magistrate Judge Arthur H. Latimer).

16. Id.

17. Alexander v. Yale University, 631 F.2d 178, 184 (2d Cir. 1980).

18. Continental Can Co. Inc. v. State of Minnesota, 291 N.W.2d 241, 250 (Minn. 1980).

19. "I'm Black and Blue from the Rolling Stones—and I Love It!," *Rolling Stone*, July 1, 1976.

20. "Hit Me with a Club," Heublein's Club Cocktail, 1975.

21. Hugh M. Hefner, "The Playboy Philosophy," 1 *Playboy* 41 (Jan. 1963).

22. This analysis was later pursued in detail in Catharine A. MacKinnon, "Not a Moral Issue," in Catharine A. MacKinnon, *Feminism Unmodified: Discourses on Life and Law* (Cambridge, MA: Harvard University Press 1987).

2. A RADICAL ACT OF HOPE

1. This event occurred in New Haven, Connecticut, on April 16, 1989.

2. As cited in Deborah Rhode, *Speaking of Sex: The Denial of Gender Inequality* 169 (Cambridge, MA: Harvard University Press 1997); Herma Hill Kay, *MacNeil/Lehrer News Hour*, Apr. 24, 1995.

3. LAW'S POWER

1. This talk was previously published as Catharine A. MacKinnon, "Graduation Address: Yale Law School, June 1989," 2 *Yale Journal of Law & Feminism* 299 (1990).

2. I remember Cher saying this around the time of this talk but can only find it documented in Cher and Robert Haas, *Cher Forever Fit: A Lifetime Plan for Health, Fitness, and Beauty* 159 (1991), discussing her Academy Award ("If I can get this from where people thought I was coming from, then anyone can do anything.").

3. Catharine A. MacKinnon, *Sex Equality* 16, 170 (3d ed., New York: Foundation Press 2016) ("*Sex Equality*") ("In 1875, the U.S. Supreme Court,

referencing the language of § 2, ruled unanimously in Minor v. Happersett, 88 U.S. (21 Wall.) 162 (1874), that voting, as a creature of state law, was not a right of national citizenship protected from denial to women by the Fourteenth Amendment"; "By material measures, women's work is not as highly valued as men's, and work less valued by every measure is assigned to women on the basis of sex").

4. Id. at 861 ("Sexual abuse ranges from undesired sexual touching, forced nudity, and molestation of children as well as adults through sexual harassment in schools, at work, and on the street to rape and attempted rape in war zones and other settings of everyday life").

5. Id. at 1689–1690 ("On the simplest descriptive level, pornography sells women or children, sometimes men, and at times transgendered people, for sexual use as objects . . . . While women compared with men are disproportionately used in the most violating ways in pornography, . . . men compared with women disproportionately consume pornography as entertainment, a trend increasing among younger Americans").

6. Id. at 1536–1537 ("How many women or men have been in prostitution as such at some point in their lives is also not reliably known. Estimates of the numbers of women in prostitution in the United States in the 1970s and '80s range from 500,000 to 1,300,000").

7. Id. at 1361 ("Legal and social arrangements throughout the world have long combined to thrust maternity on women whether they want it or not through imposed sex roles valorizing motherhood as destiny and fulfillment of women's essential function, heterosexual intercourse that is coerced, pressured, or routinized, and restricted or precluded options for ending unwanted pregnancies. While many women seek motherhood, and many women embrace it unsought, many risk and lose their lives").

8. Id. at 401 ("Many inequities remain for women and girls at all educational levels. They include unequal treatment in and out of class, widespread sexual harassment, destruction of self-confidence and self-esteem, unequal funding for athletics, textbooks that stereotype, curricula that ignore women's contributions, and the sex, race, and other biases of many teachers").

9. Id. at 498 ("The inadequate real world grounding of the legal categories of race and sex—specifically producing a male-valanced law of race and a white-valanced law of sex—combined with the perceived imperative to establish sex as a basis for discrimination by analogy to race, has often erased the inequality injuries of women of color, for whom racism and sexism can be injurious simultaneously and geometrically").

10. Id. at 873, 956–959 ("Many victims of rape anticipate, with reason, that they will not be believed by the authorities or will lose in court—perhaps because they are not believed, but also perhaps because the triers of fact value their rapist over them, blame the woman for her rape, or do not care that they were raped, thinking the harm trivial or the law against rape repressive"; "In the criminal context, rape has classically been defined by three elements: sexual intercourse by force without consent").

11. American Booksellers Ass'n, Inc. v. Hudnut, 771 F.2d 323, 329 (7th Cir. 1985), aff'd, 475 U.S. 1001 (1986).

12. Harris v. McRae, 448 U.S. 297, 317–318 (1980).

13. MacKinnon, Sex Equality 1420–1422 ("Attempting to stop the procedure by any means legally permissible, many states have passed abortion regulations that target clinics where abortions are provided, aim to restrict the licensing of physicians who perform abortions, create waiting periods for the women, and require medical procedures such as ultrasounds be taken and shown to the pregnant woman without medical reason").

14. Diana E. H. Russell and Nancy Howell, "The Prevalence of Rape in the United States Revisited," 8 Signs: Journal of Women in Culture & Society 689, 690 (1983). For a recent update see Patricia Tjaden and Nancy Thoennes, U.S. Department of Justice, National Institute of Justice, NCJ 210346, Extent, Nature, and Consequences of Rape Victimization: Findings from the National Violence Against Women Survey 7 (2006) (finding that one in six women has been raped at some time in her life).

15. United States Merit Systems Protection Board, Sexual Harassment in the Federal Government: An Update (1988); MacKinnon, Sex Equality 1011 ("Although true epidemiological studies do not exist, large-scale surveys of working women suggest that approximately 1 of every 2 women will be harassed at some point during their academic or working lives.").

16. Diana E. H. Russell, "The Incidence and Prevalence of Intrafamilial and Extrafamilial Sexual Abuse of Female Children," 7 Child Abuse & Neglect 133, 145 (1983). For a recent update see Centers for Disease Control and Prevention, National Center for Injury Prevention and Control, Adverse Childhood Experiences Study: Data and Statistics (1997), available at http://www.cdc.gov/nccdphp/ace/prevalence.htm (estimating that 24.7 percent of women were sexually abused as children).

17. G. Daniel Rath et al., "Rates of Domestic Violence Against Adult Women by Men Partners," 2 Journal of the American Board of Family Medicine 229 (finding that 28 percent of adult women reported severe physical abuse by their male partners). Mary P. Koss et al., No Safe Haven: Male

Violence Against Women at Home, at Work, and in the Community 44 (Washington, DC: American Psychological Association 1994) (estimating that one in every three women will experience at least one physical assault by an intimate partner during adulthood); Michele C. Black et al., National Center for Injury Prevention and Control Centers for Disease Control and Prevention, *National Intimate Partner and Sexual Violence Survey: 2010 Summary Report* 39 (2011) (finding that one in three women (32.9 percent) has experienced physical violence by an intimate partner in her lifetime).

18. MacKinnon, *Sex Equality* 1012 ("A 1993 survey of 800 law partners and associates revealed that 51% of the women lawyers reported that they had been sexually harassed at some point during their careers and that one in six reported incidents within the previous three years").

19. Donald J. Treiman and Heidi I. Hartmann, eds., Committee on Occupational Classification and Analysis, National Research Council, *Women, Work, and Wages: Equal Pay for Jobs of Equal Value* 13 (1981) ("In 1978 women of all races who worked full time all year earned 55 percent as much as white men, and black men earned 72 percent as much as white men"). In 2014, the median annual wage of women who worked full time was 79 percent of the median annual wage of men who worked full time. U.S. Census Bureau (2015). Current Population Survey, *Annual Social and Economic (ASEC) Supplement: Table PINC-05: Work Experience in 2014—People 15 Years Old and Over by Total Money Earnings in 2014, Age, Race, Hispanic Origin, and Sex*, retrieved March 13, 2016, from http://www.census.gov/hhes/www/cpstables/032015/perinc/pinc05_000 .htm (Unpublished calculation based on the median annual wages of all men and women who worked full time, year round in 2014).

20. MacKinnon, *Sex Equality* 1536–1537 ("How many women or men have been in prostitution as such at some point in their lives is also not reliably known. Estimates of the numbers of women in prostitution in the United States in the 1970s and '80s range from 500,000 to 1,300,000.").

21. Martha Langelan, "The Political Economy of Pornography," *Aegis: Magazine on Ending Violence Against Women*, 1981, at 5 ("[t]he actual U.S. sales volume [of pornography] may be as much as $10 to $15 billion in 1981 . . . . Hard-core bookstores alone account for at least $3 to $4 billion a year. Adding in movies, mainstream newsstand sales, mail order revenues, and paraphernalia sales, D.C. Feminists Against Pornography conservatively estimates the industry's total revenues at $7 billion in 1980"); Melinda Tankard Reist and Abigail Bray, eds., "The Global Por-

nography Industry Is Expected to Reach US $100 Billion in the Near Future," in *Big Porn Inc: Exposing the Harms of the Global Pornography Industry* xiv (North Melbourne, Vic.: Spinifex Press 2011) (citing Elliott R. Morss, "The Economics of the Global Entertainment Industry," *Elliott Morss,* June 26, 2009, http://www.morssglobalfinance.com/the -economics-of-the-global-entertainment-industry.

22. American Booksellers Ass'n, Inc. v. Hudnut, 771 F.2d 323, 329 (7th Cir. 1985), *aff'd,* 475 U.S. 1001 (1986).

4. TO QUASH A LIE

1. This talk was originally titled "Doing Something: The Situation of Women and the Possibility of Change," but I liked the title suggested by the editor of the *Smith Alumnae Quarterly,* where it was first published from a transcript of an audiotape. Catharine A. MacKinnon, "To Quash a Lie," 11 *Smith Alumnae Quarterly* 11 (1991).

2. Andrea Dworkin and Catharine A. MacKinnon, *Pornography & Civil Rights: A New Day for Women's Equality* 31 (Minneapolis, MN: Organizing Against Pornography 1988) ("*A New Day for Women's Equality*") (antipornography ordinance); Catharine A. MacKinnon, *Sex Equality* 1750 (3d ed., New York: Foundation Press 2016) ("In 1983, a sex discrimination ordinance was passed by the Minneapolis City Council that made four injuries done through pornography—coercion into pornography, forcing pornography on a person, assault due to specific pornography, and trafficking in pornography—civilly actionable as practices of sex discrimination."). Indianapolis enacted a similar ordinance. The Seventh Circuit ruled the ordinance unconstitutional, holding that pornography is speech protected by the First Amendment. American Booksellers Ass'n, Inc. v. Hudnut, 771 F.2d 323, 329 (7th Cir. 1985). The Supreme Court upheld the Seventh Circuit's ruling without comment. Hudnut v. American Booksellers Ass'n, Inc., 475 U.S. 1001 (1986).

3. American Booksellers Ass'n, Inc. v. Hudnut, 771 F.2d 323, 329 (7th Cir. 1985), *aff'd,* 475 U.S. 1001 (1986).

4. MacKinnon, *Sex Equality* 170 ("By material measures, women's work is not as highly valued as men's, and work less valued by every measure is assigned to women on the basis of sex.").

5. Id. at 1011 ("Although true epidemiological studies do not exist, large-scale surveys of working women suggest that approximately 1 of every 2 women will be harassed at some point during their academic or working lives.").

6. Id. at 1689–1690 ("On the simplest descriptive level, pornography sells women or children, sometimes men, and at times transgendered people, for sexual use as objects . . . . While women compared with men are disproportionately used in the most violating ways in pornography, . . . men compared with women disproportionately consume pornography as entertainment, a trend increasing among younger Americans.").

7. Id. at 1361, 1536–1537 ("Legal and social arrangements throughout the world have long combined to thrust maternity on women whether they want it or not through imposed sex roles valorizing motherhood as destiny and fulfillment of women's essential function, heterosexual intercourse that is coerced, pressured, or routinized, and restricted or precluded options for ending unwanted pregnancies. While many women seek motherhood, and many women embrace it unsought, many risk and lose their lives"; "How many women or men have been in prostitution as such at some point in their lives is also not reliably known. Estimates of the numbers of women in prostitution in the United States in the 1970s and '80s range from 500,000 to 1,300,000.").

8. Edgar B. Herwick III, "How One Woman Eventually Founded Smith College," *WGBH News*, Mar. 13, 2015, http://news.wgbh.org/post/how -one-woman-eventually-founded-smith-college; Maggie McLean, "Sophia Smith," *History of American Women*, Mar. 25, 2014, http://www .womenhistoryblog.com/2012/03/sophia-smith.html.

9. Richard Rorty, "Feminism and Pragmatism," 30 *Michigan Quarterly Review* 231 (1991).

10. Robinson v. Jacksonville Shipyards, Inc., 760 F. Supp. 1486, 1523 (M.D. Fla. 1991). The defendant appealed. The case was settled before the appellate decision was handed down.

11. For the record, published here for the first time, is the original submission:

It's a rare day for glacier watchers when the law recognizes a harm to women, especially a harm done by pornography.

Lois Robinson, a skilled welder in a craft with few women, sued her employer for the pornography that saturated Jacksonville shipyards. She said it was sexual harassment, specifically that it constituted a sexually hostile, intimidating, demeaning and offensive working environment that discriminated against her on the basis of sex under federal civil rights law. When she won last week—and the pornography, not the woman, had to go—those who work for sex equality saw the mountain of male dominance move, even if only a little.

The judge's opinion describes the unrelenting assault of pornography on Lois Robinson and other women workers at the shipyard. On the walls were naked women, including Black women, their breasts and genitals displayed as objects for use, presented as pieces of meat ("USDA Choice"), engaged in lesbian sex, masturbating, inviting penetration, in proffering poses of sexual submission, display, and access. Many had long blonde hair, like Lois. Some materials were forced on her individually by coworkers and supervisors who laughed at her pain and escalated when she complained.

As it always does, the pornography engendered a further onslaught of vilification and other aggression by men against women. Examples from the ten-year flood Lois recalled at trial are: "Hey, pussycat, come here and give me a whiff," "I'd like to get in bed with that," "Black women taste like sardines," "It doesn't hurt a woman to have sex right after childbirth," "That one is mine" (referring to a woman in one of the magazines), and "You rate about an 8 or 9 on a scale of 10." Graffiti created just for her said, "eat me," "pussy," and "lick me you whore dog bitch." A woman coworker testified that she was pinched and grabbed and, when she protested, told in front of a large group of male co-workers, "if you fell into a barrel of dicks, you'd come up sucking your thumb." The dart board there had a woman's breast painted on it with the nipple as the bull's-eye. Apparently by way of remedy, one thickly pornography-infested area was posted "Men Only."

These are just a few instances from the record of violation that most press reports of this case have subsumed under the euphemism "pin-ups."

To women, none of this abuse is unusual. Its misogyny is commonplace, in and out of pornography. What is unusual is that a court recognized it as real and illegal. Usually, women have no civil rights where pornography is concerned. Courts protect pornography, not women, no matter how much damage the pornography is proven to do. Indeed, one court—conceding the role of pornography in promoting rape, economic deprivation, and second class citizenship—measured its value by the harm it does and protected it for that reason. Another said that pornography cannot constitute sexual harassment at work because pornography is everywhere.

So there is no law against pornography that is demonstrated to cause rape and murder. There is no law against forcing pornography on women and children in their homes; on patients by doctors, on clients by lawyers, or on parishioners by clergymen; on children in playgrounds; on prostitutes in brothels. There is no law against coerced pornography for the women who have been abducted and tortured to make it. There is no law against saturating the entire society with pornography, a traffic in women that targets all women for sexual assault and promotes prejudice against them, like the attacks and bigotry and segregation suffered by Lois Robinson and her women coworkers. There is proof of all of it. There is nowhere to go to get away from any of it.

The court in Lois Robinson's case concluded that the shipyard was a "sexually hostile, intimidating work environment." Take the word "work" out of that and you have the rest of society. Given that backdrop, what made it possible for this court—where others have failed—to recognize the harm of pornography at work, creating a pornography-free island in a sea of abuse?

On the job, sex equality is the legal standard. Women are supposed to be equals at work. The workplace is special because we have a law against sexual subordination there, so when it happens it may be seen for what it is.

You who thought that women were supposed to be equal everywhere else too, guaranteed equal protection of the law throughout society, take note: everywhere else, this abuse is protected speech.

The self-censored version added, after all the blanks at the reference to "pin-ups:" "The mainstream media will not print what was actually done to Lois Robinson in the paragraph above. The consequence of such censorship is to make concern with the harm of pornography look exaggerated, because you are not permitted to know what it is. Imagine the reaction if the media wanted to print this and someone tried to get a court order to stop them." At the end, in reference to First Amendment protected speech, this sentence was also added: "That is, it is for those who do the harm, not for those who criticize it."

12. Leo Weinstein was Esther Cloudman Dunn Professor of Government, faculty member at Smith from 1952 to 1991, who passed away in 1999. He taught constitutional law and political theory together, emphasizing the classics, shaping the way I think about law and politics to this day.

13. The École Polytechnique Massacre, also known as the Montreal Massacre, occurred on December 6, 1989, at the École Polytechnique in Montreal, Quebec, Canada.

14. Avram Finklestein et al., AIDS Coalition to Unleash Power, "Silence=Death" (1987).

5. THE MEASURE OF WHAT MATTERS

1. People v. Burnham, 176 Cal. App. 3d 1134, 1148 (Cal. Ct. App. 1986).

2. See, e.g., Glenn Collins, "Sex Abuse: The Child's Word Isn't Enough," *New York Times*, July 11, 1983, at B4; Debra Whitcomb, U.S. Dept. of Justice, National Institute of Justice, *Prosecution of Child Sexual Abuse: Innovations in Practice* 5–7 (1985).

3. Phil Mintz, "Los Angeles Verdict: Jurors Acquit 4 Cops," *Newsday*, Apr. 30, 1992, at 5. ("Rioting erupted in Los Angeles yesterday after four white Los Angeles police officers were acquitted of nearly all charges yesterday in the videotaped beating of black motorist Rodney King.").

4. Toner v. Commissioner, 60 T.C.M. (CCH) 1016, 1019 (1990), *aff'd sub nom.* Doe v. Commissioner, 958 F.2d 362 (3d Cir. 1992) (Table) (No. 91-1678) (unpublished). The IRS did not agree with this argument; neither did the court, unfortunately.

5. See Judith Herman, *Trauma and Recovery* 7 (2d ed., New York: Basic Books 1997); Jennifer Freyd, *Betrayal Trauma: The Logic of Forgetting Childhood Abuse* (Cambridge, MA: Harvard University Press 1996); Ellen Bass and Laura Davis, *The Courage to Heal* 70 (4th ed. New York: Collins Living 2008).

6. National Conference of State Legislatures, *State Civil Statutes of Limitations in Child Sexual Abuse Cases* (2016), http://www.ncsl.org/research /human-services/state-civil-statutes-of-limitations-in-child-sexua.aspx #ATNP ("According to the National Center for Victims of Crime, nearly every state has a basic suspension of the statute of limitation ("tolling") for civil actions while a person is a minor. Many states have also adopted additional extensions specifically for cases involving sexual abuse of children. Extensions for filing civil actions for child sexual abuse are most often based upon the discovery rule—by the time the victim discovers the sexual abuse or the relationship of the conduct to the injuries, the ordinary time limitation may have expired. This "delayed discovery" may be due to emotional and psychological trauma and is often accompanied by repression of the memory of abuse. Child victims frequently do not discover the relationship of their psychological injuries to the abuse until well into

adulthood—usually during the course of psychological counseling or therapy. They may not even discover the fact of such abuse until they undergo such therapy."); National Center for Prosecution of Child Abuse, *Statutes of Limitation for Prosecution of Offenses Against Children* (2012), http://www.ndaa.org/pdf/Statute%20of%20Limitations%20for%20Pros ecution%20of%20Offenses%20Against%20Children%202012.pdf.

7. Catharine A. MacKinnon, *Sex Equality* 1003 (3d ed., New York: Foundation Press 2016) (*"Sex Equality"*) ("It was 1977 when sexual harassment was first recognized by a federal Court of Appeals as legally actionable as a form of sex discrimination at work under the sex discrimination prohibition of Title VII of the Civil Rights Act of 1964, Pub. L. No. 88-352, 78 Stat. 241. See Barnes v. Costle, 561 F.2d 983 (D.C. Cir. 1977); see also Williams v. Saxbe, 413 F. Supp. 654 (D.D.C. 1976) (Richey, J.) (marking first federal district court recognition of sexual harassment as sex discrimination). A decade later the U.S. Supreme Court adopted the same interpretation in Meritor Savings Bank v. Vinson, 477 U.S. 57 (1986). In the interim, in 1980 the Equal Employment Opportunities Commission encapsulated the basic legal understanding in guidelines that were widely followed by courts.").

8. In South Carolina in 1992, Dale Crawford was acquitted of rape after he videotaped himself having sex with his bound and gagged (with duct tape) wife, the videotape having served as evidence of his defense of a consensual sadomasochistic relationship with her. See Lucy Soto, "S.C. Man Acquitted of Marital Rape, Jury Saw Videotape, Decided Screams, Ropes Part of Sex Game," *The Charlotte Observer*, Apr. 18, 1992, at 1A; "Marital Rape Case in South Carolina Ends with Acquittal," *NPR All Things Considered*, Apr. 22, 1992; "A Controversy Over Marital Rape," *CNN Larry King Live Transcripts*, May 15, 1992. Ann Russo, *Taking Back Our Lives: A Call to Action for the Feminist Movement* 115 (New York: Routledge 2001). Mr. Crawford was convicted of killing his third wife in Virginia in 2004. See Crawford v. Commonwealth of Virginia, 686 S.E.2d 557 (Va. Ct. App. 2009).

9. MacKinnon, *Sex Equality* 1003 ("Long regarded as just life, such acts are usually beneath sanction by the criminal law, which treats them as uncoerced because the forms of power they rely upon are not exclusively physical. Sex under these conditions has also been long regarded as consensual, because acquiescence forced by inequality is typically regarded as free . . . . These acts also went unremedied by the law of tort. Sexual harassment's modern legal history began in the mid-1970s with the women's movement in the United States, when the injury became more publicly

visible as a result of its legal recognition as a civil rights violation and form of sex discrimination.").

6. INTERVENING FOR SEX EQUALITY

1. The three lectures were published as Catharine A. MacKinnon, *Sex Equality Controversies: The Formosa Lectures* (National Taiwan University Press 2015) in English and Mandarin, this one in English at 305.
2. General Recommendation No. 19: Violence against women, U.N. Doc. A/47/3 (1992).
3. See Catharine A. MacKinnon, *Sexual Harassment of Working Women: A Case of Sex Discrimination* 143–214 (New Haven, CT: Yale University Press 1979).
4. See Regina v. Butler, 1 S.C.R. 452 (1992); Regina v. Keegstra, 3 S.C.R. 697 (1990).
5. See Andrews v. Law Society of British Columbia, 1 S.C.R. 143 (1989).
6. Violence Against Women Act, 42 U.S.C. § 13981 (1994).
7. See United States v. Morrison, 529 U.S. 598 (2000).
8. This analysis is discussed in Catharine A. MacKinnon, "Rape, Genocide, and Women's Human Rights," in *Are Women Human?: and Other International Dialogues* 181 (Cambridge, MA: Belknap Press of Harvard University Press 2006).
9. For the Rwanda Tribunal's analysis of rape, see Prosecutor v. Akayesu, ICTR-96-4-T (1998).
10. See The Protocol to Prevent, Suppress and Punish Trafficking in Persons, especially Women and Children, supplementing the United Nations Convention against Transnational Organized Crime, Nov. 15, 2000, 2237 U.N.T.S. 319.
11. See Swedish law, which criminalizes sex buyers, the demand for prostitution, as well as the sellers, the pimps and traffickers, while eliminating any punishment of any kind for people in prostitution, that is, "the sold," and providing them with the services and job training they say they want. See Lag om förbud mot köp av sexuella tjänster 405 (1998) ("A person who obtains casual sexual relations in exchange for payment shall be sentenced—unless the act is punishable under the Swedish Penal Code—for the purchase of sexual services to a fine or imprisonment for at most six months"). I would have drafted it differently, as "Any person who purchases another person for sexual use is guilty of a crime," or words to that effect. For the proposal, see Catharine A. MacKinnon, "On Sex and

Violence: Introducing the Antipornography Civil Rights Law in Sweden,"
in MacKinnon, *Are Women Human?* 91, 100. See also Andrea Dworkin,
introduction to "Feminism: An Agenda," in *Letters from a War Zone* 133
(London: Secker & Warburg 1988) ("I still think that prostitution must
be decriminalized, as I say in this speech; but, increasingly, I think there
must be simple, straightforward, enforced criminal laws against exploiting
women in commercial sexual transactions. The exploiter—pimp or john—
needs to be recognized and treated as a real criminal, much as the batterer
now is.").

12. Rome Statute of the International Criminal Court, 2187 U.N.T.S. 3 (1998).
13. Andrea Dworkin, "Against the Male Flood: Censorship, Pornography, and
Equality," in *Letters from a War Zone* 273.

7. INTRODUCTION, SYMPOSIUM ON SEXUAL HARASSMENT

1. Catharine A. MacKinnon, Symposium: Sexual Harassment, 10 *Capital
University Law Review* i (Spring 1981).
2. "Pourquoi Sorcières?" in Elaine Marks and Isabelle De Courtivron, eds.,
New French Feminisms 200 (Amherst, MA: University of Massachusetts
Press 1980).
3. To my knowledge, this is true in the North American legal tradition.
4. Barnes v. Costle, 561 F.2d 983 (D.C. Cir. 1977); Tomkins v. Public Service
Electric & Gas Co., 422 F. Supp. 553 (D.N.J. 1976); Miller v. Bank of
America, 600 F.2d 211 (9th Cir. 1979), *rev'd and remanded*, 568 F.2d 1044
(3d Cir. 1977); Alexander v. Yale University, 459 F. Supp. 1 (D. Conn. 1977);
Alexander (Price) v. Yale University, 631 F.2d 178 (2nd Cir. 1980). The his-
tory of the establishment of the employment claim is discussed by Jill Laurie
Goodman, "Sexual Harassment: Some Observations on the Distance Trav-
eled and the Distance Yet to Go," in Symposium: Sexual Harassment, 10
Capital University Law Review 445, 445 (1981) ("Some Observations");
the education claim by Phyllis L. Crocker and Anne E. Simon, "Sexual
Harassment in Education," in Symposium: Sexual Harassment, 10 *Capital
University Law Review* 541 (1981) ("Sexual Harassment in Education").
5. Bundy v. Jackson, No. 79-1693, slip. op. at 21 (D.C. Cir., Jan. 12, 1981);
Continental Can Co. v. Minnesota, 297 N.W.2d 241 (Minn. 1980); Wilson
v. Northwest Publications, Inc. ("What appears most significant in this
case and what does not appear in *Continental Can Company, Inc.* is the
fact that Mlynarczyk was intimidated by her male co-workers because of
her sex. This had little to do with sexual advances or propositioning in
the sense discussed in those cases. There was never any physical touching

in a sexual sense. Instead, comments were made to, and actions taken against, Mlynarczyk that were intended to degrade, demean, or offend her because she was a woman. According to Moeller, they were the type of things a man would not say to another man. The physical abuses—the throwing of paper towels, paper clips, and the spraying of alcohol—were physical abuses against a physically weaker person. Walking by a person and saying "Horseshit" is purely an act of disdain. Standing around a woman and chanting "Fuck you, fuck you" is pure abuse. Placing a piece of Ku Klux Klan literature on Mlynarczyk's desk was also an act of intimidation."); *Report of Hearing Examiner of Human Rights*, May 10, 1979 (144479); *aff'd*, Minnesota Supreme Court (Mar. 30, 1981); E.E.O.C. Guidelines on Sexual Harassment, 29 CFR 1604.ll(a)(3); Caldwell v. Hodgeman, Civ. No. 36573, Memorandum Decision (D. Mass. Apr. 6, 1981).

6. EEOC v. Sage Realty, 507 F. Supp. 599 (S.D.N.Y. 1981). See also 87 F.R.D. 365 (S.D.N.Y. 1980).

7. Barnes v. Costle, 561 F.2d 983, 1001 (D.C. Cir. 1977) (MacKinnon, J., concurring) ("We are not here concerned with racial epithets or confusing union authorization cards, which serve no one's interest, but with social patterns that to some extent are normal and expectable."). Racial epithets probably serve the interest of racists no less than coercive sexual advances—sexual epithets—serve the interests of sexists. Sexual harassment as a concept challenges precisely "the common attitude that sexual demands [in student-teacher relations] are an ambiguous and even trivial problem, merely a complicitous game between the powerful and ambitious, in which nothing important is suffered by the victim or gained by the victimizer." Erika Munk, "A Case of Sexual Abuse," *The Village Voice* XXIV, 45, Oct. 22, 1979, at 24. The problem is moving the perceived line between normal practices and victimization in the first place.

8. Neely v. American Fidelity Assurance Co., 17 FEP Cases 482 (W.D. Okla. 1978).

9. It is much like not comprehending Blacks protesting relegation to the back of the bus, on the ground that they got where they were going, or giving protesters of lunch-counter segregation lunch as a remedy. After strenuous and costly effort (see, e.g., Crocker and Simon's account of the *Alexander v. Yale* litigation) the legal system has become somewhat more responsive, Crocker and Simon, "Sexual Harassment in Education." See Bundy v. Jackson, No. 79-1693 slip op. at 21 (D.C. Cir., January 12, 1981) (constant unsolicited and unreciprocated sexual attention is sex discrimination

in employment, even though no formal index of the job is disturbed); EEOC Guidelines on Sexual Harassment, 29 CFR 1604.ll(a)(3) (prohibiting sexual advances that create an intimidating, hostile or offensive working environment).

10. This is the upshot of Texas Department of Community Affairs v. Burdine, 49 U.S.L.W. 4214 (Mar. 3, 1981), sealing the implications of Furnco Construction Company v. Waters, 438 U.S. 567 (1978) and Board of Trustees of Keene State College v. Sweeney, 439 U.S. 24 (1979). Once the defendant "articulates lawful reasons for the action" on rebuttal, the plaintiff is returned to the status quo prior to her prima facie case—i.e., to the (hidden) presumption of a prior nondiscriminatory social universe, Burdine, 49 U.S.L.W. at 4216. This is not to say that courts should hold defendants liable on merely a prima facie showing. Rather allocations of burden of proof should give the plaintiff some benefit of the congressional recognition that discrimination against women exists, as a context within which to evaluate claims and weigh evidence. *Burdine*, to the contrary, has the effect of assessing each claim within the context of a presumption that the merit system generally works. This is a very substantive rule on an apparently technical point. Each plaintiff is prevented from having her evidence heard in the context of the findings that have prompted congressional action in the sex discrimination area—that women have often not been advanced according to ability.

11. See Crocker and Simon, "Sexual Harassment in Education."

12. Tomkins v. Public Service Electric & Gas Co., 568 F.2d 1044 (3d Cir. 1977) (consent order); Bundy v. Jackson, No. 79-1693 slip op. at 22ff (D.C. Cir., Jan. 12, 1981) (injunction).

13. See Joan Vermeulen, "Employer Liability Under Title VII for Sexual Harassment by Supervisory Employees," 10 *Capital University Law Review* 499 (1981); Jan C. Leventer, "Sexual Harassment and Title VII: EEOC Guidelines, Conditions Litigation, and the United States Supreme Court," in Symposium: Sexual Harassment, 10 *Capital University Law Review* 481 (1981).

14. Heelan v. Johns-Manville Corp., 451 F. Supp. 251 (D. Colo. 1978) (finding for the plaintiff at trial, discussing credibility in detail); Alexander v. Yale, "Memorandum of Decision" Civil No. N-77-277, at 3 (D. Conn. July 3, 1977) (Judge Ellen B. Burns, finding against the plaintiff at trial, making no reference to credibility or explicitly weighing evidence, stating only: "On the basis of all the evidence the court finds that the alleged incident of sexual proposition did not occur . . .").

15. These cases are discussed in Jill Laurie Goodman, "Some Observations."

16. Compare the opinions denying motions to dismiss in, for example, Munford v. James T. Barnes & Co., 441 F. Supp. 459 (E.D. Mich. 1977) and Alexander (Price) v. Yale University, 459 F. Supp. 1 (D. Conn. 1977) with the losses at trial in both Munford v. James T. Barnes & Co., "Judgment of District Court After Trial" (E.D. Mich. S.D. Apr. 20, 1978) and Alexander (Price) v. Yale University, "Memorandum of Decision" and "Judgment" Civil No. N-77-277 (D. Conn. July 3, 1979). Both plaintiffs were Black women.

17. Teamsters v. United States, 431 U.S. 324, 335–336, n.15 (1977). When a rule or practice is differentially applied to an individual on a prohibited basis, disparate treatment occurs. McDonnell Douglas v. Greene, 411 U.S. 792 (1973); Albermarle Paper v. Moody, 422 U.S. 405 (1975). When an action or policy is neutral on its face but adversely affects members of the plaintiff's group on a prohibited basis, disparate impact arises. Griggs v. Duke Power, 401 U.S. 424 (1971).

18. A similar argument was made in Plaintiff's Post-Trial Memorandum (Mar. 9, 1979), Price v. Yale, Civil No. N-77-277, 4 (D. Conn. 1979). Anne E. Simon helped clarify this point. The issue this formulation leaves open is whether there is also social hierarchy between men and women.

19. One consequence of the incoherence of the treatment/impact distinction has been its collapse in practice. Disparate treatment plaintiffs seem effectively to need to make what amounts to a disparate impact showing to prove that their treatment is sex based (see, e.g., Kyriazi v. Western Electric Co., 461 F. Supp. 894 (D.N.J. 1978)) unless available atrocities are unusually explicit. See, e.g., David v. Passman, 442 U.S. 228, 230 n.3 (1979) ("[O]n account of the unusually heavy work load in my Washington office, and the diversity of the job, I concluded that it was essential that the understudy to my Administrative Assistant be a man"). In light of the group showing needed to situate an individual claim, it is particularly disabling to confine a discrimination plaintiff to her facts alone. See Crocker and Simon, "Sexual Harassment in Education." Disparate impact cases need exemplarily abused individual plaintiffs, no matter how compelling the statistical disparity.

20. Teamsters v. United States, 421 U.S. 324, 335 n.15 (1977); Washington v. Davis, 426 U.S. 229 (1976); Personnel Administrator of Massachusetts v. Feeney, 442 U.S. 256 (1979).

21. Reed v. Reed, 404 U.S. 71 (1971); Frontiero v. Richardson, 411 U.S. 677 (1973); Craig v. Boren, 429 U.S. 190 (1976).

22. Examples where this is relatively clear include: Muller v. Oregon, 208 U.S. 412 (1908); Philips v. Martin-Marietta, 400 U.S. 542 (1971); Diaz v. Pan American World Airlines, Inc., 311 F. Supp. 559 (S.D. Fla. 1970), Diaz v. Pan American World Airways, 442 F.2d 385 (5th Cir. 1971) *cert. denied*, 404 U.S. 950 (1971); Geduldig v. Aiello, 417 U.S. 484 (1974); Gilbert v. General Electric, 429 U.S. 125 (1976). It is instructive to compare Geduldig v. Aiello with Michael M. v. Superior Court of Sonoma County, 450 U.S. 464 (1981). *Michael M.* challenged a statutory rape law as sex discrimination. The Supreme Court found the sexes "not similarly situated" toward the risks of intercourse (primarily pregnancy) so that the statute rationally related gender to a valid state interest in preventing teenage pregnancy. In *Geduldig*, a sex discrimination challenge to the exclusion of pregnancy disabilities from a state employee insurance plan, pregnancy was found not a sex-based distinction, its exclusion not sex discrimination, because some women as well as all men are "non-pregnant persons." *Geduldig*, 417 U.S. at 496–497 n.20. In *Michael M.*, because "only women may become pregnant," risk of pregnancy was a sex-based distinction. In *Geduldig*, because men as well as women are nonpregnant, risk of pregnancy was not a sex-based distinction. In both cases, the state's purpose in making the distinction was found valid; both turned upon pregnancy as a characteristic of gender. In *Michael M.*, it was sexually based. In *Geduldig* it was not. This is not only inconsistent, it is, if anything, reversed. Not all statutorily underage girls are even "potentially pregnant" since many have not reached puberty; not all underage girls who have intercourse conceive (the plaintiff in *Michael M.* for example); not all (or even most) unwed mothers are underage; male sterility is not a defense; and not all underage children at risk of intercourse are girls. By contrast, as a matter of rational fit between gender, the characteristic, and its application, all "persons" at risk of noncoverage for pregnancy disabilities are women and all who would receive benefits would be both pregnant and female. *Michael M.* suggests a possible need perceived by the Court for sympathetic "rational basis" law in advance of its resolution of the sex discrimination challenge to the male-only draft. Goldberg v. Rostker, No. 71-1480 (E.D. Pa. July 18, 1980), *probable jurisdiction noted*, 101 S. Ct. 563 (1980) [This became Rostker v. Goldberg, 453 U.S. 57 (1981)]. In its implication for sexual harassment law, the *Michael M.* case (together with Dothard v. Rawlinson, 433 U.S. 321 (1977) (women's rape-ability grounded a BFOQ for prison guard contact positions in all-male prisons), strengthens the notion that women's

and men's sexuality make the sexes "not similarly situated" with regard to sexual intercourse. Doing this on a purportedly biological ground, such as pregnancy potential in *Michael M.* and "her very womanhood" (sexuality as gender itself) in *Dothard*, suggests that nothing that makes this true can be changed. The same holding on a social ground could indict the context that makes women's sexuality a vulnerability or pregnancy a disability (instead of an ability). Arguably, the practice of coercive male sexual initiation toward women, particularly those perceived as vulnerable, targets young girls, even more than it does all women. This, together with women's lack of access to meaningful consent, which may vary with age (as well as economic resources and other factors), would criticize the social context of gender inequality that situates women and men nonsimilarly in the sexual arena. Such an argument would produce a very different conception of the injury of rape upon which to support a sex-specific statutory prohibition than the ones used by either the legislature or the Court in this case.

23. The social creation of biological differences is considered in City of Los Angeles Department of Water and Power v. Manhart, 98 S. Ct. 1370, 1376 n.17 (1978) [see 435 U.S. 702 (1978)].

24. The first case to decide that gay sexual harassment is sex discrimination is Wright v. Methodist Youth, 511 F. Supp. 307 (N.D. Ill. 1981). The EEOC Guidelines do not address this issue but do not preclude this result. While recognizing that same-sex discrimination can be sex-based, this is not exactly a gay rights ruling. It protects a man's right to be free from homosexuality, not to prefer it.

25. Crocker and Simon, "Sexual Harassment in Education" 541, address all these issues. Particularly useful is the consistency and insight with which they assess legal initiatives in a political context, rather than the other way around.

26. See Susan Rae Peterson, "Coercion and Rape: The State as a Male Protection Racket" in M. Vetterling-Braggin, F. A. Elliston, and J. English, *Feminism and Philosophy* (Totowa, NJ: Littlefield, Adams & Co., 1977); Janet Rifkin, "Toward a Theory of Law and Patriarchy," 3 *Harvard Women's Law Journal* 83, 83–92 (1980).

27. See Alexander Bickel, *The Morality of Consent* 133 (New Haven, CT: Yale University Press 1975).

28. Herbert Wechsler, "Toward Neutral Principles of Constitutional Law," 73 *Harvard Law Review* 1 (1959).

29. Andrea Dworkin, *Woman Hating* 202 (New York: E. P. Dutton 1974).

8. SEXUAL HARASSMENT

1. Meritor Savings Bank v. Vinson, 477 U.S. 57 (1986). Patricia Barry brilliantly argued the case for Mechelle Vinson in the Supreme Court as she had at trial (where, in an unorthodox approach that turned out to be helpful, she frequently cited my book, *Sexual Harassment of Working Women*, for her theory of the case) and in the Court of Appeals. I was principal author of the brief, on which Sarah E. Burns was of great assistance.

2. Kimberlé Williams Crenshaw is the primary theoretician of intersectionality. See Kimberlé Williams Crenshaw, "Demarginalizing the Intersection of Race and Sex: A Black Feminist Critique of Antidiscrimination Doctrine, Feminist Theory and Antiracist Politics," 1989 *University of Chicago Legal Forum* 139 (1989), and Kimberlé Williams Crenshaw, "Mapping the Margins: Intersectionality, Identity Politics, and Violence Against Women of Color," 43 *Stanford Law Review* 1241 (1991). All footnotes hereinafter are from the original brief.

3. References to the partial trial transcript that has been lodged with this Court will be preceded by TR, followed by date, volume and page. The transcript is incomplete due to respondent's lack of financial resources. Although granted permission to proceed in forma pauperis, Ms. Vinson's motion for a transcript was denied by the district court, which noted it "cannot find that this appeal presents a substantial question which requires a transcript to be furnished at taxpayers' expense." Vinson v. Taylor, 27 F.E.P. 948, 950 (D.D.C. 1980.)

4. This policy statement also notes, "there appears to be an underutilization of females in positions of higher responsibilities, particularly at the officer level." (Defendant's Exhibit 7, at 5.)

5. The parties concur with all circuit courts and all amici that quid pro quo sexual harassment is a claim for sex discrimination under Title VII. Horn v. Duke Homes, 755 F. 2d 599 (7th Cir. 1985); Crimm v. Missouri Pacific R.R. Co., 750 F.2d 703 (8th Cir. 1984); Simmons v. Lyons, 746 F. 2d 265 (5th Cir. 1984); Craig v. Y & Y Snacks Inc., 721 F. 2d 77 (3d Cir. 1983); Katz v. Dole, 709 F. 2d 251 (4th Cir. 1983); Garber v. Saxon Business Products, 552 F. 2d 1032 (4th Cir. 1977); Miller v. Bank of America, 600 F. 2d 211 (9th Cir. 1979); Tomkins v. Public Service Electric & Gas Co., 568 F. 2d 1044 (3d Cir. 1977); Barnes v. Costle, 561 F. 2d 983 (D.C. Cir. 1977). The instant case, as currently shaped by trial and appeal, does not pose a simple extreme quid pro quo of sexual compliance in exchange

for a job. Any such issues, involving for example a possible constructive discharge, remain for factual development on remand. Thus the question is not raised of whether employers, including those without notice other than to the perpetrator, are responsible under Title VII in quid pro quo situations, as they have universally been held to be in the cases referenced this note supra. Any adequacy of this record to pose these issues for review is thus irrelevant to a dismissal of the writ, since they are neither posed nor contested here. (See Petition for Writ of Certiorari at 6 n.3; Reply Brief of Petitioner at 1.)

6. Unwanted bisexual advances may mean either that both women and men are injured on the basis of their gender, or that because both are, no basis in gender exists. Title VII sets itself primarily against differential treatment. If an employer fires everyone, Black and white alike, it is regarded as improbable, although not impossible, that the reasons were racist because the treatment is racially even-handed. By the same token, a conclusion that indiscriminate treatment, however injurious, may provide a defense to a claim of group-based discrimination does not, as the Court of Appeals dissenters would have it, 760 F.2d at 1333 n.7 (App. 28a n.7) invalidate a law against conduct that is directed exclusively against members of one group.

7. A further distinction may be suggested sub rosa by the brief for the United States. It implies that while other discrimination may be done for the benefit of the company, sexual harassment is done for the personal benefit of the discriminating individual. (US, 24, 27.) Exploitation through pay inequity may be good for balance sheets, but exclusion of qualified job applicants because they are minority or female, for example, deprives companies of needed talent. Just as sexual harassment presumably gratifies harassing individuals, other forms of discrimination may subjectively benefit perpetrators, who thus express and reinforce their social superiority, regardless of objective harm to the company.

8. There is some authority, for instance EEOC 84-1 (CCH) 6839 (1983) for the view that participation in sexual harassment evidences consent, consent which must subsequently be expressly revoked before unwelcomeness will be found. The instant case is different from EEOC 84-1, where one complainant never indicated to the perpetrator that the sexual banter was oppressive to her. Here, respondent repeatedly did so.

9. Nonresistance does not always mean an absence of force and not all force is violent: "I can remember the violence, times he forced himself on me,

but all the times he forced himself on me, he wasn't violent." (TR, Jan. 23, III, 80) (Testimony of M. Vinson).

10. Because of sexual harassment, some women may be promoted who do not merit it because they comply sexually. But more evidence suggests that women are overwhelmingly not promoted who do merit it, because they were not sexually compliant. Both groups of women pay for a system under which supervisors' sexual proclivities are permitted to govern their personnel policies. See MacKinnon, 38–40.

11. Slack v. Havens reveals the falsity of the assertion by the United States that there is no racial equivalent to sexual harassment's quid pro quo. (US, 15 n.5.) "Had Polaski not discriminated against the plaintiffs by demanding they perform work he would not require of a white female employee, they would not have been faced with the unreasonable choice of having to choose between obeying his discriminatory work order and the loss of their employment." 7 F.E.P. at 890. Any time a person has to endure indignity or extra work or other workplace detriment because of their protected status, an implicit quid pro quo is involved, because their tolerance of the discrimination is the price of their job. Unless such persons are fired for resistance, the implicit bargain only becomes explicit if they sacrifice their employment opportunity and leave.

12. Mr. Taylor's individual liability for his act as the "employer" is not entirely clear under Title VII, although it would be most peculiar to found liability as an agent in one whose principal was not jointly and severally liable. Those few courts that have ruled on the issue under Title VII have properly found the agent directly liable, Padilla v. Stringer, 395 F. Supp. 495 (D.N.M. 1974); Compston v. Borden, Inc., 424 F. Supp., at 157. Yet courts at times prefer not even to permit suits against individual supervisors where full monetary relief is available from employers and injunctive relief will bind incumbent supervisors. White v. North La. Legal Assistance Corp., 19 F.E.P. 307 (W.D. La. 1979) (individual not mentioned in EEOC charge).

13. Only the employer is capable of rectifying harms like Ms. Vinson's allegedly altered work records and recommendation letters, which may be found part and parcel of an attempt to cover up sexual harassment. Mr. Taylor, if still employed by the Bank, could presumably hire her as previously; if not, he could not grant her reinstatement, should it be sought and granted. Further, if the advances were found unwelcome and environmental, and the perpetrator is found to be the procedure, the court might order an adequate procedure.

14. In amending the 1964 act by passing the Equal Employment Opportunity Act of 1972, Pub. L. No. 92-261, 86 Stat. 103 et seq., Congress elaborated its intent more explicitly than it had in 1964. The committee reports emphasize that "[d]iscrimination against women is no less serious than other forms of prohibited employment practices and is to be accorded the same degree of social concern given to any type of unlawful discrimination." H.R. Rep. 92-238, 92nd Cong., 1st Sess. 4-5 (1971); S. Rep. 92-415, 92nd Cong., 1st. Sess. 7-8 (1971).

15. Had tort been adequate to the discriminatory harm of sexual harassment, the injury would likely have been recognized prior to its address under Title VII. Before Williams v. Saxbe, 413 F. Supp. 654 (D.D.C. 1976), the first case squarely to recognize sexual harassment as a violation of anti-discrimination law, perhaps two or three cases with facts amounting to sexual harassment had been reported brought in tort. (See MacKinnon, 164–174.) Since Williams, several hundred have been reported in the federal system alone, many more under state laws, an unknown number settled or resolved by administrative agencies or internal grievance mechanisms.

16. Amicus United States appears to be of the view that the Bank may well have had adequate notice here. (US, 30).

17. In cases where a single proprietor is the perpetrator, there is no one else to whom to report. Cases governing whether a relationship is employer/employee have ruled that factors that establish an employment relationship include, inter alia, control of the conditions of employment and maintenance of employment records. Bonnette v. California Health and Welfare Agency, 704 F.2d 1465, 1469–70 (9th Cir. 1983); Hodgson v. Griffin and Brand of McAllen, Inc., 471 F.2d 235, 237 (5th Cir. 1973) cert. denied, 414 U.S. 819 (1973).

18. In a final turn on its notice argument, petitioner attempts to avoid liability by relying on the intent requirement under Title VII. The doctrine is misconstrued and misapplied. The Bank states it can not be liable for relief under 706(g) unless it knew of the discrimination, because otherwise it could not have intended to discriminate. (Bank, 12.) Intent goes to whether treatment is based on sex, not to employer liability. U.S. Postal Service v. Aiken, 460 U.S. at 715; Musikiwamba v. Essi, Inc., 760 F.2d 740, 747 (7th Cir. 1983) (intent not an employer liability issue in sexual harassment cases). Courts have treated sex basis in sexual harassment cases as essentially facial unless answered to the contrary. Instead of inquiring whether a man who engaged in coitus 40 to 50 times with a woman workplace subordinate did so with intent to gratify himself sexually with a member

of her gender, regardless of her inclinations, or whether he did so with intent to discriminate against a woman on the basis of sex, courts have approached the question as if to show the first is to show the second. See, e.g., Katz v. Dole, 709 F.2d at 256 n.7 applying precisely the approach later enunciated in Aiken.

19. Other than one common law sexual harassment case in education, Micari v. Mann, 481 N.Y.S.2d 967 (Sup. 1984), respondent is aware of only one other sexual harassment case in court in which a victim accuses a perpetrator of sexual harassment with a man with whom sex had been consummated. Cummings v. Walsh Construction Co., 561 F. Supp. 872 (S.D. Ga. 1983).

20. See generally Continental Can v. Minnesota, 297 N.W.2d 241, 246 (Minn. 1980) (defendant in sexual harassment case "wished slavery days would return so that he could sexually train [plaintiff] and she would be his bitch.") "Follow me sometimes and see if I lie. I can be coming from eight hours on an assembly line or fourteen hours in Mrs. Halsey's kitchen. I can be all filled up that day with three hundred years of rage so that my eyes are flashing and my flesh is trembling—and the white boys in the streets, they look at me and think of sex. They look at me and that's all they think . . . . Baby you could be Jesus in drag—but if you're brown they're sure you're selling!" L. Hansberry, To be Young, Gifted, and Black (1969) at 98. Ms. Vinson's predicament suggests that while such a view may be most prevalent among white men, it is not confined to them alone. Reasons are suggested in W. Jordan, White Over Black: American Attitudes Toward the Negro 1550–1812 (1968) at 150.

9. TESTIMONY ON PORNOGRAPHY, MINNEAPOLIS

1. Accounts by Andrea Dworkin and me of the ordinance process, copies of various versions of it, together with the hearings in Minneapolis held that are advocated here and those that were held elsewhere, can be found in Catharine A. MacKinnon and Andrea Dworkin, eds., *In Harm's Way: The Pornography Civil Rights Hearings* (Cambridge, MA: Harvard University Press 1998).

2. The Supreme Court of the United States summarily affirmed a Court of Appeals judgment in American Booksellers Ass'n, Inc., v. Hudnut, 771 F.2d 323 (1985), *aff'd mem.* 475 U.S. 1001 (1986), finding the ordinance violated the First Amendment. Apart from the myriad flaws in the Court of Appeals decision, see discussion in Catharine A. MacKinnon, *Sex Equality* 1757–1778 (3d ed., New York: Foundation Press, 2016), a sum-

mary affirmance does not give reasons, leaving open the terms of a later Supreme Court analysis. And its outcome is only binding in the circuit in which it was brought. The reasons a civil rights ordinance against pornography has not been reintroduced since the mid-1980s speak to the lock on public consciousness the pornographers hold and the fear they engender in anyone who challenges them.

10. TESTIMONY TO THE ATTORNEY GENERAL'S COMMISSION ON PORNOGRAPHY

1. The Charter of the Commission was "to determine the nature, extent, and impact on society of pornography in the United States and to make specific recommendations to the Attorney General concerning more effective ways in which the spread of pornography could be contained, consistent with constitutional guarantees." Attorney General's Commission on Pornography, *Final Report* 1957 (July 1986).

2. Ronald Reagan announced his intention to create the Commission in May of 1984. See "Reagan Panel Will Study Effects of Pornography," *Philadelphia Inquirer*, National, May 22, 1984, at A05. The Commission itself was established by Reagan's Attorney General William French Smith, 50 Fed. Reg. 8684 (February 25, 1985). See also 50 Fed. Reg. 21671 (announcing members appointed by Meese).

3. *Final Report of the Attorney General's Commission on Pornography* 40 (Nashville, TN: Rutledge Hill Press 1986). This volume is an abridged version of the longer complete official report.

4. For the most comprehensive up-to-the-present discussion of the evidence, see Max Waltman, "The Politics of Legal Challenges to Pornography: Canada, Sweden, and the United States," *Stockholm Studies in Politics* 90–140, 160 (Stockholm: Stockholm University 2014) (Ph.D. Dissertation) (concluding "[p]ornography produces harmful consumption effects that are significant, substantial, and independent of other causes," largely visited by men upon women).

5. Previously unpublished but recorded in the Commission's transcript, this testimony was delivered at the Chicago session on July 25, 1985 and was titled "The Civil Rights Approach to Pornography." A subsequent speech based in part on this testimony was given at the Seventh Annual Conference of the National Association of Women Judges, University of Minnesota Law School, May 1986, published as Catharine A. MacKinnon, "Pornography as Sex Discrimination," 4 *Law and Inequality: A Journal of Theory and Practice* 38 (1986), and collected in that form as "Civil Rights

Against Pornography," in Catharine A. MacKinnon, ed., *Women's Lives, Men's Laws* 492 (Cambridge, MA: Belknap Press of Harvard University Press 2005) ("*Women's Lives, Men's Laws*").

6. Commission on Obscenity and Pornography, *The Report of the Commission on Obscenity and Pornography* 27 (Washington, DC: U.S. Government Printing Office 1970) (footnote omitted) ("In sum, empirical research designed to clarify the question has found no evidence to date that exposure to explicit sexual materials plays a significant role in the causation of delinquent or criminal behavior among youth or adults.").

7. See Miller v. California, 413 U.S. 15, 24 (1973) (defining obscene material that is unprotected by the First Amendment as "works which, taken as a whole, appeal to the prurient interest in sex, which portray sexual conduct in a patently offensive way, and which, taken as a whole, do not have serious literary, artistic, political, or scientific value.").

8. See, e.g., Young v. American Mini Theatres, Inc., 427 U.S. 50 (1976).

9. See, e.g., Brockett v. Spokane Arcades, Inc., 472 U.S. 491 (1985).

10. See, e.g., MacKinnon, *Women's Lives, Men's Laws* 29 (footnote omitted) (citing to Edward Donnerstein, "Pornography: Its Effect on Violence Against Women," in *Pornography and Sexual Aggression* 53, Neil M. Malamuth and Edward Donnerstein, eds. (Orlando, FL: Academic Press, 1984) ("*Sexual Aggression*") ("Pornography: Its Effect") ("As Edward Donnerstein's data show, consumer preferences escalate toward more violent materials—a dynamic that means that new markets, hence greater profits, are created through creating community standards that tolerate more and more violating materials.").

11. See, e.g., Andrea Dworkin, "Pornography: The New Terrorism," in *Letters from a War Zone: Writings 1976–1987* 199–200 (London: Secker & Warburg 1988) ("A woman, nearly naked, in a cell, chained, ripped up from the whip, breasts mutilated by a knife: she is entertainment, the boy-next-door's favorite fantasy, every man's precious right, every woman's potential fate. The woman tortured is sexual entertainment. The woman tortured is sexually arousing. The anguish of the woman tortured is sexually exciting. The degradation of the woman tortured is sexually entrancing. The humiliation of the woman tortured is sexually pleasing, sexually thrilling, sexually gratifying.").

12. Until the hearings on the proposed civil rights antipornography ordinance in Minneapolis in December of 1983. See Catharine A. MacKinnon and Andrea Dworkin, eds., *In Harm's Way: The Pornography Civil Rights*

Hearings (Cambridge, MA: Harvard University Press 1997) (*"In Harm's Way"*) (documenting the testimony of women who have been harmed by prostitution).

13. See, e.g., New York v. Ferber, 458 U.S. 747 (1982).

14. See, e.g., MacKinnon and Dworkin, *In Harm's Way*; Catharine A. Mac-Kinnon, *Only Words* (Cambridge, MA: Harvard University Press 1994) (*"Only Words"*); Catharine A. MacKinnon, "Pornography, Civil Rights, and Speech," 20 *Harvard Civil Rights-Civil Liberties Law Review* 1 (1985) ("Pornography, Civil Rights, and Speech"); Andrea Dworkin, "Pornography Is a Civil Rights Issue for Women," 21 *University of Michigan Journal of Law Reform* 55 (1987–1988) ("Pornography Is a Civil Rights Issue for Women").

15. MacKinnon and Dworkin, *In Harm's Way* 60–66.

16. Id. at 44–60.

17. Id. at 98–99.

18. MacKinnon, "Pornography, Civil Rights, and Speech," 12 n.20.

19. MacKinnon and Dworkin, *In Harm's Way* 170–171.

20. Id. at 104–107.

21. Id. at 99–100.

22. Id. at 44–60.

23. Kathleen Barry, *Female Sexual Slavery* (New York: New York University Press 1979).

24. *Effect of Pornography on Women and Children: Hearings Before the Subcomm. on Juvenile Justice of the Comm. on the Judiciary*, 98th Cong., 2d Sess. 227–255 (1984) (testimony of Andrea Dworkin).

25. Andrea Dworkin and Catharine A. MacKinnon, *Pornography & Civil Rights: A New Day for Women's Equality* 138–142 (1988).

26. See, e.g., MacKinnon, *Only Words* 35 ("Consider snuff pornography, in which women or children are killed to make a sex film. This is a film of a sexual murder in the process of being committed. Doing the murder is sex for those who do it. The climax is the moment of death. The intended consumer has a sexual experience watching it. Those who kill as and for sex are having sex through the murder; those who watch the film are having sex through watching the murder. A snuff film is not a discussion of the idea of sexual murder any more than the acts being filmed are. The film is not 'about' sexual murder; it sexualizes murder.").

27. See, e.g., MacKinnon, "Pornography, Civil Rights, and Speech," 18 ("What pornography *does* goes beyond its content: It eroticizes hierarchy, it sexualizes inequality. It makes dominance and submission sex.").

28. See, e.g., Dworkin, "Pornography Is a Civil Rights Issue for Women," 55–56 ("In this country where I live, there is a trafficking in pornography that exploits mentally and physically disabled women, women who are maimed; there is amputee pornography, a trade in women who have been maimed in that way, as if that is a sexual fetish for men. In this country where I live, there is a trade in racism as a form of sexual pleasure, so that the plantation is presented as a form of sexual gratification for the black woman slave who asks please to be abused, please to be raped, please to be hurt. Black skin is presented as if it is a female genital, and all the violence and the abuse and the humiliation that is in general directed against female genitals is directed against the black skin of women in pornography. Asian women in this country where I live are tied from trees and hung from ceilings and hung from doorways as a form of public entertainment. There is a concentration camp pornography in this country where I live, where the concentration camp and the atrocities that occurred there are presented as existing for the sexual pleasure of the victim, of the woman, who orgasms to the real abuses that occurred, not very long ago in history."); MacKinnon, *Women's Lives, Men's Laws* 29.

29. See, e.g., American Booksellers Ass'n, Inc. v. Hudnut, 771 F.2d 323, 330 (7th Cir. 1985) ("Racial bigotry, anti-semitism, violence on television, reporters' biases—these and many more influence the culture and shape our socialization. None is directly answerable by more speech, unless that speech too finds its place in the popular culture. Yet all is protected as speech, however insidious . . . . Sexual responses often are unthinking responses, and the association of sexual arousal with the subordination of women therefore may have a substantial effect. But almost all cultural stimuli provoke unconscious responses . . . . If the fact that speech plays a role in a process of conditioning were enough to permit governmental regulation, that would be the end of freedom of speech."); see also Andrea Dworkin, "Pornography Is a Civil Rights Issue for Women," 21 *University of Michigan Journal of Law Reform* 57 (1987–1988) ("I live in a country where if you film any act of humiliation or torture, and if the victim is a woman, the film is both entertainment and it is protected speech.").

30. Attorney General's Commission on Pornography, U.S. Department of Justice, I *Final Report* 291–297 (1986).

31. MacKinnon and Dworkin, *In Harm's Way* 101–106.

32. Id. at 44–60; see also Catharine A. MacKinnon, "Trafficking, Prostitution, and Inequality," 46 *Harvard Civil Rights-Civil Liberties Law Review* 271 (2011).

33. MacKinnon and Dworkin, *In Harm's Way* 98–106, 108–109, 111–112.
34. See, e.g., Malamuth and Donnerstein, *Sexual Aggression* (social studies); id. at 157–159 (testimony of Daryl Dahlheimer, psychotherapist); id. at 149–155 (testimony of Wanda Richardson, Harriet Tubman Women's Shelter, and Sharon Rice Vaughn, Minnesota Coalition for Battered Women); id. at 155–156 (testimony of Barbara Chester, director of Rape and Sexual Assault Center); id. at 175–176 (testimony of Sue Santa, Minneapolis Youth Division); id. at 161–165 (testimony of Cheryl Champion, Washington County Human Services, Inc.); MacKinnon, "Pornography, Civil Rights, and Speech," 46–50 nn.107–108 (discussion of court cases); id. at 143–145 (testimony of Bill Neiman, assistant county attorney, Hennepin County Attorney's Office).
35. See, e.g., Donnerstein, "Pornography: Its Effect" 53; Mike Allen et al., "A Meta-Analysis Summarizing the Effects of Pornography II: Aggression After Exposure," *Human Communication Research* 258 (Dec. 1995); James Weaver, "The Social Science and Psychological Research Evidence: Perceptual and Behavioural Consequences of Exposure to Pornography," in *Pornography: Women, Violence and Civil Liberties* 284, Catherine Itzin, ed. (Oxford: Oxford University Press 1992) (summarizing studies); MacKinnon, "Pornography, Civil Rights, and Speech," 52–53 nn.116–118 (collecting studies).
36. Neil M. Malamuth, "Aggression Against Women: Cultural and Individual Causes," in *Sexual Aggression* 19, 34–39; Daniel Linz et al., "The Effects of Multiple Exposures to Filmed Violence Against Women," 34 *Journal of Communications* 130, 142 (Summer 1984).
37. See, e.g., MacKinnon and Dworkin, "The Minneapolis Hearings," in *In Harm's Way* 61 (footnotes omitted) (telling her story at the Minneapolis hearings, Linda Marchiano describes the bruises, evidence of abuse, that can be seen on her body in the pornography in which she was forced to participate).
38. See, e.g., "Minneapolis: Press Conference: Statement of Peggy," id. at 264 ("Starting at age 4, old Mr. Edwards up the street used pornography to entice me into taking baths so he could watch, had me wearing his wife[']s clothes and eventually having oral sex and being penetrated by him. This went on for five years. He used the pornography to show me how to be—and what to do—until I didn't see anything wrong—with anything he did to me—or had me do to him . . . . The man I lived with last used pornography books to sexually arouse my son so he could molest him—and my son and his friends used pornography to molest my daughter—to

experiment on her sexually—using the pornographic books as teaching guides.").

39. See, e.g., John D. Foubert, Matthew W. Brosi, and R. Sean Bannon, "Pornography Viewing among Fraternity Men: Effects on Bystander Intervention, Rape Myth Acceptance and Behavioral Intent to Commit Sexual Assault," 18 *Sexual Addiction & Compulsivity* 212, 214 (2011) (citations omitted) ("The preponderance of research suggests significant, negative impacts of pornography on men in the aggregate. Recent meta-analyses and literature reviews have revealed in both correlational and experimental studies that pornography use, acceptance of aggression, and violence towards women are linked. The strongest correlations with these violence related variables are with the more violent types of pornography; though an association with mainstream pornography is both reliable and consistent"); see also Malamuth and Donnerstein, *Sexual Aggression*.

40. See, e.g., Andrea Dworkin, "Pornography Is a Civil Rights Issue for Women," 21 *University of Michigan Journal of Law Reform* 57–58 (1987–1988) ("I live in a country where if you film any act of humiliation or torture, and if the victim is a woman, the film is both entertainment and it is protected speech. Now that tells me something about what it means to be a woman citizen in this country and the meaning of being second-class. When your rape is entertainment, your worthlessness is absolute. You have reached the nadir of social worthlessness.").

41. MacKinnon, *Women's Lives, Men's Laws* 496–497 n.22 (Model Antipornography Civil-Rights Ordinance, Section 2).

42. Id.

43. Andrea Dworkin, "Against the Male Flood: Censorship, Pornography, and Equality," 8 *Harvard Women's Law Journal* 1 (1985).

44. See, e.g., Miller v. California, 413 U.S. 15, 24–25 (1973).

45. MacKinnon, *Women's Lives, Men's Laws* 496–497 n.22 (Model Antipornography Civil-Rights Ordinance, Section 2).

46. See id. at 305 ("The legal protections for pornography are an incentive to molest and rape and run.").

47. See Ruth Colker, "Pornography and Privacy: Towards the Development of a Group Based Theory for Sex Based Intrusions of Privacy," 1 *Law and Inequality* 191 (1983).

48. See generally Catharine A. MacKinnon, "Pornography as Sex Inequality," in *Women's Lives, Men's Laws*.

49. See generally MacKinnon and Dworkin, *In Harm's Way*.

50. See Catharine A. MacKinnon, *Women's Lives, Men's Laws* 496–497 n.22 (Model Antipornography Civil-Rights Ordinance, Section 5).

51. See, e.g., Miller v. California, 413 U.S. 15 (1973); Roth v. United States, 354 U.S. 476 (1957).

52. See, e.g., Beauharnais v. People of State of Illinois, 343 U.S. 250 (1952).

53. See, e.g., New York v. Ferber, 458 U.S. 747 (1982).

54. See, e.g., Members of the City Council of Los Angeles v. Taxpayers for Vincent, 466 U.S. 789, 794 (1984) ("the District Court found that the large number of illegally posted signs 'constitute a clutter and visual blight.'").

55. See, e.g., Davis v. Passman, 442 U.S. 228, 230 (1979) (holding that firing of a female employee by a U.S. Congressman because "it was essential that the understudy to [his] Administrative Assistant be a man" is not protected by the Speech or Debate Clause of the U.S. Constitution); Pittsburgh Press Co. v. Pittsburgh Commission on Human Relations, 413 U.S. 376 (1973) (holding that sex-segregated job advertisements are not protected under the First Amendment).

56. The law was ultimately summarily found unconstitutional, although not in a way that precludes further adoption of the approach. See American Booksellers Ass'n, Inc. v. Hudnut, 771 F.2d 323, 324 (7th Cir. 1985), aff'd sub nom. Hudnut v. American Booksellers Ass'n, Inc., 475 U.S. 1001 (1986).

57. For further discussion, see Dworkin, "Pornography Is a Civil Rights Issue for Women," 21.

11. SUBSTANTIVE EQUALITY

1. Andrews v. Law Society of B.C., [1989] 1 S.C.R. 143.

2. Catharine A. MacKinnon, *Sexual Harassment of Working Women: A Case of Sex Discrimination* 116–141 (New Haven, CT: Yale University Press 1979).

3. For further development, see Catharine A. MacKinnon, "Substantive Equality Past and Future: The Canadian Charter Experience," in Richard Albert and David Cameron, eds., *Canada in the World: Comparative Perspectives on the Canadian Constitution*, in the *Comparative Constitutional Law and Policy Series*, Zachary Elkins, Tom Ginsburg, and Ran Hirschl, eds. (Cambridge: Cambridge University Press, forthcoming 2017).

4. This talk was delivered at the National Meeting of Equality-Seeking Groups sponsored by the Government Court Challenges Program, held January 13–16, 1989, in Ottawa, Canada. This is its first publication.

5. For examples of its application, see, e.g., Bliss v. Attorney General of Canada, [1979] 1 S.C.R. 183 (finding that a pregnant woman was not similarly situated to nonpregnant individuals and so not entitled to unemployment benefits); Reed v. Reed, 404 U.S. 71 (1971) (finding unconstitutional a law that provided "dissimilar treatment for men and women who are thus similarly situated."). A pair of American scholars was especially influential in furthering this idea. Joseph Tussman and Jacobus tenBroek, "The Equal Protection of the Laws," 37 *California Law Review* 344 (1949) ("The Constitution does not require that things different in fact be treated in law as though they were the same. But it does require, in its concern for equality, that those who are similarly situated be similarly treated. The measure of the reasonableness of a classification is the degree of its success in treating similarly those similarly situated."). See also Catharine A. MacKinnon, *Sex Equality* 93 (3d ed., New York: Foundation Press 2016) (*"Sex Equality"*).

6. For an example of this logic applied in Canada, see Bliss v. Attorney General of Canada, [1979] 1 S.C.R. 183. For an example of this logic applied in the United States, see Geduldig v. Aiello, 417 U.S. 484 (1974) (finding inability to work due to normal pregnancy may be excluded from coverage without discriminating because not all women become pregnant, and pregnancy is not part of sex per se because some nonpregnant persons are men). See also MacKinnon, *Sex Equality* 311.

7. Ontario Health Insurance Plan, Ontario's government-run health insurance plan.

8. For a discussion on how segregation played out in the municipal pools in the United States, see Jeff Wiltse, *Contested Waters: A Social History of Swimming Pools in America* (Chapel Hill: University of North Carolina Press 2007).

9. See Leon F. Litwack, *Trouble in Mind: Black Southerners in the Age of Jim Crow* (New York: Alfred A. Knopf, Inc. 1998).

10. Canadian Charter of Rights and Freedoms § 15 (Can. Const. (Constitution Act, 1982) Pt. 1) ("Section 15 (1) Every individual is equal before and under the law and has the right to the equal protection and equal benefit of the law without discrimination and, in particular, without discrimination based on race, national or ethnic origin, colour, religion, sex, age or mental or physical disability. (2) Subsection (1) does not preclude any law, program or activity that has as its object the amelioration of conditions of disadvantaged individuals or groups including those that are

disadvantaged because of race, national or ethnic origin, colour, religion, sex, age or mental or physical disability.").

11. Id.

12. Id.

13. See, e.g., Jane E. Larson, "'Even a Worm Will Turn at Last': Rape Reform in Late Nineteenth-Century America," 9 *Yale Journal of Law & Humanity* 1, 8–10, 53, 56–58 (1997) (describing the morality arguments used to support creation of double-standard statutory rape laws).

14. Canadian Charter of Rights and Freedoms § 32 (Can. Const. (Constitution Act, 1982) Pt. 1)(1) ("This Charter applies (a) to the Parliament and government of Canada in respect of all matters within the authority of Parliament including all matters relating to the Yukon Territory and Northwest Territories; and (b) to the legislature and government of each province in respect of all matters within the authority of the legislature of each province. (2) Notwithstanding subsection (1), section 15 shall not have effect until three years after this section comes into force.").

15. According to the Bureau of Justice Statistics, intimates were responsible for 24 percent of aggravated assaults, 22 percent of simple assaults, and 17 percent of rapes and sexual assaults committed against women in 2010. See Jennifer L. Truman, Bureau of Justice Statistics, U.S. Dep't of Justice, Criminal Victimization, 2010, at 9 tbl.5 (2011). See also *Women and Violence: Hearings on Legislation to Reduce the Growing Problem of Violent Crime Against Women Before the Senate Comm. on the Judiciary*, 101st Cong. (1990); Majority Staff of Senate Comm. on the Judiciary, 102d Cong., *Violence Against Women: A Week in the Life of America* (Comm. Print 1992); Evan Stark and Anne Flitcraft, "Violence Among Intimates: An Epidemiological Review," in *Handbook of Family Violence* 293, Vincent B. Van Hasselt et al., eds. (New York: Plenum Press 1988); MacKinnon, *Sex Equality*, 772–773.

16. MacKinnon, *Sex Equality* 862, 880 ("Most sexual abuse is not treated as, or even defined as, illegal. This has arguably occurred in part because women, those most frequently subjected to sexual abuse, have historically been excluded from the authoritative processes through which community rules are made, interpreted, and enforced."); Mary P. Koss et al., *No Safe Haven: Male Violence Against Women at Home, at Work, and in the Community* 167–171 (Washington, DC: American Psychological Association 1994) (analyzing major studies on rape prevalence done as of 1994, many showing approximately 20 percent of women raped, some lower,

some higher); Diana E. H. Russell, *Sexual Exploitation: Rape, Child Sexual Abuse, and Workplace Harassment* 35 (Beverly Hills, CA: Sage Publications 1984) (reporting large probability sample finding 24 percent of women experience rape in lifetime).

17. See, e.g., Catharine A. MacKinnon and Andrea Dworkin, eds., *In Harm's Way: The Pornography Civil Rights Hearings* (Cambridge, MA: Harvard University Press 1998) (documenting presence of pornography throughout social life in United States); MacKinnon, *Sex Equality* 1687–1688.

18. Congress passed the Violence Against Women Act ("VAWA"), 42 U.S.C. § 13981 (1994) to address and prevent violence against women (originally including a civil remedy, struck down in United States v. Morrison, 529 U.S. 598 (2000), as beyond the Commerce Clause and other constitutional authorization of Congress's legislative power). Despite these efforts, this violence still occurs. See, e.g., Jennifer L. Truman, Bureau of Justice Statistics, U.S. Dep't of Justice, Criminal Victimization, 2010, at 9 tbl.5 (2011).

19. Canadian Charter of Rights and Freedoms § 32 (Can. Const. (Constitution Act, 1982) Pt. 1) (1).

20. These arguments did win and did work. See Andrews v. Law Society of B.C., [1989] 1 S.C.R. 143. The casebook Sex Equality traces the analysis through the cases and years to follow.

12. ON TORTURE

1. See citations in note 3 below.

2. This speech was given on November 10, 1990, at Human Rights in the Twenty-First Century: A Global Challenge, an international law conference convened at Banff, Alberta, Canada. The conference was supported and organized under the auspices of the Secretary-General of the Council of Europe, The European Court of Human Rights, the European Human Rights Commission, the Strasbourg Institute of Comparative Human Rights Law, the Alberta Law Foundation and the International Centre at the University of Calgary. This talk was originally published as "On Torture: A Feminist Perspective on Human Rights" in *Human Rights in the Twenty-first Century: A Global Challenge* 21, Kathleen E. Mahoney and Paul Mahoney, eds. (Boston: M. Nijhoff 1993).

3. Path-breaking examples since involving domestic violence holding states responsible for their inaction are Maria Da Penha Fernandes v. Brazil, Case 12.501, Inter-Am. Comm'n H.R. Report No. 54/01 (2001), Lenehan

(Gonzales) v. United States, Case No. 12.626, Inter-Am. Comm'n H.R. Report No. 80/11 (2011), and Opuz v. Turkey, Eur. Ct. H.R. App. No. 33401/02 (2009).

4. See Convention Against Torture and Other Cruel, Inhuman or Degrading Treatment or Punishment, U.N. Doc. NRES/39/46 (Dec. 10, 1984).

5. See, e.g., Universal Declaration of Human Rights, General Assembly Resolution 217A (III) (Dec. 10, 1948), arts. 2 and 7; International Covenant on Civil and Political Rights, G.A. Res. 2200A (XXI), 21 U.N. GAOR Supp. (No. 16) at 52, U.N. Doc. A/6316 (1966), 999 U.N.T.S. 171, *entered into force* Mar. 23, 1976, art. 2(1). The Convention for the Elimination of All Forms of Discrimination Against Women, U.N. Doc. NRES/34/180 (1979). Many nations have explicit sex equality provisions in their constitutions. For examples, see *Constitutions of the Countries of the World*, Gisbert H. Flanz and Albert P. Blaustein, eds. (Dobbs Ferry, NY: Oceana Publications 1971–1994).

6. Since this speech was given and published, some jurisdictions have recognized that rape, at least in official custody or by potentially official forces or when ignored by official instrumentalities, can be torture. See, e.g., Aydin v. Turkey, (1998) 25 E.H.R.R. 251; Mejia v. Peru, Case No. 10.970, Inter-American Committee on Human Rights, Report No. 5196, OEA/Ser.L./V/II.91 Doc. 7 rev. (1996), available at www.cidh.org/annualrep/95eng/Peru10970.htm. See also M. C. v. Bulgaria, (2003) E.C.H.R. 646 (Dec. 4, 2003).

7. See Amnesty International, *Torture in the 80's* 18–26 (1984).

8. For an account, see Jacobo Timerman, *Prisoner Without a Name, Cell Without a Number*, Toby Talbot, trans. (New York: Knopf 1981).

9. Much of this analysis was inspired by Andrea Dworkin's essay "Pornography: The New Terrorism," in *Letters from a War Zone: Writings, 1976–1989* 199–200 (London: Secker & Warburg 1989).

10. Declaration of Defendant-Intervenor Linda Marchiano, Village Books et al. v. City of Bellingham (Marchiano Affidavit), para. 2, No. 88-14701 (unpublished) (W.D. Wash., Feb. 9, 1989). The original publisher asked me to explain the language used here. This is Linda's language. Rarely are the voices of victims of sexual abuse heard unmediated, raw, and direct. Only comparatively unspeakable language exists for women's violations. Euphemisms cover them up. To make these accounts pretty through less direct language is a kind of lie. The realities are not pretty; nobody makes them less direct for the women who live through them. A distanced

discourse removes the reader from what happened, perhaps producing comfort but also making action less likely. These accounts *should* be hard to take. Living through them was unbearable.

11. Id., ¶¶ 7–11, 15, 22–23.

12. Jayne Stamen statement, Feb. 14, 1988 (on file with author).

13. This account is drawn from the following sources: *Los Angeles Times*, May 19, 1981; *Costa Mesa Daily Pilot*, May 29, 1981; *Los Angeles Herald Examiner*, A-1, May 30, 1981; *Sun-Star* (Merced, CA), May 29, 1981; *Sun-Star* (Merced, CA), May 27, 1981; *Times-Delta* (Tulare County, CA), June 6, 1981; *Sun-Star* (Merced, CA), May 28, 1981; *Sun-Star* (Merced, CA), June 5, 1981; People v. Burnham, 222 Cal. Rptr. 630 (Cal. Ct. App. 1986), *rev.* denied (May 22, 1986).

14. See International League for Human Rights, *Human Rights Abuses Against Women: A Worldwide Survey* (May, 1990) for excerpts from the U.S. State Department's 1990 Country Reports on Human Rights (1990); Lori Heise, "The Global War Against Women," *Utne Reader*, 45 (Nov./Dec. 1989). No data are kept on the prevalence of pornography.

15. United Nations, *The State of the World's Women 1979*, quoted in Burns H. Weston, Richard A. Falk, and Anthony A. D'Amato, *International Law and World Order* 578–580 (St. Paul, MN: West 1980). See also Marilyn Waring, *Counting for Nothing: What Men Value and What Women Are Worth* (Wellington, NZ: Allen & Unwin 1988).

16. Diana E. H. Russell, *Sexual Exploitation* 35 (Beverly Hills, CA: Sage Publications 1984); Gail E. Wyatt, "The Sexual Abuse of Afro-American and White American Women in Childhood," 9 *Child Abuse and Neglect* 507 (1985). See also Senate Judiciary Committee Majority Staff Report, "Violence Against Women: The Increase of Rape in America 1990," 102d Cong., 1st Sess. (Mar. 21, 1991).

17. U.S. Department of Justice, *Crime in the United States* (Uniform Crime Reports) 13 (Aug. 6, 1989).

18. *Yearbook of Juridical Statistics*, Statistics Sweden, 1989, as cited in R. A. Elman and M. Eduards, "Unprotected by the Swedish Welfare State: A Survey of Battered Women and the Assistance They Received" 1 (unpublished paper) (1990).

19. Exceptions include, for instance, gay men, who can be seen to be feminized by this process, and so are not exceptions to the degree their abuse as gay *is* not seen as political either.

20. Even among men it is inadequate. Such a definition also excludes racist atrocities often committed against men of color, such as lynching, unless

proven done under color of law, and racism generally, and class-based oppression, which harms both men and women.

21. Noreen Burrows, "International Law and Human Rights: The Case of Women's Rights," in *Human Rights: From Rhetoric to Reality* 82, Tom Campbell et al., eds. (New York: Blackwell 1986). See Eschel M. Rhoodie, *Discrimination Against Women: A Global Survey* 92 (Jefferson, NC: McFarland 1989) ("This [public/private] dichotomy is deeply engrained in the laws of some countries and thus the law plays a critical role in maintaining gender stratification."). The Convention on the Elimination of All Forms of Discrimination Against Women covers both the conventionally public and private in its guarantees.

22. See Declaration of Defendant-Intervenor Linda Marchiano, above note 10, at ¶ 17, p. 7.

23. Id. at ¶ 21, p. 8.

24. "Public Hearings on Ordinances to Add Pornography as Discrimination Against Women," (Minneapolis, MN, Dec. 12, 1983), published in Catharine A. MacKinnon and Andrea Dworkin, eds., *In Harm's Way: The Pornography Civil Rights Hearings* (Cambridge, MA: Harvard University Press 1998).

25. American Booksellers Ass'n, Inc. v. Hudnut, 771 F.2d 323, 329 (7th Cir. 1985) ("Depictions of subordination tend to perpetuate subordination. The subordinate status of women in turn leads to affront and lower pay at work, insult and injury at home, battery and rape on the streets. In the language of the legislature, '(pornography *is* central *in* creating and maintaining sex as a basis of discrimination. Pornography is a systematic practice of exploitation and subordination based on sex which differentially harms women. The bigotry and contempt *it* produces, with the acts of aggression it fosters, harm women's opportunities for equality and rights [of all kinds].' Indianapolis Code § 16-l(a)(2). Yet this simply demonstrates the power of pornography as speech.").

26. Hudnut v. American Booksellers Ass'n, Inc., 475 U.S. 1001 (1986) (summary affirmance).

27. Personal correspondence from Jayne Stamen to the author, March 11, 1988.

28. The New York State Department of Correctional Services Web site lists Jayne Stamen as released on parole on July 17, 2003, after over fifteen years in prison.

29. People v. Burnham, 222 Cal. Rptr. 630 (Cal. Ct. App. 1986), *rev. denied* (May 22, 1986).

30. Inter-American Court of Human Rights, Velasquez-Rodriguez v. Honduras Series C, No. 4, (Judgment of July 29, 1988) (1989), 28 *International Legal Materials* 291.

31. See, e.g., Directorate of Human Rights, Council of Europe, Information Sheet No. 24 (Nov. 1988–July 1989), Appendix XXXII, Declaration on Equality of Women and Men (Nov. 16, 1988). General Recommendation No. 12, Report of the Committee on the Elimination of Discrimination Against Women on Its 8th Session, U.N. Doc. A/44/38 (1989) 81 (considering that Articles 2, 5, 11, 12, and 16 of the Convention require states parties to act to protect women against violence of any kind occurring within the family, at the workplace, or in any other area of social life, effectively reading in an obligation to take steps to address violence against women). On efforts to eradicate violence against women within society and the family, see *Report by the Secretary General*, U.N. Doc. E/CN.6/1988/6 (1987). Regarding pornography, see Directorate of Human Rights, Council of Europe, Information Sheet No. 24 (Nov. 1988–July 1989), Recommendation No. R (89) 7 (principles on distribution of violent, brutal, or pornographic videos). After this speech was given, the CEDAW Committee promulgated its General Recommendation 19, see CEDAW, General Recommendation 19 (11th Sess. 1992), Report of the Committee on the Elimination of Discrimination Against Women on Its 11th Session, U.N. Doc. A/47/38 (1992), interpreting CEDAW's antidiscrimination provision to encompass violence against women and its official condonation. The CEDAW Committee has also recognized pornography's role in violence against women in its General Comment 12: "These attitudes also contribute to the propagation of pornography and the depiction and other commercial exploitation of women as sexual objects, rather than as individuals. This in turn contributes to gender based violence." Id. at Comment 12. The Human Rights Committee's General Comment 28 on sex equality under the International Covenant on Civil and Political Rights finds that pornography is likely to promote violence or degrading and inhuman treatment. Human Rights Committee, General Comment 28, Equality of Rights Between Men and Women (Article 3), U.N. Doc. CCPR/C/2 1/Rev.1/Add.10 (2000), para. 22.

32. See, e.g., Prepared Statement of Amnesty International USA, Hearings on Human Rights Abuses Against Women, Hearing Before the Subcommittee on Human Rights and International Organizations, Committee on Foreign Affairs, U.S. House of Representatives, March 21, 1990 ("[S]ome

governments do not consider rape, sexual assault and sexual abuse as serious a crime as other types of physical assaults. This is particularly alarming when the perpetrators of the rape are government officials charged with the protection of the public"). Id. at 6. Amnesty International has, since this speech was published, increasingly taken on sexual torture in official custody as part of its mandate.

33. But see U.S. State Dept. Cable, "In recent legislative report language, the Senate Foreign Relations Committee observed that government tolerance of violence and abuse against women appears to be widely practiced and tacitly condoned in many parts of the world. Noting that such abuse is a violation of human rights as defined in existing legislation, the Committee called on the Department to pay special attention to these abuses in the cruelty reports;" International League for Human Rights, *Human Rights Abuses Against Women: A Worldwide Survey* (May 1990). See above note 11, at Appendix 2.

34. American Booksellers Ass'n, Inc. v. Hudnut, 771 F.2d 323, 329 (7th Cir. 1985).

35. In some places, there are various ingenious methods for cushioning the impact or qualifying the irrationality of the "similarly situated" test, usually by recognizing "differences" in some form, but it remains the main rule, and "difference" inscribed in law has its own hazards.

36. This critique is discussed more fully in Catharine A. MacKinnon, "Reflections on Sex Equality Under Law," 100 *Yale Law Journal* 1281 (1991), reprinted in Catharine A. MacKinnon, ed., *Women's Lives, Men's Laws* 116 (Cambridge, MA: Belknap Press of Harvard University Press 2005).

37. See Andrews v. Law Society of British Columbia, [1989] 1 S.C.R. 143; Regina v. Turpin, [1989] 1 S.C.R. 1296; Regina v. Lavallée, [1990] 1 S.C.R. 852; but compare Regina v. Hess, [1990] 2 S.C.R. 906.

38. See Richard Rorty, "Feminism and Pragmatism," 30 *Michigan Quarterly Review* 231, 234 (Spring 1991).

13. RAPE AS GENOCIDE: APPELLATE ARGUMENT

1. Each unknown to the other, a roughly contemporaneous filing of the same contention on behalf of the state was made in *Bosnia and Herzegovina v. Serbia and Montenegro* in the International Court of Justice, Application of the Convention on the Prevention and Punishment of the Crime of Genocide (Bosnia and Herzegovina v. Serbia and Montenegro, Judgment, I.C.J. Reports 2007, p. 43). For the filed documents making this claim and

an account of some of the proceedings, see Francis Anthony Boyle, *The Bosnian People Charge Genocide: Proceedings at the International Court of Justice Concerning* Bosnia v. Serbia *on the Prevention and Punishment of the Crime of Genocide* 29 (Northampton, MA: Aletheia 1996).

2. Alien Tort Claims Act, 28 U.S.C. § 1350.

3. Torture Victim Protection Act, 101 Stat. 73, printed at 28 U.S.C. § 1350.

4. Doe v. Karadžić, 866 F. Supp. 734 (S.D.N.Y. 1994), *rev'd sub nom.* Kadic v. Karadžić, 70 F.3d 232 (2d Cir. 1995).

5. Id. After winning the right to go to trial, the Does' lawyers moved to certify a class of all survivors of the Bosnian genocide, Doe v. Karadžić, 176 F.R.D. 458, 461 (S.D.N.Y. 1997), which the *Kadic* plaintiffs opposed. Judge Leisure denied our motion to leave the class, Doe v. Karadžić, 182 F.R.D. 424, 430 (S.D.N.Y. 1998), making it necessary to challenge the class certification itself, which we successfully did. See Doe v. Karadžić, 192 F.R.D. 133, 144 (S.D.N.Y. 2000). The *Kadic* plaintiffs did not wish to be represented as part of the *Doe* class; they also opposed on principle a class being asserted that included people who had no actual voice in their own representation, with whom the *Doe* lawyers had no contact. For some discussion, see Catharine A. MacKinnon, "Collective Harms Under the Alien Tort Statute: A Cautionary Note on Class Actions," 6 *ILSA Journal of International and Comparative Law* 567, 573 (2000).

6. Kadic v. Karadžić, 70 F.3d 232, 242 (2d Cir. 1995).

7. Kadic v. Karadžić, 518 U.S. 1005, 116 S. Ct. 2524 (1996).

8. See Kiobel v. Royal Dutch Petroleum Co., 569 U.S. 12 (2013) (holding the Alien Tort Act presumptively inapplicable extraterritorially).

9. Prosecutor v. Karadžić, Case No. IT-95-5/18-T, ¶¶ 2500, 5741 (Mar. 24, 2016) (convicting the defendant of mass rapes in the Bosnian conflict, and separately finding that the assaults at Srebrenica were genocidal).

10. See, e.g., Prosecutor v. Akayesu, Judgment, Case No. ICTR-96-4-T, ¶¶ 695 (Sept. 2, 1998).

11. In this transcript, the ellipses are in the original, indicating where a speaker did not finish a sentence; they do not indicate omitted material. Footnotes are, of course, added.

12. Filàrtiga v. Peña-Irala, 630 F. 2d 876 (2d Cir. 1980).

13. Terrill v. Rankin, 65 (Ky.) (2 Bush) 453 (1867).

14. Amended Complaint, Kadic v. Karadžić, 93 Civ. 1163 (PKL) (S.D.N.Y. Dec. 3, 1997).

15. Brief of Plaintiffs-Appellants, Kadic v. Karadžić, #94-9069 (2d Cir. Jan. 17, 1995).

14. RAPE AS GENOCIDE: SUMMATION TO THE JURY

1. Order, Kadic v. Karadžić, Order Entering Default on Liability, 93 Civ. 1163 (PKL) (S.D.N.Y. June 13, 2000).
2. See Convention on the Prevention and Punishment of the Crime of Genocide, art. 3(c) adopted Dec. 9, 1948, 78 U.N.T.S. 277.

15. TRAFFICKING, PROSTITUTION, AND INEQUALITY

1. Various versions of this talk were given, among other places, in Johannesburg on February 22, 2010; in Buenos Aires on June 10, 2010; in Taipei on June 3, 2013; in Tel Aviv on July 28, 2014; in Shanghai on February 5, 2015; and in the form it appears here in Perth, Australia, on February 16, 2015. In a previously published form, this speech can be found at "Trafficking, Prostitution, and Inequality," 46 *Harvard Civil Rights-Civil Liberties Law Review* 271 (2011).
2. On Sweden, see Brottsbalken [BrB] (Criminal Code) 6:1 (Sweden); Max Waltman, "The Politics of Legal Challenges to Pornography: Canada, Sweden, and the United States," *Stockholm Studies in Politics* 277–286, 294–298 (Stockholm: Stockholm University 2014) (Ph.D. Dissertation) (recounting sex equality dimensions of passage of Swedish law against prostitution). Canada passed a version of the Nordic model on prostitution in December 2014. Protection of Communities and Exploited Persons Act, S.C. 2014, c. 25, http://www.canlii.org/en/ca/laws/astat/sc-2014-c-25 /latest/sc-2014-c-25.html?resultIndex=1. France passed it in April 2016. Loi visant à renforcer la lutte contre le système prostitutionnel et à accompagner les personnes prostituées, Loi n° 2016-444 du 13 avril 2016 parue au JO n° 0088 du 14 avril 2016 (Legislation to strengthen the fight against the system of prostitution and to support prostituted persons, Legislation No. 2016-444 of April 13, 2016, appearing in Journal No. 0088 of April 14, 2016), http://www.senat.fr/dossier-legislatif/ppl13-207.html.
3. Proponents of the sex work position include the Sex Worker Education and Advocacy Taskforce ("SWEAT") in South Africa; Durbar Mahila Samanwaya Committee ("DMSC") in India; the New Zealand Prostitutes Collective ("NZPC") in New Zealand; Call Off Your Old Tired Ethics ("COYOTE") in the United States; the Initiative Against Trafficking in Persons, also based in the United States; and the international Network of Sex Work Projects ("NSWP"), founded in 1991. The sexual exploitation approach is exemplified internationally by the Coalition Against Trafficking in Women ("CATW") and Equality Now, as well as by Apne

Aap in India, Embrace Dignity in Cape Town, South Africa, and similar organizations worldwide. Some U.S. groups pursuing this work are Girls Educational & Mentoring Services ("GEMS"), New York; End Demand Illinois, a campaign of the Chicago Alliance Against Sexual Exploitation ("CAASE"); Council for Prostitution Alternatives ("CPA"), Portland, OR; Breaking Free, Minneapolis, MN; and Refuge House, Inc., Tallahassee, FL.

4. See, e.g., Jo Doezema, *Sex Slaves and Discourse Masters* (London: Zed Books 2010); Ronald Weitzer, ed., *Sex for Sale: Prostitution, Pornography, and the Sex Industry*, (2d ed., New York: Routledge 2010); Gillian Abel et al., eds., *Taking the Crime Out of Sex Work: New Zealand Sex Workers' Fight for Decriminalisation* (Bristol, UK: Policy Press 2010); Chi Mgbaka and Laura A. Smith, "Sex Work and Human Rights in Africa," 33 *Fordham International Law Journal* 1178 (2010).

5. See, e.g., Melissa Farley, *Prostitution and Trafficking in Nevada: Making the Connections* (San Francisco: Prostitution Research & Education 2007) ("*Trafficking in Nevada*"); Melissa Farley et al., "Prostitution and Trafficking in Nine Countries: An Update on Violence and Posttraumatic Stress Disorder," 2 *Journal of Trauma Practice* 33 (2003) ("Trafficking in Nine Countries").

6. See, e.g., Julie Bindel and Liz Kelly, *A Critical Examination of Responses to Prostitution in Four Countries: Victoria, Australia; Ireland; the Netherlands; and Sweden* (2003) ("*Responses to Prostitution*"); S. African Law Reform Comm'n, Sexual Offenses: Adult Prostitution 128 (2009).

7. See Lag om förbud mot köp av sexuella tjänster 405 (1998) ("A person who obtains casual sexual relations in exchange for payment shall be sentenced—unless the act is punishable under the Swedish Penal Code—for the purchase of sexual services to a fine or imprisonment for at most six months.").

8. Iceland made the purchase of sexual services illegal in 2009. See Lög um breytingu á almennum hegningarlögum, nr. 19/1940, með sí ðari breytingum [Icelandic Law No. 54 of 2009] (2009) (Ice.). As of January 1, 2009, citizens of Norway were prohibited from paying for sex domestically or abroad. See Law Amending the Penal Code and Criminal Procedure Act of 1902, No. 104 (2008) (Nor.), available at http://www.lovdata.no/cgiwift/ldles ?doc=/all/nl-20081212-104.html. South Korea's laws of March 22, 2004, are Act on the Prevention of Prostitution and Protection of Victims Thereof, Statutes of South Korea, Act No. 7212; and Act on the Punishment of Procuring Prostitution and Associated Acts, Statutes of South

Korea, Act No. 7196 (criminalizing at article 21(1) "[a]nyone who sells sex or buys sex" while exempting "victims of prostitution" from punishment, at article 6(1)). On Israel and South Africa's proposed laws, see Rebecca Anna Stoil, "Knesset Bill Seeks to Ban Hiring a Prostitute," *Jerusalem Post*, Dec. 21, 2009, at 4; Criminal Law (Sexual Offences and Related Matters) Amendment Act 32 of 2007 § 11 (S. Afr.) (criminalizing purchase of sex from persons 18 years of age and older). On Scotland's debated law, see *Scottish Parliament, Justice Committee, Official Report of 20 April 2010* (Scot.), at cols. 2919, 2937, http://archive.scottish .parliament.uk/s3/committees/justice/or-10/ju10-1302.htm. On France's law, see "France prostitution: MPs outlaw paying for sex," *BBC News*, Apr. 7, 2016, http://www.bbc.com/news/world-europe-35982929.

9. New York State, for example, moved towards the Swedish model in 2007 by legislating penalties for buyers higher than for prostituted people, by creating the class B felony for "sex trafficking," and by excluding victims from accomplice liability for trafficking. See N.Y. Penal Law §§ 230.34, 230.36 (2010). But the sold remained criminals. See id. § 230.00 (deeming "Prostitution" a class B misdemeanor).

10. See Mike Dottridge, *Kids as Commodities? Child Trafficking and What To Do About It* 28 (2004) ("The principal reason why children, as well as adults, from particular communities end up being trafficked is the lack of alternative ways of earning a living for them and their families."); Chandré Gould and Nicolé Fick, *Report to the South African Law Reform Commission: Preliminary Research Findings of Relevance to the Draft Legislation to Combat Trafficking in Persons and Legislation Pertaining to Adult Prostitution* 12 (2007) ("*Report to the SALRC*") (relating from focus group discussions with people in prostitution that "[i]n all cases financial responsibilities, or expectations from families or dependents led to entry into the industry").

11. See, e.g., Dorchen Leidholdt, "Prostitution: A Violation of Women's Human Rights," 1 *Cardozo Women's Law Journal* 133, 142 (1993) ("In the vast majority of cases, prostitution enables a woman at best to eke out a subsistence living.").

12. Special Committee on Pornography & Prostitution in Canada, 2 *Pornography and Prostitution in Canada* 350 (1985). See also John J. Potterat et al., "Mortality in a Long-term Open Cohort of Prostitute Women," 159 *American Journal of Epidemiology* 778, 783 (2004) (concluding, based on a study of prostituted women in Colorado Springs, Colo., that "[t]o our

knowledge, no population of women studied previously has had a crude mortality rate, standardized mortality ratio, or percentage of deaths due to murder even approximating those observed in our cohort").

13. Research throughout the United States shows that African American women and girls are overrepresented in the sex trade. See, e.g., Jennifer James, *Entrance into Juvenile Prostitution: Final Report* 17, 19 (1980) (*"Juvenile Prostitution"*) (finding African American girls, 4.2 percent of the population in the geographic area of the study, were 25 percent of sample of prostituted girls interviewed in Seattle area ($n=136$)). Interviews conducted with over 3,000 "streetwalking prostitutes" for an outreach project in New York City found approximately half were African American, a quarter Hispanic, and the remaining quarter white. Barbara Goldsmith, "Women on the Edge," *New Yorker*, Apr. 26, 1993, at 64, 65.

14. See Melissa Farley et al., Prostitution in Vancouver: Violence and the Colonization of First Nations Women," 42 *Transcultural Psychiatry* 242, 242, 249 (2005) (finding 52 percent of 100 prostituted women in Vancouver, British Columbia, of First Nations descent, a group constituting 1.7–7 percent of the population).

15. See, e.g., Christine Joffres et al., "Sexual Slavery Without Borders: Trafficking for Commercial Sexual Exploitation in India," 7 *International Journal for Equity in Health* 22, 24 (2008); R. C. Swarankar, "Ethnographic Study of Community-Based Sex Work Among Nats," in *Prostitution and Beyond: An Analysis of Sex Work in India* 118, Rohini Sahni et al., eds. (Los Angeles: Sage Publications 2008).

16. See, e.g., Comm. on Sexual Offenses Against Children, 2 *Sexual Offenses Against Children: Report of the Committee on Sexual Offenses Against Children* 229, 991 (1984) (conducting in-depth interviews with 229 sexually exploited youth in Canada recounting turning first trick between ages eight and nineteen—most were fifteen or sixteen, many aged thirteen or fourteen); Michelle Stransky and David Finkelhor, "Fact Sheet: How Many Juveniles Are Involved in Prostitution in the U.S.?" (2008), available at http://www.unh.edu/ccrc/prostitution/Juvenile_Prostitution_factsheet.pdf. The United Nations Office on Drugs and Crime ("UNODC") and the United Nations Interregional Crime Research Institute ("UNICRI") report on trafficking victims in the Czech Republic and Poland states, "[c]hanges in the profile of victims were characterized by the experts as follows: the age of victims is decreasing; the emphasis is particularly on young girls living in socially and economically disadvantaged conditions . . . ." Ivana Trávníéková et al., *Trafficking in Women: The Czech*

Republic Perspective 81 (Prague: Institute of Criminology and Social Prevention 2004).

17. See, e.g., Debra Boyer et al., *Survival Sex in King County: Helping Women Out* 3 (1993) (reporting from interviews with currently and recently prostituted women in Washington State, 100 percent (*n*=16) stated they had been sexually abused as girls); Mimi H. Silbert and Ayala M. Pines, "Sexual Child Abuse as an Antecedent to Prostitution," 5 *Child Abuse & Neglect* 407, 407, 409 (1981); Simons and Whitbeck, "Sexual Abuse as a Precursor to Prostitution and Victimization Among Adolescent and Adult Homeless Women," 12 *Journal of Family Issues* 361, 375 (1991) (concluding that "child sexual abuse increases the probability of involvement in prostitution irrespective of any influence exerted through other variables").

18. A strikingly convergent observation is made by Vednita Nelson concerning the role of zoning in largely Black neighborhoods in encouraging the perception that Black women and girls are available for purchase, in particular by white men: "[W]e got the message growing up, just like our daughters are getting it today, that this is how it is, this is who we are, this is what we are for." Vednita Nelson, "Prostitution: Where Racism and Sexism Intersect," 1 *Michigan Journal of Gender & Law* 81, 84 (1993).

19. According to the United Nations Population Fund ("UNFPA"), "survival sex" denotes "sex . . . exchanged for food, shelter or protection." UNAIDS Inter-Agency Task Team on Gender & HIV/AIDS, *Fact Sheet: HIV/AIDS, Gender and Sex Work* 1 (2008), available at www.unfpa.org/hiv/docs/factsheet_genderwork.pdf.

20. See, e.g., Meritor Savings Bank v. Vinson, 477 U.S. 57 (1986); Declaration on the Elimination of Violence against Women art. 2(b), G.A. Res. 48/104, U.N. Doc. A/RES/48/104, (Dec. 20, 1993); U.N. Comm. on the Elimination of Discrimination against Women, General Recommendation No. 19 to Convention on the Elimination of All Forms of Discrimination against Women, 11th Sess. (1992) (commenting on Art. 11, ¶¶ 17–18).

21. Fernando Henriques, *Prostitution and Society: A Survey* 17 (1962).

22. See, e.g., Jan Macleod et al., *Challenging Men's Demand for Prostitution in Scotland: A Research Report Based on Interviews with 110 Men Who Bought Women in Prostitution* 4, 5, 14, 20, 24 (2008) (*"Prostitution in Scotland"*).

23. See, e.g., Janice G. Raymond and Donna M. Hughes, *Sex Trafficking of Women in the United States* 11 (2001) (*"Sex Trafficking of Women"*); Susan Moore, "Characteristics, Attitudes and Risk Behaviours of Australian Men

Who Visit Female Sex Workers," 12 *Venereology* 7, 7, 13 (1999) (determining that johns engage in multiple risk-taking behaviors, particularly in relation to HIV/AIDS, that expose women they buy to extreme danger).

24. Following years of intensive investigation, Dr. Mimi Silbert concluded that prostituted women were "the most raped class of women in history." Susan Kay Hunter, "Prostitution Is Cruelty and Abuse to Women and Children," 1 *Michigan Journal of Gender & Law* 92 (1993).

25. The vast majority of prostituted people report being physically assaulted in prostitution, most often by johns. See Ruth Parriott, *Health Experiences of Twin Cities Women Used in Prostitution: Survey Findings and Recommendations* 18 (1994) (50 percent by john, 90 percent by someone other than john, over half beaten once per month or more); Ine Vanwesenbeeck, *Prostitutes' Well-Being and Risk* 91 (Amsterdam: VU Uitgeverij 1994) ("*Prostitutes' Well-Being*") (60 percent).

26. For an exemplary South African case exposing excessive force by police raiding an adult entertainment establishment, see Palmer v. Minister of Safety & Security 2002 (1) SA 110 (S. Afr.); see also Anonymous, "Bad Luck at Lucky's Or Caught Between the Rapists and Police," 1 *Gauntlet* 111, 112 (1994) ("It's hard to protect yourself from the rapists while you're busy protecting yourself from the police.").

27. See Kimberly J. Mitchell et al., "Conceptualizing Juvenile Prostitution as Child Maltreatment: Findings from the National Juvenile Prostitution Study," 15 *Child Maltreatment* 18 (2010).

28. Not surprisingly, arrests of women of color in prostitution in the United States are significantly skewed compared with their proportion of the total population. The most recent Federal Bureau of Investigation ("FBI") statistics show that prostituted African Americans constituted 40.9 percent (*n*=23,987) of those arrested in 2008; 55.7 percent (*n*=32,682) were white. See FBI, *Uniform Crime Statistics*, tbl.43 (2008), http://www2 .fbi.gov/ucr/cius2008/data/table_43.html; Marilyn G. Haft, "Hustling for Rights," in *The Female Offender* 207, 212, Laura Crites, ed. (Lexington, MA: Lexington Books 1976) (citing government statistics that African American women in early 1970s were seven times more likely to be arrested for prostitution than members of other racial and ethnic groups).

29. Studies of prostitution in the United States have long identified posting bail as among the pimp's traditional functions. See, e.g., Ben L. Reitman, *The Second Oldest Profession: A Study of the Prostitute's 'Business Manager'* 15 (New York: Vanguard Press 1931); Charles Winick and Paul M.

Kinsie, *The Lively Commerce: Prostitution in the United States* 109 (Chicago: Quadrangle Books 1971).

30. According to an authoritative Canadian study, "[m]ost prostitutes have a criminal record." Special Comm. on Pornography & Prostitution in Can., 2 *Pornography and Prostitution in Canada* 374 (1985).

31. See, e.g., Working Group on the Legal Regulation of the Purchase of Sexual Services, *Purchasing Sexual Services in Sweden and the Netherlands: Legal Regulation and Experiences* 13 (2004) (asserting that Swedish antiprostitution law has increased the risk of violence "for those who no longer work on the streets").

32. See Melissa Farley, "'Bad for the Body, Bad for the Heart': Prostitution Harms Women Even If Legalized or Decriminalized," 10 *Violence Against Women* 1099–1101 (2004) (discussing findings of violence against women engaged in street as compared to indoor prostitution); Jody Raphael and Deborah L. Shapiro, "Violence in Indoor and Outdoor Prostitution Venues," 10 *Violence Against Women* 126, 133 (2004) (presenting data from 222 women presently or recently in prostitution in metropolitan Chicago showing "violence was prevalent across both outdoor and indoor prostitution venues").

33. Prostitution has long been organized into distinct hierarchical classes. See, e.g., Vern Bullough and Bonnie Bullough, *Women and Prostitution: A Social History* 35–40 (Buffalo, NY: Prometheus Books 1987) (Greece); id. at 86–93 (India); id. at 102–103; id. at 105–108 (China).

34. See Mary Lucille Sullivan, *Making Sex Work: A Failed Experiment with Legalised Prostitution* 315 (North Melbourne, Australia: Spinifex Press, 2007) (*"Making Sex Work"*). For more on the placement of panic buttons in the rooms of many legal brothels, see Farley, *Trafficking in Nevada* 18, 21.

35. See supra notes above. As additional evidence, Farley et al. found no difference in the incidence of PTSD between street and brothel prostitution, although they, with Plumridge and Abel, examining conditions in New Zealand, found higher rates of physical violence in street than brothel prostitution. See Farley et al., "Prostitution in Five Countries," 8 *Feminism & Psychology* 405, 419 (1998); Libby Plumridge and Gillian Abel, "A 'Segmented' Sex Industry in New Zealand: Sexual and Personal Safety of Female Sex Workers," 25 *Australian & New Zealand Journal of Public Health* 78, 82–83 (2001).

36. A researcher not unfriendly to the sex work perspective observed its adherents see prostitution "by definition as a human right instead of as a

violation of human rights" and are inclined to "consider sex-work liberating, a manifestation of crossing the borders of strictly circumscribed femininity, and a possibility for women to use the (sexual) power that has been denied them by patriarchal traditions." Vanwesenbeeck, *Prostitutes' Well-Being* 7–8. So "[t]hey would rather not talk about sexual victimization at all." Id. at 7. Representatives of this camp consign prostitution's harms to the realm of phantasmagorical "moral panic." See, e.g., Gayle Rubin, "Thinking Sex: Notes for a Radical Theory of the Politics of Sexuality," in *Pleasure and Danger: Exploring Female Sexuality* 267, 297, Carole S. Vance, ed. (London: Pandora Press 1992) (arguing that panic-driven antiprostitution reforms seeking to ban such "innocuous behavior []" aim at "chimeras and signifiers" so are destined to fail).

37. See Jan Jordan, *The Sex Industry in New Zealand: A Literature Review* (2005) ("A harm minimisation approach was favoured by many, and the resultant legal changes sought to reflect such sentiments."), available at www.justice.govt.nz/assets/Documents/Publications/sex-industry-in-nz.pdf.

38. For a dialogue, see Melinda Gates from 2004 speaking of "sex workers" in India using condoms as "empowerment," Melinda French Gates, "AIDS and India," Op-Ed., *Seattle Times*, Apr. 11, 2004, available at http://community .seattletimes.nwsource.com/archive/?date=20040411&slug=gates11, and a response by Ambassador John R. Miller, then director of the Office to Monitor and Combat Trafficking in Persons, U.S. State Department, criticizing the same, when not accompanied by resistance to prostitution itself, as support for slavery. John R. Miller, "Fight AIDS, of course, but also fight prostitution," Op-Ed., *Seattle Times*, May 20, 2004, available at http:// community.seattletimes.nwsource.com/archive/?date=20040520&slug =johnmiller20.

39. See Farley et al., "Trafficking in Nine Countries," 36, 37, 56, 57 (comparing 68 percent prevalence rate of PTSD among women in prostitution in nine countries to that in combat veterans, torture victims, and rape survivors); Melissa Farley et al., "Prostitution in Five Countries," 405, 415 (finding prostituted women across five countries evidenced PTSD rates slightly above treatment-seeking Vietnam veterans in United States).

40. For major contributions to the psychology of dissociation, see generally Kathleen Kendall-Tackett and Bridget Klest, eds., *Trauma, Dissociation and Health: Causal Mechanisms and Multidimensional Pathways* (2009). For a brief introduction to the extensive literature documenting the relationship between child sexual abuse and dissociation, see Judith Lewis Herman, *Trauma and Recovery* 99–103, 110, 111 (1992).

41. No doubt addiction can make one vulnerable to entry into prostitution. Some earlier studies suggested that some women were addicts prior to entering prostitution, but more recent larger samples find more start using as a result of it. See, e.g., Janice G. Raymond et al., *A Comparative Study of Women Trafficked in the Migration Process: Patterns, Profiles and Health Consequences of Sexual Exploitation in Five Countries (Indonesia, the Philippines, Thailand, Venezuela and the United States)* 64, 171–172 (2002) (finding 60 percent of Venezuelan respondents who admitted taking drugs and alcohol to escape the reality of the sex industry abused those substances only after they had been prostituted).

42. As Melissa Farley has aptly observed, "dissociation is a job requirement for surviving prostitution." Farley, "'Bad for the Body, Bad for the Heart,'" 1106; see also id. at 1107, 1109 (quoting illustrative reflections from multiple studies).

43. See Farley et al., "Trafficking in Nine Countries," 51; see also James, *Juvenile Prostitution* 17, 69 (noting fatalism of prostituted girls in Seattle where near impossibility of exit was widely accepted); Lynda M. Baker et al., "Exiting Prostitution: An Integrated Model," 16 *Violence Against Women* 579, 588–590 (2010) (summarizing studies of barriers).

44. Kathleen Barry, *Female Sexual Slavery* 39–40 (New York: New York University Press 1984). See also U.N. ESCOR, Commission on Human Rights, "Activities for the Advancement of Women: Equality, Development and Peace, Report of the Special Rapporteur Jean Fernand-Laurent," 1st Sess., Agenda Item 12, at 7, U.N. Doc. E/1983/7 (1983) (likening prostitution to slavery).

45. Innumerable such cases underlie international reports. See, e.g., U.N. Economic & Social Council ("ECOSOC"), Commission on Human Rights ("CHR"), "Preliminary Report Submitted by the Special Rapporteur on Violence Against Women, Its Causes and Consequences," 50th Sess., Agenda Item 11(a), ¶ 211, U.N. Doc. E/CN.4/1995/42 (Nov. 22, 1994) (by Radhika Coomaraswamy) ("Women who are trafficked are by and large not aware of what awaits them; some women contact pimps or managers directly, but the larger percentage of trafficked women are sold into bondage by their parents, husbands, boyfriends, or they are deceived or coerced, sometimes by friends or elders in the village.").

46. See, e.g., Farley, *Trafficking in Nevada* 93 (describing exemplary cases of women unwittingly sold into prostitution).

47. Slavery Convention art. 1(1), Sept. 25, 1926, 46 Stat. 2183, 2191, 60 L.N.T.S. 253, 263 ("Slavery is the status or condition of a person over

whom any or all of the powers attaching to the right of ownership are exercised.").

48. See, e.g., "Special Comm. on Pornography & Prostitution in Can.," 2 *Pornography and Prostitution in Canada* 371 (1985) (observing "the ratio of female to male prostitutes is estimated to be at least four to one," with some variation among cities); Kristiina Kangaspunta, "Mapping the Inhuman Trade: Preliminary Findings of the Database on Trafficking in Human Beings," 3 *Forum on Crime & Society* 81, 95–97 (2003) ("Mapping the Inhuman Trade") (utilizing open source case information in UNODC trafficking database to show the vast majority of those trafficked for sex are women and children).

49. Shulamith Firestone called sex "the oldest, most rigid class/caste system in existence." Shulamith Firestone, *The Dialectic of Sex: The Case for Feminist Revolution* 15 (New York: Farrar, Straus and Giroux 2003).

50. As a retired madam reflected decades ago on a situation that has not changed, "No girl, as a social worker once said, sets out to be a prostitute . . . . Who wants to be a pariah, a social outcast—treated with contempt, jailed, beaten, robbed and finally kicked into the gutter when she is no longer salable?" Polly Adler, *A House Is Not a Home* 127–128 (New York: Rinehart 1953) ("*A House*").

51. As expressed by Ekberg, "What they mean, but do not say, is that prostitution is an acceptable solution for women living in poverty. Seldom do we see proposals that poor men should make their way out of poverty by welcoming the insertion of penises and other objects into them on a regular basis . . . ." Gunilla S. Ekberg, "The International Debate About Prostitution and Trafficking in Women: Refuting the Arguments" (2002) (unpublished paper presented at the Seminar on the Effects of Legalisation of Prostitution Activities, Stockholm, Sweden).

52. Nothing in this analysis turns on absolute or relative numbers, across or within borders, but gaining even a general sense of magnitudes proves complex. No transnational data on the global magnitude of prostitution or domestic trafficking exists. As to the much smaller numbers of internationally trafficked people, UNESCO finds between 500,000 and 4 million victims cross borders annually. United Nations Educ., *Scientific, & Cultural Org. ("UNESCO"), Trafficking Project, Factsheet #1: Worldwide Trafficking Estimates by Organizations* (June 2004). Notwithstanding the inevitable undercounting of a clandestine industry, since many countries are source, transit, and destination locations, the incidence of trafficking—

each act of which is a crime and a human rights violation—can be up to three times the prevalence of trafficked people.

53. A prostituted Vancouver woman put it this way: "Men who go to prosti-tutes go to prostitutes (and I've been hooking for 19 years) because it's a power trip. They pay the money, they get to call the shots. They own you for that 1/2 hour or that 20 minutes or that hour. They are buying you. They have no attachments, you're not a person, you're a thing to be used." Special Comm. on Pornography & Prostitution in Can., 2 *Pornography and Prostitution in Canada* 387 (1985).

54. See, e.g., Committee on Sexual Offenses Against Children, 2 *Sexual Offenses Against Children: Report of the Committee on Sexual Offenses Against Children* 229, 1016–1017, 1034–1035 (1984) (documenting prostituted youth who definitively indicate they neither enjoy prostitution nor recommend it as a life choice); Adler, *A House* 127 (1953) (observing, based on years of experience as New York madam, "despite all the feigned transports of ecstasy . . . to ninety-nine out of a hundred girls, going to bed with a customer is a joyless, even distasteful, experience.").

55. A recent study in London attests to johns' attitudes in this regard. "Most interviewees said they assumed that to a greater or lesser extent, women in prostitution are sexually satisfied by the sex acts purchased by buyers," believing in particular that they "were satisfied by the sex of prostitution 46% of the time." Melissa Farley et al., *Men Who Buy Sex: Who They Buy and What They Know* 19 (2009).

56. See Macleod et al., *Prostitution in Scotland* 20–21 (reporting that 73 percent of johns interviewed said that women engaged in prostitution strictly out of economic necessity and 85 percent said that prostituted sex was not pleasurable to those sold). Any tension with the finding in note 55 above is explained by the important finding that men who buy sex simultaneously hold many diametrically opposed attitudes about prostitution, including on their own roles and women's roles in it. See Melissa Farley et al., "Attitudes and Social Characteristics of Men Who Buy Sex in Scotland," 3 *Psychological Trauma* 4, 369 (Dec. 2011) ("Men Who Buy Sex in Scotland").

57. For whatever reason, johns consider the transaction consensual despite their knowledge of her actual conditions. See, e.g., Macleod et al., *Prostitution in Scotland* 20 (2008) ("Almost all (96%) of the punters interviewed in this research stated that to a significant extent (50% or more of the time) prostitution was a consenting act between two adults."); Victor

Malarek, *The Johns: Sex for Sale and the Men Who Buy It* 103 (New York: Arcade Publishing 2009) (quoting a john, "Ninety-nine per cent of mongers purchase as a willing buyer a service from a consensual adult willing seller . . . .").

58. On relative magnitudes of sex and labor trafficking, Kangaspunta finds 85 percent of women victims are trafficked for sexual purposes, 2 percent for forced labor, and 13 percent for a combination of both; 16 percent of victimized men are trafficked for sex, 24 percent for forced labor, and 60 percent for a combination of both; 70 percent of child victims are trafficked for sexual exploitation, 13 percent for forced labor, and 18 percent for both. "Mapping the Inhuman Trade" 81, 95, 97. The dynamics mentioned in the text, observed by activists, leave some trace here.

59. For instance, Martha Nussbaum asserts, "All of us . . . take money for the use of our body. Professors, factory workers, lawyers, opera singers, prostitutes, doctors, legislators—we all do things with parts of our bodies for which we receive a wage in return." Martha C. Nussbaum, "'Whether from Reason or Prejudice': Taking Money for Bodily Services," 27 *Journal of Legal Studies* 693–694 (1998).

60. When this talk was given, Amnesty International was in the process of considering its policy on prostitution. It has since disgracefully adopted, in the guise of supporting "sex workers," exactly the position criticized here: across-the-board decriminalization, meaning pimps and traffickers as well as buyers would have free rein. See the resolution at *Decision on State Obligation to Respect, Protect, and Fulfil the Human Rights of Sex Workers*, Amnesty International, https://www.amnesty.org/en/policy-on-state-obligations-to-respect-protect-and-fulfil-the-human-rights-of-sex-workers and the policy at Amnesty International, *Amnesty International Policy on State Obligations to Respect, Protect and Fulfill the Human Rights of Sex Workers*, Amnesty International (May 26, 2016) https://www.amnesty.org/en/documents/pol30/4062/2016/en/.

61. See Wendy Chapkis, *Live Sex Acts: Women Performing Erotic Labor* 17–20 (New York: Routledge 1997) (categorizing exponents of the sexual exploitation approach as "anti-sex" feminists); Carol Queen, "Sex Radical Politics, Sex-Positive Feminist Thought, and Whore Stigma," in *Whores and Other Feminists* 125, 129, Jill Nagel, ed. (New York: Routledge 1997) (disparaging ideological opponents as "anti-sex-work demagogues").

62. This is a compressed reconstruction of twenty-seven years of experience debating these issues, the atmosphere of which is evoked by literature such as Pat Califia, *Public Sex: The Culture of Radical Sex* (Pittsburgh, PA:

Cleis Press 1994); Camille Paglia, *Sexual Personae: Art and Decadence from Nefertiti to Emily Dickinson* (New Haven, CT: Yale University Press 1990); and Katie Roiphe, *The Morning After: Sex, Fear, and Feminism on Campus* (Boston: Little, Brown 1993).

63. See, e.g., Tiggey May et al., *For Love or Money: Pimps and the Management of Sex Work* 3 (2000) (distinguishing "pimps from the—largely female—managers of sex work in saunas and massage parlors" whose "relationship with their workers" tends to be "contractual rather than coercive"); Ronald Weitzer, "Prostitution as a Form of Work," 1 *Sociology Compass* 143, 143 (2007) (referring to pimps and johns respectively as "male managers and customers").

64. See Farley, "'Bad for the Body, Bad for the Heart'," 1112–1115.

65. Gloria Steinem, "Body Invasion is De-humanising," *The Hindu*, Apr. 6, 2012, available at http://www.thehindu.com/news/national/body-invasion -is-dehumanising/article3287212.ece ("What the idea of unions has done is to enhance the ability of the sex industry to attract millions of dollars from the Gates Foundation for the distribution on [sic] condoms, despite the fact that customers often pay more for sex without condoms, and it has created a big new source of income for brothel owners, pimps and traffickers who are called 'peer educators,' I understand that that the traffic of women and girls into Sonagachi has greatly increased.").

66. Other people do. Compare Vijayendra Rao et al., "Sex Workers and the Cost of Safe Sex: The Compensating Differential for Condom Use Among Calcutta Prostitutes," 71 *Journal of Developmental Economics* 585, 588 (2003), with data from a random sample of prostituted people in Sonagachi, Kolkata, India, calculating that "sex workers face between a 66% and a 79% loss in the average prices they charge by using condoms." In a study of women trafficked in the United States, 47 percent of respondents said they were often confronted with the demand for condom-free sex, 73 percent confirming that men offered to pay more for going "bare back." Raymond and Hughes, *Sex Trafficking of Women* 11.

67. An especially thorough criminalization of child prostitution is contained in recent laws of South Africa. See Criminal Law (Sexual Offences and Related Matters) Amendment Act 32 of 2007 §§ 17–22. Indicative is Priscilla Alexander's observation that "[a]dult prostitutes are concerned about adolescents and children turning to sex work to survive or being pressured to do so by parents and brokers." Priscilla Alexander, "Feminism, Sex Workers and Human Rights," in *Whores and Other Feminists* 93. The tendency to prioritize children has also been observed in the work

of governmental and nongovernmental organizations. See, e.g., David E. Guinn, "Defining the Problem of Trafficking: The Interplay of US Law, Donor, and NGO Engagement and the Local Context in Latin America," 30 *Human Rights Quarterly* 119, 124 (2008) ("Out of all forms of trafficking, child trafficking receives the greatest attention and condemnation. Countries that provide practically no programs to combat the trafficking of women or trafficking for labor exploitation nonetheless make some effort to prevent child trafficking, especially trafficking for purposes of sexual exploitation as reported in the US Trafficking in Persons (TIP) Report.").

68. See, e.g., Derek Jehu, Marjorie Gazon, and Carole Klassen, "Common Therapeutic Targets Among Women Who Were Sexually Abused in Childhood," 3 *Journal of Social Work & Human Sexuality* 25, 29, 30 (1985) (presenting results from structured interviews showing that more than three-quarters of treatment-seeking adult female subjects who had been sexually abused in childhood ($n=22$) experienced low self-esteem, with sixteen of twenty-one agreeing with the statement "I am worthless and bad.").

69. See Protocol to Prevent, Suppress and Punish Trafficking in Persons, Especially Women and Children, Supplementing the United Nations Convention Against Transnational Organized Crime art. 3(a) Nov. 2, 2000, G.A. Res. 25 (II), at 54, U.N. Doc. A/55/383:

    "Trafficking in persons" shall mean the recruitment, transportation, transfer, harbouring or receipt of persons, by means of the threat or use of force or other forms of coercion, of abduction, of fraud, of deception, of the abuse of power or of a position of vulnerability or of the giving or receiving of payments or benefits to achieve the consent of a person having control over another person, for the purpose of exploitation. Exploitation shall include, at a minimum, the exploitation of the prostitution of others or other forms of sexual exploitation, forced labour or services, slavery or practices similar to slavery, servitude or the removal of organs. . . .

70. For one use of the Palermo definition that elides these elements, see ECOSOC, "Recommended Principles and Guidelines on Human Rights and Human Trafficking," U.N. Doc. E/2002/68/Add. 1, at 7 n.6 (May 20, 2002).

71. South Africa's trafficking law defines "abuse of vulnerability" as "any abuse that leads a person to believe that he or she has no reasonable alternative but to submit to exploitation, and includes, but is not limited to,

taking advantage of the vulnerabilities of that person resulting from—(a) the person having entered or remained in the Republic illegally or without proper documentation; (b) pregnancy; (c) any disability of the person; (d) addiction to the use of any dependence-producing substance; (e) being a child; (f) social circumstances; or (g) economic circumstances[,]" unless context indicates otherwise. Prevention and Combating of Trafficking in Persons Act, 2013, Act 7-2013 (No. 36715) (S. Afr.).

72. Asserting in the Preamble that "prostitution and the accompanying evil of the traffic in persons for the purpose of prostitution are incompatible with the dignity and worth of the human person and endanger the welfare of the individual, the family and the community," adherents to the 1949 Trafficking Convention "agree to punish any person who, to gratify the passions of another: (1) Procures, entices or leads away, for purposes of prostitution, another person, even with the consent of that person; (2) Exploits the prostitution of another person, even with the consent of that person." Convention for the Suppression of the Traffic in Persons and of the Exploitation of the Prostitution of Others art. 1, Dec. 2, 1949, G.A. Res. 317 (IV), U.N. Doc. A/1251, at 33.

73. See, e.g., Protocol to Prevent, Suppress and Punish Trafficking in Persons, Especially Women and Children, Supplementing the United Nations Convention Against Transnational Organized Crime art. 3(a) Nov. 2, 2000, G.A. Res. 25 (II), at 54, U.N. Doc. A/55/383 (incorporating "slavery or practices similar to slavery" into its definition of trafficking).

74. When the Swedish Parliament voted to criminalize purchase of sexual services in 1998, it described the connection between gender-based violence and prostitution as:

> [I]ssues that in major parts pertain to relationships between men and women, relationships that have significance for sex equality, in the particular case as well as in the community at large. In this way the issues can be said to be related with each other. Men's violence against women is not consonant with the aspirations toward a gender equal society, and has to be fought against with all means. In such a society it is also unworthy and unacceptable that men obtain casual sex with women against remuneration.

Proposition [Prop.] 1997/98:55 Kvinnofrid [approx: Women's Sanctuary/Women's Peace] [government bill], 22 (Swed.).

75. The law is now found in the Criminal Code. See Brottsbalken [BrB] [Criminal Code] 6:11 (Swed.) ("[a] person who, otherwise than as previously provided in this Chapter [on Sexual Crimes], obtains a casual sexual

relation in return for payment, shall be sentenced for purchase of sexual service to a fine or imprisonment for at most six months. [This law] also applies if the payment was promised or given by another person . . . ." (passed in 2005, amending Lag om förbud mot köp av sexuella tjänster (Svensk författnigssamling [SFS] 1998:408), which took effect January 1999)).

76. On July 10, 2008, the Swedish government adopted a five-prong "National Action Plan" to combat prostitution and sex trafficking by providing "greater protection and support for people at risk, more emphasis on preventive work, higher standards and greater efficiency in the justice system, increased national and international cooperation, and a higher level of knowledge and awareness." Ministry of Integration & Gender Equality (Swed.), *Information Sheet: Action Plan Against Prostitution and Human Trafficking for Sexual Purposes* (2008), available at http://www .ungift.org/doc/knowledgehub/resource-centre/Governments/Sweden _Infosheet_National_Action_Plan_Against_Human_Trafficking_en.pdf.

77. See National Assembly (Fr.), Texte Adopté 716 Proposition de loi visant à renforcer la lutte contre le système prostitutionnel et à accompagner les personnes prostituées, Apr. 6, 2016, available at http://www2.assemblee -nationale.fr/documents/notice/14/ta/ta0716/%28index%29/ta; Alissa J. Rubin, "To Discourage Prostitution, France Passes Bill That Penalizes Clients," *New York Times*, Apr. 6, 2016, available at http://www.nytimes .com/2016/04/07/world/europe/to-discourage-prostitution-france-passes -bill-that-penalizes-clients.html?_r=0 ("Prostitutes who wish to leave the sex business will be eligible for funding to pay for training in other fields . . . . The law would also help foreign prostitutes acquire temporary residence permits and find other work, since 80 percent to 90 percent of France's prostitutes come from outside the country and are victims of human trafficking").

78. The Swedish government, in adopting its law, recognized, inter alia, that "[I]t is not reasonable also to criminalize the one who, at least in most cases, is the weaker party whom is exploited by others who want to satisfy their own sexual drive. It is also important in order to encourage the prostituted persons to seek assistance to get away from prostitution, that they do not feel they risk any form of sanction because they have been active as prostituted persons." Cf. Betänkande [Bet.] 1997/98:JuU13 Kvinnofrid [Committee on Justice parliamentary report] (Swed.) (dismissing minority motions proposing criminalizing both parties), available at http://www .riksdagen.se/webbnav/index.aspx?nid=3322&dok_id=GL01JuU13.

79. Although the National Criminal Police did not, in this instance, include an estimate of the number of girls and women trafficked in Sweden, "[f]rom telephone interception it appears that the stream of sex buyers is not often as large as desired by the pimps. A probable explanation is that the law relating to purchase of sexual services works like a barrier to the establishment of trafficking in human beings in Sweden." National Criminal Police (Swed.), *Trafficking in Human Beings for Sexual Purposes: Situation Report No. 8, January 1—December 31, 2005* 19 (2006). This conclusion was strengthened subsequently: "It is clear that the prohibition against buying sexual services, known as the sex purchase law, is still functioning as a barrier that is preventing human traffickers and pimps from becoming established in Sweden." Id. at 9.

80. The Swedish Ministry of Justice's 2010 Report concludes that the law against sexual purchase is largely working as intended. Ministry of Justice, *Prohibition of the Purchase of Sexual Services. An Evaluation* 1999–2008 (SOU 2010:49) at 120, 123, 128, 130 (Jul. 2, 2010), available at http://www.government.se/articles/2011/03/evaluation-of-the-prohibition-of-the-purchase-of-sexual-services.

81. Sweden's achievement, if incomplete, is no less impressive, given prostitution's notorious imperviousness to law. In the long history of failed efforts, Britain's Contagious Diseases Acts rank high. See, e.g., Philippa Levine, *Prostitution, Race and Politics: Policing Venereal Disease in the British Empire* (New York: Routledge 2003).

82. See Bindel and Kelly, *Responses to Prostitution* 15 (2003). In fact, all facets of the commercial sex industry have exploded as a result of the reforms implemented in Victoria. See generally Sullivan, *Making Sex Work*.

83. See, e.g., Mary Lucille Sullivan and Sheila Jeffreys, "Legalization: The Australian Experience," 8 *Violence Against Women* 1140 (2002); Mary Sullivan, *What Happens When Prostitution Becomes Work: An Update on Legalisation of Prostitution in Australia* (2005), available at https://www.feministes-radicales.org/wp-content/uploads/2012/03/Mary-Sullivan-CATW-What-Happens-When-Prostitution-Becomes-Work...-An-Update-on-Legalisation-of-Prostitution-in-Australia.pdf.

84. See Catherine Campbell, "Selling Sex in the Time of AIDS: The Psychosocial Context of Condom Use by Sex Workers on a Southern African Mine," 50 *Social Science & Medicine* 479, 487 (2000) (describing detailed life histories of twenty-one prostituted women near Johannesburg where customers "almost always" rebuffed requests to wear a condom and "would take [their] business elsewhere" if pressured). In Victoria, Australia, for

example, "illegal brothel prostitution, in particular, has burgeoned to meet buyers' demands for 'cheaper' or 'unrestricted' sexual services." Sullivan, *Making Sex Work* 202.

85. See, e.g., Donna M. Hughes, *The Demand for Victims of Sex Trafficking* 58 (2005), available at http://www.nordicbaltic-assistwomen.net/IMG/pdf /demand_for_victims_D_Hughes.pdf (reporting that in Munich, Germany, where legalization has heightened competition among brothels, brothel owners are "forcing women to engage in riskier sex acts and sex without condoms in order to attract men. Code terms and euphemisms for sex without condoms appear in advertisements").

86. Barbara Hobson found "some of the worst features of legalized prostitution in the Nevada system." Barbara Hobson, *Uneasy Virtue: The Politics of Prostitution and the American Reform Tradition* 227 (Chicago: University of Chicago Press 1990). Conditions documented there make clear that the interests of nonprostituted people, whether johns, brothel owners, or community residents, are routinely privileged over those of the women being used in the commercial sex industry. See, e.g., Farley, *Trafficking in Nevada* 9–10, 13, 16–20, 21, 23–24, 29–30, 31–32, 35–36, 40–41, 45, 46–47, 202; id. at 227–228.

87. *Report by the German Federal Government on the Impact of the Act Regulating the Legal Situation of Prostitutes* 79 (2007), available at Publikationsverstand der Bundesregierung, www.bmfsfj.de.

88. New Zealand's own assessment underscores its failure to significantly improve the lives of prostituted people. See *Report of the Prostitution Law Review Committee on the Operation of the Prostitution Reform Act 2003* (2008), available at http://www.justice.govt.nz/policy/commercial-property -and-regulatory/prostitution/prostitution-law-review-committee/ publications/plrc-report/report-of-the-prostitution-law-review-committee-on -the-operation-of-the-prostitution-reform-act-2003.

89. The information on which this analysis is based comes from discussions with hundreds of prostituted women over four decades.

90. This is by no means to substitute dignity for equality, see, e.g., M. v. H., [1999] 2 S.C.R. 3 (Can.), but compare R. v. Kapp, [2008] 2 S.C.R. 483 (Can.), but to point to dignitary loss as one part of inequality, especially in the context of prostitution. Although in prostitution, the material loss is grittily concrete, its gendered dimensions visible, supporting relief for prostituted women, dignity's avatars seldom see the dignitary loss in prostitution, or if they do, blame prostitutes. Thus Justices O'Regan and Sachs in

Jordan say that women in prostitution choose their loss of dignity. See State v. Jordan 2002 (6) SA 642 (CC) at ¶ 74 (S. Afr.).

91. Johns interviewed in Scotland said that what would most deter them from using a prostituted woman is, in order, being placed on a sex offender registry, having their patronage publicized, and serving jail time. Macleod et al., *Prostitution in Scotland* 26–27 (2008); Farley et al., "Men Who Buy Sex in Scotland" 369.

92. See, e.g., Gould and Fick, *Report to the SALRC* 12 ("The sex workers were unanimous in the view that it is not a job that they like doing or would choose to do should their range of options have been wider."); Evelina Giobbe, "Confronting the Liberal Lies About Prostitution," in *The Sexual Liberals and the Attack on Feminism* 79–80, Dorchen Leidholdt and Janis Raymond, eds. (New York: Pergamon Press 1990) (quoting a prostituted woman, "I don't think I came into this world with the desire to be a prostitute. I think that that was something that was put on me by the dynamics of society.").

16. REALITY, NOT FANTASY

1. Catharine A. MacKinnon, "Reality, Not Fantasy," *Village Voice*, Mar. 26, 1985, at 24–25 (1985). All citations here are added.

2. The ordinances can be found in the Appendix to Catharine A. MacKinnon and Andrea Dworkin, eds., *In Harm's Way: The Pornography Civil Rights Hearings* (Cambridge, MA: Harvard University Press 1998).

3. Our definition of pornography can be found in the context of the proposed ordinance of which it was a part in id. at 426–461.

4. This reference is to the following articles: Nat Hentoff, "Forbidden Fantasies: Is the First Amendment Dangerous to Women," *Village Voice*, Oct. 18, 1984, at 14; Nat Hentoff, "Censorship Unlimited," *Village Voice*, Oct. 21, 1984, at 8; Nat Hentoff, "Equal-Opportunity Banning," *Village Voice*, Oct. 30, 1984, at 8; Nat Hentoff, "The Lost and the Saved," *Village Voice*, Nov. 6, 1984, at 8.

5. See Richard Goldstein, "Forbidden Fantasies: Pornography and Its Discontents," *Village Voice*, Oct. 18, 1984, at 18.

6. Diana E. H. Russell calculated this figure at my request from her probability sample data base of 930 San Francisco households surveyed in 1977 as discussed in her *The Secret Trauma: Incest in the Lives of Girls and Women* 20–37 (New York: Basic Books 1986) and *Rape in Marriage* 27–41 (New York: Macmillan 1982). The number includes all forms of

abuse, contact as well as noncontact, from gang rape to obscene phone calls, unwanted sexual advances on the street, unwelcome requests to engage in sex for pornography, and subjection to peeping toms and sexual exhibitionists.

17. TO THE AMERICAN CIVIL LIBERTIES UNION
ON PORNOGRAPHY

1. As observed by journalist Michael McManus of the Gray & Co. campaign, "What is frightening to me as a journalist is that the public relations campaign outlined in the letter is working." Michael McManus, "Introduction," *Final Report of the Attorney General's Commission on Pornography* xlvi (Nashville, TN: Rutledge Hill Press 1986).

2. Susan B. Trento, *The Power House* 192 (New York: St. Martin's Press 1992).

3. Letter from Steve Johnson, Senior Vice President, Gray & Co., to John M. Harrington, Executive Vice President of the Council for Periodical Distributors Association, 1–2, June 4, 1986.

4. Id. at 4.

5. At this event, I was met with refusal when I asked how many. David Hamlin, Executive Director of the ACLU/Illinois from 1974 to 1978, once said the group lost 30 percent in Illinois and 10 percent nationally as a result of its position on the Skokie case. David Hamlin, "The ACLU's Stand in Skokie," *Los Angeles Times*, Oct. 12, 1988. The whispered rumor was at least one in four.

6. Collin v. Smith, 578 F.2d 1197 (7th Cir.), *cert. denied* 437 U.S. 916 (1978).

7. This talk was given at the ACLU 1985 Biennial Conference in Boulder, Colorado, June 13–16.

8. Andrea Dworkin wrote:
These are the dreaded images of terror.

—A Jew, emaciated, behind barbed wire, nearly naked, mutilated by the knife of a Nazi doctor: the atrocity is acknowledged.

—A Vietnamese, in a tiger cage, nearly naked, bones twisted and broken, flesh black and blue: the atrocity is acknowledged.

—A black slave on an Amerikan plantation, nearly naked, chained, flesh ripped up from the whip: the atrocity is acknowledged.

—A woman, nearly naked, in a cell, chained, ripped up from the whip, breasts mutilated by a knife:

she is entertainment, the boy-next-door's favorite fantasy, every man's precious right, every woman's potential fate.

The woman tortured is sexual entertainment.

The woman tortured is sexually arousing.

The anguish of the woman tortured is sexually exciting.

The degradation of the woman tortured is sexually entrancing.

The humiliation of the woman tortured is sexually pleasing, sexually thrilling, sexually gratifying.

Andrea Dworkin, "Pornography: The New Terrorism," in *Letters from a War Zone: Writings 1976–1987* 199–200 (London: Secker & Warburg 1988).

9. See, e.g., Nan D. Hunter and Sylvia A. Law, "Brief Amici Curiae of Feminist Anti-Censorship Task Force et al., in *American Booksellers Association v. Hudnut*," 21 *University of Michigan Journal of Law Reform* 69 (1987–1988); Catharine A. MacKinnon, *Sex Equality* 1783 (3d ed., New York: Foundation Press 2016) (*"Sex Equality"*).

10. This was an estimated figure at the time. *See, e.g.*, Melinda Tankard Reist and Abigail Bray, eds., "The Global Pornography Industry is Expected to Reach US$100 Billion in the Near Future," in *Big Porn Inc: Exposing the Harms of the Global Pornography Industry* xiv (North Melbourne, Australia: Spinifex Press 2011) (*"Big Porn"*) ("When the profits of the industry were being more closely and confidently tracked, the United States saw revenues of the pornography industry grow from a conservatively estimated $4 billion a year in 1978 (although some sources put 'hard core' bookstores at $3 to $4 billion a year in 1981) to a low estimate of $15 to $20 billion a year in 1998, with adult Web sites contributing an estimated $1 to $2 billion."). It is now estimated to be $10 billion, though some calculate the actual number to be from $15 to $20 billion. Frederick S. Lane III, *Obscene Profits: The Entrepreneurs of Pornography in the Cyber Age* xiv (New York: Routledge 2000) (*"Obscene Profits"*) (referring to pornography as "an industry that over the last quarter-century has grown from approximately $2 billion in total annual revenues to at least $10 billion (although some estimate that the actual total today is somewhere between $15 billion and $20 billion . . . . Of that industry total, adult Web sites contribute an estimated $1 billion to $2 billion per year)"); Frank Rich, "Naked Capitalists," *New York Times Magazine*, May 20, 2001 (estimating that Americans spend $10 to $14 billion annually on pornography). It is difficult to determine

just how much money the industry makes. MacKinnon, *Sex Equality* 1688.

11. For a full articulation of this position, see Nadine Strossen, *Defending Pornography: Free Speech, Sex, and the Fight for Women's Rights* (New York: New York University Press 1995). Nadine Strossen was President of the ACLU from 1991 to 2008.

12. Ana J. Bridges et al., "Aggression and Sexual Behavior in Best-Selling Pornography Videos: A Content Analysis Update," 16 *Violence Against Women* 1075 (2010); Robert Jensen, "Pornography Is What the End of the World Looks Like," in *Everyday Pornography* 105, Karen Boyle, ed. (New York: Routledge 2010); Meagan Tyler, "'Now, That's Pornography!': Violence and Domination in Adult Video News," in *Everyday Pornography* 50; Ana J. Bridges, "Methodological Considerations in Mapping Pornography Content," in *Everyday Pornography* 34 (finding the majority of popular pornography videos include verbal and physical abuse of women); MacKinnon, *Sex Equality* 1690–1691.

13. See, e.g., Melissa Farley, "Legal Brothel Prostitution in Nevada," in *Prostitution and Trafficking in Nevada: Making the Connections* 37 (San Francisco: Prostitution Research & Education 2007) (documenting the trauma suffered by women in pornography).

14. Aric Press et al., "The War Against Pornography," *Newsweek*, Mar. 18, 1985, at 58 ("If, as Minneapolis councilwoman Charlee Hoyt puts it, porn isn't just 'a dirty book under Daddy's mattress' anymore, then what is it? In addition to the gynecological photographs known as 'beaver shots,' the standard categories include films and magazines devoted to: group sex, oral sex, anal sex, gay and lesbian sex, sex with pregnant women, sex with crippled women, bestiality, child porn and sadomasochism.").

15. This is information that has been shared with me and Andrea Dworkin by women used in pornography.

16. See, e.g., United States v. DePew, 751 F. Supp. 1195, 1196–1197 (E.D. Va. 1990), *aff'd*, 932 F.2d 324 (4th Cir. 1991) ("Defendant [DePew] maintains that his statements and actions were merely part of a sexual fantasy and that he never intended to realize his plan or to commit any crime" despite the fact that "the undercover agents learned that defendant was interested in producing a video depicting the sexual exploitation and murder of a minor. Defendant explained to Lambey and the undercover agents that he would be willing to 'tie the kid up, suffocate him, and beat him on

film' and that he 'had no problem with snuffing [killing]' him. Defendant also expressed his desire to tie a plastic bag over the child's head, hang him, have sex with him, and watch him struggle. Defendant offered suggestions about how to dispose of the victim at the completion of the film, including dousing the body with muriatic acid to disfigure it and dumping it in a remote area of the woods. In connection with the child's abduction, defendant researched how to manufacture ether for use in subduing the child. During the planning of this crime, defendant described previous incidents in which he had attempted to molest and kill a sixteen or seventeen year old American boy in Greece and a boy from D.C. who 'looked about fifteen.'"); see also Catharine A. MacKinnon, *Only Words* 35 (Cambridge, MA: Harvard University Press 1994) ("Consider snuff pornography, in which women or children are killed to make a sex film. This is a film of a sexual murder in the process of being committed. Doing the murder is sex for those who do it. The climax is the moment of death. The intended consumer has a sexual experience watching it. Those who kill as and for sex are having sex through the murder; those who watch the film are having sex through watching the murder. A snuff film is not a discussion of the idea of sexual murder any more than the acts being filmed are. The film is not 'about' sexual murder; it sexualizes murder.").

17. See, e.g., Catharine A. MacKinnon and Andrea Dworkin, eds., "Minneapolis: Press Conference: Statement of Ms. P.," in *In Harm's Way: The Pornography Civil Rights Hearings* 265–266 (Cambridge, MA: Harvard University Press 1998) ("*In Harm's Way*") ("I saw a different side of my father, he called it his play-time. I don't know why I posed nude with my sister, but by age eight I was forced into my first pornographic movie . . . . His temper and cumulative violence convinced me that something was wrong. I'd never been told that little girls didn't star in pornographic movies and weren't supposed to be raped by their father. His pressure to be secretive alerted me, but his violence kept me quiet.").

18. See, e.g., id. at 264 ("Starting at age 4, old Mr. Edwards up the street used pornography to entice me into taking baths so he could watch, had me wearing his wife[']s clothes and eventually having oral sex and being penetrated by him. This went on for five years. He used the pornography to show me how to be—and what to do—until I didn't see anything wrong—with anything he did to me—or had me do to him . . . . The man I lived with last used pornography books to sexually arouse my son so he could molest him—and my son and his friends used pornography to molest my

daughter—to experiment on her sexually—using the pornographic books as teaching guides.").

19. See, e.g., id. at 61 (telling her story at the Minneapolis hearings, Linda Marchiano said, "He began a complete turnaround and beat me physically and began the mental abuse. From that day forward, my hell began. I literally became a prisoner . . . . In my book *Ordeal*, an autobiography, I go into greater detail of the monstrosity I was put through, from prostitution to porno films to celebrity satisfier. The things that he used to get me involved in pornography went from a .45 automatic 8 shot and M-16 semi-automatic machine gun to threats on the lives of my family. I have seen the kind of people involved in pornography and how they will use anyone to get what they want.").

20. Catharine A. MacKinnon, "Pornography, Civil Rights, and Speech," 20 *Harvard Civil Rights-Civil Liberties Law Review* 1 (1985); Andrea Dworkin, "Pornography Is a Civil Rights Issue for Women," 21 *University of Michigan Journal of Law Reform* 55 (1987–1988).

21. Code of Indianapolis and Marion County, Ind., Sec. 16-3(q) (1984) ("Pornography shall mean the graphic sexually explicit subordination of women, whether in pictures or in words, that also includes one or more of the following: (1) Women are presented as sexual objects who enjoy pain or humiliation; or (2) Women are presented as sexual objects who experience sexual pleasure in being raped; or (3) Women are presented as sexual objects tied up or cut up or mutilated or bruised or physically hurt, or as dismembered or truncated or fragmented or severed into body parts; or (4) Women are presented being penetrated by objects or animals; or (5) Women are presented in scenarios of degradation, injury, abasement, torture, shown as filthy or inferior, bleeding, bruised, or hurt in a context that makes these conditions sexual; [or] (6) Women are presented as sexual objects for domination, conquest, violation, exploitation, possession, or use, or through postures or positions of servility or submission or display").

22. Id. ("The use of men, children or transsexuals in the place of women shall also be deemed to be pornography for purposes of this definition.")

23. Miller v. California, 413 U.S. 15, 24–25 (1973) ("[T]he basic guidelines for the trier of fact must be: (a) whether 'the average person, applying contemporary community standards' would find that the work, taken as a whole, appeals to the prurient interest, . . . (b) whether the work depicts or describes, in a patently offensive way, sexual conduct specifically defined by the applicable state law; and (c) whether the work, taken as a

whole, lacks serious literary, artistic, political, or scientific value. We do not adopt as a constitutional standard the 'utterly without redeeming social value' test of *Memoirs v. Massachusetts*, 383 U.S., at 419").

24. Code of Indianapolis and Marion County, Ind., Sec. 16-3 (1984).

25. Id. sec. 16-3(5) ("Coercion into pornographic performance: Coercing, intimidating or fraudulently inducing any person, including a man, child or transsexual, into performing for pornography, which injury may date from any appearance or sale of any products of such performance").

26. Id. sec. 16-3(6) ("Forcing pornography on a person: pornography on any woman, man, child or transsexual in any place of employment, in education, in a home, or in a public place").

27. Id. sec. 16-3 (1984) ("Assault or physical attack due to pornography: The assault, physical attack, or injury of any woman, man, child, or transsexual in a way that is directly caused by specific pornography").

28. Id. sec. 16-3(4) ("Trafficking in pornography: The production, sale, exhibition, or distribution of pornography, a. City, state, and federally funded public libraries or private and public university and college libraries in which pornography is available for study, including on open shelves, shall not be construed to be trafficking in pornography, but special display presentations of pornography in said places is sex discrimination. b. The formation of private clubs or associations for purposes of trafficking in pornography is illegal and shall be considered a conspiracy to violate the civil rights of women").

29. See, e.g., Brief of American Civil Liberties Union as Amici Curiae in *Hudnut* (in support of Appellee) in American Booksellers Ass'n, Inc. v. Hudnut, 771 F.2d 323 (7th Cir. 1985) (No. 84-3147); Village Books et al. v. City of Bellingham, No. 88-1470 (W.D. Wash. Feb. 9, 1989). The ACLU's current views on pornography appear to be unchanged. According to the "Obscenity Laws" page of the ACLU website, "[a] free and democratic society should guarantee every individual the right to decide what art or entertainment they read, watch, or listen to. That also means that every individual has the right to decide what not to read or watch: to turn off the TV, leave a website, or decline to visit a particular art exhibit." "Obscenity Laws," *ACLU*, accessed July 10, 2016, https://www.aclu.org/issues/free-speech/artistic-expression/obscenity-laws.

30. See, e.g., Edward Donnerstein, "Pornography: Its Effect on Violence Against Women," in *Pornography and Sexual Aggression* 53, Neil M. Malamuth and Edward Donnerstein, eds. (Orlando, FL: Academic Press 1984); Mike Allen et al., "A Meta-Analysis Summarizing the Effects of

Pornography II: Aggression After Exposure," 22 *Human Communication Research* 258 (1995); James Weaver, "The Social Science and Psychological Research Evidence: Perceptual and Behavioural Consequences of Exposure to Pornography," in *Pornography: Women, Violence and Civil Liberties* 284, Catherine Itzin, ed. (Oxford: Oxford University Press 1992) (summarizing studies). See also MacKinnon, *Sex Equality* 1731–1736.

31. Id. at 861 n.1.

32. David Finkelhor, *Sexually Victimized Children* (New York: The Free Press 1979) ("This study should leave no doubt that a large number of children are sexually victimized. Nearly one in five girls and one in eleven boys say they have had a sexual experience as a child with a much older person. The experiences cut across social class and ethnic lines and involve children of all ages. Boys as well as girls are frequent victims.").

33. Miller v. California, 413 U.S. 15, 24–25 (1973).

34. See, e.g., Mary Beth Norton et al., "The Afro-American Family in the Age of Revolution," in *Slavery and Freedom in the Age of the American Revolution* 175–187, Ira Berlin and Ronald Hoffman, eds. (Champaign, IL: University of Illinois Press 1983) (discussing Jefferson's slave holdings and economic dependence on them); MacKinnon, *Sex Equality* 13.

35. Compare "Naked Capitalism," *Economist*, Sept. 26, 2015, http://www.economist.com/news/international/21666114-internet-blew-porn-industrys-business-model-apart-its-response-holds-lessons ("The web boasts an estimated 700m-800m individual porn pages, three-fifths in America. PornHub, Mindgeek's biggest tube, claims to have had nearly 80 billion video viewings last year, and more than 18 billion visits (see chart). In terms of traffic and bandwidth, Mindgeek is now one of the world's biggest online operators in any industry. The company says its sites serve more than 100m visitors a day, consuming 1.5 terabits of data per second—enough to download 150 feature films."); with "Time Media Kit: Print Audience," *Time*, accessed July 21, 2016, http://www.timemediakit.com/audience/ (reporting that *Time*'s total U.S. audience includes 16,414,000 people); "IBT Media: An Innovative Digital Media Company." *IBT Media*, accessed July 21, 2016. http://corp.ibt.com/brands-newsweek (reporting that *Newsweek* has over 100,000 subscribers and over three million social media followers). For more on pornography consumption by men, see Jason S. Carroll, Laura M. Padilla-Walker, Larry J. Nelson, Chad D. Olson, Carolyn McNamara Barry, & Stephanie D. Madsen, "Generation XXX: Pornography Acceptance and Use Among Emerging Adults," 23 *Journal of Adolescent Research* 18 tbl.1 (2008)

(finding 21.3 percent of 313 male university students aged eighteen to twenty-six reported using pornography "everyday or almost every" or "3 to 5 days a week"); Max Waltman, "The Politics of Legal Challenges to Pornography: Canada, Sweden, and the United States," *Stockholm Studies in Politics* 34 (Stockholm: Stockholm University 2014) (Ph.D. Dissertation).

36. This was an estimated figure at the time. See, e.g., Melinda Tankard Reist and Abigail Bray, eds., *Big Porn* xiv (North Melbourne, Vic.: Spinifex Press, 2011) (noting the growth of the pornography industry: from $4 billion per year in 1978 to $15 to $20 billion a year in 1998); Martha Langelan, "The Political Economy of Pornography," *Aegis: Magazine on Ending Violence Against Women*, Autumn 1981, at 5 ("[t]he actual U.S. sales volume [of pornography] may be as much as $10 to $15 billion in 1981 . . . . Hard-core bookstores alone account for at least $3 to $4 billion a year. Adding in movies, mainstream newsstand sales, mail order revenues, and paraphernalia sales, D.C. Feminists Against Pornography conservatively estimates the industry's total revenues at $7 billion in 1980"). It is now estimated to be $10 billion, though some calculate the actual number to be from $15 to $20 billion. Lane, *Obscene Profits* xiv (referring to pornography as "an industry that over the last quarter-century has grown from approximately $2 billion in total annual revenues to at least $10 billion (although some estimate that the actual total today is somewhere between $15 billion and $20 billion . . . . Of that industry total, adult Web sites contribute an estimated $1 billion to $2 billion per year)"). It is difficult to determine just how much money the industry makes. See also MacKinnon, *Sex Equality* 1688.

37. Alan Cowell, "Fight Apartheid, Tutu Tells Investors," *New York Times*, Jan. 3, 1985, http://www.nytimes.com/1985/01/03/world/fight-apartheid-tutu-tells-investors.html (quoting Bishop Tutu).

38. Id. The anti-Semitism of the character of Shylock, the stereotyped Jewish merchant in Shakespeare's *Merchant of Venice*, Act III, Scene I, cannot pass unremarked.

18. X-UNDERRATED

1. This analysis was first published in *Times Higher Education Supplement* (London, May 20, 2005). Citations are added.

2. "Naked capitalism," *Economist*, Sept. 26, 2015. http://www.economist.com/news/international/21666114-internet-blew-porn-industrys-business-model-apart-its-response-holds-lessons ("In America the number of porn

studios is now down from over 200 to 20, says Alec Helmy, the founder of XBiz, a trade publication. Performers who used to make $1,500 an hour now get $500—even as increased competition means they are asked to produce more extreme content. Revenues are well below their peak; how far below is hard to say, as most porn producers are private. Just before the tubes took off, plausible estimates put worldwide industry revenues at $40 billion-50 billion. Mr. Thylmann thinks they have fallen by at least three-quarters since then."); see also Frederick S. Lane III, *Obscene Profits: The Entrepreneurs of Pornography in the CyberAge* (New York: Routledge 2000).

3. The derivation of the term "obscenity" is disputed and appears not definitively established. The Oxford English Dictionary says its origins partly borrow from French and Latin, then notes: "Classical Latin obscēnus, obscaenus has been variously associated, by scholars ancient and modern, with scaevus left-sided, inauspicious . . . and with caenum mud, filth . . . . The derivation from scaena SCENE n., one of several suggested by the Latin grammarian Varro, probably represents a folk etymology." *OED Third Edition*, March 2004 updated. A thicker discussion is provided by Carolyn McKay, who begins by quoting from the fiction writer J. M. Coetzee stating in his *Elizabeth Costello*:

> Obscene. That is the word, a word of contested etymology, that she must hold on to as a talisman. She chooses to believe that obscene means off-stage. To save our humanity, certain things that we may want to see (may want to see because we are human!) must remain off-stage (Coetzee 2003: 168).

The etymology of the English word obscene is obscure, with most dictionaries referring to the French obscène and Latin obscaenus meaning from or with filth, ill-omened or abominable. The legal definitions follow this line, referencing that which may deprave or corrupt or which is offensive to decency (Osborn 2001). Like Coetzee's *Elizabeth Costello*, others suggest obscene derives from the Latin obscaena or Greek ob skene meaning off-stage, not to be seen on-stage, "scenes that do not belong in the light of day," and it is this derivation that I adopt as appropriate to my exploration of the absent crime scene in a murder trial (Coetzee 2003: 159). Carolyn McKay, Murder Ob/Scene: Seen, Unseen and Ob/scene in Murder Trials, 14 *Law Text Culture* 79–80 (2010).

Since Coetzee may have appropriated antipornography women activists as a partial model for his denigrating imagined portrayal, one statement by Andrea Dworkin on the derivation of obscene may be of interest:

> This is not a book about obscenity. For something to be obscene, a judgement must be made that it is not fit to be shown or displayed. One possible (though not generally accepted) root meaning of the word obscene is the ancient Greek for "off stage"—in effect that which should not be shown, probably for aesthetic reasons. Another possible, more likely root meaning of the word obscene is the Latin for "against filth." This suggests our own contemporary legal usage: is a given work filth and are we, the people, against it? If so, it is obscene. Obscenity is not a synonym for pornography. Obscenity is an idea; it requires a judgement of value. Pornography is concrete, "the graphic depiction of whores."

Andrea Dworkin, *Pornography: Men Possessing Women*, Preface (New York: G. P. Putnam's Sons, 1981). She, at least, is hardly holding onto it at all, far less like/as a talisman. I am unaware of anyone who works on the civil rights approach who does.

4. United States v. Roth, 237 F.2d 796, 812 (1957) (appendix to concurrence of Frank, J.) ("Echoing Macaulay, 'Jimmy' Walker remarked that he had never heard of a woman seduced by a book."); Paul S. Boyer, *Purity in Print: Book Censorship in America from the Gilded Age to the Computer Age* (2002) ("Opponents of the bill were led in the floor debate by Jimmy Walker, then the Democratic majority leader, who immortalized himself on this occasion by observing that 'No woman was ever ruined by a book.'").

5. Virginia Greendlinger and Donn Byrne, "Coercive Sexual Fantasies of College Men as Predictors of Self-Reported Likelihood to Rape and Overt Sexual Aggression," 23 *Journal of Sex Research* 1, 7 ("Results of our investigation suggest the potential importance of the tendency to engage in coercive fantasies as a predictor of both hypothetical future likelihood to rape and as a postdictor of past coercive sexuality. Just as in the studies of convicted sex offenders, those college men who indicated that fantasies of dominance, force, and rape are an important part of their erotic repertoire are those who were more likely to characterize themselves as potential rapists and as past users of coercion in sexual interactions.").

6. See, e.g., United States v. DePew, 751 F. Supp. 1195, 1196–1197 (E.D. Va. 1990), *aff'd*, 932 F.2d 324 (4th Cir. 1991) ("Defendant [DePew] maintains that his statements and actions were merely part of a sexual fantasy and that he never intended to realize his plan or to commit any crime" despite the fact that "the undercover agents learned that defendant was

interested in producing a video depicting the sexual exploitation and murder of a minor. Defendant explained to Lambey and the undercover agents that he would be willing to 'tie the kid up, suffocate him, and beat him on film' and that he 'had no problem with snuffing [killing]' him. Defendant also expressed his desire to tie a plastic bag over the child's head, hang him, have sex with him, and watch him struggle. Defendant offered suggestions about how to dispose of the victim at the completion of the film, including dousing the body with muriatic acid to disfigure it and dumping it in a remote area of the woods. In connection with the child's abduction, defendant researched how to manufacture ether for use in subduing the child. During the planning of this crime, defendant described previous incidents in which he had attempted to molest and kill a sixteen or seventeen year old American boy in Greece and a boy from D.C. who 'looked about fifteen.' "); "Ex-Banker Guilty in Sex-Bondage Death: Huntington Beach Woman, 19, Died in Bathtub Fantasy," *Los Angeles Times*, Apr. 29, 1986, http://articles.latimes.com/1986-04-29/local/me -2333_1_huntington-beach ("A former bank executive, accused of killing a 19-year-old prostitute from Huntington Beach during a sexual bondage fantasy in his bathtub, was found guilty Monday of second-degree murder . . . . According to testimony, Byrd had sexual fantasies of watching a nude woman submerged in a tub of water. Byrd admitted bringing a prostitute to his home last year and playing out his fantasy, but he claimed she died accidentally."); Byrd v. Hernandez, No. 08CV651 JM AJB, 2010 WL 5759150, at *5–6 (S.D. Cal. Aug. 6, 2010), *report and recommendation adopted*, No. 08-CV-651-JM AJB, 2011 WL 446069 (S.D. Cal. Feb. 2, 2011) (citations omitted) ("According to Petitioner [Byrd], he was engaged in bondage sex with the victim tied up in the bathtub when the victim panicked and started yelling and struggling . . . . According to the probation officer's report, there were signs of violence including bruises on her forehead, the backs of her hands, swelling over her left eye, right eye, inside her upper lip, a large area of bruising on top of her head and behind her left ear, and markings on her ankles and wrists as if something were constricting them. There was also evidence of forcible compression on the victim's neck so it was not clear whether the death was caused by strangulation or drowning . . . . At trial, it was revealed that Petitioner had homicidal hateful fantasies involving women that he discussed over several months with various prostitutes that he retained. The most graphic fantasy that he shared with a prostitute was one of watching a woman drown and seeing the fear in her eyes as the water rose up over her face.").

7. Bret Easton Ellis, *American Psycho* (New York: Vintage Books 1991).

8. Id.

9. Elizabeth Venant, "An 'American Psycho' Drama: Books: The flap surrounding Bret Easton Ellis' third novel flares again. NOW is seeking a boycott of his new publisher. Other observers raise questions of censorship," *Los Angeles Times*, Dec. 11, 1990, http://articles.latimes.com/1990-12-11/news/vw-6308_1_american-psycho ("The original publisher, Simon & Schuster, abruptly canceled the book in mid-November, just a month before its scheduled release, and Ellis kept his $300,000 advance."); Roger Cohen, "Bret Easton Ellis Answers Critics of 'American Psycho,'" *New York Times,* Mar. 6, 1991, http://www.nytimes.com/1991/03/06/books/bret-easton-ellis-answers-critics-of-american-psycho.html?pagewanted=all ("Simon & Schuster abruptly canceled the book's publication three months ago and it was resold to Vintage.").

10. Elizabeth Mehren, "Simon & Schuster Pulls the Plug on Novel: Books: Publisher says it will not market 'American Psycho.' Author Bret Ellis calls the novel's gore gruesome, but necessary." *Los Angeles Times*, Nov. 16, 1990, http://articles.latimes.com/1990-11-16/news/vw-4903_1_american-psycho ("Some women at Simon & Schuster who read 'American Psycho' were reportedly troubled by the painstaking descriptions of violence toward women. A paragraph excerpted in *Time* magazine several weeks ago described a woman being skinned alive. That was 'sort of mild compared to the first four pages of the book,' a Simon & Schuster employee said . . . . Barbara Reno, a corporate spokesman for Simon & Schuster, would not comment about when the decision not to publish "American Psycho" was made. Nor would she elaborate on the reasons for the decision. Reno did say, however, that Snyder alone had chosen not to publish the book.").

11. Andrea Dworkin, "Pornography Is a Civil Rights Issue for Women," 21 *University of Michigan Journal of Law Reform* 55, 59 (1987–1988) ("A third group that colludes to legitimize pornography are publishers and the so-called legitimate media. They pretend to believe that under this system of law there is a first amendment that is indivisible and absolute, which it has never been. As you know, the first amendment protects speech that has already been expressed from state interference. That means it protects those who own media. There is no affirmative responsibility to open communications to those who are powerless in the society at large."); see, e.g., American Booksellers Ass'n, Inc. v. Hudnut, 598 F. Supp. 1316 (S.D. Ind. 1984), *aff'd*, 771 F.2d 323 (7th Cir. 1985) (challenging the Indianapolis antipornography ordinance, the list of plaintiffs included trade associations

of publishers, distributors of books, magazines, and television broadcasts, booksellers, and video sale and rental stores.).

12. *Snuff* (August Films, Selected Pictures 1975).

13. Elizabeth Venant, "An 'American Psycho' Drama: Books: The flap surrounding Bret Easton Ellis' third novel flares again. NOW is seeking a boycott of his new publisher. Other observers raise questions of censorship." *Los Angeles Times*, Dec. 11, 1990, http://articles.latimes.com/1990 -12-11/news/vw-6308_1_american-psycho ("The novel was then picked up by Vintage Books, a trade paperback division of Random House, which plans to publish the novel by early spring.").

14. Jamie Tarabay, "Abu Ghraib Closes, Bitter Memories of Torture Remain," *Al Jazeera America*, Apr. 16, 2014, http://america.aljazeera.com/articles /2014/4/15/abu-ghraib-s-infamousend.html ("In 2004, a scandal erupted when enlisted U.S. soldiers were investigated for abusing Iraqi detainees through physical and sexual torture."); Seymour M. Hersh, "The General's Report," *New Yorker*, June 25, 2007, http://www.newyorker.com /magazine/2007/06/25/the-generals-report ("The previous week, revelations about Abu Ghraib, including photographs showing prisoners stripped, abused, and sexually humiliated, had appeared on CBS and in the *New Yorker*.").

15. Susan J. Brison, "The Torture Connection/When Photographs from Abu Ghraib Can't Be Distinguished from 'Good Old American Pornography,' It's Not Just the Torture We Should Be Questioning," *SFGate*, July 25, 2004, http://www.sfgate.com/magazine/article/The-Torture-Connection -When-photographs-from-2738847.php ("What are we to make of this: porn that looks like torture, torture that looks like porn? Some claimed the similarity revealed that what might have appeared to be torture wasn't so bad after all. Rush Limbaugh wondered what the fuss was all about, because the photos from Abu Ghraib 'look like standard good old American pornography.' That in turn led Frank Rich in the *New York Times* to ridicule this likening of 'wartime atrocities' to 'an entertainment industry that, however deplorable to Islam, has more fans in our Christian country than Major League Baseball.' Although Rich's article is steeped in irony, his determination to distinguish the Abu Ghraib photos ('atrocities') from pornography ('entertainment') suggests that pornography must be morally unproblematic—even Christians like it!—except to those morally benighted Muslims.").

16. The photos purporting to show abuse were initially published in Donovan Slack, "Councilor Takes Up Iraq Issue: Turner Releases Purported Images

of Rape by Soldiers," *Boston Globe*, May 12, 2004, http://archive.boston
.com/news/local/massachusetts/articles/2004/05/12/2; Susan J. Brison,
"The Torture Connection/When Photographs from Abu Ghraib Can't
Be Distinguished from 'Good Old American Pornography,' It's Not Just
the Torture We Should Be Questioning," *SFGate*, July 25, 2004, http://www
.sfgate.com/magazine/article/The-Torture-Connection-When-photographs
-from-2738847.php ("In this new 'theater of operations,' things are not
always what they seem. Both the *Boston Globe* and the *Daily Mirror* discovered this fact last spring, to their chagrin. The *Globe*'s publication of
what turned out to be staged pornographic photos of U.S. soldiers raping
Iraqi women led to self-castigation by the editorial board, and the *Daily
Mirror*'s unwitting publication of faked photos of British troops abusing
Iraqi prisoners forced the paper's editor to resign."); Claire Cozens, "US
Paper Says Sorry for 'Fake' Photos," *Guardian*, May 14, 2004, https://www
.theguardian.com/media/2004/may/14/pressandpublishing.iraq ("A US
newspaper has been forced to apologise after admitting that photographs
it published apparently showing US soldiers raping Iraqi women could
be fake. The *Boston Globe* said it had been wrong to publish the photographs, which appeared alongside a story about alleged abuses, because
they 'were overly graphic and the purported abuse portrayed had not been
authenticated'. 'There was a lapse in judgment and procedures, and we
apologise for it,' said the editor, Martin Baron.").

17. This is my assessment of the public response as a whole, which became
    suddenly tepid and unoutraged once the actual genealogy of the photos
    was revealed.

18. Donovan Slack, "Councilor Takes Up Iraq Issue: Turner Releases Pur-
    ported Images of Rape by Soldiers," *Boston Globe*, May 12, 2004, http://
    archive.boston.com/news/local/massachusetts/articles/2004/05/12/2_cite
    _photos_purported_to_show_abuse/ ("EDITOR'S NOTE FOR CAPTION:
    PUBLISHED CORRECTION - DATE: Thursday, May 13, 2004: Editor's
    Note: A photograph on Page B2 yesterday did not meet *Globe* standards
    for publication. The photo portrayed Boston City Councilor Chuck
    Turner and activist Sadiki Kambon displaying graphic photographs that
    they claimed showed US soldiers raping Iraqi women. Although the
    photograph was reduced in size between editions to obscure visibility of
    the images on display, at no time did the photograph meet *Globe* stan-
    dards. Images contained in the photograph were overly graphic, and the
    purported abuse portrayed had not been authenticated. The *Globe* apolo-
    gizes for publishing the photo."); Claire Cozens, "US Paper Says Sorry for

'Fake' Photos," *Guardian*, May 14, 2004, https://www.theguardian.com
/media/2004/may/14/pressandpublishing.iraq.

19. Slavefarm, http://www.slavefarm.com, last visited July 16, 2016; Lydia
Cacho, *Slavery Inc: The Untold Story of International Sex Trafficking*
213–214, Elizabeth Boburg, trans. (Berkeley, CA: Soft Skull Press 2014)
("The new pornography, not the type in *Hustler* magazine or on the
Playboy Channel, that is available free on the Internet or can be bought
for $30 in Shanghai and less than $20 in Tokyo; it mostly belongs to traffickers who have invested in the new 'pop slave culture.' Jean, a young
North American, spent two months in hospital with a head injury resulting from a punch she received while being raped in Tijuana. One year
later her brother found a photograph of her on the pornographic web site
www.deputaspormexico.com (translates as 'whoringinmexico.com'). There
are also websites such as slavefarm.com that are a shocking view of reality.
The slavery pornography is here to stay.").

20. See James Cook, "The X–Rated Economy," *Forbes*, Sept. 18, 1978, at 81
("According to the California Department of Justice, the nation's pornographers do a good $4 billion a year business . . . . That estimate may be
grossly conservative"); Frank Rich, "Naked Capitalists," *New York Times
Magazine*, May 20, 2001 (estimating that Americans spend $10 to $14
billion dollars annually on pornography); Frederick S. Lane III, *Obscene
Profits: The Entrepreneurs of Pornography in the Cyber Age* xiv (New
York: Routledge 2000) (referring to pornography as "an industry that
over the last quarter-century has grown from approximately $2 billion in
total annual revenues to at least $10 billion (although some estimate that
the actual total today is somewhere between $15 billion and $20 billion . . . . Of that industry total, adult Web sites contribute an estimated
$1 billion to $2 billion per year)"); see also Catharine A. MacKinnon, *Sex
Equality* 1688–1689 (3d ed., New York: Foundation Press 2016) (footnotes omitted) (quoting Melinda Tankard Reist and Abigail Bray, "The
Global Pornography Industry Is Expected to Reach US$100 Billion in the
Near Future," in *Big Porn Inc: Exposing the Harms of the Global Pornography Industry* xiv, Melinda Tankard Reist and Abigail Bray, eds.
(North Melbourne, Vic.: Spinifex Press 2011) ("When the profits of the
industry were being more closely and confidently tracked, the United
States saw revenues of the pornography industry grow from a conservatively estimated $4 billion a year in 1978 (although some sources put
'hard core' bookstores at $3 to $4 billion a year in 1981) to a low estimate of $15 to $20 billion a year in 1998, with adult Web sites contrib-

uting an estimated $1 to $2 billion. Pornography is beyond cavil massively lucrative, netting many times that figure each year, exploding exponentially into the twenty-first century. 'The global pornography industry is expected to reach US $100 billion in the near future.' ").

21. Gail Dines, *Pornland: How Porn Has Hijacked Our Sexuality* 51 (Boston: Beacon Press 2010) ("The economic connections between porn and mainstream industries were the focus of a 2007 article by Alex Henderson on Xbiz.com, a business website for the porn industry. Henderson begins by noting that although executives from mainstream companies don't want to talk about their connections to porn, they are indeed 'profiting nicely, consistently and discreetly from adult entertainment.' Some of the examples he gives illustrate the multiple ways that porn has increasingly become interconnected with companies that are household names. In the cable television business, for example, porn is distributed by Time Warner Cable, Cox Communications, and Comcast—the latter being the largest cable TV providers in the United States (Comcast also owns E! Entertainment, a cable station that often carries porn-friendly documentaries, such as one on Jenna Jameson, as well as the show *The Girls Next Door*).").

22. See, e.g., John D. Foubert, Matthew W. Brosi, and R. Sean Bannon, "Pornography Viewing among Fraternity Men: Effects on Bystander Intervention, Rape Myth Acceptance and Behavioral Intent to Commit Sexual Assault," 18 *Sexual Addiction & Compulsivity* 212, 214 (2011) (citations omitted) ("Fraternity Men") ("The preponderance of research suggests significant, negative impacts of pornography on men in the aggregate. Recent meta-analyses and literature reviews have revealed in both correlational and experimental studies that pornography use, acceptance of aggression, and violence towards women are linked. The strongest correlations with these violence related variables are with the more violent types of pornography; though an association with mainstream pornography is both reliable and consistent"); Neil M. Malamuth, Tamara Addison, and Mary Koss, "Pornography and Sexual Aggression: Are There Reliable Effects and Can We Understand Them?," 11 *Annual Review of Sex Research* 26, 85 (2000) ("Pornography and Sexual Aggression") ("The current findings do suggest that for the majority of American men, pornography exposure (even at the highest levels assessed here) is not associated with high levels of sexual aggression . . . But among those at the highest 'predisposing' risk level for sexual aggression (a little above 7% of the entire sample), those who are very frequent pornography users (about 12% of this high risk group) have sexual aggression levels approximately

four times higher than their counterparts who do not very frequently consume pornography. Although not nearly as dramatic an elevation, the coercion levels found for similar risk subgroups (such as the moderate risk group who are very frequent pornography consumers) suggests the need for increased research attention on the use and impact of pornography in men at elevated risk for sexual aggression."); Larry Baron and Murray A. Straus, *Four Theories of Rape in American Society: A State-Level Analysis* 185–187 (New Haven, CT: Yale University Press, 1989) (finding distribution of pornography positively correlated to increased rape rate); see also MacKinnon, *Sex Equality* 986, 1728–1750.

23. In fact, the entire body of empirical work over the last three decades on pornography consumption, capturing its harmful effects ever more conclusively, disproves the catharsis hypothesis, showing it to be a stand-in for desensitization. For documentation of all the harms of pornography as documented to date, see Max Waltman, "The Politics of Legal Challenges to Pornography: Canada, Sweden, and the United States," *Stockholm Studies in Politics* (Stockholm: Stockholm University 2014) (Ph.D. Dissertation). See also Pamela Hansford Johnson, "Peddling the Pornography of Violence: Further Thoughts on 'Iniquity,' " in *The Case Against Pornography* 195, 199, David Holbrook, ed. (London: Tom Stacey Ltd. 1972) ("Commenting on the once widely believed 'catharsis hypothesis' concerning pornography: 'Do we give a child an erector set so that he will get rid of his interest in real construction, or a chemistry set so that he gets out of his system his natural bent for science?' ").

24. See, e.g., Elizabeth Oddone-Paolucci et al., "A Meta-Analysis of the Published Research on the Effects of Pornography," in *The Changing Family and Child Development* 48, 51, 52–53, Claudio Violato et al., eds. (Aldershot, UK: Ashgate 2000) ("exposure to pornographic material puts one at increased risk for developing sexually deviant tendencies, committing sexual offenses, experiencing difficulties in one's intimate relationships, and accepting the rape myth."); William O'Donohue and James H. Geer, *Handbook of Sexual Dysfunctions* 67–68, 81 (Boston: Allyn and Bacon 1993); Edna F. Einsiedel, "The Experimental Research Evidence: Effects of Pornography on the 'Average Individual,' " in *Pornography: Women, Violence, and Civil Liberties* 589–597, Catherine Itzin, ed. (Oxford: Oxford University Press 1992); Dolf Zillmann, "Effects of Prolonged Consumption of Pornography," in *Pornography: Research Advances and Policy Considerations* 127, 144–145, Dolf Zillmann and Jennings Bryant, eds. (Hillsdale, NJ: L. Erlbaum 1989) (finding escalation from less to

more aggressive materials after two weeks of experimental exposure); *Pornography and Sexual Aggression: Assessment & Treatment* (Neil M. Malamuth and Edward Donnerstein, eds. (Orlando, FL: Academic Press 1984) (finding effects of exposure); see also MacKinnon, *Sex Equality* 1728–1750.

25. See, e.g., Foubert, Brosi, and Bannon, "Fraternity Men" 212, 225 (2011) ("This study showed that men who viewed pornography, particularly rape and sadomasochistic pornography, report a greater likelihood of raping, committing sexual assault, higher rape myth acceptance, lower willingness to intervene in a sexual assault situation, and lower efficacy to intervene in a sexual assault situation."); see generally Malamuth, Addison, and Koss, "Pornography and Sexual Aggression" 26; MacKinnon, *Sex Equality* 1728–1750.

26. See, e.g., MacKinnon, *Sex Equality* 1736 ("In this connection, consider neuroscience findings of a significant negative correlation between pornography consumption and higher brain function, pornography use changing the brain similar to the way drug addiction does, see Simon Kühn and Jürgen Gallinat, "Brain Structure and Functional Connectivity Associated with Pornography Consumption: The Brain on Porn," 71 *Journal of American Medical Association Psychiatry* 827, 833 (2014); that when men are sexually aroused by pornography, their bodies experience not only desire but also a survival need through activation of the parts of the brain that also control the drive for food and water, see Sherif Karama et al., "Areas of Brain Activation in Males and Females During Viewing of Erotic Film Excerpts," 16 *Human Brain Mapping* 1, 7 (2002); and when men are sexually aroused by pornography, the mirror neurons in the brain fire, meaning their brains imagine them into the scene being viewed, see H. Mourassa et al., "Activation of Mirror-Neuron System by Erotic Video Clips Predicts Degree of Induced Erection in fMRI Study," 42 *NeuroImage* 1143, 1149 (2008).").

27. See, e.g., Gert Martin Hald et al., "Pornography and Attitudes Supporting Violence Against Women: Revisiting the Relationship in Nonexperimental Studies," 36 *Aggressive Behavior* 14 (2010); Foubert, Brosi, and Bannon, "Fraternity Men" 212; Neil M. Malamuth, Gert Martin Hald, and Mary Koss, "Pornography, Individual Differences in Risk, and Men's Acceptance of Violence Against Women in a Representative Sample," 66 *Sex Roles* 4217 (2012); MacKinnon, *Sex Equality* 1728–1750.

28. See, e.g., MacKinnon, *Sex Equality* 862 ((footnote omitted) (quoting Kathleen Daly and Brigitte Bouhours, "Rape and Attrition in the Legal

Process: A Comparative Analysis of Five Countries," 39 *Crime & Justice* 565, 565 (2010)) ("In the past 15 years in Australia, Canada, England and Wales, Scotland, and the United States, 'victimization surveys show that 14 percent of sexual violence victims report the offense to the police. Of these, 30 percent proceed to prosecution, 20 percent are adjudicated in court, 12.5 percent are convicted of any sexual offense, and 6.5 percent are convicted of the original offense charged. In the past 35 years, average conviction rates have declined from 18 percent to 12.5 percent.' ").

29. See, e.g., Anaïs Nin, *Little Birds* (New York: Harcourt, Brace, Jovanovich 1979) (containing some short stories in which young women and girls are sexually initiated by older men); Kathryn Harrison, *The Kiss: A Memoir* (New York: Random House 1997) (describing the seduction of the author by her father when she was twenty years old); Margaret Atwood, *The Handmaid's Tale* (Toronto: McClelland and Stewart 1985) (depicting a dystopian Christian theocracy in which pornography existed in a free society and antipornography characters are tyrants).

30. This is my observed opinion, supported by the trajectory of some careers. For example, after J. M. Coetzee published *Elizabeth Costello*, showing a woman who lectures widely against pornography as being sexually repressed, he won the Nobel Prize for Literature in 2003. J. M. Coetzee, *Elizabeth Costello* (New York: Viking 2003); J. M. Coetzee—Facts, *Nobelprize.org*, last visited July 16, 2016, http://www.nobelprize.org/nobel_prizes /literature/laureates/2003/coetzee-facts.html.

31. *Basic Instinct* (Carolco Pictures, StudioCanal 1992).

32. "Apologetic Jackson says 'costume reveal' went awry," *CNN*, Feb. 3, 2004, http://www.cnn.com/2004/US/02/02/superbowl.jackson/; David Bauder, "Spike Lee says Janet Jackson's breast baring a 'new low' for entertainers," *SignOnSanDiego*, Feb. 4, 2004, http://web.archive.org/web /20040411114159/http://www.signonsandiego.com/news/features/20040 204-0213-superbowl-jackson.html.

33. "Sharon Stone 'Slapped' Director Over *Basic Instinct* Leg Cross," *N.Z. Herald*, Jan. 7, 2014, http://www.nzherald.co.nz/entertainment/news /article.cfm?c_id=1501119&objectid=11182601 ("Stone was initially reluctant to remove her underwear for the famous scene, but director Paul Verhoeven assured her that nothing would be seen. However, when she watched the movie in the cinema, the US actress was angered by how much was exposed.").

34. "Apologetic Jackson says 'costume reveal' went awry," *CNN*, Feb. 3, 2004, http://www.cnn.com/2004/US/02/02/superbowl.jackson/ ("It was

not my intention that it go as far as it did. I apologize to anyone offended—including the audience, MTV, CBS, and the NFL.").

35. Marianne Garvey, "Sex Tape Brings Paris Hilton (and Her Mom) to Tears on Piers Morgan," Today, June 1, 2011, http://www.today.com/id /43240551/ns/today-entertainment/t/sex-tape-brings-paris-hilton-her -mom-tears-piers-morgan/ ("it's hard because I'll have to live with that the rest of my life and explain it to my children. It's something that's changed my life forever and I'll never be able to erase it.").

36. See generally Nadine Strossen, *Defending Pornography: Free Speech, Sex, and the Fight for Women's Rights* (New York: New York University Press 2000). By citing this example, I do not mean to imply that she in particular does not really believe this—to the contrary.

37. See MacKinnon, *Sex Equality* 1700–1701; Catharine A. MacKinnon and Andrea Dworkin, eds., *In Harm's Way: The Pornography Civil Rights Hearings* (Cambridge, MA: Harvard University Press 1998) (*"In Harm's Way"*).

38. Andrea Dworkin and Catharine A. MacKinnon, "Appendix D: Model Antipornography Civil-Rights Ordinance," in *Pornography and Civil Rights: A New Day for Women's Equality*, 138–142 (1988).

39. Andrea Dworkin and I each predicted a burgeoning pornography industry and dire social consequences, especially for women and children, if the pornography was not stopped by an effective means, such as our antipornography ordinance. See, e.g., Catharine A. MacKinnon, "The Roar on the Other Side of Silence," in MacKinnon and Dworkin, *In Harm's Way* 23 ("Every day the pornography industry gets bigger and penetrates more deeply and broadly into social life, conditioning mass sexual responses to make fortunes for men and to end lives and life chances for women and children. Pornography's up-front surrogates swallow more public space daily, shaping standards of literature and art. The age of first pornography consumption is young, and the age of the average rapist is ever younger. The acceptable level of sexual force climbs ever higher; women's real status drops ever lower. No law is effective against the industry, the materials, or the acts. Because the aggressors have won, it is hard to believe that they are wrong."); Catharine A. MacKinnon, "Vindication and Resistance: A Response to the Carnegie Mellon Study of Pornography in Cyberspace," 83 *Georgetown Law Journal* 1959, 1959 ("Ever more women and children have had to be used ever more abusively in ever more social sites and human relationships to feed the appetite that each development [in communication technology] stimulates and profits from filling.

More women have had to live out more of their lives in environments pornography has made. As pornography saturates social life, it also becomes more visible and legitimate, hence less visible as pornography. Always the abuse intensifies and deepens, becoming all the time more intrusive, more hidden, less accountable, with fewer islands of respite. In the process, pornography acquires the social and legal status of its latest technological vehicle, appearing not as pornography, but as books, photographs, films, videos, television programs, and images in cyberspace." See generally Andrea Dworkin, "Letter from a War Zone," in Andrea Dworkin, *Letters from a War Zone: Writings 1976–1987*, 308–329 (London: Secker & Warburg 1988) and "Why Pornography Matters to Feminists," in *Letters from a War Zone*, 205 ("[P]ornography numbs the conscience, makes one increasingly callous to cruelty, to the infliction of pain, to violence against persons, to the humiliation or degradation of persons, to the abuse of women and children. Also: pornography gives us no future; pornography robs us of hope as well as dignity; pornography further lessens our human value in society at large and our human potential in fact; pornography forbids self-determination to women and to children; pornography uses us up and throws us away; pornography annihilates our chance for freedom."); and Catharine A. MacKinnon, "On Sex and Violence: Introducing the Antipornography Civil Rights Law in Sweden," in *Are Women Human? And Other International Dialogues* 103–104, Catharine A. MacKinnon, ed. (Cambridge, MA: Belknap Press of Harvard University Press 2006) ("If you do not introduce this law, what will happen is clear. There will be no real sex equality as long as pornography saturates your society.").

40. American Booksellers Ass'n, Inc. v. Hudnut, 771 F.2d 323 (7th Cir. 1985).

19. GENDER: THE FUTURE

1. This talk was given at a conference of stunning depth and erudition at the 10th Annual Gender Symposium entitled Gender: The Future, held on March 9, 2007, at the University of Cambridge, U.K., sponsored by the Cambridge University Centre for Gender Studies. It was previously published as Catharine A. MacKinnon, "Gender: The Future," 17 *Constellations* 501 (2010).

2. Marge Piercy, *Woman on the Edge of Time* (New York: Knopf 1976).

3. These developments are historicized in Shira Tarrant, *When Sex Became Gender* (New York: Routledge 2006). For a selection of exemplary read-

ings of the time, see Linda Nicholson, ed., *The Second Wave: A Reader in Feminist Theory* (New York: Routledge 1997).

4. Useful sources of global data include Stephanie Hepburn and Rita J. Simon, *Women's Roles and Statuses the World Over* (Lanham, MD: Lexington Books 2007); and Joni Seager, *The Penguin Atlas of Women in the World* (4th ed., New York: Penguin 2008). Information pertaining to individual U.S. states is available in Institute for Women's Policy Research, *Women's Economic Status in the States: Wide Disparities by Race, Ethnicity, and Region*, available at http://www.iwpr.org/pdf/R260.pdf.

5. In an official statement released to mark the twenty-fifth anniversary of the passage of the Convention on the Elimination of All Forms of Discrimination Against Women (CEDAW), the Committee tasked with overseeing that Convention stated that "no country in the world has achieved total equality between the sexes both in law and in practice." UN News Centre, "UN Committee for Women's Rights Treaty Says No Country Has Reached Full Equality" Oct. 13, 2004, available at http://www.un.org/womenwatch/daw/cedaw/anniversary25.htm. This assessment is borne out in the UN's most recent surveys of women's status worldwide. See, e.g., *The World's Women 2005: Progress in Statistics* (New York: United Nations Publications 2005); and *The World's Women 2000: Trends and Statistics* (New York: United Nations Publications 2000). For additional insight into the persistence of sex inequality focusing on economic indicators, see Mayra Buvinic et al., *Equality for Women: Where Do We Stand on Millennium Development Goal 3?* (Washington, DC: International Bank for Reconstruction & Development/World Bank, 2008).

6. I have previously explored this theme in a number of contexts, including "X Underrated," *Times Higher Education Supplement*, 20 May 2005, available at http://www.timeshighereducation.co.uk/story.asp?storyCode=196151&sectioncode=26.

7. For a superb collection of articles focusing on trauma to prostituted women, see Melissa Farley, ed., *Prostitution, Trafficking, and Traumatic Stress* (Binghamton, NY: Haworth Press 2003). For further contributions to this vast literature, see especially Melissa Farley, "Prostitution, Trafficking, and Cultural Amnesia: What We Must Not Know in Order to Keep the Business of Sexual Exploitation Running Smoothly," 18 *Yale Journal of Law & Feminism* 109 (2006); Melissa Farley and Howard Barkan, "Prostitution, Violence, and Posttraumatic Stress Disorder," 27 *Women & Health* 37–49 (1998); Evelina Giobbe, "Prostitution: Buying the Right

to Rape," in *Rape and Sexual Assault III: A Research Handbook*, 143–160, Ann Wolbert Burgess, ed. (New York: Garland Publishing 1991); Dorchen Leidholdt, "Prostitution: A Violation of Women's Human Rights," 1 *Cardozo Women's Law Journal* 133 (1993); Catharine A. MacKinnon, "Prostitution and Civil Rights," 1 *Michigan Journal of Gender & Law* 13 (1993); Mimi H. Silbert and Ayala M. Pines, "Occupational Hazards of Street Prostitutes," 8 *Criminal Justice & Behavior* 395 (1981); and Mimi H. Silbert and Ayala M. Pines, "Victimization of Street Prostitutes," 7 *Victimology* 122 (1982). That this reality survives legalization is documented in Mary Louise Sullivan, *Making Sex Work: A Failed Experiment with Legalised Prostitution* (North Melbourne, Australia: Spinifex Press 2007). See also Melissa Farley, "'Bad for the Body, Bad for the Heart': Prostitution Harms Women Even If Legalized or Decriminalized," 10 *Violence Against Women* 1087, 1087–1125 (2004).

8. For a lucid discussion of the corollary phenomena of mass pornografication and pervasive sexual violence against women, see Jane Caputi, "The Pornography of Everyday Life," in *Goddesses and Monsters: Women, Myth, Power, and Popular Culture* 74–116 (Madison: University of Wisconsin Press 2004). See also Sheila Jeffreys, *Beauty and Misogyny: Harmful Cultural Practices in the West* (New York: Routledge 2005).

9. Simone De Beauvoir, *The Second Sex*, 555, H. M. Parshley, trans. (New York: Vintage Books 1989) (1953).

10. See, e.g., Gail Dines, "The Big Business of Pornography," in *Pornography: Driving the Demand in International Sex Trafficking*, Captive Daughters Media, ed. (Philadelphia: Xlibris 2007); Gail Dines and Karla Mantilla, "Pornography and Pop Culture: Putting the Text in Context: What is Pornography Really About?" 37 *Off Our Backs* 56 (2007).

11. Research has found that between 50 and 90 percent of prostituted women had been sexually abused in childhood. See, e.g., Mimi H. Silber and Ayala M. Pines, "Sexual Child Abuse as an Antecedent to Prostitution," 5 *Child Abuse and Neglect* 407, 407–411 (1981); Ronald L. Simons and Les B. Whitbeck, "Sexual Abuse as a Precursor to Prostitution and Victimization Among Adolescent and Adult Homeless Women," 12 *Journal of Family Issues* 361, 361–379 (1991). See also Evelina Giobbe, "Confronting the Liberal Lies about Prostitution," in *Living with Contradictions: Controversies in Feminist Social Ethics* 123, Alison M. Jagger, ed. (Boulder, CO: Westview Press 1994) (reporting that 74 percent of subjects in an oral history project conducted in Minneapolis, Minnesota, by

WHISPER (Women Hurt in Systems of Prostitution Engaged in Revolt), an organization of formerly prostituted women, recalled being sexually abused between the ages of 3 and 14); and Susan Kay Hunter, "Prostitution Is Cruelty and Abuse to Women and Children," 1 *Michigan Journal of Gender & Law* 91, 99 (1993) (presenting the results of a study of 123 survivors undertaken by the Council for Prostitution Alternatives, in Portland, Oregon, in which incest histories were recounted by 85 percent of participants). Seventy percent of respondents in another survey informed researchers that their early experiences of sexual abuse had influenced their later entry into prostitution. See Mimi H. Silbert and Ayala M. Pines, "Early Sexual Exploitation as an Influence in Prostitution," 28 *Social Work* 285–289 (1983). Comparable conclusions have been drawn across cultures, with rates of child sexual abuse ranging from a recorded low of 34 percent in Turkey through a high of 84 percent in Zambia. See Melissa Farley et al., "Prostitution in Five Countries: Violence and Post-Traumatic Stress Disorder," 8 *Feminism & Psychology* 405, 405–426 (1998). An incisive examination of the link between pornography consumption and child sexual abuse is provided by Diana E. H. Russell and Natalie J. Purcell, "Exposure to Pornography as a Cause of Child Sexual Victimization," *Handbook of Children, Culture, and Violence* 59–84, Nancy E. Dowd et al., eds. (Thousand Oaks, CA: Sage Publications 2006).

12. For a few selections from this voluminous literature, see, e.g., Barbara Drinck and Chung-noh Gross, eds., *Forced Prostitution in Times of War and Peace: Sexual Violence Against Women and Girls* (Bielefeld, Germany: Kleine Verlag 2007); Cynthia Enloe, "The Prostitute, the Colonel, and the Nationalist," in *Maneuvers: The International Politics of Militarizing Women's Lives* 49–107 (Berkeley: University of California Press 2000); and Indai Lourdes Sajor, ed., *Violence Against Women in War and Armed Conflict Situations* (Quezon City, Philippines: Asian Centre for Women's Human Rights 1998).

13. For findings on girls in particular, see Diana E. H. Russell, "The Incidence and Prevalence of Intrafamilial and Extrafamilial Sexual Abuse of Female Children," 7 *Child Abuse & Neglect* 133, 137–138 (1983); and Diana E. H. Russell and Rebecca M. Bolen, *The Epidemic of Rape and Child Sexual Abuse in the United States* 163–164 (Thousand Oaks, CA: Sage Publications 2000) (both describing the results of a 1978 survey of San Francisco women in which 38 percent of respondents reported being sexually abused before reaching adulthood). See also Rebecca M. Bolen, Diana E.

H. Russell, and Maria Scannapieco, "Child Sexual Abuse Prevalence: A Review and Re-Analysis of Recent Studies," in *Home Truths about Child Sexual Abuse: Influencing Policy and Practice* 169–196, Catherine Itzin, ed. (New York: Routledge 2000).

14. Numerous studies, revealing this knowledge deficit, find variations in prevalence, with 3 percent to 31 percent of males in the United States estimated to have been sexually victimized in childhood. See Stefanie Doyle Peters, Gayle Elizabeth Wyatt, and David Finkelhor, "Prevalence," in *A Sourcebook on Child Sexual Abuse* 15–59 (Beverly Hills, CA: Sage Publications 1986). See also Gurmeet K. Dhaliwal et al., "Adult Male Survivors of Childhood Sexual Abuse: Prevalence, Sexual Abuse Characteristics, and Long-Term Effects," 16 *Clinical Psychology Review*, 619–639 (1996); and David Finkelhor, "Boys as Victims: Review of the Evidence," in *Child Sexual Abuse: New Theory and Research* 150 (New York: Free Press 1984). Nonetheless, the conclusion reached by a wide-ranging review of the psychological literature reflects a broad consensus in the field that the sexual abuse of boys is "common, underreported, underrecognized, and undertreated." William C. Holmes and Gail B. Slap, "Sexual Abuse of Boys: Definition, Prevalence, Correlates, Sequelae, and Management," 280 *Journal of American Medical Association* 1855, 1860 (1998).

15. Why and how people develop a heterosexual sexual orientation has not been the focus of intensive empirical investigation. Studies of homosexual sexual orientation, including the role of child sexual abuse, have produced suggestive if variable results and remain a subject of active investigation. See generally Louis Diamant and Richard D. McAnulty, eds., *The Psychology of Sexual Orientation, Behavior, and Identity: A Handbook* (Westport, CT: Greenwood Press 1995). Some compelling evidence shows a strong correlation between homosexual molestation in childhood and adult homosexual identity. See Marie E. Tomeo et al., "Comparative Data of Childhood and Adolescent Molestation in Heterosexual and Homosexual Persons," 30 *Archives of Sexual Behavior* 535 (2001). Yet "virtually all research that has attempted to demonstrate a causative relationship between early negative sexual experiences and homosexuality has failed to demonstrate significant findings." Kathleen Y. Ritter and Anthony I. Turndrup, *Handbook of Affirmative Psychotherapy with Lesbians and Gay Men* 57 (New York: Guilford Press 2002). That early abuse could also produce heterosexual orientation seems not to have been considered as an empirically testable hypothesis.

16. See Catherine E. Purcell and Bruce A. Arrigo, *The Psychology of Lust Murder: Paraphilia, Sexual Killing, and Serial Homicide* 6 (Burlington, MA: Academic Press 2006); Eric W. Hickey, *Serial Murderers and Their Victims* (4th ed., Belmont, CA: Thomson Higher Education 2006); Heather Mitchell and Michael G. Aamodt, "The Incidence of Child Abuse in Serial Killers," 20 *Journal of Police and Criminal Psychology* 40, 42 (2005) (finding a history of child sexual abuse in 26 percent of serial killers studied); Robert R. Hazelwood and Ann Wolbert Burgess, *Practical Aspects of Rape Investigation: A Multidisciplinary Approach* (4th ed., Boca Raton, FL: CRC Press 2008) (rapists); and Robert I. Simon, *Bad Men Do What Good Men Dream: A Forensic Scientist Illuminates the Darker Side of Human Behavior* (rev. ed., Washington, DC: American Psychiatric Publishing 2008) (findings on pedophiles/molesters).

17. A predilection to subjugate others as a means of enhancing one's own self-esteem has been associated with a range of conditions in the psychiatric and psychological literature from its early expositions as "sadism," generally understood originally to be an explicitly sexual deviation, to more expansive conceptions identifying it as a feature of various personality disorders, notably the pathological narcissism that is at the core of what in contemporary terms is called "Narcissistic Personality Disorder." See, e.g., D. Richard Laws and William T. O'Donoghue, eds., *Sexual Deviance: Theory, Assessment, and Treatment* (2nd ed., New York: Guilford Press 2008); Elsa Ronningstam, *Identifying and Understanding the Narcissistic Personality* (New York: Oxford University Press 2005).

18. See, e.g., Terri L. Messman-Moore and Patricia J. Long, "Child Sexual Abuse and Revictimization in the Form of Adult Sexual Abuse, Adult Physical Abuse, and Adult Psychological Maltreatment," 15 *Journal of Interpersonal Violence* 489 (2000); and Terri L. Messman-Moore and Patricia J. Long, "The Role of Childhood Sexual Abuse Sequelae in the Sexual Revictimization of Women: An Empirical Review and Theoretical Reformulation," 23 *Clinical Psychology Review* 537 (2003). Useful overviews of the current state and prospective direction of research on women's sexual revictimization include Catherine C. Classen, Oxana Gronskaya Palesh, and Rashi Aggarwal, "Sexual Revictimization: A Review of the Empirical Literature," 6 *Trauma, Violence, & Abuse* 6, 103 (2005); and Rebecca J. Macy, "A Research Agenda for Sexual Revictimization: Priority Areas and Innovative Statistical Methods," 14 *Violence Against Women* 1128 (2008). Diana Russell's study of revictimization, which focuses

exclusively on incest survivors, is also supportive. See Diana E. H. Russell, "Incestuous Abuse as a Contributing Cause of Revictimization," in *The Secret Trauma: Incest in the Lives of Girls and Women* 157–173 (rev. ed., New York: Basic Books 1999).

19. See, e.g., Sujata Desai et al., "Childhood Victimization and Subsequent Adult Revictimization Assessed in a Nationally Representative Sample of Women and Men," 17 *Violence and Victims* 639 (2002) (finding correlation between the sexual abuse of boys and subsequent sexual revictimization).

20. Linda Lovelace, *Ordeal* 144 (Secaucus, NJ: Citadel Press 1980).

21. Andrea Dworkin's *Pornography: Men Possessing Women* 48–69 (New York: Perigee Books 1981) contains a stunning analysis of this dynamic in her chapter "Men and Boys."

22. Worldwide pornography revenues in 2006 (the most recent year for which annual data are available) were more than $97 billion, exceeding those of the top U.S.-based technology companies, including Microsoft, Google, Amazon, eBay, Yahoo!, Apple, Netflix, and Earthlink combined. See http://intemet-filter-review.toptenreviews.com/internet-pornography-statistics.html#time. On the stunning growth of the pornography industry generally, see Frederick S. Lane III, *Obscene Profits: The Entrepreneurs of Pornography in the CyberAge* (New York: Routledge 2000).

23. Diverse empirical studies include Mike Allen et al., "Exposure to Pornography and Acceptance of Rape Myths," 45 *Journal of Communication* 5 (1995); Mike Allen, Dave D'Alessio, and Keri Brezgel, "A Meta-Analysis Summarizing the Effects of Pornography 11: Aggression After Exposure," 22 *Human Communication Research* 258 (1995); Robert Jensen, "Pornography and Sexual Violence," Applied Research Center, VAWnet: The National Online Resource Center on Violence Against Women, July 2004, available at http://www.vawnet.org/sites/default/files/materials/files/2016-09/AR_PornAndSV.pdf; Drew A. Kingston et al., "Pornography Use and Sexual Aggression: The Impact of Frequency and Type of Pornography Use on Recidivism among Sexual Offenders," 34 *Aggressive Behavior* 341 (2008); Neil M. Malamuth, Tamara Addison, and Mary Koss, "Pornography and Sexual Aggression: Are There Reliable Effects and Can We Understand Them?" 11 *Annual Review of Sex Research* 26, 26–91 (2000); Elizabeth Oddone-Paolucci, Mark Genuis, and Claudio Violato, "A Meta-Analysis of the Published Research on the Effects of Pornography," in *The Changing Family and Child Development* 48–59, Claudio Violato and Elizabeth Oddone-Paolucci, eds. (Aldershot, UK: Ashgate Publishing,

2000); and Vanessa Vega and Neil M. Malamuth, "Predicting Sexual Aggression: The Role of Pornography in the Context of General and Specific Risk Factors," 33 *Aggressive Behavior* 104 (2007).

24. Ariel Levy and others have observed that what she calls "raunch culture"— which is nothing other than what Andrea Dworkin and I predicted and Piercy foresaw in its ultimate nightmare version—is upon us. See especially Ariel Levy, *Female Chauvinist Pigs: Women and the Rise of Raunch Culture* (New York: Free Press 2005); and Pamela Paul, *Pornified: How Pornography Is Transforming Our Lives, Our Relationships, and Our Families* (New York: Times Books 2005).

25. See Proposition 1997/98: 55 § 2.3. See also Catharine A. MacKinnon, "On Sex and Violence: Introducing the Antipornography Civil Rights Law in Sweden," *Are Women Human? And Other International Dialogues* 100 (Cambridge, MA: Harvard University Press 2004) (proposing what became the Swedish model, along with the antipornography civil rights law). Data on Swedish model in operation is compiled in Kriminalstatistik 2005, Criminal Statistics-Official Statistics of Sweden, Rapport 2006:4, Brottsförebyggande rådet [Report 2006:4, National Council for Crime Prevention] (Ulla Wittrock, ed. 2006).

26. See Code of Indianapolis and Marion County, Ind., Sec. 16-3 (1984). See also Andrea Dworkin, "Against the Male Flood: Censorship, Pornography, and Equality," 8 *Harvard Women's Law Journal* 1, 1-29 (1985); Andrea Dworkin, "Pornography Is a Civil Rights Issue," in *Letters from a War Zone* 276–307 (Brooklyn, NY: Lawrence Hill Books, 1993); and Catharine A. MacKinnon, "Francis Biddle's Sister: Pornography, Civil Rights, and Speech," *Feminism Unmodified: Discourses on Life and Law* 163–197 (Cambridge, MA: Harvard University Press 1987). An audiofile of Andrea Dworkin's 1986 testimony before the Attorney General's Commission on Pornography, published as "Pornography Is a Civil Rights Issue," may be downloaded at http://andreadworkin.com/audio/attgeneralcommNYC_M .mp3.

27. Piercy, *Woman on the Edge of Time* 197.

28. This fable or folktale, which has been variously attributed to Australian aboriginal, Japanese / Indian Buddhist, Jewish, Druid, and African American sources among others, appears to define the meaning of apocryphal. The nation, ethnicity, and sex of the sage, who is sometimes an animal, and of the questioners, varies. Always it is about a bird in the hand, and the lesson that the asker controls its fate and hence the answer. See, e.g., Toni Morrison, Nobel Lecture, Dec. 7, 1993, available at http://nobelprize

.org/nobel_prizes/literature/laureates/1993/morrison-lecture.html; *Witty Tales of Japan and India*, Yoshiko Dykstra, trans., available at http://www .kanjipress.com/4-4_witty_tales_japan_india.htm; Nina Jaffe and Steve Zeitlin, *While Standing on One Foot: Puzzle Stories and Wisdom Tales from the Jewish Tradition* (New York: Henry Holt 1993); Jack Kornfield and Christina Feldman, *Soul Food: Stories to Nourish the Spirit and the Heart* (San Francisco: Harper San Francisco 1996); Gerry Spence, *How to Argue and Win Every Time: At Home, at Work, in Court, Everywhere, Every Day* 141–142 (New York: St. Martin's 1996).

20. GENDER LITERACY

1. I was charged with wrapping up the proceedings of the Conference on Gender Bias in the Law: Ideas for Education and Action held at the University of Chicago Law School, December 2–3, 1994, at its conclusion, which had just occurred. The quotations and references in this talk are all from that conference, which apparently was not recorded in its entirety, although someone taped mine. This is the first publication of these comments.

2. Lynn Hecht Schafran, "Gender Bias in the Courts: An Emerging Focus for Judicial Reform," 21 *Arizona State Law Journal* 237, 243–251 (1989); Lynn Hecht Schafran, "Educating the Judiciary About Gender Bias: The National Judicial Education Program to Promote Equality for Women and Men in the Courts and the New Jersey Supreme Court Task Force on Women in the Courts," 9 *Women's Rights Law Reporter* 109, 113–117 (1986).

3. "I seriously wonder how many men married five, four years would have the strength to walk away without inflicting some corporal punishment . . . . I shudder to think what I would do." This is the statement made by Judge Robert E. Cahill during the sentencing of Kenneth Peacock, who was convicted of voluntary manslaughter for killing his wife after catching her in bed with another man. This case is detailed in Lynn Hecht Schafran, "There's No Accounting for Judges," 58 *Albany Law Review* 1063, 1063–1064 (1994–1995), citing Judge Cahill's statement as Reporter's Official Transcript of Proceedings (Sentencing) at 20, State v. Peacock (Md. Cir. Ct. Oct. 17, 1994) (No. 94-CR-0943) (on file with the Albany Law Review) at footnote 2. Professor Martha C. Nussbaum also talks about this case in her book *Hiding from Humanity: Disgust, Shame, and the Law* 46 (Princeton, NJ: Princeton University Press 2004) citing "She Strays, He Shoots, Judge Winks," *New York Times*, Oct. 22, 1994, at A22.

4. Cass R. Sunstein, "The Anticaste Principle," 92 *Michigan Law Review* 2410, 2454 (1994).

5. Andrea Dworkin, *Our Blood* 110 (New York: Harper & Row 1976).

6. "The Phone Company," *Saturday Night*, NBC Television, New York, NY, Sept. 18, 1976.

7. United States v. X-Citement Video, Inc., 513 U.S. 64 (1994).

8. Carr v. Allison Gas Turbine Division General Motors Corp., 32 F.3d 1007, 1011 (7th Cir. 1994) (Posner, C.J.) ("Of course it was unwelcome.").

9. Meritor Savings Bank v. Vinson, 477 U.S. 57 (1986).

10. Since 1997, this topic has been more extensively studied. See Catharine A. MacKinnon, *Sex Equality* 897 (3d ed., New York: Foundation Press 2016) ("According to the National Crime Victimization Survey, roughly 9 percent of rapes and sexual assaults recorded from 1995 to 2010 were perpetrated against males. See U.S. Department of Justice, Bureau of Justice Statistics, *Female Victims of Sexual Violence, 1994–2010*, at 3, 3 fig.2 (2013). In 2010, "the male rate of rape or sexual assault was 0.1 per 1,000 males compared to a rate of 2.1 per 1,000 for females." Id. at 3, 12 app. tbl. 3. A review of a number of studies of the sexual abuse of boys has found it to be "common, underreported, underrecognized, and undertreated." William C. Holmes and Gail B. Slap, "Sexual Abuse of Boys: Definition, Prevalence, Correlates, Sequelae, and Management," 280 *Journal of American Medical Association* 1855, 1860 (1998); see also Ramona Alaggia and Graeme Millington, "Male Child Sexual Abuse: A Phenomenology of Betrayal," 36 *Clinical Social Work* 265 (2008) (underscoring the need for greater awareness of the problem of the sexual abuse of boys). On the basis of reported data, 12 percent of all boys have been abused—depending upon the study's sample, definition, and methodology—with the largest percentage reaching close to the statistics for girls. See id. at 39.

11. Andrea Dworkin, *Ice and Fire* 90 (New York: Weidenfeld & Nicolson 1986) ("I'm a feminist, not the fun kind.").

12. For a sense of Ann Scales's work on this subject, see Ann Scales, *Legal Feminism: Activism, Lawyering, and Legal Theory* (New York: New York University Press 2006); Ann C. Scales, Remarks at the University of Toronto Legal Theory Workshop: The Women's Peace Movement and Law: Feminist Jurisprudence as Oxymoron? 64 (Feb. 26, 1988) ("This is an incredibly difficult challenge, but I suspect that women are up to it.") (on file with author); Ann Scales, "Disappearing Medusa: The Fate of Feminist Legal Theory?," 20 *Harvard Women's Law Journal* 34 (1997).

21. MAINSTREAMING FEMINISM IN LEGAL EDUCATION

1. This talk was published as Catharine A. MacKinnon, "Mainstreaming Feminism in Legal Education," 53 *Journal of Legal Education* 199 (2003). Some of the thoughts in it were previously published in an earlier form in Australia in Catharine A. MacKinnon, "Feminism in Legal Education," 1 *Legal Education Review* 85 (1989) and in Japanese in *Sekai* 104 (2002). The helpful comments and support of Kent Harvey and Lisa Cardyn are gratefully acknowledged, as is the research help of the fabulous University of Michigan Law Library.

2. Aldous Huxley, *Island* 163 (New York: Harper 1962).

3. Catharine A. MacKinnon, *Feminism Unmodified: Discourses on Life and Law* (Cambridge, MA: Harvard University Press 1987).

4. For a current update on the legal side, see Martha Chamallas, *Introduction to Feminist Legal Theory*, (2d ed., New York: Aspen 2003).

5. This is argued in Catharine A. MacKinnon, *Toward a Feminist Theory of the State* (Cambridge, MA: Harvard University Press 1989).

6. This analysis is presented in more detail in Catharine A. MacKinnon, "Points Against Postmodernism," 75 *Chi-Kent Law Review* 687 (2000).

7. Having documented and discussed this pattern repeatedly for the past thirty years, yet continuing on occasion to encounter shock and incredulity over facts well documented by others, I refer the reader to evidence for the below statements to be found throughout Catharine A. MacKinnon, *Sex Equality* (3d ed., New York: Foundation Press 2016) ("*Sex Equality*").

8. For analysis see Beatrice Faust, *Apprenticeship in Liberty: Sex, Feminism, and Sociobiology* (North Ryde, NSW, Australia: Angus & Robertson 1991); Cheryl Brown Travis, ed., *Evolution, Gender, and Rape* (Cambridge, MA: MIT Press 2003).

9. Andrea Dworkin, *Woman Hating* 202 (New York: Dutton 1974) ("People are willing to think about many things. What people refuse to do, or are not permitted to do, or resist doing, is to change the way they think.").

10. The Council of Europe has taken up gender mainstreaming, meaning considering the implications of gender for every aspect of policy. See, e.g., *Rapporteur Group on Equality Between Women and Men, Gender Mainstreaming: Conceptual Framework, Methodology and Presentation of Good Practices* (Council of Europe, Mar. 26. 1998).

11. See, e.g., Mary Jane Mossman, "Feminism and Legal Method: The Difference It Makes," 3 *Wisconsin Women's Law Journal* 147 (1987).

12. See, e.g., Leslie Bender, "A Lawyer's Primer on Feminist Theory and Tort," 38 *Journal of Legal Education* 3 (1988); Leslie Bender, "An Overview of Feminist Torts Scholarship," 78 *Cornell Law Review* 575 (1993); Martha Chamallas, "Importing Feminist Theories to Change Tort Law," 11 *Wisconsin Women's Law Journal* 389 (1997); Lucinda M. Finley, "A Break in the Silence: Including Women's Issues in a Torts Course," 1 *Yale Journal of Law & Feminism* 41 (1989); Taunya L. Banks, "Teaching Laws with Flaws: Adopting a Pluralistic Approach to Torts," 57 *Missouri Law Review* 443 (1992); Regina Austin, "Employer Abuse, Worker Resistance and the Tort of International Infliction of Emotional Distress," 41 *Stanford Law Review* 1 (1988).

13. See, e.g., Barbara Y. Welke, "Unreasonable Women: Gender and the Law of Accidental Injury, 1870–1920," 19 *Law & Social Inquiry* 369 (1994); Martha Chamallas, "Feminist Constructions of Objectivity: Multiple Perspectives in Sexual and Racial Harassment Litigation," 1 *Texas Journal of Women & Law* 95 (1992); Nancy S. Ehrenreich, "Pluralist Myths and Powerless Men: The Ideology of Reasonableness in Sexual Harassment Law," 99 *Yale Law Journal* 1177 (1910). See also Caroline A. Forell and Donna M. Matthews, *A Law of Her Own: The Reasonable Woman as a Measure of Man* (New York: New York University Press 2000).

14. See, e.g., Jane Goodman et al., "Money, Sex, and Death: Gender Bias in Wrongful Death Damage Awards," 25 *Law & Society Review* 263 (1991); Martha Chamallas, "The Architecture of Bias: Deep Structures in Tort Law," 146 *University of Pennsylvania Law Review* 463 (1998).

15. Basic sources include Clare Dalton, "An Essay in the Deconstruction of Contract Doctrine," 94 *Yale Law Journal* 997 (1985); Mary Joe Frug, "Re-reading Contracts: A Feminist Analysis of a Contracts Casebook," 34 *American University Law Review* 1065, 1125–1134 (1985); Elizabeth Mensch, "Freedom of Contract Colored Band Aid—Contracts, Feminism, Dialogue, and Norms," 28 *Housing Law Review* 791 (1991). An excellent contribution to the gender critique of contractualism is Carole Pateman's *The Sexual Contract* (Stanford, CA: Stanford University Press 1988).

16. See MacKinnon, *Sex Equality* 1300–1380, for discussion of existing law of consent in the rape context.

17. For further discussion, see Catharine A. MacKinnon, "Disputing Male Sovereignty: On *United States v. Morrison*," 114 *Harvard Law Review* 135 (2000).

18. The relevance of gender for civil procedure is explored in Judith Resnik, "Revising the Canon: Feminist Help in Teaching Procedure," 6 *University*

of *Cincinnati Law Review* 1181 (1993); Elizabeth M. Schneider, "Gendering and Engendering Process," 61 *University of Cincinnati Law Review* 1223 (1993).

19. See MacKinnon, *Sex Equality* 791 n.5 (collecting studies).

20. It is estimated that between 64 and 96 percent of all rapes are never reported to criminal justice authorities. See, e.g., B. S. Fisher et al., "The Sexual Victimization of College Women" (No. NCJ-182369) Bureau of Statistics, U.S. Department of Justice (2000); National Victim Center, *Rape in America: A Report to the Nation* (Apr. 1992); C. Perkins and P. Klaus, "Criminal Victimization 1994" (Report No. NCJ-158022), Bureau of Justice Statistics, U.S. Department of Justice (1996); Diana E. H. Russell, "The Prevalence and Incidence of Forcible Rape and Attempted Rape of Females," 7 *Victimology* 81 (1982). One recent study of nonreporting among undetected rapists supports these findings. David Lisak and Paul M. Miller, "Repeat Rape and Multiple Offending Among Detected Rapists," 17 *Violence & Victims* 73 (2002).

21. An entry point to some relevant literature is Carol Smart, *Women, Crime and Criminology: A Feminist Critique* (Boston: Routledge & Kegan Paul 1976). See also the special issue on feminism and the criminal law, 4 *Buffalo Criminal Law Review* 709 (2001). Dana M. Britton, "Feminism in Criminology: Engendering the Outlaw," 571 *The Annals of the American Academy of Political & Social Science* 57 (2000); Stephen J. Schulhofer, "The Feminist Challenge in Criminal Law," 143 *University of Pennsylvania Law Review* 2151 (1995) ("Feminist Challenge").

22. Relevant literature includes Phyllis L. Crocker, "Is the Death Penalty Good for Women?" 4 *Buffalo Criminal Law Review* 917 (2001): Elizabeth Rapaport, "Staying Alive: Executive Clemency, Equal Protection, and the Politics of Gender in Women's Capital Cases," 4 *Buffalo Criminal Law Review* 967 (2001).

23. Linda Meyer Williams, "Recall of Childhood Trauma: A Prospective Study of Women's Memories of Child Sexual Abuse," 62 *Journal of Consulting & Clinical Psychology* 1167 (1994) (finding that 38 percent of women whose childhood rapes had been medically documented at the time were not recalled by victims seventeen years later).

24. South African Constitution ch.2 § 9(3).

25. For further development of this critique, see MacKinnon, *Sex Equality* 24–35, 91–94.

26. United States v. Carolene Products Co., 304 U.S. 144, 152 n.4 (1938).

27. On that experience, see Catharine A. MacKinnon, "Rape, Genocide, and Women's Human Rights," 17 *Harvard Woman's Law Journal* 5 (1994).

28. For an example, see Aviva Orenstein, "'MY GOD!': A Feminist Critique of the Excited Utterance Exception to the Hearsay Rule," 85 *California Law Review* 159 (1997). For an overview see Andrew E. Taslitz, "What Feminism Has to Offer Evidence Law," 28 *Southwestern University Law Review* 171 (1999).

29. For basic sources, see Katherine T. Bartlett, "Feminism and Family Law," 33 *Family Law Quarterly* 47 (1999); Twila L. Perry, "Family Values, Race, Feminism and Public Policy," 36 *Santa Clara Law Review* 345 (1996).

30. See, e.g., Marion Crain, "Feminism, Labor, and Power," 65 *Southern California Law Review* 1819 (1992).

31. See Edward McCaffery, *Taxing Women* (Chicago: University of Chicago Press 1997); Anne L. Alston, "Tax Policy and Feminism: Competing Goals and Institutional Choices," 96 *Columbia Law Review* 2001 (1996); Lawerence Zelenak, "Feminism and Safe Subjects Like the Tax Code," 6 *Southern California Law Review & Women's Studies* 323 (1997).

32. Theresa A. Gabaldon, "Feminism, Fairness, and Fiduciary Duty in Corporate and Securities Law," 5 *Texas Journal of Women & Law* 1 (1995).

33. An example of the approach suggested here is provided by Martha R. Mahoney et al., *Cases and Materials on Social Justice: Professionals, Communities, and Law* (St. Paul, MN: Thomson/West 2003).

34. Sometimes it is. For some considerations of the import of feminist analysis for property law, see, e.g., Carol M. Rose, "Women and Property: Gaining and Losing Ground," 78 *Virginia Law Review* 421 (1992); Katherine K. Baker, "Property Rules Meet Feminist Needs: Respecting Autonomy by Valuing Connection," 59 *Ohio State Law Journal* 1523 (1999); Margaret Davies, "Feminist Appropriations: Law, Property and Personality," 3 *Social & Legal Studies* 365 (1994); Joseph William Singer, "Re-Reading Property," 26 *New England Law Review* 711 (1992); Jeanne L. Schroeder, "Chix Nix Bundle-o-Stix: A Feminist Critique of the Disaggregation of Property," 93 *Michigan Law Review* 239 (1994).

35. See, e.g., Hilary Charlesworth and Christine Chinkin, *Boundaries of International Law: A Feminist Analysis* (Manchester, UK: Manchester University Press 2000). See also Pierrette Hondagneu-Sotelo, "Feminism and Migration," 571 *The Annals of the American Academy of Political & Social Science* 107 (2000).

36. See, e.g., Carrie Menkel-Meadow, "Portia in a Different Voice: Speculations on a Woman's Lawyering Process," 1 *Berkeley Women's Law Journal* 39 (1985); Carrie Menkel-Meadow, "Feminist Legal Theory, Critical Legal Studies and Legal Education or The Fem-Crits Go to Law School," 38 *Journal of Legal Education* 61 (1988).

37. See Phyllis Goldfarb, "A Theory-Practice Spiral: The Ethics of Feminism and Clinical Education," 75 *Minnesota Law Review* 1599 (1991).

38. For documentation of this problem, and of misogyny on law faculties, see Sheila McIntyre, "Gender Bias Within the Law School: 'The Memo' and its Impact," 2 *Canadian Journal of Women & Law* 362, 407 (1987). ("In my experience this includes being endlessly accessible, publicly and privately, supportive, emotionally engaged, and a model of uncompromising resistance. Our limited numbers and the urgency of the feminist project drive us to meet these impossible standards.").

39. See, e.g., Lani Guinier et al., *Becoming Gentlemen: Woman, Law School, and Institutional Change* (Boston: Beacon Press 1997) ("*Becoming Gentlemen*").

40. Socrates's epigram is "I know nothing except the fact of my own ignorance;" see Titus Maccius Plautus, *Bacchides*, John Barsby, trans., line 324 ("The only thing I know is that I don't know").

41. Guinier documents this clearly. Guinier et al., *Becoming Gentlemen* 59–62, 144–145 n.159.

42. An inspiring source on this subject in general remains Adrienne Rich, "Toward a Women-Centered University," in *On Lies, Secrets, and Silence: Selected Prose, 1966–1978,* 125 (New York: Norton 1979).

43. As Stephen Schulhofer puts it, without asking feminist questions, it is impossible to do criminal law well. Schulhofer, "Feminist Challenge" 2151.

22. ON ACADEMIC FREEDOM

1. The information contained in this introduction can be found at the website for the Davis, Markert & Nickerson Lecture, available at: http://www.screencast.com/t/rUr5iiEy8t. The American Association of University Professors (AAUP) censured the University of Michigan in 1957 for these actions but removed the censure in 1958 following the adoption of a new Bylaws of the Board of Regents, available at https://catalog.hathitrust.org/Record/005840237. My unpublished talk, the Twelfth Annual Lecture, was delivered on October 31, 2002.

2. The foundational case establishing academic freedom as a "special concern" of the First Amendment is Keyishian v. Board of Regents of the

University of State of New York, 385 U.S. 589, 603 (1967) (noting the "essentiality of freedom in the community of American universities" to ensure continued academic development and social progress (citing Sweezy v. State of New Hampshire, 354 U.S. 234, 250 (1957))). Academic freedom is not an independent right under the First Amendment, but is cognizable only in reference to the right to protected free speech or association. See Schrier v. University of Colorado, 427 F.3d 1253, 1266 (10th Cir. 2005).

3. John Stuart Mill, *On Liberty* 50 (2d ed. 1859). See also id. at 92 ("[I]n an imperfect state of the human mind, the interests of truth require a diversity of opinions.").

4. See, e.g., John Milton, Areopagitica 49–50, John Wesley Hales, ed., (Clarendon Press 1874) (1644) ("[T]hey who counsell ye to such a suppressing doe as good as bid ye suppresse yourselves . . . [L]iberty which is the nurse of all great wits; this is that which hath ratify'd and enlightn'd our spirits like the influence of heav'n; this is that which hath enfranchis'd, enlarg'd and lifted up our apprehensions degrees above themselves. Ye cannot make us now lesse capable, lesse knowing, lesse eagerly pursuing of the truth, unlesse ye first make your selves, that made us so, lesse the lovers, lesse the founders of our true liberty . . . Give me the liberty to know, to utter, and to argue freely according to conscience, above all liberties.").

5. The seminal case in recognizing academic freedom as grounded in the Constitution is Sweezy v. New Hampshire, 354 U.S. 234 (1957), see supra note 2. Adler v. Board of Education, 342 U.S. 485 (1952) (Douglas J., dissenting) is the first Supreme Court decision to mention academic freedom.

6. Tom Emerson taught at Yale Law School. He had been accused of being a communist during the McCarthy era. When I was his law student in the 1970s, he secured his FBI file and convened a meeting at which he read its contents aloud. One particularly memorable feature from his reading of the file was the agents' conclusion, after they reported meeting after meeting in which nothing worth reporting occurred, that since no information whatever substantiating Tom's participation in any communist activities could be found, he must be a very high and important figure in the party under especially deep cover.

7. *Keyishian* at 603.

8. See Sweezy, supra note 2, at 250 ("The essentiality of freedom in the community of American universities is almost self-evident. No one should underestimate the vital role in a democracy that is played by those who

guide and train our youth. To impose any strait jacket upon the intellectual leaders in our colleges and universities would imperil the future of our Nation. No field of education is so thoroughly comprehended by man that new discoveries cannot yet be made. Particularly is that true in the social sciences, where few, if any, principles are accepted as absolutes. Scholarship cannot flourish in an atmosphere of suspicion and distrust. Teachers and students must always remain free to inquire, to study and to evaluate, to gain new maturity and understanding; otherwise our civilization will stagnate and die."). See also *Keyishian* at 603.

9. *Keyishian* at 603 (citing United States v. Associated Press, D.C., 52 F. Supp. 362, 372 (S.D.N.Y. 1943)).

10. Regents of the University of California v. Bakke, 438 U.S. 265, 311–315 (1978) ("Academic freedom . . . long has been viewed as a special concern of the First Amendment. The freedom of a university to make its own judgments as to education includes the selection of its student body . . . An otherwise qualified medical student with a particular background—whether it be ethnic, geographic, culturally advantaged or disadvantaged—may bring to a professional school of medicine experiences, outlooks, and ideas that enrich the training of its student body.").

11. Statements to this effect are axiomatic and ubiquitous. See, e.g., Brandt v. Board, 480 F.3d 460 (7th Cir. 2007) ("[Academic freedom] also includes the authority of the university to manage an academic community and evaluate teaching and scholarship free from interference by other units of government, including the courts" (quoting Hosty v. Carter, 412 F.3d 731, 736 (7th Cir. 2005))).

12. Thomas Kuhn, *The Structure of Scientific Revolutions* (Chicago: University of Chicago Press 1962) analyzes this phenomenon in some detail.

13. University of Pennsylvania v. Equal Employment Opportunity Commission, 493 U.S. 182 (1990).

14. Prominent examples are Pittsburgh Press Co. v. Pittsburgh Commission on Human Relations, 413 U.S. 376 (1973) (declining to protect sex segregated job ads as speech) and Roberts v. United States Jaycees, 468 U.S. 609 (1984) (holding expressive association of all-male organization not protected against equal rights challenge).

15. But cf. Adams v. Trustees of the University of North Carolina-Wilmington, 640 F.3d 550 (4th Cir. 2011) (finding professor's discussions of feminism being a matter of public concern and an issue of public importance, unrelated to his teaching duties, and therefore protected under the First Amendment).

16. See, e.g., Lynn v. Regents of the University of California, 656 F.2d 1337, 1343 (9th Cir. 1981) (stating that a "disdain for women's issues, and a diminished opinion of those who concentrate on those issues, is evidence of a discriminatory attitude towards women."); Paul v. Leland Stanford University, 46 Fair Empl. Prac. Cas. 1350, 1986 WL 614 at 6–7 (N.D. Cal. 1986) (accepting as part of Plaintiff's prima facie case for sex discrimination the rejection by the chair of the Religious Studies Department to approve a course on women in religion); Kraemer v. Franklin and Marshall College, 1995 WL 672523 (E.D. Penn. 1995) (denying Defendant's Motion to preclude Defendant's disagreement with Women's Studies and feminist theory as evidence of gender-based discrimination). But see also University of Southern California v. Superior Court, 222 Cal. App.3d 1028 (1990) (ruling that University committee, although evaluating associate professor's record as feminist scholar in some detail, did not discriminate based on her gender).

17. See, e.g., Fisher v. University of Texas at Austin, 631 F.3d 213 (5th Cir. 2011), *vacated on other grounds*, 133 S. Ct. 2411 (2013) (holding that judicial deference to state university's academic decisions are supported by respect for university expertise and by educational autonomy grounded in the First Amendment).

18. A potentially telling study undertaken at the University of Southern California Dornsife found that 92 percent of white male faculty were granted tenure while only 55 percent of female and minority faculty were. Memorandum to Philip Ethington, President of the USC Dornsife Faculty Council, from Jane Junn, Professor of Political Science, USC Dornsife, *Analysis of Data on Tenure at USC Dornsife*, October 19, 2012, at 2–3 ($n=106$). This process comparison, which to my knowledge has not been duplicated on a larger scale, suggests that the right question is not, ultimately, how many members of each group survive the process, but what each individual faces in it. It suggests that, compared with white men, several women and people of color are denied tenure before one is granted, producing the overall numbers. The overall numbers of women and people of color in the higher reaches of academia have improved some from prior decades but remain low. Women accounted for 38.4 percent of the full-time faculty in 2001 and 44.8 percent in 2013. Blacks, however, represented 5.13 percent of the full-time faculty in 2001 and 5.46 percent in 2013; Hispanics 3.00 percent and 4.20 percent; Asian/Pacific Islanders 6.15 percent and 9.13 percent; and Native Americans 0.45 percent and 0.45 percent, respectively. For 2001 data, see National Center for Education Statistics,

Table 231. Full-time instructional faculty in degree-granting institutions, by race/ethnicity, academic rank, and sex: Fall 2001 (2003); for 2013 data, see National Center for Education Statistics, *Table 315.20, Full-time faculty in degree-granting postsecondary institutions, by race/ethnicity, sex, and academic rank: Fall 2009, fall 2011, and fall 2013* (2016). Tenure rates are lower and stalled in the same period. Tenured male faculty were 56.5 percent of all male faculty and 41.5 percent of all female faculty in 2001–2002. In 2013–2014, 56.6 percent of male faculty were tenured and 43.2 percent of female faculty were tenured. See National Center for Education Statistics, Digest of Education Statistics, Table 243, *Full-time instructional staff with tenure for degree-granting institutions with a tenure system, by academic rank, sex, and type and control of institution: Selected years, 1993–94 to 2003–4* (2004); National Center for Education Statistics, Digest of Education Statistics, Table 316.80, *Percentage of degree-granting postsecondary institutions with a tenure system and of full-time faculty with tenure at these institutions, by control and level of institution and selected characteristics of faculty: Selected years, 1993–94 through 2013–14,* (2016).

19. *Keyishian* at 604. The ubiquitous "chilling effect" originally referred to stifling protected speech, hence was a form of censorship. See Wieman v. Updegraff, 344 U.S. 183, 195 (1952) (Frankfurter, J., concurring) ("Such unwarranted inhibition upon the free spirit . . . has an unmistakable tendency to chill that free play of the spirit which all teachers ought especially to cultivate and practice"); Gibson v. Florida etc., 372 U.S. 539, 544 (1963) ("Freedoms . . . are protected not only against heavy-handed frontal attack, but also from being stifled by more subtle governmental interference." (quoting Bates v. Little Rock, 361 U.S. 516, 523 (1960)). It has become extended to include the assertion that a given behavior or claim imposes any burden on a speaker, for example, is critical of the speaker.

20. Ronald Dworkin, "We Need a New Interpretation of Academic Freedom" in *The Future of Academic Freedom* 184, Louis Menand, ed. (Chicago: University of Chicago Press 1996).

21. See, e.g., *Unfettered Expression: Freedom in American Intellectual Life*, Peggie J. Hollingsworth, ed. (Ann Arbor: University of Michigan Press 2000).

22. See William W. Van Alstyne, *Academic Freedom and the First Amendment in the Supreme Court of the United States: An Unhurried Historical Review*, 53 *Law & Contemporary Problems* 79 (Summer 1990) (summa-

rizing academic freedom jurisprudence in the twentieth century, showing most cases until late 1950s/early 1960s focused on speech rights of teachers and professors, then the increase from 1968 to 1978 in Supreme Court cases challenging restrictions on student speech, notably *Tinker*), available at: http://scholarship.law.duke.edu/lcp/vol53/iss3/4; C. Thomas Dienes and Annemargaret Connolly, *When Students Speak: Judicial Review in the Academic Marketplace*, 7 *Yale Law & Policy Review* 343 (1989) (discussing *Tinker*, *Fraser*, and *Hazelwood* in detail).

23. I don't know if this is true, but according to Neil W. Hamilton, "Contrasts and Comparisons Among McCarthyism, 1960s Student Activism and 1990s Faculty Fundamentalism," 22 *William Mitchell Law Review* 369 (1996), "In 1994 the American Association of University Professors (AAUP) heard from about three professors per week who believed they had been unfairly accused of sex harassment." Id. at 386. Perhaps the AAUP safeguards other rights, but the principal one is academic freedom.

24. In addition to the cases discussed in this talk, see, for example, the following line of cases relevant to this point raise a variety of issues in various postures with diverse results: Korf v. Ball State University, 726 F.2d 1222 (7th Cir. 1984); Doe v. University of Michigan, 721 F. Supp. 852 (E.D. Mich. S.D. 1989); Levin v. Harleston, 770 F. Supp. 895 (S.D.N.Y. 1991), *affirmed in part, vacated in part*, 966 F.2d 85 (2d Cir. 1992); Miles v. Denver Public Schools, 944 F.2d 773 (10th Cir. 1991); Keen v. Penson, 970 F.2d 252 (7th Cir. 1992); McDaniels v. Flick, 59 F.3d 446 (3d Cir. 1995); Booher v. Board of Regents, Northern Kentucky University, 1998 WL 35867183 (E.D. Ky. 1998); Goldbarth v. Kansas State Bd. of Regents, 269 Kan. 881 (2000); Lighton v. University of Utah, 209 F.3d 1213 (10th Cir. 2000); Bonnell v. Lorenzo, 241 F.3d 800 (6th Cir. 2001); Hardy v. Jefferson Community College, 260 F.3d 671 (6th Cir. 2001); Vega v. Miller, 273 F.3d 460 (2d Cir. 2001); Trejo v. Shoben, 319 F.3d 878 (7th Cir. 2003); Mills v. Western Washington University, 150 Wash. App. 260 (Ct. App. Wash. App. 2009); Lopez v. Fresno City College, 2012 WL 844911 (E.D. Cal. March 12, 2012); Traster v. Ohio Northern University, 2015 IER Cases 419 (N.D. Oh. 2015). See also Iota Sigma Chapter of Sigma Chi Fraternity v. George Mason University, 993 F.2d 386 (4th Cir. 1993); Urofsky v. Gilmore, 215 F.3d 401 (4th Cir. 2000). A thoughtful and informed treatment of many of the same issues discussed in this speech from a somewhat different perspective can be found in Peter Byrne, "The Threat to Constitutional Academic Freedom," 31 *Journal of College and University Law* 79 (2004).

25. See, e.g., Adams v. Trustees of the University of North Carolina-Wilmington, 640 F.3d 550 (4th Cir. 2011) (holding that to the extent the Constitution recognizes a right of academic freedom beyond every citizen's First Amendment rights, the right inheres in a university, not in individual professors); Evans-Marshall v. Board of Education of the TIPP City Exempted Village School District, 624 F.3d 332 (6th Cir. 2010) (holding the educational institution, not the individual teacher, has the right to academic freedom); Asociación de Educatión Privada de Puerto Rico, Inc. v. García-Padilla, 490 F.3d 1 (1st Cir. 2007) (holding academic freedom establishes zone of First Amendment protection for educational process which includes host institutions, including private schools); Faghri v. University of Connecticut, 621 F.3d 92 (2d Cir. 2010) (holding state university did not violate professor's First Amendment free speech rights by demoting him from deanship for voicing opposition to university policies). But see Emergency Coalition to Defend Educational Travel v. United States Department of the Treasury, 545 F.3d 4, 12 (D.C. Cir. 2008) (stating the professor's right to academic freedom under the First Amendment can be invoked only to prevent governmental effort to regulate content of professor's academic speech).
26. *Keyishian* at 603.
27. Id.
28. Mount Healthy City School District Board of Education v. Doyle, 429 U.S. 274 (1977) (holding unanimously that untenured teacher could not be terminated for constitutionally protected speech on a matter of public concern unless the school could show he would have been fired anyway for other unprotected activity).
29. Edwards v. California University of Pennsylvania, 156 F.3d 488, 491 (3d Cir. 1998).
30. Bishop v. Aronov, 926 F.2d 1066, 1075 (11th Cir. 1991).
31. Id. at 1076. This continues to be the legal position in other circuits as well. See, e.g., Lee v. York County School Division, 484 F.3d 687 (4th Cir. 2007); Axson-Flynn v. Johnson, 356 F.3d 1277 (10th Cir. 2004).
32. Silva v. University of New Hampshire, 888 F. Supp. 293 (D.N.H. 1994).
33. See, e.g., William H. Honan, "Professor Ousted for Lecture Gets Job Back," *New York Times*, Sept. 17, 1994, available at: http://www.nytimes.com/1994/09/17/us/professor-ousted-for-lecture-gets-job-back.html.
34. *Silva* at 299.
35. Id.
36. Id. at 302.

37. Id. at 314. This is the *Hazelwood* test from the Supreme Court's epony-mous case. Hazelwood School District v. Kuhlmeier, 484 U.S. 260, 273 (1988) (holding that educators exercising editorial control over the style and content of student speech in school-sponsored expressive activities is permitted if reasonably related to legitimate pedagogical concerns).

38. *Silva* at 313 (concluding that the six complainants were "under the mis-taken impression that the word 'vibrator' necessarily connotes a sexual device"). Silva had said in class that "Belly dancing is like jello on a plate with a vibrator under the plate." Id. at 299.

39. Id. at 330.

40. Bethel School District No. 403 v. Fraser, 478 U.S. 675 (1986).

41. Id. at 683.

42. Id. at 683–684.

43. Cohen v. San Bernardino Valley College, 92 F.3d 968, 971 (9th Cir. 1996).

44. Id. at 970.

45. Id.

46. Id. at 971.

47. Id. This decision reverses a cogent analysis by the district court in Cohen v. San Bernardino Valley College, 883 F. Supp. 1407 (C.D. Cal. 1995).

48. 29 C.F.R. § 1604.11(a)(3) (1999).

49. See, e.g., Meritor Savings Bank, FSB v. Vinson, 477 U.S. 57, 65 (1986).

50. *Cohen* at 972 (concluding that Cohen was without notice that the policy would be applied to punish his "longstanding" teaching method).

51. Id. (calling "a legalistic ambush" the college officials' "ad hoc" applica-tion of the policy's "nebulous outer reaches" to Cohen's teaching methods that he had used for many years).

52. Id.

53. 933 F. Supp. 1425 (C.D. Ill. 1996). This case was, from all indications, not appealed.

54. Id. at 1440.

55. Id. at 1441.

56. Id.

57. Id. at 1448.

58. Id. at 1441.

59. Id.

60. Id. at 1440.

61. *Silva* at 316 (finding that Silva's First Amendment interest in the speech at issue is "overwhelmingly superior" to the university's interest in regulating such speech); *Cohen* at 972 (concluding that the college's approach was

ad hoc and a legalistic ambush to punish Cohen's longstanding teaching methods).

62. *Rubin* at 1443.

63. For the basic law of this area focusing on the "matter of public concern," see Pickering v. Board of Education, 391 U.S. 563 (1968) and Connick v. Myers, 461 U.S. 138 (1983). A large body of case law continues to rely on this distinction. See, e.g., Garcetti v. Ceballos, 547 U.S. 410 (2006) (holding that public employers may not restrict employees' free speech rights by creating excessively broad job descriptions, such that listing a given task as within the employees' job description is not enough to show that conducting it is within their professional duties). Working for a candidate's political campaign is protected speech. Nagle v. Marron, 663 F.3d 100 (2d Cir. 2011). Congress, however, can require that law schools, including private ones, allow military recruiters (who at the time discriminated against gay men and lesbian women) the same access to campus and students as nonmilitary recruiters without violating the law schools' First Amendment rights of expressive association. See Rumsfeld v. Forum for Academic and Institutional Rights, Inc., 547 U.S. 47 (2006) (upholding Solomon Amendment against law schools' claim it forced them to discriminate, against their convictions and educational objectives). Instructive cases illustrating the parameters of "matter of public concern" for present purposes include Decotiis v. Whittemore, 635 F.3d 22 (1st Cir. 2011) (holding speech therapist spoke as citizen rather than as employee, providing information the public had a nontrivial interest in, when she provided information to clients' parents about their rights in potentially illegal denial of special education services), cf. Alberti v. Carlo-Izquierdo, 548 F. App'x 625 (1st Cir. 2013) (holding statements by director of nursing program complaining of an alleged Health Insurance Portability and Accountability Act (HIPAA) violation was pursuant to her official duties, hence not protected academic freedom for purposes of grounding First Amendment retaliation complaint).

64. *Rubin* at 1444 (quoting Eberhardt v. O'Malley, 17 F.3d 1023, 1027 (7th Cir. 1994)).

65. Title IX of the Education Amendments of 1972, Pub. L. No. 92-318, 86 Stat. 373 (codified at 20 U.S.C. §§ 1681–88 (1972). See Alexander v. Yale University, 631 F.2d 178 (2d Cir. 1980).

66. This continues to be the case. See, e.g., DeJohn v. Temple University, 537 F.3d 301, 318–319 (3d Cir. 2008) (holding that prohibiting expressive conduct of a "gender-motivated nature" that had the purpose or effect of

unreasonably interfering with work or educational performance, or of creating an intimidating, hostile, or offensive environment, was unconstitutionally overbroad under First Amendment). The *DeJohn* court also held that because overbroad harassment policies can suppress protected speech and are susceptible to selective application amounting to content-based or viewpoint discrimination, the overbreadth doctrine may be invoked in students' free speech cases. Id. at 314. The Third Circuit held in 2010 that a policy against "offensive" and "unauthorized" speech without demonstrating that the speech objectively and subjectively created a hostile environment or substantially interfered with work or study, was facially overbroad in violation of the First Amendment. McCauley v. University of the Virgin Islands, 618 F.3d 232 (3d Cir. 2010). This exception was effectively a sexual harassment standard, although this was not noted. Another case held that "courts must defer to colleges' decisions to err on the side of academic freedom." Rodriguez v. Maricopa County Community College District, 605 F.3d 703, 709 (9th Cir. 2010). In this case, a professor's website and subscriber-based emails that asked readers to celebrate "the superiority of Western Civilization" and argued "[t]he only immigration reform imperative is preservation of White majority," id. at 705, was deemed pure speech and not unlawful harassment in violation of Hispanic employees' equal protection right to be free from unlawful workplace harassment.

67. For one pointed instance, see Esfeller v. O'Keefe, 391 F. App'x 337 (5th Cir. 2010), in which a state university's code of conduct prohibiting extreme, outrageous or persistent acts or communications intended to harass, intimidate, harm, or humiliate was found not explicitly viewpoint-based because it did not prohibit such speech or conduct based on race, religion, color, national origin, gender, sexual orientation, disability or other characteristics. The law on this subject is relatively settled: see, e.g., O'Brien v. Welty, 818 F.3d 920 (9th Cir. 2016) (finding that a California regulation authorizing state universities to discipline students for harassment was not an unconstitutionally overbroad or vague limitation on speech) and Piggee v. Carl Sandburg College, 464 F.3d 667 (7th Cir. 2006) (holding a community college's sexual harassment policy that prohibited commenting or acting on one's sexual orientation or religion was not an unconstitutional prior restraint on speech). See also Brown v. Chicago Board of Education, 2016 WL 3094438 (7th Cir. 2016) (holding that because public school teacher was speaking as a teacher and an employee and not as a citizen when he used the N-word in violation of school policy during classroom discussion on why such words must not be used, teacher's suspension on

versity Press 1993), focusing on pornography. This trend has become clearer in Supreme Court cases into the present, as money has become defined as speech and corporations have become defined as possessing speech rights. See Buckley v. Valeo, 424 U.S. 1 (1976) and Citizens United v. Federal Election Commission, 558 U.S. 310 (2010).

23. ENGAGED SCHOLARSHIP AS METHOD AND VOCATION

1. This speech was given on January 7, 2005, and previously published in Catharine A. MacKinnon, "Engaged Scholarship as Method and Vocation," 22 *Yale Journal of Law and Feminism* 193 (2011). The title draws inspiration from Max Weber, "Politics as a Vocation," in *The Vocation Lectures*, David Owen and Tracy B. Strong, eds., Rodney Livingstone, trans. (Indianapolis: Hackett 2004) and Sheldon S. Wolin, "Political Theory as a Vocation," 63 *American Political Science Review* 1062 (1969). Thanks are owed to Kent Harvey, Lisa Cardyn, Marc Spindelman, Lindsay Waters, and Lori Watson for critical readings. Maureen Pettibone provided excellent research assistance.

2. See Catharine A. MacKinnon, *Feminism Unmodified: Discourses on Life and Law* (Cambridge, MA: Harvard University Press 1987).

3. Peter Novick, *That Noble Dream: The "Objectivity Question" and the American Historical Profession* (Cambridge: Cambridge University Press 1988). Novick's lucid tracing of objectivity as a norm in historical scholarship clarifies the intellectual history and dimensions of this imperative.

4. See Karl Mannheim, *Ideology and Utopia* 137 (New York, Harcourt, Brace 1936). Mannheim was attempting to get beyond relativism toward objectivity. One means he offered was an "unanchored, *relatively* classless stratum [called], to use Alfred Weber's terminology, the 'socially unattached intelligentsia' *(freischwebende Intelligenz)*," a group supposedly less subject to social influence than lesser mortals. Id.

5. Paul W. Kahn, *The Cultural Study of Law: Reconstructing Legal Scholarship* 3 (Chicago: University of Chicago Press 1999).

6. Id. at 7 ("A new discipline of legal study must abandon the project of reform."). He further argues, "From the very beginning, the study of law is co-opted by legal practice. The independence of the discipline will never be possible unless the understanding deployed in theoretical inquiry can be distinguished from the reason deployed in legal practice." Id. at 18. He concludes that legal scholars must "marginaliz[e] ourselves, if the study of law is to free itself from the practice of law." Id. at 139.

7. Id. at 3 (footnote omitted). On the separation approach, see Charles Beard, *The Nature of the Social Sciences in Relation to Objectives of Instruction* 19–20 (New York: Scribner's 1934).

8. See, e.g., Ian Hacking, *Historical Ontology* (Cambridge, MA: Harvard University Press 2002); Ian Hacking, *The Social Construction of What?* (Cambridge, MA: Harvard University Press 1999); Helen E. Longino, *Science as Social Knowledge: Values and Objectivity in Scientific Inquiry* 231–322 (Princeton, NJ: Princeton University Press 1990); Thomas Nagel, *The View from Nowhere* (New York: Oxford University Press 1989); Sally Haslanger, "On Being Objective and Being Objectified," in *A Mind of One's Own: Feminist Essays on Reason and Objectivity* 209 Louise M. Antony and Charlotte E. Witt, eds. (Boulder, CO: Westview Press 2002).

9. See, e.g., Catharine A. MacKinnon, *Toward a Feminist Theory of the State* (Cambridge, MA: Harvard University Press 1989). The parts most responsive to Kahn's points were written in 1972–1973.

10. Harold D. Lasswell, *Politics: Who Gets What, When, How* 133 (New York: Meridian Books 1958) ("The politician displaces his private motives upon public objects, and rationalizes the displacement in terms of public advantage.").

11. See generally Jerome Frank, *Law and the Modern Mind* (New York: Anchor Books 1970). Jerome Frank, who sat on the Second Circuit Court of Appeals, is often said to have contended that legal decisions may be less determined by legal texts than by what the judge had for breakfast. My contention is formally similar but substantively much tighter in terms of the relevance nexus: legal texts involving structural inequalities may be strongly determined by the status location and pertinent experiences, hence views, of the legal actor involved.

12. For some documentation and analysis, see Victor Farís, *Heidegger and Nazism* 59–67, Joseph Margolis and Tom Rockmore, eds., Paul Burrell, trans. (Philadelphia: Temple University Press 1989). See also Martin Heidegger, *Being and Time* (1927).

13. Kingsley Amis, *Lucky Jim* 226–231 (Garden City, NY: Doubleday 1953).

14. I had thought this turn of phrase came from Mark Twain, but it seems Konrad Lorenz said it of the smaller question of specialization: "The specialist comes to know more and more about less and less, until finally he knows everything about a mere nothing." Konrad Lorenz, *Behind the Mirror: A Search for a Natural History of Human Knowledge* 33 Ronald Taylor, trans. (1997); see also Nicholas Murray Butler, Commencement

Address at Columbia University, in *Bartlett's Familiar Quotations* 625, Justin Kaplan, ed. (17th ed., Little, Brown 2002) ("An expert is one who knows more and more about less and less.").

15. Stanley Fish, "Theory's Hope," 30 *Critical Inquiry* 374, 377 (2004) ("Theory's Hope").

16. Sheldon Wolin didn't say exactly this in his 1969 *Political Theory as a Vocation*, but I came to understand it better from his stunning analysis of "the behavioral revolution," one feature of which is disengagement, and his defense of epic theory, one feature of which is engagement. See Wolin, supra note 1, at 1062–1082.

17. See Thomas S. Kuhn, *The Structure of Scientific Revolutions* 38–39 (3d ed., Chicago: University of Chicago Press 1996).

18. Robert Frost, "A Considerable Speck," in *A Witness Tree* 57, 58 (New York: Holt 1942).

19. Barbara Johnson, *Mother Tongues: Sexuality, Trials, Motherhood, Translation* 3 (Cambridge, MA: Harvard University Press, 2003).

20. Fish, "Theory's Hope" 378.

21. Kadic v. Karadžić, 70 F.3d 232 (2d Cir. 1995); Catharine A. MacKinnon, "Rape, Genocide and Women's Human Rights," 17 *Harvard Women's Law Journal* 5 (1994).

22. See Catharine A. MacKinnon, "The Roar on the Other Side of Silence," in Catharine A. MacKinnon and Andrea Dworkin, eds. *In Harm's Way: The Pornography Civil Rights Hearings* 3–24 (Cambridge, MA: Harvard University Press 1998).

23. The book is Catharine MacKinnon, *Sexual Harassment of Working Women: A Case of Sex Discrimination* (New Haven, CT: Yale University Press 1979). The prior student paper of the same title is on file in my archive at the Schlesinger Library, Radcliffe College, with a copy in the Lillian Goldman Law Library at Yale Law School.

24. Conservative commentator David Brooks helped me find some of the words for this. See David Brooks, "The Wonks' Loya Jirga," *New York Times*, Dec. 14, 2004, at A33 ("[Y]ou have to remember that Republicans have a different relationship to ideas than Democrats. When Democrats open their mouths, they try to say something interesting. If the true thing is obvious and boring, the liberal person will go off and say something original, even if it is completely idiotic. This is how deconstructionism got started.").

25. Robert Frost, "For Once, Then, Something," in *New Hampshire* 88 (New York: Holt 1923).

26. Gerald Torres, "Why the World Ain't Obvious" (1976) (unpublished poem) (on file with author) (published by permission).

24. DEFYING GRAVITY

1. "Defying Gravity," from the Broadway musical *Wicked*, Music and Lyrics by Stephen Schwartz, Copyright © 2003 Stephen Schwartz, All rights reserved. Used by permission of Grey Dog Music (ASCAP).
2. For a little information on Ann C. Scales, 1952–2012, see Catharine A. MacKinnon, "Raising Hell, Making Miracles: The Everlovin' Legal Imagination of Ann Scales," 91 *Denver University Law Review* 1 (2014). The entire symposium on her in which this tribute appears is worth reading.
3. Jane E. Larson, Voss-Bascom Professor of Law, University of Wisconsin, 1958–2011. See www.feministlawprofessors.com/2012/01/memory-jane-larson-1959-2011. Jane stood out as formidable, creative, and a riveting speaker even as my student at the University of Minnesota Law School.

25. RAPE REDEFINED

1. Catharine A. MacKinnon, "Rape Redefined," 10 *Harvard Law and Policy Review* 431 (2016) develops these ideas with full footnote support.
2. See, e.g., R. v. Osolin [1993] 4 S.C.R. 595, 669 (Canada) ("sexual assault is in the vast majority of cases gender based. It is an assault upon human dignity and constitutes a denial of any concept of equality for women."); Inter-American Convention on the Prevention, Punishment and Eradication of Violence Against Women (Convention of Belem do Para), June 9, 1994, Preamble ("CONCERNED that violence against women is an offense against human dignity and a manifestation of the historically unequal power relations between women and men."); id. art. 1 ("For the purposes of this Convention, violence against women shall be understood as any act or conduct, based on gender, which causes death or physical, sexual or psychological harm or suffering to women, whether in the public or the private sphere."); Protocol to the African Charter on Human and Peoples' Rights on the Rights of Women in Africa (African Protocol), art. 1, July 11, 2003 ("'Violence against women' means all acts perpetrated against women which cause or could cause them physical, sexual, psychological, and economic harm, including the threat to take such acts; or to undertake the imposition of arbitrary restrictions on or deprivation of fundamental freedoms in private or public life in peace time and during situations of armed conflicts or of war."); Council of Europe Convention on Preventing and Combating Violence against Women and Domestic

Violence, art. 3, May 11, 2011, C.E.T.S. No. 210 ("'Violence against women' is understood as a violation of human rights and a form of discrimination against women and shall mean all acts of gender-based violence that result in, or are likely to result in, physical, sexual, psychological or economic harm or suffering to women, including threats of such acts, coercion or arbitrary deprivation of liberty, whether occurring in public or in private life.").

3. For examples of gender crimes as prohibited by the International Criminal Court, see Rome Statute of the International Criminal Court Treaty, art. 7, ¶ 1(g), July 17, 1998, 2187 U.N.T.S. 3 (defining "crime against humanity" to include "[r]ape, sexual slavery, enforced prostitution, forced pregnancy, enforced sterilization, or any other form of sexual violence of comparable gravity"); id. art. 7, ¶ 1(h) (recognizing persecution based on gender as a "crime against humanity"); id. art. 8, ¶ 2(b)(xxii) (defining "war crimes" perpetrated during international armed conflicts to include "rape, sexual slavery, enforced prostitution, forced pregnancy, as defined in article 7, paragraph 2(f), enforced sterilization, or any other form of sexual violence also constituting a grave breach of the Geneva Conventions"); id. art. 8, ¶ 2(e)(vi) (extending definition to encompass noninternational armed conflicts); id. art. 6(b) (defining "genocide" to include "[c]ausing serious bodily or mental harm to members of [a] group," which has been interpreted to apply to sexual atrocities in genocides).

4. See Wayne Lafave, *Criminal Law* 894 (5th ed., St. Paul, MN: West/Thomson 2010).

5. Sexual Offenses Act 2003, c. 42, § 1 (UK).

6. Code Pénal [C. Pén.] arts. 222-223 (Fr.).

7. See, e.g., Ga. Code Ann. § 16-6-1 (West, Westlaw current through Act 317 of the 2016 Reg. Sess. of the Georgia General Assembly) (defining rape as "carnal knowledge of: (1) A female forcibly and against her will; or (2) A female who is less than ten years of age. Carnal knowledge in rape occurs when there is any penetration of the female sex organ by the male sex organ."); Mass. Gen. Laws Ann. ch. 265 § 22 (West, Westlaw current through Chapter 85 of the 2016 2d Ann. Sess.) (defining rape as "(a) Whoever has sexual intercourse or unnatural sexual intercourse with a person, and compels such person to submit by force and against his will . . . .").

8. Liz Kelly, Jo Lovett, and Linda Regan, *Home Office Research Study 293: A Gap or a Chasm? Attrition in Reported Rape Cases* 28 (2005), available at http://webarchive.nationalarchives.gov.uk/20110218135832/rds.homeoffice.gov.uk/rds/pdfs05/hors293.pdf.

9. Marcelo F. Aebi et al., *European Institute for Crime Prevention & Control, European Sourcebook of Crime and Criminal Justice Statistics* 163 (5th ed. 2014), http://www.heuni.fi/material/attachments/heuni/reports/qrMWoCVTF/HEUNI_report_80_European_Sourcebook.pdf; J. M. Jehle, *Attrition and Conviction Rates of Sexual Offences in Europe: Definitions and Criminal Justice Responses, European Journal Criminal Policy & Research* 18, 145–161 (2012). An updated edition of *European Sourcebook* is due out this year.

10. See Majority Staff of Senate Committee on the Judiciary, 103d Cong., *The Response to Rape: Detours on the Road to Equal Justice* 1–13 (Comm. Print 1993), https://www.ncjrs.gov/pdffiles1/Digitization/145360NCJRS.pdf (providing statistics on attrition at each step). According to the White House Council on Women and Girls, while national prosecution data is not available, regional studies indicate that "two thirds of survivors [of rape] have had their legal cases dismissed, and more than 80% of the time, this contradicted her desire to prosecute . . . . Prosecutors were more likely to file charges when physical evidence connecting the suspect to the crime was present, if the suspect had a prior criminal record, and if there were no questions about the survivor's character or behavior." White House Council on Women & Girls, *Rape and Sexual Assault: A Renewed Call to Action* 17 (2014), available at https://www.whitehouse.gov/sites/default/files/docs/sexual_assault_report_1-21-14.pdf.

11. Diana E. H. Russell, *Sexual Exploitation: Rape, Child Sexual Abuse, and Workplace Harassment* 31 (Beverly Hills, CA: Sage Publications 1984) (documenting 9.5 percent of rapes reported); Mary P. Koss, "The Hidden Rape Victim: Personality, Attitudinal and Situational Characteristics," 9 *Psychology of Women Quarterly* 193, 206 (1985) (determining that of 38 percent of randomly selected college women whose experiences met the legal definition of rape or attempted rape, only 4 percent had reported the assault to the police); Crystal S. Mills and Barbara J. Granoff, "Date and Acquaintance Rape Among a Sample of College Students," 37 *Social Work* 504, 506 (1992) (noting among twenty student rape victims, none told police and only 15 percent told anyone).

12. See Jill Elaine Hasday, "Contest and Consent: A Legal History of Marital Rape," 88 *California Law Review* 1373, 1375 (2000). This consent rationale in the marital context was repudiated, with others, in the breakthrough state case of People v. Liberta, 474 N.E.2d 567, 573 (1984) ("Any argument based on a supposed consent . . . is untenable.").

13. The trend may be toward "no" meaning lack of consent, although the verbal "no" from the victim is usually discussed with evidence of physical resistance and threats as well. See, e.g., State v. Gatewood, 965 S.W.2d 852, 857 (Mo. Ct. App. W.D. 1998). For discussion of the potential scope of "no means no" in application, see the comparison of New York, where the victim must express lack of consent clearly and such that the reasonable person in the accused's situation would understand it as such; with Nebraska, where the victim can prove she said "no" but the statute allows the defendant to argue that this is not, in context, what she meant; with Massachusetts, where, once the victim says no, any other implication as to her consent must be considered legally irrelevant. Model Penal Code, Statutory Commentary, Sexual Assault and Related Offenses at 26–27 and n.68 (American Law Institute, Preliminary Draft No. 4, Oct. 3, 2014).

14. Usually, such cases are not brought at all, particularly not as rape. For example, "[i]n Florida, Jonathan Bleiweiss of the Broward Sheriff's Office was sentenced to a five-year prison term . . . for bullying about 20 immigrant men into sex acts. Prosecutors said he used implied threats of deportation to intimidate the men," Matt Sedensky and Nomaan Merchant, "AP: Hundreds of Officers Lose Licenses over Sex Misconduct," *Associated Press: The Big Story*, Nov. 1, 2015, http://bigstory.ap.org/article/5a66f0898 7f445d9ba9253ba3d706691/ap-hundreds-officers-lose-licenses-over-sex -misconduct. In another case of forced sexual acts by a police officer, the defendant was found guilty of battery, stalking, and false imprisonment. See Jason Silverstein, "Florida Cop Who Was Once 'Employee of the Year' Pleads Guilty to Forced Sex Acts with Undocumented Immigrants," *New York Daily News*, Feb. 21, 2015, http://www.nydailynews.com/news /national/employee-year-fla-prison-sentence-article-1.2123778.

15. Sexual assault in multiple forms and iterations was charged, and much of it found, in the Holtzclaw case in Oklahoma, where the defendant police officer repeatedly used his power to intimidate Black women into sexual acts. See Jessica Testa, "The 13 Women Who Accused a Cop of Sexual Assault, in Their Own Words," *Buzzfeed News*, Dec. 9, 2015, http://www .buzzfeed.com/jtes/daniel-holtzclaw-women-in-their-ow#.fqezA4y22; Oklahoma v. Holtzclaw, CF 2014-5869 (Okla. Dist. Ct. Jan. 21, 2016) (Bloomberg Law). If charged with anything, it is not uncommon for police officers to be accused and convicted for acts other than rape for using their authority to force others to engage in sex acts with them. See, e.g., State v. Moffitt, 801 P.2d 855, 856 (Or. Ct. App. 1990) (defendant who

picked up a woman and drove her to a location where he demanded she fellate him claimed she initiated the sexual contact and was convicted of sodomy and official misconduct).

16. A range of views on this question are visible in the ALI process. The Reporters propose that when an act of sex otherwise violates its prohibitions, the fact it is commercial, defined as an act "in exchange for which any money, property, or services are given to or received by any person," results in an offense one degree higher than otherwise provided. Model Penal Code §§ 213.0(2), 213.8, Sexual Assault and Related Offenses at Appendix 18, 21 (American Law Institute, Preliminary Draft No. 6, Feb. 29, 2016). This proposal is tantamount to a sentencing enhancement, not a redefinition of forced sex in inequality terms.

17. Canada wrestles with this issue this way:

> When belief in consent not a defence (5) It is not a defence to a charge under this section that the accused believed that the complainant consented to the activity that forms the subject-matter of the charge if (a) the accused's belief arose from the accused's (i) self-induced intoxication, or (ii) recklessness or wilful blindness; or (b) the accused did not take reasonable steps, in the circumstances known to the accused at the time, to ascertain that the complainant was consenting.
>
> Accused's belief as to consent (6) If an accused alleges that he or she believed that the complainant consented to the conduct that is the subject-matter of the charge, a judge, if satisfied that there is sufficient evidence and that, if believed by the jury, the evidence would constitute a defence, shall instruct the jury, when reviewing all the evidence relating to the determination of the honesty of the accused's belief, to consider the presence or absence of reasonable grounds for that belief.

Canada Criminal Code, R.S.C. 1985, c. C-46, § 153.1 (Canada).

18. See George E. Buzash, "The 'Rough Sex' Defense," 80 *Journal of Criminal Law & Criminology* 557, 568 (1989).

19. Rousseau's view was that authority constituted by popular consent was essentially unlimited. Jean-Jacques Rousseau, "On the Social Contract," in *The Basic Political Writings*, Donald A. Cress, ed. and trans. (Indianapolis: Hackett 1987). Other liberals opposed this view and saw this authority as limited, including Adam Smith, who opposed division of society into relations of domination and submission even if legitimated by consent of equal individuals. See Adam Smith, *Wealth of Nations* Book I,

ch. 2:15 and Book III, ch. 4:385 (however women are not mentioned); see also John Stuart Mill, *On Liberty* 10–11, David Spitz, ed. (New York: Norton 1975) (1859), who thought that harm to others justifies the exercise of sovereign power over someone against their will.

20. David Hume was vividly clear on this. See David Hume, "Of the Original Contract," in *Essays: Moral, Political, and Literary* 465, 473–474, Eugene F. Miller, ed. (Indianapolis: Liberty Classics 1985) (1777).

21. See John Locke, *Two Treatises of Government* 349, Peter Laslett, ed. (Cambridge: Cambridge University Press 1988) (1690). For a distinct but related doctrine, see Thomas Hobbes, *Leviathan: Or the Matter, Forme & Power of a Commonwealth, Ecclesiasticall and Civill* 520–522, A. R. Waller, ed. (Cambridge: Cambridge University Press 1935) (1651).

22. In one ALI draft revised definition of consent, "although silence or passivity does not 'by itself' constitute consent, such inaction is a form of 'conduct' that can be sufficient, in appropriate circumstances, to communicate positive willingness." Model Penal Code, Reporters' Memorandum, Sexual Assault and Related Offenses at xii (American Law Institute, Preliminary Draft No. 5, Sep. 15, 2015) (emphasis omitted).

23. Another use of consent in law is to allow medical intrusions to be inflicted upon a person that are injurious, but are being allowed for some other benefit. Does this sound like sex to you? Apparently, it doesn't sound foreign to women's situation in sex to a lot of men.

24. Canada's basic definition of consent is "the voluntary agreement of the complainant to engage in the sexual activity in question." Canada Criminal Code, R.S.C. 1985, c. C-46, § 273.1 (Canada). See also, e.g., State *ex rel.* M.T.S., 609 A.2d 1266, 1277 (N.J. 1992).

25. M. C. v. Bulgaria, 2003-XII Eur. Ct. H.R. 1. This opinion contains the statement regarding a U.S. case, Commonwealth v. Berkowitz (*Berkowitz II*), 641 A.2d 1161 (Pa. 1994), that "Pennsylvania courts held that the victim's repeated expressions of 'no' were sufficient to prove her nonconsent." *Bulgaria*, 2003-XII Eur. Ct. H.R. at 31–32. As to rape, this is not the case. The appeals court held that her statements of "no" would be relevant to the issue of non-consent, but were not relevant to the issue of forcible compulsion, the requirement for rape in Pennsylvania. Commonwealth v. Berkowitz (*Berkowitz I*), 609 A.2d 1338, 1347–1348 (Pa. Super. Ct. 1992). The jury conviction for rape was accordingly overturned. See id. at 1352. The case was remanded for retrial on "indecent assault," which requires nonconsent, a conviction the appeals court upheld. *Berkowitz II*, 641 A.2d at 1166. No discussion of equality occurred in the case.

26. *Vertido v. The Philippines* contains excellent equality analysis of rape myths and misogynistic stereotypes. U.N. Doc. CEDAW/C/46/D/18/2008, ¶¶ 8.4–8.6 (July 16, 2010), https://opcedaw.files.wordpress.com/2012/02/vertido-v-the-philippines.pdf. However, it does not consider inequality as a form of coercion, but challenges the force-only law in the Philippines as lacking the "essential element" of rape law: "lack of consent," which it redefines to mean "unequivocal and voluntary agreement." Id. at ¶¶ 8.7–8.9.

27. See, e.g., Model Penal Code § 213.1 (American Law Institute, Proposed Official Draft 1962). Lesser forms of the offense recognized less brutal forms of violence as well as some nonphysical threats. See generally, id.

28. Prosecutor v. Akayesu, Case No. ICTR-96-4-T, Judgment, ¶ 598 (Sept. 2, 1998).

29. The impression should not be left that international courts uniformly or fully grasp and apply the *Akayesu* breakthrough, understanding the irrelevance of consent in contexts of extreme inequality, including pervasive violence. The ICTY in particular adheres to nonconsent, although it acquiesces in the Appeals Chamber's ruling that this be determined circumstantially. See Prosecutor v. Kunarac, Case No. IT-96-23 & 23/1-A ¶¶ 127–133 (Int'l Crim. Trib. For the Former Yugoslavia June 12, 2002) ("The coercive circumstances in this case made consent to the instant sexual acts . . . impossible."); see also Prosecutor v. Karadžić, Case No. IT-95-5/18-T, ¶¶ 511–513 (Int'l Crim. Trib. for the Former Yugoslavia Mar. 24, 2016). The International Criminal Court has been more contextually realistic in its treatment of its distinct statute, noting that since nonconsent is not an element of rape as an act of genocide, crime against humanity, or war crime under the Rome Statute, nonconsent need not be proven by the prosecution. Prosecutor v. Jean-Pierre Bemba Gombo, Case No. ICC-01/05-01/08, ¶¶ 105–106 (Mar. 21, 2016) ("The Chamber notes that the victim's lack of consent is not a legal element of the crime of rape under the Statute. The preparatory works of the Statute demonstrate that the drafters chose not to require that the Prosecution prove the non-consent of the victim beyond reasonable doubt, on the basis that such a requirement would, in most cases, undermine efforts to bring perpetrators to justice. Therefore, where 'force', 'threat of force or coercion', or 'taking advantage of coercive environment' is proven, the Chamber considers that the Prosecution does not need to prove the victim's lack of consent.").

30. See, e.g., Model Penal Code, Statutory Commentary, Sexual Assault and Related Offenses at 34 (American Law Institute, Preliminary Draft No. 4, Oct. 3, 2014).

31. Many survivors have said this to me. See also, e.g., Evelina Giobbe, "Prostitution: Buying the Right to Rape," in *Rape and Sexual Assault III: A Research Handbook* 144, Ann Wolbert Burgess, ed. (New York: Garland 1991) ("Prostitution is like rape . . . it felt like rape. It was rape to me."); Melissa Farley, "Prostitution Is Sexual Violence," *Psychiatric Times*, Oct. 1, 2004, http://www.psychiatrictimes.com/sexual-offenses/prostitution-sexual -violence (referring to prostitution as "'paid rape,' as one survivor described it").

32. For more on this, see sources cited in Catharine A. MacKinnon, "Trafficking, Prostitution, and Inequality," 46 *Harvard Civil Rights-Civil Liberties Law Review* 271 (2011).

33. Protocol to Prevent, Suppress and Punish Trafficking in Persons, Especially Women and Children, Supplementing the United Nations Convention Against Transnational Organized Crime art. 3(a)–(c), Nov. 15, 2000, TIAS 13127, 2237 U.N.T.S. 319, http://www.ohchr.org/EN/Professional Interest/Pages/ProtocolTraffickingInPersons.aspx.

34. Id.

35. See, e.g., Proposition [Prop.] 1997/98:55 Kvinnofrid [approx: Women's Sanctuary/Women's Peace] [government bill], 22 (Sweden) ("Men's violence against women is not consonant with the aspirations toward a gender equal society, and has to be fought against with all means. In such a society it is also unworthy and unacceptable that men obtain casual sex with women against remuneration.").

36. Ane Brun, "One," in *It All Starts with One* (Balloon Ranger Recordings 2011).

26. RESTORING INSTITUTIONAL ACCOUNTABILITY
FOR EDUCATIONAL SEXUAL HARASSMENT

1. Gebser v. Lago Vista Indept. Sch. Dist., 524 U.S. 274, 290 (1998) (deciding that the correct school officials must have notice of sexual harassment incidents and that their response "must amount to deliberate indifference to discrimination" for monetary damages to be available under Title IX).

2. This testimony, slightly modified here, was submitted to the Department of Education on May 28, 2013, at their request for submissions on Title IX. A fully developed version of this argument can be found at Catharine A. MacKinnon, "In Their Hands: Restoring Institutional Liability for Sexual Abuse in Education," 125 *Yale Law Journal* 2037 (2016).

3. Gebser, supra note 1.

4. Id. at 287–288.

5. 20 U.S.C. § 1681(a) (2006) ("No person in the United States shall, on the basis of sex . . . be denied the benefits of . . . any education program or activity receiving Federal financial assistance . . . .").

6. Alexander v. Yale University, 631 F.2d 178, 182, 185 (2d Cir. 1980) (affirming district court finding that plaintiff Price, who alleged that sexual harassment by a faculty member violated her sex equality rights under Title IX, could sue Yale University).

7. See, e.g., Billie Wright Dziech and Michael W. Hawkins, *Sexual Harassment and Higher Education: Reflections and New Perspectives* 31–32 (New York: Garland 1998) ("[B]y now most [colleges and universities] can claim to meet the basic standards of good policy and practice: (1) provide the campus community with a coherent and comprehensive definition of sexual harassment (most use the EEOC definition as a base), (2) issue a strong policy statement expressing disapproval of the behavior, (3) establish an accessible grievance procedure that allows for both formal and informal complaints, (4) conduct student, faculty, and staff programs that educate all constituencies about the problem, and (5) employ multiple sources (catalogues, posters, campus newspaper and radio and television presentations) to communicate policies and procedures."); Robert O. Riggs et al., *Sexual Harassment in Higher Education: From Conflict to Community* 33 (Washington, DC: George Washington University 1993) ("It was not until the early 1980s that sexual harassment was recognized as a problem of significant dimensions in higher education and incidents of harassment on campuses were documented by survey and published. Since that time, . . . the potential for institutional and individual liability has prompted colleges and universities to adopt policies to avert such problems.").

8. Franklin v. Gwinnett County Public Schools, 503 U.S. 60, 63–64, 72, 76 (1992) (holding that the implied private right of action under Title IX supports a claim for monetary damages).

9. See Gebser, 524 U.S. at 292–293 (creating deliberate indifference standard for faculty-student sexual harassment); Davis v. Monroe County Board of Education, 526 U.S. 629, 648 (1999) (applying same to peer sexual harassment).

10. A school can be "far from thorough," Thomas v. Board of Trustees of the Nebraska State Colleges, No. 8:12-CV-412, 2015 WL 4546712, at *13 (D. Neb. July 28, 2015), need not "use[] the best practices," Harden v. Rosie, 99 A.3d 950, 964 (Pa. Commw. Ct. 2014), can respond with "[n]egligent or careless conduct," T.L. ex rel. Lowry v. Sherwood Charter

School, 68 F. Supp. 3d 1295, 1309 (D. Or. 2014), and not be deliberately indifferent.

11. See, e.g., Roe v. St. Louis University, 746 F.3d 874, 883–884 (8th Cir. 2014) (citing the victim's stated desire for confidentiality as a factor in finding no deliberate indifference). OCR's encouragement of confidential reporting sources, predictably embraced by schools and trumpeted as an advance for survivor sensitivity, exacerbates this situation. Schools are now being "strongly encouraged" by OCR to designate virtually everyone that a survivor of sexual assault is likely to approach or trust as a "confidential source[]" for reporting. Office for Civil Rights, "Questions and Answers on Title IX and Sexual Violence," *U.S. Department of Education* 5–6 (Apr. 29, 2014), http://www2.ed.gov/about/offices/list/ocr/docs/qa -201404-title-ix.pdf. How a school as such becomes aware of a report for purposes of legal notice if it is provided to a "confidential source" is unclear. How schools can investigate allegations they cannot discuss—for example with the alleged perpetrator, which in most instances will identify the victim—is similarly unclear. "Confidentiality" means that even the fact of the allegations being made cannot be disclosed, although there are always exceptions for exigent circumstances and danger to others, meaning that the reassurance given to survivors may also be illusory. In the Q&A, OCR takes the position that confidential resource employees are not "responsible employees" within the meaning of Title IX. Id. This, combined with an earlier explanation that confidential sources are not responsible employees, seems to mean that the school does not have "notice" of sexual harassment that is reported only to a confidential resource, producing no obligation under Title IX to pursue such an investigation and no liability for failing to respond to a report. Thus, hiding behind sensitivity to survivors, who generally are responding to shame and a culture of blame and reflecting the stigma attached to them by their environments, produces what for OCR and victims, but not for schools, are doubtless unintended consequences for private litigation as institutional lack of accountability.

12. Alberto R. Gonzales et al., National Institute of Justice, U.S. Department of Justice, *Sexual Assault on Campus: What Colleges and Universities Are Doing About It*, 3, 6, 11 (2005), available at https://www.ncjrs .gov/pdffiles1/nij/205521.pdf; see also "Sexual Assault on Campus: A Frustrating Search for Justice," *Center for Public Integrity*, Feb. 24, 2010, http://www.publicintegrity.org/investigations/campus_assault/

(documenting procedural lapses and lack of consequences imposed by schools on perpetrators of sexual assault).

13. Its use for diverse claims across the legal system indicates just how not specifically equality-oriented the standard is. Deliberate indifference is used as a constitutional liability standard under § 1983 for the First Amendment, see, e.g., Schroeder *ex rel*. Schroeder v. Maumee Bd. of Education, 296 F. Supp. 2d 869, 877 (N.D. Ohio 2003), Fifth Amendment, see, e.g., Bistrian v. Levi, 696 F.3d 352, 367 (3d Cir. 2012), Eighth Amendment, see, e.g., Estelle v. Gamble, 429 U.S. 97, 106 (1976), and Fourteenth Amendment, see, e.g., City of Canton v. Harris, 489 U.S. 378, 388 (1989) (using it in the due process context); Gant *ex rel*. Gant v. Wallingford Board of Education, 195 F.3d 134, 140 (2d Cir. 1999) (using it in the equal protection context). It is also used for a range of claims in the criminal intent context. See, e.g., United States v. Threadgill, 172 F.3d 357, 368 (5th Cir. 1999); United States v. Jewell, 532 F.2d 697, 702–703 (9th Cir. 1976). Equality does not belong on a one-size-fits-all list.

14. The "due diligence" standard originated in international human rights law in Velásquez Rodrigues v. Honduras, Merits, Judgment, Inter-Am. Ct. H.R. (ser. C) No. 4, ¶ 172 (July 29, 1988), and has been widely accepted in many settings as the global standard for state accountability for violations of human rights by nonstate actors when state entities fail to prevent human rights violations or to respond to them effectively after the fact. The standard was adopted for sexual violations that discriminate against women on the basis of sex in Comm. on the Elimination of Discrimination Against Women, General Recommendation 19, ¶ 9, U.N. Doc. CEDAW/C/1992/L.1/Add. 15 (1992). An informative recent discussion, providing a basis for consideration of potential applications to U.S. law, can be found in Yakin Ertürk, "15 Years of the United Nations Special Rapporteur on Violence Against Women (1994–2009)," *Office of the High Commissioner for Human Rights*, http://www.ohchr.org/Documents/Issues /Women/15YearReviewofVAWMandate.pdf.

15. See Gebser, 524 U.S. at 292–293 (stating that the Court would apply the deliberate indifference standard "[u]ntil Congress speaks directly on the subject" of school district liability for sexual harassment). The Court stated it came to its conclusion "in the absence of further direction from Congress." Id. at 290.

16. See Franklin, 503 U.S. at 71–72, 76 (1992) (finding a "lack of any legislative intent to abandon the traditional presumption in favor of all available remedies" when Congress enacted Title IX).

17. "A Title IX Primer," *Women's Sports Foundation*, http://www.womens sportsfoundation.org/home/advocate/title-ix-and-issues/what-is-title -ix/title-ix-primer ("Despite the fact that most estimates are that 80 to 90 percent of all educational institutions are not in compliance with Title IX as it applies to athletics . . . withdrawal of federal moneys has never been initiated. When institutions are determined to be out of compliance with the law, the United States Department of Education Office for Civil Rights (OCR) typically finds them 'in compliance conditioned on remedying identified problems.'").

18. Violence Against Women Reauthorization Act of 2013, Pub. L. No. 113-4, sec. 304, 127 Stat. 54, 89–92 (2013) (requiring federally funded schools to institute certain response procedures and develop and distribute policy statements on sexual assault and related conduct).

19. See Letter from Russlynn Ali, Assistant Secretary for Civil Rights, U.S. Department of Education, Office of Civil Rights, Apr. 4, 2011, available at http://www2.ed.gov/about/offices/list/ocr/letters/colleague-201104.pdf (outlining schools' Title IX obligations with respect to sexual harassment and other sexual violence).

20. See, e.g., Diane L. Rosenfeld, "Changing Norms? Title IX and Legal Activism," 31 *Harvard Journal of Law & Gender* 407 (2008).

27. TOWARD A RENEWED EQUAL RIGHTS AMENDMENT

1. This analysis was given as the opening remarks on September 28, 2013, to the New ERA Brainstorming Session at Harvard Law School's conference "Celebrating 60 Years of Alumnae," together with Jessica Neuwirth, chair and animating force of the ERA Coalition, and former Congresswoman Elizabeth Holtzman, who was instrumental in the most recent previous ERA effort, particularly its time extension. It was previously published as Catharine A. MacKinnon, "Toward a Renewed ERA: Now More Than Ever," 37 *Harvard Journal of Gender and Law* 569 (2014). Some prior thoughts on the issues raised here can be found in Catharine A. MacKinnon, "Not by Law Alone: From a Debate with Phyllis Schlafly (1982)," in Catharine A. MacKinnon, *Feminism Unmodified: Discourses on Life and Law* 21 (Cambridge, MA: Harvard University Press 1987), and Catharine A. MacKinnon, "Unthinking ERA Thinking," in Catharine A. MacKinnon, ed., *Women's Lives, Men's Laws* 13 (Cambridge, MA: Belknap Press of Harvard University Press 2005).

2. See generally Catharine A. MacKinnon, "Reflections on Sex Equality Under Law," 100 *Yale Law Journal* 1281 (1991).

3. See, e.g., U.N. Development Program, Human Development 2013: The Rise of the South: Human Progress in a Diverse World 156–159, tbl.4 (2013); U.N. Department of Economic & Social Affairs, The World's Women 2010; Trends and Statistics, U.N. Doc. ST/ESA/STAT/SER.K/19, U.N. Sales No.E.10.XVII.11 (2010).

4. U.S. Constitution amend. XIV, § 1.

5. Civil Rights Act of 1964, 42 U.S.C. §§ 2000e-2000e-17 (2006).

6. Prominent examples are the combat exclusion, see, e.g., Press Release, U.S. Department of Defense, "Defense Department Rescinds Direct Combat Exclusion Rule; Service to Expand Integration of Women into Previously Restricted Occupations and Units," Jan. 24, 2013, archived at http://perma.cc/TW3Z-Z5EV, and gay and lesbian rights, see, e.g., United States v. Windsor, 133 S. Ct. 2675 (2013); Hollingsworth v. Perry, 133 S. Ct. 2652 (2013).

7. Equal Rights Amendment, H.R.J. Res. 208, 92d Cong. § 1 (1972) ("Equality of rights under the law shall not be denied or abridged by the United States or by any State on account of sex.").

8. H.R.J. Res. 56, 113th Cong. § 1 (2013).

9. Craig v. Boren, 429 U.S. 190, 211 n.* (1976) ("[Our] decision today will be viewed by some as a 'middle-tier' approach.") (Powell, J., concurring). Since VMI, United States v. Virginia, 518 U.S. 515, 557 (1996) (finding exclusion of women from military academy unconstitutional although very few women would be qualified: 'Women seeking and fit for a VMI-quality education cannot be offered anything less, under the Commonwealth's obligation to afford them genuinely equal protection"), it might be observed that sex is being strictly scrutinized, even if "strict scrutiny" has not been so declared.

10. "Strict scrutiny" originated in *Korematsu*, where the Supreme Court announced the requirement that "legal restrictions which curtail the civil rights of a single racial group" must be subjected to "the most rigid scrutiny." Korematsu v. United States, 323 U.S. 214, 216 (1944). With race the paradigm for constitutional strict scrutiny from the outset, the Court has come to apply "intermediate" or "second-tier" scrutiny to gender, with the Frontiero plurality momentarily mandating strict scrutiny of sex-based classifications based on the ill-fated premise that ERA would succeed in ratification. Frontiero v. Richardson, 411 U.S. 677, 688 (1973) (concluding that "classifications based upon sex, like classifications based upon race, alienage, or national origin, are inherently suspect, and must therefore be subjected to strict judicial scrutiny").

11. See Aristotle, *The Nicomachean Ethics*, 1131a–1131b, at 112–117, J. L. Ackrill and J.O. Urmson, eds., David Ross, trans. (Oxford: Oxford University Press 1980) (1925).

12. The deployment of the Aristotelian model throughout U.S. equality law is exhaustively demonstrated in Catharine A. MacKinnon, *Sex Equality* (3d ed., New York: Foundation Press 2016).

13. See, e.g., Washington v. Davis, 426 U.S. 229 (1976) (originating the constitutional intent requirement under the Fourteenth Amendment); Personnel Administrator v. Feeney, 442 U.S. 256 (1979) (applying a constitutional intent requirement to sex).

14. For example, the plaintiff/appellee in Town of Castle Rock v. Gonzales, 545 U.S. 748 (2005) had no remedy, and the case was not even brought as sex discrimination, perhaps for the reasons mentioned above. See also, e.g., Soto v. Flores, 103 F.3d 1056 (1st Cir. 1997) (affirming no intentional sex discrimination by police in failure to respond effectively to domestic violence calls); Hynson v. City of Chester Legal Department, 864 F.2d 1026 (3d Cir. 1988) (finding no equal protection violation absent clear evidence that intent to discriminate against women motivated differential treatment by police to victims of domestic versus nondomestic violence).

15. See generally Barbara A. Brown et al., "Equal Rights Amendment: A Constitutional Basis for Equal Rights for Women," 80 *Yale Law Journal* 871 (1971). Intent, as a constitutional requirement, was nowhere on the minds or in the field of vision of these authors because it had yet to be invented and imposed by the Supreme Court.

16. Economic Equity Act, H.R. 3117, 97th Cong. (1981); Economic Equity Act, S. 888, 97th Cong. (1981); see also Patricia A. Seith, "Congressional Power to Effect Sex Equality," 36 *Harvard Journal of Law & Gender* 1 (2013).

17. See American Association of University Women, *The Simple Truth About The Gender Pay Gap* 3, 3 fig.1 (Fall 2013).

18. See id. at 3; National Partnership for Women & Families, *Fact Sheet: America's Women and the Wage Gap* (Apr. 2013); see also Jessica Arons, Center for American Progress Action Fund, *Lifetime Losses: The Career Wage Gap* 2 (Dec. 2008) (relying on data from 2007, when women were earning 78 cents to every dollar earned by a man, to conclude that "the average full-time female worker loses approximately $434,000 in wages over a 40-year period as a direct result of the gender pay gap").

19. Data from 2012 show that 56.1 percent of poor children lived in female-headed households, while 13.2 percent of single mothers employed

year-round in full-time jobs were living in poverty. Joan Entmacher et al., National Women's Law Center, *Insecure and Unequal: Poverty and Income Among Women and Families 2000–2012* 4 (2003). Additionally, the poverty rate for female-headed families with children was 40.9 percent, compared to 22.6 percent for male-headed families with children, and 8.9 percent for families with children headed by a married couple. Poverty rates were about one in two for Black female-headed families with children (46.7 percent), Hispanic female-headed families with children (48.6 percent), foreign-born female-headed families with children (47.1 percent), and Native American female-headed families with children (56.9 percent). Id. This pattern is also borne out in research on the extreme poor. See H. Luke Shaefer and Kathryn Edin, National Poverty Ctr., Policy Brief No. 28, *Extreme Poverty in the United States, 1996 to 2011* 1, 4 tbl. 1 (2012) (finding that the percentage growth in extreme poverty—defined as those living on $2.00 or less per person, per day—between 1996 and 2011 was highest among single female households (190.6 percent)).

20. Shawn Mcmahon and Jessica Horning, Wider Opportunities for Women, *Living Below the Line: Economic Insecurity and America's Families* 5 (2013).

21. A recent study by the National Equal Pay Task Force, while noting progress over the past half century, underscored the persistence of occupational sex segregation despite efforts aimed to eliminate it. National Equal Pay Task Force, *Fifty Years After the Equal Pay Act: Assessing the Past, Taking Stock of the Future* 24 (2013) (*"Fifty Years After"*). Among the illustrative data set forth in support of this assertion is the striking finding that 44 percent of working men are employed in occupations that are over three-quarters male, compared to a mere 6 percent of women working in those same occupations. Id. See also Ariane Hegewisch et al., Institute for Women's Policy Research, Briefing Paper: *Separate and Not Equal? Gender Segregation in the Labor Market and the Gender Wage Gap* 13 (2010) (analyzing occupational data showing that "after a steady trend towards a more even distribution of men and women across occupations during the 1970s and 1980s, there has been no further progress since the late 1990s . . . [T]he data clearly confirm that gender is the predominant factor in occupational segregation in all major race and ethnic groups."); Jan Diehm and Margaret Wheeler Johnson, "Gender Wage Gap Heavily Influenced by Occupation Segregation (INFOGRAPHIC)," *Huffington Post*, June 1, 2013, http://www.huffingtonpost.com/2013/06/11/gender -wage-gap_n_3424084.html, archived at https://perma.cc/A3QZ-5HYG

(providing a visual representation of sex segregation in the contemporary U.S. workforce).

22. The Center for American Progress attributes 41 percent of the wage gap to "gender-based discrimination," in which they do not include occupational segregation. Sarah Jane Glynn, Center for American Progress, *Fact Sheet: The Wage Gap for Women* 3 (2012).

23. See National Equal Pay Task Force, *Fifty Years After* 24 (stating that "occupational segregation has important implications for closing the pay gap, because women are segregated into low-paying occupations and also typically earn less than men in the same field"); Institute for Women's Policy Research, *The Gender Wage Gap by Occupation* 1 (2010) (arguing that the pay differential that exists between male-dominated occupations and those that are predominantly female make "tackling occupational segregation . . . an important part of tackling the gender wage gap").

24. Rexroat v. Arizona Department of Education No. CIV. 11-1028-PHX-PGR, 2013 WL 85222, at 6 (D. Ariz. Jan. 7, 2013) (discussing Kouba v. Allstate Insurance Co. 691 F.2d 873, 876–877, 878 (9th Cir. 1982)). The case was appealed but appears to have settled in January, 2014, before the appeals court decision was issued.

25. See, e.g., Young v. United Parcel Service, Inc., No. DKC 08-2586, 2011 WL 665321 (D. Md. Feb. 14, 2011), *aff'd*, 707 F.3d 437 (4th Cir. 2013), *vacated and remanded*, 135 S. Ct. 1338 (2015), *opinion amended and superseded*, 784 F.3d 192 (4th Cir. 2015) (continuing to hold for UPS). The Docket Sheet shows the case dismissed with prejudice after a settlement conference following the Fourth Circuit decision. The line of cases finding denial of alternative job assignments for pregnant women not a violation of the Pregnancy Discrimination Act includes Anzanovska v. Wal-Mart Stores Inc., 682 F.3d 698 (7th Cir. 2012), Serednyj v. Beverly Healthcare, LLC, 656 P.3d 540 (7th Cir. 2011). Reeves v. Swift Transp. Co., 446 F.3d 637 (6th Cir. 2006), Spivey v. Beverly Enterprise, Inc., 196 F.3d 1309 (11th Cir. 1999), and Urbano v. Continental Airlines, Inc., 138 F.3d 204 (5th Cir. 1998).

26. See, e.g., Wiseman v. Wal-Mart Stores, Inc., No. 08-1244-EFM, 2009 WL1617669, at *1 (D. Kan. June 9, 2009) (holding pregnant plaintiff's claim that firing due to "insubordination" for drinking from a water bottle to prevent urinary and bladder problems from dehydration not discriminatorily based on pregnancy and attendant medical conditions).

27. See, e.g., Greg J. Duncan and Saul D. Hoffman, "Economic Consequences of Marital Instability," in *Horizontal Equity, Uncertainty, and Economic Well-Being* 449–450, Martin David and Timothy Smeeding, eds. (Chicago:

University of Chicago Press 1985) (illustrating how the movement of women and children in and out of marriage parallels their entrance to and exit from poverty); Saul D. Hoffman and Greg J. Duncan, "What Are the Economic Consequences of Divorce?," 25 *Demography* 641, 644 (1988) (concluding that creditable "estimates suggest a decline in (divorced women's) economic status of about one third"); Richard R. Peterson, "A Re-evaluation of the Economic Consequences of Divorce," 61 *American Social Review* 528, 534 (1996) (finding a 27 percent decline in women's post-divorce standard of living as compared to a 10 percent increase in men's).

28. See, e.g., City of Washington v. Gunther, 452 U.S. 161 (1981); American Federation of State, County, & Municipal Employees v. Washington, 770 F.2d 1401, 1407 (9th Cir. 1985); Lemons v. City of Denver, No.76-W-1156, 1978 WL 13938, at *13 (D. Colo. Apr. 17, 1978).

29. Geduldig v. Aiello, 417 U.S. 484, 496 n.20 (1974).

30. Pregnancy Discrimination Act, Pub. L. No.95-SSS, 92 Stat. 2076 (1978) (codified at 42 U.S.C. § 2000e(k) (2006)).

31. Patient Protection and Affordable Care Act, 42 U.S.C. § 711 (Supp. V 2011) (establishing maternal, infant, and early childhood home visiting programs); id. § 712 (providing funds for research on post-partum conditions and programs for women and families of women experiencing post-partum conditions); id. §§ 18202–18203 (funding both pregnancy assistance programs at educational institutions and services for pregnant women who have been subjected to sexual or domestic violence).

32. See Majority Staff of Senate Committee on the Judiciary, 102d Cong., *Violence Against Women: A Week in the Life of America* (Comm. Print 1992); see also Okin v. Village of Cornwall-on-Hudson Police Department, 577 F.3d 415, 442 (2d Cir. 2009) (upholding victim's right to sue police on due process but not equal protection grounds when they did not respond to reports of ongoing domestic violence); Soto v. Flores, 103 F.3d 1056, 1072 (1st Cir. 1997) (supra note 14); McKee v. City of Rockwall, 877 F.2d 409, 416 (5th Cir. 1989) (rejecting claim of gender-based discrimination in officers' refusal to arrest as insufficient to prove policy in domestic violence cases); Watson v. City of Kansas City, 857 F.2d 690, 696–697 (10th Cir. 1988) (holding insufficient evidence of sex as motive for discrimination in police failure to provide equal protection of the law in rape and stabbing of wife of police officer).

33. Violence Against Women Act of 1994, Pub. L. No. 103-322, 108 Stat. 1902 (1994) (codified as amended in scattered sections of the U.S. Code).

NOTES TO PAGES 302–303

34. United States v. Morrison, 529 U.S. 598, 627 (2000).
35. See, e.g., Diana E. H. Russell, *Rape in Marriage* 303 (expanded and rev. ed., Indianapolis, IN: Indiana University Press 1990) (1982) (finding that 9.5 percent of extramarital rapes committed were ever reported to authorities); Michael Planty et al., U.S. Department of Justice, Ncj 240655, *Special Report: Female Victims of Sexual Violence, 1994–2010* 6 (2013) (identifying significant fluctuations in rates of rape reporting over time, with 29 percent of victims reporting the crime to police in 1995, 56 percent in 2003, and 35 percent in 2010).
36. For a range of outcomes, see Rebecca Campbell, "The Psychological Impact of Rape Victims' Experiences with the Legal, Medical, and Mental Health Systems," 63 *American Psychologist* 702, 704 (2008) (reporting that "overall, case attrition is staggering: For every 100 rape cases reported to law enforcement, on average thirty-three would be referred to prosecutors, sixteen would be charged and moved into the court system, twelve would end in a successful conviction, and seven would end in a prison sentence"), and Patricia A. Frazier and Beth Haney, "Sexual Assault Cases in the Legal System: Police, Prosecutor, and Victim Perspectives" 20 *Law & Human Behavior* 607, 622 (1996) (finding that "substantial attrition continues to occur in the prosecution of rape cases" with most "occur[ring] in the initial stages of the process" such that fewer than 25 percent of reported cases are referred for prosecution). See also Sharon B. Murphy et al., "Exploring Stakeholders' Perceptions of Adult Female Sexual Assault Case Attrition," 3 *Psychology of Violence* 172 (2013) (examining potential causes of and remedies for persistently high levels of rape case attrition).
37. See, e.g., "Backlog of Untested Rape Kits Drawing Attention of U.S. Legislators," *The Guardian*, Feb. 24, 2014, http://www.theguardian.com /world/2014/feb/24/untested-rape-kits-backlog-us-legislators, archived at http://perma.cc/N4SQ-YV89 (reporting that around 400,000 untested rape kits have been counted nationwide.); Mario Garcia et al., "Prosecutor Leads Effort to Test Long-Abandoned Rape Kits, Brings Justice to Victims," *NBC News*, Feb. 15, 2013, http://rockcenter.nbcnews .com/_news/2013/02/15/15848051-prosecutor-leads-effort-to-test-long -abandoned-rape-kits-brings-justice-to-victims?lite, archived at https:// perma.cc/BP2C-6VRJ.
38. H.R.J. Res. 56, 113th Cong. § 1 (2013).
39. Id.

40. See generally MacKinnon, supra note 12, at ch. 8; Catharine A. Mac-Kinnon, *The Road Not Taken: Sex Equality in* Lawrence v. Texas, 65 *Ohio State Law Journal* 1081 (2004).

41. On the intersection of race and sex, see generally Kimberlé Williams Crenshaw, "Demarginalizing the Intersection of Race and Sex: A Black Feminist Critique of Antidiscrimination Doctrine, Feminist Theory and Antiracist Politics," 1989 *University of Chicago Legal Forum* 139 (1989), and Kimberlé Crenshaw, "Mapping the Margins: Intersectionality, Identity Politics, and Violence Against Women of Color," 43 *Stanford Law Review* 1241 (1991).

42. See supra note 13.

43. Catharine A. MacKinnon, "Gender in Constitutions," in *The Oxford Handbook of Comparative Constitutional Law* 397, 404, Michel Rosenfeld and András Sajó, eds. (Oxford: Oxford University Press 2012).

44. Id. at 405.

45. "The Originalist: Justice Antonin Scalia," *California Lawyer*, Jan. 2011, archived at http://perma.cc/X7Z4-MTQ6. In response to a question posed by Sen. Dianne Feinstein in a hearing before the Senate Judiciary Committee, he later said his remarks were meant only to apply to private discrimination. See Ian Millhiser, "Justice Scalia Appears to Back Off His Claim That the Constitution Does Not Prevent Gender Discrimination," *Think Progress*, Oct. 7, 2011, http://thinkprogress.org/justice/2011/10/07 /337419/scalia-and-women, archived at http://perma.cc/W2V3-XD63. Such a statement, as well as its purported clarification, reveals (inter alia) the presuppositions of the negative state in full force.

28. SEX EQUALITY IN GLOBAL PERSPECTIVE

1. Much was learned delivering parts of this discussion at The European International University in 2011, in French at The Sorbonne, Paris, in January 2013, and at the Knesset, Jerusalem, during bombardment on July 23, 2014. The discussion of it at Fordham Law School, October 29, 2014, was unusually vibrant and acute. This version was delivered at the University of Western Australia, Perth, Australia, on February 17, 2015, co-sponsored by John Toohey Chambers. Gratitude goes to Christopher Kendall for his support, brilliance, and friendship.

2. See, e.g., Yoav Dotan, "The Boundaries of Social Transformation Through Litigation: Women's and LGBT Rights in Israel, 1970–2010," 48 *Israel Law Review* 3 (2015).

3. Aristotle, *Nicomachean Ethics* 1131a–1131b, 112–114, J. L. Ackrill and J. O. Urmson, eds., David Ross, trans. (Oxford: Oxford University Press, 1980).

4. Aristotle, *The Politics* 232, Benjamin Jowett, trans. (Oxford: Clarendon Press, 1885).

5. See Catharine A. MacKinnon, "Gender in Constitutions," in *The Oxford Handbook of Comparative Constitutional Law* 397, Michel Rosenfeld and András Sajó, eds. (Oxford: Oxford University Press, 2012).

6. In Israel, since independence in 1948, with the formal guarantees of the Women's Equal Rights Law in 1951, sex equality has been extended legislatively in 1998 and in the 2000 amendments; specific legislation on pay, sexual harassment, and stalking have been added. Sex equality has been interpreted under the Basic Law as a dimension of the dignity guarantee; see HCJ 4541/94 Alice Miller v. Minister of Defence 49(4) PD 94 (1995) (Isr.).

7. See Catharine A. MacKinnon, *Sexual Harassment of Working Women: A Case of Sex Discrimination* (New Haven, CT: Yale University Press 1979), on the analysis that sexual aggression is a practice of sex discrimination.

8. Andrews v. Law Society of B.C., [1989] 1 S.C.R. 143 (Can.).

9. See infra notes 39–43, 46, 47, 49, 51, 52, 60, 65–67.

10. For further documentation and analysis, see Catharine A. MacKinnon, "Creating International Law: Gender as Leading Edge," 36 *Harvard Journal of Law & Gender* 105 (2013).

11. See, crucially, M. C. v. Bulgaria, 15 Eur. Ct. H.R. 627 (2003).

12. This began with Ontario v. M. & H. [1999] 171 D.L.R. 4th 577 (Can.), has gone more or less viral, and was repudiated in R. v. Kapp, [2008] 2 S.C.R. 483 (Can.).

13. Basic Law: Human Dignity and Liberty, 5752-1992 (Isr.); HCJ 4541/94 Alice Miller v. Minister of Defence 49(4) PD 94 (1995) (Isr.).

14. See M. C. v. Bulgaria, 15 Eur. Ct. H.R. 627 (2003); Vertido v. The Philippines, Communication No. 18/2008, U.N. Doc. CEDAW/C/46/D/18/2008 (Sept. 22, 2010).

15. This is explored in Catharine A. MacKinnon, "Sex Equality: On Difference and Dominance," in *Toward a Feminist Theory of the State* (Cambridge, MA: Harvard University Press 1989), and throughout Catharine A. MacKinnon, *Sex Equality* (3rd ed., New York, Foundation Press 2016).

16. File No. 23834-04-13 District Court (Jerusalem), State of Israel v. Ras (Apr. 24, 2013), Takdin Legal Database (by subscription) (Isr.), translation

available at http://womenofthewall.org.il/wpcontent/uploads/2012/06
/Final-File_Women-of-the-Wall-Ruling_April-25-2013-2.pdf (holding that
the Women of the Wall could not have committed a breach of the peace
by wrapping themselves in prayer shawls and reading aloud from the Torah
at the Western Wall in violation of local custom, recognizing that they had
acquired the right to pray according to their own custom). This dispute is to
a considerable extent ongoing.

17. See Geduldig v. Aiello, 417 U.S. 484 (1974). The Pregnancy Discrimination Act (PDA) in 1978 amended Title VII to include discrimination
"because of or on the basis of pregnancy" as a form of discrimination on
the basis of sex. 42 U.S.C. § 2000e(k) (1978). This overruled the *Geduldig*
result but did not and could not change its constitutional reasoning for
situations that the PDA does not reach.

18. For constitutional sex equality doctrine on sex classifications, see Reed v.
Reed, 404 U.S. 71 (1971) (subjecting sex to rational basis review); Frontiero v. Richardson, 411 U.S. 677 (1973) (plurality subjecting sex to strict
scrutiny, not legally in effect); and Craig v. Boren, 429 U.S. 190 (1976)
(subjecting sex to middle tier scrutiny).

19. This becomes especially vivid upon observing that affirmative action is
more difficult to justify for race, which receives strict scrutiny, and easier
to justify for sex, which receives intermediate scrutiny.

20. See Maloney v. The Queen [2013] HCA 28 (upholding conviction for possession of alcohol above legislative restrictions on Palm Island, a location
with an almost entirely indigenous population, found justified as "special
measure" under Racial Discrimination Act 1975).

21. See Town of Castle Rock, Colo. v. Gonzales, 545 U.S. 748 (2005); Lenahan (Gonzales) v. United States, Case 12.626, Inter-Am. Comm'n H.R.,
Report No. 80/11 (2011).

22. See World Economic Forum, *The Global Gender Gap Report 2013* 8
tbl.3a (Geneva: World Economic Forum 2013), accessed August 7, 2016,
http://www3.weforum.org/docs/WEF_GenderGap_Report_2013.pdf.

23. For a vivid illustration, compare the opinions of Justice Spina and Justice
Cordy in Goodridge v. Department of Public Health, 798 N.E.2d 941, 974
(Mass. 2003) (Spina, J., dissenting); id. at 983 (Cordy, J., dissenting).

24. Plessy v. Ferguson, 163 U.S. 537, 559 (1896) (Harlan, J., dissenting) ("Our
constitution is color-blind").

25. Andrews v. Law Society of B.C., [1989] 1 S.C.R. 143 (Can.).

26. An example is the test in Law v. Canada, [1999] 1 S.C.R. 497, 523–524
(Can.).

27. R. v. Kapp, [2008] 2 S.C.R. 483, 504 ¶ 22 (Can.).
28. Id.
29. Peter W. Hogg, *Constitutional Law of Canada*, vol. 2 55-53 (5th ed. Supp., Toronto: Carswell 2007), as quoted in *Kapp*, at 511 ¶ 37. One pertinent example involving domestic violence is R. v. Lavallee, [1990] 1 S.C.R. 852, 871–889 (Can.).
30. See Immanuel Kant, *Grounding for the Metaphysics of Morals* 39–41, James W. Ellington, trans. (3rd ed., Indianapolis, IN: Hackett Publishing Co., 1993) (1785).
31. Not being used as a mere means to another's ends—a Kantian notion of dignity not explicitly used in most law—could help women in some situations. It might forthrightly condemn prostitution, for example, although dignity's enthusiasts have not seemed to notice. Yet many women dedicate themselves to being instruments to the ends of others with whom they are in relation, such as their children, as do many people of both sexes, such as police officers or soldiers, who understand the purpose of their lives in communal terms as giving them dignity rather than sacrificing it. Perhaps "mere" makes a difference here?
32. Brown v. Bd. of Ed. of Topeka, Shawnee Cty., Kan., 347 U.S. 483, 494 (1954).
33. See also HC 6698/95 Ka'adan v. Israel Lands Administration, 54(1) PD 258 ¶ 30 (2000) (Isr.) (citing to Brown v. Bd. of Ed. of Topeka, Shawnee Cty., Kan., 347 U.S. 483 (1954)) (noting that "[a]t the core of this approach is the notion that separation conveys an affront to a minority group that is excluded, sharpens the difference between it and others, and cements feelings of social inferiority" and finding that because Israel has policies regarding allocation of state land for Jewish communal settlements but not for Arab communal settlements, the effect "of the separation policy, as practiced today, is discriminatory, even if the motive for the separation is not the desire to discriminate. The existence of discrimination is determined, inter alia, by the effect of the decision or policy, and the effect of the policy in the case before us is discriminatory.").
34. This is expressly recognized in R. v. Turpin, [1989] 1 S.C.R. 1296, 1330–1334 (Can.).
35. Herbert Wechsler, "Toward Neutral Principles of Constitutional Law," 73 *Harvard Law Review* 1, 33–34 (1959) (quoting Plessy v. Ferguson, 163 U.S. 537, 551 (1896) ("In the context of a charge that segregation *with equal facilities* is a denial of equality, is there not a point in *Plessy* in the statement that if 'enforced separation stamps the colored race with a

badge of inferiority' it is solely because its members choose 'to put that construction upon it'?").

36. See People v. Superior Court (Hartway), 562 P.2d 1315, 1319–1320 (Cal. 1977). For a contrast between the formal equality approach and the substantive equality approach of the dissent on the subject of prostitution, see also S v. Jordan and Others 2002 (6) SA 642 (CC) at 44–45 para. 73 (S. Afr.) (O'Regan, J., and Sachs, J., dissenting), available at http://www .saflii.org/za/cases/ZACC/2002/22.pdf.

37. See Brottsbalken [BrB] [Criminal Code] 6:11 (Swed.) ("[a] person who, otherwise than as previously provided in this Chapter [on Sexual Crimes], obtains a casual sexual relation in return for payment, shall be sentenced for purchase of sexual service to a fine or imprisonment for at most six months. [This law] also applies if the payment was promised or given by another person . . . ." (passed in 2005, amending Lag om förbud mot köp av sexuella tjänster (Svensk författnigssamling [SFS] 1998:408), which took effect January 1999)); Law Amending the Penal Code and Criminal Procedure Act of 1902, No. 104 (2008) (Nor.), available at http://www .lovdata.no/cgiwift/ldles?doc=/all/nl-20081212-104.html (As of January 1, 2009, citizens of Norway were prohibited from paying for sex domestically or abroad); Lög um breytingu á almennum hegningarlögum, nr. 19/1940, með sí ðari breytingum [Icelandic Law No. 54 of 2009] (2009) (Ice.) (Iceland made the purchase of sexual services illegal in 2009); National Assembly (Fr.), Texte Adopté 716 Proposition de loi visant à renforcer la lutte contre le système prostitutionnel et à accompagner les personnes prostituées, Apr. 6, 2016, available at http://www2.assemblee -nationale.fr/documents/notice/14/ta/ta0716/%28index%29/ta; "France prostitution: MPs outlaw paying for sex," *BBC News*, Apr. 7, 2016, http://www.bbc.com/news/world-europe-35982929; Protection of Communities and Exploited Persons Act, Bill C-36, 41st Parliament (2d Sess. 2014) (Can.) (passing Commons); Rebecca Anna Stoil, "Knesset Bill Seeks to Ban Hiring a Prostitute," *Jerusalem Post*, Dec. 21, 2009, at 4.

38. For further discussion and documentation, see Catharine A. MacKinnon, "Trafficking, Prostitution, and Inequality," 46 *Harvard Civil Rights-Civil Liberties Law Review* 271, 301–304 (2011).

39. As to violence against women, for example, this is true in the United States, even if no authority has denied that violence against women is sex discriminatory, and the U.S. Congress once adopted the theory argued here. See, e.g., H.R. Rep. No. 103-711, at 152 (1994) (Conf. Rep.); S. Rep. No. 102-197, at 42 (1991). The case that invalidated the civil remedy af-

forded by the Violence Against Women Act (VAWA) did so for impermissible use of the federal legislative power—wrongly in my view—but did not question that violence against women may be cognized as sex discrimination. See United States v. Morrison, 529 U.S. 598, 617–620 (2000).

40. Recommendation No. 19, ¶ 6, U.N. Doc. A/47/38 (Feb. 1, 1992). CEDAW has always been broad-gauged socially, economically, and culturally, but largely formal and conventional so far as its concept of equality itself is concerned, and did not originally mention violence against women.

41. Protocol to the African Charter on Human and Peoples' Rights on the Rights of Women in Africa, O.A.U. Doc. CAB/LEG/66.6, adopted July 11, 2003, entered into force Nov. 25, 2005, http://www.achpr.org/files /instruments/women-protocol/achpr_instr_proto_women_eng.pdf [Maputo Protocol].

42. See Maria da Penha Fernandes v. Brazil, Case 12.051, Inter-Am. Comm'n H.R., Report No. 54/01, OEA/Ser.L./III.111, doc. 20 (2001), http://cidh .org/annualrep/2000eng/ChapterIII/Merits/Brazil12.051.htm.

43. Inter-American Convention on the Prevention, Punishment and Eradication of Violence Against Women, June 9, 1994, 33 I.L.M. 1534, http://www .oas.org/juridico/english/treaties/a-61.html. The Maputo Protocol, supra note 40, also includes economic harm. See also U.N. Secretary-General, *In-Depth Study on All Forms of Violence Against Women*, U.N. Doc. A/61/122/Add. 1 (July 6, 2006).

44. Opuz v. Turkey, App. No. 33401/02 Eur. Ct. H.R. ¶ 153 (2009), http:// hudoc.echr.coe.int/sites/eng/pages/search.aspx?i=001-92945.

45. Id. at ¶ 200.

46. Id.

47. Final Observations Regarding the Merits of the Case at 149, Lenahan (Gonzales) v. United States, Case 12.626, Inter-Am. Comm'n H.R., Report No. 80/11 (2011).

48. See Rome Statute of the International Criminal Court, art. 7, ¶ 1(g), July 17, 1998, 2187 U.N.T.S. 3 ["Rome Statute of the International Criminal Court"] (defining "crime against humanity" to include "[r]ape, sexual slavery, enforced prostitution, forced pregnancy, enforced sterilization, or any other form of sexual violence of comparable gravity"); id. art. 7, ¶ 1(h) (recognizing persecution based on gender as a "crime against humanity"); id. art. 8, ¶ 2(b)(xxii) (defining "war crimes" perpetrated during international armed conflicts to include "rape, sexual slavery, enforced prostitution, forced pregnancy, as defined in article 7, paragraph 2 (f), enforced sterilization, or any other form of sexual violence also constituting

a grave breach of the Geneva Conventions"); id. art. 8, ¶ 2(e)(vi) (extending definition to encompass noninternational armed conflicts); id. art. 6(b) (defining "genocide" to include "[c]ausing serious bodily or mental harm to members of [a] group," which has been interpreted to apply to sexual atrocities in genocides). Almost all the first cases prosecuted include gender crimes in some form. See, e.g., Prosecutor v. Katanga, Case No. ICC-01/04-01/07, Decision on the Confirmation of Charges, ¶¶ 339–354 (Sept. 30, 2008), https://www.icc-cpi.int/CourtRecords/CR2008 _05172.PDF.

49. See Rome Statute of the International Criminal Court at art. 21 ¶ 3.

50. Prosecutor v. Akayesu, Case No. ICTR-96-4-T, Judgment, ¶ 688 (Sept. 2, 1998), http://www.unictr.org/Portals/0/Case/English/Akayesu/judgement /akay001.pdf.

51. Id.

52. M. C. v. Bulgaria, 15 Eur. Ct. H.R. 627 (2003).

53. Vertido v. The Philippines, Communication No. 18/2008, U.N. Doc. CEDAW/C/46/D/18/2008 (Sept. 22, 2010).

54. Id. at ¶ 8.9 (b)(i). See also id. at ¶ 8.7.

55. Penal Law, 5737-1977, § 345 (Isr.).

56. Liz Kelly, Jo Lovett, and Linda Regan, *Home Office Research Study 293: A Gap Or A Chasm? Attrition In Reported Rape Cases* 28 tbl.3.3 (2005), http://webarchive.nationalarchives.gov.uk/20110218135832/rds .homeoffice.gov.uk/rds/pdfs05/hors293.pdf. See also Jessica Harris and Sharon Grace, *Home Office Research Study 196: A Question of Evidence? Investigating and Prosecuting Rape in the 1990s* (1999), http://webarchive .nationalarchives.gov.uk/20110220105210/rds.homeoffice.gov.uk/rds /pdfs/hors196.pdf.

57. David Hume was vividly clear on this; see David Hume, "Essay XII: Of the Original Contract," in *Essays: Moral, Political, and Literary* vol. 1 450, ed. T. H. Green and T. H. Grose (London: Longmans, Green, and Co., 1875) ("My intention here is not to exclude the consent of the people from being one just foundation of government where it has place. It is surely the best and most sacred of any. I only pretend that it has very seldom had place in any degree, and never almost in its full extent. And that therefore some other foundation of government must also be admitted.").

58. See John Locke, *Two Treatises on Government* 293, ¶ 121 (London 1821). For a distinct but related doctrine, see Thomas Hobbes, *Leviathan: Or the Matter, Forme & Power of a Commonwealth, Ecclesiasticall and Civill* 521–522, A. R. Waller, ed. (Cambridge: Cambridge University Press, 1904).

59. See Stephen J. Schulhofer, *Unwanted Sex: The Culture of Intimidation and the Failure of Law* (Cambridge, MA: Harvard University Press 1998); Catharine A. MacKinnon, "Unequal Sex: A Sex Equality Approach to Sexual Assault," in *Women's Lives, Men's Laws* 240 (Cambridge, MA: Belknap Press of Harvard University Press 2005).

60. See, e.g., George E. Buzash, "The 'Rough Sex' Defense," 80 *Journal of Criminal Law & Criminology* 557, 557 (1989) ("The 'rough sex' defense in murder cases has displayed the potential to become both the updated 1990s version of the 'she asked for it' defense and a formidable obstacle to prosecutors trying to secure a murder conviction in a homicide involving a male offender and a female victim."). For a recent selection of voluminous press reports of the "rough sex" defense in sexual assault cases, see, e.g., "Airport Workers Stop Alleged Rape," *Charleston Gazette*, June 15, 2011, at C4; M. L. Nestel, "War Machine Mocks Rape Case in Court," *Daily Beast* (Nov. 26, 2015), http://www.thedailybeast.com /articles/2015/11/26/war-machine-mocks-rape-case-in-court.html; Jim Phillips, "Defense Attorney in Rape Case: Alleged Victim Wanted 'Rough Sex,' " *Athens News* (Oct. 29, 2009), http://www.athensnews.com/news/local /defense-attorney-in-rape-case-alleged-victim-wantedrough-sex/article _c51ddeea-c3f2-5b47-a2ba-9625a4fb8018.html.

61. Protocol to Prevent, Suppress and Punish Trafficking in Persons, Especially Women and Children, Supplementing the U.N. Convention Against Transnational Organized Crime, G.A. Res. 55/25, 55 U.N. GAOR Supp. (No. 49), U.N. Doc. A/45/49 (Vol. I) (2001).

62. Rantsev v. Cyprus & Russia, App. No. 25965/04 Eur. Ct. H.R. (2010).

63. Id. at 8 ¶ 41.

64. Id. at 76 ¶ 316.

65. Id. at 70 ¶ 293, 76 ¶ 318.

66. Id. at 49–50 ¶ 220–223.

67. For a substantive equality analysis of gender-based killing of women in Ciudad Juarez, Mexico, and surrounding area, see González ("Cotton Field") v. Mexico, Preliminary Objection, Merits, Reparations, and Costs, Judgment, Inter-Am. Ct. H.R. (ser. C) No. 205 (Nov. 16, 2009).

68. S/Res/2122 (Oct. 18, 2013); see also Valerie M. Hudson, Bonnie Ballif-Spanvill, Mary Caprioli, and Chad F. Emmett, *Sex and World Peace* (New York: Columbia University Press 2012).

69. For developments on the Security Council's Intervention Brigade, see S/ RES/2098 (March 28, 2013); S/RES/2147 (March 28, 2014); S/RES/2211 (March 25, 2015).

70. General Recommendation No. 30 on Women in Conflict Prevention, Conflict and Post-Conflict Situations, U.N. Doc. CEDAW/C/GC/30 (Oct. 18, 2013).

INTERVENING FOR CHANGE, 1976–2016

1. The paper can be found at Catharine A. MacKinnon Papers, 1946–2008; Paper: "Political Lawyers: Theories of Their Practice," 1976. MC 703, folder 15.3v. Schlesinger Library, Radcliffe Institute, Harvard University, Cambridge, Mass. (hereinafter, Political Lawyers).

2. Id. at 1.

3. Id. at 11.

4. Id. at 6.

5. Id. at 12.

6. Id. at 8.

7. Id. at 21.

8. Id. at 18.

9. Patty Reinert et al., "Jasper Killer Gets Death Penalty," *Houston Chronicle*, Feb. 26, 1999, at A1 and Lee Hancock, "Jasper Man to Die for Murder—Justice Is Served, Victim's Kin Say," *Dallas Morning News*, Feb. 26, 1999, at 1A (reporting on trial of John William King and death sentence, documenting that the jury consisted of eleven white members and one African-American member who was elected foreperson); Bruce Tomaso, "2nd Jasper Killer Sentenced to Death," *Dallas Morning News*, Sept. 24, 1999, at 1A (reporting Lawrence Russell Brewer, the second defendant in Mr. Byrd's murder, was sentenced to death by a jury of eleven white members and one Hispanic member); C. Bryson Hull, "Third Dragging Death Defendant Convicted, Sentenced to Life in Prison," *Associated Press*, Nov. 19, 1999 and Barry Schlachter, "Berry Gets Life Sentence in Jasper Dragging Death," *Fort Worth Star-Telegram*, Nov. 19, 1999, at 1 (reporting on Shawn Allen Berry, the third defendant in Mr. Byrd's murder, sentenced to life in prison with eligibility for parole after forty years by a jury of all white members).

10. After Pinochet arrived in the UK in 1998, he was arrested on a warrant from Spanish authorities for alleged torture and murder of Spanish citizens in Chile while he was a Chilean dictator. During sixteen months of legal proceedings, he unsuccessfully argued he was entitled to former head-of-state immunity. See R. v. Bartle and the Commissioner of Police for the Metropolis, Ex Parte Pinochet [1998] UKHL 41 (holding Pinochet not entitled to state immunity as former head of state for internationally recog-

nized crimes). His appeals failed when the House of Lords decided in March 1999 that he could be extradited to Spain for alleged crimes committed after September 1988, when UK legislation implemented the UN Convention Against Torture. See R. v. Bartle and the Commissioner of Police for the Metropolis, Ex Parte Pinochet [1999] UKHL 17. Ultimately, in March 2000, UK Home Secretary Jack Straw decided not to extradite Pinochet to Spain on account of his health and medical conditions, and he was released back to Chile. Warren Hoge, "After 16 Months of House Arrest, Pinochet Quits England," *New York Times*, March 3, 2000 at A6.

11. In light of the focus over the years to come, surprisingly little attention was devoted to women in the 1976 paper. One exception is an application of a distinction made by Robert Dahl between incremental, comprehensive, and revolutionary change at Robert A. Dahl, *Pluralist Democracy in the United States: Conflict and Consent* 236 (1967):

> [G]uaranteeing legal equality for women through affirmative action, the Equal Rights Amendment, equal protection attacks, and so forth is no change at all, or an incremental change, to those who think women are already better than equal or essentially equal already. [I]t is a comprehensive change to those who see barriers to women's equal advancement as backward widespread unjustifiable irrationalities and qualifications upon merit. It is revolutionary to those who see women's legal inequality as integral to their social oppression and economic exploitation [.]

Political Lawyers at 9.

12. Id. at 8.

13. This is considered in detail in Catharine A. MacKinnon, "Afterword," in *Directions in Sexual Harassment Law*, Catharine A. MacKinnon and Reva B. Siegel, eds. (New Haven, CT: Yale University Press 2004).

14. That men's sexual access to women is supported by legal recognition of the abortion right is argued in Catharine A. MacKinnon, "Abortion: On Public and Private," in *Feminism Unmodified: Discourses in Life and Law* (Cambridge, MA: Harvard University Press 1987).

15. Political Lawyers at 26, 28.

16. Id. at 25.

17. Id. at 17.

18. Some of the ideas and language in this and the foregoing paragraph draw on Catharine A. MacKinnon, "Women and Law: The Power to Change," in *Sisterhood Is Forever: The Women's Anthology for a New Millennium*, Robin Morgan, ed. (New York: Washington Square Press 2003) 447, 453–454.

ACKNOWLEDGMENTS

Each of the pieces in the forty years spanned by this volume mentions its own story and its own people. Short of listing everyone who has made my life possible and beautiful during that time, a few stand out, Kent Harvey, Jerry Minkoff, Harvey Schwartz, George McCann, Randy Benway, Adolfo Rico, Lisa Cardyn, Nancy Ruth, Natalie Hanson, and Diane Ellis prominently among them.

Those who helped with this volume specifically—for research, Seth Quidachay Swan and Victoria Neisler of the indispensably stellar University of Michigan Law Library; for endnotes, Madeline Buck, Matthew Lindgren, Nayoung Kim, and Mary Shelly—have my eternal gratitude.

When other obligations seemed overwhelming, Amelia Vander-Laan's inquiries after the health of this volume let me know that one young reader looked forward to its emergence. The friendship and acuity of Marcela Rodriguez and Lori Watson, their excitement over this book and its prospects for reaching its audience, have been sustaining during its gestation as a collection.

Lindsay Waters made this book possible. Because of him, my work lives in the world.

The incomparable Andrea Dworkin and the valiant Linda Boreman inspire me every day. We go on.

INDEX

AAUP (American Association of
University Professors), 262, 430n1
Abortion, in Ireland, 137
Abu Ghraib incident and scandal,
201–202
Academia: discriminatory tenure
decisions in, 247–248; pressures for
conformity in, 246; sexual politics
in, 279–281; women in, 39–40
Academic freedom: core principle of,
242–243, 262; as defense to student
claims of discrimination, 253–262;
feminism and, 248–249; First
Amendment and, 244, 253; as
freedom to be academic, 252–253;
intellectual freedom and, 242–243,
249–250, 253; literature on, 242;
orthodoxies and, 245–247; paradox
of, 243, 245, 253; in practice, 247;
purpose of, 243–245; self-censorship
and, 249–251; tenure and, 251–252;
trajectory of, 242
Academic publishing, 252
Accountability: avoidance of, 31; due
diligence standard and, 291, 293,
294
ACLU (American Civil Liberties
Union): speech given to, 189–198;
views on pornography of, 401n29
Affirmative action, 116, 245, 310
Affirmative diversity, 297
Agency and "sex work" model of
prostitution, 163–164, 179
Akayesu (Prosecutor v. Akayesu) case,
289, 319, 335–336n21
Alexander v. Yale University, 18–19,
292

Alienated scholarship, 268–269
Alien Tort Claims Act, 140–145
American Association of Law Schools:
award from, 278; job fair, 249;
speech on method of work at,
263
American Association of University
Professors (AAUP), 262, 430n1
American Booksellers Ass'n,
Inc. v. Hudnut, 343n3, 360n2,
364n29
American Civil Liberties Union
(ACLU): speech given to, 189–198;
views on pornography of, 401n29
American Law Institute, Model Penal
Code, 285
American Psycho (Ellis), 201
Amnesty International, 374–375n32
Andrews v. Law Society of British
Columbia, 138–139, 370n20
Anglo-Canadian-American approach
to equality, 110–116
Antipornography civil rights ordinance
and approach: anticipation of,
11; appropriateness of, 103–106;
opposition to, 186, 189; overview
of, 206; reaction to, 34–35; reasons
to adopt, 108; to zoning ordinance,
96–98
Apne Aap, 162
Aristotelian (formal) equality, 110,
137–138, 296, 297, 306, 308–312
Armanda, Asja, 282
Assault, definition of, 195
Attitudes toward women and sex,
effects of exposure to pornography
on, 103, 203, 205

Attorney General's Commission on Pornography, testimony to, 99–108
Audience, interactive dynamics of, 2
Australia: gender gap in, 310; prostitution in, 177; "special measures" in, 310

Babcock, Barbara, 26
Bakke (Regents of the University of California v. Bakke) case, 245
Barnes v. Costle, 88–89
Barry, Kathleen, 170
Barry, Patricia, 356n1
Bartow, Ann, 282
Basic Instinct (film), 204
Bethel (Bethel School District No. 403 v. Fraser) case, 255–256
Black men: rape convictions of, 16; white women and, 61
Black women: prostitution of, 381n18, 382n28; rape of, 14–15; sexual harassment of, 95
Blind sage fable, 214
Bollinger, Lee, 279
Boreman, Linda. See Marchiano (Boreman), Linda
Bosnia-Herzegovina, 153–154. See also Kadic v. Karadžić
Boys, effects of childhood sexual abuse of, 210–212, 222
Brennan (Justice), 244
Brown v. Board of Education, 314–315
Bundy v. Jackson, 73, 89
Burnham (People v. Burnham) case, 131, 135–136, 137
Butterfly effect, 1, 207, 331
Byrd, James, Jr., 326–327
Bystander mentality, 150–151

Calabresi, Guido, 23
Campus SaVE Act, 293

Canada: Charter of Rights and Freedoms, 110, 111, 120–121, 123–124, 125; constitutional equality in, 6; dignity deprivation and, 306–307, 313–314; substantive equality and, 306, 312–313
Capital University Law Review symposium on sexual harassment, 57
Carr v. Allison Gas Turbine Division General Motors Corp., 221–222
Catharsis hypothesis, 203
Causality, 4, 7, 26
CEDAW Committee, 288–289, 317, 320, 324
Change. See Social change
Chaos theory: butterfly effect and, 1; complexity, causality, and, 4; sensitivity to initial conditions and, 5
Character assassination, 91, 93
Charter of Rights and Freedoms, Canada, 110, 111, 120–121, 123–124, 125
Chen, Chao-ju, 47
Childbearing and childrearing, 300–301
Child pornography, 100, 107, 221
Child prostitution, 163, 168, 175–176
Children, sexual abuse of: outcomes of, 210–212, 222; pornography and, 192–193; statutes of limitations for, 236
"Chilling effect," 251
Civil procedure law and sex inequality, 233–234, 235
Civil rights antipornography ordinance and approach. See Antipornography civil rights ordinance and approach
Clark, Ramsey, 152
Class and sex inequality, 49
Clients: choosing, 44; finding, 52; humility with, 53

Clinical education in law schools, 239
Clothing, as sexual communication, 63, 91–94
Coercion: assault, police, and, 447–448n15, 447n14; definition of, 195; inequality and, 319; rape and, 289–290
Coetzee, J. M., *Elizabeth Costello*, 404n3, 414n30
Cohen v. San Bernardino Valley College, 256, 257, 259, 262
Collective, inequalities as, 120
"Colorblindness," 312
Comparison groups, in legal concept of equality, 113–114
Condoms, in prostitution, 175
Conference on Gender Bias in the Law, summation of proceedings of, 217–224
Confidential sources/confidentiality, in sexual violence on campuses, 453n11
Conflict, gender inequality as, 324
Consent: assumptions of, 286–287; as autonomy concept, 319–320; breaking under torture and, 136; definitions of, 286; desire and, 288–289, 321; dominance and, 287; in equality framework, 307–308; inequality and, 321–322; mistaken belief in, 137; pornography and, 202; prostitution and, 172–173; rape and, 13, 137, 221, 285–286; sex trafficking and, 322–323; standards of, as putting women on trial, 320–321; survival necessity and, 209; as unequal concept, 287–288
Conservatives, in legal scholarship, 274–275
Constitutional law and gender status, 236–237

Continental Can Corp. Inc. v. State of Minnesota, 19–20, 350–351n5
Contract law and sex inequality, 233
Convention on the Elimination of All Forms of Discrimination Against Women (CEDAW), 47–48, 374n31. *See also* CEDAW Committee
Copelon, Rhonda, 140
Coughenour, Beulah, 184
Council of Europe and gender main-streaming, 426n10
Courts: as forums for women, 21, 152; receptivity of, to new ideas, 250; talking reality to judges about sexual assault, 329–330
Co-worker sexual harassment, 88
Credibility at trial, implicit standards for, 58
Criminal law and sex inequality, 235–236
Curriculum, structural divisions in, 231

Dahl, Robert A., 279
Damages awarded for rape in Bosnia-Herzegovina, 153, 160–161
Davis, Karen, 40
Davis (Washington v. Davis) case, 292
Death penalty, 236
De Beauvoir, Simone, 209
Decriminalization of pornography, 137, 177–179
Deep Throat (film), 20, 96, 211. *See also* "Linda Lovelace"
De facto equality, 309
DeGrace v. Rumsfeld, 83
Deliberate indifference, liability standard of, 292–293
Demand for prostitution, 167–168
Difference, sex as socially constructed as, 309
Differential treatment, 59

Dignity, deprivation of, 306–307, 313–316

Disadvantaged groups: equality law and, 112–116, 124–125; prostitution and, 166; social definition of, 112

Discrimination: academic freedom as defense to student claims of, 253–262; in Bosnia-Herzegovina, 154; differential treatment, disparate impact, and, 59; failure to act as, 310; as pervasive behavior, 16–17; sexual abuse as form of, 47; sexual harassment as, 6, 19–20, 48, 71–72, 74–82, 105; in tenure decisions, 247–248. *See also* Sex discrimination

Disengaged scholarship, 264, 265–267, 269–271, 272–273, 274, 275–276

Disparate impact, 59, 298

Dissociation in prostitution, 170

Diversity, deliberations on, 25–27

Does v. Karadžić, 140

Domestic violence, 126, 131–132, 235, 301–302, 460n32

Dominance: consent and, 287; inequality question and, 118–119. *See also* Male dominance

Dothard v. Rawlinson, 354–355n22

Due diligence standard of accountability, 291, 293, 294

Dworkin, Andrea: acknowledgment of, 282; on changing ways of thinking, 62; death of, 206; on derivation of obscene, 405n3; equality approach to pornography and racist hate speech of, 48; on harm of pornography, 192, 194; on MacKinnon, 50; pornographic portrayals of, 205; pornography and, 100; pornography course taught by, 96; on sexual polarity, 219. *See also* Antipornog-

raphy civil rights ordinance and approach; Swedish model of prostitution

Dworkin, Ronald, 251

Economic inequality, 295–296, 299–301

Education: about gender bias, 219–223; quality of, and student strikes at Yale, 24. *See also* Legal education

Educational sexual harassment, 240, 291–294

EEOC *Guidelines on Discrimination Because of Sex,* 69, 84, 88

Effectiveness, measures of, 44–45

Emerson, Thomas I., 244, 279

Employer liability for sexual harassment by supervisors, 64–65, 72–73, 76, 82–91

Engaged scholarship: conservatives, liberals, and, 274–275; critique of, 264; determinants and, 269; direct involvement and, 264–265; as grounded and theoretical, 275–276; as intrinsic, 272; legal practice and, 273–274; as method, 267, 274; overview of, 263–264; social reality and, 271–272, 276–279

Entitlement assumption, 25

Environmental sexual harassment, 64, 71–73, 76, 86–88. *See also* Employer liability for sexual harassment by supervisors

Equal Employment Opportunity Act of 1972, 359n14

Equal Employment Opportunity Commission, 248

Equality: de facto, 309; disadvantaged groups and, 112–116, 124–125; formal, 110, 137–138, 296, 297, 306, 308–312; as ideal, 305; litigating for, 47–54; substantive,

110, 177, 306, 312–317; taking
seriously, 40–41
Equality, approaches to: Anglo-
Canadian-American, 110–116;
Aristotelian, 110, 137–138, 296,
297, 306, 308–312; as biased,
116–117; dissident or alternative
view, 118–125; dominant point of
view and, 117–118; overview of,
111–112; as positive right, 303–304.
See also Equal Rights Amendment
Equal Pay Act, 300
Equal protection law, 221
Equal Rights Amendment (ERA),
50–51, 295–304
Equitable estoppel theory, 256
ERA (Equal Rights Amendment),
50–51, 295–304
"Ethnic cleansing" and rape. See *Kadic
v. Karadžić*
European Court of Human Rights,
288–289, 318, 319, 322
Evidence law and sex inequality,
237–238

Fable of blind sage, 214
Fair treatment, 116, 117
Fantasy: as evidence in sexual harass-
ment case, 91–94; pornography as,
183, 200–201
Feinberg, Wilfred, 140
Fellows, Mary Lou, 218
Female, as form of powerlessness, 29
Femicide, 323
Femininity, 209, 210
Feminism: academic freedom and,
248–249; misconceptions about,
225–227; overview of, 227–228;
women's point of view and, 57–58.
See also Mainstreaming feminism
Feminism Unmodified (MacKinnon),
225, 263, 279

Feminist scholarship, 269–270
Feminist theory of state, 12–13
Filàrtiga v. Peña-Irala, 142
Finley, Lucinda, 218
First Amendment: absolutist approach
to, 221; academic freedom and, 244,
253; free speech and pornography,
195–198; inequality and, 197;
pornography and, 106–108; sexual
harassment and, 258–259; speech of
teachers and, 254; trend in, 262;
women and, 21
Fish, Stanley, 269, 271
Force: definition of, 195; prostitution
and, 163; rape and, 13–14, 136–137,
289; sexism and, 187–188; torture
and, 190
Force of law, 234
Foreign Sovereign Immunities Act, 150
Formal (Aristotelian) equality, 110,
137–138, 296–297, 306, 308–312
Fourteenth Amendment, Equal
Protection Clause, 295–299, 304
Frank, Jerome, 268
Franklin v. Gwinnett Public Schools,
292, 293
Free speech and pornography,
195–198
Frost, Robert, 270, 276

Gates, Bill, 175
*Gebser v. Lago Vista Independent
School District*, 292, 293
Geduldig v. Aiello, 354n22, 368n6,
464n17
Gender: mainstreaming in legal
education, 230–239; as social
construction, 222; as social meaning
of sex, 316. *See also* Men; Women
Gender bias, 134, 217–224
Gender blindness, in sex equality
jurisprudence, 312

Gender crime: development of concept of, 6; International Criminal Court and, 49; rape as, 285; Rome Statute of International Criminal Court and, 319; substantive equality and, 324; violence against women as, 306, 317

Gender equality and pornography, 207–214

Gender hierarchy: in popular culture, 209; in society, 297

Gender illiteracy, 226–227

Gender inequality: as approach to sexual abuse, 47; complex causality and, 7; conflict and, 324; gender differences, sexual harassment, and, 60–61; sexual objectification and, 57–58

Gender literacy, 217–224

Gender neutrality, 300, 312

Gender relations through law, activism in, 1–2

Gender: The Future conference, speech given at, 207–214

Genocide: definition of, 314; jurisdiction in cases of, 141–142; rape as act of, 48, 155–159. See also *Kadic v. Karadžić*

Germany, prostitution in, 178

Ginsburg, Ruth Bader, 278

Girls, effects of childhood sexual abuse of, 210, 211

Goldstein, Richard, 186

Gonzales, Jessica, 318

Grounded theory, 275–276

Group libel laws, 107

Harm: of obscenity, 196–197; of pornography, 34–35, 100–104, 135, 192–193, 195; of prostitution, 175–176, 178–179; of racial segregation, 313–315; of sexual

assault, nature of as injury, 58; of sexual harassment, 94–95

Harm minimization/reduction approach to prostitution, 169

Harvey, Kent, 282

Hearsay rule, 237–238

Hentoff, Nat, 186

Hierarchy: gender, 209, 297; inequality as, 313; sex inequality as, 138–139

Hilton, Paris, 205

Hirschman, Linda, 224

HIV/AIDS and prostitution, 169, 175

Holtzman, Elizabeth, 455n1

Hope, 330–331

Horizontal rights, 236–237

Human being, definition of, 198

Human Rights in the Twenty-First Century conference, 370n2

ICC (International Criminal Court), 49, 317, 318–319

ICTR (International Criminal Tribunal for Rwanda), 140, 289, 319

ICTY (International Tribunal for Former Yugoslavia), 140

Illegal prostitution, 163

Immortality, assumption of, 32

"Impact litigation," 52

Indianapolis: city council of, 101; support of antipornography civil rights law from progressive neighborhood groups in, 184

Inequality: Charter of Rights and Freedoms (Canada) and, 120–121; as collective, 120; commonalities among types of, 119–121; dignity deprivation in, 307; dominance and, 118–119; economic, 295–296, 299–301; grounds as interconnected, 121; hierarchy and, 313; injury done by, 315–316; respect for precedent

and, 237; as systemic and systematic, 120. *See also* Equality, approaches to; Gender inequality; Sex inequality
Intellectual freedom: academic freedom and, 242–243, 249–250, 253; sexual harassment and, 259
Intent: in sex inequality, 298–299, 304; in sexual harassment, 59–60
Inter-American Commission on Human Rights, 318
International Criminal Court (ICC), 49, 317, 318–319
International Criminal Tribunal for Rwanda (ICTR), 140, 289, 319
International law: outrages taken seriously in, 126; rape in, 6, 285, 319; sex equality in, 317–324; substantive equality in, 306; women and, 238–239
International Tribunal for Former Yugoslavia (ICTY), 140
Intersectionality, 11, 63, 356n2
Intimate partner violence, 126, 131–132, 235, 301–302, 460n32
Ireland, abortion in, 137
Israel: consent and rape in, 320–321; gender gap in, 310; substantive equality in, 306, 307; Women of the Wall cases in, 309

Jackson, Janet, 204
Jail, rape in, 15
Jasper, Texas, 326–327
Johnson, Barbara, 271
Judges, talking reality of sexual assault to, 329–330
Jurisdiction: in cases of genocide, 141–142; as division of power, 234; sex inequality and, 234
Justice, law as instrument for, 45–46

Kadic v. Karadžić: appellate argument, 141–151; summation to jury, 153–161
Kahn, Paul, 265–267, 270
Karadžić, Radovan, 140, 152. See also *Kadic v. Karadžić*
Keyishian v. Board of Regents of the University of the State of New York, 244–245, 254, 430–431n2
Knowledge: personal, 267–268; sociology of, 268

Larson, Jane E., 282
Law: as fitting life, 43–44; gender bias in, 217–224; hope and, 330–331; as instrument for justice and redistribution of wealth, 45–46; male ignorance in, 220–221; power of, 28–33, 326; practice of, and scholarship, 265–266, 273–274; reasons for study of, 42–43; reasons for working with, 49–50; social reality and, 271–272; use of, for real change, 325–331; views of, 12
Law practice, relation between legal education and, 239
Law schools: clinical education in, 239; sexual harassment in, 240, 291–294. *See also* Legal education; *specific law schools*
The Law Society of British Columbia v. Andrews, 110
Lawyer: goal for life as, 43; as neutral instrument, 11, 22, 218–219; as social activist, 12
Legal education: exclusion of women from, 239–240; mainstreaming feminism in, 230–239, 241; sexual harassment in, 240; Socratic method in, 240–241
Legalization of prostitution, 137, 177–179

Legal scholarship: alienated, 268–269; contempt for, 273; disengaged, 264–276; feminist, 269–270; law practice and, 265–266; personal and, 267, 268. *See also* Engaged scholarship

Legal system: courts, 21, 152, 250; judges, 329–330; legitimacy of, 124; role of, for women, 22

Lessig, Larry, 223

Lessons learned: clients will find you, 52; fight to win, 54; getting something is better than nothing, 53–54; hold your position, 50–51; it is not about you, 53; life is short, 51; stay grounded, 43; support and care for yourself so as to be ready, 52–53; use everything you've got, 51; what is good for one is often good for all, 51–52

Liability: attachment and scope of, 58; in cases of genocide, 142; of educational institution for sexual harassment, 291–294; of employer for sexual harassment by supervisors, 64–65, 72–73, 76, 82–91

Libel laws, 107

Liberals and legal scholarship, 274–275

Liberation of women, male dominance as obstacle to, 208

"Linda Lovelace," 128–130, 134–135. *See also* Marchiano (Boreman), Linda

Lorenz, Edward, 1

Los Angeles County, Commission for Women of, 101

Mahoney, Kathleen, 218, 221

Mainstream approach to equality. *See* Aristotelian (formal) equality

Mainstreaming feminism, 225, 230–239, 241

Mainstream media: as credentialing intelligentsia, 250; pornography and, 183, 199–202

Male dominance: consent and, 321; exposure of, 220–221; feminism and, 227–228; gender bias in law and, 219, 223; as learned, 222; as obstacle to liberation of women, 208; prostitution and, 316; sexuality as vector for, 211–213; in society, 15, 208–209

Male form, power as taking, 29

Maloney, Carolyn, 296, 302–303

Mannheim, Karl, 265

Marchiano (Boreman), Linda: legal concept conceived for, 96; as "Linda Lovelace," 128–130, 134–135; on oppression, 211; *Ordeal*, 400n19; testimony of, 365n37

Marital rape, 14, 135–136

Marshall, Burke, 279

Martin, Sheilah, 220

Masculinity, as learned, 222

M.C. v. Bulgaria, 288–289, 319–320, 323–324

Meares, Tracy, 223

Media. *See* Mainstream media

Media Coalition, 189

Meiji University Law School, 225

Men: Black, and rape convictions, 16; Black, and white women, 61; as gender group, 229–230; sexuality and inequality of women to, 13. *See also* Male dominance; White men

Meritor Savings Bank, FSB v. Vinson: discriminatory working environment argument, 82–91; evidence of dress argument, 91–94; questions presented, 65; sexual harassment argument, 74–82; statement of case, 65–70; summary of argument,

64–65; writ of certiorari argument, 70–74

Method, as way to truth, critique of, 265

Michael M. v. Superior Court of Sonoma County, 354–355n22

Midwest Regional Women and the Law Conference, speech given at, 11–22

Mill, John Stuart, 12

Mindgeek, 402n35

Minneapolis: city council of, 101; request for help with pornography from neighborhood groups in, 184

Minor v. Happersett, 339–340n3

Misogyny, 217

Morality in Media, Minneapolis, 184

Moran, Beverly, 218

Moreno Ocampo, Luis, 49

Mt. Healthy v. Doyle, 254

Narcissistic personality disorder, 421n17

National Taiwan University College of Law, 47

Negative state, concept of, 236, 303

Nenadic, Natalie, 282

Neutrality: as constitutional law principle, 237; lawyer as neutral instrument, 11, 22, 218–219; trap of, 26

Neuwirth, Jessica, 282, 455n1

Newman, Jon O., 140

New York Times, op-ed piece for, 37, 344–346n11

Nonlinear processes, tolerance built into, 6–7

Nonreporting of sexual abuse/assault, 236, 302, 428n20

Objectification. *See* Sexual objectification

Objectivity, as norm in scholarship, 265–267

Obscenity: definition of, 21, 99–100, 404–405n3; First Amendment and, 106–107; harm as irrelevant to, 196–197

Occupational sex segregation, 299–300, 459n23

Office of Civil Rights (OCR), "Questions and Answers on Title IX and Sexual Violence," 453n11

Oncale v. Sundowner Offshore Servs., Inc., 335n20

Opuz v. Turkey, 318, 323–324

Organized crime, pornography as industry of, 102

Organizing, with legal initiatives, 61–62

Ormerod, Paul, *Butterfly Economics*, 4

Orthodoxies in academia, 245–247

Ostracism, punishment by, 251

Outdoor/street prostitution, 163, 168–169

Palermo Protocol definition of trafficking, 176, 176n69, 290

Paul, Weiss, Rifkind, Wharton & Garrison, 153

Pay gap, by sex, 299–300

PDA (Pregnancy Discrimination Act), 301, 464n17

Peace, equality as precondition for, 305, 324

Peacock (State v. Peacock) case, 218

Penthouse magazine, 189

Piercy, Marge, *Woman on the Edge of Time*, 207, 213

Pinochet, Augusto, 327

Playboy magazine, 21

Plessy v. Ferguson, 315

Police: assault, coercion, and, 447–448n15, 447n14; domestic violence and, 460n32; sex business and, 168

Political, definition of, 133–134
"Political Lawyers" (MacKinnon), 325–326, 330
Pope, Alexander, 226
Popular culture: audience for, 203–204; gender hierarchy in, 209
PornHub, 402n35
Pornography: abusive sexuality and, 212; as causing aggression toward women, 195–196; as changing culture, 205–206; consent and, 202; conservatism, feminism, and, 184–186; definition of, 104–105, 194; effects of exposure to, 103–104, 203, 205, 209; equality approach to, 48; as "fantasy," 183, 200–201; First Amendment issues with, 106–108; as form of sexual harassment, 37; free speech and, 195–198; gender equality and, 207–214; harm caused by, 34–35, 100–104, 135, 192–193, 195; legal approach to, 20–22, 184; mainstream media and, 183, 199–202; opposition to law on, 186; protection of, in U.S., 137; publishing industry and, 201; reasons for doing nothing about, 35–38; as sex discriminatory practice, 96–98, 194; sex equality and, 106, 135, 184–186, 207–214; sex inequality and, 190–191, 193; sexual violence and, 99, 187–188, 192–193; snuff pornography, 211, 363n26, 398–399n16; soft-core, 191, 209–210; sphere of, 199–200; talking about harms to women of, 34–35; testimony to Attorney General's Commission on Pornography, 99–108; as torture, 190–192, 197–198; ubiquity of, 200; as violation of civil liberties, 194. See also Antipornography civil rights ordinance and approach

Pornography industry, profits of, 197, 202, 397–398n10
Positive right to equality, 303–304
Postmodernism, 276, 277
Post Traumatic Stress (PTSD) and prostitution, 170
Poverty: prostitution and, 165; sex-based, 209; women in, 457–458n19
Power: academic freedom and, 243–244, 253, 259, 262; accountability toward, 31; calling out, 249–250, 251; dominance, inequality, and, 118–119, 229–230; of law, 28–33, 326; of political law for women, 329; resistance to change in distribution of, 327–329; seeing things from point of view of, 25–27; sexualization of, 209
Precedent, respect for, and inequality, 237
Pregnancy Discrimination Act (PDA), 301, 464n17
Priest v. Rotary, 93
Privacy laws and pornography, 105
Proportionality trick, 25–26
Prostitution: age of entry into, 166; Black women in, 381n18, 382n28; childhood sexual abuse and, 166, 176, 418–419n11; condoms and, 175; as consensual sex, 286; consent and, 172–173; as contested, 162–163; demand for, 167–168; denial of harm of, 175–176; disadvantaged groups and, 166; dissociation and, 170; force and, 163; harm of, 178–179; HIV/AIDS and, 169, 175; indoor vs. outdoor/street, 163, 168–169; legal approaches to, 164–165; legalization of, 137, 177–179; moralist view

of, 163; pornography and, 97–98; Post Traumatic Stress and, 170; poverty and, 165; race and, 168; as serial rape, 290; sex and, 166–167; sex inequality and, 171–172; as sex trafficking, 176–177; sexual exploitation view of, 164–165, 169; sexual slavery and, 170–171; "sex work" view of, 163–165, 169–170, 173–175; substantive equality perspective on, 316–317; trafficking for, 322; violence and, 165–166, 169, 177. *See also* Swedish model of prostitution

PTSD (Post Traumatic Stress) and prostitution, 170

Public concern, matters of, 257–258, 260

Public employee speech, standards for, 258–260

Publishing, academic, 252

Publishing industry and pornography, 201

Quid pro quo sexual harassment, 76–78, 85–86

Race: colorblindness in equality jurisprudence, 312; prostitution and, 168; sex discrimination and, 63; sex inequality and, 49; sexual harassment and, 95; sexual harassment based on, 78–79; white supremacy in society, 15

Racial hatred, sexualization of, 191

Racial segregation, 114, 116–117, 313–315

Racist abuse of cause of action, 61

Racist hate speech, equality approach to, 48

Rae, Doug, 279

Rantsev v. Cyprus & Russia, 322–324

Rape: abdicating state as recourse for, 16; as act of genocide, 48, 155–159; appearance in court after, 152; Black women and, 14–15; in Bosnia-Herzegovina, damages awarded for, 153, 160–161; case attrition, 302, 321; consent and, 13, 137, 221, 285–286; conviction rate for, 285–286; definition of, 13, 16; difficulty of winning cases of, 17–18; force and, 13–14, 136, 137, 289; as human rights violation, 136–137; in international law, 6, 285, 319; jail and, 15; marital, 14, 135–136; nonreporting of, 428n20; prostitution as serial rape, 290; redefined in sex equality term, 285–290; reform of law regarding, 11, 13–16; reporting of, 14, 15; sexual harassment analogies to, 92–93; statistics on, 132–133; as torture, 126, 140; trials for, 14; weaponized, 319. *See also* Consent; *Kadic v. Karadžić*

Rape kits, untested, 302

Rationality review, 296, 300

Reasonable accommodation doctrine, 112–113, 116

Redistribution of wealth, law as instrument for, 45–46

Remedy, adequacy of, 58

Reproductive rights, 122

Resistance, as not permitted, 36–37

Robinson, Lois, 37, 344–346n11

Robinson v. Jacksonville Shipyards, Inc., 344n10

Rome Statute of International Criminal Court, 318–319

Rorty, Richard, 36, 139

Rosenfeld, Diane, 293

"Rough sex" defense, 286, 469n60

Rovner, Ilana, 223

Rubin v. Ikenberry, 257–258, 259, 262
Ruth Bader Ginsburg Lifetime Achievement Award, speech upon receiving, 278–282

Sadism, 421n17
Sameness/difference approach to equality. *See* Aristotelian (formal) equality
Scales, Ann, 220, 223, 224, 282
Scalia, Antonin, 304
Schafran, Lynn, 218
Scholarship. *See* Disengaged scholarship; Engaged scholarship; Feminist scholarship; Legal scholarship
Schroer v. Billington, 335n20
Scienter requirement in child pornography law, 221
Scientific metaphors in legal thinking, 3–5
Scrutiny, in Equal Protection law, critique of, 309–310, 456n10
Segregation: racial, 114, 116–117, 313–315; of workforce, 299–300, 459n23
Self-censorship and academic freedom, 249–251
Sensitive dependence in chaos theory, 5
Sex: attitudes toward, and effects of exposure to pornography, 103, 203, 205; definition of, 166–167; as difference, 309; social meaning of, 316
Sex discrimination: gender-motivated violence as, 301–302, 317–318; legal absence and, 310; pornography as, 96–98, 194; race and, 63; sexual harassment as, 6, 19–20, 48, 71–72, 74–82, 105
Sex equality: as dream, 282; international law and, 317–324; as legal

guarantee, 305; need for Equal Rights Amendment, 295–304; pornography and, 106, 135, 184–186, 207–214; prostitution and, 177; rape redefined in terms of, 285–290. *See also* Sex inequality
Sex inequality: civil procedure law and, 233–234, 235; as complex and unstable domain, 3; consent and, 321–322; contract law and, 233; criminal law and, 235–236; evidence law and, 237–238; gender literacy and, 218; as hierarchy, 138–139; intent requirements and, 298–299, 304; other inequalities in issues of, 49; pornography and, 190–191, 193; prostitution and, 171–172; race and, 49; state and, 134; in terms of male power, 229–230. *See also* Sex equality
Sexism: force and, 187–188; pornography and, 193
Sex trafficking: consent and, 322–323; definitions of, 176–177, 290; legalization of prostitution and, 177
Sexual abuse: accounts of, 128–131; in childhood, and prostitution, 166, 176, 418–419n11; gendered, 133; gender inequality approach to, 47; issues of, as inequality questions, 122; state and, 134–137; statistics on, 132–133; as torture, 131–134
Sexual assault: consequences of, 155; nonreporting of, 236, 302, 428n20; talking reality to judges about, 329–330. *See also* Rape
Sexual exploitation view of prostitution, 164, 165, 169
Sexual harassment: academic freedom as defense to student claims of, 253–262; challenges to law of, 11; definition of, 17; design of federal

cause of action, 44–45; difficulty of
winning cases of, 17–19; dignity
deprivation and, 314; as discrimination, 6, 19–20, 48, 71–72, 74–82,
105; educational, 240, 291–294;
employer liability for, 64–65, 72–73,
76, 82–91; First Amendment and,
258–259; first case to reach Supreme
Court, 63; injury from, and likelihood of suing for, 94–95; institutional liability for, 291–294;
intellectual freedom and, 259; in law
schools, 240, 291–294; legal claim
for, 3, 6, 57–62; pornography as
form of, 37; quid pro quo, 76–78,
85–86; race and, 95; reform of law
regarding, 16–21. See also Meritor
Savings Bank, FSB v. Vinson
Sexual Harassment of Working
Women (MacKinnon), 110, 356n1
Sexuality and inequality of women to
men, 13
Sexualization of power, 209
Sexually explicit, definition of, 194
Sexual objectification: abuse and, 228;
pornography and, 103, 104, 194,
200, 206; progress against cultural
forms of, 209; prostitution and,
316; sexual harassment and, 19,
57–58, 59
Sexual slavery, 170–171, 174, 202
Sexual violence: on campuses, and
confidential sources/confidentiality,
453n11; inequality and, 122; in
mainstream cinema, 204–205;
pornography and, 99, 187–188,
192–193
Sex work view of prostitution,
163–165, 169–170, 173–175
Silencing women, 36–39, 41
Silva v. University of New Hampshire,
255, 256, 257, 259, 262

"Similarly situated" assumption,
112–115, 138
Skokie (Collin v. Smith) case, 189
Slavery, sexual, 170–171, 174, 202
Smith, William French, 99
Smith College Medal, 34
Snuff (film), 201
Snuff pornography, 211, 363n26,
398–399n16
Social activist, lawyer as, 12
Social change: as fast, 45; speaking
out/town meetings and, 24–25; use
of law for, 325–331
Social construction, gender as, 222
Sociology of knowledge, 268
Socratic method in legal education,
240–241
"Soft-core" pornography, 191,
209–210
"Special measures," 310
Speech: pornography and, 195–198;
public employee, standards for,
258–260; racist hate, equality
approach to, 48; of teachers,
in-class, 254–255
Speeches, writings as spoken first, 2.
See also specific speeches
Stamen, Jayne, 130–131, 135
St. Antoine, Ted, 242
State: abdicating, as recourse for rape,
16; abuse of women and, 133–135;
feminist theory of, 12–13; negative
state concept, 236, 303; sex
inequality and, 134; sexual abuse
and, 134–137
Status quo: change and, 326, 327;
defended as freedom, 186–187;
equality doctrine and, 115, 119,
123–124, 300; legal, and pornography, 106; as natural, 3; scholarship and, 265, 270, 272; sex equality
and, 296, 311

Statutes of limitations for sex crimes against children, 236
Stein, Robert, 279
Stevens, Beth, 140
Stone, Sharon, 204, 205
Strategy: content as key to, 329; dissection and abstraction as, 26; trial, 61
Strict scrutiny, 456n10
Strike for Faculty Diversity, Yale Law School, 23–27
Student claims of sexual harassment, academic freedom as defense to, 253–262
Subordination: attributed to nature and body, 229; definition of, 104, 194; inequality question and, 118–119; of women, 35–36, 123–124
Substance, as key to process, 329–330
Substantive equality: as alternative to Aristotelian equality, 306, 312–317; Swedish model of prostitution as, 177; theory of, 110
Sunstein, Cass, 218, 219, 221
Supervisors. *See* Employer liability for sexual harassment by supervisors
Supreme Court (Canada): *The Law Society of British Columbia v. Andrews*, 110; substantive equality and, 313
"Survival sex," as prostitution, 167
Swedish model of prostitution: adoption of, 165; equality and, 162; influence of, 290; initiation and implementation of, 48–49; overview of, 7; substantive equality and, 177, 213, 316–317

Teachers, in-class speech of, 254–255, 258–260. *See also* Academic freedom
Tenure and academic freedom, 247–248, 251–252

Texas Department of Community Affairs v. Burdine, 58n10
Third-party involvement as defining trafficking, 177
Thomas, James, 279
Times Higher Education Supplement, article in, 199–206
Title VII, Civil Rights Act of 1964: definition of "employer," 83; economic equality and, 301; employment relationship and, 86–87; intent under, 298; *Meritor Savings Bank, FSB v. Vinson* and, 65, 74–75; need for ERA and, 295; sex equality principle and, 296
Title IX, Education Amendments of 1972, 258, 260, 291–294
Tolstoy, Leo, 5
Toohey, John, Chambers of, 462n1
Torres, Gerald, 263, 276–277
Torts: sex inequality and, 231–233; sexual harassment and, 86–87
Torture: Abu Ghraib incident and, 201; consequences of, 127–128; by intimates, 131–132; by Pinochet, 327; pornography as, 190–192, 197–198; profile of, 127; purpose of, 190; rape as form of, 126, 140; sexual abuse as, 131–134; views of, 189–190; as violation of human rights, 127, 128, 139
Torture Victim Protection Act (TVPA), 140, 146, 149–150
Toward a Feminist Theory of the State (MacKinnon), 11
Town meetings, 24–25
Trafficking: definition of, 195; pornography and, 105, 202; third-party involvement as, 177; views about prostitution and, 163. *See also* Sex trafficking
Traynor, Chuck, 128–139

Tutu, Desmond, 198
TVPA (Torture Victim Protection Act), 140, 146, 149–150

United Kingdom (UK), consent-only rape law in, 321
United Nations (U.N.) Security Council, 324
United States v. DePew, 398–399n16, 405–406n6
University of California, Davis, Law School, commencement address at, 42–46
University of Michigan Senate, Davis, Markert & Nickerson Lecture on Academic and Intellectual Freedom, 242. *See also* Academic freedom
University of Minnesota School of Law, pornography course at, 96
University of Western Australia, speech given at, 462n1

Value, equality as not a, 315
Velasquez-Rodriguez v. Honduras, 136
Velazquez, Lisa, 153
Vertical rights, 237
Vertido v. Philippines, 288–289, 320
Village Voice, The, response to, 183–188
Vinson, Mechelle, 63, 94. See also *Meritor Savings Bank, FSB v. Vinson*
Vinson case, 221–222. See also *Meritor Savings Bank, FSB v. Vinson*
Vinson v. Taylor, 69
Violence: as core of sex inequality, 305; gender-based, 209, 295–296, 299, 301–302, 317–318; intimate partner, 126, 131–132, 235, 460n32; pornography exposure and, 103; prostitution and, 165–166, 169, 177. *See also* Sexual violence; Torture

Violence Against Women Act, 11, 48, 301–302, 370n18
Voluntariness of sexual encounters, 80–82, 93. *See also* Consent; Welcomeness in sexual encounters
Vullo, Maria, 153

Wage gap, 299–300
Walker, John M., Jr., 140
War against women, 36
Waters, Lindsay, 279
Wechsler, Herbert, 315
Weiler, Joseph, 279
Weinstein, Leo, 38, 279
Welcomeness in sexual encounters, 80–82. *See also* Consent; Voluntariness of sexual encounters
White men: equal treatment of, 138; homosocial subordination by, 222; power and, 29; prostitution and, 381n18; sex discrimination in education and, 18; sexual harassment and, 360n20; tenure granted to, 433n18; wage gap for, 342n19
White people: equality approach and, 113, 308–309; equating Black people with, 25; segregation and, 114, 116–117, 315; standards for, 117; strikes to change relations between Black people and, 24; of Yale Law School faculty, 23. *See also* White men; White women
White supremacy, 15, 46, 250, 326–327
White-valanced law of sex, 340n9
White women: Black men and, 61, as judge in *Alexander v. Yale*, 19; pornography and, 101; as slaves, 197
Wicked (play), 278
Woman on the Edge of Time (Piercy), 207, 213

Women: attitudes toward, and effects of exposure to pornography, 103, 203, 205; Black, and rape, 14–15; Black, and sexual harassment, 95; Black, in prostitution, 381n18, 382n28; courts as forums for, 21, 152; First Amendment and, 21; as gender group, 229–230; international law and, 238–239; law from viewpoint of, 12–13, 28–33; obligation to silence, 36–39, 41; obstacle to liberation of, 208; reasons for working with law, 49–50; sexuality and inequality of, 13; status of, 228–229; as students, equality interests of, 258; war against, 36; work that impacts, 278–282. *See also* White women

Women's Legal Education and Action Fund (LEAF), 110

Women's movement and sexual harassment, 19. *See also* Feminism

Women writers, 204

Workforce, segregation of, 299–300, 459n23

Working environment. *See* Employer liability for sexual harassment by supervisors

Writ of certiorari argument in *Meritor Savings Bank, FSB v. Vinson,* 70–74

Yale Law School: commencement address at, 28–33; stained glass in front door of, 277; Strike for Faculty Diversity, 23–27

Young v. Southwestern Savings & Loan Assn., 83–84

Zoning ordinance: antipornography civil rights ordinance and, 96–98; attempts to confine pornography with, 100